CANADIAN
FAMILY HISTORY

Selected Readings

Edited by
Bettina Bradbury
Université de Montréal

Copp Clark Pitman Ltd.
A Longman Company
Toronto

ISBN: 0-7730-5194-5

editor: Barbara Tessman, Melanie Sherwood
design: Susan Hedley, Liz Nyman
cover: Kyle Gell
N5 1/12/94
cover illustration: Jenny Duda
typesetting: Andrea Weiler
printing and binding: Metropole Litho Inc.

Canadian Cataloguing in Publication Data

Main entry under title:

Canadian family history

Includes bibliographical references.
ISBN 0-7730-5194-5

1. Family – Canada – History. I. Bradbury, Bettina, 1949 –

HQ559 C35 1992   306.85'0971   C92-093077-8

Copp Clark Pitman Ltd.
2775 Matheson Blvd. East
Mississauga, Ontario
L4W 4P7

associated companies: *Longman Group Ltd., London* • *Longman Inc., New York* • *Longman Cheshire Pty., Melbourne* • *Longman Paul Pty., Auckland*

Printed and bound in Canada

1 2 3 4 5   5194-5   96 95 94 93 92

FOREWORD

o

For years, critics maintained that the study of Canada's past was unsophisticated and immature, its practitioners trapped in a "colony to nation" syndrome or imprisoned by the "great man" school of biography. If that was ever so, it is so no longer. Today Canadian scholars work on every area of the historical frontier, probing into cliometrics, examining the role of ideology, or tracing the myriad parts played by women, both elite and ordinary. Nowhere has this increasing sophistication been more in evidence than in the area of family history.

A generation ago, family history was a term that was scarcely even heard in this country. Today, there are skilled practitioners of this genre in almost every university, all grappling with the complex questions that shaped—and still shape—our lives. This collection of essays, carefully selected by Bettina Bradbury, herself one of the leading practitioners in the field, is striking testimony to how far we have come. It is no criticism at all to say that these essays also show how much further we must go to understand this critical area of our past. Young scholars using this book should remain confident that there is ample place for them in a field that is not yet crowded and in a genre that still has many important questions to answer.

J.L. Granatstein
General Editor

CONTENTS

o

INTRODUCTION

o

The family is both an ideal and a lived reality that is invariably charged with emotion. It is at once the space where love between adults and between parents and children is cultivated and nurtured and the site of some of society's most disturbing violence. The feelings and images that come to mind when individuals think about their own families vary immensely depending on the history of their relationships with their mothers, fathers, siblings or members of their extended family. The kinds of family that people grow up in also vary greatly. Some are large, some small. Some children have only one parent, some two, some more. Growing proportions of parents divorce and many remarry, so that while adults may experience what sociologists call serial monogomy, children may live with a variety of parents and step- or surrogate parents. Some adults choose never to marry, some never to have children. Some live in permanent relationships with adults of the same sex, some with a member of the opposite sex. While the reality of what constitutes a family in terms of its structure, emotional content, or demographic characteristics is clearly varied, this diversity has only recently begun to be recognized in the ideals projected by the state, popular magazines, and much contemporary discourse.

More major changes in family life have occurred in the last twenty or thirty years than in almost any other time in history. Women have sought a different role within the family and in society. Successive generations of feminists have succeeded in opening up many new areas of paid work and education to women, in encouraging the state to provide day care for mothers who worked outside the home, and in making growing numbers of women understand the inequalities and oppression that they face in a patriarchal society. Over the last twenty years, divorce rates in Canada and other countries have increased, releasing some couples from the agonies of destructive relationships, sometimes causing major trauma for their children and leading to new types of custody arrangements. In the same period, new forms of birth control have revolutionized sexuality within and outside marriage, allowing women to make love without fear of pregnancy and accelerating the decline in the birth rate that had already been underway in most western countries for over a century. Largely released from the fear of unwanted pregnancies, growing numbers of couples have chosen to live together prior to marriage or not to marry at all. Some do so because they see marriage as an oppressive, constraining institution. Others, because it makes sense to get to know someone before making a long-term commitment. Still others because heterosexual marriage holds no interest for them.

In the face of such changes, proponents of a return to traditional values have constructed two versions of the history of the family that correspond in many ways to received popular wisdom. In one version, families were made up of a husband and a wife, who married for life. He had a job, while she was a full-time housewife and mother, caring for their children. In the other, the family included grandparents who lived with their grown children and grandchildren, often on a farm. While these ideals do correspond to the reality of many family histories, they are neither traditional, in the sense of having always existed, nor has either ever represented the majority of families in a society for more than a small slice of historical time.

History teaches us that there are no traditional families. Rather, there are certain kinds of relationships, family structures, and demographic patterns that have predominated in specific historical periods, in specific cultures, and within particular classes. Some patterns, structures, and relationships characterized most families for longer periods than others. And the pace of change has varied dramatically across time. Some features of families have changed as a result of forces that are largely outside the control of individuals. The decline in death rates among children and adults since the nineteenth century, for example, has reshaped both the structure and some of the emotional meaning of families. Fewer marriages are broken by death, fewer young children lose parents, or parents their young children. Periods of major economic transformation like the Industrial Revolution, of contact with other cultures, as in the occupation of Canada by the French and later the English, or of intense ideological ferment have provoked other kinds of changes. When large numbers of people question the nature of their relationships with members of the other sex, with spouses, or with children, they prompt change in the meaning attached to families. When economic transformations alter the kinds of work that men, women, or children perform, the places they labour, or the way they are rewarded for work, the material basis of family life is restructured. Other changes follow. Yet the impact of such changes invariably differs depending on the economic situation of families and the age and sex of family members. For families, it is important to underline, are usually made up of men, women, and children. Power within families and relations with the wider economy and society vary with age and gender.

The more rapidly economic, social, or ideological changes occur, the more likely the kinds of family that are believed to have predominated before will appear to be traditional. When traditional images are presented as ideal, a simplification invariably occurs. The complexity of historical reality is denied. Denying past diversity is too often coupled with a refusal to admit variety today. Difference becomes a source of discrimination. To understand the flexibility of families as institutions and the variety of different forms families can take without society collapsing, it is essential to study their history.

This book brings together seventeen essays that help us to see the diversity of the family as an institution in the past, and some of the ways in which families have changed over the years since Europeans initially occupied what has become Canada. It aims firstly to show how important the family has been as an institution in Canadian history. At the same time, the articles demonstrate clearly that the structure, ideological content and demographic characteristics of Canadian families have varied across time and region, and between classes and ethnic groups. Thirdly, most of the articles underline the fact that the family has never meant the same thing to men as it has to women. Finally, I have chosen articles that illustrate many of the different sources, methods, and interpretive frameworks historians use to try to understand the history of families.

The limitations of space, the high costs of republishing some articles, and the existing state of research in Canada have dictated a narrowing of focus within these overriding goals. Most of the articles included here deal with marriage and family formation, the work of family members, or the links between families and the economy or between families and the legal system or the state. I have attempted to include research covering the period from the initial settlement by Europeans to the 1980s. The articles are grouped both chronologically and thematically, starting with marriage and unwed mothers in New France, then looking at the confrontation of family norms and practices among native peoples and fur-trading families, at rural and fishing families in the nineteenth century, and then at working-class families in the nineteenth and twentieth centuries. I have attempted to cover different regions and hence to look at how the nature of local economies and labour markets influenced the sexual division of labour within families. I have tried, too, to chose papers that cover most periods of the family life cycle. Articles deal with premarital sex, marriage, divorce, inheritance, children's work roles, and men and women's work.

Most of the articles in one way or another make the family the focus of the analysis, although many draw as much on approaches in women's history or labour history as they do on the traditions and methods of family history as a field. I have consciously attempted to push beyond the limits of that field to demonstrate the growing contribution of feminist work to the history of the family. Thus, this collection should complement existing collections on women's history,[1] and histories of childhood, education, and the family.[2] Many aspects of family history are missing here. I have not included chapters from books, in part because I wanted complete articles, but also in the hope that readers would consult some of the excellent monographs that now exist in this area and that are listed in the further reading section at the back of this volume. No articles deal with courtship,[3] sexuality within marriage,[4] family violence,[5] emotional relations between husbands and wives, child rearing,[6] or gay relationships. Most of these subjects have only just begun to receive attention in Canada. More articles deal with working-class or agricultural families than with the middle-class or more wealthy families, a fact that largely reflects the current state of research in Canada.

Just as the family has a history, so too does the writing of family history. What we now know about the past of Canadian families has been influenced by the questions historians have posed, the interpretive frameworks they have used, and the kinds of sources they have turned to. The history of the family is an international and interdisciplinary field.[7] Canadian practitioners have drawn on traditions developed in our intellectual metropoli—France,

England, and the United States. The particular nature of the subjects studied reflects both the influence of approaches originating in those countries and the nature of sources available here.

The articles included broadly reflect the major currents of family history as it has been written in Canada, and in some ways as it has been written elsewhere. Writing in 1980, Michael Anderson outlined what he saw as the major ways in which European and North American historians had treated the family. He identified three broad approaches: those focussing on demographic behaviour and family and household structures; those concerned with household economics, including inheritance, the family economy, and the process of proletarianization; and those stressing sentiments and attitudes within families.[8] Subsequent scholarship in the field makes it important to add two other approaches: those focussing on gender relations within families and those interested in the interactions between families and other institutions, particularly the state.[9] While some Canadian historians of the family fit neatly into one or another of these categories, the best works combine different approaches, drawing on a variety of methods and sources to paint a complex portrait of families in the place and period studied.

In Canada the earliest works of family history fell squarely within the demographic approach. In the 1950s, Quebec demographers, who had trained in France with pioneers of techniques such as reconstituting families from parish birth, death, and marriage registers, began the task of uncovering the population history of the province.[10] Demographers working at the University of Montreal (Programme de recherche en démographie historique—PRDH) and at the University of Quebec at Chicoutimi (Programme de recherche sur la société Saguenayenne—SOREP) have subsequently taken advantage of the unique richness of Quebec's population records, refined the methodologies initiated in France, and utilized contemporary computer technology to undertake massive projects reconstructing the history of the entire population of New France[11] and of the Saguenay Region.[12] Understanding demographic behaviour—the age at which people decide to marry, the number of children they have, the likelihood of males and females dying at different ages, and the patterns of migration—is an essential base to understanding the family. Yet demographic details and their major source—parish registers—offer only the skeleton of family history. The flesh, heart, and soul are missing. Luckily few Canadian historians have examined only demographic behaviour. The article in this collection by Yves Landry on the marriages of the *filles du roi*, which is based on the data-base created by the PRDH, demonstrates the usefulness of combining demographic material with other sources, in this case marriage contracts, to better understand people's motivations. Gérard Bouchard's article, based on some of the early material collected for the SOREP project, is typical of much Canadian work in combining several approaches and a variety of sources. Here he argues convincingly that inheritance practices in Quebec were very different from those prevalent in many parts of Europe. The fact of living in a region where land was still available made different fertility patterns and different inheritance strategies possible. The intricacies of the connections between demography, land availability, family ideals, and the economic goals of farmers are pursued further in the three major book-length studies of Canadian rural families: Louise Dechêne's detailed study of merchants and habitants in seventeenth-century Montreal, Alan Greer's investigation of rural society in three Quebec parishes between 1740 and 1840, and David Gagan's work on families, land, and social change in Peel County, Canada West, in the mid-nineteenth-century. All of these works go far beyond a study of demography, integrating questions of family structure, economic motivations, and analysis of the economy to portray the characteristics of families and the changes occurring in the periods studied.[13]

Outside Quebec, the major source for family history has until recently been the forms that families filled out every ten years for the census takers, and the main intellectual influences have been from the United States and England. This has meant that historians of English Canada have paid more attention to family and household structures and what Anderson calls household economics than their colleagues in Quebec, where parish registers have been so much better kept. The first major study of urban families in Canada, Michael Katz's *The People of Hamilton, Canada West*, published in 1975, recreated the population of Hamilton between 1851 and 1871, not by combining births, deaths, and marriages, but by linking together the censuses taken during that period and combining them with other sources.[14] The questions that preoccupied Katz and his colleagues—social and geographical mobility, family structures, and the patterns of growing up—were influenced strongly by research on social mobility[15] and life-cycle patterns in the United States,[16] and by English studies of family and household structures.[17] The schedules of the censuses allow historians to analyse residential groups, offering a snapshot of who is living with whom at the moment the census was taken. Reconstructing family history from parish registers, in contrast, offers a picture of patterns over time. The great advantage of the censuses is that they show us people in their households and they give some idea of the formal jobs people held. However, unless they are combined with other sources, the picture risks remaining static, the dynamics of family relationships or the evolution and change of patterns over time is missing.

The articles by Chad Gaffield and Bettina Bradbury in this collection demonstrate how the censuses can be used to recreate not just the structure of families, but also to see what kinds of jobs family members had. Here again there are problems. Only specific kinds of work were recognized by census takers. Women's work in the home is rarely acknowledged. The casual labour of children on farms, city streets, or in the home is also invisible. By combining reports of school inspectors with government investigations and newspaper reporting from the period, John Bullen is able to describe the types of unpaid tasks school children in Toronto performed at the end of the nineteenth century.

Until the late 1970s most histories of the family, whether they focussed on demography, household and family structures, or even sentiments and ideas, paid little attention to the particular role that women played within the family. Demographers might talk about rates of illegitimacy, but what it meant to be an unmarried mother in specific societies was not addressed or, worse, was celebrated as evidence of sexual liberation.[18] While those using the manuscript censuses to talk about family structures or the family economy might discuss the jobs that women reported, they seldom attempted to think about work that was not visible, or about what the dynamics of family relationships meant for men, women, and children. And they often had problems fitting women's jobs into classification schemes that worked for male occupations.[19] Almost all the practitioners of family history were men, perhaps because it had become an extremely quantitative field of history. At the same time, women's history was developing as a separate field. In Canada, as in other countries, initial research in women's history focussed largely on the early feminist movements, on middle-class women and their careers, or on working-class women and their paid labour. Early feminist scholarship generally steered clear of the family, seen as the source of women's oppression.

By the 1980s, however, feminist work by historians and sociologists was offering new ways of understanding families and the potential of integrating family history and women's history.[20] In Canada, Meg Luxton's *More than a Labour of Love* built on theoretical debates about the role of domestic labour to describe and underline the importance of women's unpaid labour in the home. Her article in this collection examines similar questions for the contemporary period. Historians began to pay more explicit attention to the sexual division of labour within families, examining how the particular nature of local economies influenced not only the paid labour but also the domestic labour of men and women. Joy Parr's "Rethinking Work and Kinship," reproduced here, forms part of her wider study, *The Gender of Breadwinners: Women, Men, and Change in Two Industrial Towns, 1880–1950,* in which these questions are central. Consideration of the sexual division of labour in communities with diverse economic bases is equally the concern of the articles included here by Marilyn Porter, Mark Rosenfeld, Bettina Bradbury, and Franca Iacovetta. Other historians began to confront the pervading ideologies about women and their role within the family with the realities of their lives.[21] And a few feminist historians and lawyers began to expose the extreme historic legal inequality of women.[22] Considerations of *gender,* the concept developed by women's historians to explain how the nature of being female or male has been socially determined, were gradually incorporated into some studies of the family, while women's historians were beginning to pay more attention to the family.

Historians interested in understanding inequality, the dynamics of power, of dependence and independence, or relations between husbands and wives had to find sources that were more eloquent than the parish registers, censuses, and land records on which earlier family historians largely relied. It is no coincidence that all the articles included here that deal with the sexual division of labour within families in the twentieth century are based partially on interviews. Oral history offers new possibilites and poses challenges that are somewhat different from those associated with more traditional sources. When done with sympathy and skill, it makes possible the kinds of detail found in Mark Rosenfeld's study of class and gender in the rhythms of a railway town. Legal records have also proved to be an extremely rich source for understanding some aspects of past family life. Created when individuals stepped outside or contested community norms or the law, court records and law reports generally deal with conflict between individuals. As a result they permit us to see families where all was not harmonious, countering the consensual vision of early family history. And, because the law represents a formalized coding of a society's dominant norms and its application involves the ideological beliefs of lawyers and judges, we see the dialectic between the claims of individuals and dominant ideologies. Thus Marie-Aimée Cliche's examination of unmarried women in New France who pursued the men who had got them pregnant reveals much about the prevailing norms concerning how females were expected to act. Similarly, Constance Backhouse's careful study of changes in married women's property law underlines the profound fear that many judges had of releasing women from their totally subordinate legal state and hence removing what they saw as a linchpin of family stability.

Once those interested in the history of families turned their attention away from questions that focussed inward on the family, such as who lived with whom or how many children couples had, it became vital to consider the nature of interactions between the family and other institutions.[23] The relationship between families, education, and the school system was one of the areas that received attention earlier in Canada than in some other countries, in large part because of the importance of research done by historians like Michael Katz, Alison Prentice, and others at the Ontario Institute for Studies in Education. Chad Gaffield's monograph on rural families in eastern Ontario and his article in this collection represent examples of the kind of careful consideration given to the links between families, the economy, and the education system among such scholars.[24] Historians who examined the paid work of family members could not avoid treating the links between what American historian Tamara Hareven has aptly referred to as family time, industrial time, and historical time.[25] Bettina Bradbury investigates how the particular configurations of the family economy varied with the class position of family heads in industrializing Montreal.[26] And Michael Katz and his colleagues have tied changes in the patterns of growing up to the industrialization of Hamilton.[27] Pursuing in a different way the link between the nature of workplace cultures and the wider economy, Suzanne Morton draws on work in labour history and women's history in her article in this collection to show how the rituals linked to the weddings of young working-class women in early twentieth-century Halifax gradually changed as couples were subjected to the pressures of the advertising that accompanied the expansion of mass consumption. Examination of the impact of the law on women and families and the pressures exerted by women to change the law is another fruitful area where historians have begun to analyse relations between women, the family, and other institutions. Constance Backhouse's article included here not only describes married women's limited legal rights in the nineteenth century, but also the attempts to change them.[28]

Since the 1980s more attention has also been paid to the role of the state in structuring family life or attempting to control family behaviour. Some writing, especially by sociologists and political economists, describes a one-way relationship in which the state is seen to have exercised fairly unilateral control over family behaviour through schools, legislation, and policing. James Snell's article makes very clear how male, largely middle-class legislators increasingly used the state to defend marriage, restrict divorce, and perpetuate their vision of the family in the years leading up to World War I.[29] Other recent work attempts to portray a more complex dynamic between individuals, families and the state, in which some policies are welcomed, even promoted, and some modified by the recipients. Dominique Jean's article examining "Family Allowances and Family Autonomy" is a good example of this approach. It also demonstrates the richness of largely untapped government records.

Families are clearly not simple institutions, whether we consider the complexities of relations between spouses or parents and children or their links with schools, the economy, and the state. Families are social institutions woven in a variety of ways into the society and economy of their times. They contain, sometimes in uneasy tension, the particular beliefs and practices of the individuals living together and the wider norms about the rights, responsibilities, and roles of each member. Norms and practices vary with people's gender, class, and ethnic tradition. This collection, unfortunately renders little justice to the ways families have functioned among either the indigenous peoples or immigrant groups, largely because historical research in this area is scarce.[30] Jennifer Brown and Sylvia Van Kirk describe some aspects of the conflict between native and white cultural norms about what constituted a family, a marriage, or acceptable child-rearing techniques. Most successive waves of immigrants to Canada have experienced some kind of similar disjunction between their practices and beliefs about the family and those of the dominant culture. For some groups there were radical breaks, involving much agony and often conflict between generations. For others, like the postwar Italians described by Franca Iacovetta in this collection, a more complex combination of tradition and innovation enabled economic and perhaps psychological survival.

Those studying the family are only just beginning to unearth the diversity and the richness of past family life. To date, research has revealed more about work patterns, family structures, and demographic behaviour than it has about either ties of love and affection or the agonies of conflict and sorrow. Peter Ward's *Courtship, Love, and Marriage in Nineteenth-Century English Canada* is the first book-length study in Canada that falls within the "sentiments" approach to family history. It is also one of the few monographs to

focus largely on middle-class families. His study reveals the richness of letters and diaries as a source for understanding the hopes and feelings of those literate groups whose records have survived.

Feminist scholarship is pushing family historians to see the family as an institution in which legal and economic rights and power have always been unequal. Husbands have historically enjoyed legal rights and economic possibilities denied to their wives. Sons and daughters have had very different roles to play. Pressure by different generations of feminists has eliminated many of these inequalities. Yet, in many ways, it has been easier to change public aspects of women's rights, like the right to vote, to hold property, or to keep their wages, than the more private aspects of inequality embedded in relationships within families and households. Meg Luxton's examination of changing patterns in the gendered division of labour in the home underlines both the agonies that are involved when people attempt to modify responsibilities and work patterns within families, and the diversity of beliefs held among women in one small town about the proper roles and work of husbands and wives. If we want to forge a new kind of family that promotes the equality of men and women and girls and boys without stifling diversity and denying difference, we clearly need to continue to work for change both in the public world of politics and in the more private sphere of the home.

NOTES

1. Veronica Strong-Boag and Anita Clair Fellman, eds., *Rethinking Canada: The Promise of Women's History* (Toronto: Copp Clark Pitman, 1986; 2nd ed. 1991); Katherine Arnup, Andrée Lévesque, and Ruth Roach Pierson, eds., with Margaret Brennan, *Delivering Motherhood: Maternal Ideologies and Practices in the Nineteenth and Twentieth Centuries* (London: Routledge, 1990); Alison Prentice and Susan Mann Trofimenkoff, eds., *The Neglected Majority: Essays in Canadian Women's History*, 2 vols. (Toronto: McClelland and Stewart, 1977, 1985); Marie Lavigne and Yolande Pinard, eds., *Travailleuses et féministes: aspects historiques* (Montreal: Boréal Express, 1983); Jean Burnet, ed., *Looking into My Sister's Eyes: An Exploration in Women's History* (Toronto: Multicultural History Society of Ontario, 1986); Linda Kealey and Joan Sangster, eds., *Beyond the Vote: Canadian Women and Politics* (Toronto: University of Toronto Press, 1989); Franca Iacovetta and Mariana Valverde, eds., *Expand-ing the Boundaries: New Essays in Women's History* (Toronto: University of Toronto Press, 1991).

2. Joy Parr, ed., *Childhood and Family in Canadian History* (Toronto: McClelland and Stewart, 1982); Patricia T. Rooke and R.L. Schnell, eds., *Studies in Childhood History: A Canadian Perspective* (Calgary: Detselig Enterprises, 1982); Nadia Fahmy-Eid and Micheline Dumont, eds., *Maîtresses de maison, maîtresses d'école: Femmes, famille et éducation dans l'histoire de Québec* (Montreal: Boréal Express, 1983); Micheline Dumont and Nadia Fahmy-Eid, *Les Couventines: L'éducation des filles au Québec dans les congégations religieuses enseignantses, 1840–1960* (Montreal: Boréal Express, 1986).

3. On this see Peter Ward, "Courtship and Social Space in Nineteenth-Century English Canada," *Canadian*

Historical Review 68, 1 (1987): 35–62,
and especially his book, *Courtship,
Love, and Marriage in Nineteenth-
Century English Canada* (Montreal:
McGill-Queen's University Press,
1990).

4. Angus McLaren and Arlene Tigar
McLaren, *The Bedroom and the State:
The Changing Practices and Politics of
Contraception and Abortion in Canada,
1880–1980* (Toronto: McClelland and
Stewart, 1986); Serge Gagnon, *Plaisir
d'amour et crainte de Dieu: Sexualité et
confession au Bas-Canada* (Sainte Foy:
Les Presses de l'Université Laval,
1990).

5. Research on this topic is just begin-
ning. See especially Kathryn Harvey,
"To Love, Honour and Obey: Wife-
battering in Working-Class
Montreal, 1869–79," *Urban History
Review* 19, 2 (1990); James Snell,
"Marital Cruelty: Women and the
Nova Scotia Divorce Court, 1900–
1939," *Acadiensis* 18, 1 (1988); and
Constance Backhouse, *Petticoats and
Prejudice: Women and Law in
Nineteenth-Century Canada* (Toronto:
Women's Press, 1991), 167–99.

6. See, for example, Veronica Strong-
Boag, *The New Day Recalled: Lives of
Girls and Women in English Canada,
1919–1939* (Toronto: Copp Clark
Pitman, 1989), 145–77; Denise
Lemieux and Lucie Mercier, *Les
Femmes au tournant du siècle,
1880–1940: Ages de la vie, maternité et
quotidien* (Ville Saint-Laurent,
Institut québécois de recherche sur
la culture, 1989), 67–108.

7. On this theme and on the development of family history as a field see
especially Michael Anderson,
*Approaches to the History of the
Western Family, 1500–1914* (London:
Macmillan Press, 1980); Lawrence
Stone, "Family History in the 1980s,"
Journal of Interdisciplinary History 12
(1981): 41–87; Martine Ségalen,
"Sous les feux croisés de l'histoire et
de l'anthropologie: La famille en
Europe," *Revue d'histoire de l'Amérique
française* (hereafter *RHAF*) 39, 2
(1985); Tamara Hareven "Les grands
thèmes d'histoire de la famille aux

Etats-Unis," *RHAF* 39, 2 (1985);
Tamara Hareven, "Family History at
the Crossroads," *Journal of Family
History* 12, 1–3 (1987).

8. Anderson, *Approaches to the History
of the Western Family.*

9. Louise Tilly and Miriam Cohen
argue for adding the political/insti-
tutional approach, which emphasizes "connections between family
and other processes and institutions," in "Does the Family Have a
History? A Review of Theory and
Practice in Family History," *Social
Science History* 6 (1982). In
"Women's History and Family
History: Fruitful Collaboration or
Missed Connec-tion?" Louise Tilly
discusses both the points of convergence between women's history and
family history and the characteristics
that keep the two fields apart.
Journal of Family History 12, 1–3
(1987).

10. Jacques Henripin, *La population
canadienne au début du XVIIIe siècle:
nuptialité, fécondité, mortalité infantile*
(Paris: Presses universitaires de
France, 1954).

11. For a recent description of the work
of the PRDH see Jacques Légaré, "A
Population Register for Canada
under the French Régime: Context,
Scope, Content and Applications,"
Canadian Studies in Population 15, 1
(1988).

12. Gérard Bouchard, "Introduction à
l'étude de la société saguenayenne
aux XIXe et XXe siècles," *RHAF* 31, 1
(juin); Christian Pouyez et al., *Les
Saguenayens: Introduction à l'historie
des populations du Saguenay, XVIe–
XXe siècles* (Quebec: Presses de
l'Université du Québec, 1983).

13. Louise Dechêne, *Habitants et
marchands de Montréal au XVIIe siècle*
(Paris: Plon, 1974); Allan Greer,
*Peasant, Lord and Merchant: Rural
Society in Three Quebec Parishes,
1740–1840* (Toronto: University of
Toronto Press, 1985); David Gagan,
*Hopeful Travellers: Families, Land, and
Social Change in Mid-Victorian Peel
County, Canada West* (Toronto:

Ontario Historical Studies Series, 1981).

14. Michael B. Katz, *The People of Hamilton, Canada West: Family and Class in a Mid-Nineteenth-Century City* (Cambridge: Harvard University Press, 1975) and Michael B. Katz, Michael Doucet, and Mark J. Stern, *The Social Organization of Early Industrial Capitalism* (Cambridge: Harvard University Press, 1982).

15. Especially the questions posed by urban historians following the early work of Richard Sennett, *Families against the City: Middle-Class Homes of Industrial Chicago* (Cambridge: Harvard University Press, 1970), and Stephan Thernstrom, *Poverty and Progress: Social Mobility in a Nineteenth-Century City* (Cambridge: Harvard University Press, 1964); Stephan Thernstrom and Richard Sennett, eds., *Nineteenth-Century Cities: Essays in the New Urban History* (New Haven: Yale University Press, 1969).

16. Lutz K. Berkner and Tamara K. Hareven were especially influential in promoting use of the concept of the family life cycle. Hareven would subsequently insist on the importance of considering the life course as well. See Lutz K. Berkner, "The Stem Family and the Developmental Cycle of the Peasant Household: An Eighteenth Century Austrian Example," *American Historical Review* 77 (1972) and, for example, Tamara K. Hareven, "Cycles, Courses, and Cohorts: Reflections on the Theoretical and Methodological Approaches to the Historical Study of Family Development," *Journal of Social History* 12, 1 (1978). This approach appears to have been more widely embraced by American historians than by their colleagues in Europe.

17. The most important early studies were Peter Laslett with Richard Wall eds., *Household and Family in Past Time* (Cambridge: Cambridge University Press, 1972), which presented the influential work underway by the Cambridge Group for

the History of Population and Social Structure on the question of how family structures had changed across time, and Michael Anderson, *Family Structure in Nineteenth-Century Lancashire* (Cambridge: Cambridge University Press, 1971), which was a detailed study of the changes occurring among working-class families in an industrial city.

18. This is Edward Shorter's argument in his *The Making of the Modern Family* (New York: Basic Books, 1975). His arguments have been convincingly critiqued by feminist historians. See, especially, Joan W. Scott and Louise A. Tilly, "Women's Work and Family in Nineteenth-Century Europe," *Comparative Studies in Society and History* 17 (1975).

19. See especially Michael Katz who created a special category, of "unclassifiable occupations," that listed charwomen, dressmakers, nurses, and indeed most women's occupations, along with lunatics, the deceased, and the handicapped. *The People of Hamilton*, 348.

20. Outside Canada some of the most important works by women's historians that reflect this convergence have been Mary Ryan, *Cradle of the Middle Class: The Family in Oneida County, New York, 1780–1865* (New York: Cambridge University Press, 1981); Bonnie Smith, *Ladies of the Leisure Class: The Bourgeoises of Northern France in the Nineteenth Century* (New Jersey: Princeton University Press, 1981); Jane Lewis, ed., *Labour and Love: Women's Experience of Home and Family, 1850–1940* (Oxford: Basil Blackwell, 1986); and more recently Leonore Davidoff and Catherine Hall, *Family Fortunes: Men and Women of the English Middle Class, 1780–1850* (Chicago: University of Chicago Press, 1987).

21. See especially Andrée Lévesque, *La Norme et les déviantes: Des femmes au Québec pendant l'entre deux guerres* (Montreal: Les éditions du remue-ménage, 1989).

22. Jennifer Stoddart, "The Dorion Commission, 1929–1931: Quebec's Legal Elites Look at Women's Rights" in *Essays in the History of Canadian Law*, ed. David H. Flaherty (Toronto: University of Toronto Press, 1981); Constance Backhouse, "Nineteenth-Century Canadian Rape Law, 1800–1892," ibid.; Constance Backhouse, "Nineteenth-Century Canadian Prostitution Law: Reflections of a Discriminatory Society," *Histoire sociale/Social History* 18, 36 (1985).

23. In all fairness, these studies were never detached from a concern with the economy. Indeed the huge question of what changes the Industrial Revolution had brought to the structure of families was behind much of the research on changing patterns of marriage and family structure. Broadly speaking, however, there has been a shift from "the study of discrete domestic family or household structures to the nuclear family's interaction with the wider kinship group; and from the study of the family as a separate domestic unit to an examination of its interaction with the worlds of work, education, and correctional welfare institutions." Tamara Hareven, "Family History at the Crossroads," x.

24. Chad Gaffield, *Language, Schooling and Cultural Conflict: The Origins of the French-Language Controversy in Ontario* (Montreal: McGill-Queen's University Press, 1987). See also Susan Houston and Alison Prentice, *Schooling and Scholars in Nineteenth-Century Ontario* (Toronto: University of Toronto Press, 1988); Alison Prentice and Susan E. Houston, eds., *Family, School, and Society in Nineteenth-Century Canada* (Toronto: Oxford University Press, 1975).

25. See especially her *Family Time and Industrial Time: The Relationship between the Family and Work in a New England Industrial Community* (New York: Cambridge University Press, 1982).

26. Bettina Bradbury, *Working Families: Age, Gender, and Daily Survival in Industrializing Montreal* (forthcoming).

27. Katz, *The People of Hamilton*; Katz, Doucet, and Stern, *The Social Organization of Early Industrial Capitalism*.

28. While Constance Backhouse's book *Petticoats and Prejudice* is largely framed within a women's history approach, every subject relates to the history of the family.

29. For a much more wide-ranging discussion of divorce see his *In the Shadow of the Law: Divorce in Canada, 1900–1939* (Toronto: University of Toronto Press, 1991).

30. For a good introduction to studies of immigrant women, many of which deal with women's roles in the family, see Jean Burnet, ed., *Looking into My Sister's Eyes: An Exploration in Women's History*. See also Bruna Ramirez and Michele Del Balzo, "The Italians of Montreal: From Sojourning to Settlement, 1900–1920" in *Little Italies in North America*, ed. Robert Harney and Vincenze Scarpaci (Toronto: Multicultural History Society, 1981); and Franca Iacovetta, *Such Hard-working People: Italian Immigrants in Postwar Toronto* (forthcoming); Varpu Lindstom-Best, *Defiant Sisters: A Social History of Finnish Immigrant Women in Canada* (Toronto: Multicultural History Society of Ontario, 1988).

NEW FRANCE: FORMING FAMILIES IN A NEW LAND

GENDER IMBALANCE, LES FILLES DU ROI, AND CHOICE OF SPOUSE IN NEW FRANCE[◇]

YVES LANDRY[✦]

○

The early European settlement of New France is an important period for family history. The vast majority of immigrants in the early years of settlement were men. The gender imbalance in the marriage market prior to 1680 created an unusual situation that led to variations in customary marriage practices.[1] These can be studied thanks to the historical and demographic data reconstructed from seventeenth- and eighteenth-century parish registers that are contained in the Population Register of Old Quebec.[2]

Over 700 women, known as the *filles du roi*, were sent to populate the St. Lawrence valley between 1663 and 1673. The mechanisms of Canadian family formation in the seventeenth century cannot be discussed without examining their role. In only eleven years, the number of *filles du roi* crossing the Atlantic represented almost half the total number of women immigrants arriving in the 150 years between the earliest settlement and the Conquest. Yet, because men dominated among immigrants, the *filles du roi* represented only 8 percent of all immigrants who settled in Canada under

[◇] This article has not been previously published. It summarizes the results of the analysis of the marriage rate of the *filles du roi* published in my book *Orphelines en France, pionnières au Canada: les Filles du roi au XVIIe siècle* (Montreal: Leméac, 1991). This work was produced within the Programme de recherche en démographie historique de l'Université Montréal which is subsidized by the Social Sciences and Humanities Research Council of Canada, the Fonds FAR, and the Université de Montréal.

[✦] Translated by Jane Parniak.

the French Regime. Their arrival got the young colony started demographically and socially. In less than ten years following their arrival, average annual population growth almost doubled, increasing from 5 to 9 percent, while the total population almost tripled to approximately 8500 people in 1673. But most importantly, between 1660 and 1670, the natural growth rate rose sharply from less than one-third to more than three-quarters of the total growth rate. This dramatic demographic shift was entirely contingent on the rapid marriage rate of the *filles du roi*. Analysis of how these women chose their husbands helps to illustrate the atmosphere of urgency and haste that characterized marital matters in the colony at the time. It also shows how these women acted in a situation where the gender balance was decidedly in their favour. First, however, it is important to look at their background and the state of the marriage market prior to 1680.

THE BACKGROUND OF THE FILLES DU ROI

The life of most of the *filles du roi* had been marked by both economic and cultural poverty before leaving France. More than a third of them came from the Hôpital général de Paris, where the diet was meagre enough to cause stunted growth. Only 36 percent were able to sign their name on their marriage act, despite the fact that writing was supposed to have been taught at the Hôpital général and that they came from Paris, a city that was intellectually far ahead of the rest of France, and where the literacy rate has been reported at 75 percent. Even among the *filles du roi* who came from noble or bourgeois background, only half could write their names, although historians suggest that the upper classes were 100 percent literate in France by the end of the seventeenth century.[3]

The lot of these women was undoubtedly tied to their tragic family lives. Declarations on their marriage certificates and contracts suggest that close to 65 percent of them had lost their fathers before they reached adulthood. This percentage indicates a paternal mortality rate almost 20 percent higher than the French averages during this period. Orphaned, usually illiterate, and often having spent years within the Hôpital général du Paris, the *filles du roi* clearly bore the scars of past misfortune when they left their native land.

THE MARRIAGE MARKET

A thorough reconstruction of the marriage market in New France prior to 1680 would require knowing the exact annual numbers of men and women in the colony as well as their age and marital status. These conditions are satisfactorily fulfilled for the women, very few of whom escaped observation, but the situation is less clearcut for the men, many of whom were casual immigrants with demographically indeterminate profiles. However, current research, combined with some hypotheses allows for annual estimates of the numbers of marriageable men and women.[4] Comparison of the numbers in figure 1 with the historical censuses of 1666 and 1667, and with Marcel Trudel's reconstitution of the 1663, 1666, and 1667 censuses,[5] suggests that my estimates of the single male population are low, so that the discrepancy between marriageable men and women would in fact have been even greater than the figures suggest.

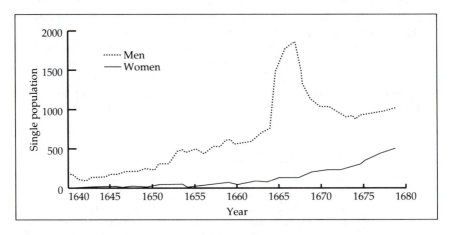

FIGURE 1 *CHANGES IN THE ANNUAL NUMBERS OF SINGLE MEN AND WOMEN IN THE MARRIAGE MARKET, NEW FRANCE, 1640–79*

Despite the gaps in the data, figure 1 clearly depicts the predominance of male immigrants and, by implication, the tremendous value of women in the Canadian marriage market prior to 1680. There were always far more single men than women, particularly between 1665 and 1668, when the troops from the Carignan regiment were stationed in the colony. Until the beginning of the 1670s, there were between six and fourteen times more eligible men than women (figure 2). Analysis of the workings of the marriage market suggests that approximately nine out of ten of the marriageable men in New France during this period were immigrants. Many returned to France precisely because of the shortage of women. Women also entered the marriage market of New France by immigrating. In contrast to men, however, they left it by marrying.

As female immigration ceased at the beginning of the 1670s, this pattern changed radically. More and more young men and women who had been born in the colony began to enter the marriage market. The proportion entering through immigration fell proportionately. As more men were able to find spouses, the numbers returning to France fell off and some of the pressure on women to marry rapidly gradually eased. By 1680, the ratio of marriageable women to men had dropped to approximately two to one.

The *filles du roi* clearly played a fundamental role at a time when first-generation *Canadiennes* were still scarce and hundreds of men were obliged either to take work in the fur trade or to return to France. It would clearly have been in the interest of the authorities to continue the immigration of the *filles du roi* for several more years to produce a more balanced number of men and women within the colony. This would have reduced the surplus of single males, of whom there were still at least five hundred in 1679. Furthermore, immigrant women would have provided spouses of a more appropriate age than the *Canadiennes*, many of whom were barely pubescent when they married.

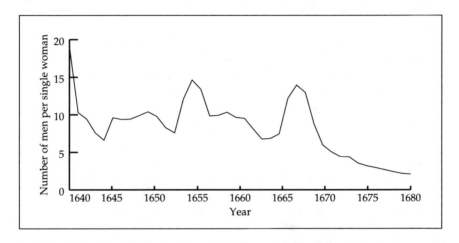

F I G U R E 2 *PERCENTAGE OF MEN IN THE MARRIAGE MARKET, NEW FRANCE, 1640–79*

MARRIAGE RATES AMONG THE FILLES DU ROI

The *filles du roi* were sent to New France primarily to satisfy the colony's need for marriageable women. Did they fulfil these expectations? To answer this question we must look at how many married and how quickly they married as well as at the numbers who either died or returned to France without marrying.

Without thorough immigration records, a list of the *filles du roi* has to be culled from other references to women who arrived between 1663 and 1673. Single persons were less conspicuous than those who lived in families and appeared regularly in parish registers, so it is impossible to make a precise count of single women and widows who did not marry. However, genealogical research reveals that at least thirty-two *filles du roi* came to Canada but did not marry. Most of them are mentioned either as witnesses at the marriages of their fellow immigrants or as parties in marriage contracts that were subsequently annulled. There are no further references in the archives, so we assume that the vast majority returned to France, most of them during the first year of their arrival, some after three or even four years. Only one, Madeleine de Roybon d'Alonne, a lady of minor nobility and a famous adventurer, remained in Canada until she was elderly; she was still single when she died in Montreal in 1718 at the age of seventy-two.

The estimate that thirty-two *filles du roi*, or 4 percent of the total, did not marry in New France, is definitely conservative, since other immigrants could have lived for a short time in the colony without appearing in official documents. Nevertheless, this figure does signify that the marriage market exerted a strong pull on single women during this period of marked imbalance of the sexes. The full significance of the calculation becomes apparent if we consider only the *filles du roi* who settled in the colony. Only one out of 738, or 0.14 percent, died single at age fifty or over, compared to close to 10 percent of *Canadiennes* born at the end of the seventeenth and beginning of the eighteenth centuries or to approximately 7 percent of French women born between 1660 and 1664.[6] It is quite likely, moreover, that the pressures of the marriage market compelled the *filles du roi* not only to marry in great numbers, but also to marry soon after their arrival.

MARRIAGE SCHEDULE

Investigation of the schedule of first Canadian marriages of the *filles du roi* requires precise calculation of the interval between their arrival in the country and the celebration of their first marriage. We first had to determine, for each year between 1663 and 1673, the exact arrival date of the first ships transporting these immigrants or, failing that, of the first ship that anchored outside of Quebec. This procedure is not ideal, as some women may have travelled on other ships that arrived later in the season. Comparison of the intervals calculated for each annual arrival with the observations of contemporaries does, however, substantiate our overall results. The *filles du roi* waited an average of five months to marry, and more than 80 percent of them married within the first six months. These figures may be surprising at first glance, since the marriages of these women are notorious in historiography and folklore for being extremely hasty. The King's orders were in fact formal: courtships were to be kept to a strict minimum. A ruling handed down in 1670 and repeated the following year enjoined "all Voluntary Companions and other persons old enough to enter into marriage to marry within fifteen days of the arrival of the ships carrying the *filles* under Pain of being deprived of the rights to any kind of fishing, hunting, and trading with the natives."[7] Writing in 1703, the Baron de Lahontan is responsible for spreading the idea that all *filles du roi* married within fifteen days of their arrival.[8] Our analysis shows that this was not the case, even though they married much more quickly than the women who immigrated between 1632 and 1656, who waited roughly one year before marrying.[9]

The first official act publicizing a promise of marriage between a man and a woman was usually the betrothal, "carried out in the Church, in the presence of the Priest and Witnesses."[10] Before this custom was practically prohibited at the end of the seventeenth century,[11] most future spouses apparently used it to formalize their intentions for close to 60 percent of the marriage certificates registered in the parish of Notre-Dame-de-Québec from July 1659 until the end of 1662 mention the betrothal ceremony.[12] A random one-fifth sampling of all the 565 acts for first marriages of the *filles du roi* in the colony shows that the betrothal was mentioned in more than 65 percent of the cases, increasing to 92 percent in certificates of the Quebec register alone. Despite, or perhaps because of, the brevity of courtships, future spouses were anxious to formalize their relationship in an attempt to reinforce the tenuous bonds between them.

Alongside this ritual verbal promise, the couples could also make a written promise and stipulate the material terms of their union in a marriage contract. This procedure was not strictly necessary, since the *Coutume de Paris* made provisions for its absence, but most of the future spouses went to a notary in a gesture that betokened both social conformity and goodwill.[13] The data compiled by Marcel Trudel for the period from 1632 to 1662 suggest that marriage contracts were drawn up for more than 65 percent of marriages.[14] This percentage is consistent with Hubert Charbonneau's calculation for the seventeenth century as a whole.[15] In the following century, roughly 80 percent of couples signed a marriage contract, a rate comparable with those observed in France during the same era.[16] Among the *filles du roi*, 82 percent signed a contract for their first marriage, while 62 percent did so for subsequent marriages. The last figure may seem normal for the time, but the first is definitely high and, like the betrothal ceremony, could reflect a desire to create a bond between two people who hardly knew each other and to confirm a decision that the vagaries of time and chance might alter.

Almost all the marriage contracts were signed prior to the religious ceremony. Roughly half were concluded in the ten days preceding the wedding; in almost nine cases out of ten, the interval was one month or less. These results corroborate Charbonneau's results for the entire seventeenth century, but the average interval of nineteen days calculated for unions in which a contract preceded the marriage represents less than half of the forty-one-day interval calculated by Trudel for the period from 1632 to 1662.[17] The discrepancy could be explained in two ways. Firstly, Trudel looked at both rural and urban marriages, while 83 percent of the *filles du roi* had their first marriage entered in an urban register. Secondly, there was intense pressure on the *filles du roi* when they arrived in Canada, which reduced the interval between the marriage contract and the wedding to an average of seventeen days, or one week less than for subsequent marriages. Once the marriage agreements were signed, the *filles du roi* and their future husbands had literally promised to solemnize the eagerly awaited marriage before the Church "as soon as possible."

Before they could be blessed in marriage, the couple had to wait for the publication of the banns, to take place three times as stipulated by the Council of Trent. Table 1 shows that here again, the *filles du roi* clearly diverged from common practice. Prior to 1663, only one out of four cases were granted a dispensation from publishing their banns, but the ratio rose to more than half for the wards of the King. This was most likely due to the relative isolation of the *filles du roi*: their lack of connections with other immigrants meant there were no potential objections regarding their liberty to marry, often making it futile to go through the long process of publishing the banns.

TABLE 1   *PUBLICATION OF BANNS FOR A SAMPLE OF FIRST MARRIAGES OF FILLES DU ROI, 1632–62*

	1632–62		Filles du roi	
	Number	Percentage	Number	Percentage
Publication of 3 banns	278	76	48	47
Publication of 2 banns	51	14	22	21
Publication of 1 bann	27	7	28	27
Dispensation from 3 banns	9	3	5	5
Total	365	100	103	100
Undetermined	41		10	
Combined	406		113	

Sources: 1632–62: Trudel, *Histoire de la Nouvelle-France*, 538. *Filles du roi*: random one-fifth sample.

A quarter of the marriage certificates in our sampling specify the exact dates of publication of the banns. This information, coupled with the dates of marriage contracts, makes it possible to establish the typical chronology of the days preceding the wedding. In almost every case (26 of 27), the banns were published only after the marriage contract was signed. The publications then followed in quick succession (table 2), sometimes (in 8 out of 36 cases) even in violation of the rule "that there shall be at least two or three clear days between each, by three Sundays or Holidays."[18]

TABLE 2   *INTERVAL BETWEEN MARRIAGE CONTRACT, BANNS, AND WEDDING FOR FIRST MARRIAGES OF FILLES DU ROI*

	Interval in days			
Interval	Between contract and first bann	Between first and second bann	Between second and third bann	Between third bann and marriage
Average	16	5	5	5
Median	2	6	4	2
Modal	1	1	3	1
Number	26	20	16	28

Source: random one-fifth sample.

Given the hastiness with which they chose partners when they arrived in Canada, it is hardly surprising that many of the *filles du roi* regretted their decision before it had been made official by the priest. Figure 3 illustrates the complicated path followed by many immigrant women prior to their first marriage in the St. Lawrence valley. If all *filles du roi*, including those who returned to France or died without marrying, are considered, it can be seen that more than 15 percent of the women who concluded a first marriage contract (96 of 621) did not ultimately marry their fiancé. If only the immigrants who settled in the colony are considered, the rate of first marriages preceded by at least one cancellation of the marriage contract comes to 11 percent (79 of 737), which is double the rate for subsequent marriages (11 of 218, or 5 percent) and triple the rate calculated from Trudel's data for 1632 to 1662 (15 of 449, or 3.3 percent).[19] These results, which highlight the instability of the prenuptial relations of the *filles du roi*, are all the more striking in that, even after a first rupture, close to 13 percent of the women who concluded a second marriage contract (8 of 63) quickly cancelled it.[20] The time taken in choosing a candidate was a decisive factor in the outcome of the relationship. After a first marriage contract was cancelled, a second contract was concluded after an average interval of only twenty-two days (N = 7) if the second contract was also cancelled. By contrast, there was an average interval of more than 111 days (N = 62)[21] if the two parties ending up getting married.

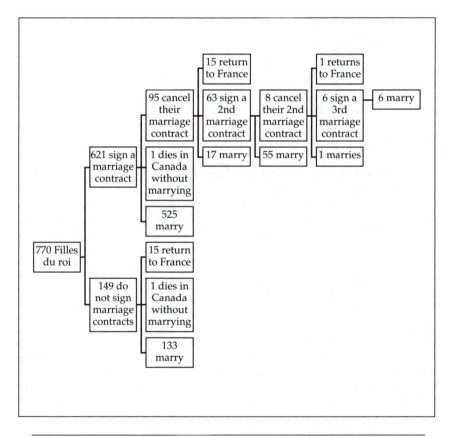

F I G U R E 3 *NUMBER OF MARRIAGE CONTRACTS SIGNED BY FILLES DU ROI BEFORE THEIR FIRST MARRIAGE*

Given the demand for women on the marriage market, it might be supposed that, if the first relationship failed, it would have been easier for the *filles du roi* than for the men to find a new partner. The results presented in table 3 substantiate this hypothesis. Once freed from an earlier promise, the women were back before the notary or priest seven times faster than were the men. From this it seems plausible that the women were primarily responsible for revoking marriage promises, since they had little to risk in looking for a better partner.[22] However, the archives have little to say on this point.

TABLE 3   *DISTRIBUTION OF CANCELLED MARRIAGE CONTRACTS ACCORDING TO FATE OF THE PARTIES*

Fate	Women	Men
Signs a new marriage contract (or marries without a contract) after waiting:		
0–30 days	48	31
31–90 days	15	5
91–365 days	11	10
more than 365 days	4	29
Total	78	75
Average wait	108 days	741 days
Marries at an undetermined date	9	3
Dies in Canada (without marrying)	1	6
Returns to France	16	20
Combined	104	104

The Diocesan Tribunal had sole legal jurisdiction for dissolving marriage promises, whether it was a matter of amicable settlement or an actual trial in case of disagreement.[23] Since freedom of consent was required for the marriage to be valid, the official could not force recalcitrant partners to make good their promises if there was disagreement between the parties.[24] However, the civil judge could order a man who backed out of his commitment to pay the woman a sum of money for damages and interest. The recalcitrant woman usually escaped this sanction but, in return, had to give back to the man the deposit he had made as security on his promise.[25] It's not surprising that nothing is found in the religious archives of New France about cancelled engagements and marriage contracts, since the Diocesan Tribunal was established around 1685 and the first preserved marriage files date back only to the nineteenth century. Yet even the legal archives yield practically no information about possible disagreements between the *filles du roi* and their rejected or fickle fiancés.[26] This suggests that the rejected partner usually agreed to the breakup, which would only be normal after such brief courtships that hardly gave two people a chance to become attached to each other. The guilty party could not have made much restitution in any case; the man was often so poor that he would have been unable to pay any monetary compensation whatsoever, and a woman who had received no deposit had nothing to return. In forty-two out of 104 cancelled contracts, the notary added a footnote to the agreement, usually stating that the two partners "were voluntarily released from and acquitted of any claims they might have had with respect to each other," all without "any expenses for damages and interest."[27]

We know nothing about why these promises of marriage were broken. Jean-Louis Flandrin simply imputes it to lack of love.[28] This is a reasonable hypothesis, given the hastiness with which most relationships were formed and sometimes dissolved, but it would be risky to assume that every couple who ultimately sanctioned their promise by marrying did so out of love, especially in view of the cultural, social, and age differences between many spouses.

CULTURAL DIFFERENCES

As they crossed the Atlantic, the *filles du roi* might have thought that in adopting a new country, they would have to choose a husband from among the men born in the colony. In fact only 3 percent of the women married men born in New France; more than 95 percent married French immigrants like themselves. This situation apparently reflects the composition of the male marriage market, which largely consisted of single male immigrants.

The marriage of spouses who were both born in France is significant only in light of their regional and environmental background. Table 4 gives a breakdown of first marriages of French spouses according to their regions of origin. There is a relatively low rate of endogamy, which can be traced to differences in the areas of origin of male and female immigrants. Among individuals whose regional background is known, close to half of the women came from the Paris region and less than 15 percent came from the west of France, whereas almost 43 percent of the men were born in the west and only 8 percent came from the Paris region. The endogamy rate is only 18.7 percent compared to 33 percent for other pioneer couples who settled before 1680.[29] Marcel Trudel did a similar calculation for marriages that took place between 1632 and 1662; based on smaller geographical units: the provinces of France. He found that only 12.7 percent of marriages (52 of 408) brought together spouses who came from the same province or who were born in Canada.[30]

Shared regional background bore little weight when the *filles du roi* chose their marriage partners. If cases of indeterminate regional origins are excluded, the rate of homogamy, or marriage to those of similar origins, is low (0.116).[31] It is less than half that observed in the marriages of other pioneers who settled before 1680.[32] Heterogeneity of background does not seem to have been an obstacle in choosing a spouse. In this the marriages of these women do not seem very different from those observed by Jean Quéniart in the eighteenth and nineteenth centuries in coastal regions of Brittany, Normandy, Maine, and Anjou. He did not find that provincial boundaries in and of themselves defined limits when it came to choosing a spouse. Rather, he argued, they "played a role only insofar as provincial identity helped in constructing a network of relationships that went beyond the bonds of proximity."[33]

TABLE 4   DISTRIBUTION OF MARRIAGES OF FILLES DU ROI BASED ON REGION OF ORIGIN OF SPOUSES

Man's region of origin	Woman's region of origin												
	Brittany	Normandy	Paris	Loire	North	East	West	Centre	South	Total	Undetermined	Combined	%
Brittany	0	2	16	0	0	3	1	1	0	23	3	26	3.9
Normandy	3	32	46	11	5	9	12	1	0	119	7	126	19.0
Paris	0	15	28	1	2	3	5	0	0	54	0	54	8.2
Loire	2	4	35	4	2	5	4	0	1	57	2	59	8.9
North	0	5	12	2	1	1	4	0	0	25	1	26	3.9
East	0	5	5	1	1	0	3	2	0	17	0	17	2.6
West	6	44	123	14	5	22	54	1	3	272	11	283	42.8
Centre	1	3	9	2	0	1	2	0	0	18	0	18	2.7
South	1	9	23	3	0	8	6	1	0	51	2	53	8.0
Total	13	119	297	38	16	52	91	6	4	636	26	662	100.0
Undetermined	0	5	6	1	1	1	4	0	0	18	19	37	
Combined	13	124	303	39	17	53	95	6	4	654	45	699	
%	2.0	19.0	46.3	6.0	2.6	8.1	14.5	0.9	0.6	100.0			

Nor did whether the partners came from a rural or an urban background make much difference. Given the predominantly urban background of the *filles du roi*, and the largely rural origins of the men, it is not surprising that in more than half of the marriages (348 of 626, or 55.6 percent) the spouses came from different backgrounds. After their marriage, nearly one in five couples would lead an essentially rural life, despite their lack of experience in such an environment.

TABLE 5 *DISTRIBUTION OF FIRST MARRIAGES OF FILLES DU ROI BASED ON RURAL OR URBAN BACKGROUND OF FRENCH SPOUSES*

Man's background	Woman's background							
	Urban		Rural		Total		Undeter-mined	Com-bined
	N	%	N	%	N	%	N	N
Urban	140	22.4	57	9.1	197	31.5	9	206
Rural	291	46.5	138	22.0	429	68.5	11	440
Total	431	68.9	195	31.1	626	100.0	20	646
Undeter-mined	15		7		22		31	53
Combined	446		202		648		51	699

Literacy was a slightly more important factor than region of origin or rural or urban background in determining who would marry whom. Still, the level of homogamy (0.258) was much lower among these couples than those found in seventeenth- and eighteenth-century European populations. Overall roughly one quarter of men and women were able to write their names on their marriage acts or contracts. While this figure seems low for the women given their largely urban backgrounds, it does seem to correspond with the data pertaining to the overall French male population during the same period.[34]

TABLE 6 *DISTRIBUTION OF FIRST MARRIAGES OF FILLES DU ROI BASED ON SPOUSE'S SIGNING ABILITY*

Men	Women							
	Able to sign		Unable to sign		Total		Undeter-mined	Com-bined
	N	%	N	%	N	%	N	N
Able to sign	58	9.7	107	18.0	165	27.7	4	169
Unable to sign	67	11.3	363	61.0	430	72.3	13	443
Total	125	21.0	470	79.0	595	100.0	17	612
Undetermined	34		65		99		26	125
Combined	159		535		694		43	737

SOCIAL DIFFERENCES

Chance, rather than shared literacy, illiteracy, or geographical origin, thus seems to have dictated these women's choice of husband. Or was a shared class background important? The abundance of sources generated by these first Canadians (especially parish registers, censuses, and notarial acts) makes it possible to determine the social origins of 95 percent (700 of 737) of the first husbands of the *filles du roi*. In contrast, because so many of these women were orphans and far from their families of origin, it is only possible to identify the occupation of 23 percent of their fathers. As a result, the occupations of a woman's spouse and father are known for less than 22 percent of the marriages (164 of 737).

Despite these shortcomings in the data, the figures in table 7 do suggest several conclusions. Similarity of social background was not much more important than the other factors already considered. Only 25 percent of the *filles du roi* (42 of 164) married husbands of similar social background to their fathers. This compares with Marcel Trudel's finding that 60 percent of all marriages celebrated in the colony in the years before their arrival (between 1632 and 1662) were among couples of similar standing.[35] In France, historians have found 44 percent homogamy at Tourouvre-au-Perche between 1665 and 1770,[36] 57 percent at Vraiville, a small Normandy parish in the eighteenth century,[37] and 52 percent in the Basse-Meuse of Liège in the nineteenth century.[38] Clearly this high incidence of social intermingling was quite unusual during the Ancien Régime, a product of the arrival of the *filles du roi* into the particular frontier conditions and demographic imbalance of New France. Over a longer period, people were more likely to marry those of similar origins. A study of Quebec City in the period leading up to 1760, for instance, shows that occupational endogamy was a widespread practice, particularly among the children of military officers, civil officials, and merchants.[39]

AGE DIFFERENCES

Large age gaps between most *filles du roi* and their husbands added to the differences of social, economic, and geographical background that distinguished their marriages from those of other settlers or from their French compatriots. Six out of ten of the *filles du roi* were between the ages of fifteen and twenty-four when they married for the first time in Canada. A similar proportion of husbands was between twenty and twenty-nine years old. The average age at which women married was twenty-four, whereas for men it was twenty-eight, a difference of four and a half years. There was little difference in the age of men and women at the time of migration. This difference, then, is essentially a function of the time these men, who were mostly hired civilians or soldiers, had to wait before marrying, either because there were few available women or because they had not yet acquired the material basis necessary for marriage. Obtaining a land grant or buying a piece of land, clearing it, and constructing the necessary buildings all took time.

TABLE 7 *SOCIO-ECONOMIC CATEGORY OF HUSBAND*

Socio-economic category of father	Socio-economic category of husband											Undetermined	Combined
	Aristocracy		Professionals		Farmers		Tradesmen		Total			
	N	%	N	%	N	%	N	%	N	%		
Aristocracy	26	15.9	17	10.4	42	25.6	3	1.8	88	53.7	5	93
Professionals	5	3.1	12	7.3	37	22.6	2	1.2	56	34.2	2	58
Farmers	1	0.6	2	1.2	4	2.4	1	0.6	8	4.8	0	8
Tradesmen	0	0.0	2	1.2	10	6.1	0	0.0	12	7.3	1	13
Total	32	19.6	33	20.1	93	56.7	6	3.6	164	100.0	8	172
Undetermined	21		94		398		23		536		29	565
Combined	53		127		491		29		700		37	737

The resulting age gap between these women and their husbands is greater than that observed in seventeenth-century France, but is less than that estimated for all first marriages occuring in New France either between 1640 and 1679 or 1680 and 1699.[40]

Some of the age gaps between the *filles du roi* and their husbands were extremely large. In almost one-fifth of the unions more than ten years separated the spouses. In over half the cases the disparity was greater than five years. Some of the gaps were closer to what would have been expected among the first generation of native born *canadiennes* who married in a period of extreme imbalance between the sexes. One *fille du roi* for instance, married an immigrant thirty-two years her senior.[41] Marguerite Charpentier, in contrast, was nearly sixty when she married a man thirty-six years younger than herself.[42]

TABLE 8   DISTRIBUTION OF AGE DIFFERENCES BETWEEN PREVIOUSLY UNMARRIED SPOUSES FOR FIRST MARRIAGES OF FILLES DU ROI

Age difference in years*	Number	Percentage
−11 or less	8	1.6
−6 – −10	27	5.4
−1 – −5	86	17.1
0	26	5.2
1–5	131	26.1
6–10	140	27.9
11–15	52	10.3
16–20	22	4.4
21–25	6	1.2
26 or more	4	0.8
Combined	502	100.0
Average difference	4.5 years	
Median difference	4.2 years	

*Age of husband minus age of wife

CONCLUSION

This study of the first marriages of the women known as the *filles du roi*, who arrived in the New World between 1663 and 1673, shows that their marriage practices diverged in a number of ways from nuptial behaviour observed throughout the seventeenth century, both in France and in New France. Cultural and social endogamy, whether measured by region of origin, rural or urban background, literacy, or socio-economic status was unusually low. The intense intermixing that characterized these marriages is inextricably tied to the sexual imbalance in the colony and the related atmosphere of urgency that accompanied the arrival of the women. The short interval between their arrival in Canada and the religious ceremony, and the frequency of dispensation from banns point to the precipitous nature of these marriages. The fact that spouses were chosen in haste highlights the state of expectancy of the male population—many of whom had long been deprived of women—and the women's apparent acceptance of their mission as future wives. On the other hand, lacking both kinship ties in the colony and experience in a frontier-type situation, it would have been difficult for most of these women to survive for long without a spouse. The large number of cancelled marriage contracts suggests that they could take some advantage from their situation and not necessarily accept just any partner. It would be interesting to know whether the haste of marriage meant that more ended up separating from their husbands than other immigrant or locally born women. Research currently underway using judicial archives and notarial minutes should soon provide us with answers to this question.[43]

The *filles du roi* were clearly instrumental in establishing a more equal balance of the sexes in the marriageable population of mid- to late seventeenth-century New France. Had they not been sent to the colony, the marriage rate could not have increased as it did during the early years of royal government.[44] The scarcity of wives, far more than the Iroquois threat, would have kept the population as low as it had been at the beginning of the century.

NOTES

1. Hubert Charbonneau, Bertrand Desjardins, André Guillemette, Yves Landry, Jacques Légaré, and François Nault, *Birth of a Population: The French who Settled in the St. Lawrence Valley in the XVIIth Century* (Newark: University of Delaware Press, 1991) Raymond Roy and Hubert Charbonneau, "La nuptialité en situation de déséquilibre des sexes: le Canada du XVIIe siècle," *Annales de démographie historique* (1978): 285–94.

2. Jacques Légaré, "A Population Register for Canada Under the French Regime: Context, Scope, Content and Applications," *Canadian Studies in Population* 15, 1 (1988): 1–16. Yves Landry, "Le registre de population de la Nouvelle-France: un outil pratique au service de la démographie historique et de l'histoire sociale," *Revue d'histoire de l'Amérique française* (hereinafter *RHAF*) 38, 3 (Winter 1985), 423–26.

3. Alain Blum and Jacques Houdaille, "L'alphabétisation aux XVIIIe et

XIXe siècles: l'illusion parisienne?" *Population*, 40th year, no. 6 (Nov.–Dec. 1985), 951.

4. For each year, boys and girls living in the country (born in Canada or not) who had reached the ages of 14 and 12 respectively, unmarried immigrants at least 14 and 12 years old when they arrived in Québec, and widowed persons enter the marriage market. Single persons who marry, enter a religious institution, die, or emigrate during that year withdraw from the market. For a discussion of methodological problems related to the statistical estimate of the number of single immigrants (unmentioned in the population register), see Landry, *Orphelines en France*.

5. Hubert Charbonneau and Jacques Légaré, "La population du Canada aux recensements de 1666 et 1667," *Population*, 22nd year, no. 6 (Nov.–Dec. 1967): 1047–54. Marcel Trudel, "Le recensement de 1666 et l'absence du quart de la population civile,"

Mémoires de la Société généalogique canadienne-française 40, 4 (Winter 1989): 258–69.

6. Hubert Charbonneau, *Vie et mort de nos ancêtres. Etude démographique* (Montreal: Les Presses de l'Université de Montréal, 1975) 154–58. Lorraine Gadoury, Yves Landry, and Hubert Charbonneau, "Démographie différentielle en Nouvelle-France: villes et campagnes," *RHAF* 38, 3 (Winter 1985), 366. Louis Henry and Jacques Houdaille, "Célibat et âge au mariage aux XVIIIe et XIXe siècles en France. I.—Célibat définitif," *Population*, 33rd year, no. 1 (Jan.–Feb. 1978), 50.

7. Ruling to force single men to marry the women who arrive from France. . . , Quebec, 20 Oct. 1671, in Pierre-Georges Roy, *Inventaire des ordonnances des intendants de la Nouvelle-France conservées aux Archives provinciales de Québec*, vol. III, (Beauceville: L'Eclaireur, 1919), 266. See also Mémoire de Talon sur le Canada au ministre Colbert, Quebec, 10 Nov. 1670, in *Rapport de l'Archiviste de la province du Québec pour 1930–1931* (Quebec: Paradis, 1931), 132, and lettre du ministre Colbert à Talon, 11 Feb. 1671, ibid., 145.

8. "There wasn't even one left after 15 days." *Nouveaux Voyages de M. le Baron de Lahontan, in l'Amérique Septentrionale*, vol. I, La Haye, Frères l'Honoré, 1703, p. 11 (Lahontan, *Oeuvres complètes*, annotated ed. by Réal Ouellet and Alain Beaulieu (Montreal: Les Presses de l'Université de Montréal, 1990), 1: 266).

9. Marcel Trudel, *Histoire de la Nouvelle-France*, vol. 3; *La seigneurie des Cent-Associés (1627–1663)*, tome 2; *La société* (Montreal, Fides, 1983), 78.

10. *Ritual du diocese de Québec publié par l'ordre de Monseigneur l'evêque de Québec* (Paris: Simon Langlois, 1703), 339.

11. Following, it seems, infringements of the rule prohibiting "fiancés to live in the same house [and] to consort familiarly with each other." Ibid. Additions to the Synodal Statutes, settled in the third meeting of the synod held in Quebec on 27 Feb. 1698, in *Mandements, lettres pastorales et circulaires des évêques de Québec*, edited by H. Têtu and C.-O. Gagnon (Quebec: Coté, 1887), 376.

12. Trudel, *Histoire de la Nouvelle-France*, 537.

13. Louise Dechêne, *Habitants et marchands de Montréal au XVIIe siècle* (Paris: Plon, 1974), 418–19. Trudel, *Histoire de la Nouvelle-France*, 517–34.

14. Trudel, ibid., 518.

15. Charbonneau, *Vie et mort de nos ancêtres*, 151–52.

16. Louis Lavallée, "Les archives notariales et l'histoire sociale de la Nouvelle-France" *RHAF* 28, 3 (Dec. 1974), 388–89. Louis Lemoine, *Longueuil en Nouvelle-France* (Longueuil: Société d'histoire de Longueuil, 1975), 47. Yves Landry, *Quelques aspects du comportement démographique des troupes de terre envoyées au Canada pendant la guerre de Sept Ans* (M.A. thesis, Université de Montréal, 1977), 99.

17. Trudel, *Histoire de la Nouvelle-France*, 535.

18. *Rituel du diocese de Quebec*, 340.

19. Trudel, *Histoire de la Nouvelle-France*, 518.

20. Take, for instance, the inordinate case of Marie Ducoudray, who on 25 Aug. 1670, concluded a marriage contract with Jean Jouanne (notary Romain Becquet); the fact that neither signature appears on the document would seem to indicate that the parties immediately revoked their decision. Three days later, before the same notary, Marie Ducoudray got engaged to Robert Galien, but once again the relationship was shortlived: before the end of the day, the notary added a footnote to the contract rendering it "null and void." The next day, Ducoudray came to an agreement

with François Grenet and ended up marrying him 17 days later.

21. This result incorporates the period of almost six years that Marguerite Jasselin waited to marry after breaking off an earlier engagement with Robert Gaumond (notary Romain Becquet, 8 Nov. 1670). Before marrying Mathurin Lelièvre in Oct. 1674, she gave birth in March 1674 to an illegitimate child whose fate was not settled until January 1676 by the Sovereign Council. If this long interval had not been retained, the average waiting period would have been 78 days.

22. The converse was observed in trials for breach of contract in the Cambrai diocese in the seventeenth and eighteenth centuries: "Who initiates the suit in rupture petitions? We cannot proffer an exact percentage, but clearly the man takes the initiative in petitions for breakups," A. Lottin and K. Pasquier, "Les fiançailles rompues ou empêchées," in *La désunion du couple sous l'Ancien Régime: L'exemple du Nord*, ed. Alain Lottin (Villeneuve d'Ascq and Paris: Université de Lille III and Editions universitaires, 1975), 58.

23. Jean Gaudemet, *Le mariage en Occident: Les moeurs et le droit* (Paris: Cerf, 1987), 362.

24. Although in the fifteenth and sixteenth centuries judges ordered the fiancés to marry, they revised this procedure in the following century in compliance with the Tametsi decree of the Council of Trent except, in rare cases, to force a man to marry woman if he had had sexual relations with her. Claude-Joseph de Ferrière, *Dictionnaire de droit et de practique, contenant l'explication des termes de croit, d'ordonnances, de coutumes & de practique. Avec les jurisdictions de France* (Paris: Barrois, 1771), tome 2, pp. 447–48. Jean-Louis Flandrin, *Le sexe et l'Occident: Evolution des attitudes et des comportements* (Paris: Seuil, 1981), 75–78. Gaudemet, *Le mariage en Occident*, 363.

25. Ferrière, *Dictionnaire de droit*, 447–48. F.B. de Visme, *La science parfaite des notaires, ou le parfait notaire, contenant les ordonnances, arrêts & Réglemens rendus touchant la Fonction des Notaires, tant Royaux qu'Apostoliques . . .* (Paris: Desaint, 1771), tome 1, pp. 316–17. Flandrin, *Le sexe et l'Occident*, 72–74.

26. The only case we came across was that of Madeleine Plouard and Jean Cosset, who cancelled their marriage contract subsequent to a trial before the Provostship of Québec. Silvio Dumas, *Les filles du roi en Nouvelle-France. Etude historique avec répertoire biographique* (Quebec: Société historique de Québec, 1972), 314.

27. Marriage contract between Adrien Lacroix and Marie Hué, 18 Oct. 1667, notary Romain Becquet.

28. "Whereas in the fifteenth and sixteenth centuries [promises of marriage] were usually not dissolved except for serious and canonical reasons, in this second half of the seventeenth century the causes of dissolution are far more numerous, sometimes futile, or even unexpressed. . . . Whereas in the fifteenth and sixteenth centuries fiancés who did not love each other were forced to marry, the judges in the seventeenth century recognize the impossibility of marrying without love." Flandrin, *Le sexe et l'Occident*, 75–78.

29. Charbonneau et al., *Birth of a Population*. Unions of single pioneers excluding single *filles du roi* are 118 of 353, or 33.4 percent.

30. Trudel, *Histoire de la Nouvelle-France*, 511.

31. The homogamy index is based on the general formula devised by Albert Jacquard and Martine Segalen. The method consists of comparing marriages in the target population to marriages that would have taken place in a competely intermixed population and to marriages that would have taken place in a completely homogeneous population. The index summarizes the comparison so that 1 equals total

homogamy and 0 complete intermixing. Martine Segalen and Albert
Jacquard, "Choix du conjoint et
homogamie," *Population*, 26th year,
no. 3 (May–June 1971): 487–98. For a
critique of this index, see Mark
Lathrop and Gilles Pison, "Méthode
statistique d'étude de l'endogamie:
Application à l'étude du choix du
conjoint chez les Peul Bandé,"
Population, 37th year, no. 3 (May–
June, 1982), 522.

32. For unions of single pioneers excluding the *filles du roi*: = 0.272.

33. Jean Quéniart, "Le choix du conjoint
dans une région de frontiére provin-
ciale," in *La France d'Ancien Régime.
Etudes réunies en l'honneur de Pierre
Goubert* (Paris: Société de démographie historique et Privat, 1984), tome
2, p. 613.

34. Jacques Houdaille, "Les signatures
au mariage, 1670–1739," *Population*,
43rd year, no. 1 (Jan.–Feb. 1988), 209.

35. Trudel, *Histoire de la Nouvelle-France*,
512–13.

36. Hubert Charbonneau, *Tourouvre-au-
Perche aux XVIIe et XVIIIe siècles:
Etude de démographie historique* (Paris:
PUF, 1970), 283.

37. Martine Segalen, *Nuptialité et
alliance: Le choix du conjoint dans une
commune de l'Eure* (Paris: Maison-
neuve et Larose, 1972), 133.

38. Leboutte and Hélin, "Le choix du
conjoint," 449.

39. Danielle Gauvreau, "Nuptialité et
catégories professionelles à Québec
pendant la régime français,"
Sociologie et sociétés 19, 1 (April 1987),
33–34.

40. Age difference in the countryside of
the Bassin parisien, according to
Dupâquier's estimates: 2.1 years. In

Canada, according to Charbonneau's
estimates: generations 1640 to 1679,
7.9 years; generations 1680 to 1699,
5.3 years; generations 1700 to 1729,
3.8 years; together, 5.7 years. Jacques
Dupâquier, ed., *Histoire de la population française*, vol. 2, *De la Renaissance
à 1789* (Paris: PUF, 1988), 305.
Charbonneau, *Vie et mort de nos
ancêtres*, 165.

41. Barbe Duchesne was 23 and André
Badel (known as Lamarche) 55 years
old. The advanced age of the husband, who apparently had not been
married before, did not stop the
couple from having eight children,
and the husband even outlived his
wife. The fact that the couple were
both of Swiss background might
explain this somewhat unusual
match.

42. Margeurite Charpentier was 59 and
Toussaint Lucas 23 years old. The
marriage apparently produced no
offspring and the woman outlived
her husband.

43. Sylvie Savoie, *Les couples en difficulté
aux XVIIe et XVIIIe siècles: les deman-
des de séparation en Nouvelle-France*
(M.A. thesis, Sherbrooke University,
1986). Hélène Lafortune and
Normand Robert: "Parchemin: une
banque de données notariales du
Québec ancien (1635–1885)," *Archives*
20, 4 (Spring 1989): 51–58. France
Parent, *Entre le juridique et le social: Le
pouvoir des femmes à Québec au XVIIe
siècle* Cahier 42, Les cahiers de
recherche multidisciplinaire femi-
niste, Université Laval, 1991.

44. Hubert Charbonneau and R. Cole
Harris, "Resettling the St. Lawrence
Valley," in *Historical Atlas of Canada*,
vol. 1, *From the Beginning to 1800*, ed.
R. Cole Harris (Toronto: University
of Toronto Press, 1987), plate 46.

UNWED MOTHERS, FAMILIES, AND SOCIETY DURING THE FRENCH REGIME ◇

MARIE-AIMÉE CLICHE ✦

o

Changing times and attitudes have largely eradicated the older meanings of terms like *unwed mother*, *bastard*, or *seducer*, each of which denoted specific sexual transgressions. However, the sexual realities they encompassed have not disappeared. Rather they have become commonplace with the emergence of different value systems and the acceptance of radical changes in sexual morals. It is interesting, therefore, to return to the past to study the attitudes and reactions of the parties involved in premarital conceptions and to identify the sexual norms that were imposed in different historical periods.

Researchers in several disciplines have explored such questions. Sociologists concentrate on the present. Demographers map out the statistical patterns of some aspects of sexuality in the past. Historians are more concerned with understanding the context of such sexual behaviour. They have sought to understand some of the familial and social strategies devised to cope with extramarital pregnancies and to trace the evolution of sexual norms and behaviour. In Quebec, sexuality was initially examined within the moralizing and didactic framework of historians like Lionel

◇ *Histoire sociale/Social History* 21, 41 (May 1988): 39–69. Research was made possible by a grant from the Social Sciences and Humanities Research Council of Canada. The author would like to thank the evaluators of *Histoire sociale/Social History* and Professor Jacques Mathieu of Laval University for their invaluable comments.

✦ Translated by Jane Parniak. The title of the original article is "Filles-mères, familles et société sous le Régime français." The term *filles-mères*, the French expression for unwed mothers, did not exist during the French Régime. Its appearance in Quebec around the 1870s or 1880s indicates a hardening of society's attitudes towards women who got pregnant outside marriage.

Groulx or Jean-Baptiste-Antoine Ferland. By contrast, Robert-Lionel Séguin, who wrote in the 1970s, took a more revisionist approach.[1] More recently, demographers have taken a fresh approach. The work of Lyne Paquette and Réal Bates, which focusses on illegitimate births and premarital conceptions prior to 1730, gives us a much better measurement of the extent of these two phenomena,[2] providing a context for looking in more detail at specific cases as I do here.[3]

TABLE 1   NUMBER OF ILLEGITIMATE PREGNANCIES AND TRIALS INVOLVING UNWED MOTHERS (to 1759)

| | Illegitimate births | Premarital conceptions◇ | Judicial and notarized acts | | | | |
			Proceedings for illicit paternity	Abductions	Infanticides	Miscellaneous	Total
Before 1680	40	44	1		1	2	4
1680–89	41	32	1	2		6	9
1690–99	101	64	5	1	1	5	12
1700–09	170	104	6	4	1	6	17
1710–19	162	118	9	3		6	18
1720–29	233	74✦	9	6	1	2	18
1730–39			7	4	2	3	16
1740–49			14	1	1	6	22
1750–59			17	2		2	21
Undetermined	2						
Total	749	436	69	23	7	38	137

◇ The number of illegitimate births and premarital conceptions is taken from the article by Lyne Paquette and Réal Bates, "Les naissances illégitimes sur les rives du Saint-Laurent avant 1730," *Revue d'histoire de l'Amérique française* (*RHAF*) 40 (Autumn 1986): 243; and Réal Bates, "Les conceptions prénuptiales dans la vallée du Saint-Laurent avant 1725," ibid., 259. The remaining data was taken from legal documents preserved at the Archives nationales du Québec. These documents were used to prepare all the other tables.

✦ 74 premarital conceptions between 1720 and 1724.

The registers of births, deaths, and marriages that constitute the basis of demographers' estimates provide little detail on the individuals involved and nothing on the norms of the period. Judicial sources, in contrast, contain a wealth of information, although they deal only with extreme cases. When a women became pregnant outside marriage, for example, they reveal whether the primary concern of her family and the wider society was the child's welfare, the mother's future, family honour, or masculine privilege. They can also tell us whether blame for the sexual transgression was laid mostly on the man or on the woman and can indicate its consequences. In short, the study of premarital conceptions reveals much about the social-situation of women, men and women's roles within sexual relations, and social and moral values surrounding sexuality in the past.

TABLE 2   *LEGAL DOCUMENTS USED FOR THIS STUDY*

	Number of cases
Legal proceedings	
Proceedings for civil damages and illicit paternity	69
Abductions	23
Declarations of pregnancy without trial	7
Infanticides	7
Found child statements	7
Concubinage	3
Opposition to marriage	2
Marriage *à la gaumine*◇	1
Obligatory marriage	1
Cross-examination following a clandestine birth	1
Security in case of proceedings for illicit paternity	1
Declaration of paternity	1
Mention in another trial	1
Breaking of bann (obligatory marriage)	1
Flight (testimony rejected)	1
Notarized acts	
Agreements	5
Wills	3
Hiring wetnurse	1
Marriage contract	1
Amiable agreement	1
Total	137

◇ Illicit marriage celebrated without the priest's knowledge. See Pierre-Georges Roy, "Les mariages à la gaumine," *Rapport de l'archiviste de la province de Québec,* 1920–1921, 366–407.

Since sexual practices are intimate personal matters, it is important to pay special attention to the silences when exploring the subject. Most cases of premarital pregnancy produced no documentation. Many women solved the problem by marrying hastily. In other cases, a private settlement determined the future of the mother and child. Very few cases, probably about 10 percent, led to court appearances or formal arrangements with a notary (see table 1).

It is also essential to decipher the discourse surrounding extramarital pregnancies. Modesty, real or manufactured for the occasion, meant that women sometimes avoided describing the circumstances of the "mishap." And ambiguity is rife in the use of words such as "solicitation," "seduction," or "abduction." Over and above the objective facts, the words used to describe the circumstances are charged with meaning.

A painstaking search uncovered a total of 126 cases of court proceedings and eleven notarized acts concerning unwed mothers in the districts of Quebec, Montreal, and Trois-Rivières from the establishment of the settlements until 1759.[4] In addition, there are many documents on related subjects, such as opposition to marriages, demands for reparation for loss of honour, and placement of illegitimate children. The files range in size from around ten lines to 500 pages. The mothers and their parents commonly appear as plaintiffs in trials for abduction or illicit paternity, but in cases of infanticide or concubinage, the women are usually in the position of defendant (see table 2). Complete files contain the declaration of pregnancy, the petition filed by the mother or her parents, the alleged putative father's speech for the defence, the testimony of witnesses, the cross-examination, the confrontation of the two parties, the King's attorney's speech for the prosecution and, lastly, the sentence. In the ten most interesting trials, a number of witnesses were summoned.

Despite their inevitable limitations, the richness and diversity of these judicial documents allow us to see the institutional responses to these kinds of situations. Thanks to the arguments made by the litigants, the motives evoked by the attorneys, and the sentences delivered by the judges, we see society's choices through the legal system. This documentation is always subjective, but it clarifies what kinds of behaviour were best received in the society of the time, providing the context for facts presented from a variety of perspectives.

Several well-known French historians have already discussed unwed mothers.[5] Some of them (Lefebvre-Teillard, Phan, Logette) have examined the spirit of legislation pertaining to illegitimate births. Others (Flandrin, Lottin, Depauw, Laget) have analysed the social status of unwed mothers. These works will serve as methodological guidelines for this study. However, since my sources are both less abundant and more diverse than those of these authors, who have largely relied on declarations of pregnancy, I chose to do a case analysis rather than a serial study of the documentation.

THE MOTHERS AND FATHERS OF ILLEGITIMATE CHILDREN

Persons who appeared in court were required to state their name, age, occupation, and place of residence. This identification process can be used to reconstitute some characteristics of the "illicitly pregnant women and girls," as they were labelled at the time, and of the alleged fathers of their children.

The mothers of illegitimate children were almost all single women, although several widows and even a few married women appear in the records. Their average age was 22.5. Most of the accused fathers were single, but on the average they were six years older than the women (see tables 3 and 4). Both their average age and their marital status is similar to that described in Lyne Paquette's study for all parents of illegitimate children in the colony in the period before 1730.[6]

The young women were usually escorted by a parent, most often their father, when they went to see the magistrate. If the father had died or was absent, either their mother or a male relative stepped in, even when the women was of age. Men usually managed on their own, although most minors (22 out of 24) were accompanied by a parent or guardian (see tables 5 and 6). Girls, perhaps because they were so young, seem to have been more sheltered and protected by their families than were the men.

TABLE 3   *AVERAGE AGE OF FATHERS AND MOTHERS OF ILLEGITIMATE CHILDREN (1670–1759)*

Mothers	Age	Fathers	Age
Single	21.4 years	single	25.9 years
Married, widowed	29 years	married, widowed	36.3 years
Average	22.5 years	average	28.3 years

Sources: Legal archives, Cyprien Tanguay, *Dictionnaire généalogique des familles canadiennes* (Quebec: Eusèbe Senécal, 1878), 7 vol. René Jetté, *Dictionnaire généalogique des familles canadiennes* (Montreal: Presses de l'Université de Montréal, 1983).

N.B. In all, we found the ages of 99 mothers and 73 fathers out of 137. We have shown the age of parents at the time of birth.

TABLE 4   *BREAKDOWN OF MARITAL STATUS OF MOTHERS AND FATHERS OF ILLEGITIMATE CHILDREN (1670–1759)* ⬦

Mothers	Number	Percentage	Fathers	Number	Percentage
Single	110	80.3	Single	72	52.6
Married	9	6.6	Married	15	11
Widowed	8	5.8	Widowed	3	2.1
Unknown	10	7.3	Unknown	47	34.3
Total	137	100		137	100

⬦ This table shows marital status at the beginning of pregnancy.

TABLE 5   *PERSON ACCOMPANYING THE PLAINTIFF DURING PROCEEDINGS (1670–1759)* ⬦

Relation	Number of cases
Father alone	31
Mother alone	16
Both parents	9
Brother	5
Uncle	5
Stepfather	4
Sister	3
Husband	1
Brother-in-law	1
Master or mistress	2
Guardian	1
Alone or not specified	31
Total	109

⬦ This table does not include trials for infanticide or cases where the girl did not appear in court.

TABLE 6 *PERSONS ACCOMPANYING THE DEFENDANT DURING TRIALS (1670–1759)*

Relation	Number of cases
Father alone	7
Mother alone	2
Both parents	4
Brother	2
Stepfather	3
Guardian	3
Master	1
Total	22

TABLE 7 *BREAKDOWN OF TRIALS BY REGION*

	Judicial and notarial interventions		Population (%) in 1739◇	Population (%) in 1765◇
	Number	Percentage		
District of Montreal	65	53.7	41.5	38.8
District of Quebec	46	38.0	48.8	47.6
District of Trois-Rivières	10	8.3	9.7	11.6
Total of known cases	121	100		

◇ These percentages are from an unpublished article by Fernand Ouellet, "Origine de l'industrialisation et développement régional au Québec avant 1850."

Of the 91 cases where the mother's place of residence when she became pregnant is known, 56 cases (62 percent) came from rural areas rather than from the cities. However, since by 1765 only 22 percent of the enumerated population was living in urban areas, towns to seem to have been a more conducive milieu for premarital pregnancies.[7] And, while the district of Quebec had a greater population than that of Montreal, a disproportionate number of judicial and notarial proceedings concerning pregnancy out of wedlock occurred within the Montreal district (see table 7).

It is highly tempting to establish a link between the over-representation of trials for illicit pregnancy and the mobility of the male population in the Montreal region due to the fur trade. But to confirm this correlation, we would have to compare the respective number of illegitimate births in each area and try to find out whether the fathers were in fact explorers and trappers. Our sources show that only six defendants ever did this kind of work, but all six lived in the Montreal region.

The occupation or social background of the two partners is known in approximately 75 percent of the cases, making it possible to pinpoint some of their characteristics (see tables 8 and 9). Firstly, the high percentage of domestic servants clearly shows that their work exposed them to certain risks, a phenomenon observed in several French cities at the same time period, and in Quebec until the mid-twentieth century.[8] Secondly, 25 percent of the men were members of the upper classes—military officers, high government officials, members of the liberal professions, merchants, or traders—despite the fact that this group represented only 10 percent of the total population and only 5 percent in rural areas. This might suggest that seduction was the result of such men too readily taking advantage of girls from the lower classes. Certainly when one partner in these liasons was socially superior to the other, it was almost always the man (26 of 32). Yet in most liaisons where the social status of both partners is known (76 of 136), they came from similar social backgrounds (44 out of 76).

TABLE   8   *OCCUPATION OF THE MOTHERS (OR THEIR FATHERS OR HUSBANDS) OF ILLEGITIMATE CHILDREN ACCORDING TO JUDICIAL AND NOTARIAL ARCHIVES (1670–1759)* ◇

Occupation	Number	Percentage
1. Of the father (or husband) of a mother without occupation		
• Professional (military officer, high-ranking civil servant, member of a likeable profession, merchant)	8	7.8
• Artisan	16	15.7
• "Habitant"	39	38.2
• Other	1	1.0
2. Of the mother		
• Servant, slave	33	32.3
• Barmaid	1	1.0
• Laundress	1	1.0
• Seamstress	1	1.0
• Beggar	2	2.0
Total of known cases	102	100

◇ The classification method is modelled on that of Lyne Paquette and the Programme de recherche en démographie historique to facilitate comparisons.

Sources: Cyprien Tanguay, *Dictionnaire généalogique des familles canadiennes* (Quebec: Eusèbe Senécal, 1878), 7 vol. René Jetté, *Dictionnaire des familles canadiennes* (Montreal: Presses de l'Université de Montréal, 1983).

A portrait of the unwed mothers emerges from this quantitative data. They were young and of modest background. The men were older and a good number of them occupied positions of prestige or authority. Presumably, marital status and social similarities or differences between the couple had a bearing on why the affair took place and on the reactions of families when the pregnancy became known.

TABLE 9   *OCCUPATION OF THE FATHERS OF ILLEGITIMATE CHILDREN ACCORDING TO JUDICIAL AND NOTARIAL ARCHIVES (1670–1759)*

Occupation	Number	Percentage
• Professional (military offices, high-ranking civil servant, member of the liberal professions, merchant)	26	25.0
• Artisan	10	9.6
• "Habitant"	42	40.4
• Writer, clerk	2	2.0
• Servant, soldier, vagrant, explorer, slave	24	23.0
Total of known cases	104	100

THE CONTEXT OF SEXUAL RELATIONSHIPS

The circumstances of the sexual relationships were usually described by the girls themselves or their parents in declarations of pregnancy and illicit paternity suits. Further details are found in the testimony of witnesses and the judge's cross-examination of the two parties. The inquiry was especially rigorous if the girl was charged with infanticide or concealment of pregnancy. These trials give us a glimpse into the homes where the love affairs were kindled, and an idea of how the families reacted when they found out. The circumstances of ninety-nine affairs can be partly identified in court testimony, and a major distinction can be made between affairs that were conducted with marriage in mind and those that could never have led to marriage.

PUTTING THE CART BEFORE THE HORSE

Unwed mothers usually explained their pregnancy by arguing that their lover had promised to marry them (55 cases). While this may have been done at the King's attorney's suggestion, the fact that it was so commonly made shows that the girls considered it the most normal explanation and the best excuse for their behaviour. The men most often denied this charge, although some did acknowledge these promises either during the trial or when drawing up their marriage contract or even their will.[9] The economic and family pressures the young people mention in these documents help to explain why they exchanged such promises but did not always keep them.

In traditional society, marriage was, among other things, an economic institution.[10] Before marrying, a man had to be able to support a family. For a farmer, this meant being settled on land that was at least partly cultivated; for a craftsman, being able to make a living at his trade. A twenty-seven-year-old peasant, when reprimanded by a neighbour who told him that "they'd be better off marrying instead of hugging and kissing all the time," replied that "he had to have something to live on and then he'd get married."[11] At the other end of the social scale, similar comments were heard:

the lieutenant of the Prévôté of Quebec, Sieur de Leigne, rejected one of his daughter's suitors because he had "no property, no fortune, no employment that would enable him to support a wife."[12]

While waiting for the work or wealth that would enable him to marry, a man would court his girlfriend, sometimes giving her a ring or other jewellery "as a token of his good faith" (4 cases). In at least a dozen trials, there is mention of quite long courtships, lasting from two to seven years. Naturally, the young people became increasingly intimate during these long waiting periods. Witnesses reported that some couples exchanged signs of familiarity in full public view: playing around and teasing (2 cases), or hugging and kissing (3 cases). Some couples took advantage of their parents' absence and made love on a bed in the presence of friends their own age.[13] The clergy, particularly Bishop de Saint-Vallier, was quick to condemn these "overly free courtships,"[14] characterized by Jean-Louis Flandrin as a waiting technique in rural areas where people married at a later age. While waiting to marry his sweetheart, a man might make love to her. So it was that an outraged father declared to a judge that "all the neighbours were aware that the defendant loved the plaintiffs' daughter and had made love to her."[15]

In addition to the economic difficulties that sometimes held up marriage plans, another major obstacle was parental opposition (14 cases). Opposition might be reinforced with economic sanctions, with parents threatening to cut off their rebellious son's means of subsistence. Pierre Demers, for instance, declared that if he married Marie-Josephe Roussiard, his father would throw him out and disinherit him. Such a threat was carried out in the cases of Joseph Rouffio and Jean-Christophe Decoste.[16] The young people had some legal means to overcome this problem: they could contact a judge, formulate the three required summonses, and assemble a meeting of friends and relatives whose opinion would be decisive. But the announcement of an imminent birth spoke heavily in favour of marriage. Apparently, some couples deliberately resorted to this tactic. Thérèse Brossard, for instance, could not marry Pierre Coquillard because her brother and guardian were opposed to it, so she made a declaration of pregnancy to the Crown prosecutor. The older brother continued to oppose the marriage, but the assembled relatives agreed to the marriage to save the family's honour.[17] Similarly, the pregnancy announced by Thérèse Willis was taken into consideration by the judge of the Prévôté of Quebec when he authorized her marriage with Claude Louet despite the opposition of the boy's father.[18] For the same reason, and after the intendant's intervention, Pierre Auger and his wife finally allowed their son to marry, but only with great reluctance and after severely reprimanding him.[19]

This ploy was not always successful, however. Olivier Morel de La Durantaye and his wife managed to stop two of their sons from marrying, even though the girls were pregnant.[20] Worse yet, the man sometimes went back on his word. Madeleine Duclos pleaded that Jacques Diel "always told her that unless he slept with her, he could not marry her otherwise because neither his relatives nor his master would give their consent."[21] Nicolas Lemoyne assured Elisabeth Campeau that his sister and other relatives would have to "agree to their marriage since he had made her pregnant."[22] François Albert and René Lefebvre[23] employed the same argument, according to the girls' parents, and afterwards refused to keep their promises. Finally, paternal authority could form a convenient shield for young men who had no desire to see a fling turn into marriage. Pierre Dubro, for instance, signed a marriage promise with Marguerite Bouchard, but when it came time to act on his promise, he refused on the pretext that "he [was] under his father's power, being only twenty years of age, that his father [ordered] him to return to France and that he [could] not disobey him."[24] The father was in fact opposed to the marriage, but even had the son been able to have his own way, it seems quite unlikely that this well-bred boy, whose father was a market vendor, would willingly have married a maid-servant who already had an illegitimate child. As for Marguerite Bouchard, perhaps she was hoping that her pregnancy and a written marriage promise would guarantee her a good settlement, but the obstacles (opposition of her lover's father and difference in social status) defeated her.

Many sexual relationships (a little more than half of those that can be studied in detail; 55 out of 99) were conducted with marriage in mind, either because the couple really intended to get married or the girl alone cherished such hopes. But in many other cases, marriage plans were not mentioned at all during the trial, and the litigants gave very different versions of what happened.

AFFAIRS WITH NO HOPE OF MARRIAGE

Often there was but a slim difference between the intimate relationships of future spouses and passing liaisons. A married man might promise to marry his mistress as soon as his wife died,[25] or he might keep his marital status a secret. This was particularly easy to do if his legitimate wife was living in France.[26] Not all men even bothered to make promises of marriage: they had plenty of other arguments at their disposal.

Merchants won the favours of their customers by offering them merchandise from their store (2 cases). It's easy to understand how tempting a silk sash or a pair of gloves could be for poor girls.[27] Jean-Baptiste Mailhot did not consider it necessary to give anything to Marie, for she was a slave— "One day when she was walking by his house, Jean-Baptiste Mailhot invited her in and had his way with her, which he has again done twice since then."[28] It didn't take long for masters to break down their maids' resistance; all they had to do was "throw their power onto the scale."[29] Some men did not scruple to use brute force (13 cases), and hit the girl or threaten to kill her. It is easy to imagine how men treated the "Pépin girl," an imbecile who bore five or six children, but could not say who the fathers were.[30]

In these liaisons—for they were indeed liaisons—only two of the thirty-six girls imputed their pregnancy to only one sexual encounter. All the others mentioned several encounters. Cases of rape by strangers are exceptional. Most relationships took place between people who lived in the same area, often involving neighbours or family friends (9 cases) or members of the same household. In 18 percent of the trials (25 cases), pregnancy was the result of having sex with someone in the same household. Most often this was the classic case of a master, or his son, seducing the maid (12 cases). Less frequently (2 cases), the daughter of the house had intimate relations with her parents' servant. The other cases involved servants and boarders.

Sexual intimacy may have been facilitated by the lack of privacy that reigned in Canadian households, where it seems that the universal custom was for several people to share a room or even a bed. This custom, which was quite widespread in France,[31] persisted in the colony because of the harsh climate. Poverty was also a factor: Pierre Bourgoin, for instance, reserved his only bed and one blanket for his sick wife; he himself slept by the fire with the neighbour who acted as nurse.[32] But it was not poverty that induced Lady Veillon to share her bed with her maid when her husband was absent.[33] Jean Bouchard was not poor either—he had more than one servant on staff—yet he argued that it was normal to share a bedroom with his two maids since his house was so cramped.[34]

Were orphans and housemaids more susceptible to sexual exploitation, as some authors have argued?[35] Parental supervision may well have restricted the sexual freedom of daughters. And for supervision to be effective, the girl had to live under the same roof as her family. The slightly higher rates of conception outside marriage among widows may in part have been because most no longer lived with their parents.[36] Yet living at home was no absolute guarantee of sexual purity. Some particularly bold lovers did manage to get around the restrictions of the parental home. Pierre de Saint-Ours entered the bedroom of Hélène Céloron while her father slept in the next room, and François Campot joined Marie Monnet at home while her father and brothers were out working in the fields or attending Mass.[37] But significant differences come to light if the affairs of girls who lived at home are systematically compared with those of women who lived elsewhere.

Out of twenty-seven girls who lived at home (with their two parents or a remarried parent) at the time of their affair, 74 percent declared that they yielded to a man who promised to marry them. The rest had affairs with a neighbour (5 cases), a hired hand, or a cousin. On the other hand, of the thirty-four who lived away from home, all but one of whom were housemaids, only nine (26.5 percent) mentioned a promise of marriage; more than a third (12 of 34) had slept with their master or his son; the other thirteen had affairs with a neighbour (10 cases) or some other members of the household. We should add that in the fourteen cases where the seducer was socially superior, the girl was usually a housemaid (11 of 14 cases), not counting the twelve affairs between masters and maids.

In three exceptional cases the affair lasted for months or even years, in time becoming true common-law arrangements with no prospect of marriage. The women who found themselves in this situation were all married but separated from their husbands. To all appearances, they had freely opted for this kind of sexual life without being misled, bribed, or forced like many unwed mothers.

Sexual relationships that culminated in extramarital pregnancies were clearly quite diverse in character, running the gamut from rape all the way to affairs willingly pursued by adult women. Without exception, they fell under a category of sexual activity prohibited by the Church, but society laid the blame differently depending on the circumstances.

EXTRAMARITAL PREGNANCY: A FAMILY AFFAIR

There was little chance of an illegitimate pregnancy going unnoticed either in small cities like Montreal and Quebec or in the countryside. Rumours spread quickly (17 mentions in the trials) about an expectant mother's condition,[38] and gossip flew about the father's identity.

Families reacted differently depending on the circumstances. Upon learning that their daughter had had a clandestine love affair against their express injunction, some parents gave their anger free rein and sometimes even beat the girl, as was the case with both Augustin Cadet and his daughter Louise and Urbain Brossard and his younger sister Thérèse.[39] However, if they thought that the girl had fallen prey to a lecherous man, they turned their anger against him, especially if the girl was "an imbecile and feeble-minded."[40] Pregnant housemaids ran the risk of being dismissed, because they could not work in their condition, because the mistress of the house was concerned with appearances, or because she had found out that her own husband was responsible for the pregnancy.[41]

Shame and fear drove some girls to such desperate measures as abortion, sometimes at their lover's instigation,[42] or infanticide. Geneviève Gaudreau secretly gave birth and immediately disposed of her child after her first employer dismissed her, for fear that her second employer would follow suit. Françoise Duverger did likewise, not daring to admit her condition to her mistress "for fear that she would rebuke her." In fact, this girl declared that "if her employer had found out that she was pregnant, she would have thrown her out of her house."[43] The seven trials for infanticide and the few proceedings concerning the discovery of corpses of newborns give a very sketchy idea of how common these practices were.

Other girls tried to hide their condition while still giving their child a chance to survive. They secretly gave birth and afterwards left the newborn in a public place—at the gate of the Montreal seminary on the doorstep of a midwife's house[44]—where it would soon be found. At least one country girl brought her child to the city: Elisabeth Campeau gave birth at Saint-Pierre River and, a few hours later, on a cold February night, walked to Montreal with her baby in her arms.[45] Conversely, city dwellers would retire to the country to give birth.[46] Women were anxious to preserve their reputation: out of 749 illegitimate births recorded before 1730, 249 certificates (33.2 percent) state "unknown mother."[47]

Not all unwed mothers were reduced to despairing solitude. Some of them found support from their priest, their mistress, or a friend.[48] But those who could turned to their families, for it was not just the woman's problem; many plaintiffs declared that their disgrace was a stain on the family name.[49] In addition, the girl risked becoming a burden on the family. Her misconduct reduced her chances of finding employment or a husband, and the father might worry about having her on his hands forever.[50] This argument, raised three times in court, may have been exaggerated but was not entirely groundless; in six other trials, the boys, or their parents, refused to consent to marriage with a girl "who had been with" someone else, and a judge confirmed this fear when he declared that a seduced girl suffered a serious and even irreparable wrong.[51] Most unwed mothers probably ended up getting married,[52] but how many had to settle for what would have been looked on as inferior partners? Marie-Anne Baudet's marriage to a Panis Indian, for instance, was unlikely to have been considered a step up the social ladder.[53]

If the father had been seeing the pregnant women regularly, or was considered a suitable partner (though marriage might not have been in his plans), he was expected to marry without delay to salvage her honour.[54] Thus, on hearing the gossip that was circulating about her stepdaughter and Pierre de Saint-Ours, Madame de Blainville declared "that if anything happens to her, he'll have to marry her for sure."[55]

Some men were slow to keep their promises, in which case neighbours (1 case) or the priest (6 cases) joined forces with the girl's parents to apply pressure.[56] When a man's parents opposed the marriage, the same people stepped in to elicit their consent. Often, social pressures sufficed. A comparison of the number of premarital conceptions and illegitimate births shows that in 36.8 percent of the cases, the expectant mother got married before the child was born.[57] A further 29.3 percent of the unwed mothers recorded by demographers before 1730 married the father after the birth of their child.[58]

Even when marriage was impossible for one reason or another—the marital status of one of the partners, difference in social status, or lack of love—an amicable settlement could still be concluded. A number of men promised to provide for the needs of the women they had made pregnant, though they sometimes forgot their promises later.[59] Some parents agreed to keep their daughter and her child in exchange for monetary compensation.[60] Some women raised a child on their own or with their lover's assistance, all the while nursing the vain hope that they would eventually marry the father.[61] Priests, who the girls confided in and who registered declarations of pregnancy, were in a good position to direct negotiations. They sometimes obtained a cash settlement for the girl (1 case), or discreetly placed her as a wetnurse (2 cases).[62] Occasionally, in an attempt to atone for the sins of youth, in later life men left wills with private legacies to the women they had wronged.[63]

When patience and diplomacy failed, some girls and their families resorted to more blatant pressure tactics, such as leaving the child on the father's doorstep to publicize his paternity. "Here you go, here's your child, do what you want with it," said Charlotte Préquet as she laid her bundle at the feet of Henri Cattin.[64] This practice, which was quite common in France, was apparently reminiscent of the *ius tollendi* of ancient Rome.[65]

Some men turned a deaf ear to pleas and remonstrances alike. Some (6 cases) even tried to flee. Rarely, it was the girl who refused to get married.

Cécile Saint-Yves, for instance, told her priest "that she wanted nothing to do with this marriage, and that it was pointless to make such a fuss about it."[66] There was quite a fuss in fact; Cécile's brothers tried every trick in the book to force their sister's lover to marry her. Blinded by the thought of protecting their family honour, they simply forgot to ask the principal party how she felt about it. In extreme cases, the quarrel between the two families heated up to the point where they threatened to kill each other.[67] Then it became advisable to consult a judge.

BEFORE THE COURT

Three kinds of legal appeals—religious, civil, and criminal—were available to unwed mothers. In all three cases, proceedings could be instituted as a last-ditch attempt to force the man to marry if he were single. If he still refused, he was required to pay in some other way for the injury he had caused the woman (33 mentions in the trials).

All of the petitions presented to the Quebec Diocesan Council (6 cases) aimed to oblige the man to honour his promise of marriage. But since the Catholic Church considered absolute freedom of consent an essential condition for the validity of marriages, the ecclesiatical judge never forced a man to marry. At most, if the man admitted that he had made such a promise, the judge would order him to give alms to the poor to compensate for "the violation of his word."[68]

Civil proceedings had three objectives: firstly, to obtain payment of the birthing fees and a provision to meet the basic needs of mother and child; secondly, to make the putative father assume the costs of child support and education; finally, to claim civil damages to compensate for loss of virginity and breach of the marriage promise.[69] According to some authors, it was assumed that girls "succumbed" only after a promise of marriage. It was violation of this condition that led to civil action on behalf of the seduced girl.[70] The accused always had the alternative of marrying the girl and making the child legitimate. Since the Middle Ages, theologians and confessors had ordered men who were guilty of deflowering a virgin to atone for their sin by marrying her or giving her a dowry.[71] In this they acknowledged that the seduced girl suffered a greater social injury than her seducer, and that men had the economic resources necessary to raise a child.

Criminal proceedings could also be instituted for abduction. French legislators drew a distinction between abduction by violence and abduction by seduction. The first consisted in "forceably removing a person of either sex for purposes of abuse."[72] The second was defined as follows under section 42 of the Ordinance of Blois in 1576:

> Let it be known that those who are found guilty of seducing a son
> or daughter under twenty-five years of age, under the pretext of
> marriage or for any other reason, without the express agreement,
> acknowledgement, desire, or consent of the fathers, mothers, and
> guardians, shall be sentenced to death without hope of grace and
> pardon.[73]

A Quebec prosecutor very clearly outlined the difference between the two kinds of abduction:

> Abduction may be committed in two ways. Firstly, by force and against the abducted person's will. Secondly, without force and with the consent of the abducted person, who is taken off guard and extorted through seduction. In the first case, the victim is the abducted person; in the second case it is the parents, guardians or family of the abducted person. In both cases, abduction is a capital crime.[74]

The historians Flandrin and Gaudement have shown that the concept of "abduction by seduction" was conceived to prevent young people from marrying against their parents' will. The Church recognized the validity of marriages concluded with the consent of the spouses even if the parents withheld their consent. On the other hand, it "had long since proclaimed the invalidity of marriages made by abduction, and civil law punished the abductor by death."[75] Imposing the death penalty on persons guilty of abduction by seduction was therefore a way of breaking up such marriages: "There's no marriage so good that a rope can't sunder it."[76] In New France, however, the death penalty was very rarely claimed for this sort of offence,[77] and only two trials were held with a view to annulling or preventing a marriage that was contracted despite parental opposition.[78] In the other cases, it was more a question of forcing the seducer to marry (8 cases) or otherwise atone for his offence. Finally, it should be noted that during these proceedings, judges had the task of distinguishing between abductions by seduction, as defined above, and illegal sex, which was not punishable by death.[79]

Legislators also foresaw that some unwed mothers would try to save their reputation by concealing the pregnancy and birth. To prevent infanticide, which was considered especially serious because the child might die before it was baptized, the authorities in New France published in 1708 the Edict of Henri II, which stipulated that this crime was punishable by death.[80] And in 1722 the declaration of pregnancy became obligatory for "illicitly pregnant girls and women."[81]

These laws aimed to offer some protection to unwed mothers and illegitimate children by making the presumed father assume full responsibility for a deed (an offence?) committed by two. It remains to be seen how judges enforced these laws; that is, whether the plaintiff won or lost her case. The arguments raised during the trials give an idea of the code of sexual behaviour society imposed on young women (and young men) at the time.

UNWED MOTHER: VICTIM OR WHORE?

The girls who confessed an illicit pregnancy to the court were not proud of their exploit. On the contrary, they claimed to be unhappy (6 cases) and dishonoured by their condition (20 cases), feelings that were shared by their families (6 mentions) and even by some judges. One judge asked the defendant why he did not want to marry a young girl "after having brought disgrace upon her and made her odious to all her family."[82] To excuse their behaviour, the girls most often cited their youth (5 cases) and the weakness and fragility of their sex (19 cases). Being "of a tender age when girls are easily led astray," they had found it all too easy to fall for declarations of love (8 cases) and, especially, promises of marriage (55 cases).

Aside from the girls who alluded to "feminine weakness," common ground at that time, others claimed that they had been taken "by force and violence" (13 cases, including 3 where the girl was described as "an imbecile and simpleminded"). It might well be asked why these girls did not charge the man with rape from the very first in cases of sustained affairs. The answer is provided by the girls themselves. Marie Monnet, a "very simple" girl according to her father, did not dare complain about a neighbour's assaults because of the threats he made and the shame she felt.[83] Lord d'Arpentigny apparently also threatened to kill his maid, Anne Lugré, if she told anyone about their intimate relations.[84] As for Brigitte Morel, she did indeed complain to her priest that her master had raped her, but the priest refused to believe her and sent her away.[85] If she had taken her complaint to the Crown prosecutor, what are the chances that he would have believed her? Unwilling to take the risk, she returned to her master's house, where she remained until she became pregnant. The girls invariably insisted that they had been with no man apart from the accused (in other words, that they were virgins before the affair) and that he was indeed the father of the child they were expecting.

The male defendants had quite a different attitude. With one or two exceptions, men did not claim to be dishonoured by this charge.[86] If by chance they considered it a weakness to have slept with a girl (3 cases), they were referring to strictly personal behaviour; none of them took refuge behind allusions to the innate weakness of the male sex. If they deplored their misfortune, it was for quite another reason. Some men were imprisoned while awaiting the verdict, depriving the poorest of them of the means of making a living,[87] and all of them were afraid of being ordered to pay civil damages and child support, a fear shared by the relatives who stood by them.[88]

Nevertheless, twenty-five men admitted that they had "known" the plaintiff (in the biblical sense of the word); two even acknowledged that they had promised marriage. Among them, of course, were those men who wanted to marry the girl despite the opposition of her parents or guardians. But most defendants tried to escape marriage or sentencing. Accordingly, the most common line of defence was to deny that an affair had ever taken place. Sometimes the man admitted that he had slept with the girl, but without promising marriage (8 cases), which in itself lessened his responsibility.

Other men tried to blame the girl for what happened, maintaining that she had made advances to him (7 cases), or that she had known many other men (17 cases), which would invalidate the accusation of deflowering. This allegation was enough to destroy the girl's honour forever; she would henceforth be known as "a whore . . . at anyone's disposal."[89] Worse still, one girl had enjoyed making love. She would forthwith be accused of "wanton appetites," of sinking to the "lowest depths of lust," conduct for which she deserved to be "thrown into prison."[90] As a logical consequence of such charges, the accusation was sometimes turned back against the plaintiff, reproaching her for seducing a naïve and inexperienced young man. This tactic was mainly used by parents in defending a minor son against an older woman. For instance, Suzanne Beaujean accused Marie Brazeau, a twenty-nine-year-old married woman, of seducing her twenty-four-year-old son and making him spend all the proceeds of his trading expedition to the Ottawa valley.[91] Similarly, Pierre Dubro claimed that Marguerite Bouchard, the twenty-two-year-old mother of an illegitimate child, committed abduction when she seduced his twenty-year-old son.[92]

Men who had had several mistresses and seemingly enjoyed the sexual act were not criticized; quite the contrary. The aunt of Nicolas Giroux openly stated that "her nephew had made love to the said Savaria from on top, from below, from the sides, on his belly and in every position, even holding a candle in his hand . . . *that the best men acted like that.*"[93] Some men (4 cases), fully aware of this approbation, were quick to boast of their good fortune, but in private only, since it was in their interest to deny the facts in court.

Faced with accounts that were often contradictory, how was the judge supposed to decide the question? He started by questioning the parties, then summoned witnesses, took account of what the mother said when in labour,[94] and finally attached considerable weight to the mother's sworn declaration.[95] Out of sixty-nine trials where the outcome is known, the defendant was sentenced to pay the birthing fees in thirty-one cases and to compensate the girl in forty-one.

It was in the more unusual circumstances—when the plaintiff was a widow, a married woman separated from her husband,[96] a woman who was having a second child,[97] or a woman whose reputation was highly suspect[98]—that judges decided they were not entitled to civil damages. None of these women were virgins when the affair took place, so they could not sue for loss of virginity. In the eyes of society and the magistrates, they had fallen into the ranks of "loose women," and the judge exhorted them in plain words to mend their wicked ways. It is hardly necessary to add that this counsel was never addressed to a man, even in cases where he was the father of three or four illegitimate children.[99]

One other group of women seemed to have difficulty winning their case in court: women who were of much lower social standing than their lovers, but were not their servants. Out of fourteen cases of this kind, we did not come across one sentence obliging the man to pay damages to the woman. However, in eleven cases involving masters who had had sexual relations with their maids, the men were sentenced to pay the women civil damages or provisions of an equal amount. The judge even imposed an additional fine in the form of alms for the poor on one man.[100] This attitude fits with the socio-religious context of the colony. A master was supposed to keep an eye on his servants' conduct like a good father. A man who wielded his power to abuse his housemaid was doubly guilty.

When they delivered the verdict, judges treated girls they felt were victims (victims of their own naïveté or of an abuse of power by their master) quite differently from women who could not provide excuses that were valid in the eyes of society. It was the woman, however, who got the benefit of the doubt.

THE WEIGHT OF MALE RESPONSIBILITY

The law made men assume most of the responsibility for the sexual act. However, although seducers were forced to face the consequences of their actions, judges imposed sentences that ranged from mild to harsh, depending on the circumstances. The most severely punished seducer was the Indian Panis Jacques, who was sentenced to penal servitude for life. This sentence partly reflects the fact that the accused had committed a typical abduction with violence: young Marie-Josephe Durand, fourteen years old, had certainly not gone willingly when he abducted her with the intention of taking her to Acadia and making her his wife.[101] The other defendants, all of them European, got off more easily. For instance, Pierre Rouffio, who had abducted Louise Cadet with her consent, had a penal sentence commuted to nine years exile and 10 000 francs in damages and interest.[102]

The Price of Virginity

The sum set by the judge to compensate for loss of feminine honour ranged from 40 to 10 000 francs (table 10), but the fine imposed most often throughout the eighteenth century was in the area of 150 francs. The money was supposed to provide a dowry for the woman so that she could marry "in keeping with her station," notwithstanding the stain on her reputation. Consequently, fines levied reflected social rank. Agathe Petit, for instance, asked for "the equivalent of the satisfaction due to an upper-class daughter."[103] She was awarded 500 francs, which was higher than usual. But other factors explain diverging fines: the girl's age, what a man admitted to, and his ability to pay.

The harshest penalties were inflicted on certain defendants found guilty of abduction, but their financial resources were undoubtedly taken into consideration. The merchant Pierre Rouffio (or his brothers) could handle a fine of 10 000 francs, but this was certainly not true of simple habitants. François Albert, was declared acquitted of the charge of abduction but was nonetheless fined 3000 francs in civil damages and interest, "in view of the social equality between the woman and himself, the girl's minority, and the considerable, even irreparable, damage done to her reputation."[104]

Equality or difference in social status was a significant factor. In cases where the girl was of markedly inferior social status, we found no sentence ordering the man to pay civil damages and interest. A Montreal magistrate's comment to Pierre de Saint-Ours is quite revealing in this context; he asked him why he had set his sights on the Céloron daughter when there were "plenty of girls of lower birth at his beck and call with little risk involved."[105] This seduction of Hélène Céloron de Blainville cost him 1000 francs.

TABLE 10 *DAMAGES IMPOSED BY THE JUDGE*

Fine (in livres)	Proceedings for illicit paternity	Abductions
10 000		1
3 000	1	
1 000	1	1
800		1
600		1
500	2	
400	1	
300	4	
230	1	
200	2	1
150	7	
120	1	
100	6	2
60	1	
50	6	
40	1	

Differences in social standing could also work to the disadvantage of men. When soldiers or vagrants of no fixed address took it upon themselves to seduce daughters, even habitant daughters, they paid dearly for their boldness. Jean-Baptiste Dubord, François Bosne, Antoine Bonin, and Simon Bergeron[106] were promptly imprisoned to stop them from fleeing and were sentenced to pay fines ranging from 200 to 1000 francs to the compromised girls. Simon Bergeron poured fuel on the fire by boasting that he had enjoyed every possible intimacy with the daughter of Louis Truchon while in his service. The indignant father let it be known that "if they didn't make an example of a hired hand who took every liberty in a household, daughters would be at constant risk of losing their reputations." The judge was of the same mind.

Finally, the defendant's admission of guilt could lead to a harsher sentence. Judges cited this reason, among others, when they sentenced five men to pay amounts ranging from 300 to 1000 francs.[107] In these circumstances, it is understandable that so many men vehemently denied having "known" the woman.

When the defendants were single, judges sometimes offered them the option of marrying the girl (8 cases). Some men resigned themselves to this fate to escape ruin. Simon Bergeron offered to marry the Truchon girl rather than have his property seized. François Bosne, who had declared during his trial that he did not want to marry Marie-Anne Lalande because he simply did not like her, was forced to relent when faced with the prospect of paying her 1000 francs. René Lefebvre married Gabrielle Foucault the day after the sentence was delivered, four days before their child was born.[108] Pierre de Saint-Ours ended up marrying Hélène de Blainville,[109] and Joseph Ruffio probably married Louise Cadet, who had been abducted by his brother Pierre, in order to recuperate the 10 000 francs his family had paid her.[110]

Seducing a girl of good reputation could be a costly proposition, especially as the defendant was usually ordered to pay court costs (41 cases). These usually came to less than 40 francs, but could rise as high as 100 francs if a number of witnesses were summoned.[111]

Throughout the French Regime, judges applied legislation that held the man primarily responsible for the affair and obliged him to compensate the woman. Aside from civil compensation, the guilty parties were sometimes ordered to pay alms to the poor in hospitals (7 cases), ostensibly to atone for their "moral" infraction. Prior to 1740, this fine was imposed only three times—twice on the man alone and once on both partners, since the woman was married. However, during the last twenty years of the French Regime, it was imposed four times, in three cases on both partners. Significantly, in 1747, the magistrates of the Prévôté of Quebec sentenced the defendant Saint-Louis to make such a donation because he had impregnated his housemaid,[112] but the Superior Council, which heard the appeal, ordered both servant and master to pay the fine. Apparently this tribunal had reached the conclusion that both partners were equally guilty of the moral infraction, although civil damages continued to be paid by the man alone.

Foster Fathers Despite Themselves

Civil proceedings always included a petition that aimed to make the defendant take charge of the illegitimate child. The old French adage, "He who engenders a child must feed it,"[113] applied in the colony, where it was reflected in both popular custom and judicial practice.

The man was ordered to provide for the child's needs more often than to pay damages to the woman (61 cases to 41). The man might be exempt from civil reparation for one reason or another, but as soon as it was proven that he had had sexual relations with the plaintiff, he became responsible for the resulting child. Accordingly, neither Nicolas Lemoyne nor Pierre Hervé, who both admitted to "carnally enjoying" Elisabeth Campeau, was sentenced to compensate the young woman, whose reputation was already suspect, but they were held jointly responsible for the support and education of the child that either one of them might have fathered.[114] If the putative father was a minor, his parents or guardian had to share this responsibility with him.

If a judge ordered a presumed father to provide for a child's needs, he usually obliged him to personally assume the responsibility (49 cases); in other words, the father had to take the child from the mother at birth, give it to a nurse and pay for her services, regularly take a health certificate signed by a priest to the Crown prosecutor, and keep an eye on the child until it was old enough to earn a living. If the mother nursed the child herself (9 cases), the father had to pay for this service just as he would have paid a wetnurse.[115]

Most of the putative fathers tried to shirk this responsibility by denying that they had fathered the child. Accordingly, they declared that they had never known the woman (34 cases), blamed the pregnancy on another man (17 cases), or performed complicated calculations to prove that the beginning of the pregnancy did not coincide with the time of the affair (7 cases). Some men who were sentenced to take care of the child accepted the verdict with great reluctance. For instance, when his offspring was brought to him, François Beauchamps cried, "I want nothing to do with the b—— of a child."[116] Other men had stronger paternal instincts: nine of them acknowledged their fatherhood in court and five others, who had not been brought to trial, voluntarily placed their children with nurses or drew up legacies to ensure that they would be provided for.[117]

A practical consideration made some fathers look at the bright side of things. The child would be a financial burden during the early years, but after the age of twelve or thirteen represented considerable working potential. The child then became more than just another mouth to feed; she or he had a pair of arms that could be put to work. That's why Claude Nau agreed to take the child he was accused of producing with Geneviève Meran, "on condition that neither the woman nor anyone else would be permitted to take it back, since it seemed fair that to repay him for the cost of food, board, and education, the child would render the services of which he was capable until the age of 18."[118] From this perspective, it seems likely that boys would have been somewhat more welcome than girls, since they could do more work. The child that Claude Nau agreed to take was a boy. And, Louis Briquet, who had stated that he was ready to take a child under the same conditions, suddenly changed his tune when his mistress gave birth to a daughter.[119] But judges took no account of the child's sex when delivering their verdict. Boy or girl, it was up to the father to take care of the child.

The custom of taking a child from its mother to entrust it to a paid wetnurse seems surprising, going against maternal feelings and even basic common sense. First, it should be pointed out that not all unwed mothers spontaneously exhibited maternal love. Geneviève Picoté de Belestre, for instance, declared to the Montreal bailiff "that she would not care for her offspring, that she would rather die than nurse it."[120] In this particular case, it was surely better to hand the child over to a nurse. But the general attitude of judges, who entrusted almost all the children to the fathers, was shaped by other forces, including the patriarchal ideas of the time, which attributed a more important role to the man in the procreative act,[121] and economic conditions, which made it easier for men to provide for the needs of the children. During the French Regime, rare was the woman who could earn an independant living and still raise a child. Louise Savaria, a widow who worked as a seamstress, was able to keep her child until she remarried.[122] Some women who could count on the support of their families did likewise. But women who were completely alone could not manage. Marguerite Vanier, for instance, placed her three-year-old child because she could not afford to feed and raise it.[123]

Not all the mothers who gave up their children were indifferent or without feelings. Marguerite César provided her son with a bed and clothing and continued to look out for him after she had turned him over to the Crown prosecutor who placed him with a bootmaker. When she realized that he was not being properly cared for, she arranged to have him returned to her.[124]

Did the judges who were so concerned with ensuring the material and spiritual well-being of the illegitimate children consider the possibility of emotional ties between mother and child? There are signs of progress in this respect. In the seventeenth century, each time that a magistrate left an illegitimate child with the mother for a major reason (only 4 cases), he simultaneously enjoined her to take good care under pain of punishment.[125] Clearly, the law put no stock in maternal instinct. Perhaps they even suspected that these poor women would let their children perish from negligence because the burden would be too heavy for them. In the eighteenth century, however, these exhortations disappeared. On one hand, two unwed mothers who had nursed their children themselves appeared in court, in 1725 and 1741, to seek custody. The judge granted their requests, but on condition that they no longer expect any support from the father.[126] This suggests that if they wanted to replace the father in the role of supporting parent, they were expected to assume the concomitant disadvantages as well as the advantages. In one case in 1723, the intendant decided that the unwed mother would retain custody of the child, but the father would pay her an allowance.[127] Judges were not completely indifferent to maternal feelings. But until the end of the French Regime, they continued to put the child into the father's care in most cases.

CONCLUSION

The most striking fact that emerges from the study of judicial proceedings concerning unwed mothers is how infrequently these women instituted proceedings even though the law tended to be in their favour. Clearly, they were averse to flaunting their disgrace. The unwed mothers and their families preferred to try and settle the problem as discreetly as possible, using the courts only as a last resort. Nonetheless, the impact of judicial measures in settling these matters should not be underestimated. The threat of a trial convinced more than one man to assume his responsibilities. On the other hand, the number of trials did not increase in proportion to the population, which stood at 15 000 toward 1700 but had risen to 55 000 at the end of the French Regime. This clearly indicates that as the population grew and stabilized, social control mechanisms outside the court system became increasingly efficient.

Although only a limited number of cases were studied, the breakdown of sentences delivered by judges allows us to partially reconstitute society's scale of tolerance for extramarital sexual relations. Notwithstanding religious precepts, it seems to have been tacitly accepted that men could have affairs with women who were "up for grabs," meaning prostitutes or even slaves. In fact, not one man incurred legal sanctions for this type of conduct. Some tolerance was also displayed toward upper-class men who seduced working-class girls as long as they were not their servants. When these girls found themselves in an embarrassing situation, the seducers were subtly urged to provide for their needs, but legal proceedings were rarely successful. Affairs between future spouses were excused, provided that marriage ensued. Here, a combination of familial, social, and legal pressures forced the young man to marry. However, it was imperative to respect the social hierarchy, and young men were strictly forbidden to disgrace a young woman of good family. Men who did so had to make reparations. The seduction of housemaids was punished. Society therefore imposed limits on male sexual freedom; men were allowed to sow their wild oats with prostitutes, but could not bring disgrace upon respectable families. Men who *abused* their privileges by tampering with a prohibited class of girls were required to pay civil damages.

Society was much less permissive toward women. While men could enjoy amorous escapades without losing their honour, a girl who had more than one lover was immediately branded a loose woman. In addition, even if a woman had had only one affair, loss of virginity was synonymous with loss of honour and reputation. Declarations to this effect by unwed mothers, their families and even judges are confirmed in some fifteen trials instituted by girls falsely accused of being pregnant or having a lover, who demanded reparations of honour.[128] We found no case where a man sought reparations for similar reasons. Civil and religious law obliged men to compensate seduced women because they suffered a much greater social handicap than did men.

Society during the French Regime may have been slightly more indulgent toward widows. Certainly Louise Savaria, the widow of Louis Métivier, managed to retain custody of a child fathered by Nicolas Giroux without losing the respect of her neighbours.[129]

Unwed mothers, who faced harsher social censure than the fathers, tried to mitigate their offence by describing their adventure so that it diverged as little as possible from the code of behaviour, society imposed on young women. And the judge, in delivering his verdict, always signalled what was acceptable or blameworthy in their behaviour, and indicated just how far the man had overstepped his limits. In the arguments raised in court by plaintiffs, defendants, witnesses and judges alike, we can clearly discern how society expected young men and women to behave sexually.

From the facts as stated by the girl and her parents, the following behavioural norms can be deduced. The young man took the initiative. He pestered the woman with his attentions, declared his love to her, gave her presents, and promised to marry her. Sometimes he threatened her or used force, and finally he had his way with her. The woman initially resisted his overtures, but gradually she gave in and fell for his promises.[130] From start to finish, the man acted and the woman reacted. He played an essentially active role (the seducer); she was more passive (the seduced). If the judge was persuaded that this was the course of events, he decided in the girl's favour. But if the man managed to convince the judge that the girl's actions diverged from this pattern, that she made advances or had had more than one affair,[131] or in other words, that she behaved like a man, she was instantly condemned for her misconduct. For a woman, behaving like a man meant misbehaving. Gender roles in sexual matters were thus clearly defined in New France, and women who stepped outside them faced social ostricization.

Responsibility for illegitimate children was also clearly defined. The man had to provide for the needs of the child he had fathered. If his paternity were proven (by whatever means were available at the time), the judge almost never allowed him to shirk his obligation. However, law and custom attributed an auxiliary role to the woman. In the father's absence, the court could entrust the mother with childcare "as she is obliged by every kind of law," and women who requested custody of their child easily won their case. So it seems that maternal rights could override paternal obligations. If judges continued to turn newborns over to the fathers, it was clearly because the women themselves accepted it, and because the men were usually better equipped to support their offspring.

Legislation that obliged men to compensate for the injury caused to seduced girls was reminiscent of Church teachings. On the other hand, the social attitude that granted men greater sexual freedom diverged from Christian doctrine. The clergy attempted to palliate the resulting injustices by intervening to organize marriages of reparation or to help the mother and child. Unable to change social norms, priests and later religious communities adapted their action to the needs of society with important results. Not until the late twentieth century did a radically transformed view of gender roles and the demand for equal sexual freedom for men and women succeed in quelling the discredit implicit in the term "unwed mother."

NOTES

1. Jean-Baptiste-Antoine Ferland, *La France dans l'Amérique du Nord* (Tours: Mame, 1929), tome II, p. 8. Lionel Groulx, "La famille canadienne-française, ses traditions, son rôle," *Semaines sociales du Canada*, 4th session, Montreal, 1923, on "The Family," (Montreal: bibliothèque de l'Action française, 1924), 337. Robert-Lionel Séguin, *La vie libertine en Nouvelle-France au dix-septième siècle* (Montreal: Leméac, 1972), 2 vols. See also Jean Blain, "La moralité en Nouvelle-France: les phases de la thèse et de l'antithèse," *Revue d'histoire de l'Amérique française* (hereinafter *RHAF*) 27 (Dec. 1973): 408–16.

2. Lyne Paquette and Réal Bates, "Les naissances illégitimes sur les rives du Saint-Laurent avant 1730" *RHAF* 40 (Autumn 1986): 239–52. Réal Bates, "Les conceptions prénuptiales dans la vallée du Saint-Laurent avant 1725," *RHAF* 40 (Autumn 1986): 253–72.

3. Demographers carefully distinguish between premarital conceptions and illegitimate births. In the first case, there was a sexual relationship between a man and

woman who were not married to each other, but the couple married before the birth and the child is legitimate. In the second case, the man and woman do not marry before the birth of the child, who is born out of wedlock and is therefore illegitimate. In judicial and notarial acts we find both cases, but there are more illegitimate births. The women may be single, widowed, or married. For the sake of brevity, we will use the term "unwed mother" in this article to designate any "illicitly pregnant" women, if necessary, pointing out the special instances of widows and married women. Likewise, we will use the term "illegitimate children" even if ten of them were legitimized because their mother married before giving birth.

4. The research was carried out at the Archives nationales de Québec (ANQQ), Montréal (ANQM), and Trois-Rivières (ANQTR). ANQM Archives judiciares (AJ), Registres des audiences (Reg. aud.), Juridiction du bailliage de la seigneurie de Montréal (Jur. bailliage), 1665–1693, vol. 1–6; Juridiction royale (Jur. royale), 1693–1760, vol. 1–28; Documents judiciares en pièces détachées (Doc. jud.), 1644–1760, boxes no. 39–168. ANQTR, Archives judiciaires (AJ), Juridiction royale de Trois-Rivières, 1655–1759, vol. 1–14. Juridiction du Cap-de-la-Madeleine, 1659–1685; Juridiction seigneuriale de Batiscan, 1662, 1742–1753; Juridiction seigneuriale de Champlain, 1669–1684. The archives of the seigneuriale courts were inventoried in the *Rapport de l'archiviste de la province de Québec*, t. 49 (1971), 6–35. ANQQ, Archives de la Prévôté de Québec, Registres des causes criminelles, des sentences extraordinaires, des documents épars, des pièces détachées, des causes civiles. In the last case (and for civil cases only), we used a sampling corresponding to years 1, 3, 6, and 9 of each decade. (Henceforth, Prév. Q., Reg. civil, Reg. crim., Petit crim., Grand crim. ou Doc. épars.)

Dossiers du Conseil supérieur. Precédures judiciaires, Matières criminelles, 1665–1759, 6 vol. Collection of judicial and notarial documents, including the registers of hearings of the seigneury of Notre-Dame-des-Anges (inventoried by Pierre-Georges Roy) (henceforth CPJN). Registres des jugements du Conseil supérieur (c.S), 1717–1759 (inventoried by Pierre-Georges Roy). Ordonnances des Intendants, 1666–1760, (inventoried by Pierre-Georges Roy) (henceforth OI). *Jugements et délibérations du Conseil souverain, 1663–1716* (Quebec, 1891), 6 vols. (henceforth JDCS). We found several useful references in: Séguin, *La vie libertine*; André Lachance, "*La justice criminelle du roi au Canada au XVIIIe siècle*" (Ph.D. thesis, University of Ottawa, 1974). Raymond Boyer, *Les crimes et les châtiments au Canada française du XVIIe au XXe siècles* (Montreal: Le Cercle du livre de France, 1966). We also checked all the record offices from the time of the French Regime.

5. Jean-Louis Flandrin, *Les amours paysannes (XVIe–XIXe siècle)* (Paris: Gallimard-Julliard, 1975), 200–35. Jacques Depauw, "Amour illégitime et société à Nantes au XVIIIe siècle," *Annales, Economie, Société, Civilisation* (1972): 1155–83. Mireille Laget, "Déclarations de grossesse et accusations d'infanticide devant la châtellenie de Pézenas au XVIIIe siècle" in *Pézenas. Ville et campagne. XIIIe–XXe siècles* (Montpellier: Fédération historique du Languedoc méditerranéen et du Roussillon, 1976), 185–96. Marie-Claude Phan, "Typologie d'aventures amoureuses d'après les déclarations de grossesse et les procédures criminelles enregistrées à Carcassone de 1676 à 1786" in *Aimer en France, 1760–1860* (Colloque international de Clermond-Ferrand, Association des publications de la Faculté des lettres et sciences humaines, 1977, 1980), 503–11. Alain Lottin, "Naissances illégitimes et filles-mères à Lille au XVIIIe siècle," *Revue d'histoire moderne et contemporaine* 17 (April–June

1970): 278–322. Jacques Depauw, "Les filles-mères se mariaient-elles? L'exemple de Nantes au XVIIIe siècle," *Aimer en France, 1760–1860*, 525–31. Legal appeals available to unwed mothers in French law are outlined in the following articles: Anne Lefebvre-Teillard, "L'enfant naturel dans l'ancien droit français," *Recueils de la société Jean Bodin pour l'histoire comparée des institutions*, tome 36, *L'enfant* (1976), 251–69. Marie-Claude Phan, "Les déclarations de grossesse en France (XVIe–XVIIIe siècles): essai institutionnel" *Revue d'histoire moderne et contemporaine*, tome 22 (1975), 61–88. Aline Logette, "Naissances illégitimes en Lorraien dans la première moitié du XVIIIe siècle d'après les déclarations de grossesse et la jurisprudence," *Annales de l'Est* (1983), no. 2: 91–125; no. 3: 221–45. Arlette Farge, "Séduite et abandonnée" in *La vie fragile: Violence, pouvoir et solidarités à Paris au XVIIIe siècle* (Paris: Hachette, 1986), 37–54.

6. Paquette and Bates, "Les naissances illégitimes," 248, 250.

7. The figures pertaining to the Canadian population, the percentage of upper-class people, and the breakdown by government are taken from an unpublished article by Fernand Ouellet, "Origine de l'industrialisation et developpement régional au Québec avant 1850."

8. Logette, "Naissances illégitimes," 99; Phan, "Typologie," 505; Depauw, "Amour illégitime," 1163; Lottin, "Naissances illégitimes," 310. We are currently doing research on the status of unwed mothers in Québec, from 1850 to 1970, and we have observed that many of the patients at the Hôpital de la Miséricorde de Québec were unwed mothers.

9. ANQQ, Report of Pierre Rousselot, no. 246, 4 July 1744, Jacques Rodrigue and Madeleine Lemieux promised to marry and make their child who had been born two

months earlier legitimate; Record office of J. Pinguet, 10 Nov. 1742, will of Philibert Mahon, known as Champagne, who bequeathed 500 francs to Catherine Friscot "to compensate the wrong he had done her under a promise of marriage, which he could not fulfill."

10. Flandrin, *Les amours paysannes*, 74–75.

11. ANQQ, Dossiers du C.S., Prpc., jud., Mat. civ., vol. 1. f. 7–15, 5 June 1700. Trial between Jean Foucault and Elisabeth Provost, representing their daughter Gabrielle, and René Lefebvre.

12. ANQQ, Dossiers of C.S., Proc. jud., Mat. civ., vol. 2 f. 146–52. Trial between Sieur André de Leigne and Madame de Rouville, 1741.

13. ANQQ, CPJN, no. 408, Aug.–Sept. 1707. Trial between Madeleine Maugras and Jean-Baptiste Dubord, known as Latourelle.

14. Jean-Baptiste de la Croix de Chevrière de Saint-Vallier, *Catéchisme du diocèse de Québec 1702* (Montréal: Editions franciscaines, 1958), 188.

15. Jean-Louis Flandrin, *Le sexe et l'Occident: Evolution des attitudes et des comportements* (Paris: Seuil, 1987), 285–91; ANQQ, OI, vol. 30, 18 April 1742.

16. ANQM, AJ, Rég. aud. jur. royale, vol. 24, f. 87, 4 Feb. 1747; *Dictionnaire biographique du Canada* (DBC), 3: 617–18; 4: 216–17.

17. ANQM, AJ, Reg. aud. jur. royale, vol. 21 (1741–43) f. 241 v., 9 Nov. 1742; f. 259. 29 Nov. 1742. Doc. jud., b. 149, 26 Nov. 1742. Trial between Urbain and François Brossard concerning the marriage of their sister Thérèse and Pierre Sera, known as Coquillard.

18. ANQQ, Prév. A., Reg. civil, vol. 70, f. 83, 27 Jan. 1733; f. 89. 3 Feb. 1733; Trial between Jean Willis and Claude Louet.

19. ANQQ, OI, 7 March 1747.

20. ANQQ, Prév. Q., Reg. Petit Crim., vol. 44, f. 4, 25 June 1704; JDCS, 4: 1072–73, trial between Olivier Morel de la Durantaye and Robert Mossion; Reg. civil, v. 47, f. 39–40, 6 March 1705; JDCS 5: 56, 16 March 1705, trial between Gabrielle Thivierge and Françoise Morel Sieur de Boisbrillant de la Durantaye.

21. ANQM, AJ, Doc. jud., b. 84, 9–25 Oct. 1713. Trial between André Poutret Lavigne and his brothers representing Madeleine Duclos, their niece, and Jacques Diel.

22. ANQM, Aj, Doc. jud. b. 67, 11 March–15 April 1701. Trial between Catherine Paulo, Campeau widow and mother of Elisabeth, and Nicolas Lemoyne.

23. ANQQ, Prév. Q., Reg. civil, vol. 52, f. 132 v., 15 March 1718; v. 53, f. 60, 10 Aug. 1718; v. 53, f. 81, 6 Sept. 1718; v. 53, f. 175, 18 April 1719; v. 55, f. 28–30, 21 Feb. 1720; Jugements du C.S., 15 July 1720, f. 90. Trial between Guillaume Levitre, father of Madeleine, and François Albert. ANQQ, Dossiers du C.S., Proc. jud. Mat. civ., vol. I, f. 7–15, June 1700; ANQTR, AJ de Trois-Rivières, v. 6, f. 349, 14 June 1700; f. 356, 6 July 1700 trial between Jean Foucault and Elisabeth Provost, parents of Gabrielle, and René Lefebvre.

24. ANQQ, Prév. Q., Doc. épars, vol. 24, f. 28, 11 Sept. 1696. Trial between Michel Bouchard, father of Marguerite, and Pierre Dubro. Reg. civil, v. 32, f. 93, 18 Sept. 1696.

25. ANQM, AJ, Doc. jud., b. 60, 12 July–3 Sept. 1697. Trial of Madeleine Gibault for infanticide.

26. ANQQ, Prév. Q., Doc. épars, vol. 24, f. 27, 30 July 1696. Jouineau–Bonamy trial.

27. ANQM, AJ, Doc. jud., b. 82, 12 Sept. 1712. Petition of Joseph and Barbe Chevalier against Pierre de l'Estage, merchant. ANQM, AJ, Doc. jud., b. 88, 11 Dec. 1715. Declaration of pregnancy by Madeleine Clignancourt. The seducer was Renéde Couagne, merchant.

28. ANQM, Doc. jud., b. 121, 14 July 1730. Declaration of pregnancy by Marie Panise.

29. Phan, "Typologie," 505.

30. ANQQ, Dossiers du C.S., Proc. jud., Mat. crim., vol. 3, f. 70 v., 1707. Cross-examination of Potier.

31. Jean-Louis Flandrin, *Familles, parenté, maison, sexualité dans l'ancienne société* (Paris: Seuil, 1984), 97–104.

32. ANQQ, CPJN, no. 465 1/2. 1712. Trial between Louise Savaria and Nicolas Giroux. Testimony of Pierre Bourgoin.

33. ANQQ, CPJN, no. 739b, 1726. Trial of Geneviève Gaudreau for infanticide.

34. ANQQ, OI, v. 38, 14 Feb. 1750.

35. Depauw, "Amour illégitime," 1163; Lottin, "Naissances illégitimes," 305; Phan, "Typologie," 505; Logette, "Naissances illégitimes," 99; Laget, "Déclarations," 169.

36. Bates, "Les conceptions prénuptiales," 262.

37. ANQQ, Dossiers du C.S., Proc. jud., Mat. crim., vol. 2, f. 163–413, 1705, proceedings against Sir de Saint-Ours; ANQM, AJ, Doc. jud., b. 84, 30 Nov. and 31 Dec. 1713, petition of Jean Monnet, father of Marie, against François Campot.

38. ANQQ, CPJN, no. 293, 8 July 1701, directive against Suzanne Jouineau (Larose) for concealing her pregnancy; Dossiers du C.S., Proc. jud., Mat. Crim., vol. 3, f. 159 and 164, trial of Barbe Dupont for infanticide.

39. ANQM, AJ, Reg. aud. jur. royale, vol. 21 (1741–43), f. 241 vol., 9 Nov. 1742, trial between François and Urban Brossard; ANQQ, Dossiers du C.S., Proc. jud., Mat. crim., vol., 5. 275–403, 1753, trial between Augustin Cadet and Pierre Rouffio.

40. ANQM, AJ, Doc., b. 84, 30 Nov. and 31 Dec. 1713, petition of Jean

Monnet, father of Marie, against François Campot; Reg. aud. jur. royale, vol. 27, f. 154, 16 Nov. 1754, Dany–Louveteau trial.

41. ANQM, AJ, Doc. jud., b. 49, 6 May 1686, declaration of Jeanne Guitet concerning her pregnancy; ANQQ, CPJN, no. 730 and 739, Jan. 1726, trial of Geneviève Gaudreau for infanticide; Prév. Q., Reg. civil, vol. 91, f. 288, 12 Dec. 1747, trial between Louis Roy, father of Marie-Josephe, and François Fabas (Saint-Louis).

42. Allusions to attempted abortions appear in six trials. In particular, ANQQ, Prév. Q., Doc. épars, vol. 24, f. 20, 14 Nov. 1693; JDCS 3: 816–18, 1 Jan. 1694, Bouchard–Gagnon trial.

43. ANQM, AJ, Doc. jud., b. 40, 9 July 1671. Cross-examination of Françoise Duverger.

44. ANQM, AJ Doc. jud., b. 92, 3 Oct. 1717; ANQQ, CPJN, no. 847, 19 Feb. 1730.

45. ANQM, AJ, Doc. jud., b. 67, 11 March to 15 April 1701. Trial of Elisabeth Campeau. Recounted in detail in Séguin, *La vie libertine*, 264–67.

46. Sieur de Blainville sent his daughter Hélène to the country "because he did not want her to suffer or be seen in Montreal while she was pregnant." ANQQ, Dossiers du C.S., Proc. jud., Mat. crim., vol. 2, f. 214, trial Blainville–Saint-Ours. The granddaughter of the widow Pinel (who lived in Quebec) said that her mother would be disgraced when she gave birth and that she would give birth in the country. ANQQ, Dossiers du C.S., Proc. jud., Mat. crim., vol. 3, f. 165, 1708. Trial of Marie-Barbe Dupont the Pinel widow for infanticide.

47. Paquette and Bates, "Les naissances illégitimes," 242.

48. ANQM, AJ, Doc. jud., b. 49, 6 May 1686, declaration of Jeanne Guitet concerning her pregnancy; b. 121, 14 July 1730, declaration of preg-

nancy of the bonded servant, Marie; ANQQ, Dossiers du C.S., Proc. jud., Mat. crim., vol. 4, 3 May 1732, f. 174–89, trial of Marie-Anne Sigouin.

49. In eight cases, the family declared that they were dishonoured, notably: ANQM, AJ, Reg. aud. jur. royale, vol. 21 (1741–73), f. 241 v., 9 Nov. 1742, trial between François and Urbain Brossard concerning the marriage of their sister Thérèse; Doc. jud., b. 84, 9–25 Oct. 1713, trial between André Poutret and his brothers, representing their niece Madeleine Duclos, and Jacques Diel; another example of family solidarity: Elisabeth Campeau's brothers threatened to kill Pierre Hervé if he spoke badly of their sister when making his deposition to the judge. Record office of Adhémar, 25 May 1701, declaration of Pierre Hervé.

50. ANQM, AJ, Reg. aud. jur. royale, vol. 21 (1741–43), f. 241 v., 9 Nov. 1742, trial between Urbain and François Brossard; v. 24 (1746–49), f. 340–41, 18 Nov. 1748, trial between Louis Truchon, known as Léveillé, and Simon Bergeron.

51. ANQQ, Jugements du C.S., 15 July 1720, f. 90. Levitre–Albert trial.

52. Demographers Paquette and Bates have estimated that 23 percent unwed mothers remained single. Paquette and Bates, "Les naissances illégitimes," 249–50.

53. René Jetté, *Dictionnaire généalogique des familles canadiennes* (PUM, 1983), 142.

54. ANQQ, OI, vol. 26, 10 May 1738.

55. ANQQ, Dossiers du C.S., Proc. jud., Mat. crim., vol. 2, 1705. Blainville– Saint-Ours trial, f. 207 v.

56. During the trial of René Lefebvre, a witness declared to have told Lefebvre "that he should restore the honour of the girl everyone knew he had abused." Another witness supposedly told Lefebvre "that since he had abused [the girl], he should marry her." ANQQ,

Dossiers du C.S., Proc. jud., Mat. civ., vol. 1, f. 7–15, 5 June–6 July 1700. Trial between Jean Foucault and his wife, parents of Gabrielle, and René Lefebvre. The Bigot father spoke to Jean-Baptiste Dubord about Madeleine Maugras's pregnancy and asked him if he didn't want to marry her. ANQQ, CPJN, no. 408, 1707. Trial between Madeleine Maugras and J.-B. Dubord. A confessor made Pierre Dubro sign a written marriage promise. ANQQ, Prév. Q., Doc. épars, vol. 24, f. 28, 11 Sept. 1696; Reg. civil, vol. 32, f. 93, 18 Sept. 1696. Trial between Michel Bouchard, father of Marguerite, and Pierre Dubro.

57. See table 1. However, the pregnant woman did not necessarily marry the father of her child. Anne Lugré, for instance, who was made pregnant by Sieux de Repentigny, married Gilles Gadiou. ANQM, AJ, Doc. jud., 8 July 1686. Quoted by Séguin, *La vie libertine*, 326. (We did not however find this document in the archives).

58. Paquette and Bates, "Les naissances légitimes," 249.

59. ANQM, AJ, Doc. jud., b. 82, 12 Sept. 1712, trial between Barbe Chevalier and the master of l'Estage; b. 82, 30 Oct. 1712 and Reg. aud. jur. royale, vol. 7, f. 883–84, 6 Nov. 1712, trial between Marie Hébert and Hertel de Rouville.

60. ANQM, Report of Simon Sanguinet senior, 20 Nov. 1742, agreement between Jean Arnaut and his wife, parents of Marguerite, and Christophe Lussier, on behalf of Jacques Chaleu, his son-in-law; Record-office of Adhémar, 8021 a, 17 July 1708, agreement between the parents of Medeleine Drousson and Lord de La Découverte.

61. ANQQ, CPJN, no. 465 1/2, 1712, trial between Louise Savaria and Nicolas Giroux; Dossiers du C.S., proc. jud., Mat. crim., vol. 1, 12

Aug. 1682, cross-examination of Marguerite Boissel, widow of Bouchard.

62. ANQQ, OI, 15 Dec. 1709; ANQM, AJ, Doc. jud., b. 78, 29 Dec. 1709; Reg. aud. jur. royale, vol. 5, f. 606–7, 5 June 1705.

63. See our article "Les attitudes devant la mort d'après les clauses testamentaires sous le Régime français," *RHAF* 32 (June 1978), 62.

64. ANQQ, Prév. Q., Reg. Petit Crim., vol. 13, f. 6, 29 July 1678, trial of Charlotte Préquet; the father of Louise Quay sent a child to Antoine Bonnin "as his progeny," CPJN, no. 3564-1, 21 April 1721, petition of Louis Quay, father of Louise, against Antoine Bonnin; Pierre Bourgoin, finally, threatened to greet with gunshot anyone who brought him Louise Savaria's child, CPJN, no. 465, 1712, Savaria–Giroux trial. Deposition of François Traversy.

65. In Roman society, the newborn would be laid on the ground at his father's feet. If he picked it up, the father expressed his intention to raise it. If he left it on the ground, he abandoned it. See Jacques Gélis, *L'arbre et le fruit: La naissance dans l'Occident moderne, XVIe–XIXe siècle* (Paris: Fayard, 1984), 422. Also see Laget, "Déclarations," 192; Lefebvre-Teillard, "L'enfant naturel," 259; Phan, "Les déclarations," 82.

66. ANQM, AJ, Doc. jud., b. 102, 21 June and 18 July 1722. Saint-Yves and Lajeunesse trial.

67. ANQQ, OI, 5 Jan. 1722. A young girl from La Chevrotière, Geneviève Méran, had given birth to a child and named Claude Nau as the father. He denied the charge. This led to a feud between the two families, who threatened to shoot one another. Worried, the priest alerted the intendant.

68. CNQQ, CPJN, no. 720 B, 21 Oct. 1724. Excerpt from the registers of the Quebec Diocesan Council. The research we did at the Archives de

l'Archevêché de Québec to find further information on the six cases was fruitless.

69. We should point out that breach of the marriage promise alone could entail the obligation to compensate the injured party (man or woman), even if the woman was not pregnant. ANQM, AJ, Reg. bailliage 1687–90, f. 176–78, 18 Nov. 1687, breach of a marriage promise; Doc. jud., b. 77, 26 May 1708, breach of a marriage contract.

70. Lefebvre-Teillard, "L'enfant naturel," 260.

71. Flandrin, *Les amours paysannes*, 38–39.

72. François Serpillon, *Code criminel ou commentaire sur l'ordonnance de 1670* (Lyon, 1784), tome 1, 97.

73. François-André Isambert, *Recueil des anciennes lois françaises depuis l'an 420 jusqu'à la Révolution de 1789* (Paris, 1827–29), tome 14, 392, quoted in Flandrin, *Les amours paysannes*, 43–44.

74. ANQQ, CPJN, no. 720E, 5 Jan. 1725. Petition of François Janis to the lieutenant general of the Provostship of Quebec.

75. Flandrin, *Les amours paysannes*, 43–44. Jean Gaudemet, "Législation canonique et attitudes séculières à l'égard du lien matrimonial au XVIIe siècle," *XVIIe siècle* 102–3 (1974): 15–31.

76. Flandrin, *ibid.*, 44 and Serpillon, *Code criminelle*, 100.

77. In 1701, the substitute for the Crown prosecutor, Raimbault, demanded the death penalty for Nicolas Lemoyne, charged with abduction, ANQM, AJ, Doc. jud., b. 72, 4 April 1701; in 1734, the Crown prosecutor at Trois-Rivières also demanded the death penalty for Panis Jacques who was accused of abduction, ANQQ, Dossiers du C.S., Proc. jud., Mat. crim., 4: 233, 14 July 1734. Neither man was put to death.

78. See note 20. Trial involving the De La Durantaye sons.

79. Serpillon, *Code criminelle*, 98–99, and Jean-François Fournel, *Traité de la séduction considerée dans l'order judiciaire* (Paris, 1781), 322, quoted in Phan, "Les déclarations," 82.

80. JDCS, 5: 895–99, 905, 20 Aug. 1708. Trial of Barbe Dupont for infanticide and order to read from the pulpit the edict of Henri II, once a month for one year.

81. ANQ, OI, 8: 16, Ordonnance de Bégon, 6 Feb. 1722. Extensive excerpts from this ordinance are printed in la Broquerie Fortier's article, "Les enfants trouvés sous les Régimes français et anglais au Canada français, 1608–1850," *Laval médical* 33 (Sept. 1962): 530–37; 34 (April 1963): 442–53 (Dec. 1963): 1242–54; 35 (March 1964): 335–47; (April 1964): 469–80; 36 (April 1965): 351–59; (May 1965): 466–76.

82. ANQQ, CPJN, no. 408, 31 Aug. 1707. Maugras–Dubord Latourelle trial.

83. ANQM, AJ, Doc. jud., b. 84, 30 Nov.–31 Dec. 1713. Trial between Jean Monet, father of Marie, and François Campot.

84. ANQM, AJ, Doc. jud., 8 July 1686. Charge made by Marie Lugré against Lord d'Arpentigny. Quoted in Séguin, *La vie libertine*, 326.

85. ANQM, AJ, Reg. aud. jur. royale, vol. 19, f. 100, 17 Sept. 1739. Trial between Louis Morel, father of Brigitte, and Paul Cristin.

86. For instance, the mother of Antoine Beaujean accused Marie Brazeau of having "caused a scandal and disgraced their family" by seducing her minor son, ANQM, AJ, Doc. jud., b. 55, Oct. 1692, Brazeau–Beaujean trial. Lord de Rouville stated that "as he feared the disgrace of being brought before the court for such a base reason," he would agree to compensate the girl; ANQM, AJ, Reg. aud. jur. royale, vol. 7, f. 833–34, 6 Nov. 1712, Hébert–Rouville trial.

87. ANQQ, Prév. A., Reg. civil, v. 31, f. 332–33, 24 Dec. 1699. Boucher-Aubert trial.

88. Damages could also be required from a guardian or master in the case of a slave. ANQM, AJ, Doc. jud., b. 78, 30 Jan.–16 Feb. 1709, trial between Angéline Chapacou, mother of Marie Boutillié, and Urbain Gervaise, brother-in-law and guardian of Pierre Perthuis; Reg. aud. jur. royale, vol. 21 (1741–43), f. 32 v., 9 Feb. 1742, Doc. jud., b. 148, 20 April 1742, trial between Bleury de Sabrevois, master of the maid-servant Charlotte Rondeau, and Antoine Ménard, owner of the slave Charles.

89. ANQM, AJ, Doc. jud., b. 67, 11 March–15 April 1701. Trial between Catherine Paulo, mother of Elisabeth Campeau, and Nicolas Lemoyne. Confrontation of Elisabeth Campeau and Nicolas Lemoyne on 17 March.

90. ANQQ, Dossiers du C.S., Proc. jud., Mat. crim., vol. 2, 1705. Blainville–St-Ours trial, f. 211 v. ss and 194.

91. ANQM, AJ, Doc. jud., b. 55, Oct. 1692. Brazeau–Beaujean trial.

92. ANQQ, Prév. Q., Teg. civil, vol. 32, f. 93, 18 Sept. 1696; vol. 35, f. 102–103, 9 Oct. 1696. Bouchard–Dubro trial.

93. ANQQ, CPJN, no. 4651/2, 1712. Savaria–Giroux trial. Our italics. We should add that Giroux's mother called Louise Savaria a "slut."

94. ANQQ, CPJN, no. 465, March–July 1712, trial between Louise Savaria and Michel Giroux and Thérèse Prévost, parents of Nicolas Giroux, deposition of Jean Baugy; and ANQM, AJ, Reg. aud. jur. royale, vol. 27 (1749–55), 23 May 1755, trial between Jean Aubain, father of Angélique, and Joseph Delcourt. In France, consideration was also given to this declaration made "in doloribus partus." See Logette,

"Naissances illégitimes," 222; Lottin, "Naissances illégitimes," 280–81.

95. The father of Marie-Anne Trudel even maintained that "in matters like this, the declaration of the abuse girl accompanied by the religion of the oath sufficed, for all that it was followed by the slightest presumptions to condemn the accused." ANQQ, OI, vol. 30, 18 April 1742.

96. ANQM, Reg. aud. jur. royale, vol. 25 (1749–54), f. 163–164, 8 June 1751, trial between Marguerite Bissonnet, widow, and Maurice Vincent; ANQQ, Prév. Q., Reg. Petit Crim., vol. 13, f. 6, 29 July 1678, trial between the Crown prosecutor and Charlotte Préquet, wife of René Richard, who was out of the country; Reg. Petit Crim., vol. 13, f. 15, 10 June 1679, trial held at the request of the Crown prosecutor against Marie Loubier, wife of Simon Simard, who was out of the country.

97. Marguerite Bouchard obtained damages in 1693 when she was seduced for the first time by Jean Gagnon, but not in 1696 when she became pregnant the second time, by Pierre Dubro. ANQQ, Prév. Q., Doc. épars, vol. 24, f. 20, 14 Nov. 1693; JDCS 3: 793, 809, 816, 23 Nov. 1693–1 Jan. 1694, trial between Michel Bouchard, father of Marguerite, and Jean Gagnon; ANQQ, Prév. Q., Doc. épars, vol. 24, f. 28, 11 Sept. 1696; Reg. civil, vol. 32, f. 93, 18 Sept. 1696; vol. 35, f. 102–103. 9 Oct. 1696, trial between Michel Bouchard, father of Marguerite, and Pierre Dubro.

98. Elisabeth Campeau apparently had two lovers. She was not awarded civil damages, but the two men had to take joint charge of the child. ANQM, AJ, Doc. jud., b. 67, 11 March–15 April 1701, trial between Catherine Paulo, mother of Elisabeth Campeau, and Nicolas Lemoyne; Record-office of Adhémar, no. 5264, 19 May 1701, agreement between Lemoyne and

Hervé to support Elisabeth Campeau's child.

99. This was the case with Gabriel Duprat and François Albert. Jetté, *Dictionnaire* 7, 389, 617, 733.

100. ANQQ, Prév. Q., Reg. civil, vol. 91, f. 288, 12 Dec. 1747, Roy–Saint-Louis trial.

101. ANQQ, C11A, vol. 62, f. 136 v. Hocquart to the Minister, 19 Oct. 1734; Dossiers de C.S., Proc. jud., Mat. crim., vol. 4, f. 213 to 241, in part. f. 215 v. and 239 r.

102. ANQQ Prév. A., Reg. crim., vol. 105A, f. 17 v.-19r., 27 Aug. 1753; Jugements du C.S., vol. 37, 28 Sept. 1753.

103. ANQQ, OI, vol. 26, 10 May 1738.

104. ANQQ, Prév. Q., Reg. civil, vol. 55, f. 28030, 21 Feb. 1720, Lévine–Albert trial. The judges also cited the girl's minority when they fined Charles Comtois and Michel Billy 200 and 300 francs in damages respectively. ANQTR, AJ, vol. 10, f. 263, 16 March 1747, Turbal–Billy trial; ANQQ, AJ, Prév. Q., Reg. civil, vol. 57, f. 32–33, 13 Aug. 1721; Jugements du C.S., 26 1721, f. 45.

105. ANQQ, Dossiers du C.S., Proc. jud., Mat. crim., v. 2, 1705, f. 281 and 388.

106. ANQQ, CPJN, no. 408, 31 Aug. 1707, trial between Madeleine Maugras and Jean-Baptiste Dubord; ANQM, AJ, Reg. aud. jur. royale, vol. 7 (1709–13) f. 684 v., 24 April 1711, trial between Guillaume Roussel, stepfather of Marie-Anne Lalande, and François Bosne; ANQQ, CPJN, no. 3564, 1721–22, trial between Louis Quay, father of Louise, and Antoine Bonin; ANQM, Reg. aud. jur. royale, vol. 24, f. 340–41, 18 Nov. 1749; f. 348–49, 7 Dec. 1748, trial between Louis Truchon and Simon Bergeron.

107. ANQM, AJ, Reg. aud. jur. royale, v. 7 (1709–13), f. 684 v. 24 April 1711, trial between Guillaume Roussel, stepfather of Marie-Anne Lalande, and François Bosne; ANQQ, OI, 15 March 1752, sentence against Nicolas Moaran; ANQM, AJ, Doc. jud., b. 84, Cot. 9–25, 1713, trial between André Poutret representing his niece Madeleine Duclos, and Jacques Diel; ANQQ, Dossiers du C.S., Proc. jud., Mat. civ., v. 1, f. 7–15, June–July 1700, trial between Jean Foucault and his wife, parents of Gabrielle, and René Lefebvre; ANTQR, AJ, vol. 10, f. 263, 16 March 1747, Turbal–Billy trial.

108. ANQTR, AJ de Trois–Rivières, vol. 6, f. 349, 14 June 1700; f. 356, 6 July 1700. Trial between Jean Foucault and his wife parents of Gabrielle, and René Lefebvre. Jetté, *Dictionnaire*, 689.

109. Jetté, *Dictionnaire*, 1029.

110. This was the explanation given by José Igartua and it seems likely enough to us, given the importance of the economic factor in choosing spouses. "Joseph Rouffio," DBC 3: 617–18.

111. The exact amount of court costs is indicated in 22 cases and is broken down as follows: 2 to 40 francs (16 cases); 51 to 71 francs (3 cases); 100 to 158 francs (3 cases).

112. ANQQ, Prév. Q., Reg. civil, vol. 92, f. 288, 12 Dec. 1747. Trial between Louis Roy, father of Marie-Joseph, and François Fabas, known as Saint-Louis. Jugements du C.S., vol. 63, f. 71 ss, 15 Jan. and 19 Feb. 1748.

113. Phan, "Les déclarations," 66, and Logette, "Naissances illégitimes," 238.

114. See note 98.

115. ANQQ, OI, 18 April 1723. Ordinance concerning Madeleine Chamberlain and Jean-Baptiste Bissonnet.

116. ANQM, AJ, Doc. jud., b. 164, 20 July 1754. Inquiry made upon the request of Pierre Forget [the midwife's husband] against François Beauchamp.

117. ANQQ, Dossiers du C.S., Proc. jud., Mat. crim., vol. 1, 12 Aug. 1682,   cross-examination   of

Marguerite Boissel; ANQM, AJ, Reg. du bailliage, 1687–1690, f. 140–43, 18 Sept. 1687. "Jean Leroy, known as Lasserene, gave a little girl who was his bastard to Louis Guibaut and his wife to feed and raise for three years"; ANQQ, record-office of J. Pinguet, 10 Nov. 1742, will of Philibert Mahon, known as Champagne; record-office of Barbel no. 549, 3 Jan. 1721, will of René Frérot; record-office of Grenaple, 21 Jan. 1688, will of Jacques Bertet, "Wills to provide for and ensure subsistence for Jacques and Charles Bertet, his illegitimate twin sons, aged approximately 4 $\frac{1}{2}$, as he believes this is his obligation by conscience, honour and piety." This man was certainly not in regular touch with his two sons, who were 9 years old in 1688.

118. ANQQ, OI, 5 Jan. 1722.

119. ANQM, AJ, Reg. aud. jur. royale, vol. 18 (1738–39), f. 117–18, 8 July 1738. Proceedings between the Crown prosecutor and Louis Briquet, known as Lefebvre.

120. ANQM, AJ, Reg. du bailliage, 1 May 1686, f. 368–69. Quoted in R. - L. Séguin, *La vie libertine*, 333.

121. Elisabeth Badinter, *L'un est l'autre: Des relations entre hommes et femmes* (Paris: Ed. Odile Jacob, 1986), 123–24; Simone de Beauvoir, *Le deuxième sexe* (Paris: Gallimard, 1949), 103–104.

122. ANQQ, CPJN, no. 465 1/2, 1712. Savaria–Giroux trial.

123. ANQQ, record-office of Chambalon, 27 Oct. 1694. Placement of the illegitimate child of Marguerite Vanier. In 1730, the Crown prosecutor also placed an 18-month-old illegitimate child whose father was a vagrant on the run in Mississippi and whose mother was extremely poor and reduced to begging. ANQM, record-office of Raimbaut, 19 Sept.

1730. Placement of an illegitimate child named Simon.

124. ANQM, AJ, Reg. aud. jur. royale, vol. 7 (1709–13), f. 770, 22 March 1712; f. 789, 10 June 1712; Doc. jud., b. 82, 15 and 20 July 1712; JDCS 6: 537, 5 Dec. 1712; p. 551, 30 Jan 1713; trial between Marguerite César and Jacques Séguin and his wife.

125. ANQQ, Prév. Q., Petit Crim., vol. 13, f. 6, 29 July 1678. Proceedings against Charlotte Préquet.

126. ANQQ, OI, 1 June 1725; ANQM, AJ, Reg. aud. jur. royale, v. 20 (1740–41), f. 36–37, 25 Jan. 1741, trial between Madeleine Charon and Joseph Faignant.

127. ANQQ, OI, 18 April 1723.

128. The following cases are examples: Jean Larchevêque accused Michel Parant of having spread "atrocious calumny and insults against the reputation and honour of this niece Catherine when he . . . accused her of having had a child." (ANQQ, record-office of Chambalon, 24 Feb. 1700). Jeanne Couc complained that two women "had accused her in the presence of several other people of having had a baby . . . slander that was extremely injurious to the honour of her family and herself." (ANQM, AJ, Doc. jud., b. 42, 27 July 1677).

129. ANQQ, CPJN, no. 465 1/2, 1712. Trial between Louise Savaria and Nicolas Giroux. Louise Savaria was even deemed worthy of praise for raising her child on her own.

130. Declaration of Agathe Petit, OI, vol. 26, 10 May 1738; ANTQR, AJ, 14 Nov. f. 20, 8 March 1756, Cantara–Petit trial; ANQM, AJ, Doc. jud., b. 84, Oct. 9–25, 1713, Duclos–Diel trial.

131. This happened to Marguerite Bouchard, Elisabeth Campeau, and others. See notes 97 and 98.

section

2

NATIVE PEOPLES AND
OCCUPIERS: CONFRONTATIONS
OF FAMILY NORMS AND
ECONOMIC SYSTEMS

"THE CUSTOM OF THE COUNTRY": AN EXAMINATION OF FUR TRADE MARRIAGE PRACTICES*

SYLVIA VAN KIRK

೦

Although extensive work has been done on the economic and political aspects of the fur trade in Western Canada, historians in the past have neglected the important social side of this far-flung enterprise. From the interaction between two very different cultures—European and Indian—grew an early Western society that was a blend of Indian, British, and French attitudes and traditions. Little appreciated has been the extent to which this society developed its own mores and customs in response to the particular needs of the environment that gave it birth. This paper will attempt to trace the evolution of a fundamental institution in fur trade society—marriage *à la façon du pays*.[1] It was according to this rite that hundreds of fur traders formed unions with Indian and, later, mixed-blood women.

If the concept of marriage *à la façon du pays* is not actually articulated in the early annals of the Hudson's Bay Company, it is because of the official policy formulated by the remote London Committee that prohibited any social contact between its servants and the Indians. Almost as soon as posts were established on the Bay, the men showed a tendency to form relationships with Indian women, but to the Committee this seemed a reprehensible practice that could only result in the debauching of its servants, the wasting of provisions, and illicit trade. The London Committee admonished its governor on the Bay in 1683:

> We are very sensibly [sic] that the Indian Women resorting to our Factories are very prejudiciall to the Companies affaires. . . . It is

* From L.H. Thomas, ed., *Essays on Western History* (Edmonton: University of Alberta Press, 1976), 49–68. This chapter was read by Dr. Van Kirk at the annual meeting of the Canadian Historical Association, University of Toronto, 1974.

therefore our possitive order that you lay your strict Commands on every Chiefe of each Factory upon forfiture of Wages not to Suffer any woman to come within any of our Factories.[2]

Although similar remonstrances were to be sent out many times in future, the Committee's regulation remained only loosely or, at best, sporadically enforced. However sensible the official policy may appear in theory, in practice it proved largely unworkable because it failed to make allowances for the realities of fur trade life.

Sex was, of course, a motivating factor in the development of intimate ties between white men and Indian women. No white women were permitted to accompany their men to Hudson Bay, a situation that precluded the possibility of connubial comforts in the conventional European sense.[3] It is apparent, however, that many Englishmen found Indian females not unattractive representatives of their sex. According to James Isham, Cree maidens were most enticing: "very frisky when Young & . . . well shap'd . . . their Eyes Large and Grey yet Lively and Sparkling very Bewitchen."[4]

It was certainly within the context of their own moral code for the Indians to sanction liaisons between their women and the Company's men. As Richard White, a witness at the parliamentary enquiry of 1749, put it: "The Indians were a sensible people, and agreed their Women should be made use of."[5] Both the Cree and the Chipewyan practised the custom, common among primitive people, of offering their wives or daughters to strangers as a token of friendship and hospitality.[6] To an Englishman, it appeared that an Indian took a wife with scant ceremony and a rather shocking disregard for the precepts of chastity and fidelity.[7] However, the Indian was not without his own standards. When found guilty of a clandestine amour, a wife could expect violent punishment or even death, but a husband deemed it perfectly proper to lend his wife to another man for anywhere from a night to several years, after which she was welcomed back together with any children born in the interim.[8]

If the sexual mores of the Indians encouraged the growth of intimate relations, the development of a body of "Home" Indians around each post meant that frequent contact was unavoidable. Traders on the Bay, who soon appreciated the essential role to be played by the women in making mocassins and netting snowshoes, defended the necessity of admitting women to the factories: "we cannot do without Snowshoes & other Necessarys for our Men who are always abroad & requires a Constant Supply of Shoes for the winter otherwise we can Kill no partridges nor, be able to provide our Selves with fireing."[9] In spite of the Committee's ruling, the governors or chief factors themselves took the lead in forming unions with Indian women. Such alliances, they realized, helped to cement trade ties. Among the Cree, a daughter was esteemed because, once married, her husband was obliged to contribute to the maintenance of her parent's household.[10] To have a fur trader for a son-in-law would thus be seen to promise unlimited security and prestige. Although the specific identity of most of the Indian women kept by the early H.B.C. factors remains unknown, it appears that they were usually the daughters or wives of leading "Home" Indians. During his governorship of Albany in the 1760s, Humphrey Marten formed a union with Pawpitch, a daughter of the "Captain of the Goose Hunters."[11] Several decades earlier, another factor, Joseph Adams, had had a child by a Cree women described as being of "ye blood Royal."[12]

Among the Cree, as in most Indian tribes, polygamy was an economic necessity, and a man's prestige was enhanced by the number of wives he could support. Significantly, a number of H.B.C. factors appear to have adopted the practice that, however contrary to European morality, would have found favour in Indian eyes. James Isham, described as the "Idol of the Indians" during his rule at York Factory in the 1740s and 1750s, maintained more than one Indian lady.[13] Similarly, Robert Pilgrim kept two Indian women with their children in his apartments at Fort Prince of Wales in the 1740s.[14] One of his successors, Moses Norton, who assumed command of Churchill in 1762, was reputedly a most notorious polygamist. If the very unsavory character sketch written by his archenemy Samuel Hearne is to be believed, Norton kept a selection of five or six of the finest Indian girls to satisfy his passions, being quite ready to poison anyone who dared refuse him their wives or daughters.[15]

By the mid-eighteenth century, it had become an established practice for a Company governor to take an Indian "wife." Andrew Graham, who himself fathered at least two children during his time on the Bay, affirmed that "the Factor keeps a bedfellow within the Fort at all times."[16] The term "wife" is not inappropriate when one considers that from the Indian point of view these unions would have been seen as marriages. Furthermore, the appearance of such phrases as "father-in-law" and "son-in-law" in the post journals indicates that the English themselves were beginning to acknowledge a marital relationship.[17] Children were a strong factor in cementing ties between mother and father, and the resulting domesticity must have done much to alleviate the loneliness of life on the barren shores of Hudson Bay. Humphrey Marten's intense concern for the Indian girl Pawpitch, for example, was revealed when she fell ill of a fever. He must have been watching over her when she died, for he records her death, an unusual step in itself, as occurring at precisely ten minutes to three on the morning of 24 January 1771. The father worried about the fate of his "poor Child" now motherless. He feared to entrust the little boy to his in-laws, as would have been customary, because Pawpitch's father was now old and already burdened with a large family.[18]

The extent to which the Committee's policy was applied to the lower ranks of the service varied with the capability and inclination of each individual governor, most of whom had exempted themselves from the ruling. The situation at York Factory in the mid-eighteenth century is illustrative. James Isham, one of the Company's most successful governors during the early period, readily permitted his men to have the company of Indian women outside the fort at the goose hunters' tents or on short journeys where they were especially useful. Some women were allowed to reside with servants inside the factory as well, since Isham undoubtedly observed that such liaisons had a conciliating effect upon the men. His successor Ferdinand Jacobs, however, roundly denounced such license when he took over in 1761, declaring that "the worst Brothel House in London is Not So Common a Stew as the men's House in this Factory." He refused to admit Indian women to men they regarded as husbands, a move so unpopular that several servants feigned sickness and refused to work.[19] This vacillation in enforcing the rules led to a good deal of resentment on the part of both the men and the Indians.[20]

Although its prohibition regarding Indian women was frequently ignored, the official policy of the Hudson's Bay Company during its first century did work to prevent the widespread development of marriage relationships between its servants and Indian women. As a general rule, only a chief factor was permitted to keep a woman permanently within the factory. "At proper times," a factor might allow an officer to entertain an Indian lady in his apartment provided she did not stay there overnight, but ordinary servants were usually limited to chance encounters and took to sneaking over the walls at night.[21] Even these restrictions were to break down when the Company began to move inland to confront a powerful Canadian rival that actively encouraged the formation of intimate ties with the Indians.

The men of the Montreal-based North West Company, inheritors of the framework and traditions of the French colonial fur trade after the conquest of 1763, readily adopted the attitudes of their predecessors with regard to Indian women. The coureur de bois had realized that his adaptation to, and understanding of, Indian society, on which his success depended, could be greatly facilitated by an Indian mate. Besides helping to secure trade ties and familiarizing the trader with the customs and language of her tribe, the Indian woman performed a myriad of domestic tasks essential to wilderness survival.

The North West Company, therefore, gave its sanction to unions between its employees and Indian women, and it was among the Nor'-Westers that marriage à la façon du pays first developed into a recognized and widespread custom. All ranks, bourgeois, clerk, and engagé, were allowed to take a women, and the Company accepted the responsibility for the maintenance of Indian wives and families.[22] It irked more than one H.B.C. officer to observe the high style in which his Canadian counterpart travelled. The bourgeois always had "his girl" who was carried in and out of his canoe and shared the luxury of his tent and feather bed; furthermore, if a clerk "chuses to keep a girl which most of them does the Master finds her in Apparel so that they need not spend one farthing of their Wages."[23] The only restriction placed on an engagé taking an Indian wife was that he had to obtain the consent of his bourgeois to his proposed match.[24]

It is important to emphasize the extent to which "the custom of the country" derived from Indian marriage rites. The active involvement of the Indians in securing unions between their women and the Nor'Westers is much in evidence. According to one observer, many among the Cree kept one or more of their daughters specifically to offer as wives "for the white

People."[25] Simple as the Indian notions of matrimony appeared to the Nor'Westers,[26] a trader could not take a wife without giving credence to the customs of her people. Of fundamental importance was the consent of the girl's parents. In the words of an old voyageur:

> On ne se joue pas d'une femme sauvage comme on veut . . . . Il y aurait du danger d'avoir la tête cassée, si l'on prend la fille dans ce pays, sans le consentement des parents. C'est le père et la mère qui donnent les femmes, et s'ils sont morts, ce sont les plus proches parents.[27]

To obtain the consent of the parents, the Nor'Wester was required to make a suitable present. This bride price could vary considerably, but it usually took more than a few trifles to gain the hand of an Indian maiden. At Fort Alexandria in 1801, Payet, one of Daniel Harmon's interpreters, gave the parents of his Cree bride rum and dry goods to the value of two hundred dollars.[28] According to the younger Henry, the common medium of exchange was a horse for a wife.[29] On the Pacific coast, the marriages of several Nor'Westers to the daughters of the powerful Chinook chief Concomely involved more elaborate ceremony with a mutual exchange of gifts. In July 1813, for instance, a rich dowry of pelts accompanied the bride of proprietor Duncan McDougall, but it took McDougall until the following April to discharge his part of the bargain: "Mr. D. McDougall this afternoon completed the payment for his wife . . . he gave 5 new guns, and 5 blankets, $2\frac{1}{2}$ feet wide, which makes 15 guns and 15 blankets, besides a great deal of other property, as the total cost of this precious lady."[30]

Before being consigned to her new husband, it became common for an Indian woman to go through a "ritual," performed by the other women of the fort, designed to render her more acceptable to a white man. She was scoured of grease and paint and exchanged her leather garments for those of a more civilized style. At the Nor'Wester posts, wives were clothed, usually at the expense of the Company, in "Canadian fashion" which consisted of a shirt, short gown, petticoat, and leggings.[31] The trader then conducted his bride to his quarters and, without further ado, the couple was considered man and wife. The women assumed their husbands' last names, and the engagés respectfully addressed the wives of the bourgeois as "Madame."[32]

Initially marriage *à la façon du pays*, in accordance with Indian custom, was not viewed as a binding contract.[33] Should the relationship prove unhappy, both parties were free to separate and seek a more congenial union. Even a moralist such as Daniel Harmon, as he became more familiar with the ways of the fur trade, conceded that this attitude had merit: "for I cannot conceive it to be right for a Man & Woman to cohabit when they cannot agree, but to live in discontent, if not downright hatered [sic] to each other, as many do."[34] In contrast to Indian practice, however, the Nor'-Westers appear to have taken a definite stand against polygamy both for moral and economic reasons. The Indian was understandably slow to comprehend white man's morality since in his view "all great men should have a plurality of wives." Such was the argument used by Alexander Henry the younger's father-in-law, himself the husband of three sisters, when he pressed the trader to take his second daughter.[35] The reluctance evinced by Henry in taking his first Indian wife and his adamant refusal of a second typifies the attitude of many bourgeois, and polygamy was never part of "the custom of the country" as practised by the Nor'Westers.[36] While H.B.C. officers, in their isolation on the Bay, appear to have been susceptible to polygamy, the economic implications of such a practice when moving into the interior served to reaffirm the desirability of monogamy. By 1780, according to Philip Turnor, English officers stationed inland from York Factory found themselves besieged with offers of wives:

> The Masters of most of your Honors Inland settlements . . . would Labour under many difficulties was they not to keep a Woman as above half the Indians that came to the House would offer the master their Wife the refusal of which would give great offense to both the man and his Wife; though he was to make the Indian a present for his offer the Woman would think her self slighted and if the Master was to accept the offer he would be expected to Cloath her and by keeping a Woman it makes one short ready answer (that he has a Woman of his own and she would be offended) and very few Indians make that offer when they know the Master keeps a Woman.[37]

Thus marriage à la façon du pays was essentially an adaptation and not an adoption of Indian marriage rites. In particular, the Indian attitude that marriage did not constitute a union for life was corrupted to suit the needs of the transient fur trader. The men of both companies never intended to remain permanently in the Indian Country, but the growth of family ties during their sojourn placed many traders in an agonizing dilemma when it came time to retire. After the unhappy experience of one of its officers, the Hudson's Bay Company actively discouraged any attempt on the part of its servants to remove their families from Rupert's Land. In 1750, Robert Pilgrim had taken his Indian wife Thu a Higon and their infant son to England. Unfortunately, Pilgrim died within a few months of his arrival, having stipulated in his will that, while the child was to remain in England with his brother, Thu a Higon was to be properly looked after until she could be sent back to Churchill.[38] An irritated London Committee, fearing that dependents brought to Britain might easily become a burden on the Company, sent Thu a Higon back to Hudson Bay accompanied by a strict order forbidding all ship's captains to allow any native man, women, or child to be brought to Great Britain without its express written consent.[39]

Whether Thu a Higon could have overcome the almost insuperable problems of adjustment she would have had to face in England is doubtful. This consideration helps to explain the action of most early bourgeois. Many of the Nor'Westers were men of education who, having won sizeable fortunes, intended to retire to enjoy the fruits of civilization in Eastern Canada or Britain. An Indian family had little place in such a design; the wife especially would have to cope with an alien way of life where too often she might meet with "impertinent insult" and "unmerited obloquy."[40] While many of the early wintering partners sent their children east to be educated, most forsook the Indian mothers of these children and felt at liberty to marry white women upon retirement.[41]

Yet until the founding of the Red River settlement in the early 1800s, even the most devoted father could not have remained in Rupert's Land with his family after his contract had expired.[42] It distressed more than one H.B.C. officer to witness the suffering caused by the breakup of families owing to "the want of an Asylum in this part of the Country to which a Parent might retire with a prospect of supporting his Family and which would prevent the Miseries of a Separation and check the Increase of a Burden on the Factories."[43] Before the creation of the colony, it had of necessity become customary to leave one's Indian family behind. Although the unions between H.B.C. men and Indian women had shown an increasing tendency to last for the duration of the husband's stay on the Bay, the usual and accepted course had always been for an Indian wife and her offspring to return to her own relations in the event of his death or departure. An Indian husband, whether old or new, readily adopted "the Englishman's children," an act which reflected the strong kinship ties and great love of children characteristic of Indian society.[44]

While the London Committee had tacitly had to accept that it could do little to prevent its men from having native families, it refused to assume any official responsibility for their maintenance. This accounts for the fact that the Indian families of H.B.C. men were absorbed back into the "Home Guard" bands, but it was also a spur to conscientious fathers to make some provision for their families. Many of the officers' and servants' wills that have survived from the late eighteenth and early nineteenth centuries clearly reveal the growth to definite family ties and a marked concern for the welfare of native dependents. The action of John Favell, an early inland officer in the Albany district, is typical. Upon his death in 1784, Favell left an annuity for his Indian wife Tittimeg and their four children, earnestly requesting "the Honorable Company" to implement this part of his will so that his family would receive an annual supply of goods from the Company's warehouse.[45]

Similarly, an Indian woman who had formed a union with a Nor'Wester could expect to be taken back into her tribe. According to the elder Henry, Cree women who had been kept by the men received a ready welcome along with their progeny: "One of the chiefs assured me, that the children borne by their women to Europeans were bolder warriors, and better hunters, than themselves. The women, so selected, consider themselves as honoured."[46] However, there was less impetus for a family of a Nor'Wester to return to live with the Indians. The Company itself accepted the responsibility for at least feeding the families of its servants who had died or left the country, and some traders did provide their wives with a small annuity to purchase cloth and other goods from the company stores.[47] Furthermore, the Nor'Westers were not insensible to the problems that could arise from divorcing an Indian wife and her children from the life of a fur trade post to which they were accustomed. A concomitant of marriage *à la façon du pays*, therefore, was the growth of another custom, known as "turning off," whereby a trader leaving the country endeavoured to place his spouse under the protection of another. Ross Cox declared that many a voyageur for "a handsome sum" would be happy to take over *"la Dame d'un Bourgeois."*[48] On his wedding day in 1806, Daniel Harmon was obviously expressing a contemporary attitude when he confided to his journal that he intended to keep his wife,

> as long as I remain in this uncivilized part of the world, but when I return to my native land shall endeavour to place her into the hands of some good honest Man, with whom she can pass the remainder of her days in this Country much more agreeably, than it would be possible for her to do, were she to be taken down into the civilized world, where she would be a stranger to the People, their manners, customs & Language.[49]

Although Harmon, like others, may be accused of wanting to enjoy the best of both worlds, there was a good deal of truth in the generally held view that this was the kinder course of action.

Since the late eighteenth century, the men of both companies had, in fact, been espousing the daughters of their predecessors, an action that emphasizes the extent to which micegenation had taken place. Owing to the restriction of marital unions in the Hudson's Bay Company, most of the marriageable mixed-blood girls were initially daughters of former officers.[50] Of Matthew Cocking's daughters, for example, the eldest, Ke-the-cow-e-com-e-coof, became the country wife of Thomas Staynor, governor at Churchill in the 1790s, while another, Agathas, married William Hemmings Cook who took charge of York Factory in the early 1800s.[51] As the British moved inland, the pattern of intermarriage spread among the servants. Although Neskisho, the wife of Orkney servant James Spence, is referred to as "Indian" like many other daughters of H.B.C. men, she was actually a daughter of the early inlander Isaac Batt.[52]

The daughters of the French-Canadian engagés, on the other hand, constituted the largest group of eligible females of the Nor'Westers. Many of the bourgeois wed the daughters of voyageurs or freemen in unions that cut across both class and racial lines. Ross Cox tells the story of one doughty old voyageur Louis La Liberté who felt he could address himself with familiarity to one of the Company's proprietors because he was father-in-law to three wintering partners.[53] Like Indian girls, the daughters of the men of both companies were given in marriage when very young. To cite a famous instance, Daniel Harmon took his Métis bride Elizabeth Duval when she was only fourteen years old.[54]

By the early 1800s, the replacement of the Indian wife by one of mixed-blood had become a widespread phenomenon in fur trade society. As the mixed-blood population grew, it naturally evolved that wives should be drawn increasingly from its ranks. In the first place, a fur trader's daughter possessed the ideal qualifications to become a fur trader's wife. A very child of the fur trade, she knew no other way of life. From her Indian mother, the mixed-blood girl learned those native skills so valuable to the trade such as making moccasins, netting snowshoes, and preparing pemmican. Her familiarity with Indian language and customs enabled her to act as an interpreter,[55] and on more than one occasion, her timely intervention reputedly saved the life of a white husband.[56] The mixed-blood wife was thus in a position to adequately perform the functions that had made the Indian woman such a useful helpmate but, unlike the Indian woman, there was little danger of her becoming a source of friction between Indian and white. In fact, by the turn of the century, partly because of the violence and drunkenness occasioned by the trade war, Indian–white relations had seriously deteriorated. In well-established areas, marriage alliances were no longer so important, and many Indians deeply resented the flagrant way in which the Nor'Westers in particular now abused their women.[57]

Secondly, the white man generally evinced a decided personal preference for a mixed-blood wife whose lighter skin and sharper features more closely approximated his concept of beauty. Many, according to Alexander Ross, were captivating with "their delicacy of form," "their nimble movements," and "the penetrating expression" of their bright black eyes. The officers especially considered the greater potential of a mixed-blood girl for adapting to "civilized ways" as increasingly desirable. "With their natural acuteness and singular talent for imitation," Ross declared, they could acquire considerable grace and polish.[58]

Furthermore, the fur traders had a collective responsibility for the fate of their daughters. They were not Indian; even those raised among the "Home Guard" were taught that their paternity gave them a definite superiority.[59] But they were not white; fathers were actively discouraged from sending their daughters to the civilized world to be educated.[60] Being women, however, the only way in which mixed-blood girls could remain an integral part of fur trade society was through marriage, either to new men coming in or at least to fur traders' sons. This consideration can be seen in the ruling introduced by the North West Company in 1806 that prohibited men of all ranks from taking any more pure-blooded Indian women as wives. Although primarily instigated to reduce the enormous cost of maintaining the growing families of its servants, the resolution can also be seen as encouraging Nor'Westers to marry "the Daughter of a white man" in an effort to ensure them husbands.[61]

Significantly, as mixed-blood wives became the rule, the "custom of the country" increasingly evolved towards white concepts of marriage. There is much evidence to suggest that the men of both companies came to view a union contracted *à la façon du pays* as a union for life. A respected H.B.C. officer, J.E. Harriott, explained that "the custom of the country" involved a solemn agreement between the father of the girl and the man who was taking her to wife. When Harriott espoused Elizabeth, a daughter of Chief Trader J.P. Pruden, he "made a solemn promise to her father to live with her and treat her as my wife as long as we both lived. I kept this promise until her death." He further declared that he considered his union as binding as if celebrated by an archbishop:

> It was not customary for an European to take one wife and discard her, and then take another. The marriage according to the custom [of the country] was considered a marriage for life . . . I know of hundreds of people living and dying with the women they took in that way without any other formalities.[62]

Although it was more difficult for the lower ranks to maintain permanent unions, the engagés, in general, recognized the permanency of the marriage bond. According to one old voyageur Pierre Marois, whose marriage à la façon du pays lasted over twenty years, "nous regardons cette union comme union de mari et femme . . . et union aussi sacrée."[63]

Within fur trade society, "the custom of the country" was undoubtedly regarded as a bona fide marriage rite. As one clerk declared, "I never knew or heard of a man and woman living together in the North-West without being married."[64] Although the actual ceremony remained simple, the union was accorded public recognition through festivities similar to those found at European weddings. It became customary to celebrate a fur trade marriage with a dram to all hands and a dance that might see the fun-loving engagés jigging till norning.[65] When the young clerk Robert Miles took Betsey Sinclair as "a Femme du Pays" at York Factory in the fall of 1822, a friend recorded, "we had a Dance & supper on the occasion, when no one but the happy Swain was allowed to go sober to bed."[66] Whereas initially a trader had been required to make a substantial present to his Indian in-laws for his bride, it was now not unusual for a fur trader to provide his own daughter with a handsome dowry.[67]

Numerous examples of the development of lasting and devoted relationships between white men and their mixed-blood wives could be cited. H.B.C. officer George Gladman, for instance, emphasized that he considered Mary Moore to be his "lawful wife."[68] Like many of his contemporaries, he made generous provision for her in his will, specifically entreating his sons to see that their mother was well cared for in her old age.[69] Significantly, growing numbers, especially among the Nor'Westers, now took their wives and families with them when they retired to the East. A most famous example is that of Daniel Harmon who took his wife back to his home in New England in 1819. Although the deeply religious Harmon could never deny the sanctity of a church marriage, he, like others before him, had come to realize that something much deeper than mere ceremony bound him to his wife:

> Having lived with this woman as my wife, though we were never formally contracted to each other, during life, and having children by her, I consider that I am under a moral obligation not to dissolve the connexion, if she is willing to continue it. The union which has been formed between us, in the providence of God, has . . . been

cemented by a long and mutual performance of kind offices.
. . . How could I spend my days in the civilized world, and leave my
beloved children in the wilderness? The thought has in it the bitter-
ness of death. How could I tear them from a mother's love, and
leave her to mourn over their absence, to the day of her death?
. . . On the whole, I consider the course which I design to pursue, as
the only one which religion and humanity would justify.[70]

Once outside fur trade society, though some maintained it was unnecessary,[71] most submitted to a church ceremony if only to conform to "civilized"
convention. Such action was seen, however, as merely "un bénédiction" and
not an admission that no marriage had existed before. J.E. Harriott maintained that he would have gone through "the civilized form of solemnizing
marriage . . . to please people and to conform to the custom of society. I
would not consider myself more strongly bound to that women than
before."[72]

Within fur trade society, however, one was expected to conform to its
own social norm with regard to marriage, that of "the custom of the country." While no laws existed to enforce morality in the Indian Country, it is
evident that the society itself exerted considerable pressure on a newcomer
to adopt a code of behaviour that had gained its own legitimacy through
long usage. One can observe this social conditioning working on Nor'-
Westers such as Daniel Harmon, Alexander Henry the younger, and George
Nelson. Arriving fresh from a society that recognized only the legitimacy of
church marriage, these young men were initially shocked by "the custom of
the country" that seemed only a form of concubinage. They therefore began
by refusing all the offers of wives made to them, but eventually an
increased understanding of the ways of the fur trade, coupled with the
loneliness and the attractiveness of the girls themselves, led them to follow
in the footsteps of their predecessors and take a wife *à la façon du pays*.[73] As
James Douglas very perceptively observed, only through such adaptation
could one become reconciled to fur trade life:

> There is indeed no living with comfort in this country until a per-
> son has forgot the great world and has his tastes and character
> formed on the current standard of the stage. . . . To any other
> being . . . the vapid monotony of an inland trading post would be
> perfectly unsufferable, while habit makes it familiar to us, softened
> as it is by the many tender ties, which find a way to the heart.[74]

Even though the desirability of a lasting union had become widely
acknowledged, the security of a native wife ultimately depended upon individual conscience. Because "the custom of the country" had evolved from
two very different sets of attitudes towards marriage, it was inevitable that
irregularities should persist. "Turning off" remained a problem, it being not
uncommon for a mixed-blood woman to have two or three husbands in her
lifetime.[75] After the amalgamation of the two companies in 1821, the
Hudson's Bay Company took definite steps to regulate country marriages

by introducing marriage contracts that were signed by both parties in the presence of witnesses. In 1824 the Council of the Northern Department further resolved:

> That no Officer or Servant in the company's service be hereafter allowed to take a woman without binding himself down to such reasonable provision for the maintenance of the women and children as on a fair and equitable principle may be considered necessary not only during their residence in the country but after their departure hence.[76]

Since marriage *à la façon du pays* contained all the elements of "civilized" marriage except the blessing of the church, it might be supposed that the arrival of missionaries in Rupert's Land would have been welcomed. In fact, the intolerant and unsympathetic attitude of particularly the Protestant missionaries toward "the custom of the country" provoked a good deal of hostility. The Reverend John West, the first Anglican chaplain of the Hudson's Bay Company who arrived at Red River in 1820, refused to acknowledge that marital relationships already existed. In his view, all couples were merely "living in sin" and too often a man might "turn off" his woman after having enjoyed the morning of her days.[77] While abuses undeniably existed, West in seizing upon the exception rather than the rule encountered much resentment. To many an old trader, the pronouncement of a clergyman could add no more legality or sanctity to a country union that had existed for decades. Although West, who firmly believed that "the institution of marriage and the security of property were the fundamental laws of society," performed a total of sixty-five marriages before his departure in 1823, it is clear that he had had to force his view in many cases.[78] Resistance seems to have come from some of the most prominent settlers in Red River such as James Bird and Thomas Thomas, retired H.B.C. chief factors, who continued to live with their Indian wives *à la façon du pays*. West, being especially concerned that such men set an example to the rest of the community, was much gratified when both couples agreed to take the vows of the Church of England on 30 March 1821.[79]

West's successors, David Jones and William Cockran, continued to rail against the immoral habits of the fur traders. Jones's dogmatic stance was hardly conciliating. It had been West's custom to baptise traders' wives immediately before the marriage ceremony, but Jones was adamant that it would be a sacrilege to pronounce "our excellent Liturgy" over persons entirely ignorant of its meaning. When several traders maintained that there would be little point in having a church marriage since their wives would still be regarded as "heathens" unless baptised, Jones declared they were merely looking for an excuse to continue "living in sin."[80]

By the end of the 1820s, however, Cockran, the assistant chaplain, was optimistic about the changing attitude in Red River:

> It is encouraging to view the growing attention of the people to divine ordinance. Many that could not be prevailed upon formerly

to marry their women have now seen the sin of despising the ordinance, and have felt truly sorry for the contempt and neglect of it.[81]

Equally gratifying to the missionaries was the spread of the church rite along the route between the colony and York Factory. On his way out to England in 1828, Jones was rejoiced "to unite two officers of high standing to their partners" at Oxford House. These proved to be Chief Factor Colin Robertson and his half-breed wife Theresa Chalifoux, and Clerk James Robertson and Margaret, a daughter of Chief Factor Alexander Stewart and his half-breed wife Susan Spence.[82]

In the post-1821 period, the Red River colony became the hub of fur trade society since increasing numbers retired there with their families, and schools were established for the children of the men in the field. Thus, the doctrines of the missionaries gained widespread acceptance. In 1835 Parson Jones jubilantly observed that it had become customary for traders passing through Red River to seek religious sanction for their unions: "This laudable practice is now becoming General, in fact the revolution in these respects during the past ten years had been immense."[83]

Indeed, the mid-1830s mark a definite change in attitude toward "the custom of the country" in the environs of the settlement. Chief Trader Archibald McDonald emphasized that the acceptance of the church rite was now the only proper course for an honorable gentleman:

> All my colleagues are now about following the example, & it is my full conviction few of them can do no better—the great mistake is in flattering themselves with a different notion too long—nothing is gained by procrastination, but much is lost by it.[84]

After attending the annual meeting of Council, McDonald himself had had his union with his half-breed wife Jane Klyne blessed by the church in a well-attended ceremony at the parsonage in Red River on 9 June 1835. Yet he could not resist pointing out the humour in the solemn pronouncements of the clergy as he and his beloved Jane had lived in a most exemplary fashion since he had wed her *à la façon du pays* ten years before:

> [we] were joined in Holy wedlock & of course declared at full liberty to live together as man & wife & to increase & multiply as to them might seem fit—And I hope the validity of *this* ceremony is not to be questioned though it has not the further advantage of a Newspaper Confirmation.[85]

Even old die-hards eventually gave in. Although William Hemmings Cook had retired to Red River with his wife Mary [Agathas] and family in 1815, it took till 1838 before he could be persuaded to tie the solemn knot. As one of the guests at his wedding feast sarcastically observed, old Cook had "stood manfully forth . . . bringing his 35 years courtship to an early close."[86]

Just at the time when Red River was becoming firmly reconciled to the European form of marriage, a bitter feud over this issue erupted at Fort Vancouver, the headquarters of the Columbia district. The desirability of a mission to the Columbia had been suggested as early as 1824, but Governor Simpson, in enumerating the qualities such a missionary should possess, issued a prophetic warning: "he ought to understand in the outset that nearly all the Gentlemen & Servants have Families altho' Marriage ceremonies are unknown in the Country and that it would be all in vain to attempt breaking through this uncivilized custom."[87] Simpson appears to have forgotten his own advice, however, when selecting the Company's first Pacific coast chaplain because, in spite of his name, the Reverend Herbert Beaver could not have been a more unfortunate choice. According to Beaver, Fort Vancouver, upon his arrival in the fall of 1836 with his English wife Jane, presented a "deplorable scene of vice and ignorance."[88] He refused to give any credence to "the custom of the country," styling the trader's wives as concubines and chastizing the men for indulging in fornication.[89] This most insulting and inappropriate assessment of the well-regulated domestic situation at the fort provoked much hostility.

No one resented Beaver's slanders on his wife's character more than the fiery-tempered ruler of Fort Vancouver, Chief Factor John McLoughlin. Around 1811, while a young Nor'Wester in the Rainy Lake area, McLoughlin had wed Margeurite Wadin McKay à la façon du pays. Four children were born to the couple, and when McLoughlin assumed charge of the Columbia district in 1824, Margeurite and the youngest children made the long journey overland with him.[90] McLoughlin treated his wife with respect and devotion and the remarks of contemporaries indicate that she played her role as first lady of Fort Vancouver well. According to Chief Trader James Douglas, Madame McLoughlin was respected by all for "her numerous charities and many excellent qualities of heart."[91] Narcissa Whitman, the wife of one of the first American missionaries to reach the post, is unlikely to have been guilty of bias in describing Margeurite as "one of the kindest women in the world."[92]

But to Beaver, good Mrs. McLoughlin was only a "kept Mistress" who could not be allowed to associate with respectable married females such as Mrs. Beaver.[93] He demanded that McLoughlin set an example by entering into a legal union with Margeurite. This, McLoughlin, who had Catholic predilections, absolutely refused to do. However, in order to silence once and for all any charge of illegality against his union, he had James Douglas, acting in his capacity of Justice of the Peace, perform a civil ceremony.[94] When Beaver and his wife, therefore, continued to heap invective upon Mrs. McLoughlin, her husband's anger reached such a pitch that on one occasion he could not refrain from giving the parson a sound drubbing with his own cane.[95]

Beaver also encountered stiff opposition when he attempted to prevent the "country marriage" of the clerk A.C. Anderson to a daughter of Chief Trader James Birnie. Anderson, at this time stationed in New Caledonia, had commissioned Chief Factor Peter Skene Ogden to conduct the girl north with the annual brigade. Beaver refused to baptise the girl prior to her departure and wrote a scathing letter to Anderson denouncing the contemplated union as "immoral and disgraceful"; he threatened to deny Anderson the church's blessing forever if he persisted in wilfully denying God's ordinance.[96] Ogden paid no heed to Beaver's rantings, declared that he would have the girl baptised by the American missionaries en route or do it himself and, as a Justice of the Peace, ultimately presided over Anderson's marriage.[97] Anderson himself wrote a spirited letter to Beaver giving a sophisticated defence of his action. In the first place, he claimed, legal authorities acknowledged that marriage was essentially a civil contract, the religious ceremony being merely a social convention. Scottish law, he pointed out, did not require church rites for marriages to be considered legal.[98] Furthermore, laudable as Beaver's presence at Fort Vancouver might be, he was of little use to Anderson hundreds of miles away. Even Church authorities had previously recognized that, "marriages contracted in these wild and secluded regions in positions where the intervention of a person duly ordained may not be immediately available are valid and irreproachable."[99]

While few officers actually denied the desirability of a church marriage when a clergyman was present, Beaver's insufferable attitude alienated even the most devout. Such was the case of James Douglas who had wed Amelia, a daughter of Chief Factor William Connolly and his Cree wife, according to "the custom of the country" at Fort St. James in 1828. Douglas was anxious to have his marriage recognized by the church, however, and on 28 February 1837 Beaver performed the Church of England rite for the first, and almost last, time.[100] Even though she was now regularly married, Beaver still regarded the kind and gracious Mrs. Douglas as "little calculated to improve the manners of society."[101] Douglas, who was extremely sensitive to such unjust slanders, stoutly defended the honour of the ladies of the country when he assumed temporary command of Fort Vancouver in 1838. To Beaver's accusation that the Factor's house was "a common receptacle for every mistress of an officer in the service, who may take a fancy to visit the Fort," Douglas retorted that only the wives and officers visited the fort when their husbands were on brigade business: "I neither have nor would suffer any person, of whatever rank, to introduce loose women into this Fort, an attempt which, to the honor of every gentlemen here, was never made."[102] Beaver and his wife created such friction that all were gratified when he was relieved of his post and the haughty pair departed in the fall of 1838.

The dismal failure of Beaver was in sharp contrast to the success of the Pacific Mission established by the Catholic missionaries F.N. Blanchet and Modeste Demers who travelled overland to the Columbia in 1838. Although the majority of the populace at Fort Vancouver were Catholic, the priests' conciliatory attitude toward "the custom of the country" also contributed to their welcome. The Protestant missionaries in Red River had denounced their Catholic counterparts for refusing to marry persons of different religious persuasions "as though it were better for them to live in fornication, than that they should violate the rigid statutes of the Papal see."[103] Blanchet and Demers, however, had received special dispensation, and the records show that a considerable number of the marriages they performed in their progress across the country were between Protestant and Catholic. Although the Catholic Church did not recognize the sanctity of a "country marriage," the priests did acknowledge the existence of a marital bond by considering that every cohabiting couple were living in a state of "natural marriage." The only children stigmatized with illegitimacy were those whose parents could not be identified. Furthermore, the general tenor of the Catholic rite was that the parties were "renewing and ratifying their mutual consent of marriage" and formally recognizing the legitimacy of their children.[104] On 19 November 1842, to the priests' undoubted satisfaction, McLoughlin, who had just turned Catholic, had his union with Margeurite "his legitimate wife," blessed by the church: "wishing to renew their consent of marriage in order to discharge the grave bonds on receiving the sacrament of marriage, we priests . . . have received the renewal of their consent of marriage and have given them the nuptial benediction."[105]

The coming of the missionaries to Rupert's Land with their insistence on the prerogative of the church in the sphere of marriage made it inevitable that "the custom of the country" would become a thing of the past. Even the "civil" contracts enacted by the Hudson's Bay Company contained the proviso that the marriage would receive the sanction of the church at the first possible opportunity.[106] The slow spread of missionary activity to more remote areas, however, meant that for many this opportunity never actually arose. As a result, official civil powers were granted to the chief officers of the Company; in 1845 the Council of the Northern Department resolved that, in the absence of a clergyman, chief factors only could solemnize marriages, but no person could take a wife at any establishment without the sanction of the gentleman in charge of the district.[107]

If the missionaries introduced "civilized" conventions into Rupert's Land, it was not without painful repercussions for fur trade society. "The custom of the country" had been regarded as a bona fide marriage rite, entailing all the obligations toward wife and children that marriage implies. Around the time of the union of the two companies, however, a significant change in the behaviour of newly arrived men toward native women can be observed. The stand of the church, it can be argued, worked to block the traditional conditioning process by which a newcomer had adapted to fur trade custom. The native woman was now often reduced to the status of mistress or even prostitute—someone with whom to gratify one's passions but never actually marry.

Unfortunately, the classic practitioner of this new attitude was the Governor himself, George Simpson, a man who had only wintered one year in Rupert's Land before assuming control of the Northern Department. Simpson showed little sympathy for the marital concerns of his associates, partly because he did not recognize "the custom of the country." His lack of understanding is shown in his initial liaison with Betsey Sinclair, a daughter of the late Chief Factor William Sinclair and his native wife Nahovway. While Betsey was acknowledged as "Mrs. Simpson" by his contemporaries, the Governor treated her as a casual mistress and felt little compunction in getting rid of her when he tired of her charms.[108] Simpson, in fact, gained a notorious reputation for his womanizing,[109] and his behaviour is not typical of officers who had had long experience in the fur trade.

He further shattered the norms of fur trade society by bringing a British wife out to Red River in 1830, even before he had severed his connection with Margaret Taylor whom all had come to regard as his "country wife."[110] Although none dared openly criticize the Governor for this action, widespread shock was expressed when a former Nor'Wester John George McTavish followed suit and renounced Nancy McKenzie, his "country wife" of long-standing. His unfeeling violation of fur trade custom provoked one old comrade John Stuart to declare their friendship at an end:

> what could be your aim in discarding her whom you clasped to your bosom in virgin purity and had for 17 Years with you, She was the Wife of your choice and has born you seven Children, now Stigmatized with ognominy ... if with a view to domestick happiness you have thus acted, I fear the Aim has been Missed and that remorse will be your portion for life.[111]

That white women might become the wives of fur traders had been a possibility ever since the founding of the Red River settlement. But, because her numbers were so few, the white woman tended to be put on a pedestal, to be regarded as a "lovely tender exotic."[112] The presence of white women helped to reinforce the attitudes and customs of the society their men had previously left behind, that made native women appear less desirable as marriage partners. As the clerk James Hargrave observed in 1830, "this influx of white faces has cast a still deeper shade over the faces of our Brunettes in the eyes of many."[113] Hargrave himself, however was not immune to "the fascinations of dark-eyed beauty,"[114] but studiously avoided any permanent attachment, ultimately bringing a Scottish bride Letitia Mactavish out to York Factory in 1840.

Significantly, the church gave support to this trend. William Cockran, who actively discouraged young officers from marrying mixed-blood girls, upheld Chief Factor Duncan Finlayson as worthy of emulation since he, though almost alone, had managed to evade "the snare which has ruined many of our countrymen."[115] So great was the Rev. Beaver's concern to prevent his wife from being tainted by association with "loose females" that he actually proposed that all who had not been married by a clergyman should be barred from Fort Vancouver. They might, however, be maintained outside the walls where the men could visit them on the sly to at least conform with the "outward decorum" that men in civilized societies observed in relation to their mistresses.[116] Such a plan, which would have completely subverted the existing state of morality, provoked an angry rebuttal from Chief Trader Douglas. A *wife* according to "the custom of the country" bore no resemblance to a prostitute in European society:

> The woman who is not sensible of violating [any] law, who lives chastely with her husband of her choice, in a state approved by friends and sanctioned by immemorial custom, which she believes

strictly honorable, forms a perfect contrast to the degraded creature who has sacrificed the great principle which from infancy she is taught to revere as the ground work of female virtue; who lives a disgrace to friends and an outcast from society.[117]

Native women were particularly victimized by the introduction of the Victorian double standard. While men might indulge their pleasure without obligation, women were now expected to abide by rigid European standards of propriety. It was grossly unfair to blame native women for perpetuating immorality, even though they were influenced by Indian sexual mores that were much more lenient compared to those of white society.[118] Beaver, for example, proposed to punish the women directly for the sinful state of affairs at Fort Vancouver by denying them rations and medical attention to bring them to a sense of their shame.[119] A major concern of the boarding school established in Red River in the 1820s for the daughters of officers was to estrange them from their Indian heritage and inculcate proper notions of feminine virtue, particularly chastity.[120] After the stern disciplinarian John MacCallum took over the school, the children were even forbidden any contact with their mothers if they had not had a church marriage. One tragic victim of this situation was the poor Indian wife of a trader Kenneth McKenzie who had gone off to join the American Fur Company. She never saw her two daughters who had been placed in the school, except when they, at risk of severe punishment, would sneak out to visit their mother. Wives who could claim "benefit of clergy" were taught to look upon those who could not as most debased creatures. But Letitia Hargrave, though not always charitable in her remarks about native women, protested against such hypocrisy:

> This may be all very right, but it is fearfully cruel for the poor unfortunate mothers who did not know that there was any distinction & it is only within the last few years that anyone was so married. Of course had all the fathers refused, every one woman in the country wd have been no better than those that are represented to their own children as discreditable.[121]

Although "the custom of the country" had fallen into disrepute in fur trade society by the mid-nineteenth century, the purpose of this paper has been to show that it was in itself an honourable and recognized marriage rite. In spite of increasing pressure to conform to the norms of white society, there were a few notable traders who insisted upon living with their wives *à la façon du pays* as they had always done.

The romantic story of how the young Nor'Wester John Rowand was rescued after a serious fall from his horse by the native girl who became his wife has become legend.[122] Rowand took Lisette Umphreville for his country wife sometime around 1811, and their relationship through the years, as Rowand rose to become the most prominent officer on the Saskatchewan, appears to have been a devoted one. Significantly, while the Catholic priests baptised four of his daughters and solemnized the marriage of one on their visit to Fort Edmonton in 1838,[123] Rowand did not feel that his "natural marriage" needed further benediction. Perhaps there is no greater testimony to the bond that existed between them than Rowand's simple lament when he learned that Lisette had died while he was returning to Fort Edmonton with the brigades in the summer of 1849: "my old friend the Mother of all my children was no more."[124] According to tradition, Chief Factor Peter Skene Ogden continually refused the church's sanction for his union with his remarkable Indian wife, known as "Princess Julia." "If many years of public recognition of the relation and of his children did not constitute sufficient proof," he declared, "no formal words of priest or magistrate could help the matter."[125]

This argument was to be used to uphold the validity of marriage *à la façon du pays* in the famous Connolly case of the late 1860s in which the judges of Lower Canada displayed a degree of tolerance and humanity in sharp contrast to the pious denunciations of the clergy.[126] In 1803 William Connolly, a newly appointed clerk in the North West Company, had contracted an alliance with Suzanne Pas-de-Nom, the fifteen-year-old daughter of a Cree chief, partly to secure his influence with this band in the Athabasca country. For the next twenty-eight years, the couple had lived together as man and wife, and at least six children were born to them. According to one H.B.C. officer:

> I often saw Suzanne at his house at different posts and he introduced her to me as Mrs. Connolly. She passed and was universally acknowledged as his wife at different posts where I met her . . . her children by William Connolly were always acknowledged in public as the lawful issue of their marriage.[127]

Connolly had, in fact, earned a reputation as one who stoutly maintained that it would be "a most unnatural proceeding" to desert the mother of one's children,[128] and he took Suzanne and his family east with him in 1831. The family was first settled in Saint Eustache where two of Connolly's daughters were baptised and Suzanne was introduced to the community as Mrs. Connolly. Shortly after the Connollys moved to Montreal, however, Connolly inexplicably repudiated his Indian wife and married his cousin Julia Woolrich in a Catholic ceremony on 16 May 1832. Nevertheless, Connolly, now stationed at Tadousac, continued to support Suzanne in Montreal until 1840 when he arranged for her to return to a convent in Red River where she remained until her death in 1862. Connolly himself had died in 1849, but his second wife, who had always known of the existence of Suzanne and even cared for some of the children, continued to make annual payments for the Indian woman's support. Then in 1867, Connolly's eldest son by Suzanne instituted a suit against Julia Woolrich as Connolly's executor, claiming that the marriage of his mother and father had been legal and that, therefore, by law Suzanne had been entitled to one-half of his father's estate. Upon her death, this inheritance would have passed to her children, and John Connolly maintained that, as a legitimate heir, he was entitled to one-sixth of the estate.

The question as to whether a valid marriage had existed between Connolly and his Indian wife was thus the central issue of the case. On the basis of the testimony of numerous witnesses who had lived in Rupert's Land and an extensive examination of the development of marriage law, Chief Justice Monk ruled that their union constituted a valid marriage: firstly, because Suzanne had been married according to the custom and usages of her own people and secondly, because the consent of both parties that was the essential element of civilized marriage had been proved by twenty-eight years of repute, public acknowledgement and co-habitation as man and wife.[129] Connolly had further given his name to Suzanne and shown considerable concern for the care and education of his offspring.

In a moving vindication of "the custom of the country," the Chief Justice summed up:

> It is beyond all question, all controversy, that in the North West among the Crees, among the other Indian tribes or nations, among the Europeans at all stations, posts, and settlements of the Hudson's Bay, this union, contracted under such circumstances, persisted in for such a long period of years, characterized by inviolable fidelity and devotion on both sides, and made more sacred by the birth and education of a numerous family, would have been regarded as a valid marriage in the North West, was legal there; and can this Court, after he brought his wife and family to Canada, after having recognized her here as such, presented her as such to the persons he and she associated with, declare the marriage illegal, null and void? Can I pronounce this connection, formed and continued under such circumstances, concubinage, and brand his offspring as bastards. . . . I think not. There would be no law, no justice, no sense, no morality in such a judgment.[130]

NOTES

1. Variations of this phrase, which means "after the fashion of the country," are also found, such as *en façon du nord* and "after the fashion of the North West."

2. E.E. Rich, ed., *Copy-Book of Letters Outward, 1680–1687* (Toronto: Champlain Society, 1948) 11: 40–41.

3. In the 1680s, a governor at Albany had been allowed to bring out his wife and her companion. They proved such a nuisance, however, that the London Committee soon withdrew this privilege and ordered all captains to make sure that no women were aboard its ships when they departed from Gravesend.

4. E.E. Rich, ed., *James Isham's Observations and Notes, 1743–1749* (London: Hudson's Bay Record Society, hereinafter HBRS, 1949), 12: 79.

5. Hudson's Bay Company Archives, *Report from the Committee, appointed to inquire into the State and Condition of the Countries Adjoining to Hudson's Bay and of the Trade carried on there, 24 April 1749*, p. 219.

6. Samuel Hearne, *A Journey to the Northern Ocean, 1769, 1770, 1771, 1772*, ed. Richard Glover (Toronto, 1958), 82; W. Kaye Lamb, ed., *The Journals and Letters of Sir Alexander Mackenzie* (Cambridge England, 1970), 134.

7. Rich, *Isham's Observations*, 101: "When a Young Man has a mind for a Wife, they do not make Long tedious Ceremony's nor yet use much formalities." Glyndwr Williams, ed., *Andrew Graham's Observations on Hudson's Bay, 1767–1791* (London: H.B.R.S., 1969), 27: 153: "I cannot with propriety rank fornication and adultery (though very frequent amongst them) among their vices as they think no harm in either."

8. Rich, *Isham's Observations*, 95; Hearne, *Journey to Northern Ocean*, 83–84; Williams, *Graham's Observations*, 57–58. It was usually the failure of the white man to respect Indian mores, even though they were much more lenient than his own, which led to hostility.

9. H.B.C.A., Churchill Journal, 27 November 1750, B.42/a/36, f. 23. For a summation of the important economic role played by native women in the fur trade, see Sylvia Van Kirk, "Women and the Fur Trade," *The Beaver* (Winter 1972), 4.

10. J.B. Tyrell, ed., *Documents Relating to the Early History of Hudson's Bay* (Toronto: Champlain Society, 1931), 28: 229–30. See also Joseph Robson, *An Account of Six Years Residence in Hudson's Bay from 1733 to 1736, and 1744 to 1747* (London, 1752), 52.

11. H.B.C.A., Albany Journal, 24 Jan. 1771, B.3/a/63, f. 18d.

12. H.B.C.A., Moose Journal, 4 March 1744, B.135/a/14, f. 32.

13. *Parliamentary Report*, 1749, 224; Rich, *Isham's Observations*, 322, 325.

14. H.B.C.A., London Committee to R. Pilgrim, 6 May 1747, A.6/7, f. 110d.

15. Hearne, *Journey to Northern Ocean*, 39–40.

16. Williams, *Graham's Observations*, 248.

17. H.B.C.A., T. Mitchell to G. Spence, 3 Feb. 1745, B.3/b/2, f. 12; Moose Journal, 16 May 1742, B.135/a/11, f. 64.

18. Albany Journal, 18–24 Jan. 1771, B.3/a/63, fos. 18–18d. Marten eventually succeeded in sending his son to England, having implored the London Committee to make an exception to the ruling passed in 1751 that no person of Indian or part-Indian extraction be allowed passage to Britain.

19. H.B.C.A., York Journal, 22–24 Sept. 1762, B.239/a/50, f. 5–5d.

20. Numerous examples could be cited. Part of Samuel Hearne's hatred for Moses Norton undoubtedly stemmed from the fact that Norton went to great lengths to prevent any of his subordinates from having any dealings with Indian women (Hearne, *Journey to Northern Ocean*, 39–40). A servant at Moose Fort in the 1740s, Augustin Frost, became very refractory when the tyrannical James Duffield cut him off from his Indian family (Moose Journal, 16–18 May 1742, B.135/a/11, fos. 64–66). Indian resentment at being barred from Henley House while their women were kept there by the master resulted in an attack on the post in 1755 (George Rushworth to London Committee, 8 Sept. 1755, A.11/2, fos. 173–74).

21. Williams, *Graham's Observations*, 248; H.B.C.A., Churchill Journal, 2–4 Nov. 1751, B.42/a/38, fos. 13–15.

22. W.S. Wallace, ed., *Documents Relating to the North West Company* (Toronto: Champlain Society, 1934), 20: 211.

23. J.B. Tyrell, ed., *Journals of Samuel Hearne and Philip Turnor, 1774–1792* (Toronto: Champlain Society, 1934), 21: 252–53.

24. "Connolly vs. Woolrich, Superior Court, 9 July 1867," *Lower Canada Jurist*, 11: 228; hereafter cited as "Connolly Case, 1867."

25. Toronto Public Library, George Nelson Papers, Journal 1810–11, pp. 41–42. This phenomenon is also seen among the Chinooks,

Frederick Merk, ed., *Fur Trade and Empire: George Simpson's Journal, 1824–25* (Cambridge, MA, 1931), 99.

26. L.R. Masson, ed., *Les Bourgeois de la Compagnie du Nord-Ouest* (New York, 1960 [reprint]), 251–52; Richard Glover, ed., *David Thompson's Narrative, 1784–1812* (Toronto: Champlain Society, 1962), 40: 82, 255; Lamb, *Journals of Mackenzie*, 151–52.

27. "Johnstone et al. vs. Connolly, Appeal Court, 7 Sept. 1869," *La Revue Legale*, 1: 280–81; hereafter cited as "Connolly Appeal Case, 1869."

28. W. Kaye Lamb, ed., *Sixteen Years in the Indian Country: The Journal of Daniel Williams Harmon, 1800–1816* (Toronto, 1957), 53.

29. Elliot Coues, ed., *New Light on the Early History of the Greater Northwest: The Manuscript Journals of Alexander Henry and of David Thompson, 1799–1814* (Minneapolis, 1965 [reprint]), 1: 228.

30. Ibid., 11: 901.

31. Ross Cox, *The Columbia River*, ed. Edgar and Jane Stewart (Norman, OK, 1957), 209–11; Lamb, *Harmon's Journal*, 28–29.

32. "Connolly Appeal Case, 1869," 280–82: "Une homme engagé respectait la femme d'un bourgeois comme si elle eute été la première femme dans ce pays."

33. Glover, *Thompson's Narrative*, 82.

34. Lamb, *Harmon's Journal*, 53.

35. Coues, *New Light on the Greater Northwest*, 1: 211.

36. "Connolly Case, 1867," 239: "I never heard of any of the men keeping two women at a time, it was not customary. A man could only have one wife at a time."

37. Tyrell, *Journals of Hearne and Turnor*, 275.

38. Public Record Office, England, Will of Robert Pilgrim, 23 Nov. 1750, Prob. 11/784, f. 396.

39. Sailing Orders, 16 May 1751, A.6/8, f. 54d. See also Williams, *Graham's Observations*, 145.

40. Cox, *Columbia River*, 224.

41. Numerous examples of early bourgeois who followed this course of action could be cited, i.e., Roderick Mackenzie of Terrebonne, Patrick Small, William McGillivray, Charles Chaboillez, and Nicholas Montour. For an account of the fêting of the retired Nor'Wester by eastern society, see Cox, *Columbia River*, 361–62.

42. The exception to this general statement would be the action of old N.W.C. engagés who became "freemen" rather than leave their Indian families. They, however, had little prospect of returning to a comfortable life in eastern Canada and were the only group prepared to live a semi-nomadic life akin to that of the Indians. In the early 1800s, the North West Company had developed a plan for a settlement at Rainy Lake for superannuated engagés and their families, but this came to naught owing to the bitter trade struggle (Lamb, *Harmon's Journal*, 5–6).

43. Thomas Thomas to George Gladman, 3 March 1813, B.3/b/49a, f, 10d.

44. H.B.C.A., *Andrew Graham's Observations, 1771*, E.2/7, f. 5d; Williams, *Graham's Observations*, 145.

45. P.R.O., England, Will of John Favell, 19 Feb. 1784, Prob. 11/1785, f. 551. The London Committee, which had received similar requests before, readily complied with Favell's wish. In fact, the administration of annuities for native families was to become a regular duty of the Company secretary in London. Many other examples could be cited of H.B.C. men who left detailed instructions in their wills for the care of their native families, i.e., William Bolland, Robert Goodwin, Matthew Cocking, and James Spence.

46. Alexander Henry, *Travels and Adventures in Canada and the Indian Territories, 1760–1776* (Edmonton, 1969 [reprint]), 248.

47. The continuing support given to the families of N.W.C. servants, plus the growth of a body of "freemen," helps to account for the fact that the mixed-blood progeny of the Nor'Westers were early identifiable as a group distinct from the Indians. It took much longer for the mixed-blood offspring of H.B.C. men to become a recognizable group because they were absorbed directly into Indian society. In the eighteenth century, no distinction was made between "half-breed" and "Indian," and it appears that many of the "Home" Indians around H.B.C. posts were actually first or second generation mixed-bloods. This phenomenon has been elaborated by anthropologist Jennifer Brown in an unpublished manuscript entitled "Halfbreeds: The Entrenchment of a Racial Category in the Canadian Northwest Fur Trade" (University of Chicago, 1973).

48. Cox, *Columbia River*, 361; "Connolly Appeal Case, 1869," 289: "L'habitude de quitter les femmes est très-commune dans les pays sauvages, et j'ai même connu des personnes qui donnaient de l'argent à d'autres pour prendre ces femmes comme leurs propres personnes, et aussi les charger le leur soutien et de leur famille."

49. Lamb, *Harmon's Journal*, 98.

50. Graham's Observations, 1771, E.2/7, f. 27.

51. P.R.O., England, Will of Matthew Cocking, 27 Jan. 1797, Prob. 11 1322, f. 256; H.B.C.A., W.H. Cook to R. Miles, 25 May 1825, B.239/c/1, f. 201.

52. H.B.C.A., Will of James Spence, 6 Nov. 1795, A.36/12.

53. Cox, *Columbia River*, 306. This is an important aspect of the pattern of intermarriage that developed among the Nor'Westers; a long list of officers who married Métis women could be cited, such as Peter and John Warren Dease, Colin Robertson, Francis Heron, William McIntosh, and Thomas McMurray.

54. Lamb, *Harmon's Journal*, 98. See also John Franklin, *Narrative of a Journey to the Shores of the Polar Sea, 1819–22* (London, 1824), 86: "The girls at the forts, particularly the daughters of Canadians, are given in marriage very young; they are very frequently wives at 12 years of age, and mothers at 14."

55. E.E. Rich, ed., *Simpson's Athabasca Journal and Report, 1821–22* (London: H.B.R.S., 1938), 1: 245: Simpson was anxious to secure a match between one of his clerks and the daughter of an old voyageur Cayenne Grogne because she spoke French, Cree, and Mountainy [Chipewyan] fluently.

56. Charles Wilkes, *Narrative of the United States Exploring Expedition, 1838–1842*, 5 vols. (Philadelphia, 1845), 4: 396–97.

57. By the late eighteenth century, the Nor'Westers on Lake Athabasca appear to have built up a nefarious traffic in Chipewyan women. When finally in 1800, a delegation of Chipewyan begged the bourgeois James Mackenzie that no more women should be traded "on any account," they received the curt reply that "it was not their business to prescribe rules to us." (Masson, *Les Bourgeois*, 11: 387–88). See also Tyrell, *Journals of Hearne and Turnor*, 446, 449.

58. Alexander Ross, *The Fur Hunters of the Far West*, ed. Kenneth Spaulding (Norman, OK, 1956), 191.

59. Williams, *Graham's Observations*, 145.

60. H.B.C.A., A. Graham to London Committee, 26 Aug. 1771, A.11/115, f. 114d; London Committee to J. Hodgson, 25 May 1803, A.6/16, fos. 159d–160.

61. Wallace, *NWC Documents*, 211. A change in attitude can also be noted on the part of H.B.C. officers, partly because of the coming of settlement: "As the Colony is at length set on foot and there is a prospect of Civilization diffusing itself among Us in a few years I would not advise you for the sake of the rising Generation to consent to either Officers or Men contracting Matrimonial Connections unless with the Daughters of Englishmen. (W.H. Cook to J. Swain, 17 Dec. 1811, B.239/a/82, fos. 9d–10.)

62. "Connolly Appeal Case, 1869," 286–87.

63. Ibid., pp. 284–85. Marois' testimony was corroborated by another engagé, Amable Dupras, 282.

64. Ibid., 284.

65. George Nelson, Journal 1808, Fort Dauphine: "we were obliged to leave off and prepare for a dance . . . in honour to Mr. Seraphim's wedding—Mr. McDonald played the violin for us"; Coues, *New Light on the Greater Northwest*, 1: 571: "My neighbour [H.B.C. at Fort Vermilion] gave a dance in honour of the wedding of his eldest daughter to one of his men."

66. H.B.C.A., George Barnston to James Hargrave, 1 Feb. 1823, B.235/c/1, fos, 3d–4.

67. H.B.C.A., G. Simpson to J.G. McTavish, 7 Jan. 1824, B.239/c/1, f. 134.

68. H.B.C.A., Eastmain Register, 1806–26, B.59/z/1.

69. P.R.O., England, Will of George Gladman, 25 March 1820, Prob. 11, 1663, f. 585.

70. Lamb, *Harmon's Journal*, 194–95. Other Nor'Westers who took their mixed-blood wives to eastern Canada in the early 1800s were David Thompson, John "Le Prêtre" Macdonell, and John "Le Borgne" McDonald. According to Ross Cox, those with means on coming to Canada with their families "purchase estates, on which they live in a kind of half-Indian, half-civilized manner, constantly smoking their calumet and railing at the fashionable frivolities of the great world," 361.

71. "Connolly Appeal Case, 1869," 287.

72. Ibid., 285–87.

73. Lamb, *Harmon's Journal*, 62–63, 93–99; Coues, *New Light on the Greater Northwest*, 1: 58, 162, 211; George Nelson, Journal 1803–1804, 51 and *Reminiscences*, Part 5, 206–207.

74. G.P. de T. Glazebrook, ed., *The Hargrave Correspondence, 1821–1843* (Toronto: Champlain Society, 1938), 24: 381.

75. Ross Cox tells the story of Françoise Boucher, the daughter of a Canadian, who was married at 14 to an interpreter. After he died, she was taken by a bourgeois in the Athabasca country, but when he left the district, she was handed on to his successor with whom she remained permanently, pp. 363–64. Although in a minority, one witness at the Connolly appeal case declared: "It was very common to change women in the Indian country. The French Canadians, in the North-West Company's employ and the English, did it too" (287).

76. E.E. Rich, ed., *Minutes of Council of the Northern Department of Rupert's Land, 1821–31* (London: H.B.R.S., 1940), 3: 94–95.

77. John West, *The Substance of a Journal during a residence at the Red River Colony, 1820–23* (London, 1827), 51–52.

78. West, *Red River Journal*, 26: "having frequently enforced the moral and social obligation of marriage."

79. H.B.C.A., Red River Register, E.4/1b, f. 195d; Nicholas Garry, *Diary of* . . . (Ottawa: Transactions of the Royal Society of Canada, Series 2, Vol. 6, 1900), 137: "Mr. West has done much good in per-

suading these Gentlemen to marry."

80. Church Missionary Society Archives (C.M.S.A.), England, David Jones to Rev. Pratt, 24 July 1824, CC1/039.

81. C.M.S.A., William Cockran, Journal, 3 March 1829, CC1/018, Vol. 3.

82. C.M.S.A., Jones, Journal, 25 Aug. 1828, CC1/039, f. 35; CC1/018, Marriage Register.

83. C.M.S.A., Jones, Journal, 9 June 1835, CC1/039.

84. B.C. Provincial Archives, Arch. McDonald to Edward Ermatinger, 1 April 1836, AB40 M142A.

85. Ibid. My emphasis.

86. B.C.A., Thomas Simpson to Donald Ross, 20 Feb. 1836, AE R73 Si5.

87. Merk, *Fur Trade and Empire*, 108.

88. Thomas E. Jessett, ed., *Reports and Letters of Herbert Beaver, 1836–38* (Portland, OR, 1959), 2.

89. Ibid., 86.

90. For details of McLoughlin's family life, see T.C. Elliott, "Margeurite Wadin McKay McLoughlin," *Oregon Historical Quarterly* 36 (1935): 338–47.

91. Jessett, *Beaver's Reports and Letters*, 141.

92. C.M. Drury, *First white women over the Rockies. . .* , 3 vols. (Glendale, CA, 1963), 1: 111.

93. Jessett, *Beaver's Reports and Letters*, 58.

94. Ibid., 77. Marriage by a Justice of the Peace had, in fact, been made legal by a law of 1836 in Canada and England, xxi, 46, 116.

95. Jessett, *Beaver's Reports and Letters*, 93.

96. Ibid., 48–50.

97. Ibid., 50–51.

98. H.B.C.A., A.C. Anderson to H. Beaver, 1838, B.223/b/20, fos.

62–66d. It is significant that in Scotland it was possible for a legal marriage to be contracted without the sanction of either civil or religious authority, see F.P. Walton, *Scottish Marriages, regular and irregular* (Edinburgh, 1893). The fact that most of the fur traders were of Scottish origin may, therefore, help to explain their acceptance of "the custom of the country."

99. B.223/b/20, fos. 62–66d; H.B.C.A., Company Secretary to Rev. W. Hamilton of Orkney, 17 March 1823, A.5/7, fos. 78d–79: It was the opinion of "one of the Highest Dignitaries of the Church of England" that "the Custom of living together in Hudson's Bay be to all intents and purposes a valid marriage."

100. Marion B. Smith, "The Lady Nobody Knows," *British Columbia: A Centennial Anthology* (Vancouver, 1958), 473–75; "Cathedral of the Pioneers," *The Beaver* (Dec. 1940), 12.

101. Jessett, *Beaver's Reports and Letters*, 35.

102. Ibid., 120, 143–45.

103. West, *Red River Journal*, 75–76; C.M.S.A., CC1/039, Jones, Journal, 13 Sept. 1824, f. 11.

104. For numerous examples, see M.L.W. Warner and H.D. Munnick, eds., *Catholic Church Records of the Pacific Northwest* (St. Paul, OR, 1972).

105. Ibid., Vancouver, 11: 5, 6, 7.

106. H.B.C.A., Marriage contract between Magnus Harper and Peggy La Pierre, Oxford House, 18 Aug. 1830, B.156/z/1, f. 96. As has been seen, those with commissions as J.P.s were allowed to perform marriages in accordance with the law of Lower Canada that "a civil contract of marriage, executed before competent witnesses, and in the presence of a J.P., shall be perfectly valid in all respects, if no clergyman within 10 French leagues" (B.223/b/20, fos. 62–66d).

107. H.B.C.A., Minutes of Council, 7 June 1845, B.239/k/2, f. 183d.

108. Van Kirk, "Women and the Fur Trade," 11.

109. "Connolly Appeal Case, 1869," 288.

110. For a more detailed account of the story of Simpson and McTavish and their country wives, see Van Kirk, "Women and the Fur Trade," 11–18.

111. H.B.C.A., J. Stuart to J.G. McTavish, 16 Aug. 1830, E.24/4.

112. Glazebrook, *Hargrave Correspondence*, 311.

113. Public Archives of Canada, James Hargrave to Charles Ross, 1 Dec. 1830, MG19 A21(1), Vol. 21.

114. P.A.C., Thomas Simpson to J. Hargrave, 27 Jan. 1839, MG19 A21(1), 7: 1574; J. Hargrave to Cuthbert Grant, 30 Nov. 1828, Vol. 21.

115. P.A.C., Wm. Cockran to J. Hargrave, 8 Aug. 1835, MG19 A21(1), 5: 1078. According to Hargrave, while there were still some young gentlemen who married daughters of officers for money or perhaps "Kinder Motives," "a different tone of feeling on these matters had gradually come around." (Hargrave to Letitia Mactavish, 24 July 1838, MG19 A21(1), Vol. 21.

116. Jessett, *Beaver's Reports and Letters*, 57.

117. Ibid., 147–48.

118. Cox, *Columbia River*, 359.

119. Jessett, *Beaver's Reports and Letters*, 141.

120. C.M.S.A., Wm. Cockran to London Secretary, 30 July 1827, CC1/018, Vol. 1; G. Simpson to D. Jones, 14 July 1832, CC1/039.

121. Margaret A. Macleod, ed., *The Letters of Letitia Hargrave* (Toronto: Champlain Society, 1947), 28: 177–78.

122. W.S. Wallace, "Lefroy's Journey to the North-West" (Ottawa: T.R.S.C., Sec. 11, 1938), 32: 93.

123. *Catholic Church Records*, Vanc., 1: 8, 9.

124. H.B.C.A., John Rowand to George Simpson, 14 Sept. 1849, D.5/25, f. 82d.

125. "Indian Women Rise to Social Eminence," 14 Dec. 1913, Spokane, Wash. (Newspaper clipping courtesy of Mrs. Jean Cole, Peterborough, ON); see also Archie Binns, *Peter Skene Ogden: Fur Trader* (Portland, OR, 1967), 355.

126. The following account has been constructed from the testimony given in the original case of 1867 and the appeal case of 1869, see *Lower Canada Jurist*, 11: 197–265 and *La Revue Legale*, 1: 253–400.

127. "Connolly Case, 1867," 231.

128. H.B.C.A., G. Simpson to J.G. McTavish, 2 Dec. 1832, B.135/c/2, f. 96.

129. "Connolly Case, 1867," 230, 248.

130. Ibid., 257. The decision was appealed by the associates of Julia Woolrich who had died in the interim before 1869. Four of the five appeal judges upheld the original decision. Plans were then made for an appeal to the Privy Council, but the parties ultimately settled out of court.

A CREE NURSE IN A CRADLE OF METHODISM: LITTLE MARY AND THE EGERTON R. YOUNG FAMILY AT NORWAY HOUSE AND BERENS RIVER ⬦

JENNIFER S.H. BROWN

○

In the last decade of his life, the Reverend E. Ryerson Young, a retired United Church minister in Toronto, Ontario, put on record two reminiscences that recounted his early experiences as the son of a Methodist missionary to the Indians in northern Manitoba. These documents reveal the domestic life and circumstances of a northern mission family in unusually rich and personal detail. More particularly, they highlight the central and formative role that Little Mary, a Cree woman who served the Youngs as their children's nurse from 1869 to 1876, played in E. Ryerson Young's upbringing during his first seven years of life.

It is a commonplace that older people remember their childhood most vividly, and Young was evidently no exception. The earlier of his reminiscences, "A Missionary and his Son," which he probably composed when in his eighties, deals entirely with his first seven years of life at the Cree and Northern Ojibwa (Saulteaux) missions conducted by his father, the Reverend Egerton R. Young. The second, dated 1962, attempts a full autobiography, but fifty-one pages (over two-thirds of the text) are in fact devoted to the author's first decade of life—his years in the Canadian northwest and the major adjustments he went through thereafter, on becoming a schoolboy in rural Ontario in the late 1870s.[1]

There is no question that the content and details of these early experiences stood out strongly in Young's mind. One may question, however, the

⬦ From Mary Kinnear, ed., *First Days, Fighting Days: Women in Manitoba History* (Regina: Canadian Plains Research Centre, 1987), 19–40.

accuracy and selectivity of such recollections, recorded so many decades after the events. One control is to compare other available records to Young's to assess his historical accuracy and consistency with other portraits of Northern Algonquian Indian and mission life in the region; this has been done as far as possible, with results that seem to confirm the validity of his accounts. Another response is to note what one might describe as the psychic validity of these texts. Setting his memories down at the end of a long life, without any traceable ulterior or publicist motive, Young centred on those events and persons having the greatest hold on him. The structure and emphases of his autobiography have their own authenticity as a personal statement of what he finally selected as the most meaningful and significant influences in his early development.

Egerton Ryerson Young II, known to his parents as Eddie or Ed, was the first white child born at the Methodist mission of Rossville near the Hudson's Bay Company post of Norway House beyond the north end of Lake Winnipeg. He was the eldest child of Egerton R. and Elizabeth Bingham Young, who had travelled from Ontario in the summer of 1868 to begin their first experience in charge of an Indian mission. His birth was to lead the Young family into a close association with "Indian Mary," or "Little Mary," as she was more often called, who became Eddie's "nurse" or nanny when he was a few months old, and remained with the Youngs throughout their mission years at Rossville (1868–73) and Berens River on the east shore of Lake Winnipeg (1874–76).[2]

Of the several Cree and Saulteaux women mentioned in the Young family's writings about their mission days, Little Mary emerges as the strongest and most vivid personality, the Indian whom they all knew best. Other Indian women appear briefly in the books that Egerton R. Young Senior later wrote about the Cree and Saulteaux and Methodist missions, and in a two-part article, "The Transformed Indian Woman," which Mrs. Young published in 1898.[3] But most of these women were merely included to help make larger points about the progress benefits of Christian missions. They included, for example, Ookemasis, the "Saulteaux Chieftainess; or a Searcher after the Truth," who on her own initiative visited the Youngs at Berens River to learn about the book of the Great Spirit and persuaded the missionary to visit her people and preach.[4] Then there was Astumastao, a little orphan girl who learned Christianity when James Evans was establishing Methodism at Norway House in the early 1840s, and who, when readopted by pagan relatives, carried the new religion in her heart until her uncle, on his deathbed, asked her to tell him about Jesus.[5]

More frequent than the chieftainess or secret convert was the archetype of what we would now call the "battered wife" saved by Christianity, or more precisely, by the conversion or removal of her pagan husband. Thus went the story, for example, of "Betsy the Indian wife" who conveyed her distress at her hard lot to the Youngs at Norway House, and whose husband was thereupon firmly and effectively instructed by Mr. Young and some of his male converts in the duties and respect that Christians owed to their wives.[6] Such too was the theme of the story of Susewist, wife of the

Plains Cree chief Maskepetoon. "A man of ungovernable temper in his wild pagan days," he scalped his wife in a rage. She survived, however, as a living reproach to her husband after he converted to Methodism; "the memory of this and other terrible crimes . . . was a great sorrow to him."[7]

These accounts of abused women and of missionary seriousness in remedying such situations point to a factual reality that has its own importance; there are no strong grounds for idealising Northern Algonquian societies as egalitarian in gender relations or as especially free from domestic abuse and strife.[8] At the same time, however, such brief vignettes of females do not provide great insight into the complexities of Northern Algonquian women's values, their individuality and self-expression, their methods of socialising and enculturating children (both male and female), and their ways of handling conflict and stress. The woman cast as exploited victim is also, in a sense, sometimes exploited by persons who write about her in that vein, to promote with vigour their own religious and social remedies. She may be simplified and stereotyped for the purposes of a morality play that is, in its content, aims, and audience, far removed from her own situation.

Little Mary, in contrast, thanks to her years of association with the Youngs, emerges as far more substantial than the shadowy, two-dimensional women who populate most mission literature or, for that matter, most of the historical record pertaining to native women. The starting point of her story parallels those just mentioned; she came to the Youngs as a battered wife. Her husband, an Indian named Robinson, got drunk while trading with some free traders in the Norway House area sometime in 1868–69. Details vary in the versions written by the senior and junior Youngs; but father and son agree that Robinson, in a rage, attacked his wife with an axe that lodged in her back, and then fled the scene and disappeared.[9]

The injured woman was brought to an Indian house at Rossville the next spring and was slowly nursed back to relative health with Mrs. Young's help, although her back remained deformed like a hunchback's. Meanwhile, on 11 June 1869, E. Ryerson Young was born. "Little Eddie's" arrival stirred much interest among the local Cree, and the chief of the Rossville Indians conferred on him the name Sagastaookemou, "little gentleman from the sunrise land" or "sunrise gentleman," as the Youngs translated it, which the Indians shortened to Sagastao.[10]

A few months later, when the invalid Indian woman regained the ability to walk, she came to the Rossville mission home to express gratitude for the Young's assistance and "installed herself as [Eddie's] nurse."[11] E. Ryerson Young in both his reminiscences recorded his parents' memory of the event:

> When in the mission house she looked around to see if there was anything she could do to express her thanks. She saw a little black-haired boy in his cradle and she exclaimed, 'Oh, I'll take care of him,' and she constituted herself as my nurse.[12]

Little Mary, as she became known to the Youngs, showed initiative and strength of personality in many ways as the family got to know her better. She would never speak English (although she learned to read Cree syllabics),

and it was mainly to her that Eddie and his younger sister Lilian or
"Minnehaha" ("laughing waters"), born on 10 March 1871, owed their
childhood fluency in Cree. She became the children's staunch protector and
advocate. Her particular attachment to Eddie was clear, however, and probably reflected a Cree preference for male children. Her reaction when Lilian
was born demonstrated her bias and required Mr. Young to clarify the
range of her future responsibilities:

> Little Mary felt her [Lilian] carefully all over then she laid her back
> in mother's arms saying, 'girl very nice but I like boy better.' She
> wished to take all the care of the little boy and some one else could
> look after the little sister. Father had some difficulty in making her
> understand that he could not support a nurse for each child, and if
> she would take care of the boy she must take care of the little girl
> too.[13]

Mary's strong opinions emerged most strikingly, however, in the
domain of discipline and punishment. Among the Youngs' later memories
of her, Mary's Cree abhorrence for Euro-Canadians' corporal punishment
or confinement of naughty children stood out most vividly. Two themes of
intercultural conflict were clearly blended here. Mary the Cree brought to
her new position no concept of arbitrary authority. Cree cultural values did
not confer coercive powers on parents and certainly provided no equivalent
to the Euro-Canadian master–servant relationship.[14] Mary, then, was dismayed to see her charges punished or confined, and doubly offended (and,
no doubt, puzzled) at being expected to comply with or abet such punishment as a dutiful servant of the parents. As her master, Egerton Young,
recalled in 1903:

> At times, especially in the matter of parental discipline, there
> would be collisions between Mary and the mother of the children;
> for the nurse, with her Indian ideas, could not accept of the posi-
> tion of a disciplined servant, nor could she quietly witness the pun-
> ishment of children whom she thought absolutely perfect.[15]

Eddie Ryerson had vivid childhood memories of how these fundamental conflicts were acted out in the household, and of how Mary used the
occasions to teach him her own basic lessons about how a Cree male should
behave, assert himself, and endure pain and punishment:

> I was soon made to understand that there were different ways to
> raise children, the Indian and the English, which said "little chil-
> dren should be seen and not heard" and "spare the rod and spoil
> the child." Little Mary was always ready to serve me as quickly as
> possible but I would protest often very loudly if I were not quickly
> served. On such occasions father or mother would try to make me
> more reasonable and if I did not cease my shouting and demonstra-
> tions they would whip me. Little Mary on her part thought I was
> perfectly justified in raising a clamor; "you want him to be a leader

then he must learn to insist on having his way." Father and mother didn't see it that way, so, to please Mary they tried every way to soften their punishment. But I was not easily conquered and so when Mary saw she could do nothing to soften their punishment she would say to me, "don't let them know they hurt you when they beat you, then they will quit beating you" In this way she tried to make a spartan out of me and on their part my parents learned that whipping did little to improve my conduct and they were always on the hunt for other methods to chastise me.[16]

Eddie learned Mary's lesson well and, as we shall see, carried it over with effect into his later Ontario school experiences.

E. Ryerson Young also recorded two specific occasions when Little Mary actually intervened to forestall his physical punishment. At Berens River, when Eddie was about five, he was "a little too demonstrative in church" one Sunday. Afterwards, his father approached him with a birch switch. Mary pressed herself between father and son. When Mr. Young asked her to stand back, she quickly asked him, "Missionary, haven't you said to us Indians you should not do unnecessary work on Sunday or any work you could do just as well some other day?"

"What's that got to do with us today?" asked Mr. Young in return.

"Why," said Mary, "you could whip this boy some other day and so it is unnecessary work for you to do today."

Mr. Young relented, but told Mary to bring Eddie to him on Monday morning. She of course did not. When Mr. Young asked for him, Mary inquired if he still planned to whip the boy. When he answered yes, she replied, "Does it do any good, Missionary, to whip a child when it does not know for what it is being whipped?"

"Why, no," Mr. Young responded.

"Well," Mary said, "little boys have short memories and if you whip this little boy now he won't know for what he's being whipped and it won't do any good."

"Well, take him away," replied Mr. Young, "and tell him if he misbehaves again I will thrash him on the spot."[17]

Another incident illustrated the rubs that could develop between Mrs. Young and Mary over the issue of punishment. When Eddie, one time, slapped his little sister, Mrs. Young quickly reached for a clothes brush to strike him. Mary as quickly intervened, and caught the blow herself. As Eddie recalled,

Mother was very angry and said, "Stand back. I'll not let any one come between me and my child," and struck me again with the brush. Little Mary left the room as much annoyed as mother was. She went to a peg in the kitchen, took down her shawl, and left the house.

Mary did not return for the rest of the day. Early the next morning, Eddie went hunting for her and found her in the bush behind the mission.

Rushing to her, "he put his arms around her neck and dragged her into the house." Mary showed a stoical Cree response; putting her shawl back on its peg, she began her cooking and other work as if nothing had happened. Eddie later sensed that the occurrence, though never discussed, was instructive to both Mary and his mother. "Neither woman so far as I know," he wrote, "ever referred to the incident again. Each learned something of the character of the other."[18]

When the senior Youngs chose confinement over whipping as a means of punishing their children, Little Mary had her own remedy for that as well. The Rossville mission house had a dark closet under the stairs, and on one occasion Mr. Young shut his little boy into it saying, "you can stay there until you promise to behave yourself." After some time, he opened the door and asked, "are you ready to behave yourself and come out?"[19]

"Oh no," was the son's recollection of his reply to his father. "Not as long as Little Mary would stay here and tell me Indian stories." Mary had crept into the closet and was sitting on the floor consoling and cheering her devoted protégé.[20]

Egerton R. Young Senior recorded a similar incident at Berens River sometime between 1873 and 1875. Eddie and his younger sister sneaked out of bed early one morning to visit an old Saulteaux named Souwanas, of whose Nanahboozhoo stories they were very fond. They were found on the trail being threatened by Indian dogs. As punishment for running away, their distraught parents confined them to their room for the next night and day on a diet of bread and water. Mary took her bedding into their room that night and slept on the floor between their beds. When the children were released at six the next evening, their father greeted them with a rather formal statement of regret at their punishment and yet of the need for it. Reportedly, the brother and sister quickly answered that their father need not feel badly; Mary had been with them all day telling stories, and had brought them "taffy candy . . . and some currant cakes and other nice things, so we got along very well after all." The parents began to wonder if the punishment had any effect, but the children later told them they had talked the whole affair over with Mary and she had "shown us that it was naughty on our parts to run away as we did" and to cause such anxiety.[21]

The storytelling theme in these two incidents draws attention to a domain in which Mary's role was active and positive rather than simply reactive and defensive. When Mary told the children stories (which she evidently did all the time, not just when they were confined), she was not only teaching them Cree and amusing them; she was, in a sense, bringing them up as Cree, introducing them at an impressionable age to her people's world view, culture, and prime mode of instruction.

During the Norway House years, Eddie and his infant sister Lilian were too young to absorb the full richness of Northern Algonquian culture that Mary could teach them. At Berens River, however, they became old enough both to undergo some instruction from their parents and to assimilate Indian ways of thought and behaviour. Several circumstances worked together to heighten Indian influences upon them (and particularly on Eddie as he approached his seventh year) and to channel those influences through the storytelling medium in this new setting.

Berens River was a new mission, among a Saulteaux (Northern Ojibwa) rather than a Cree population. Egerton R. Young saw agricultural possibilities in the land at the mouth of the river, and his superiors hoped that he would there be able to minister both to the local Saulteaux and to Cree who would follow him from the Rossville mission at Norway House, thus relieving the pressures on Rossville subsistence resources that had suffered as that community grew. At Berens River, the Youngs found themselves among a mainly non-Christian population interested in what the mission had to offer but strong in its own ways and traditions. The Hudson's Bay Company presence was also weaker here; Berens River was a small outpost, not a major depot like Norway House.[22]

Some Norway House Cree Methodists indeed soon joined the Youngs at Berens River, and among the first to arrive was Little Mary.[23] While resuming her familiar household position, however, she faced fresh challenges to her special relationship with the Young's children.

Like the Rossville Cree, the Saulteaux took a great interest in the children. When on 9 May 1875 a daughter, Florence, was born to the Youngs, the first white child born at Berens River, the Saulteaux held a naming ceremony for her (minus "pagan" elements), and adopted her into the tribe with the name Souwanaquenapete, "voice of the south wind birds." Deliberately incorporated in the name itself was that of Souwanas (South Wind), the Berens River elder who became, through his storytelling powers and his interest in drawing the children into Saulteaux life, a rival figure to Mary the Cree.[24] Souwanas actively engaged the attentions of Egerton Young himself in the mission context; Young featured him in both his book *Algonquin Indian Tales* and his personal records of Berens River and sought to convert him, apparently without success. Under the date of 26 February 1875, for example, Young wrote a description of a conversation with Souwanas on religion, with a vivid postscript on the man and his character:

> Souwanas is a noble old Saulteaux Indian. He is an *honest trusty truthful pagan* Indian. I have long coveted him for the Lord. He is a noted old conjurer, and by his incessant attention to his pagan religious rites often shames us for the briefness of the time we spend in sweet communion with our God.[25]

It was with Souwanas and his fellow pagan Saulteaux, Jakoos, that Egerton Young opened the narrative in *Algonquin Indian Tales*. As Young put it, the Indians had decided among themselves to test the missionary's purported trust and love towards them; "If the white father and mother love us as they say they do we will test them by taking away their children without asking permission." And so, one day, much to the concern of Little Mary, Souwanas and Jakoos carried Eddie and Lilian off to their camp to initiate them to stories about Nanahboozhoo, the major Northern Ojibwa mythological personage, distinct from his Cree analogue, Wisahkecahk. When the children returned, the senior Youngs welcomed them quietly, not wishing "to lessen their influence by finding fault with them [Souwanas and Jakoos] for carrying off the children."[26] Eddie himself retained fond memories of other fishing and storytelling excursions with Jakoos.

Little Mary, however, was impelled to strengthen her own hold on Eddie and Lilian whom she had been rearing, in a sense, as Cree, and disparaged the Saulteaux stories and story hero.[27] Much of the elder Young's book of tales turns on the rivalry between Mary and Souwanas as they engaged in a kind of Cree/Saulteaux story duel. There evidently was mutual respect in the relationship; the Berens River Indians knew of Mary's history and her survival after her terrible injury, and they attributed special powers to her. As Young expressed it, "she was considered to be under the special care of the Good Spirit, so that even the most influential chiefs or hunters had a superstitious fear of showing any temper, or any bitter retort, no matter what she might say."[28] But this did not keep Souwanas from reminding Eddie and Lilian (and Mary) that they were, after all, "only Crees" whereas Florence, the youngest sister, was "pure Saulteaux."[29] Egerton Young, who himself became known as an effective storyteller, may have played up this Cree/Saulteaux rivalry to heighten the interest of his book of Algonquian stories. But it is a rivalry well documented in other Manitoba historical sources,[30] and Mary's discomfiture among the Saulteaux is convincingly reported.

Exposure to two Northern Algonquian storytelling traditions strengthened Eddie's involvement in Indian life and culture more than his parents probably realized at the time. He not only learned the subject matter and form of the stories; he acquired an informal understanding about the value of storytelling as a means of instruction and education, and showed a budding skill in that direction. One Christmas at Berens River, Eddie received a child's Bible with full-page pictures that fascinated and puzzled him. He absorbed his father's explanations of them with enthusiasm. One spring Sunday morning, he was sitting on a rock near the church steps with his book when the Indians began to arrive for the service. They stopped to look at its pictures, and soon Eddie was telling the story of Isaiah to an assemblage of forty or more. Mr. Young came along and entered the church, which was the usual signal for the Indians to enter as well. When none followed him in, the missionary was obliged to tell his son to "quit talking," and Little Mary was called "to take the boy and his book into the mission house and let the Indians come into the church." The Indians entered, but as Eddie recalled, they "said they would rather hear me talking in straight ahead Cree than to hear him [Mr. Young] stumbling over interpreters."[31]

Even if Eddie was learning his Bible, his Indianisation was proceeding apace on other fronts. During one winter (probably 1875–76), he set out more than fifty rabbit snares which he checked every other day, using skills that he had begun to learn at Norway House under the tutelage of Sandy

Harte, a Cree boy from Nelson House who lived for some time with the Youngs. Once in a while he caught an ermine and Little Mary showed him how she would stretch the skin and rub it until it was clean and as soft as silk. When the local Hudson's Bay Company trader heard that the Youngs had some ermine skins he accused them of trading privately with the Indians and had to be convinced that the furs were taken by their own son.[32] Eddie and Lilian were of course at ease with canoes and dog sleds, and Little Mary kept them dressed in skilfully made "deerskin" clothing. As infants, they had been carried in moss bags; and as they grew the Indians made them gifts of their own handiwork. Souwanas, for example, made Eddie a bow and quiver full of arrows, while his wife made for Lilian "an elaborate baby cradle, of the Indian pattern" so that she could carry her doll in Indian style.[33]

Eddie also increasingly sought out Indian company on his own. He enjoyed spending time at the Hudson's Bay Company post at Berens River, where he met visiting Indians and was sometimes called upon as a "serviceable go-between" because of his skill in their language. Without his parents' knowledge, as he recalled, some of these visitors "thought it sport to paint my face, stick feathers in my hair and teach me their dances."[34] These experiences paved the way for an event that was momentous and rather traumatic for both father and son.

One time, Mrs. Young complained that in nearly eight years of life in the north, she had not seen an Indian dance performance. Mr. Young sent a dance request with some tobacco to a chief who had just come down the river with his followers, and that afternoon the Youngs were invited to a Bear Dance. As they approached the chief's tent, which was open at the bottom, Mrs. Young saw, among the legs of the other dancers, "a pair of little legs that were familiar to her." Although anxious, she held her peace as the chief seated his guests with great courtesy. The sequel is best told in the words of E. Ryerson Young himself:

> When the youngsters came in with their hops, steps and jumps, the Missionary remarked to his wife that he did not know that such little boys were called upon to perform. This remark made my mother tremble.
>
> My disguise was fairly complete, but in the gyrations of the dance there was a good deal of stamping. The stockings I had on were dark brown and not unlike the colour of an Indian's legs. Fate, however, was against me, for in doing the extra stamping before the "honoured guests" a garter gave out and a brown stocking fell down, exposing a white leg! I caught sight of my mother's face and it was so full of dismay that I seemed to realize instantly that I was in the wrong place and immediately sought refuge at her feet. My father's face appeared to turn all colours, my mother said; but whatever he felt, he knew that he was the guest of an Indian Chief and there was a decorum that must be observed. But, as soon

as he could, he thanked the Chief for his entertainment, and, taking his wife by one hand, he seized his boy with the other and marched them as quickly as he could to the Mission House.

After securing a long birch rod he took me into the dining-room the largest room in the house. Mother and Little Mary were asked to leave the room. He shoved the table against the wall and sat down in a rocking chair, shook the gad at me and said:

"Dance"!

I was somewhat relieved at the command, for I thought then that he only wanted to see the manner of the dance. So for him I went through the whole performance, and then said:

"That's the way of it."

But he did not seem to appreciate my performance, and, shaking the rod ominously near my legs, he repeated the command "Dance!"

Fear crept into my heart and I began to wonder what he wanted, but I went through the dance again. Still he said "Dance!" and that gad played near my legs, both of which were now bare.

Whenever I showed any sign of stopping he shook the rod and ordered sternly "Dance!"

At last, tired out, I crumpled to the floor.

He then dropped the rod, sprang to his feet, and, taking me into his arms, sank back into the chair. He held me passionately to his breast and I felt the beating of his heart. He just sat and rocked and held me as tightly as he could. I even forgot my own fears as I felt the beating of his heart and wondered at his silence.

"My boy, my precious boy!" he said, or rather murmured, at last.

Then his words came like a flood. He told me all about his early home, his conversion and success in his early ministry, how he and mother had left home, city church and loving friends to come out to preach the Gospel to the Indians, that they might be lifted from heathenish practices and degradation. Mother and he had endured all manner of hardships—cold, hunger and loneliness—all to do Christ's work. Had all those prayers, sacrifices and sufferings been in vain? God had given them a little boy, who was more precious to them than their own lives, and, instead of their lifting up the Indians, the Indians were dragging down their precious boy to their heathenish ways.[35]

Interestingly, Eddie's following comments on this event indicate that the main message he retained from it was of his father's overpowering love and concern for him ("I could never free myself from the impression made upon me by that beating heart"), rather than of a proscription against all things Indian. From his father's viewpoint, however, the accumulating influences of Eddie's Indian environment were becoming too deep and powerful. Mr. Young decided that the family should return to Ontario in mid-1876. The official reason for cutting short his five-year term of engagement at Berens River was the deterioration in Mrs. Young's health—and indeed her condition alone was evidently reason enough to leave the mission field. But his son, in later life, was fairly certain that "after what he [Mr. Young] had seen in that pagan Chief's tent he was almost as deeply concerned about me" as about his wife.[36]

Eddie had poignant memories of leaving his mission home. In particular, "It was very difficult for me to say Good By to Little Mary. Mother would like to have taken her home to Ontario but father said, 'we cannot think of it; if anything happened to Mary, the Indians would not believe anything else but that we had mistreated her.'" Mr. Young was promised by his native helper at Berens River, Timothy Bear, that "he would do his best to see that Little Mary was well cared for." Understandably, though, "the last parting of Mary and her beloved protégé was almost tragic."[37]

The arrival in Ontario was equally trying, in Eddie's memory. He had been in Ontario once before, during the family's furlough in 1873, and had learned in a couple of incidents that childhood and family life in Ontario were very different from his own. But the reality of those contrasts struck him indelibly in June of 1876 when his mother's relatives in Bradford, north of Toronto, gave a birthday party for his seventh birthday, at which he found his "Indian-ness" (as on other occasions in Ontario) had become a weapon to be used against him. His description in "A Missionary and his Son" aptly conveys how the encounter between his young cousins and himself shattered family harmony and caused in him a deep anger that he proceeded to express in a rather evocative (as well as provocative) way:

In my mother's home town my grandmother and aunts had a party in my honour and several cousins were there. Perhaps these young relatives did not like to see so many amenities and favours showered upon me and sought means to have revenge. Discovering in some way that I disliked being called "Indian," they seemed to think that they would be safe from punishment if they called this out in public. They made a mistake, for then and there, defying all the rules of grace and etiquette, I fought one after another until my aunts laid forceful hand upon me. Then the question was, "What shall we do with him? Where shall we put him?" In those days there were a sort of "holy of holies" in the "big houses." It was the parlor and it was usually kept closed and dark, from week-end to week-end. What wonderful haircloth furniture those parlors had, and heavy drapes hanging down in front of the great windows, and the wool or fuzzy ropes that tied those curtains and drapes back! It seemed to my aunts the only place for my incarceration, and so I was put in the parlor. All was quiet there for a while. Then there was a loud "whack! whack! whack!" and the aunts hastened in to see what was happening. I had dragged the sofa from its moorings and placed the chairs in front of it. The sofa was my cariole and the chairs were my dogs. I had somehow got those curtain ropes off and had them around the chairs as dog harness and was using the curtain pole as a whip on the "dogs!" My aunts quickly decided that it was better for me to pound my young cousins if they persisted in calling me names than to bruise their precious furniture. So I was permitted to rejoin my party.[38]

Soon thereafter, Egerton Young was appointed to Port Perry on the west side of Lake Scugog, and the family took up residence in its Methodist parsonage. At school there, Eddie was pursued by the "Indian" label and became very sensitive to the disparaging way in which the term was used (across the lake from Port Perry was an Ojibwa reserve, and the local white community, like many others near reserves, had its share of racial prejudice). It did not help much that the school's only two male teachers, the principal and assistant principal, showed interest in Eddie, saying that his English was better than that of the local people and asking him to translate words into Cree. When they were not present, Eddie's schoolmates "would point their fingers and say, Indian, Indian."[39]

Eddie's special background also set him apart when it came to school punishments. The "lady teachers," in particular, usually gave a naughty child blows with a bamboo rod or a strap until the recipient cried; but Eddie was a problem, for he didn't cry. One time he and three other boys were to have eight blows each with the strap for their misdeeds. Eddie was the last. It seemed to him "that the other fellows cried very easily, they didn't have any Little Mary to train them." Eddie took his blows from the woman teacher, then simply "looked her in the face. So she gave me eight more and still I looked at her, perhaps a little defiantly or scornfully as I remembered Little Mary."

Finally, as the teacher sat looking him over, she said, "I think you would like to be a gentleman." As Eddie recalled, "that was something different, I thought, than straps and it was something that mother had tried to instill into me as Mary did that of physical endurance." Eddie "listened carefully and humbly to what she had to say and told her I certainly did wish to be a gentleman, my eyes moistened with my repentance." Thereafter, that teacher disciplined him only by saying, "that is not gentlemanly or that doesn't become a gentleman and she knew that it meant more to me than all the straps in the bellroom."[40] The incident was rich in meanings. Eddie had received from the two adult women in his life, his mother and Cree nurse, sets of concepts about "manliness" that were evidently congruent in some key ways. Control, self-restraint, a sense of independence, and a capacity to endure and stand up for himself seem to have been qualities that Eddie had deeply internalized. Little Mary had left her mark. But so too, no doubt, had the fact that in the northwest, Eddie had been his mother's first-born and only son, early having a certain freedom and responsibility, while being subject (in the manner of first-borns) to parental anxieties and high expectations. The Port Perry teacher finally saw that he already had a sense of self that only needed to be channelled and directed. Academically, he soon took top place among the boys in his class.[41]

The schoolyard harassments continued, however. Eddie's parents hoped that he would keep speaking Cree at home and retain his bilingualism, and

Mr. Young urged that the family use Cree in its morning prayers. But Eddie had been too deeply injured. "I came to hate almost anything and everything that was Indian," he wrote, "and my usage on the school grounds seemed to be more and more unpleasant until one day in the fight my school bag was torn and slate broken." That evening his endurance cracked, and he fell to sobbing during his evening prayers. His father, hearing him, came to console him and they had a long and close conversation that strengthened the bond between them, and the son's religious convictions as well. Eddie vividly recalled the feeling it engendered: "No rebuke, no threat, only quiet understanding and inspirations, if my earthly father could actually speak like that, whatever must our heavenly father be like."[42]

In June of 1879, Egerton Young was given a new station at Colborne near the north shore of Lake Ontario. It was a new beginning for Eddie and he and the family temporarily let their years with the Indians drop from view: "There was no more talk about trying to keep up Cree in our morning prayers and nobody called me in school or out, 'Indian.' "[43] In later decades, both the Young parents and their eldest son could and did speak and write about their experiences at the missions among the Cree and Saulteaux Indians. But it seemed that they at first had to affirm their own identity and standing in Ontario's country churches and schools so that no one could suspect them of being Indian or heathenized. A Colborne lady once said to the Youngs, "We do not want the returned missionaries here; they have lived so long among the heathens that they do not know how to appreciate the amenities of civilization."[44] There were pressures, it seems, on all of the family to "cover their tracks" during these first few years, and camouflage their rich and instructive experiences at Norway House and Berens River. Eddie's exposure to "culture shock" in small-town Ontario was only the most traumatic and best recorded, he being in the most formative stages of his growth, and being of school age, the most exposed to harassment and the conflicting values of parents and peers.

The record of Eddie and Little Mary has not only its intrinsic human interest but a wider relevance for studies of the multifarious encounters and relationships between Northern Algonquians and people of European origin. With regard to missions, for example, we often tend to reconstruct missionary values and attitudes from their voluminous and accessible printed works, that were generated for a general or church audience, often a considerable period after the events they recorded, and tended greatly to simplify and romanticize the missionaries' experiences. We too seldom have private and personal records that focus on day-to-day Indian–white interactions in all their complexity, indeterminacy, and ambiguity, and that trace the growth of bonds among individuals. E. Ryerson Young, however, writing of his childhood, reminds us of these formative, on-the-ground relationships that were learning experiences for all involved, and without which no mission community could have been founded. Similarly, too, although formal mission history is largely a history of men, Little Mary, Mrs. Young, and other examples demonstrate that women's activities, support, and communication networks (Indian *and* white, in the instances of E.R. Young and other married Protestant missionaries) were fundamental to the households involved and to mission communities as they took shape.

Little Mary and Eddie also have much to suggest about the dynamics, complexities, and problems of fur trade familial relations. The recently developed field of research on traders and their native wives and children in the northwest has been handicapped by the lack of testimony from those wives and children.[45] The internal workings of these families, in which differing cultures and values met, melded, or conflicted in the intimate lives of individuals, were rarely recorded or revealed in any detail. The clues that we may gather from such a narrative as E. Ryerson Young's are therefore of great use. The working out in the Young household of such issues as the discipline and punishment of children, the character traits that were to be promulgated in them, and the modes of their enculturation and socialisation as males and females was a process surely parallelled in many a fur trader's household.

On the basis of Eddie's experiences, we also, perhaps, need to consider that the children of mixed descent born and raised in a fur trade context may have become more "Indian" (less British or Canadian) than we have sometimes assumed. Eddie, even with his Ontario-born mother constantly on hand, came close to maturing as an at least adequate Northern Algonquian, thanks mainly to Little Mary. Most traders' native offspring, typically unexposed to any women (or missionaries) from Europe or eastern Canada, would surely have been less bicultural than Eddie.

For those fur trade children who travelled to eastern Canada or Britain after an early upbringing in the northwest, the trauma of the transition (usually made without the mother's presence, and often occurring in the father's absence as well) may have been more severe than has been realised before. Two factors might have tended to reduce the visibility of such trauma in the written record (aside from the fact that few such children ever set down their experiences of these transitions). One may wonder how many of them had learned, like Eddie, to endure pain and stress in silence, in Northern Algonquian fashion. The other factor may have been that such children, and those relatives or friends who took them in, may have learned, like the Youngs in Colborne, to obscure as quickly and quietly as possible the youngsters' Indian heritage. The North West Company native children who were baptised in Montreal's St. Gabriel Street Presbyterian Church between the 1790s and early 1820s, for example, left the northwest at an average age of six, as did Eddie.[46] We do not know how they celebrated their seventh birthdays. But one fact is certain: we lose sight of the great majority of these children very quickly as they were quietly dispersed among the homes and schools of the Nor'Westers' relatives and friends. The only two categories of offspring who were traceable after baptism were those who turned up soon thereafter in church burial registers (on child out of every eight—a rate itself suggestive of some physical and mental trauma), and those few individuals who returned to the northwest to be marked as Métis or half-breed.[47] In eastern Canada (or Britain, for that matter), intermediate racial/ethnic categories were not operative, and strong pressures operated to quickly "whiten" children who brought from the northwest any sign of Indian behaviour, upbringing, and culture. Eddie's experience reminds us that these eastern prejudices went beyond matters of "race" and "blood," even if expressed in those convenient terms; there was no possible doubt about his white parentage.

E. Ryerson Young learned to adapt and succeed in Ontario society; he had a long and respected career as a Methodist and United Church minister.[48] Little Mary and the years at Norway House and Berens River left profound personal impressions, however. When, as an old man, he reviewed his life, Little Mary was restored to prominence as a central and formative personage. It is unfortunate that social prejudices in eastern Canada operated so forcefully (as they continue to do in so many settings) to suppress the biculturalism of those children (whether white or of mixed descent) privileged enough to have learned wisdom, language fluency, and other skills from native women and men in the northwest, as well as from their white parents and relatives. But we may be grateful that one such child, near the end of his life, felt compelled to put on record the details of his own experience with a Cree upbringing in Manitoba.

NOTES

1. The earlier undated reminiscence, "A Missionary and his Son," consists of eighty-one typed pages and bears the Toronto address, 96 Cranbrooke Avenue, at which Young was living in the 1950s. Since he had lost his sight in the early 1940s, the text was probably typed by his assistant, Harry Smith. The second reminiscence, untitled and seventy-five typed pages in length, was probably dictated to Young's housekeeper at the same address, and was completed shortly before his death on 5 March 1962 at the age of ninety-two; a note on page one reads, "started Jan. 16/1962," and a statement on page seventy reads, "This is February 10/62. I am 92 years old and the only living Minister of my [ordination] class." The originals are in the possession of Young's son, the Reverend H. Egerton Young of Toronto, to whom I am most grateful for permission to use these texts. Other familial data, oral, written, and photographic, were also freely made available to me by H. Egerton Young, by Mr. and Mrs. R. Allen Young, and by Harcourt Brown. They have done all they could to ensure accuracy in personal and family history; any persisting errors of fact or interpretation are my responsibility.

2. The papers of the Reverend Egerton Ryerson Young Senior, many of which bear on this mission period, are in the provincial Archives of Ontario in Toronto.

3. This article appeared in *The Indian's Friend*, a monthly publication of the Women's National Indian Association, Philadelphia, Pennsylvania, vol. 10, nos. 6, 7, Feb. and March 1898, and the manuscript is among the Young papers. Specific relevant books by E.R. Young are cited below.

4. E.R. Young, *By Canoe and dog-train among the Cree and Salteaux Indians* (New York: Hunt and Eaton,1891), 262–64; *On the Indian Trail: Stories of Missionary Work among the Cree and Salteaux* (New York: Fleming H. Revell Company, 1897), 194–202.

5. Young, *On the Indian Trail*, 52–68.

6. Ibid., 174–86.

7. Elizabeth Bingham Young, "The Transformed Indian Woman"

(manuscript), p. 4. The second half of this article also contains a battered wife story, with reference to an unconverted Berens River Saulteaux couple.

8. Neither the sources nor their interpretations afford an easy consensus on these matters. For studies affirming that Northern Algonquian women had roles of considerable importance in their communities and in social organization, see, for example, Eleanor Leacock, "Montagnais Women and the Jesuit Program for Colonization" in *Women and Colonization: Anthropological Perspectives*, ed. Mona Etienne and E. Leacock (New York: Praeger, 1980) reprinted in Veronica Strong-Boag and Anita Clair Fellman, eds., *Rethinking Canada: The Promise of Women's History*, 2nd ed. (Toronto: Copp Clark Pitman, 1991), 11–27; and Charles A. Bishop and Shepard Krech III, "Matriorganization: the Basis of Aboriginal Social Organization," *Arctic Anthropology* 17, 2 (1980): 35–35. Yet many fur trade and mission records detail incidents in which Northern Algonquian women suffered abuse and harm from males. Patterns of historical change may emerge as the records from the 1600s into the 1900s are scrutinised more closely for relevant data. It should also be noted that the battered woman was not necessarily a weak or subservient woman; we need further work on the nature of Algonquian male and female subcultures and gender relations and antagonisms.

9. Egerton Ryerson Young, *Algonquin Indian Tales* (New York: Fleming H. Revell Company, 1903); E. Ryerson Young, untitled reminiscence, 9–10. See also, Young, "A Missionary and his Son," 4–5.

10. Young, *Algonquin Indian Tales*, 31–34, 18; Young, untitled reminiscence, 11.

11. Young, *Algonquin Indian Tales*, 34.

12. Young, untitled reminiscence, 11. See also, Young, "A Missionary and his Son," 6.

13. Young, untitled reminiscence, 11; See also, Young, "A Missionary and his Son," 41.

14. James G.E. Smith, "Western Woods Cree" in *Subarctic*, ed. June Helm, vol. 6 of *Handbook of North American Indians* (Washington: Smithsonian Institute, 1981), 260, for example, discusses both the lack of leaders' coercive power over individuals' behaviour, and the absence of corporal punishment of children—patterns characteristic of Northern Algonquians generally.

15. Young, *Algonquin Indian Tales*, 34–35.

16. Young, untitled reminiscence, 12.

17. Ibid., 28, from which the reconstructed dialogue is quoted. See also, Young, "A Missionary and his Son," 14–16.

18. Young, untitled reminiscence, 29. In "A Missionary and his Son," 18, Young described such episodes as recurrent.

19. Ibid. In *Algonquin Indian Tales*, E.R. Young portrayed Mary's responses to such situations in more dramatic terms: "If she could not have things exactly as she wanted them, Mary would now and then allow her fiery temper to obtain the mastery, and springing up in a rage and throwing a shawl over her head she would fly out of the house and be gone for days" (35). Eddie's low-key description seems more convincingly in line with Northern Algonquian response patterns and etiquette. See, for example, "Respectful Talk, " in *Proceedings of Conference on Native North American Interaction Patterns*, ed. Regna Darnell (Ottawa: National Museums, 1985).

20. Young, untitled reminiscence, 12–13. See also, Young, "A Missionary and his Son," 16–17. The latter text linked this incident to the beginning of the senior Young's interest in Algonquin tales.

21. Young *Algonquin Indian Tales*, 60–61, 64–65, 67.

22. Young, "A Missionary and his Son," 37. For a history of the early fur trade in the Berens River area, see Victor P. Lytwyn, *The Fur Trade of the Little North: Indians, Pedlars, and Englishmen East of Lake Winnipeg, 1760–1821* (Winnipeg: Rupert's Land Research Centre, University of Winnipeg, 1986). John Maclean in *Vanguards of Canada* (Toronto: The Missionary Society of the Methodist Church, 1918), 124–25) noted an earlier Methodist contact with Berens River. Jacob Berens, who later became the first post-treaty chief at Berens River, frequently visited Norway House as a trapper for the Hudson's Bay Company in the early 1860s, and was baptised there by the Reverend George McDougall on 25 Feb. 1861. Rossville (Norway House) Wesleyan Methodist baptismal register, no. 1110, Provincial Archives of Manitoba, Winnipeg. Young described his mission hopes for Berens River in a letter from Norway House misdated 27 January 1863 [1873?] (Papers, Archives of Ontario).

23. Young, untitled reminiscence, 27.

24. Ibid., 34; Young, *Algonquin Indian Tales*, 124–27.

25. Egerton R. Young, manuscript copybook (Papers, Archives of Ontario), 123. In a letter of 7 April 1875 that Young wrote to Lieutenant Governor Alexander Morris representing the Indians' need for tools and agricultural implements, Souwanas was described as Chief (Mary Black-Rogers, personal communication, 1985). However, when Treaty Number 5 was signed on 20 September 1875, Nah-wee-kee-sick-quah-yash (Jacob Berens) signed as chief. Alexander Morris, *The Treaties of Canada with the Indians of Manitoba and The North-West Territories* (Toronto, 1885).

26. Young, *Algonquin Indian Tales*, 19, 31. For discussion and comparative references on Cree and Ojibwa myths and culture heroes, see Jennifer S.H. Brown and Robert Brightman, *The Orders of the Dreamed: George Nelson on Cree and Northern Ojibwa Religion and Myth, 1823* (Winnipeg: University of Manitoba Press, 1988), and A. Irving Hallowell, *The Ojibwa of Berens River, Manitoba: Ethnography into History*, ed. Jennifer S.H. Brown (Fort Worth: Holt, Rinehart and Winston, 1991). Young, "A Missionary and his Son," 21–26, described Eddie's excursions with Jakoos. E.R. Young did not identify Jakoos, but he may have been Jacob Berens, disguised for literary effect as a pagan storyteller. Jacob had a brother named Souwanas (Cauwanas, in Hallowell's spelling). For further information on the Berens family, see also Jennifer S.H. Brown, "'A Place in Your Mind for Them All': Chief William Berens" in *Being and Becoming Indian: Biographical Studies of North American Frontiers*, ed. James A. Clifton (Chicago: Dorsey, 1989), 204–25.

27. Young, *Algonquin Indian Tales*, 37.

28. Ibid., 31; see also 37.

29. Ibid., 237–38.

30. The Lake Winnipeg journals and reminiscences of North West Company trader George Nelson, covering the years 1807–13, document a non-violent but lively maintenance of boundaries between the two, particularly on the part of the Saulteaux (Nelson Papers, Metropolitan Public Library of Toronto).

31. Young, untitled reminiscence, 34–35. See also, Young, "A Missionary and his Son," 53.

32. See Young, untitled reminiscence, 37–38 and Young, "A Missionary and his Son," 8–10, on Eddie's trapping. The story of Mr. Young's meeting Sandy Harte or Pe-pe-qua-na-pu-a at Nelson House where the boy lay crippled by a gunshot wound to his hip, and of the Youngs later taking him into their home at Rossville where he was educated and became able to return to his people as a

teacher, was a favourite one in Young's later books. See, for example, Young, *On the Indian Trail*, 94–125; *Indian Life in the Great North-West* (London: S.W. Partridge and Co., nd), 9–49.

33. Young, *Algonquin Indian Tales*, 22.

34. Young, "A Missionary and his Son," 76–77.

35. Ibid., 78–80. See also, Young, untitled reminiscence, 35–37.

36. Young, "A Missionary and his Son," 81.

37. Young, untitled reminiscence, 38–39.

38. Young, "A Missionary and his Son," 44–45. See also, Young, untitled reminiscence, 39.

39. Young, untitled reminiscence, 39–40.

40. Ibid., 42. In this little room under the school belltower was "a big bookcase with a glass door. The shelves had been taken out and a rod fastened in there from end to end. This rod was decorated with instruments of torture of various lengths. At the left were two long bamboo rods and a raw hide whip with leather straps of various lengths and thickness some having several lashes" (41).

41. Ibid., 43–43.

42. Ibid., 49.

43. Ibid., 51.

44. Ibid.

45. Sylvia Van Kirk, *"Many Tender Ties": Women in Fur-Trade Society, 1670–1870* (Winnipeg: Watson and Dwyer, 1980); Jennifer S.H. Brown, *Strangers in Blood: Fur Trade Company Families in Indian Country* (Vancouver: University of British Columbia Press, 1980).

46. Jennifer S.H. Brown, "Ultimate Respectability: Fur Trade Children in the Civilized World," *The Beaver* (Winter 1977): 4–10, and (Spring 1978): 48–55; "Children of the Early Fur Trades" in *Childhood and Family in Canadian History*, ed. Joy Parr (Toronto: McClelland and Stewart, 1982), 54.

47. For several articles on the varied paths of such children towards or away from Indian or Metis identities and communities, see Jacqueline Peterson and Jennifer S.H. Brown, eds., *The New Peoples: Being and Becoming Metis in North America* (Winnipeg/Lincoln, Neb.: University of Manitoba Press/University of Nebraska Press, 1985).

48. E. Ryerson Young's later life is sketched briefly in his untitled reminiscence, 68–75.

3

RURAL AND FISHING FAMILIES: PRODUCTION AND REPRODUCTION

TRANSMISSION OF FAMILY PROPERTY AND THE CYCLE OF QUEBEC RURAL SOCIETY FROM THE SEVENTEENTH TO THE TWENTIETH CENTURY[*]

GÉRARD BOUCHARD[+]

o

The study of phenomena related to social reproduction is central to historical science. How, and to what extent, does a population in a given area perpetuate its collective structures and relations? For pre-industrial rural societies, analysis of the transmission of patrimony or of family property should be a major focus of this exploration. Here is a sort of crossroads, since family mechanisms of social reproduction are directly related to such fundamental realities as the birthrate, marriage rate, geographic mobility, the agrarian system, socio-economic inequality, and the evolution of landed property. Furthermore, in certain particular contexts, these mechanisms can provoke imbalances, tensions, and major changes in existing social structures. Here we consider the family from one point of view: the systems of transmission. In a general way, transmission is defined as the aptitude for

[*] This article was presented at the symposium "Twenty Years of Social History in Canada: From the Socio-economic to the Sociocultural," held at Carleton University in June 1982. We would like to thank our colleagues, including Jacques Mathieu, Louis Michel, Louise Dechêne, and Fernand Ouellet, for their helpful comments and suggestions. We would also like to acknowledge the invaluable contribution of all the students who helped collect data, particularly Gilles Tremblay, Denise Bouchard, and Rémi Grenon. Lastly, we would like to acknowledge that this research was carried out as part of the Programme de recherches sur la société saguenayenne, which is subsidized by the Fonds F.C.A.C., Université du Québec à Chicoutimi and the Social Sciences and Humanities Research Council of Canada.

[+] Translated by Jane Parniak.

building up capital and passing it from one generation to the next, in order to establish descendants and to place them in the social hierarchy. We are primarily interested in landed property, although goods were also an important component of family wealth, as we shall see.

Recent work on the transmission of family wealth has not always followed this approach. Many authors have sought to construct broad typologies of family structures based on linking analysis of household types with systems of inheritance. We have chosen to bypass this avenue of research, as we feel it tends to limit understanding to purely academic considerations. We also tried to steer clear of certain concepts and models drawn from studies of European peasant societies. The study of patterns of transmission in areas of low population density—as was the case for most of North American rural areas until the early twentieth century—calls for its own models and procedures.

This article aims to outline the system of transmission in the Saguenay and some other regions of Quebec in the nineteenth and twentieth centuries drawing upon empirical research. Using the perspective outlined above, we will show the impact of this system on the structure and genesis of these regional societies.[1] We conclude by laying the groundwork for a comparative study. From the early nineteenth century onwards, transmission of property in rural Quebec promoted the gradual settlement of unused land, and ultimately gave rise to a set of contradictions and of economic and social transformations. There is a potentially fruitful analogy with the colonization of the St. Lawrence Valley, and the evolution of old rural French-Canadian society in the seventeenth and eighteenth centuries. Here, too, useful land was quickly settled, leaving society susceptible to radical transformation. In both cases, this approach calls for considering the evolution of the ecosystem[2] and of rural social structures together.

TRANSMISSION OF PATRIMONY IN THE SAGUENAY

In pre-industrial rural societies, each generation was faced with the contradictory and potentially critical problem of population growth. For families, this involved determining how to establish several children when there was only one estate. By studying transmission patterns, we can try to determine how this problem was resolved from one generation to the next. The difficulties were particularly acute in the Saguenay, with its high birthrate and scarcity of professional outlets, for there were few towns and it was remote from major Quebec urban centres. Families had long viewed colonization as a solution to the problem. Efforts to settle as many offspring as possible therefore propelled the expansion of farmland, and governed the workings of the inheritance system.[3]

EXPANSION AND DISTRIBUTION STRATEGIES

Attempts to increase the size of the patrimony that could be passed on to children included such diverse strategies as clearing, purchasing, renting, and inheriting, the first two being by far the most common. These strategies often entailed intraregional migration. Sons emigrated to settle on newly opened land and the family helped with the initial clearing; in this way, older settlements defrayed the cost of expansion to the "periphery" or "frontier." In addition, entire families emigrated after cashing in their old property to purchase much larger tracts of cheap new land. This is consistent with what is known about the progress of Saguenay settlement, which proceeded in an east–west direction and then, skirting Lake St. Jean in the south, retraced its steps.[4] Thus we see the development of a series of microcycles in which a nucleus was consolidated and then spilled over, in a geographical progression that was far from linear. As a result, family property in the Saguenay was relatively unstable; the exigencies of expansion took precedence over the integrity of the family estate. The biological and social continuity of the family was guaranteed to the detriment of the physical continuity of the estate.[5]

Transmission methods were as disparate as strategies of expansion. In almost nine out of ten cases, however, property was not transferred through inheritance; most commonly, it was deeded to children during their parents' lifetime or sold. Loans were granted (usually of money and on very liberal terms) and lastly, wills were made. There were several *ab intestat* inheritances, but no verbal agreements. The marriages of children governed the transmission process, which extended over several years and can be divided into three phases: a) the establishment of older sons as they married, on lots acquired by the father for this purpose; b) transmission of paternal property, or "old family property," to a descendant appointed to take the father's place when he retired; c) transmission by inheritance of other family wealth after the death of the parents. The last process is important; it mainly involved goods rather than land, and was often complementary or compensatory in relation to the other two methods. For instance, it was used to compensate sons who remained single in order to work on the family farm, or daughters who did not marry advantageously.[6] Transmission, therefore, started quite early in the father's life, sometimes as soon as he turned forty, and there seemed to be no rule of primogeniture for "old family property"; older and younger siblings were on the same footing. Analysis of this system fits uneasily with the standard notions of patrimony. Family property was composed of different parts, generally one piece of land that the father had inherited from his family and had, perhaps, cleared to increase its arable surface, and several others that the father himself, or his sons with his assistance, had acquired. In the cases of transmission studied, the father managed to increase the estate in three out of five cases. However, it is difficult to say how many sons were settled on such additional properties, since family memory retains little about transactions involving land other than the ancestral home.[7] During the father's lifetime, the patrimony expanded and contracted in a way that is reminiscent of, but not identical to, Léon Gérin's "full estate,"[8] the expansion and contraction being mainly due to family mobility. In this way, the Saguenay pattern of transmission provided for the establishment of two or three sons per family on average—a minimum figure, since the precise number of sons who settled on additional properties is unknown.

In these conditions, questions related to inheritance laws and provisions lose their relevance, since the transmission of landed property had essentially been completed by the time the father died. The purchase or clearing of additional land noticeably reduced the stakes for the children, all of whom would otherwise have been dependent on the fate of the "old family property."

THE FATE OF THOSE EXCLUDED FROM THE SYSTEM

It is important to keep in mind that our enquiry relates primarily to the working of the transmission system, and so gives an incomplete picture. Clearly, the system did not always operate harmoniously, and farmers did not always manage to keep, let alone increase, their property. This hidden side of transmission systems has never before been studied, since the outcasts of the system were almost by definition migrants who escape observation. Non-inheriting daughters and sons have also been excluded from studies. What became of them? Here again, the problems of reconstructing geographical and socio-economic patterns make it difficult to assess the social implications of the transmission of landed property. We do know, however, that emigration to the United States was a major outlet for many non-inheriting children. We will return to this point.

The effect of "land-grabbers" is more visible. In itself, the system did not promote the lasting accumulation of capital or the introduction of agrarian capitalism since, in many cases, accumulation was governed, not by capitalsm, but by a family ethic that made hard-working fathers strive to adequately establish their children. So, at best, property was accumulated and subdivided with each generation. The system promoted the physical expansion of rural society and the reproduction of its structures, but it hindered the long term accumulation of land. The guiding values revolved around protection and solidarity of the family: support of elderly members, settlement of sons, marriage of daughters, and compensation of non-inheriting members. This is hardly surprising; in unsettled territory, the egalitarian aims of parents are more easily expressed, while the rudimentary social organization may provoke a retreat into fundamental solidarities.

The close-knit family that provided for the needs of its members was well served by an open and advancing frontier, until just after 1920 when virgin land became scarce in the Saguenay, and American legislation put an end to Canadian emigration. The system then slowed down; social reproduction mechanisms were gradually checked; the old balances of rural society, now contradictory, gave way to change.[9] Simultaneously, the transmission system changed and closed off; its major function became exclusion rather than establishment, making it possible to preserve estates that were becoming fully market-integrated units of production.

Thus the transmission of property is at the core both of processes of social reproduction and of changes in social structure. But observing it entails considerable methodological problems. Firstly, the system created a wide range of situations: stay-at-home farmers who just managed to maintain the "old family property," that they then passed on to a descendant; stay-at-home farmers who increased their estates, accumulated property, and kept their sons close to home; stay-at-home farmers who supported themselves but whose sons settled farther away; migrant families who traded their "old family property" for new land; migrant families who gave up farming; non-inheriting stay-at-home or migrant sons or daughters. Secondly, in order to account for this diversity, to trace those who settled and those excluded, and to cover the three phases of transmission outlined above, it is imperative to go beyond village limits and notarial sources; this is a problem that has yet to be resolved.

PATTERNS OF TRANSMISSION

The pattern outlined above was, until fairly recently, governed by a non-Malthusian dynamic, played out in a setting where uncleared land was still abundant and settlers were few. In contrast, it is useful to review the main features of the European context from the seventeenth to the nineteenth century. For, the models and terminology used in studies of family transmission methods were devised in relation to this context.[10] We think that, in important ways, they are not applicable to the situation in Quebec, Canada, or even North America.

THE EUROPEAN CONTEXT OR, THEORIES BASED ON LAND SHORTAGES

Generally, studies done since Frédéric Le Play's have focussed on villages or regions where there was little unsettled, habitable land, where settlement was old and property was relatively expensive. From this perspective, it is significant that researchers have so often concentrated on Pyrenean families.[11] Historical demographers' studies of modern European populations have generally demonstrated that birthrates were quite high, although lower than that of nineteenth-century Quebec, and that population growth was considerably diminished, if not altogether checked, by high mortality rates, especially among infants and children. The problem of settling adult sons and daughters, therefore, took quite a different form. In sum, according to E. Le Roy Ladurie, "the average number of a couple's children who did not die in infancy or in childhood and who lived long enough to marry barely exceeded two individuals, who statistically, according to biological probability, would be a brother and sister."[12] We should also point out that for non-inheriting persons, these old societies always offered professional outlets in the urban network, itinerant trades, apprenticeships, seasonal farm work, the army, and so on. Poor though they might be, alternatives to inheritance had long since been developed.

In these conditions, the transmission system was designed to prevent subdivision even in regions where laws and customs were egalitarian,[13] and to ensure material security for aged parents. We could almost speak of a system of exclusion, accompanied by compensation, of non-inheriting children. The family estate, which consisted entirely of the ancestral property, was not readily increased; it was often old, fairly stable, and well defined. These conditions favoured the bequeathing of unpartitioned property to one heir (especially evident in the case of the Pyrenean house or *ostal*). There are no signs of expansion or of the three phases of the Saguenay system. Even children endowed during their father's lifetime might still have to return their portion to the family holdings when the father died (rule of forced or optional "return"). All this increased the stakes and importance of inheritance customs and practices. Questions about the fate of the "old family property" (will it be divided or rest intact? will it go out of the family), about when the transmission takes place (age of the father and children), and about choice of an heir (aptitude for managing family wealth) are pivotal. Lastly, in a society where the family cycle is determined by the patrimony—understood here in the limited sense—and where material assets are relatively stable, it is clear that methods of devolution influence residential units, justifying the search for associations between household types, family structures, and inheritance practices.

These features contrast noticeably with the Saguenay pattern of transmission; we consider that the differences call for methodological adjustments.

A SHIFT IN PERSPECTIVE[14]

Firstly, the definition of patrimony should be extended to include landed property that the father acquired for himself or for his sons during his lifetime. This of course includes wooded lands bought explicitly to clear. Patrimony should not be equated with "old family property," and we should be wary of the durability that is often associated with it; survival or longevity is not always synonymous with geographical stability. Likewise, we should focus as much attention on the evolution (growth or disintegration) of the patrimony as on its transmission; the two processes are mutually determining. All this is clearly not conducive to the construction of typologies. The instability, diversity, and, often, precariousness of family strategies hardly allow observation of residential results of transmission strategies, greatly reducing the interest of attempting such links.[15] The relation between the rate of settlement and its geographical limits is the pivotal issue. Once these limits are reached, both the pattern of transmission and the social structures it helped to perpetuate will lose their equilibrium and undergo changes.

In light of these observations, it seems worthwhile to propose some definitions that take account of the constraints implicit in the type of region under study:

- *Patrimony* (or *estate*): All of the landed property owned by the father (or the mother) or acquired, with his or her assistance, by the children at any time during the parents' lifetime. It is divided into two parts:

  1. *Family property* or "paternal land": property that the head of the family acquired when he married or settled.

2. *Additions* or *acquisitions*: anything that is added to the "family property" during the lifetime of the father or mother. Additions or acquisitions may be indirect, for instance, money given to a son who intends to buy land.

- *Transmission*: The set of operations by which ownership of the estate or patrimony is transferred to the children.

- *Assignor*: The father or mother, head of the farming operation.

- *Beneficiary*: Any child who in some way during the lifetime or upon the death of the assignor receives a piece of land to settle on.

What we know about European systems of inheritance should be revised. We suspect that past models have exaggerated the cohesion and specificity of inheritance rules and practices. This might be blamed on the rigidity of legal sources,[16] on conditions of observation that inevitably highlight the stable elements of peasant society, or on the influence of the school of Le Play and his disciples, who were so concerned with continuity and order. Whatever the case may be, some works, published[17] and in progress,[18] on modern and contemporary France, clearly show how complex these models of transmission are, without really calling into question the general tendencies outlined above.

OVERVIEW OF TRANSMISSION PATTERNS IN QUEBEC, CANADA, AND THE UNITED STATES

So far, we have suggested that the Saguenay system was not specific to that region; that, on the contrary, it reflected a North American pattern. We will now attempt to illustrate this statement with data from scientific works, concentrating on the following points: family instability, expansion strategies (including subdivision of patrimony and migration for the settlement of children), diversity and flexibility of the forms, and methods of land transmission. For now, we will consider only nineteenth- and twentieth-century data.

QUEBEC DATA

Various authors have shed light on the mobility of families or on the forms of transmission. For instance, L.-E. Hamelin has shown the unusual mobility of farmers from the village of St. Didace in the upper valley of Maskinongé on the north bank of the St. Lawrence in the nineteenth century.[19] Over almost a century, less than 10 percent of the families kept their land.[20] For the same period on the south bank of the St. Lawrence east of Quebec, F. W. Remiggi has carefully reconstructed coastal migratory patterns, in particular the migration of farming families in search of new land where their children could settle.[21] There are similar examples for Lower Canada. R. L. Jones cites cases of fathers who sold their land in old settlements to move to the frontier, where their sons could settle.[22] Gauldrée-Boileau observed similar patterns in Charlevoix.[23] In addition, a number of anthropologists have defined the two phases of transmission and the two corresponding types of distribution.[24]

In addition to these indications, it is worth taking a closer look at two villages that have been treated in well-known and very controversial monographs. We are referring to Léon Gérin's study of the village of St. Justin and Horace Miner's study of St. Denis.[25] Both works present a summary and model of French-Canadian peasant society and its method of reproduction. We will briefly outline and discuss the two models, stressing the aspects that are of interest to us.

Léon Gérin and the "Full Estate"

Towards the end of the nineteenth century, Gérin concluded that the Casaubons of St. Justin represented a particular form of stem family, characterized by an extended household and a single inheritor. For various reasons, Gérin's painstaking study was instrumental in spreading the over-simplified image of the settled French-Canadian farmer, closely tied to the "old family property" and practising subsistence farming. For Gérin, the "full estate" represented an operation that corresponded perfectly in size to traditional family aspirations; once these were achieved, the family strove to maintain its position. Once the survival of the estate and lineage was ensured, a secondary function of family solidarity was to amass surplus property, if possible, to provide for non-inheriting children. The objectives of the "full estate" were, in order, to ensure daily existence, to "ensure maintenance of the original home and support of the elderly," and to "subsidize children who leave the family centre to establish new homes."[26] Thus defined, the "full estate" was said to be the "cornerstone of the French-Canadian social edifice."[27]

This simplistic version of the model is clearly vulnerable, and it drew considerable criticism, including many well-founded remarks by P. Garigue, who accused Gérin of underestimating the mobility of the rural population.[28] Two points should be raised here. Firstly, in later works, Gérin extended his field of study and redefined his model. These amendments add nuances, but also confusion. For instance, some passages clearly define the "full estate" in terms of self-sufficiency.[29] Elsewhere, it is characterized as "corresponding in size to family needs";[30] but it is also said to be "directly proportionate to the sum of the labour provided by its members,"[31] or both at once.[32] These references to family needs and labour bring to mind Chayanov and his model of the peasant family economy.[33] But the comparison goes no further. Unlike the Russian economist, Gérin has not constructed a rigorous and sophisticated model, and this aspect of his work is disappointing.

Secondly, to be fair to Gérin, we must look beyond the St. Justin monograph. Possibly misled by the model of his mentors Le Play, Demolins, and Tourville, Gérin was also victim of his method of observation that led him to take a "stable" family as his model at a time when rural Quebec populations were more mobile than ever before as a result of the colonization movement, the acceleration of Montreal's urbanization, and emigration to the west and to the United States. A careful reading of "L'Habitant de Saint-Justin" clearly reveals that the "full estate" model, basis of the stem family, is fragile. Gérin himself shows that the Casaubon estate is recent; its owner initially received forty acres and subsequently added 79 more. Why would this estate have become permanent after Casaubon? His neighbour François Gagnon received sixty acres; he and his whole family worked to build up a 300-acre estate, making it possible for at least three sons to settle on the land. Other passages in the monograph clearly point to a much less stable and more varied reality.[34]

Family instability and the extreme diversity of family reproduction patterns are more apparent in his series of essays[35] devoted to the study of five habitant families from different regions of Quebec. Here, Gérin clearly shows that the determination to settle sons on the land, and their need to increase the patrimony, was a driving force in the evolution of estates, but at the cost of an instability that contrasts with the calm continuity associated with stem families. This Gérin willingly acknowledges.[36] Garigue shows that even in St. Justin, only eight out of 174 farms built during the initial settlement period still belonged to descendants in 1955.[37] As for the Casaubon farm, it did not remain in the family for more than two generations.

In conclusion, the "full estate" model remains useful,[38] provided that it is not linked with the stem-family thesis, and if three basic elements, that Gérin himself mentioned without drawing out their full implications, are introduced:

a)   constant efforts were made to increase the estate for the settlement of children because of the large size of families and the scarcity of professional openings in the Quebec countryside, and even in the towns ("lack of patronage," in Gérin's words);

b)   the mobility that often resulted may be blamed on economic failure, but is also inherent in expansion and transmission strategies;

c)   the fragility and diversity of these transmission and reproduction patterns.

So, behind the "stem family" of St. Justin, Léon Géron in fact shows us the polymorphous, close-knit, and unpredictable family of the pre-1920 Saguenay.

Horace Miner and the Rural Ecosystem

Miner's works on rural Quebec have occasioned a misunderstanding that is interesting in itself. Commonly identified with the "Chicago school,"[39] Miner has been criticized for representing St. Denis society as a typical "folk society."[40] He was also accused of cultural determinism.[41] On the first point, it must be admitted that Robert Redfield's introduction to Miner's book contains some very debatable passages.[42] Yet, in Redfield's, Miner's, and E.C. Hughes's works on French Canada,[43] the concept of "folk society" is never applied to rural Quebec society.[44] Garique, who made this charge, admits as much.[45] In the minds of these American anthropologists, Quebec rural society during the 1930s was a "peasant society," a sort of middle point between "folk society" and "urban society." This concept is certainly open to criticism, but no more so than the almost synonymous concept of "traditional society," that can still be usefully applied to pre-industrial rural societies, provided that the term is well defined.

The flaws in Miner's concept and model are nonetheless well-known: over-generalization, overemphasis on integration, cohesion, and consensus, failure to recognize the specificities of time and place. Miner has also been charged, and rightly so we believe, with encouraging a cultural interpretation or reading of collective facts. In his book (written in 1937–38), as in his articles, Miner proposes a wholly non-culturalist interpretation; in fact, he emphasizes geographic, demographic, and economic factors that together comprise what Hughes calls the "ecosystem." This system purportedly arbitrates between transmission practices and rural society's method of reproduction. In certain conditions, as in those that converged in St. Denis just before the Second World War, it can also govern radical sociocultural changes.[46] Miner believed that the rural Quebec transmission system could function only in the context of abundant vacant land, since two out of three descendants had to leave their parish each generation. As soon as land became scarce and expensive, it became necessary to find other professional outlets, to keep farms intact and restructure their management, instill other values in descendants, modify institutions, and so on. This aspect of the St. Denis monograph offers an exemplary analysis of the structural imbalances and variations caused by blockage of the system; we see a society in the process of changing its reproduction mechanisms.[47]

It is also worth noting that the methods of transmission applied in St. Denis in a context of overpopulation—single heir, indivisibility of the estate, compensation for non-inheriting children—are identical to the methods common in the Saguenay after the crisis of 1930.

CANADIAN AND NORTH AMERICAN DATA

We will discuss only a few cases, quickly outlining points where data from the Saguenay and Quebec converge. For English Canada, we will refer to two studies of Peel County in Southern Ontario.[48] David Gagan's study[49] presents two different viewpoints of the pattern of transmission that prevailed among Peel families in the mid-nineteenth century. First, in the county itself, where arable land had been completely settled, farmers practised a closed system. They did not divide their land but bequeathed it to one heir while insisting on generous compensation for those who did not inherit. This put a tremendous economic strain on the inherited farming operations. This is what Gagan, drawing on A.R.M. Lower,[50] calls the

"English Canadian system,"[51] or the "impartible/partible system."[52] In fact, this system has frequently been observed elsewhere,[53] and clearly illustrates the flexibility and practicality of transmission strategies. It should be mentioned that Gagan's data is taken from land registry archives and wills.[54] He was therefore unable to observe forms of transmission other than inheritance, the inclusion of which might have noticeably changed the appearance of the "Canadian system."[55]

His work also shows that a second system of transmission operated alongside the first, but on the Canadian level and in the context of available land. The Canadian West offered vast open territories. The westward migratory movements also penetrated transmission systems and shifted the rules.[56] We also see whole families selling their family property and acquiring stretches of land in the west, to accommodate their children.

The second work is Mays's study of Gore Township in Peel county.[57] His results partly overlap with Gagan's, but the enquiry is conducted from a different perspective. Mays looks at farmers who did not move, who became the established families of the township. Their transmission strategies were almost without exception accumulation strategies that were integrated with the transmission of property. Farmers other than this established core followed more familiar patterns: in each decade from 1850 onwards, half of the households left the township. These data, the result of extensive research and analysis, highlight another aspect of transmission systems: the migration of families in search of larger tracts of land helped fuel the acquisition strategies of those who stayed put.

A word about the United States. Studies on the mobility of families and households in the nineteenth century have proliferated since James Malin's pioneering study.[58] He showed that only 4 to 8 percent of the families who were settled in five Kansas counties in 1860 still had descendants there seventy-five years later. In keeping with the "frontier" model, many studies have centred on the migration of families in search on new land. Some authors have given detailed analyses that integrate family migrations with the workings of the transmission system. This is true of J.A. Henretta[59] and especially of R.A. Easterlin,[60] who proposed a comprehensive model that ostensibly accounted for the economic and demographic behaviour of American peasant families. In an effort to maintain their own standard of living, but still leave their children well-off, parents living in old settlement zones could either limit the number of births or sell their property and purchase a larger piece of land in a frontier region.

These data, especially Gagan's and Mays's, bring us back to the Saguenay phenomena of two overlapping systems of transmission within a single population. One system is closed and operates within bounded limits; the other is open and is deployed on a geographical scale that can be extended. At the same time, several basic questions arise: How should full settlement be defined? How do patterns of transmission change? At what point does overpopulation trigger social change?

COMPARATIVE STUDY OF THE RURAL SYSTEM IN THE ST. LAWRENCE VALLEY AND OTHER REGIONS OF QUEBEC

The foregoing studies suggest that pre-industrial rural societies are characterized by different reproduction patterns, depending on whether or not they are undergoing geographical expansion. When land remained available we see diverse patterns of transmission that tended to change as new settlement zones fill up and that are quite different from the models developed on the basis of areas where land was fully settled. In this section, we will consider what happens to a society when reproduction methods are checked by overpopulation. This will provide the basis for a comparative study of the evolution of rural Laurentian society from the seventeenth century onwards, and of other regions of Quebec from the outset of the nineteenth century.[61] In both cases the colonizing movement comprised three phases: a short period of initial settlement, bounded at one or more points and characterized by a favourable settler/land ratio; a long period during which a series of saturation movements took place in micro-regions and an overflow gave rise to a twofold evolution characterized both by consolidation and concentration in centres and an outflow towards the frontier; a stagnant period corresponding to full settlement of arable land.

During each phase, a relation forms between the ecosystem and social structures. It is not a simple relation; at any time, blockage of the transmission system in a given area may give rise to another outflow, that will redefine the physical limits of settlement. The following data, although very disperse, show that, in this and other ways, colonizing movements in the St. Lawrence Valley and other regions have followed similar patterns, so it is well worth studying them in tandem. We have already outlined the social changes that occur when rural society can no longer expand; geographically it would also be worthwhile to reconstruct from the same perspective the evolution of Quebec rural society on the banks of the St. Lawrence until the outset of the nineteenth century.

PROGRESS OF SETTLEMENT IN THE ST. LAWRENCE VALLEY

The following is not intended to be a comprehensive summary of findings on the topic; we will simply draft some guidelines based on well-established data.

From the mid-seventeenth century onwards, original settlements were spreading out from Quebec City, Trois-Rivières, and Montreal, and the geographical framework of Laurentian Quebec was established. The long St. Lawrence Valley corridor constituted a settlement zone that would not be fully occupied for almost two centuries. The contours of the corridor are clearly marked off from one end to the other along both sides of the river by two mountainous elevations that yield only narrow strips of farmland. At

Trois-Rivières the valley stretches south to Drummondville. Higher up, flat land runs from St. Hyacinthe and St. Jean all the way to Ottawa; consequently, in the Montreal region, a 150-mile plain runs from one mountainous area to the other. This contrasts with the east, particularly the north bank, where the villages back onto the hills. The Laurentians are a short distance north of Montreal; from every point, the relief rises sharply by 300 to 600 metres.

East from Quebec City, settlement advanced in a narrow line as far as the Lower St. Lawrence, where it stopped temporarily.[62] Expansion progressed mainly in a south-west direction towards the Montreal plain in successive leaps that recently described by Courville.[63] For the plain itself, Courville posits three stages: a linear settlement movement along the principal waterways (seventeenth to eighteenth centuries); a flow towards the interior (late eighteenth century); and then a runoff into the inland townships (1830–40). This invites a search for micro-cycles of settlement—movement out from the parishes, starting with those of longest settlement—and, secondly, reconstruction of migratory chains running along the coast and on the plain. Given the characteristics of the Laurentian region and the fertility of the population, the movement finally broke when the last waves of settlement hit the plateaus and hills in the north and south.

There are considerable problems involved in mapping and dating these phenomena, as can well be imagined. Some of these difficulties have to do with the collection and interpretation of data, but there are also methodological problems involved in establishing the periods and thresholds of occupation and saturation. There is a considerable body of data pertaining, for the most part, to the final stage of settlement in the St. Lawrence region, and to signs of scattered overpopulation.[64] We know that the population of Quebec increased fivefold between 1761–70 and 1821–30,[65] and that expansion was then much more intense than during the clearing stage. In the areas of seigneurial tenure, land was noticeably scarce after 1812 at least, according to J.-P. Wallot and G. Paquet,[66] and even earlier, according to F. Ouellet and J. Hamelin.[67] We should also point out that the subdivision of land began before the end of the eighteenth century and continued until 1830–40.[68] It would be worth carefully mapping and dating these processes in order to pinpoint possible displacements, for instance, between the Quebec City and Montreal regions.[69]

Settlement in the Montreal region continued during the early nineteenth century, after which time the need to keep farms intact triggered an exodus.[70] Ouellet has argued that before this time there already were clear signs of overpopulation in the Laprairie seigneurie.[71] In the Lower St. Lawrence, according to contemporary accounts, the saturation point had been reached well before the mid-nineteenth century.[72]

Once again, we would have to map saturation points throughout the entire valley to gain a better understanding of the sharp increase in Laurentian colonization that started towards 1820, and that was a fundamental historical experience for Quebec society. In one century, settlement spilled out beyond the coastal foothills from every point, creating about a dozen regions, almost all of which are now equated with the Quebec periphery.[73] The importance of the spatial and temporal cleavage between Laurentian Quebec and the other regions started to emerge clearly. Thus, as we mentioned previously, it may well be worth considering the evolution of Laurentian rural society in conjunction with these transformations of the ecosystem.

TRANSMISSION IN THE ST. LAWRENCE VALLEY

Variations in the pattern of transmission signal that tensions and changes are underway. As later in the Saguenay and other regions of Quebec, the Laurentian system initially seemed adapted to establishing as many children as possible. Paradoxically, this seems to have had little relation to the egalitarian provisions and proclivities of the Custom of Paris. Y. Zoltvany's useful account[74] should not give rise to preconceived notions about habitant practices. A number of sources do mention widespread subdivision of land that could result from following legal prescriptions.[75] Painstaking reconstructions have shown, however, that the Quebec habitant also knew how to bend the laws to family goals.[76] Louise Dechêne has demonstrated that the Custom did not really stop fathers from bestowing a dowry, bequest, or gift on a child, and that very pragmatic motives dictated whether or not land would be divided.[77] Similar indications are found in the work of Pauline Desjardins, Fernand Ouellet, Jacques Mathieu, and others.[78] Of course, this pragmatic attitude explains the slightly chaotic diversity found in R.-L. Séguin's account of transmission in New France;[79] he juxtaposes a series of contracts, the terms of which differ so widely from case to case that the reader is left quite confused.

Overall, the seventeenth- and eighteenth-century Laurentian family seems to approximate the Saguenay family and conform to the pattern of the so-called close-knit family. Different data, provided by Jacques Mathieu and his colleagues—Courville, Ouellet, Hamelin, Joulia, to mention just a few[80]—confirm some features: land expansion strategies aimed at settling as many children as possible; migratory patterns based on family and kinship; dissociation between continuity of the estate and of the family group. Otherwise, nowhere did we find detailed accounts of co-existing transmission patterns shaped by the twofold process of consolidation and expansion. But the basic idea is found in Dechêne and Mathieu.[81]

In her study of the Montreal region in the seventeenth and early eighteenth century, Louise Dechêne wrote:

> Thus, the very large properties of one or more tenants are rarely transferred as a whole. The accumulation of land should be seen not as a trend towards large-scale farming, but as a way to establish children. The well-off habitant does not accumulate, but automatically buys land for his sons and sons-in-law. Large families went hand in hand with greater fragmentation of the inheritance, but it is also true that the presence of several grown children stimulated and influenced the expansion of paternal property.[82]

For all intents and purposes, this passage might be describing the Saguenay system. The author then refers to the same "ebb and flow of landed property, [that] is repeated each generation" and that, as we saw, impeded the accumulation of capital and the introduction of agrarian capitalism in the nineteenth century. Finally, the consolidation–colonization cycle is clearly portrayed[83] along with variations in the overall transmission pattern in the early nineteenth century: exclusion of already established children; rule of one heir; relative stability of families and estates.[84] It is worth repeating Dechêne's conclusions about the seventeenth-century Montreal family. She concludes that patrimony or paternal land was not the cornerstone of the family, and that keeping it intact was not the predominant concern. Material assets were, of course, fundamentally important, but their management was based on a value system, "a collective mental attitude" that thwarted official rules and underlaid a wide range of behaviour.

Jacques Mathieu and his colleagues, who studied several parishes in Quebec in the eighteenth century, propose a settlement model that prominently features family migrations, the transmission system (that purportedly did not favour the formation of landed capital), and expansion–saturation–expansion cycles.[85]

All these data indicate noticeable points of convergence between the patterns of transmission in the St. Lawrence Valley until the early nineteenth century and those in other regions. These points of convergence in turn suggest discontinuities and particularities. In this context, a comparative analysis of saturation conditions, on no matter what scale, could advance the study of social change.

SATURATION PROCESSES AND THEIR SOCIAL IMPLICATIONS

As we have pointed out, this avenue of research invites a comparison of variations in both the ecosystem and social structures. Thus, it goes beyond the limits of other models and does not grant a priori special status to ecological constraints. Analysis of the ecosystem is simply an efficient point of reference and departure. Excellent examples have already been provided by American historians.[86] Think of what a similar analysis of changes in French-Canadian society might yield. Firstly, at the level of the family and its demographic behaviour, goals, parent–children relations[87] and, secondly, at the level of the village and seigneury, institutions and social relations. For instance, in the conflicts over parish affairs and in quarrels about tithing or schooling, why did many habitants support their secular elites in opposition to the priest? What led to the higher school rates observed in 1829–30?[88] The campaigns conducted by local proponents of liberalism (physicians, notaries, and so on) do not give the whole answer.[89] Likewise, mapping and dating of the contractions or rural society as revealed by the evolution of transmission patterns would shed light on the disruptions that led to the confrontations of 1837–38.

Taking a more general look at the long-term evolution of rural society in the St. Lawrence Valley, we conclude with a hypothesis. It should be possible to pinpoint a series of contractions within parishes or micro-regions until the outset of the nineteenth century.[90] These contractions would have had major local implications, but would not really have affected rural society as a whole, as long as it was still able to expand and thereby ensure its reproduction. From this perspective, the full occupation of Laurentian territory during the first quarter of the nineteenth century marked a decisive stage. The problems of overpopulation that then cropped up here and there might have shattered the old framework of rural society and radically reformed its socio-economic and cultural balances. It seems, however, that with the exception of the Montreal plain, the turning point was considerably deferred. After the 1830s, emigration to the United States and the creation of colonization regions opened up extensive outlets for surplus population and permitted the reproduction of traditional rural society that was granted a reprieve of sorts.[91] This emigration progressed in spurts and continued for another century in outlying regions. For much of rural Quebec, this was a major missed opportunity. The conditions for radical change did not converge again until the 1920s, when these two outlets were blocked with the cessation of emigration to the United States and full occupation of arable land in frontier regions.[92] In new regions and in the old Laurentian countryside, this marked the beginning of the decisive redevelopments that culminated a few decades later in the Quiet Revolution, where the common folk may well have preceded the ruling elite.[93]

CONCLUSION

We have attempted to show the potential of an enquiry based on microscopic observation that seeks in rural society itself the principle of structures and social transformations. Beside the flux of politics, ideologies, and official society, mechanisms of social reproduction govern rhythms, continuities, and ruptures that are clearly exemplified in aspects of Quebec society. The evolution of this society seems to follow a lengthy cycle that completed two revolutions in three centuries. The first took place in the St. Lawrence Valley and ended at the beginning of the nineteenth century. The second, which lasted about one hundred years, took place inland and created frontier regions. Each cycle shows a population setting out to conquer virgin territory that is rapidly settled, compelling a restructuring of the patterns and methods of social reproduction. We then see a large part of old Laurentian society outside of the Montreal region temporarily escape the nineteenth-century breaking point, saved by the twofold outlet of emigration, either outward to the United States or inward with the colonization of new regions. In the Quebec context, this rural society could be called traditional. Until the 1920s or thereabouts, it was unable to invent or to adopt patterns that would have guaranteed its reproduction and enabled it to thrive in a confined space.

The foregoing remarks also invite, perhaps, another dating of the history of rural Quebec. In the final analysis, its slow pace of development seems quite unrelated to the political crisis of 1837–40 and the long domination of conservative elites until the mid-twentieth century.

NOTES

1. The Saguenay data is taken from a) a questionnaire set up to reconstruct the history of landed inheritances; about one hundred copies were distributed (cf. Working document no. 76 of the Programme de recherches sur la société saguenayenne); b) a data bank of one thousand family histories drawn up between 1930 and 1980 deposited in the Archives nationales du Québec à Chicoutimi; c) various printed sources: regional newspapers (including *Le Lac-Saint-Jean*, a weekly newspaper published at the end of the last century that dealt with colonization), theses, reports of governmental inquiries, etc. For the other regions of Quebec, we used published studies that are cited in the article.

2. This refers to the set of relations among the system of inheritance; the evolution of population in the target zone; and formulas for environmental development.

3. The following results are from a study of 100 Saguenay descendants, representing a total of 194 families over four generations. They are also based on partial analysis of a collection of 1000 life histories assembled by the Société historique du Saguenay. These results will be presented in detail in a later article.

4. *La société de recherches sur les populations* has published preliminary data on this subject. See Christian Pouyez, Raymond Roy and Gérard Bouchard, "La mobilité géographiques en milieu rural: le Saguenay, 1852–1861," *Histoire sociale/Social History* 14, 27 (May 1981): 123–55. More in-depth analyses will soon be published in a collective work currently in press.

5. One couple out of two changed residence in the Saguenay from 1852 to 1861 (ibid., 139). On the mobility of Saguenay families, see also Gérard Bouchard, "Démographie et société rurale au Saguenay, 1851–1935," *Recherches sociographiques* 19, 1 (Jan.–April 1978): 12–18, and Normand Seguin, *La conquête du sol au 19e siècle* (Quebec: Boréal Express, 1977), 186–87.

6. Daughters were almost always excluded from the first two phases of transmission and, at the same time, from the transmission of landed property.

7. In two lineages of three generations that were studied in more detail, 12 sons were established on paternal land and 11 on additions. Cf. Denyse Girard, "Familles and patrimoines fonciers dans un canton du Haut-Saguenay depuis la fin du 19e siècle" (M.A. thesis, Université du Québec à Chicoutimi, 1980).

8. Léon Gérin, "L'Habitant de Saint-Justin: Contribution à la géographie sociale du Canada" (1898); reprinted in *Léon Gérin et l'Habitant de Saint-Justin*, ed. Jean-Charles Falardeau and Philippe Garigue (Montreal: Les Presses de l'Université de Montréal, 1968), 49–128.

9. These changes range from demographic behaviour to agrarian reform, schooling, and urbanization. We have outlined a few examples in "Anciens et nouveaux Québécois? Mutations de la société rurale et problème d'identité collective au 20e siècle" (Paper presented to a conference on Cultural Changes in Rural and Urban Settings in Quebec from 1760 to 1930, Institut québécois de

recherche sur la culture, Feb. 1982). To be published with the records of the conference.

10. Obviously, it is not possible to give the entire corresponding bibliography here. The reader will, however, find essential references in Gérard Bouchard, "L'étude des structures familiales pré-industrielles: pour un renversement des perspectives," *Revue d'histoire moderne et contemporaine* 18 (Oct.–Dec. 1981): 544–71. (See under Laslett, Berkner, Collomp, Fine-Sourian, Glandrin, Yver, Habakkuk, Mendels, Bourdieu, Le Play, etc.).

11. Recall that Le Play himself, in his most famous monograph, studied a family in the Cauterets valley: Frédéric Le Play, *L'organisation de la famille, selon le vrai modèle signalé par l'histoire de toutes les races et de tous les temps* (Paris, 1871).

12. Emmanuel Le Roy Ladurie, "Structures familiales et coutumes d'héritage en France au XVIe siècle: Système de la coutume," *Annales ESC* 27, 4 (July–Oct. 1972), 829.

13. See for example Pierre Bourdieu, "Les stratégies matrimoniales dans le système de reproduction," *Annales ESC* 27, 4 (July–Oct. 1972): 1105–27; Pierre Lamaison, "Les stratégies matrimoniales dans un système complexe de parenté," *Annales ESC* 34, 4 (July–Aug. 1979): 721–43; Georges Augustins, "Reproduction sociale et changement social: l'exemple des Baronnies," *Revue française de sociologie* 18, 3 (July–Sept. 1977): 465–84.

14. On this subject, see also Bouchard, "L'étude des structures," 564–70.

15. See Bouchard, "Démographie et société rurale," 24–28.

16. See for instance Jean Yver, *Egalité entre héritiers et exclusion des enfants dotés: essai de géographie coutumière* (Paris: Sirey, 1966); and Le Roy Ladurie, "Structures familiales," 825–46.

17. For instance, the works of Marie-Claire Pingaud, "Terres et familles dans un village du Châtillonnais," *Etudes rurales* 42 (April–June 1971): 52–104, and *Paysans en Bourgogne: Les gens de Minot* (Paris: Flammarion, 1978).

18. Joseph Goy, "Norme et pratiques successorales dans la France paysanne des XVIIIe et XIXe siècles. Propositions pour une enquête" in *Société rurale dans la France de l'Ouest et au Québec (XVIIe–XXe siècles): Actes des colloques de 1979 et 1980*, ed. Joseph Goy and Jean-Pierre Wallot (Université de Montréal et Ecole des Hautes Etudes en Sciences Sociales, 1981), 71–92; M. Papy, "Problèmes de mobilité: l'étude des familles rurales à partir des listes nominatives," *Annales de démographie historique 1980*, 253–70; Jacques Poumarede, "Famille et tenure dans les Pyrénées du Moyen-Age au XIXe siècle," *Annales de démographie historique 1979*, 347–60.

19. Louis-Edmond Hamelin, "Emigration rurale à l'échelon paroissial," *The Canadian Geographer/Le géographe canadien* 5 (1955): 53–61.

20. See also Raoul Blanchard, *Le Canada français. Province de Québec étude géographique* (Paris and Montreal: A. Fayard, 1960), 82.

21. Frank W. Remiggi, "Patterns of Migration on the Gaspé North Coast: A Preliminary Study of the 19th Century Settlement of the Communities between Cap-des-Rosiers and Cap-Chat" (Department of Geography, McGill University, 1977). See in particular pp. 24–37.

22. Robert Leslie Jones, "French Canadian Agriculture in the St. Lawrence Valley, 1815–1850," *Agricultural History* 16, 3 (July 1942): 137–48, and "Agriculture in Lower Canada, 1792–1815," *Canadian Historical Review* 27, 1 (March 1946): 33–51. We also know that these family migrations could follow entirely opposite directions. In *L'Emigration des Canadiens aux Etats-Unis avant 1930. Mesure du phénomène* (Montreal: Les Presses de l'Université de Montréal, 1972), 58–61, Yolande

Lavoie uses a study of Champlain Country by E.-Z. Massicotte to illustrate that the flow of emigration towards the United States mainly carried away "family clusters."

23. C.-H.-P. Gauldrée-Boileau, "Paysan de Saint-Irénée de Charlevoix en 1861 et 1862" in *Paysans et ouvriers québécois d'autrefois*, ed. Pierre Savard (Quebec: Les Presses de l'Université Laval, 1968), 30, 41, 59–60.

24. For example P. Nadon, "La Serpentine (Québec): Etude des principaux mécanismes d'intégration d'une communauté canadienne-français" (M.A. thesis, Université de Montréal, 1970), 102.

25. Léon Gérin, "L'Habitant de Saint-Justin"; Horace Miner, *St. Denis: A French Canadian Parish* (1939) (Chicago: University of Chicago Press, 1963).

26. Léon Gérin, *Le type économique et social des Canadiens: Milieux agricoles de tradition française*, 2nd ed. (Montreal: Fides, 1948), 84.

27. Ibid., 83.

28. Philippe Garigue, "Saint-Justin: Une réévaluation de l'organisation communautaire" in *Léon Gérin et l'Habitant de Saint-Justin*, 129–46.

29. La tendance de l'habitant à se constituer, même lorsque les circonstances s'y prêtent mal, un domaine plein, c'est-à-dire un domaine sur les diverses parties duquel il puisse obtenir directement toutes les denrées qu'il consomme, tous les matériaux qu'il utilise." Gérin, "L'Habitant de Saint-Justin," 72.

30. Gérin, *Le type économique*, 83.

31. Ibid., 118.

32. Ibid., 24–25, 85.

33. The model Chayanov proposes is a set of relations whereby production and cultivated surface depend both on the needs and amount of labour of the family; it is of course understood that the latter two factors do not vary in direct proportion. Aleksandr Vasil'evich Chaianov, *The*

Theory of Peasant Economy, ed. Daniel Thorner, Basile Kerblay, and R.E.F. Smith (Homewood, IL: R.D. Irwin, 1966).

34. See Gérin, "L'habitant de Saint-Justin," 74, 78, 80.

35. Gérin, *Le type économique*.

36. Ibid., 39–40 in particular.

37. Garigue, "Saint-Justin. Une réévaluation," 138. It is true that these figures should be revised, as pointed out by H. Guindon, who questions Garigue's interpretation and proposes another set of data based on farms that have remained "intact": *La société canadienne-française*, ed. Marcel Rioux and Yves Martin (Montreal: Hurtubise HMH, 1971), 156–57. But what exactly does this mean? And isn't it just as important to take farms that are not intact into account?

38. For the sake of brevity, we had to reach this conclusion as quickly as possible. To give just one example, the model takes full account of a major Saguenay phenomenon, namely, obstacles the inheritance system presents for the accumulation of capital: "La race se décapite à chaque génération." Gerin, *Le type économique*, 40.

39. See especially Robert Redfield, "The Folk Society," *American Journal of Sociology* 52, 4 (Jan. 1947): 293–308.

40. See for instance Philippe Garigue, "The French Canadian Family" in *Canadian Dualism: Studies of French–English Relations/La dualité canadienne: Essai sur les relations entre Canadiens français et Canadiens anglais*, ed. Mason Wade (Toronto: University of Toronto Press, and Quebec: Presses universitaires Laval, 1960), 186–93 in particular, and Guindon, "Réexamen," 159 and 60.

41. Seguin, *La conquête du sol*, 177 and 180.

42. In particular, certain analogies with archaic society, or the hypothesis that the society of St. Denis resembles societies have been built "on the

fringe of expanding civilization,"
Miner, *St. Denis*, preface, xvii.

43. Redfield, introduction to Miner, *St. Denis*; see also Horace Miner, "The French Canadian Family Cycle," *American Sociological Review* 3, 5 (Oct. 1938): 700–708; and "A New Epoch in Rural Quebec," *American Journal of Sociology* 56, 1 (July 1950): 1–10; and "Le changement dans la culture rurale canadienne-française" in *La Société canadienne-française*, ed. Rioux and Martin, 77–89; Everret C. Hughes, "Industry and the Rural System in Quebec," *Canadian Journal of Economics and Political Science* 4, 3 (Aug. 1938): 341–49; and "Programme de recher-ches sociales pour le Québec," *Cahiers de l'Ecole des Sciences sociales, politiques et économiques de Laval*, 2, 4, pp. 1–41; and *Recontre de deux mondes: La crise de l'industrialisation du Canada français* (1944, Montreal: Boréal Express, 1972); translation of *French Canada in Transition* (Chicago: University of Chicago Press, 1943).

44. However, the expression "folk culture" is used once by Redfield in his introduction to Miner, *St. Denis*, xix.

45. Philippe Garigue, "Mythes et réalitiés dans l'étude du Canada français," *Contributions à l'étude des sciences de l'homme* 3 (1956), 123.

46. In fact, the charge would much more appropriately be directed at Léon Gérin's "full estate" and his stem-family thesis that posits a set of directions, models, and needs that are culturally defined and shaped.

47. Miner, *St. Denis*, 269: "The seeds of change were in the local system itself."

48. We could, of course, find useful information in the works of a number of authors (for instance Chad M. Gaffield, "Canadian Families in Cultural Context: Hypotheses from the Mid-Nineteenth Century," *Canadian Historical Association, Historical Papers* (1979): 48–70; Robert Leslie Jones, *History of Agriculture in Ontario, 1613–1880* (Toronto: University of Toronto Press, 1946). The

scope of this article does not allow for discussion.

49. David Gagan, "The Indivisibility of Land: A Microanalysis of the System of Inheritance in Nineteenth-Century Ontario," *Journal of Economic History* 36, 1 (March 1976): 126–41, followed by comments by Marvin McInnis, 142–46; and "Land, Population and Social Change: The 'Critical Years' in Rural Canada West," *Canadian Historical Review* 61, 3 (Sept. 1978): 293–318; and *Hopeful Travellers, Families, Land and Social Change in Mid-Victorian Peel County, Canada West* (Toronto: University of Toronto Press, 1981).

50. A.R.M. Lower, *Canadians in the Making: A Social History of Canada* (Toronto: Longmans, Green, 1958), 366.

51. Gagan, "Land, Population and Social Change," 303–304.

52. Gagan, "The Indivisibility of Land," 129.

53. Namely, in France, New France, and the United States. See for example Michèle Salitot-Dion, "Evolution économique, cycle familial et transmission matrimoniale à Nussey," *Etudes rurales* 68 (Oct.–Dec. 1977): 23–53; Louise Dechêne, *Habitants et marchands de Montréal au XVIIe siècle* (Paris: Plon, 1974), 271–98 and 414–49; Robert-Lionel Séguin, *La civilisation traditionnelle de l'"habitant" aux 17e et 18e siècles: Fonds matériel* (Montreal: Fides, 1967), 269–304; Serge Courville, "La crise agricole du Bas-Canada, éléments d'une réflexion géographique (deuxième partie)," *Cahiers de géographie du Québec* 24, 63 (Dec. 1980): 385–428; Marvin McInnis, "Comment on Paper by Gagan," *Journal of Economic History* 36, 1 (March 1976): 142–46; Richard A. Easterlin, "Population Change and Farm Settlement in the Northern United States," *Journal of Economic History* 36, 1 (March 1976): 45–83.

54. See for example, Gagan, "The Indivisibility of Land."

55. See also Gagan, *Hopeful Travellers*, chap. 3 and tables 13–14.

56. David Gagan and Herbert Mays, "Historical Demography and Canadian Social History: Families and Land in Peel County, Ontario," *Canadian Historical Review* 54, 1 (March 1973): 35–45; Gagan, "Land, Population and Social Change."

57. Herbert J. Mays, "A Place to Stand: Families, Land and Permanence in Toronto Gore Township, 1820–1890," *Canadian Historical Association, Historical Papers* (1980): 185–211.

58. James C. Malin, "The Turnover of Farm Population in Kansas," *Kansas Historical Quarterly* 4 (1935): 339–72.

59. James A. Henretta, "Families and Farms: *Mentalité* in Pre-Industrial America," *William and Mary Quarterly* 3rd series, 35, 1 (Jan. 1978), 27 in particular.

60. See in particular Richard A. Easterlin, "Population Change."

61. We define "regions" as space that was open to settlement beyond the banks of the St. Lawrence after the first third of the nineteenth century.

62. On this subject, see Marcel Trudel's maps, *Atlas historique du Canada français: Des origines à 1867* (Quebec: Les Presses de l'Université Laval, 1961), 67–80.

63. Courville, "La crise agricole (deuxième partie)," 391–97.

64. We are thinking in particular of the debates opened for some years now on changes in Lower Canadian rural society, by F. Ouellet, J.-P. Wallot, G. Paquet, and their disciples or colleagues. Obviously, the articles on this question are subject to caution as they have given rise to controversy.

65. Jacques Henripin and Yves Peron, "La transition démographique de la province de Québec," in *La population du Québec: études rétrospectives*, ed. Hubert Charbonneau (Montreal: Boréal Express, 1973), 28.

66. Jean-Pierre Wallot and Gilles Paquet, "Crise agricole et tensions socio-ethniques dans le Bas-Canada, 1802–1812: éléments pour une réinterpretation," *Revue d'histoire de l'Amérique française* 26, 2 (Sept. 1972): 216–18.

67. Fernand Ouellet and Jean Hamelin, "La crise agricole dans le Bas-Canada, 1802–1837," La Société Historique du Canada, *Rapport 1962*, 17–33; Fernand Ouellet and Jean Hamelin, "Les rendements agricoles dans les seigneuries et les cantons du Québec: 1700–1850" in *France et Canada français du XVIe au XXe siècle. Colloque d'histoire*, ed. Claude Galarneau and Elzéar Lavoie (Quebec: Les Presses de l'Université Laval, 1963), 81–120.

68. Courville, "La crise agricole (deuxième partie)," 339 and 425.

69. In this respect, Courville suggests that land-lease statistics could yield relevant information. Ibid., 400–401.

70. Ibid.

71. Fernand Ouellet, "Répartition de la propriété foncière et types d'exploitation agricole dans la seigneurie de Laprairie durant les années 1830" in *Eléments d'histoire sociale du Bas-Canada* (Montreal: Hurtubise HMH, 1972), 126–28.

72. See for example Jean Hamelin, and Yves Roby, *Histoire économique du Québec, 1851–1896* (Montreal: Fides, 1971), 161–62.

73. From 1851 to 1901 alone, more new land was developed than during the whole period prior to 1850. Ibid., 163.

74. Yves F. Zoltvany, "Esquisse de la Coutume de Paris," *Revue d'histoire de l'Amérique française* 25, 3 (Dec. 1971): 365–84.

75. Joseph Bouchette, *The British Dominions in North America* 2 vol. (London, 1832), II: 379–80; Blanchard, *Le Canada français*, 289; Garigue, "Mythes et réalités," 130–31, etc.

76. Once again, the behaviour of Pyrenean families is exemplary in

this respect. See Bourdieu, Goy, Lamaison, and Augustins, in notes 13 and 18.

77. Dechêne, *Habitants et marchands*, 271–98 and 414–49.

78. Pauline Desjardins, "La Coutume de Paris et la transmission des terres: Le rang de la Beauce à Calixa-Lavallée de 1730 à 1975," *Revue d'histoire de l'Amérique française* 34, 3 (Dec. 1980): 331–39; Fernand Ouellet, *Histoire économique et sociale du Québec, 1760–1850* (Montreal: Fides, 1966), 346 and 470–71; Jacques Mathieu et al., "Peuplement colonisateur au XVIIIe siècles dans le gouvernement de Québec" (Lecture presented at the History Department of Université de Montréal, 1981); information given to the author by Louis Michel, for the villages of Varennes and Verchères, and by Louise Desjardins-MacGregor, for the coast of Beaupré and Isle-aux-Coudres.

79. Séguin, *La civilisation traditionelle*, 290–303.

80. Jacques Mathieu et al., "Les alliances matrimoniales exogames dans le gouvernement de Québec, 1700–1760," *Revue d'histoire de l'Amérique française* 35, 1 (June 1981): 3–32; Serge Courville, "La crise agricole du Bas-Canada, éléments d'une réflexion géographique (première partie)," *Cahiers de géographie du Québec* 24, 62 (Sept. 1980): 193–223; and "La crise agricole (deuxième partie)"; Ouellet, *Histoire économique et sociale*, chap. 10 and 12; Louis-Edmond Hamelin, "La marche du peuplement à l'intérieur du diocèse de Joliette," La Société Canadienne d'Histoire de l'eglise Catholique, *Rapport 1949–50*, 13–21; Dominique Joulia, "Practiques successorales en milieu rural, 1795–1870: étude comparative de cas de France de l'Ouest-Québec," in *Société rurale*, ed. Goy and Wallot, 93–140.

81. Dechêne, *Habitants et marchands*; Mathieu et al., "Peuplement colonisateur."

82. Dechêne, *Habitants et marchands*, 297.

83. "From a very stable rural nucleus, a mobile fringe pushes further and further towards the lowlands. The nucleus is destined to remain economically weak since it assumes the cost of this peripheral colonization." Ibid., 298.

84. Ibid., 424–33.

85. Mathieu et al., "Peuplement colonisateur." The authors suggest that saturation of an uncleared area would occur during the third generation. Based on a solid corpus of data, D.B. Rutman reaches the same conclusion: ". . . a full three generations to move from the initiation of a population to excessive density and out-migration." Cf. Darrett B. Rutman, "People in Process: The New Hampshire Towns of the Eighteenth Century," in *Family and Kin in Urban Communities, 1700–1930*, ed. Tamara K. Hareven (New York: New Viewpoints, 1977), 29.

86. Kenneth Lockridge, "Land, Population, and the Evolution of New England Society, 1630–1790," *Past and Present* 39 (April 1968): 62–80; James A. Henretta, "The Morphology of New England Society in the Colonial Period," *Journal of Interdisciplinary History* 2, 2 (Autumn 1971): 379–98; Rutman, "People in Process."

87. Greven again sets a good precedent, showing for Andover how the growing scarcity of good land in the seventeenth and eighteenth centuries put an end to an egalitarian inheritance system, undermined the foundations of patriachal authority and led to a redefinition of intra-familial relations. Philip J. Greven, *Four Generations. Population, Land and Family in Colonial Andover, Massachusetts* (Ithaca: Cornell University Press, 1969).

88. Fernand Ouellet, "L'enseignement primaire: responsabilité des Eglises ou de l'etat," in *Eléments d'histoire sociale du Bas-Canada*, 266.

89. Richard Chabot, *Le curé de campagne et la contestation locale au Québec de 1791 aux troubles de 1837–38* (Montreal: Hurtubise HMH, 1975), chaps. 1 and 2.

90. It is understood that these phenomena could have been artificially induced, for instance, by the seigneurial concessions policy.

91. In the Joliette diocese, there were four emigrants for each colonist. Hamelin, "La marche du peuplement," 17. In 1832, J. Bouchette observed "a diminution of those neighbourly and social habits that characterize the honest and virtuous peasantry of the country." Bouchette, *The British Dominions*, 2: 380.

92. On the cessation of emigration, see Lavoie, *L'émigration des Canadiens*. On the stabilization of farmland in Quebec from 1931 onwards, see Everett C. Hughes, *Rencontre de deux mondes*, 37–46.

93. See Bouchard, "Anciens et nouveaux Québécois."

CANADIAN FAMILIES IN CULTURAL CONTEXT: HYPOTHESES FROM THE MID-NINETEENTH CENTURY◇

CHAD M. GAFFIELD

○

High fertility, extended structure, cohesive organization, and an other-worldly focus: these are some of the characteristics usually associated with the French-Canadian family in Canadian history. Contrastingly, the English-Canadian family is assumed to historically exhibit average fertility, nuclear composition, detached interpersonal relationships, and a strong material focus. This juxtaposed image is often at least implicit in the ways in which historians view the evolution of Canadian society in the nineteenth century. A consistent association is seen to exist between the respective cultural dimensions of the family and, in the first example, French-Canadian group consciousness, communal attachment, and acceptance of subsistence; and, in the second example, English-Canadian individualism, pioneering spirit, and entrepreneurial initiative.

Within the emerging historiography of the family in Canada, the traditional image has heretofore not come under systematic scrutiny. Historians have focussed specifically on either the English-Canadian or French-Canadian context. In the first instance, the work of Michael Katz, David Gagan, Susan Houston, Alison Prentice, and Neil Sutherland has helped open this historical topic. Their writings have revealed much, for example, about English-Canadian family structure in south-central Ontario,[1] the idea of the family in the minds of nineteenth-century social leaders,[2] and the changing concepts of childhood in late Victorian Canada.[3] In the second instance, the research of Hubert Charbonneau, Louise Dechêne, Gérard Bouchard, and Tamara Hareven has significantly advanced our knowledge of

◇ Canadian Historical Association *Historical Papers* (1979): 49–70.

the French-Canadian family in various historical periods. As a result of their research, the demographic history of French Canada is increasingly clear,[4] the nature and importance of the family in early Montreal well-established,[5] and the character of population patterns and kinship in specific areas identified in great detail.[6] Despite the conceptual and methodological achievements of these and other scholars, however, systematic comparative analysis is not yet available and the established stereotypes linger on. No research has forced Canadian historians to specifically reconsider the comparison between English-Canadian families as loose federations of individuals seeking material betterment and French-Canadian families as cohesive units with members collectively seeking other-worldly reward.

The importance of reconsidering this issue is suggested by the experience of two townships in Prescott County, Ontario, during the mid-nineteenth century. In these years, the cultural geography of Prescott was radically changed by the settlement of French Canadians from Quebec. The two specific townships under study were selected for both substantive and technical reasons. On the substantive side, Alfred was selected as an example of a township that did not have any significant English-Canadian settlement at the time of heavy French-Canadian immigration. Caledonia, in contrast, had a substantial English-Canadian presence at the time of Quebec settlement. For methodological reasons, Alfred and Caledonia were suitable because the manuscript census returns for these townships are very legible and the enumerators appear to have carried out their duties quite carefully. Consequently, these sources, as well as literary evidence, are available for systematic examination.

The experience of these two townships suggests that the nature of English-Canadian and French-Canadian families need not be analysed from two fully distinct perspectives. Specifically, comparative analysis of three fundamental aspects of family life reveals significant similarities and unexpected differences between the two cultural groups. The three aspects examined are familial activity and domestic organization, family and household structure, and the material perspectives of families in terms of land use and soil conditions. Within these examples, the cultural dimensions of Alfred and Caledonia families appears substantially more subtle and complex than heretofore suggested.

Substantial French-Canadian immigration to Alfred and Caledonia followed an initial settlement of Irish and Scottish pioneers who had firmly established themselves by the early decades of the nineteenth century. Local histories of Prescott County record that David Holmes and Thomas Pattee took up land just after 1800 near the trail that was later named Alfred Road, while James Proudfoot arrived in Caledonia township from Scotland in 1831. The Humphrey Hughes family came to Alfred township from Ireland in 1823 and settled on the south side of Lake George. These pioneers were followed by Thomas and John Brady, Irish immigrants in 1830, who established the tiny community of Bradyville with several other frontier families.[7]

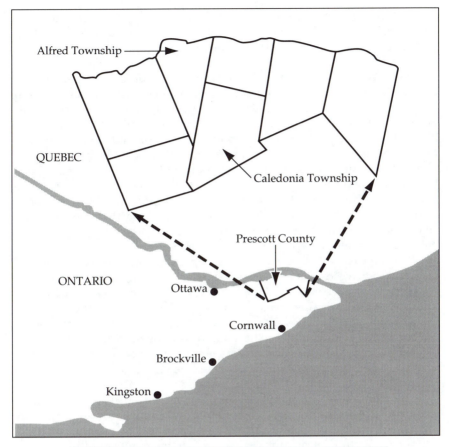

F I G U R E   1   *MAP OF PRESCOTT COUNTY*

Early settlers in Alfred and Caledonia also came from the northern United States or were descendants of United Empire Loyalists. John Cashion was the son of a New England colonist who had settled in Ontario during the late eighteenth century. Cashion came to Alfred in 1823 where he married and established his own household in 1837. Many Americans immigrated to Prescott County during the 1820s and 1830s, including Charles Gates who came with his father to Caledonia from Massachusetts. Frequently, immigrants from the United States were joined in the journey to Prescott County by pioneers who had temporarily settled in more southern Ontario counties. Duncan McLeod settled in the southwestern corner of Caledonia township after immigrating from Scotland and first residing in Glengarry County. Similarly, while Archibald McLeod immigrated through Glengarry to Caledonia in 1844, Thomas Lytle permanently settled in Alfred in 1831 after arriving in Cornwall from Ireland.

Population turnover undoubtedly characterized the British-origin and American presence in Alfred and Caledonia. Systematic analysis is not yet complete, but it is already clear that individuals and families arrived in and departed from these townships throughout the nineteenth century. However, two specific trends are particularly important: the continuance and sometimes enlargement of homesteads in Alfred and Caledonia by one and sometimes two descendants, and the emigration of other offspring. Daniel McCusker, son of James McCusker who had emigrated from Ireland and settled in Alfred in 1830, took up the family farm and developed it into one of the most successful operations of the township by the 1870s. Similarly, Abraham Hughes, the youngest son of Humphrey Hughes, continued on the homestead after his father's death, "erecting a fine brick residence and outbuildings." His success was duplicated by John Holmes, son of the pioneer Thomas Holmes, who was born in Alfred in 1841. He purchased land adjacent to his father's property in 1870 and, after clearing the soil and building his own residence, he married and established a successful farm.

While the early settlement of a British pioneer was often continued and sometimes enlarged by a particular son, other offspring migrated to different parts of Ontario or to the United States. The land settled in Caledonia by Philip Downing was inherited by his son, John, while another son emigrated to the United States. The third son of James Proudfoot remained on the homestead while his six siblings left to seek their fortune in other parts of Ontario. Similarly, the pioneer Cashion family included nine children, seven of whom migrated to neighbouring Russell County or to the United States, while two continued the family farm.

The continuance of many early settlements and the out-migration of surplus offspring combined to maintain a relatively constant number of English-speaking residents in Alfred and Caledonia throughout the mid-nineteenth century. During the 1851–71 period, the number of British-origin residents slowly declined in Caledonia and slowly increased in Alfred; no general trend is evident. The English Canadians in Caledonia decreased from 970 at mid-century to 817 in 1871 while their Alfred counterparts increased from 265 to 348 during the same period.

After 1840, French-Canadian immigration radically changed the cultural complexion of these townships. While the number of British-origin residents remained about constant, the proportion of French-Canadian settlers increased dramatically. The first French Canadians apparently came from adjoining areas of Canada East in the late 1830s and 1840s. Damase Brunet arrived in Alfred township from Saint-Clet in 1830, while Michel Parisien came from Vaudreuil in 1835 and Joseph D'Aoust from Saint-Benoit in 1840. The village of Lefaivre in Alfred was first settled by H. Lefaivre, who migrated with his family from Saint-Hermas in 1848.[8] The settlement of these and other French Canadians lowered the English-speaking residents to minority status in Alfred in 1851 and increased the French-Canadian presence in Caledonia to 35 per cent in 1871 (see figure 2).

French-Canadian settlement in Alfred and Caledonia was substantially the result of the immigration of families rather than of individuals. The dimensions of this form of migration are indicated by the proportion of French-Canadian families in the townships that included at least one Quebec-born child at the time of the mid-century enumerations. In 1851, for example, 38 percent of the settled French-Canadian families in Alfred included Quebec-born children; this proportion was 54.6 percent in 1861 and 45.3 percent in 1871. These percentages are significant in that families with Quebec-born children represent a minimum estimate of this form of migration. Many other French-Canadian families may have immigrated to Alfred with children who subsequently left their parents before a census year. Clearly, therefore, this evidence suggests that French Canadians maintained familial stability and continuity in coming to eastern Ontario.

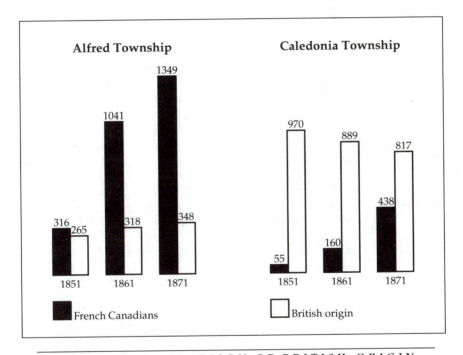

FIGURE 2 *COMPARISON OF BRITISH-ORIGIN AND FRENCH-CANADIAN POPULATION FIGURES, 1851–71*

Similar estimates of the importance of family settlement are not available for the English-Canadian example, since the birthplaces of their children are almost uniformly Upper Canadian. Nonetheless, it is clear that, however they arrived in Alfred and Caledonia, both cultural groups characteristically resided as members of assembled families during the mid-nineteenth century. In most cases, these families were nuclear in form. In the 1851–71 period, the number of households in Alfred and Caledonia that included relatives outside the conjugal family unit was never very substantial, although an upward trend is evident. In Alfred, the proportion of French-Canadian households with such relatives rose slightly from 9.5 percent in 1851 to 12.8 percent in 1871. Similarly, English-Canadian households with relatives increased from 5 percent in 1851 to 14.5 percent in 1871 (see table 1). These increases appear to have been related to the growing stability and more established nature of the township, and perhaps to the subsequent immigration of kin. In either instance, no cultural difference is evident.

TABLE 1	PERCENTAGE OF HOUSEHOLDS WITH RELATIVES OUTSIDE THE CONJUGAL FAMILY UNIT, ALFRED TOWNSHIP	
	French Canadian	British origin
1851	9.5	5.0
1861	11.8	10.0
1871	14.5	12.8

The economic activity of the nuclear families in Alfred and Caledonia during the mid 1800s was based on two forms of land exploitation: first, the use and sale of lumber and other wood products and, second, the establishment of agriculture. In Alfred and Caledonia, economic security for most resident families was afforded by participation in both these forms of land exploitation. While households were characteristically established by those with primarily agricultural ambitions, the successful lumber industry had a significant impact on the households. Lumbering offered seasonal employment for certain family members, a market for agricultural produce, and an important reward for the onerous task of land clearing. All able family members were expected to participate in some form of agriculture or lumbering and, by pooling the contribution of each member, many families were able to survive the frontier conditions.

TABLE 2	OCCUPATIONAL STRUCTURE OF ALFRED TOWNSHIP. AGE OF FARMERS AND LABOURERS BY CULTURAL ORIGIN				
		French Canadians		British Origin	
	Age	Labourer	Farmer	Labourer	Farmer
1851	10–24	34	0	27	0
	over 24	29	31	7	32
1861	10–24	27	6	22	0
	over 24	58	102	15	43
1871	10–24	20	81	0	25
	over 24	38	174	2	65

The importance of land is suggested by the occupational structures of Alfred township during 1851–71 period. Within Alfred, the character and distribution of occupational titles reflect the fully rural nature of society in eastern Ontario at this time. In each year of census enumeration, farmers and labourers predominate among those residents listed with occupations. For both English- and French-Canadian males, these titles were closely associated with age. Labourers were mostly younger than age twenty-five, while farmers were characteristically older (see table 2). While census evidence cannot be used to infer developmental patterns without the support of other sources, the relationship of age and occupation does suggest that work as a labourer normally preceded status as a farmer for young males in Alfred.

While experience as a labourer appears to have been a life course phase for both cultural groups, the continued importance of the labouring group among the French Canadians after age twenty-five is somewhat distinct. Particularly in 1861, French-Canadian adult males more frequently retained a labourer designation than did their English-Canadian counterparts. The apparently weak movement of French Canadians away from "labouring" after early adulthood was also evident in the 1871 census from Alfred. It should be noted, however, that the enumerator of this census considered males to be farmers whether or not they farmed on their own behalf or simply as younger members of a family effort. Whereas the 1851 and 1861 census enumerators followed instructions to describe the son of a farmer as a "labourer" if he "works for the benefit of his parent,"[9] the 1871 enumerator listed all such sons as farmers. Consequently, farmers predominate among working males in 1871, even during the teenage years. Conversely, individuals listed as labourers were undoubtedly wage-earners principally employed outside their own household or engaged to farm the land of someone else. This distinction makes clear that French Canadians more frequently than English Canadians did not assume the farmer title as they grew older, but rather continued as wage-earners or tenants. English Canadians who did not acquire land in early adulthood apparently left their families in Alfred and sought their fortune elsewhere.[10]

The life course experience of status as a labourer for young men was related to the opportunity for seasonal employment in some aspect of the lumber industry, either in local saw mills during the summer months or in the shanties during winter. This kind of temporary employment was an important source of supplementary income for family economies, but it also had special significance for the process of family formation itself. Labouring in saw mills or shanties provided adolescent males with the opportunity to acquire enough capital for marriage and formation of a separate household. The household structure of Alfred and Caledonia indicates that enough capital had to be saved to cover both these events before marriage could be considered. Among both English Canadians and French Canadians, marriage appears to have been dependent upon the ability to establish a separate household. Households in these townships that included more than one conjugal family unit appear to have been serving only as temporary residences for immigrating families. Heavy immigration at mid century pushed the proportion of such households to over 10 percent in 1861 Alfred and Caledonia, but this increased proportion was only temporary. By 1871, as both townships grew in stability, the proportion of households with more than one family did not even approach 5 percent (see table 3). These trends emphasize the importance of a young couple's ability to establish a separate household as a condition for marriage among both English Canadians and French Canadians. In this process of family formation, seasonal employment in the lumber industry played an important role and appears to explain the relationship of age to occupational status during the 1851–71 period.

TABLE 3 PERCENTAGE OF HOUSEHOLDS WITH MORE THAN ONE CONJUGAL FAMILY UNIT

	Alfred	
	French Canadian	British Origin
1851	9.5	7.5
1861	16.5	15.0
1871	3.4	.0

	Caledonia	
	French Canadian	British Origin
1851	.0	4.3
1861	10.3	10.4
1871	1.6	2.3

The number of males in Alfred and Caledonia who were not labourers or farmers was never significant during the mid-nineteenth century and, in fact, diminished after 1851. Most non-agricultural occupations involved woodworking; there were carpenters, shingle-makers, sawyers, wood dealers, and lumberers. By 1871, however, labourers and farmers completely dominated the occupational structure of these townships, despite the rapid population growth of the 1850s and 1860s. The lack of occupational diversity in Alfred and Caledonia resulted from the growth of specific centres of economic activity outside these townships. The development of particular villages as service points centralized the residences of carpenters, sawyers, coopers, and other artisans. This centralization engendered a reciprocal decline in artisanal work outside villages and caused a simplification of occupational structures in hinterland areas despite increased settlement. As villages such as L'Orignal and Hawkesbury expanded,[11] Prescott townships in which no real villages developed became increasingly "rural." In this way, the importance of land became even greater among families in Alfred and Caledonia during the course of the mid-nineteenth century. This development emphasized the inter-relationships of family formation, household structure, and occupational experience for both English Canadians and French Canadians.

The proportion of females with occupational titles in Alfred and Caledonia was never significant, but the occupational structures of these townships represent only part of the actual dimensions of labour in the mid-nineteenth century. Contemporary observations and local historical accounts agree that all men, women, and children actively contributed to the well-being of both English-Canadian and French-Canadian families whether or not they were "employed" or perceived themselves to have occupations. Full family participation was characteristic of all phases of settlement in eastern Ontario beginning with the initial stages of land clearing and continuing thereafter. Each family member had specific tasks throughout this process.

Land clearing first involved the cutting of underbrush and small trees, a job accomplished by the adolescents of settling families. Younger children supervised by mothers then piled the small trees, underbrush, and branches into heaps where they remained until sufficient decay facilitated "burning off."[12] As this work progressed, the father and older sons commenced chopping the large trees that were afterwards stripped of their branches and cut into logs. Once a piece of land was available, planting was begun immediately. As in land clearing, each member of a settling family contributed to the growing of agricultural produce. The female head of the household organized the planting of vegetables such as turnips, potatoes, and peas that would supply new families with initial food requirements.[13] The men of the family concentrated on hay and oats, the products most easily grown during the first years of settlement.[14] This work was paralleled by the labour of younger children who began cultivation of other fruits and vegetables including "bluets, fraises, frambroises, et groseilles sauvages." The produce of the children's gardens was then made into "des plats exquis, des confitures et des liqueurs" by the female household head.[15]

During the winter months, land was further cleared and threshing and milling was accomplished usually by the male household head and one or two of the family's male adolescents. During this time, women and children continued the domestic economic activity, often including the production of textile articles for family use. As soon as possible after settlement, women began weaving blankets, rugs, and fabrics for clothing. These materials were produced in response to the needs of their families. Women organized this domestic industry on the basis of full participation by their sons and daughters. Younger children frequently contributed by spinning. The majority of Alfred and Caledonia families produced their own fabric for clothing, generally about twenty-five yards of "home-made cloth and flannel."[16]

This kind of economic contribution was vital to the welfare of families in eastern Ontario in the mid-nineteenth century. Although rarely included in the occupational structures of townships such as Alfred and Caledonia, the participation of women and children was a crucial cog in the domestic wheel of economic survival. By contributing to land clearing, agricultural production, and domestic industry, the "unemployed" were responsible for a large part of the material well-being of frontier families. Without this help, the lives of those persons listed in the census with occupational titles would have dramatically altered.[17]

In this sense, both English-Canadian and French-Canadian families in Alfred and Caledonia conform to the classic analysis of peasant society suggested by the Russian economist, A.V. Chayanov.[18] His analysis posits that each family member in such societies is called upon to actively contribute to the material well-being of the family as a collective unit. Children are accepted as purely "consumers" only in their early years: they are expected to become "producers" and, thereby, contributors to the family economy as soon as they are physically able. In Chayanov's theory, families in peasant societies are economic units composed of individual members collectively working for the material benefit of the units themselves. There are no single breadwinners; rather, there are family economies.

The need for full family participation in the pursuit of material well-being undoubtedly helps explain why school attendance rates in Alfred and Caledonia lagged behind urban centres such as Hamilton in the mid-nineteenth century. The nature of the family in Hamilton appears to have been quite different from the Chayanov-type families in rural eastern Ontario. Perhaps most significantly, families in Hamilton were not primarily economic units. Increasingly during the nineteenth century, the place of work for most residents was distinct from the household. The potential labour-value of children and youths could not always be immediately realized within the family context and the opportunities for youngsters of employment outside household were not equal to the number of possible young workers.[19] As a result, school attendance in Hamilton, as in other urban centres, was much greater than, for example, in Alfred (see figure 3).

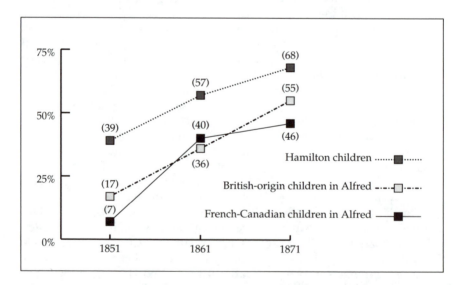

FIGURE 3   *PERCENTAGE OF CHILDREN AGES 5 TO 16 ATTENDING SCHOOL IN ALFRED TOWNSHIP AND HAMILTON, 1851–71*

Source for Hamilton data: Ian Davey, "Educational Reform and the Working Class: School Attendance in Hamilton Ontario, 1851–1891" (Ph.D. diss., University of Toronto, 1975).

The connection between schooling and the life-cycle transition of children from "consumers" to "producers" in rural societies is further suggested by the age structure of the population of school attenders in Alfred township. As shown on figure 4, only a small group of parents sent their children to school beyond the age of twelve. This pattern is similar for both English Canadians and French Canadians, and is apparent in the evidence of 1851, 1861, and 1871, despite the fact that attendance among children increased significantly. Thus, while the mid-nineteenth century promotion of schooling evidently engendered much greater attendance among young children by 1871, the need for collective endeavour within individual family economies in Alfred and Caledonia meant that teenagers remained unavailable for the classroom.

In emphasizing the importance of full family participation in rural contexts of labour-intensive production, Chayanov further suggests that family size plays a major role in determining the level of economic activity that families can achieve.[20] This relationship certainly existed in Alfred and Caledonia. The difficulty and cost of hiring wage labour as well as the non-mechanized nature of production meant that the contribution extended from participation in land clearing, spinning, and gardening to later employment in the shanties, the number of able-bodied members upon which each family could draw determined the scope of their economic activities and the extent to which they could profit from the material possibilities of residence in Alfred and Caledonia at mid century.

The role of family size in regulating economic activity appears to have been recognized positively by both English-Canadian and French-Canadian families. Throughout mid century, married women of both cultural groups gave birth at regular intervals throughout their child-bearing years. This demographic pattern can be shown by dividing the number of unmarried and resident children by the number of families in various age groups of married women. The division produces an average number of children for families at different stages in the life course of mothers (see figure 5). Clearly, families began at an earlier age for French-Canadian women, and their families consistently included a somewhat greater average number of children throughout the mothers' life course. However, the general demographic curves are remarkably similar, particularly for families of women in the twenty to thirty-nine age group. Both English-Canadian and French-Canadian families appear to have been enlarged with regularity: the average established family within either cultural sector could have drawn upon the labour of several younger teenagers. French-Canadian families usually had an advantage of one child but, especially in families with mothers younger than age forty, this was simply the result of earlier family formation.

The way in which the timing of family formation relates to the variation in family size between English Canadians and French Canadians is illustrated by the relationship of age to marital status during the mid-nineteenth century (see figure 6). In general terms, French Canadians married earlier than English Canadians. Among males, most French Canadians were married by their late twenties, while English Canadians did not reach the same proportion until their early thirties. The cultural discrepancy is similar for females, although brides appear to have married two or three years younger than their husbands. It is this cultural difference that undoubtedly explains why French-Canadian families were slightly larger than English-Canadian families with mothers in the same age cohort. Once marriages were formed, however, the families of both cultural groups grew steadily.

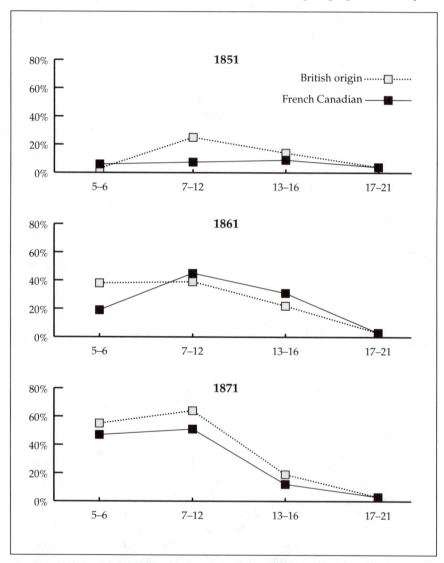

FIGURE   4   *AGE STRUCTURE OF SCHOOL ATTENDANCE IN ALFRED TOWNSHIP, 1851–71*

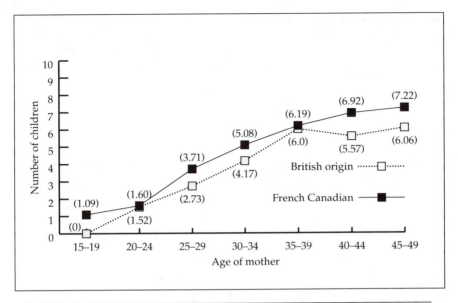

FIGURE 5 *FAMILY SIZE BY AGE OF MOTHERS IN ALFRED AND CALEDONIA TOWNSHIPS, 1851–71*

The dimensions of family size in Alfred and Caledonia may have been at least in part the result of an energetic response among both English and French Canadians to economic possibilities during the mid-nineteenth century. In Chayanov's terms, families that were able to draw upon the productive contribution of several offspring were at a distinct advantage. As earlier suggested, this was particularly apparent in the processes of land clearing and improvement. For most families in Alfred and Caledonia during the 1851–71 period, these were sizeable undertakings. Among farming families, the vast majority of English-Canadian and French-Canadian families owned land of more than fifty acres. The population of agricultural families in Caledonia with lots of less than fifty acres never exceeded 10 percent. In Alfred, a slightly larger proportion of French-Canadian families owned land of between twenty and forty-nine acres, but a substantial majority held parcels of fifty or more acres (see table 4).

Improvement of the sizeable lots was undertaken enthusiastically by families of both cultural groups; there seems to have been no satisfaction with subsistence. In this sense, the communities of Alfred and Caledonia deviated sharply from the Chayanov model of peasant society. In this model, family economies do not actively pursue more than subsistence. However, in Prescott County both English Canadians and French Canadians continued to respond to economic opportunity; they did not curtail activity once basic needs were met. In terms of material ambition, the Chayanov peasant concept does not apply. By pooling the contributions of individual members, families characteristically laboured not only to provide for themselves, but also to produce surplus crops. It was in this way that families in Alfred and Caledonia took advantage of the lumber shanty markets that throughout the mid-nineteenth century relied significantly on the lower Ottawa Valley.

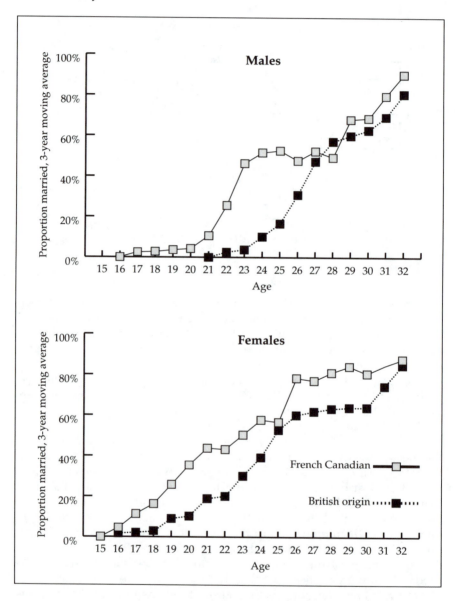

FIGURE 6 *AGE BY MARITAL STATUS, ALFRED AND CALEDONIA*

TABLE 4   LOT SIZES HELD BY FARMERS WHO
OWNED THEIR OWN LAND IN
ALFRED AND CALEDONIA, 1861–71

	French Canadian			British Origin		
	0–19 acres	20–49 acres	50 and over	0–19 acres	20–49 acres	50 and over
Caledonia 1861	1	0	10	0	3	103
Caledonia 1871	0	3	41	0	10	109
Alfred 1861	1	15	75	0	1	39
Alfred 1871	0	20	132	2	3	58

The precise proportion of Alfred and Caledonia agricultural produce not required for local family consumption is impossible to estimate in the absence of studies on the annual needs of nineteenth-century families. However, families in these townships certainly appear to have been striving to produce beyond the subsistence level. By 1871, both English-Canadian and French-Canadian farming families held proportions of cleared land that exceeded their own requirements. In Alfred and Caledonia, the earlier settlement of British-origin immigrants is clearly illustrated by the proportion of farms that included more than twenty acres of cleared land in 1861 as well as in 1871. Throughout this period, the vast majority of English-Canadian farmers held land that appears to have been used for commercial purposes. This pattern is slightly different for French Canadians in 1861, many of whom had not yet had sufficient time to establish commercial farms. In Caledonia, only one French Canadian held a sizeable portion of improved land while in Alfred less than half the *habitant* farmers cultivated twenty or more acres. By 1871, however, French-Canadian farm units in these townships had moved significantly into larger scale production. A full 43 percent of Quebec-origin farming families in Caledonia had achieved parcels of at least twenty or more improved acres while almost two-thirds of their Alfred counterparts now cultivated similarly large parcels of land (see table 5). All these families were capable of producing surplus crops.[21]

TABLE 5   PERCENTAGE OF ACRES IMPROVED ON
THE LOTS OF FARMERS WHO OWNED
THEIR OWN LAND IN ALFRED AND
CALEDONIA

	French Canadian				British origin			
	N	0–19 acres Improved	20–49	50 and over	N	0–19 acres Improved	20–49	50 and over
Caledonia 1861	11	90.9	9.1	.0	106	19.8	49.1	31.1
Caledonia 1871	44	56.8	34.1	9.1	119	16.0	41.2	42.8
Alfred 1861	91	52.7	45.1	2.2	40	10.0	65.0	25.0
Alfred 1871	152	34.9	52.0	13.1	63	25.4	60.3	14.3

The similarly positive response of English-Canadian and French-Canadian families to economic opportunity in eastern Ontario during the mid-nineteenth century further supports the suggestion that, at least in certain basic ways, the cultural dimension of social evolution during this period is not yet properly understood. The apparently similar economic ambition of families in Alfred and Caledonia is consistent with the earlier analysis of family and household structure, occupation and family formation, and the literary descriptions of family economies. While variations and distinctions are evident in the specific cultural patterns, general similarity is the more important characteristic.

Nonetheless, one crucial issue must still be addressed. If economic opportunity was offered to families in Alfred and Caledonia during the mid-1800s, why did the number of English-Canadian households not increase during the 1851–71 period? What inspired surplus English-Canadian adolescents to seek economic opportunity outside their native area? Does this emigration support the traditional notion that English Canadians, in contrast to French Canadians, actively sought to participate in the supposedly progressive urban and industrial development represented by cities such as Hamilton? Did the emigrants shun the prospect of continued existence in the labour-intensive economy of eastern Ontario and, therefore, seek more "modern" livelihoods?

The answer to these questions appears to be no. Rather, a more subtle and complex phenomenon obtained; it is in this context that a significant cultural dimension divided English and French Canadians. Specifically, differences in the interpretation of land value and soil fertility appear to have been crucial in attracting or repelling aspiring heads of household in townships such as Alfred and Caledonia. The observations of contemporary writers and the actual location of individual settlements show that English-Canadian and French-Canadian families differed dramatically in their opinion of favourable land conditions. Consequently, the availability of certain soil types significantly affected the cultural pattern of settlement in these townships.[22]

The importance of soil type is illustrated clearly by the ways in which specific kinds of land in the Ottawa Valley were viewed and settled by English Canadians and French Canadians. Most geographers consider the eastern counties to have been under glacial coverage well after the land of central and western Ontario had surfaced. As a result, soil development in this region is "several thousand years" behind the rest of the province.[23] In Prescott County, for example, sand and gravelly soils compose over half of the county's land. Most of this less fertile soil is associated with the higher plains of the county. In lower regions, the land is largely clay loams, a soil type with great productive potential. However, these loams are "water-laid, have level topography, and are stone free," consequently having very poor natural drainage.[24] This land must be drained artificially before its potential productivity can be realized. Geographers, therefore, emphasize that most Prescott soil requires preparation before cultivation can begin; moist clay soils must be drained while the higher, drier, sandy land must be improved by fertilization.[25]

The cultural pattern of English-Canadian and French-Canadian settlement in Prescott was closely related to this topography and soil composition. British-origin settlers consistently displayed a distinct preference for dry sandy plains while French Canadians readily took up wet clay lands. In 1881, The *Dominion Atlas* observed that "vast tracts of low lying land" had been "shunned by settlers of the Anglo-Saxon race." Rather, these settlers had chosen the land of regions that reached an "altitude of some dignity."[26] It was in these regions that early English-speaking settlers had established communities. For example, Simeon Vankleek, a United empire Loyalist from New York, was travelling in "the Laurentian hills north of the Ottawa when he noticed high land on the south side of the river." He crossed the Ottawa and became the first settler in Prescott's township of West Hawkesbury.[27]

Vankleek's decision to settle on "high land" may have been influenced by the many English-Canadian settlers's guides which warned pioneers to avoid swampy land. These guides emphasized the importance of limiting the initial time and effort needed for cultivation and consequently discouraged settlers from acquiring land that needed drainage. English-Canadian advisors felt that the frequent need to fertilize sandy soil, though not desirable, was far less time-consuming and less laborious than the digging of trenches on marshy fields.[28]

Contrastingly, French Canadian leaders urged *habitants* to take up tracts of wet land. In encouraging settlement in the Ottawa Valley, French-Canadian writers described the land being ignored by the British-origin settlers as a "magnifique région."[29] While the *Dominion Atlas* reported that "very extensive areas in Prescott and Russell approach so nearly the definition of the term 'swampy' as to render them almost unfit for cultivation."[30] French Canadians were describing the "grande fertilité" of the same counties.[31] Even later in the nineteenth century, one Quebec leader estimated that "la région des belles terres est très considérable" in the Ottawa Valley.[32]

The perceptions of French-Canadian leaders concerning the value of moist lands in the eastern counties were apparently shared by Quebec immigrants who came to settle in the mid-nineteenth century. The geographer, Donald Cartwright, has systematically examined the land records of Prescott and Russell counties and concluded that the characteristic French-Canadian colonist exhibited a "preference . . . to settle on the wetter clay soils. . . . " Cartwright also found that British settlers showed a "preference for the high and drier lands associated with the sand and till plains."[33] This distinction is clearly illustrated by the settlement patterns of Alfred and Caledonia townships. The 1851 enumerators of these townships emphasized the predominance of low-lying clay soil. Albert H. James, the Alfred enumerator, noted that:

> part of the township bordering on Longueil is of a clay soil and the west part of the township is for the most part sandy and the southern part of the township across which runs Horse Creek which empties itself into the South Petite Nation River is low and swampy, a portion of that section from the Part of the Great

Tamrock Marsh which pervades this township. . . . Alfred is generally considered to be a township of the most inferior in regard to
the quality of soil but parts of it is good land and produces pretty
good crops.[34]

The enumerator suggested that the "parts of good land," defined as the
sandy areas, had already been fully taken up by British-origin settlers and
that no more English-Canadian arrivals should be expected. He predicted
that whenever Alfred "becomes settled to any further extent or importance,
it will be settled by the French Canadians of Lower Canada mainly—or
rather it is most like such to be the case."

Philip Downing, the 1851 enumerator for Caledonia township, also recognized the relationship of soil type to patterns of settlement. He similarly
estimated the Caledonia land to be of very inferior quality. He described
Caledonia as having "generally swampy and cold soil—it embraces on the
North for several concessions, the great Caledonia marsh which pervades 3
or 4 townships and is of no value."[35] However, Downing noted that a "tract
in this township called the Caledonia Flats through which runs Caledonia
Creek is well settled and the soil is of superior quality." It was here that
English Canadians had established significant settlements. They were
attracted to the "soil of this lay of land which is a sandy loam. "As in
Alfred, the full settlement of this kind of land in Caledonia by mid-century
meant that the future of the township was not promising in the mind of the
enumerator. After describing the unsettled land as "of little value,"
Downing concluded that "it appears useless to make any further remarks in
regard to this township."

The 1851 enumerators' predictions that further English-Canadian settlement would not occur in Alfred and Caledonia were fulfilled during the
later decades of the nineteenth century when the number of British-origin
residents remained almost constant, despite the rapid growth of French-
Canadian settlement.[36] The *Dominion Atlas* of 1881 explained that the "peculiarities of soil and surface" characteristic of Alfred township had "militated
against the rapid development" of this township by English Canadians.
Instead, these "peculiarities" had militated for the heavy immigration of
French Canadians. The *Atlas* writers analysed this phenomenon in terms of
the importance of cultural tradition. They explained that French Canadians
had been "long accustomed to life on the flat lands of the Lower Province,"
and were thereby prepared for the "cultivation of the semi-swamps" that
the early British settlers had ignored.[37] French-Canadian heritage also was
said to have provided immigrant *habitants* with appropriate techniques of
land clearing. The *Atlas* writers admitted that French Canadians had
"proven their efficiency" in the "preliminary clearing" of the difficult low-
lying land. In the *Atlas'* analysis, this kind of "efficiency" resulted from
French Canada's specific agricultural tradition that had evolved in the fertile but very moist St. Lawrence Valley. The *Atlas* compilers thereby
explained the willingness of Quebec immigrants to settle in Alfred on the

basis of the appropriateness of this agricultural tradition to the available land in the township.[38]

The extent to which the *Dominion Atlas'* analysis is accurate has yet to be fully investigated, but the general approach does indeed appear promising. Viewed in this way, analysis of settlement patterns rises well above the level of physical determinism. Each family's decision to settle can be examined in the context of a judgment of advantage based on marital and fertility expectations, commitment to a family economy, and familiarity with specific agricultural skills. It was the appropriate combination of these elements that made settlement in Alfred and Caledonia attractive to some and unattractive to others. In turn, the culturally induced soil preferences of settlers related to agricultural tradition, family ideology, and demographic patterns. These preferences undoubtedly explain, at least in part, why the number of English-Canadian families remained relatively constant in Alfred and Caledonia during 1851–71 period. An inheriting offspring remained to take over each English-Canadian farm, but other siblings, faced with the prospect of only low-lying land, decided to seek their fortune elsewhere. This phenomenon also appears to explain the variation in age-at-marriage and therefore family size between English Canadians and French Canadians. As has been shown, marriage in Alfred and Caledonia was dependent upon the ability of aspiring couples to form separate households and, in rural eastern Ontario, land acquisition was the basic necessity. However, the shortage of land attractive to English Canadians as early as mid century meant that aspiring couples who wished to stay in their native townships would have to wait for an inheritance or a vacancy in some other established household. As a result, wedlock was often delayed, much as it was among couples in traditional European peasant society.

In this sense, there was a very significant cultural dimension to the history of the family in Alfred and Caledonia. Tradition and heritage were indeed important in differentiating population patterns in these townships. It is extremely important to note, however, that the basis of this differentiation is not as straightforward as traditionally depicted. Not only were many aspects of English-Canadian and French-Canadian families substantially similar but, in addition, the complexity of the issue of land evaluation suggests that demographic differences may be much more subtle than has yet been appreciated.

At this point, the implications of the experience of Alfred and Caledonia for the larger analysis of the family in Canadian history are no more than suggestive. The nature of the evidence thus far examined and the size of the sample offered by these townships limit the conclusions that can be drawn. Moreover, the experiences of Alfred and Caledonia were the result of a particular convergence of historical forces and the representativeness of the preceding comparative analysis cannot be estimated in even general terms. Nonetheless, it is clear that systematic examination of the families in Alfred and Caledonia has produced findings which do not conform to hitherto accepted images. Empirical comparisons do not support established stereotypes of cultural behaviour and ideologically laden judgments of social patterns. The suggested avenue of research is one that questions the conventional underpinnings of much Canadian historiography, that discards assumptions about distinct and timeless culturally defined *mentalités,* and that subjects qualitative observations and aggregate patterns to the scrutiny of empirical evidence at the level of individual families. The similarities and differences of English-Canadian and French-Canadian families in terms of structure, function, and economy suggest the need for a fresh interpretation of this important dimension of the historical process.

NOTES

1. Michael Katz, *The People of Hamilton, Canada West: Family and Class in a Mid-Nineteenth Century City* (Cambridge, MA, 1975); David Gagan and Herbert Mays, "Historical Demography and Canadian Social History: Families and Land in Peel County, Ontario," *Canadian Historical Review* (1973); and David Gagan's other articles emerging from the Peel County History Project.

2. Alison Prentice, "Education and the Metaphor of the Family: The Upper Canadian Example," *History of Education Quarterly* (May 1972); and Susan Houston, "The Victorian Origins of Juvenile Delinquency," *History of Education Quarterly* (1973).

3. Neil Sutherland, *Children in English-Canadian Society: Framing the Twentieth-Century Consensus* (Toronto, 1976).

4. Hubert Charbonneau, *Vie et mort de nos ancêtres: étude démographique* (Montreal, 1975); and Hubert Charbonneau, ed., *La population du Québec: études rétrospectives* (Quebec, 1973).

5. Louise Dechêne, *Habitants et marchands de Montréal au XVIIe siècle* (Paris, 1974).

6. Tamara Hareven and Randolph Langenbach, *Amoskeag: Life and Work in an American Factory City* (New York, 1978); and Gérard Bouchard, "Family Structures and Geographic Mobility at Laterrière, 1751–1835," *Journal of Family History* (Winter 1977).

7. These and the following examples of this section are drawn from two very helpful local histories of Prescott County: C. Thomas, *History of the Counties of Argenteuil, Quebec and Prescott Ontario form the earliest settlement to the present* (Montreal, 1896), 621–38; and Lucien Brault, *Histoire des comtés unis de Prescott et de Russell* (L'Orignal, ON, 1965), 189–207.

8. Thomas, *History,* 631–33. The circumstances which motivated French-Canadian emigration from nineteenth-century Quebec developed from the interaction of severe economic difficulties and population pressure. See W.H. Parker, "A New Look at Unrest in Lower Canada in the 1830s," *Canadian Historical Review* 40 (1959). Also see Robert Leslie Jones, "French-Canadian Agriculture in the St. Lawrence Valley, 1815–1850," *Agricultural History* (1942); and Fernand Ouellet, *Histoire économique et sociale du Québec 1760–1850* (Montreal/Paris, 1966).

9. For a discussion of the enumerators' instruction in 1851 and 1861, see David Gagan, "Enumerator's Instructions for the Census of Canada, 1852 and 1861," *Histoire Sociale/Social History* (Nov. 1974).

10. Record-linkage for the manuscript enumerations of 1851, 1861, and

1871 has not yet been accomplished, so this possibility must remain speculative. However, the records of local histories do lend supporting evidence. For Alfred and Caledonia townships, see Thomas, *History*, 621–38; and Brault, *Histoire*, 189–207.

11. By 1881, the villages of L'Orignal and Hawkesbury were enumerated separately from the townships in which they were located. At that time, L'Orignal included 853 residents while the established centre of Hawkesbury had a population of 1920. See *The Report on the Fourth Census of Canada*, 1881.

12. The process of settlement in the Ottawa Valley is described in various contemporary and historical works; see J.L. Gourlay's well-known *History of the Ottawa Valley* (Montreal, 1896); E.C. Guillet's *The Pioneer Farmer and Backwoodsman* (Toronto, 1963); Joshua Fraser's *Shanty, Forest, and River Life* (Montreal, 1883); and A.R.M. Lower, *Settlement and the Forest Frontier in Eastern Canada* (Toronto, 1936). The memoirs of a mid-nineteenth century resident indicate that immigrant families in Prescott and Russell Counties also depended on the help of previously established settlers. Mrs. Ennid Christie wrote in 1860 that settlement had a collective dimension: "the neighbours would all help one another. . . . As a rule, as each house was done they would have a little party"; see Public Archives of Ontario, "A Narrative Account of Farm Life Along the South Nation River. . . ," (manuscript), 1860, p. 2.

13. William Greening, *The Ottawa* (Toronto, 1961), 69.

14. Robert Leslie Jones, *History of Agriculture in Ontario, 1613–1830* (Toronto, 1946), 114.

15. Alexis de Barbezieux, *Histoire de la province ecclésiastique d'Ottawa* (Ottawa, 1897), 1: 287.

16. Manuscript Census, 1871; also see Greening, *The Ottawa*, 70.

17. The importance to the family economy of the labour of "housewives" has been the focus of several recent studies. For example, see the debate that emerged among contributors to the *New Left Review*: Wally Secombe, "The Housewife and Her Labour under Capitalism," no. 83; and Margaret Coulson, Branka Magas, and Hilary Wainwright, "The Housewife and Her Labour under Capitalism: A Critique," no. 89. Also see Vanier Institute of The Family, *The Family in the Evolution of Agriculture* (Ottawa, 1986).

18. A.V. Chayanov, "On the Theory of Non-Capitalist Economic Systems," trans. Christel Lane, and *Peasant Farm Organization*, trans. R.E.F. Smith in *A.V. Chayanov on the Theory of Peasant Economy*, ed. D. Thorner, B. Kerblay, and R.E.F. Smith (Homewood, IL, 1966).

19. Katz, *The People of Hamilton*, passim.

20. Chayanov, *Peasant Farm Organization*, especially ch. 1.

21. Scholars often use the amount of land under crops to indicate the level of agricultural activity. In one study, Cole Harris analyses the experience of Petite-Nation, a seigneury located on the edge of the Canadian Shield north of the Ottawa River across from Alfred township. Harris suggests that farming in this region was primarily a "subsistence activity." To illustrate his argument, Harris offers several examples of what he intends by both subsistence and commercial farming. Harris describes subsistence farming by the example of one farm in which only seven of one hundred acres had been cleared, and another farm in which seven of 120 acres had been improved. In contrast, Harris indicates the presence of commercial farming in the example of one large 1229 acre farm in which 320 acres were cleared, and another smaller farm in which 40 of 90 acres were in use. See "Of Poverty and Helplessness in Petite-Nation," *Canadian Historical Review* (March 1971).

22. In describing the way in which agricultural settlement occurred in nineteenth-century Ontario, Kenneth Kelly lists settler evaluation of land as the first step in this process; see "The Impact of Nineteenth Century Agricultural Settlement on the Land" in *Perspectives on Landscape and Settlement in Nineteenth-Century Ontario*, ed. J. David Wood (Toronto, 1975). For a general discussion of the importance of custom and tradition to the assessment of ecological characteristics, see A. Spoehr, "Cultural Differences in the Interpretation of Natural Resources" in *Man's Role in Changing the Face of the Earth*, ed. W.L. Thomas (Chicago, 1956).

23. See L.S. Chapman and J.G. Putnam's "The Soils of Eastern Ontario," *Scientific Agriculture* (March 1940). The geographical context of eastern Ontario is examined in J.R. Mackay, "The Regional Geography of the Lower Ottawa Valley" (Ph.D. diss., University of Montreal, 1949).

24. Donald G. Cartwright, "French-Canadian Colonization in Eastern Ontario to 1910" (Ph.D. diss., University of Western Ontario, 1973), 201.

25. See Chapman and Putnam, "The Soils of Eastern Ontario."

26. *The Dominion Atlas of the Counties of Prescott and Russell* (1881), 58.

27. Max Rosenthal, "Early Post Offices of Prescott County," B.N.A. *Topics* (Jan. 1967), 21.

28. See Guillet, *Pioneer Farmer* 1: 274; and Kelly, "Impact of Nineteenth Century Agricultural Settlement," English-Canadian writers may also have been concerned about the health implications of settlement in marshy areas. A malaria-type fever named ague was known to be fatal and was associated with regions of wet soil. In 1851, thirty-six people died from ague in Ontario; see the *Census of Canada*, 1851.

29. Joseph Tassé, *La vallée de l'Outaouais: sa condition géographique* . . . (Montreal, 1973), 7.

30. *Dominion Atlas*, 58.

31. Tassé, *La Vallé de l'Outaouais*, 9.

32. See A. Labelle, *Projet d'une Société de Colonisation du diocèse de Montréal pour coloniser la vallé de l'Ottawa et le nord de ce diocèse* (Montréal, 1879).

33. Cartwright, "French-Canadian Colonization," 230–31.

34. Manuscript Census for Alfred Township, 1851.

35. Manuscript Census for Caledonia Township, 1851.

36. By the mid-nineteenth century, the farmland of almost all south-central Ontario had been taken up and, at this time, British-origin immigrants must have been forced to at least consider settlement in the easternmost counties. The land shortage in Ontario was the result of "persistent immigration from the British Isles, high rates of natural increase, and exaggerated man–land ratios": see David Gagan "Geographic and Social Mobility in Nineteenth-Century Ontario: A Microstudy," *Canadian Review of Sociology and Anthropology* 12 (1976), 152–53. This evidence suggests that British-origin immigrants made a conscious decision to settle in easternmost Ontario, despite the fact that land was still available.

37. *Dominion Atlas*, 60. The French-Canadian ability to cultivate lands previously considered useless by English Canadians gives an ironic twist to the traditional claim of British agricultural superiority. For example, Lord Durham had observed that the "English farmer carried with him the experience and habits of the most improved agriculture in the world. . . . He often took the very arm which the [French] Canadian settlers had abandoned,

and, by superior management, made that a source of profit which had only impoverished his predecessor." Durham's observation may have been accurate but, at least in eastern Ontario, the reverse was also true: cited in Jones, "French-Canadian Agriculture in the St. Lawrence Valley," 138. An exceedingly promising systematic analysis of agricultural patterns in Canada East is offered in "The Efficiency of the French-Canadian farmer in the Nineteenth Century" by Frank Lewis and Marvin McInnis, Depart-

ment of Economies, Queen's University, (unpublished paper).

38. Ibid. The strong attraction of land for French Canadians in the mid-nineteenth century suggests that Quebec immigrants to Ontario conform to Cole Harris's analysis of the phenomenon of "land hunger" at that time. He argues that immigrants to Ontario at mid-century "craved land"; see Cole Harris and John Warkentin, *Canada Before Confederation* (New York, 1974), 128.

"SHE WAS SKIPPER OF THE SHORE-CREW": NOTES ON THE HISTORY OF THE SEXUAL DIVISION OF LABOUR IN NEWFOUNDLAND [*]

MARILYN PORTER

o

Our current inadequate knowledge of the generation and maintenance of the sexual division of labour has generally limited the discussion either to broad generalizations or to extrapolation based on highly specific examples.[1] What we do know suggests that there is a tension between the remarkable consistency of the *general* lines of the sexual division of labour and the degree of variation that prevents the establishment of "universal" rules. Within the broad patriarchal relations of dominance and subordination, there is an almost infinite variation in both gender relations and the sexual division of labour. Nor is the pattern fixed in any single society. Sexual divisions are constructed, negotiated, and endlessly challenged. Recent work by anthropologists and sociologists has focussed on ways in which patriarchal relations operate through the institutions of marriage and the family and in relation to capitalist productive relations.[2] Historians have contributed a growing body of detailed studies that show subordination mediated through family patterns, economic studies that show subordination mediated through family patterns, economic and technological organization, religious and political ideology, and many other factors.[3]

Newfoundland rural outports are maritime communities, dominated economically and ideologically by fishing. While fishing is no longer the mainstay of the province's economy,[4] it is the mainstay (together with fishing-related government transfer payments) of the 900-plus outports scattered along the 6000 miles of island coastline and the Labrador coast— that

[*] *Labour/Le Travail* 15 (Spring 1985): 105–23.

is, of the rural population.[5] Despite an offshore fishery and the increasing numbers of longliners and small privately owned trawlers (some 800), which can venture further from their home ports, most outports are still dominated by a traditional inshore fishery carried out in small boats (usually crewed by male agnates) operating close to their home ports. A few exceptional women take an active part in fishing,[6] and many more are involved in the fishery— processing fish in the fish plants or providing supplementary services. But by and large, the traditionally rigid sexual division of labour is unbreached. In addition, physical conditions in the outports are tough, and "male" activities such as hunting and woodcutting still play a large part in the rural economy. In short, the ethos of "fishermen" is a rugged *male* identity, and it is clamped firmly over the image of outport life.

This association of maritime communities with a rigid and extreme sexual division of labour is a commonplace of anthropological literature,[7] yet studying gender relations and the sexual division of labour in Newfoundland rural communities raises certain problems. Rigid and extreme sexual divisions have been traditionally interpreted as giving rise to oppressive male dominance. J. Tunstall gave a classic account of the negative consequences of seafaring domestic relations among the Hull fishermen and similar tendencies have been reported from Aberdeen and San Diego. J. Zulaika, writing about Portuguese fishermen, describes similar manifestations but makes some interesting and sensitive comments on the relationship between the demands of a tough seaman identity and its expression in sexual relations. Male anthropologists working in Newfoundland with this implicit understanding have stressed women's heavy work load, male authority in the family, male-biased inheritance rules, and the practice of exogamy.[8]

Yet it is not quite like that. Recent feminist studies[9] have found outport women to be relatively independent, politically and economically, and to suffer apparently little marital violence or overt male hostility outside the home, and moreover, to be in possession of a vibrant and positive women's culture. In puzzling this apparent contradiction in previous papers, I have focussed on a number of countervailing forces, of which the women's considerable economic leverage deriving from their continued share in the fishery seemed to me the most salient. However, it is also noticeable that all of the studies of male oppression associated with maritime activities have been based on communities where men are at sea for considerable periods of time. This is not true of most Newfoundland fishermen, and is certainly not true of the traditional inshore cod fishery. P. Thompson,[10] working in Scotland, has argued forcibly that the considerable variations in gender and family relations between Scottish communities are associated with different patterns of childrearing practices and economic adaptations. In this research note, I have approached the problem more circuitously: to see if it is possible, by using historical material, to clarify how current gender relations and sexual divisions of labour arose. A number of caveats have to be entered.

There is a considerable quantity of material on the early history of Newfoundland (from the sixteenth to the eighteenth century), but no serious work has been done on women in this period, and we are left with tantalizing glimpses, extrapolation, and plain guesswork about the lives of the early female settlers. All that we can be sure about is that women *did* come from the times of the earliest settlements, both as wives and daughters, and as single women who came as servants. Inevitably all their lives were both hard and hard working, and there are indications that certain traditions and divisions of labour that are current on the island today originated then. But the argument that follows is based on the more certain evidence of demography and patterns of settlement, until we reach the better-documented nineteenth and twentieth centuries.

The island of Newfoundland has always been characterized by considerable variation in climate and geography, which dictates variations in fishing patterns and strategies. There are also variations relating to the relative strengths of different denominations and sects in different areas, and to the origins of the first settlers and subsequent arrivals. All this has consequences for gender relations and the sexual division of labour, but because of the paucity of the material on women we cannot, as yet, make province-wide generalizations. I have, therefore, indicated which area of the island each piece of evidence relates to and how far it can be taken to be generally applicable. Most evidence comes from the northeast coast, and can only be applied with caution to the south coast, the southern shore, or the northern peninsula.

Nevertheless, I would argue that it is only by taking a larger perspective that we may be able to understand the current negotiation of gender relations.

"SO LONG AS THERE COMES NOE WOMEN THEY ARE NOT FIXED": SETTLEMENT, EXPANSION, AND PERMANENCE

Although European fishermen from England, France, the Basque Country, Portugal, and Spain were exploiting the bountiful supplies of cod over the Grand Banks in the summer months by the end of the fifteenth century, if not earlier, there was no attempt at permanent settlement until 1610 when the London and Bristol Company of the Colonization of Newfoundland established a settlement of forty men at Cupids, Conception Bay. Manifestly women were needed to establish a settlement and in August 1611, sixteen women arrived, and by March 1613 the first recorded child was born.[11] Apart from that we know little of who they were, why they came, or what their lives were like—save that in prevailing conditions there was no room for slackers of either sex. The story is repeated for the Welsh settlements at Renews (1618), the Bristol settlement at Harbour Grace (1618), and Calvert's more successful venture at Ferryland (1620). Throughout it is arguable that tough and hard working though the women were, it was less relevant to the development of their economic independence and mutual respect than their role in settlement as such.

A signal feature of settlement in Newfoundland up to the end of the eighteenth century was the demographic sexual imbalance and the effect the absence of women had on the speed and success of settlement. There was a huge preponderance of men on the island, especially in summer when the seasonal migrants (wholly men) far outnumbered the winter residents. Small groups of men (and a very few families) wintered over for one or two seasons. Even among the permanent residents the number of male apprentices and servants far outnumbered the imported women. Significant as they were, the servant girls were in no way sufficient to produce a balanced population. It produced problems of order in St. John's[12] and prevented further settlement on the frontiers. As a naval captain put it succinctly in 1684, "soe long as there comes noe woman they are not fixed." This situation was a double-edged sword to the authorities. Those on the ground complained bitterly about disorder "for the permanent growth of a colonial population every single man who is sent out in excess of the number of single women is absolutely useless."[13] On the other hand, the English government did not want growth of the colony and was reluctant to admit that it had grown as much as it had, in which case the answer was simple— restrict the number of women immigrants. While there seems to be no evidence that this measure was ever tried, it does seem to have been on the agenda for some time.[14]

In any event, the pattern of a large summer (male) immigration and a much smaller resident population continued through the eighteenth century, and so did the friction between them. In 1675, 1200 people wintered on the island; by 1730 it was 3500; by 1750 it was 7300, and by 1753 it has risen tenfold to 12 000. The proportion of women at the beginning of the century was only 10 percent (instead of a "normal" 25 percent) and children only accounted for 25 percent (instead of 50 percent). By the end of the century these proportions had risen to 13 percent and 33 percent respectively and they climbed to normal proportions a few years later. As G. Head puts it, "the wintering population was approaching normal characteristics and no longer contained an overwhelming mass of single male labourers. With women and children the attachment to the island was firmer."

The necessity of women to settlement was clear, but the growth in the number of women had another important consequence. The "planters" (established fishermen with their own boats) ceased to import large numbers of "youngsters" (servants from Europe) and relied instead on their families. It is likely, given the tradition of active female involvement, that wives had always helped out on shore at peak times, but evidence suggests that the heyday of family production began in the late eighteenth century.[15]

I will examine the Newfoundland family fishery in more detail below, but first I want to complete the record of women's more basic contribution to the colony—as sexual partners and founders of families. Bonavista Bay and Trinity Bay had had scattered settlements in the eighteenth century (of 450–900 and 1500 respectively in 1772) and a few pioneers had already moved north to Notre Dame Bay and Fogo. On the south coast, settlement was centred on St. Jacques, Fortune, and Grand Bank at the east end, and on Port aux Basques in the west, and these gradually extended to meet at Burgeo and Ramea, although the total resident population of the south coast continued to be small (about 600 in 1763).

By the beginning of the nineteenth century, new settlements were established not by new immigration from England but by families moving to a "summer station" on a less frequented stretch of the coast—as far as the northern peninsula, and later Labrador.[16] If the family was happy, they might well settle there. Those families then had children and the ensuing marriageable girls attracted further settlement. In one example, on the extreme northwest tip of the island, a tiny group of Englishmen in a merchant's employment survived until the Watts family arrived, with two sons and two daughters. One daughter married William Buckle in the late 1890s and they founded the Buckle family that spreads across Labrador to this day. The other daughter, Mary, married a naval deserter, Alexander Duncan, who changed his name to his mother's maiden name of Gould. They had three sons (from whom are descended the numerous and powerful Goulds of the Flowers Cove/Port au Choix area) and nine daughters "who grew into beautiful girls" providing a sudden bonus supply of eligible wives for the young English settlers. These couples spread along the coast from Eddie's Cove to St. Margaret's Bay, populating all the coves.[17]

The demographic contribution of women to settlement has been recognized both by contemporary authorities and spelt out in recent studies,[18] although the feminist implications have not been. But the economic contribution of "the skipper of the shore crew" has been more slowly recognized. It is to her that we now turn.

WOMEN'S WORK IN THE FISHING SETTLEMENTS

The best documented area is the northeast coast and much of the discussion that follows is taken from there. The situation, for example, on the south coast where the trap fishery never developed, was significantly different. Moreover, the evidence is too sparse for any legitimate conclusions to be drawn as to whether the consequences of women's different roles in the fishing economy were as great as might be expected. At this point, all I am attempting is a description of the sexual division of labour as it developed, especially on the northeast coast, together with certain congruences with women's position as observed today.

A further caveat needs to be entered when collapsing such a long period as that between the beginning of the nineteenth century and Confederation (1949). Clearly there were profound technical changes (such as the introduction of the cod trap, and of engines), social changes (such as the more widespread education), and political changes (such as the rise and fall of the Fishermen's Protective Union in the early twentieth century).[19] Nevertheless it seems that the essential pattern of sexual division of labour did remain relatively constant, and in this discussion I shall stress that continuity. It is in this context that I am using material such as Greta Hussey's

autobiography to illustrate patterns that existed long before. It should, however, be reiterated that the context in which they occurred was changing.

The outport communities were always (up to the influx of federal money
in 1949)[20] on the brink of survival. A bad year could push whole settlements
into starvation or emigration. I stress this because it was women who, as
always, had the prime responsibility for feeding, cleaning, and caring for
themselves, the men, and the children. It would have been hard in those wild
conditions even in prosperity: in poverty it was an enormous task.

A complication that affected many families was a pattern of transhu-
mance. Families who lived out on the exposed headlands would often
"winter in" the head of the bay where there was more shelter and more
wood. They lived in "tilts"—crude shacks which nonetheless, women had
to make habitable. Conversely, many families lived "at home" in the winter
but moved in the summer to "summer stations" or "outside" to fish. These
places were often hundreds of miles away "on the Labrador." Greta Hussey
describes her mother packing everything the family might need in "the
Labrador box" for four or more months. They took "pots, pans, dishes,
cooking gear and most of the rough grub that we lived on, such as salt beef,
dried peas, dried beans, hard bread, sugar, butter and salt pork."[21]

The range of domestic activities Newfoundland women undertook as a
matter of course accords closely with descriptions given of the lives of rural
women in the nineteenth and early twentieth centuries in other parts of
America and Europe.[22] Feeding the family included most of the care of the
animals—a few cows, sheep, goats, horses, and later chickens, who needed
hay and roots to help them survive the winter. The garden was a major
responsibility. Men usually did the actual digging, but women cleared or
"picked" the ground of stones, planted and weeded it, and defended it
against animals. Then they gathered the vegetables and dried them or preserved them (sometimes in salt) in a root cellar, as they are recorded as
doing in Edward Winne's letter from Ferryland in 1622. [23] They practised
rotation of crops and despised shop-bought seed because "the flies would
eat it." Besides, a woman was considered lazy "if she did not grow her own
seeds."[24]

If the family kept cows or goats, then the wife made butter. A major
food gathering activity was berry picking, and while men sometimes did
this, it was primarily the task of the women and children. Most of them rel-
ished the opportunity to get out on the barrens and the marshes. Blueberries,
partridge berries, the succulent bake apples, marsh berries, currants and
cranberries, raspberries and blackberries were all gathered on different
parts of the island. Many of them were sold, and a family might well provide itself with its winter supplies of flour, margarine, sugar, molasses,
beef, and port with its "berrynote."[25] In passing we should note that this is,
in effect, a cash contribution to the family income. The rest were bottled or
"jammed down." And so we enter the kitchen. The Newfoundland housewife was honour-bound to set a meal before any member of the family (or
visitor) the moment they entered the house. Like many of the practices
noted here, it survives today. Everyone had at least four meals a day, and in

summer it often rose to seven or eight—a man's light snack in the early morning, breakfast about 7:30–8:00, a mug-up at 10:30–11:00, dinner at 12:00–1:00 PM, mug-up at 3:30–4:00, tea at 5:30–6:00 PM, and a mug-up before bedtime at 10:30–11:00 PM. "Mug-ups" consisted of tea, bread, and butter, and "relish"—left over fish or home-made jam, and the last meal of the day, "the night-lunch," was often quite substantial. Main meals, not surprisingly, revolved around fish and potatoes, but salt pork, salt beef, figgy duff and pease pudding, thick soups, and dumplings were common. Game-meat or birds were a coveted extra. A glance at any traditional Newfoundland cookbook will show that housewives stressed quantity and weight above all else, but they were ingenious in ringing the changes on limited ingredients.

Breadmaking was both a major chore and a women's pride: "the knowledge of breadmaking was one skill all marriageable girls were expected to possess" and little girls would stand on chairs to make the "barm" or dough. Most housewives baked at least once a day; large families needed two bakings.[26] Before commercial yeast was introduced in the 1920s, women grew their own hops. Greta Hussey made her own yeast from hops and raw potato because she was dissatisfied with the bread made from shop-bought yeast. In times of dire poverty they would mix potatoes with the flour to eke it out.

Men's suits always seem to have been bought when possible, but most other clothes were homemade. It was another task made more obviously complicated by poverty. Coats had to be "turned," flour sacks had to be transformed into pillow cases, aprons, and tablecloths, and in the poorer families, into dresses and shirts brightened by embroidery. "The coloured thread was inexpensive and with a bit of skill and a few hours work, plain flour sacking was made very attractive."[27] Quilting was less developed than it was in the United States, but hooking mats developed into a folk art.[28] This developed because the women covered bare floors with mats of brin "hooked" with pictures or designs using any brightly coloured rags they could find, thus saving the last scraps of an old garment. The results fetch high prices today and are an enduring testimony to the skill and resourcefulness of Newfoundland housewives.

Some women made sails or "twine" for the nets but such work is usually conspicuous by its absence in women's tasks—a sign and a symbol of the separation of worlds that began exactly at the shoreline, or landwash. Some women could card and spin wool straight from the sheep; but all women could knit and the list of garments that had to be turned out is staggering. Murray cites "knitted petticoats, long stockings, vamps (ankle length socks), corsocks (balaclavas), mittens, cuffs, gloves, vests, long johns and sweaters." In addition, there was the mending, a much less attractive task and one heartily hated by the young cooks who went on the Labrador fishery.[29]

Washing started with carrying water and splitting wood—both women's tasks. Before the 1930s, they made their own soap from rotten cod livers and wood ash. They took care to "blue" and bleach their whites—and even after scrubbing boards were introduced, some women would not use them because they were "hard on the clothes." The production of a faultless line of washing was another indication of woman's pride. Even today there is a correct order in which to hang clothes on the line that newcomers flout at their peril. Health was another female concern, and most women knew some folk remedies, but the real skill resided with the midwives. Two or three women in each community won the confidence of the women with their skill and patience, at a time when doctors were frequently unavailable. Their work needs a separate account.[30]

Houses gradually became more complex (and larger) but some features endured (and still endure today). They were made of wood by the men of the family. A man's pride rested on his ability to build his own boat and house as surely as the woman's did in her "domestic" skills. The central room was the kitchen in which virtually all family activity took place, and in which the many visitors were received. Houses were kept spotless. They were repainted or repapered inside at least once a year and the kitchen was done spring and fall including repainting the floor linoleum. G. Hussey records repapering their Labrador house with newspaper or religious tracts each year when they arrived. Floors and steps were scrubbed daily. Mats and bedding were aired. One of the heaviest and least popular jobs was washing the heavy winter bed covers when summer eventually released them. Lamps were trimmed and polished, stoves polished. There is an endless list of such recurring tasks.

The enormous extent and weight of the work, as well as the variety of the skills and the standards of excellence the women maintained are impressive, but they are not unique. What marks out the Newfoundland women was that into this crowded schedule came the fishing. The timing and length of the fishing season varied around the coast as did the species pursued and the methods used. The south coast, for instance, could pursue a winter fishery free of ice. Its proximity to the Grand Banks also made it a natural headquarters for the banking schooners.[31] On the northeast coast, the seal hunt was an important part of the economy. Herring were important on the south and west coasts. Shellfish were increasingly caught, and lobster-canning factories were established on the northern peninsula in the nineteenth century.

But these were all supplementary to the inshore pursuit of "King Cod." In most parts of the island, cod came inshore in pursuit of caplin in early summer and remained until fall. The traditional English approach had always focussed on this catch, taken from small boats first with hook and line, and later in cod traps.[32] Boats were under pressure to catch as much as possible in the short season—up to five boatloads a day. The crews did not have time to deal with the much more complex and time-consuming operation of drying the fish onshore. While the shore operation never became "women's work" the way baking was, it did become an area in which women developed skills and expertise. Above all, in the context of the full-fledged trap fishery it involved considerable authority as the "skipper," that is, the fisherman's wife, had charge of the whole process, including the hiring and supervision of labour.

Essentially, the fish, each one of which could weigh up to ten pounds or more, were processed along an assembly line. Each load was pitchforked up onto the stage. There the "cut throat" began the operation, the "header" removed the head and guts, and "splitter" (the most skillful operator) removed the backbone. The fish were then washed and the "salter" put them in layers into barrels of salt. After a few weeks, the fish were "made." First they were washed and then carried out to the flakes where they were dried and stacked. It was an operation calling for timing and experience to spread the fish out at the correct time and then build stacks of the right size so that the fish stayed in perfect condition throughout the process:[33]

> It was first taken up with a small fish placed over a large one, both back up. Care had to be taken with the big "pickle" fish when taking them up for the first time, especially if it were a Saturday. Sunday might be hot and the big ones might sunburn if left unshielded. Next evening we put four fish together, head and tails. Then small "faggots," then larger "faggots" [that is rectangular piles nicely rounded on the top]. When the fish dried hard they were put in a big round pile.[34]

While this process was carried out by all fishing families, the degree of division of labour and the timing varied according to whether the crew was a hand-lining crew or a trap crew. It was immensely hard work. Wilson reports one woman saying, "If I had but two hours sleep in 24, I could stand the week's labor; but to do without rest for nearly a week is too much for my strength."[35] This was in addition to their usual work, which at this time of year included the preparation and clearing of seven meals a day for the equally exhausted fishermen. Luckily this intensity only lasted for two to three months with a gradual tailing off in the fall.

ECONOMY AND AUTHORITY: "THE WOMAN WAS MORE THAN 50 PER CENT"

Not suprisingly, male writers have largely failed to recognize the strategic importance of women's economic contribution to the fishery until Ellen Antler made a serious effort to estimate the cash value of the women's contribution to the fishery. She argued that the drying of the fishing added $2400 to the value of the season's catch in Labrador, $1500–$2000 in Conception Bay. Other writers have tried to put monetary or proportional values on the total amount that women's work contributed to the family income. Alexander reckoned it was at least half.[36] But to most outside authorities, this was an invisible reality. The economic unit was the family, and the head of that unit was the fisherman. Combined with ideological pre-eminence of the fisherman as a catcher of fish, it has helped to obscure not only the real contribution of women but also our understanding of the sexual division of labour in the outports.

Josiah Hobbs, who gave the title to Hilda Murray's book, was not alone in his estimation that "the woman was more than 50 per cent . . . I should say, a woman, in a fisherman's work, was half the procedure." Whenever they are asked, Newfoundland men unhesitatingly credit women with at least half the work of the family. There is an air of something like awe in the folklore descriptions older men give of the women of their youth.

The handling of what little cash actually passed in outport families reflects this trust. Women handled the "berry money," as we have seen. They also bartered the occasional dry fish for something they needed at the store. The end of the season reckoning when the fish were "shipped," that is sold to the local fish merchant, was in the hands of the man, but when he had "settled up" he gave this money to his wife.[37] Money earned "away" was passed to the wife and all household transactions were handled by her. Contemporary evidence bears this out. D. Davis working on the south coast records women handling all the domestic finances, referring major decisions to their husbands as a formality to rubber stamp their approval. Furthermore, they consider wages that they earn "theirs to spend as they see fit."[38]

All this suggests that women have earned, and been granted, a place in the economic unit of the family as nearly equal partners. Yet, much evidence in the handling of family budgets suggests that while women often "manage" money it need not necessarily imply real control.[39] This suspicion is reinforced in Newfoundland by the fact that whatever arrangements were made within the family, external economic relations were carried out by, or in the name if, men.

There is, in addition, the tradition of male-dominated fishing communities, the "authoritarianism" of Newfoundland fathers and the extreme sexual division of labour. Both historically and in contemporary Newfoundland there are particular difficulties in establishing the dimensions of "power" and its relation to "authority." The pervasive egalitarian ethic and the consequent avoidance of authority in outport communities have often been remarked on.[40] Coupled with a stress on individualism (which is interpreted as individual families) this means that there is virtually no possibility for leadership or the exercise of power within the community. Even minor success is penalized, but on the other hand, if an individual or a family (or a community) feels wronged then voluble public protest is in order. When we look at the distribution of power in Newfoundland it is also important to remember that prior to Confederation, outport communities, in common with rural communities elsewhere, were not only politically powerless but economically marginal, with each individual family equally exploited by merchant interests.

Some writers suggest that women (partly because of their stronger status) are less susceptible to the egalitarian ethic. In a previous paper, I pointed to one way that women had found of defining to the ethic but escaping its consequences. D. Davis, who worked in a community that was not characterized by exogamy, found women powerful in defence of their families and their own positions in the house, but less effective in public associations and penalized if they trespassed into the male sphere.[41] Even today it makes little sense to talk of either men or women having power in a situation when the communities themselves have such a minimal public voice.

Patriarchal assumptions permeate nineteenth-century accounts and later anthropological work. Faris, for instance, simply states, "In a fishing community one might reasonably expect a sharp division of labour along sexual lines, and Cat Harbour is certainly no exception," going on to observe that virilocal residence and exogamy reinforce such divisions. Faris has been criticized for his assumption on a number of grounds. Stiles[42] and Davis, who worked on the south coast, which never operated the trap fishery in family units as they did on the northeast coast, both point to much closer and more reciprocal husband/wife relationships. Regional differences are certainly important, but here I want, rather, to stress Faris's dubious assumption that the people of Cat Harbour, especially the women, gave priority to men's work in the same way that Faris himself does.

Both Firestone and Faris produce some evidence for what they see as extreme male authority in the home. It is worth quoting the passage in which Firestone states:

> The family is patriarchal. Decisions pertaining to family activities are ultimately those of the father . . . and plans of a group of brothers working under their fathers are finalized by him. In the house the woman gets a drink for her husband from the water barrel or food on demand. . . . The man tells his wife to do whatever it is that he wants in a matter of fact way—neither a command nor a request—and she complies.

He concludes "there is no question as to the man's authority nor to the woman's subordination."[43] He cites as corroborative evidence a woman saying, "it is best when the wife does what the husband wants." But in the very next quotation we hear a woman saying "a good woman here is one who is obedient and doesn't try to tell the man what to do . . . at least the men would say that." Thus, even on the evidence Firestone gives us, there are some contradictions. Firstly, economic decisions relating to the fishing crew might well have been taken by the skipper without infringing on the way in which domestic decisions were taken. Secondly, the apparent servitude of women in the matter of providing food applies not just to the men of the house, but to everyone, including female visitors. I suggest that rather than reflecting subordination, it arises out of poverty and the extreme skill needed to produce sufficient food and drink. It has become part of the housewife's pride that she can, and does, supply what is necessary. When I see it today, I do not notice subjugation, but rather a sense of quiet confidence in the women's control of the kitchen and the house. Thirdly, it is hard for a feminist to escape intimations of connivance in the last quotation. She was, after all, talking to a man, Firestone, who would, she assumed, also "say that."

A more overt example of patriarchal practice is that of remuneration within the family for women's work in the shore crew. Women who were hired from outside the family were paid, but while the sons who fished received a share (or more likely a part share) of the voyage, the daughters who worked on shore got nothing. On the other hand, girls who worked outside the home did not have to contribute to the household, whereas boys did.[44] Again it was part of the economic structure organized around a patrilocal fishing crew. As Faris's unsympathetic male informant puts it, "Maids leave, so why should they get anything." What we see here seems to reflect an awkward transition from the time that a household is dependent on a daughter's labour to the time when another household is dependent on her labour as a wife. At this level, the Newfoundland situation seems to confirm the stress that Levi Strauss and his followers put on "the exchange of women" as fundamental to the social organization of male dominance. Yet, as M. Mackintosh has pointed out in connection with Meillassoux's arguments, because he regarded female subordination as a fact and not a problem, he slipped into illegitimate theoretical assertions that confused the relations of human reproduction with the process of the reproduction of the whole society, and this led to a deduction of social relations from production relations.[45] Mackintosh, rightly, insists that we "should seek rather to grasp the way in which specific forms of these oppressions operate, how they are maintained and reinforced, how they are overthrown or why they are not overthrown,"[46] and this brings us back to the women of Newfoundland and the problem of an extreme sexual division of labour.

In many ways, this seems to be the crux. Partly because it is so expected in a maritime society, both male and female writers have tended to take it for granted. There are, and probably always have been, exceptions, but the sexual division of labour in the outports is now and always has been extreme. There are clearly and geographically limited spheres of activity. Lists of "man's tasks" and "women's tasks" hardly overlap at all. Social, cultural, and political life is largely carried out in single sex groups.[47] Responsibilities within the household are quite separate. The problem lies in assessing what the consequences of this are, and this is compounded by the primacy accorded to the male activity of fishing. Because of the patriarchal structure of the wider society from which the outports come and in which they continue to be embedded, this carried with it (and still carries) various overt indications of dominance over the female spheres.

As the material under discussion has indicated, however, the extreme sexual division of labour in Newfoundland communities has been combined with women's vital and acknowledged economic contributions to the household economy, with the tradition of their vital role in settlement and with an ideology of egalitarianism. One consequence of this has been that women express their autonomy, control, and authority within "separate spheres." These spheres are not coterminous with the usual delineations of "public" and "private." Indeed, the whole concept rests on the interrelationship and interdependence of men's and women's economic efforts in both

the household and the fishery. Rather there are various physical boundaries, which, together with the sexual division of labour, allow women both
the physical and ideological space they need. One of these is the shoreline,
or "landwash." Men controlled the fishery at sea; women the fishery on
shore. I would suggest that the acceptance of that boundary in such matters
as women not going in the boats, or even making the nets, reinforces their
control of the shorework and its importance in the recognition of their economic co-operation. Even more important was women's control of the
house and everything in it, including the kitchen. The distinction between
"public" and "private" in Newfoundland outports did not happen between
"outside" and "inside" but between the kitchen, which was public, and the
rest of the house, which was private. The kitchen was not just an extension
of the community, but in effective terms, the centre of it. No one knocked at
a kitchen door. Anyone could come and go as they pleased—but were forbidden to pass into the "private" areas of the house. Only "strangers" or
those in authority knocked (and sometimes entered by another door). In the
absence of community meeting places, the kitchens were the places in
which the community met, that is, publicly interacted, held discussions, and
came to decisions. Even where alternatives were available, the absence of
any effective heating except the kitchen stove would not encourage much
conversation to take place there.[48] In this context it is vital that the kitchen
was readily and obviously acknowledged to be the women's domain. It was
impossible to exclude them in those circumstances. Present-day observation
shows male conversation being carefully monitored by the women who
often disguise their interest behind ceaselessly working hands. Coupled
with the egalitarian ethic it helps to explain the much-noticed practice of
"waiting-on-men." In this way, the women can easily intervene in the men's
conversation without apparently leaving their own sphere and thus can
exert a correct authority of their own.

In assessing this somewhat contradictory material the most useful
comparison is with the material gathered in Scottish fishing communities
by P. Thompson. The crux of his argument is that the very different gender
relations and economic attitudes (past and present) in Buckie, Lewis,
Aberdeen, and Shetland are inextricably linked. In particular, the "moral
order" of a community, its interpretation of religion, its child-rearing practices, and its attitudes to gender affects its ability to adapt and survive in
different economic conditions. Regional differences have also played a com-
plicating part in the study of Newfoundland, although it would be hard to
find such overall contrasts as there are in Scotland. However, the parallels,
especially the social practices described in Buckie and Shetland, are illumi-
nating. Shetland represents the high point in both gender relations and economic success, perhaps exemplified by their positive handling of the oil
activity. The situation of women there is characterized by a degree of economic involvement and genuine equality, a lack of male authority in the
home, sexual freedom, and political and intellectual energy, which it would
be hard to equal in Newfoundland. Nevertheless, some similarities with
Shetland support the argument that women's economic participation in the

fishery and the non-authoritarian domestic relations in Newfoundland are integrally connected.

In Buckie, which Thompson characterizes as "the moral order of free enterprise," individualism, a greater separation of gender spheres, greater male authority, and a more deferential religious observance, create a more immediately recognizable comparison with Newfoundland. The most notable contrast is that, in the absence of an egalitarian imperative, highly capitalized Buckie boats are currently among the most successful fishing enterprises in Britain. As in Newfoundland, however, Buckie women have asserted control over their own sphere, and the house operates similarly as the centre of a warm and egalitarian community—"Strangers knock, friends come in." It was an open-door community; and as today, food was always offered to a visitor—"the table was always laid for anyone who came in."[49]

Too much can be made of these comparisons, but they help to set the material presented here in context. While Newfoundland outports are not unique and their experience is paralleled elsewhere, they operate in a specific historical, economic, and ideological situation and aspects of these may vary from community to community, making generalization even within Newfoundland difficult. The eventual gender relations and sexual division of labour will be the result of complex interaction of economic and ideological forces, not least of which will be women's active participation in their own lives.

What I want to suggest here is that women in Newfoundland—at least the wives of fishermen, that is the owners of boats (and that is a considerable caveat), have used their vital roles in initial settlement and in the fish-producing economy not to destroy the sexual division of labour but to establish its boundaries in such a way as to confirm their control over at least their own spheres. Inheritance did not matter if a woman gained a "woman's sphere" by marriage; nor did the ownership of a share if she controlled the household budget. Nor, and this is also important, did either matter in conditions of bare survival, when there was no surplus to be appropriated.

CONCLUSION

We can speak of "traditional outport life" at least in the sense that the outlines of the sexual divisions of labour and the basis for the negotiation of gender and power come into sharpest focus at the end of the eighteenth century with the establishment of the Planter's household unit with its inshore fishing crew and shore crew as the key unit in the fishing economy. And these outlines remain until the demise of sun-dried fish as a product in the 1950s and the access of modern goods, services, cash, and opportunities in the heady post-Confederation days after 1949. Much of what is evident today is rooted in that long experience, but the precise connections still need to be specified. Here I have restricted myself to an examination of the context of the male domination of the fishery in which the signal fact of women's contribution as both settlers and shore crew served to alert us that women were in a position to negotiate actively in the formation and development of the relations of production. In its turn, this forces a reconsideration of the consequences of the sexual division of labour and its relationship with other areas of women's interest.

We are still a long way from a wholly adequate theory of the subordination of women. But the route lies through careful examination of the evidence of different women's lives. The fishing communities of Newfoundland offer a perspective that sharpens our view of certain aspects of the sexual division of labour, and, I hope, contributes to the gradual filling out of the complex picture of negotiation, and adaptation that constitutes the reality of gender divisions.

NOTES

1. The latter is probably the most useful to the development of theory. Some of the best work has been done by anthropologists, for example, essays in the collections of R. Reiter, *Toward an Anthropology of Women* (New York, 1975); M. McCormack and M. Strathern, *Nature, Culture, and Gender* (Cambridge, 1980); K. Young, *Of Marriage and the Market* (London, 1981). The former is often restricted by its dependence on the somewhat arbitrary comparisons thrown up by Murdock and White's (1969) Standard Cross Cultural Sample, for example, M.K. Whyte, *The Status of Women in Pre-industrial Societies* (London, 1978); P. Danday, *Female Power and Male Dominance* (Cambridge, 1981).

2. See C. Delphy, *The Main Enemy* (London, 1978); J. Finch, *Married to the Job* (London, 1983); S. Walby, "Patriarchal Structures: the Case of Unemployment" in *Gender, Class, and Work*, ed. E. Garmarnikow, (London 1983).

3. Recent examples would include B. Taylor, *Eve and the New Jerusalem* (London, 1983); S. Oldfield, *Spinsters of this Parish* (London, 1984); D. Gittins, *Fair Sex, Family Size and Structure 1900–1939* (London, 1982); and P. Summerfield, *Women Workers in the Second World War* (London, 1982).

4. Today fishing only contributes 12 percent of the net value of production (Economic Council of Canada, 1980) and employs only 13 percent

of the labour force (G. Munroe, St. John's, 1980). For statistics on the composition of the fishing fleet see *Setting a Course*, Government of Newfoundland and Labrador (St. John's, 1978).

5. This essay ignores the growing proportion of the population who live in St. John's and the other urban centres. In 1981, out of a total population of 567 681, 332 898 were classified as dwelling in urban areas, 154 820 in St. John's. The position of women in St. John's is also interesting historically, but I have not had space to investigate it here.

6. Estimates vary, but there are probably not more than a couple of dozen full-time fisherwomen. Nearly all of them do it because of unusual family circumstances, for example, a family of daughters with no close relatives to take over the boat and gear. A few wives fish with their husbands in the smaller crews; more since a recent change in UIC regulations made this a profitable adaptation.

7. For example, see R. Firth, *Malay Fishermen: Their Peasant Economy* (London, 1946); M.E. Smith, *Those Who Live from the Sea* (New York, 1977); R. Andersen, *North Atlantic Maritime Cultures* (The Hague, 1979); J.A. Acheson, "The Anthropology of Fishing," *Annual Review of Anthropology* (1981).

8. See J. Tunstall, *The Fishermen* (London, 1962); M. Gray, *The Fishing*

Industries of Scotland (London, 1978); P. Thompson, *Living the Fishing* (London, 1983): M. Orbach, *Hunters, Seamen and Entrepreneurs* (Berkeley, 1977); J. Zulaika, *Terra Nova* (St. John's, 1981). For male anthropological accounts of Newfoundland outports, see J. Faris, *Cat Harbour* (St. John's, 1972); M.M. Firestone, *Savage Cove* (St. John's, 1978); for a more questioning perspective see R. Andersen and C. Wadel, eds., *North Atlantic Fishermen* (St. John's, 1972).

9. The explicitly feminist academic studies are few. I would include D. Davis, "Social Structure, Sex Roles and Female Associations in a Newfoundland Fishing Village" (unpublished paper, 1979); D. Davis, *Blood and Nerves* (St. John's, 1983); D. Davis, "The Family and Social Change in the Newfoundland Outport," *Culture* 3, 1 (1983); E. Antler, "Women's Work in Newfoundland Fishing Families" (unpublished paper, 1976); E. Antler, "Maritime Mode of Production, Domestic Mode of Production or Labour Process: An Examination of the Newfoundland Inshore Fishery," (unpublished paper, 1977); C. Benoit, "The Poverty of Mothering," (M.A. thesis, Memorial University); C. Benoit, "The Politics of Mothering in a Newfoundland Village," (unpublished paper, 1982); A. Matthews, "The Newfoundland Migrant Wife" in *People, Power, and Process*, ed. A. Himelfarb and J. Richardson (Toronto, 1980); M.B. Porter, "Women and Old Boats: The Sexual Division of Labour in a Newfoundland Outport" in *The Public and the Private*, ed. E. Garmarnikow (London, 1983); M.B. Porter, "The Tangly Bunch: the Political Culture of Avalon Women," *Newfoundland Studies* (forthcoming). There is also considerable descriptive evidence in autobiographies and folklore accounts, for example, Greta Hussey, *Our Life on Lear's Room* (St. John's, 1981); H. Murray, *More than 50%* (St. John's, 1979); H. Porter, *Below the Bridge* (St. John's, 1979); E. Goudie, *Women of Labrador* (St. John's, 1973).

10. P. Thompson, et al., *Living the Fishing* (London, 1983).

11. A son, to Nicholas Guy, related to John Guy, but the mother's name is not recorded.

12. In 1766 St. John's, the rate of single Irish men to available women was as high as 17:1, quoted in C. Grant Head, *Eighteen Century Newfoundland* (Toronto, 1976), 87.

13. Quoted in J. Mannion, ed., *The Peopling of Newfoundland* (St. John's, 1977), 19.

14. See J. Halton and M. Harvey, *Newfoundland, the Oldest British Colony* (London, 1883), 43.

15. Similar arrangements in family economics have been documented in pre-industrial France and England by, for example, L.T. Tilly and J.W. Scott, *Women, Work and Family* (New York, 1978). For citations see C. Grant Head, *Eighteenth Century Newfoundland*, 141, 232, 82, 218.

16. There are several excellent first-hand accounts of the Labrador summer fishery, one especially by G. Hussey, *Our Life*, who did not settle there, but makes clear the process by which it happened. See also F. Barbour, *Memories of Life on the Labrador and Newfoundland* (New York, 1979).

17. M. Firestone, *Savage Cove*, 23.

18. See Mannion, *Peopling of Newfoundland*: Head, *Eighteenth Century Newfoundland*: G. Handcock, "English Migration to Newfoundland" in *Peopling of Newfoundland*.

19. The cod trap is recorded as early as Bonne Esperence 1868 and seems to have been widespread by the later 1870s. Inboard engines did not become common until 1920s. Social changes arose mainly as a consequence of missionary activity. See W. Wilson, *Newfoundland and Its Missionaries* (Cambridge, 1866); D.W. Prowse, *A History of Newfoundland from English Colonial and Foreign Records* (London, 1895). For various interpretations of the Fisherman's

174 *R U R A L   A N D   F I S H I N G   F A M I L I E S*

Protective Union see W.F. Coaker, *The History of the FPU in Newfoundland 1909–29* (St. John's, 1930); B. Neis, "Competitive Merchants and Class Struggle in Newfoundland," *Studies in Political Economy* 5 (1981); J. Feltman, "The Development of the Fishermen's Union in Newfoundland" (M.A. thesis, Memorial University, 1959); I. McDonald, "W.F. Coaker and the Fishermen's Protective Union in Newfoundland Politics, 1908–25" (Ph.D. thesis, London University, 1971).

20. Even then their economic vulnerability made them liable to various "rationalizations," for example, J. Smallwood's Resettlement Programme in the 1960s which resulted in the extinction of several hundred of the smaller or more remote outports and the relocation of the inhabitants to more "convenient" locations. See C. Wadel, *Marginal Adaptations and Modernization in Newfoundland* (St. John's, 1969); N. Iverson and R. Matthews, *Commun-ities in Decline* (St. John's, 1968).

21. G. Hussey, *Our Life*, 5.

22. For example see M. Chamberlain, *Fenwomen* (London, 1975); F. Thompson, *Lark Rise to Candleford* (London, 1945); S. Van Kirk, "*Many Tender Ties*": Women in the Fur Trade, 1670–1870 (Winnipeg, 1980); B. Light and A. Prentice, *Pioneer and Gentle Women of British North America 1713–1867* (Toronto, 1980).

23. Quoted in G.T. Cello, *Newfoundland Discovered: English Attempts at Colonization, 1610–1630* (London, 1972).

24. H. Murray, *More than 50%*, 18.

25. Ibid., 23.

26. Ibid., 121.

27. Ibid., 29.

28. See G. Pocius, "Hooked Rugs in Newfoundland," *Journal of American Folklore* 92, 365 (1979).

29. Hussey, *Our Life*, 44.

30. In comparing Chamberlain's material (*Fenwomen*) with my own, I tentatively put forward two generalizations. Firstly, Newfoundland midwives never developed as many erudite skills, either herbal or surgical. They managed on commonsense and humility. Their hallmark was their accessibility. They would willingly buckle down and sort out the rest of the family or climb into bed with the mother for a warmup and a giggle. See Benoit, "The Politics of Mothering," for some further comments.

31. While this was the original method of exploiting the cod resource, it seems to have been neglected by the English settlers until its revival in the eighteenth century (Head, *Eighteenth-Century Newfoundland*, 203–206). Andersen has studied it in its heyday at the end of the nineteenth century. R. Andersen, "The 'Count' and the 'Share': Offshore Fishermen and Changing Incentives" in *Canadian Ethnology*, ed., R.J. Preston, 40 (Ottawa 1978); R. Andersen, "The Social Organization of the Newfoundland Banking Schooner Cod Fishery" (unpublished paper, 1980).

32. There are numerous accounts of both the technology and the economics of the inshore cod fishery. See, for example, M. Firestone, *Savage Cove*; NORDCO, *It Were Well to Live Mainly Off Fish* (St. John's, 1981).

33. There are excellent descriptions of the first stage in Hussey, *Our Life*, 38, and Wilson, *Newfoundland and its Missionaries*, 211, which shows the continuity of the methods used.

34. Murray, *More Than 50%*, 16.

35. Wilson, *Newfoundland and Its Missionaries*, 212.

36. Estimates of both the quantity and the value of the family catch appear in E. Antler, "Women's Work in Newfoundland Fishery Families" (unpublished, 1976), Head, *Eighteenth-*

Century Newfoundland; Alexander, *The Decay of Trade: An Economic History of the Newfoundland Salt Fish Trade, 1935–1965* (St. John's, 1977), and O. Brox, *The Maintenance of Economic Dualism in Newfoundland* (St. John's, 1969). The whole exercise is more ideologically useful than analytically pertinent in that under conditions of simple commodity production, the "value" is embodied in the product, rather than in the direct remuneration (via the wage). Nevertheless the effort to demonstrate that women's (and children's) labour contributes specifically to the value realized by the family unit was an important contribution.

37. Murray, *More Than 50%*, 24.

38. Davis, *Blood and Nerves*, 101.

39. See J. Humphries, "Class Struggle and the Persistence of the Working Class Family," *Cambridge Journal of Economics* 1, 3 (1977); R. Pahl, *Divisions of Labour* (London, 1984).

40. In, for example, Faris, *Cat Harbour*; Davis, *Blood and Nerves*; L. Chiaramonte, *Craftsman–Client Contracts: Interpersonal Relations in a Newfoundland Fishing Community* (St. John's, 1970).

41. Davis, *Blood and Nerves*.

42. G. Stiles, "Fishermen, Wives and Radios: Aspects of Communication in a Newfoundland Fishing Community" in *North Atlantic Fishermen*.

43. Firestone, *Savage Cove*, 77.

44. Ibid., 42.

45. M. Mackintosh, "Reproduction and Patriarchy: A Critique of Meillassoux," *Capital and Class* 2 (1977), 121.

46. See M. Molyneux, "Beyond the Housework Debate," *New Left Review* 116 (1979) for a similar prescription. This brief reference makes a connection with a substantial theoretical debate, contributions to which have been made by V. Beechey, "On Patriarchy," *Feminist Review* 3 (1979); F. Edholm et al., "Conceptualizing Women," *Critique of Anthropology* 3 (1977); L. Bland et al., "Relations of Production: Approaches Through Anthropology" in Women's Studies Group, *Women Take Issue* (London, 1978). This research note is an attempt to provide the kind of substantive data the debate calls for.

47. It should be noted that Thompson's evidence from Scotland, and all the material gathered on fishing communities elsewhere, stresses the sexual division of labour and separation of sexual spheres. What varies are the consequences. See P. Thompson, paper presented to ASA Symposium on Women in Fishing Economies, Nov. 1983.

48. For a discussion of the role of the kitchen as the boundary between public and private, see L. Dillon, "Black Diamond Bay: A Rural Community in Newfoundland" (M.A. thesis, Memorial University, 1983). Other confirmation can be found in Faris, *Cat Harbour*; Murray, *More Than 50%*; Davis, *Blood and Nerves*; P. Thompson, paper to Women in Fishing Economies, records the same open access to the kitchen in Buckie and Shetland. Faris, *Cat Harbour*, stresses that men also met in the shop in the evenings, an arena most other observers, for example, K.K. Szala, "Clean Women and Quiet Men: Courtship and Marriage in a Newfoundland Fishing Village," (M.A. thesis, Memorial University, 1978), allocate to the young unmarried of both sexes. Traditionally, the "stores"—sheds on the stages—were men's meeting places, but these were (and are) untenable for most of the colder months of the year.

49. Thompson, *Living the Fishing*, 250.

section

4

THE SEXUAL DIVISION OF LABOUR WITHIN URBAN FAMILIES

Cities

GENDER AT WORK AT HOME:
FAMILY DECISIONS, THE LABOUR
MARKET, AND GIRLS' CONTRIBUTIONS
TO THE FAMILY ECONOMY*

BETTINA BRADBURY

o

INTRODUCTION

"Gender at work" can be read in two ways. In the first, work is a noun, and
the central question is "How do definitions of skill, of appropriate work for
men and women get negotiated within the workplace by men and women,
workers and capital?" Recent discussions of the sexual division of labour in
diverse industries, of "gender at work," the social construction of skill and
of the role of unions in perpetuating women's unequal position in the workforce have made major contributions to our understanding of the complexities of the relationships between gender and class, between patriarchy and
capitalism. Historical research in this field is rich and fascinating, and is
reshaping both women's history and working-class history in Canada as
elsewhere.[1]

"Gender at work" can also be read, if my grammar is correct, as a verb.
Here the question posed would be "How does gender work as a process in
society which means that men and women end up with different work and
life experiences?" To answer this question involves consideration of factors
other than those found in the workplace. In this paper I would like to argue
that while workplace centred approaches go a long way toward explaining
sex segregation within specific trades, they ignore different levels of decision
making and other institutions that have already gendered the workforce
before it arrives at the factory gate.[2] Equally, while approaches stressing the

---

* From Gregory S. Kealey and Greg Patmore, eds., *Canadian and Australian Labour
History* (Sydney: Australian–Canadian Studies, 1990), 119–40.

strength of patriarchal ideology or the importance of domestic labour help explain why married women remained out of the workplace they fail to grasp the complex interactions between patriarchy and capitalism. Furthermore they are more difficult to apply when dealing with the work of daughters rather than their mothers.

Within families decisions were made about who should stay home to look after children and do housework and who should earn wages which had wide reaching impact on the composition of the workforce. Such decisions were never made in an ideological or economic vacuum, they represented a complex and often unconscious balance between basic need, existing ideology and practise regarding gender roles, the structure of the economy, and the particular economic conjuncture. Schools taught specific skills and implanted tenacious ideas about future roles. At its broadest level this paper represents a simple plea to those looking at divisions of labour in the workplace to also consider the work done by historians of the family and education. In Canada such work offers some clues about this broader process, although little research systematically examines the question.[3] To the extent that historians interested in how gender is worked out within the workplace and in the unions ignore what happens prior to men and women's arrival at work, their explanations will fail to consider the wider and deeper sexual division of labour, which not only relegated women to jobs defined as less skilled in workplaces shared with men and to feminine ghettos, but also determined that large numbers would simply not enter the workforce or would do so only sporadically.

More specifically the paper focusses on one aspect of the question, namely how family decisions in interaction with the nature of local labour markets influenced sons' and in particular daughters' contribution to the family economy.[4] The paper concentrates on the micro-level, examining what I have been able to deduce about family decision-making processes regarding which family members should seek wage labour in two Montreal working-class wards between the 1860s and 1890s. A brief description of the major sectors employing males in Montreal is followed by an assessment of the importance of additional wage earners to working-class families. The respective work of sons and daughters within the family economy is evaluated.

The sexual division of labour within the family, and the need for additional domestic workers as well as extra wage labourers, I argue meant that the context, timing, and contours of boys' and girls' participation in wage labour were different. By looking at the role of girls in the family economy and not just in the labour market,[5] we can better see how the major changes accompanying the emergence of industrial capitalism in Montreal did not modify the dominant sexual division of labour.

MONTREAL FAMILIES AND WAGE LABOUR, 1860–90

The years 1860 to 1890 were characterised by the growing dominance of industrial capital in the economic structure of Montreal, the increasing dependence on wage labour of a major proportion of its population.

Canada's first and largest industrial city, "the workshop" of Canada, had a wide and complex array of industries. Most important were those relating to rail and water transportation, shoemaking, clothing, and food and beverages. The metallurgy sector, dominated by production for the railroads, provided jobs for skilled immigrants from Great Britain, and some French Canadians with a long tradition of working in metal. In shoemaking and dressmaking, as in numerous other smaller trades, artisanal production was rapidly, if unevenly giving way to production in large factories. Minute divisions of labour accompanied the utilisation of new types of machinery throughout the period, drawing immigrants and French Canadians new to the city into the myriad of largely unskilled jobs that were being created. Broadly speaking, the male workforce was divided into four groups. Best paid and most secure were the relatively skilled workers involved in the new trades that emerged with the industrial revolution—the engineers, machinists, moulders and others who worked in the foundries and new factories. More subject to seasonal and conjunctural unemployment were skilled workers in the construction trades. A third group comprised those workers in trades undergoing rapid deskilling and re-organisation, most important amongst these were the shoemakers. General unskilled labourers made up the other major sub-group within the working class. About twenty-five cents a day separated the average wage of each of these groups, setting the stage for potential differences in their standard of living, and their family economy.[6] Women and girls worked largely in separate sectors of the economy, particularly as domestic servants, dressmakers and in specific kinds of factory work. In virtually every sector, their wages were half those of males or less.[7]

THE IMPORTANCE OF ADDITIONAL EARNERS IN THE FAMILY WAGE ECONOMY

These disparities of approximately twenty-five cents a day had the potential to separate the working class into identifiable fractions each capable of achieving a different standard of living in good times, each vulnerable in diverse ways to the impact of winter, cyclical depressions and job restructuring. Throughout most of the period the most skilled had more flexibility in their budget and a greater chance of affording to eat and live at a level that may also have helped to ward off the diseases that spread only too quickly through the poorly constructed sewers and houses of the City. This greater margin of maneouvre which higher daily wages, greater job security, and the possession of skills that were scarce and usually in demand gave to the skilled, was not constant. It was particularly likely to be eroded in times of economic depression or of rapid transformations in the organisation of work.

While some skilled workers organised successfully during this period, the major element of flexibility in the family income, for skilled and unskilled alike, lay not so much in the gains that organisation could offer, but in the ability to call on additional family members to earn wages, to gain or save money in other ways, or to limit the necessity of spending cash.

Decisions about who additional family workers would be, were therefore crucial in determining the contours of the family economy and of the labour force. An examination of the importance of secondary wage earners, and of who they were in terms of their age and sex allows a better grasp of the interaction between family labour deployment decisions, the "gendering" of the workforce and the structure of the economy. This section therefore assesses the importance of additional wage earners in families headed by men in different types of occupations.[8] The following section then attempts to determine who such workers were.

The average number of workers reported by the families of the two working-class areas studied here, Ste. Anne and St. Jacques wards, fluctuated over the family life cycle. Amongst young couples who had not yet borne children, the wife would occasionally report an occupation, sometimes another relative lived with the couple, contributing to the number of workers in the household, so that until 1881 families averaged just over one worker at this first stage of a couple's married life. Most families then passed through a long period of relative deprivation as children were born, grew, and required more food, clothing and larger living premises. Between the time when the first baby was born and some children reached twelve or thirteen, the families of Ste. Anne and St. Jacques continued to have only slightly more than one worker. Then children's contribution began to make up for the difficult years. In 1861, families where half the children were still under fifteen averages 1.34 workers; once half were fifteen or more they averaged 1.97. In subsequent decades the expansion of wage labour made children's contribution even more important. Whereas in 1861 the average family with children over the age of eleven had only .48 of them at work, in 1881 it had 1.16. By 1871 the average family with offspring aged fifteen or more had nearly as many children living at home and working as there had been total number of workers a decade earlier. From .85 children at work, the number reported increased to 1.85. The total number of family workers increased from an average of under two at this stage in 1861 to nearly three a decade later. Children's wages became more and more important as children came to constitute a wage-earning family's major source of security.

The prosperity that this number of workers could have secured was temporary. It depended largely on the ability of parents to keep their wage earning children in the household. As older sons or daughters began to leave home to work or marry, the average dropped down again. If both members of a couple survived they would find themselves struggling again in their old age on a single wage, or no wage at all. For aged working-class widows and widowers, the situation was particularly bleak if there were no children able to help.[9]

Over these years the patterns of the working-class and non-working-class families diverged. In 1861 the non-working class, particularly in St. Jacques, included a high proportion of artisans and shopkeepers, men whose family economy required not the wages, but the work of wives and children. As a result, the average number of workers and of children at work in their families was higher than in all other groups except the unskilled. Over the next two decades, artisans became less and less common. Family labour was increasingly limited to enterprises like small corner groceries. Professionals and some white collar workers became more important among the non-working-class populations. After 1871, the reporting of jobs by children was least likely amongst this group.

It was within the working class family economy that the most dramatic changes occurred over this period, although there were significant and changing differences between the skilled, the unskilled and those in the injured trades. The inadequacy of the $1.00 a day or less that a labourer could earn remained a constant throughout this period. As a result, unskilled families consistently relied on additional workers when they were able to. In 1861 they averaged 1.45 workers, compared to 1.27 among the skilled. Over the next two decades the growing number of jobs available allowed them to increase the average number of family workers to 1.62 then 1.66. Amongst those with working age offspring, the average number at work increased by 123 percent from .60 in 1861 to 1.34 two decades later.

For these unskilled workers the period before children were old enough to work was the most difficult. It is worth examining how some such families managed at the critical stage of the family life cycle and later as children matured. Olive Godaire, wife of labourer Pierre, worked, probably at home as a dressmaker in 1861, to help support their three children aged two to eight. Ten years later, it was her eighteen-year-old daughter who was taking in sewing, while a ten-year-old boy was apprenticed to be a tinsmith.[10] In the case of labourer John Harrington's family, the period when the father was the only earner within the nuclear family lasted for at least eighteen years. When John and Sarah's children were under ten, they took in boarders and had John's fifty-year-old father, also a labourer, living in the household. Whatever money these extra family and household members contributed would have helped compensate for John's low wages or irregular work and they continued to take in boarders over the next ten years. Their oldest son, Timothy was still going to school in 1871 and the family was cramped in a rear dwelling where rent was minimal. Somewhere between 1871 and 1881, the boys joined their father in seeking general labouring jobs. For the first time the family lived alone, without additional household members, and with three wage earners, even three labourers, must have enjoyed a standard of living that was relatively high compared to the previous year.

The degradation of work conditions and lower wages that typified trades like shoemaking appear to have been counteracted by sending growing numbers of family members to seek steady work. In 1861 such families had only 1.08 workers—fewer than any other group. By 1881 they averaged 1.62 workers. Most dramatic was the increased importance of the contribution of children resident at home. The average number of children reporting a job amongst those families with children of working age, nearly tripled over the two decades from .55 to 1.51. At that date a few families like that of Angeline and Alexis Larivière had four workers. Their two daughters, twenty-two-year-old Josephine and sixteen-year-old Marie-Louise worked as general labourers. The twenty-year-old son Charles was a stone-cutter.[11]

The relative superiority of the wages of skilled workers seems clear in 1861 when they appear to have been able to manage with fewer workers than other groups—averaging only 1.27. A decade later, with 1.5 workers, they still needed fewer than the rest of the working class. The depression that hit in 1874, however, appears to have eroded much of the superiority of the skilled workers. In 1881 after seven years of major depression, which was only just lifting and which must have left many a family heavily indebted, the pattern of family labour deployment was similar to that of the unskilled and those in the injured trades.

This convergence of experiences within the working class over this period is not surprising, given the impact of the depression, combined with the degeneration of work conditions in some skilled trades. In the metal-working trades, for example, trade was said to be dead in the winter of 1878. Half the local unionised workers were said to be "working at any kind of labouring work." Two years earlier, a moulder drew attention to the desperate condition of Montreal mechanics, "working on a canal at 60 cents per day, men who have served years in securing a trade, the wages they receive being only a mockery of their misery."[12]

Families clearly attempted to shape their own economies by adjusting the numbers of wage earners to fit their expenses when they were able to do so. Additional wage earners were not only needed, but were used by all fractions of the working class, with differences stemming from the economic conjuncture, the nature of the labour market, their own life cycle and earning power. In so doing, they influenced the city's labour pool and enhanced their own survival. The increasing availability of wage labour in the factories, workshops, and construction sites of Montreal meant that even in times of depression more and more sons and daughters could and did find work. The reliance of employers in certain sectors on women and youths resident at home depressed male wages generally, while offering families the opportunity to counter a father's low earnings.

Economic transformation thus interacted dialectically with family needs, reshaping the labour market, the family economy, and the life course of children. This interaction is clearest in the case of workers in those sectors undergoing most dramatic transformation. The continued re-organisation of production in trades like shoemaking was reflected not only in the greater increase in the number of their children seeking waged work over the period, but also in a tendency to delay marriage and reduce family size. In the labour market in general, children living at home became a much more significant proportion of workers.[13] In the sewing trades, for example, one quarter of the workers had been co-resident children in 1861, by 1881, 55 percent were.

AGE, GENDER, AND ADDITIONAL FAMILY EARNERS

To try to grasp the decision-making processes behind these patterns of change in the average numbers of family members reporting work over this period, it is necessary to determine who the family workers were in terms of age and gender, and to examine the families from which they came.

Older sons still living at home were the most usual second earners in a family. The number of really young children or married women reporting a job was insignificant beside the importance of children in their late teens or twenties, despite the attention focussed on such young workers by contemporaries.[14] Once sons in particular reached fifteen or sixteen, they were expected to work. "In our culture," reported Alice Lacasse, the daughter of a French-Canadian immigrant to New Hampshire, "the oldest children always went to work."[15] Wage labour for boys over fifteen became the norm in this period, as more and more were drawn into the labour force. Growing numbers of girls did report a job, but the proportion of boys at work remained consistently higher than that for girls in all age groups. And, the pattern of involvement over a girl's life course continued to be completely different from a boy's.

By the age of fifteen or sixteen, 30 percent of the boys who lived at home in these two wards were reporting a job in 1861. Others no doubt sought casual labour on the streets, working from time to time, at other times roaming together in the gangs of youths that dismayed middle-class contemporaries, and filled up the local police courts. In 1871, when times were good, and industrial capitalism more entrenched, nearly 46 percent of boys this age could find a job, while in the depression of the 1870s and early 1880s, the percentage dropped back to 37 percent. After the age of sixteen, and increasingly over the period, boys' involvement with wage labour or other work would grow steadily as they aged. At ages seventeen to eighteen, 50 percent reported a job in 1861, nearly 68 percent two decades later. By age twenty-one nearly 90 percent of boys listed a job at the end of the period.

Among the girls of Ste. Anne and St. Jacques wards, the work found and the pattern of job reporting over their lives was very different from that of the boys. Once boys passed their early teens they found work in a wide variety of jobs in all sectors and workplaces of Montreal. Girls, in contrast, remained concentrated within specific jobs and sectors. For girls as for boys, the chances of finding work clearly expanded with the growth of Montreal industry. At ages 15 to 16, for instance, only 13 percent reported a job in 1861 compared to 30 percent in 1881. At the peak age at which girls reported working, nineteen to twenty, 25 percent worked in 1861, nearly 38 percent did so in 1871, then 35 percent in 1881. Even then, however, the visible participation rate of girls was only half that of boys.[16] After age twenty, the experiences of boys and girls diverged quickly and dramatically, as most, but never all women, withdrew from the formal labour market while most men found themselves obliged to seek work for the rest of their lives.

For those girls who did earn wages, then, paid labour was apparently undertaken for a brief period of their lives prior to marriage. At any one time, most girls aged fifteen or more who remained at home with their parents in these wards reported no job at all. Joan Scott and Louise Tilly have suggested that within the "industrial mode of production" "single women are best able to work, since they have few other claims on their time."[17] The discrepancy in the formal wage labour participation rates for boys and girls in these two Montreal wards suggests to me that single women did, in fact, have other claims on their time. In particular, the heavy and time consuming nature of nineteenth century housework, the prevalence of disease, the wide age spread amongst children in most families, and the myriad of other largely invisible pursuits and strategies necessary to survival for the working-class family, meant that many of these girls were needed by their mothers to help with work at home. Their role in the division of labour within the family is highlighted on one census return where members' roles were explicitly described. Louis Coutur, a carter who was fifty in 1861, reported that his twenty-one-year-old son was a shoemaker, his wife's job was "housework."[18] It seems fair to assume, making allowance for the under-enumeration of steady labour and casual work among daughters, that most of the girls who listed no job or school attendance, worked periodically, if not continually, at domestic labour as mother's helpers in and around the home. It is thus in the light of family decisions about the allocation of labour power at home, as well as in the structure of jobs available in the marketplace, that the patterns of children's wage labour as well as of their schooling must be interpreted.

At home, girls served an apprenticeship in the reproduction of labour power—in babysitting, cleaning, mending, sewing, cooking, and shopping, and by the end of the century in nursing and hygiene.[19] Religious leaders were explicit about the need for mothers to educate their daughters in their future roles. "Apply yourselves especially to the task of training your daughters in the functions they will have to perform for a husband and family, without neglecting your other children," wrote Père Mailloux in a manual for Christian parents that was republished several times between the middle and end of the nineteenth century.[20] When girls attended school, the subjects learned were not very different. Education for females, except in a few expensive academies, out of reach of the working class, taught only the most basic and general of subjects and housekeeping-type skills. Whereas boys' schools offered bookkeeping and geography, girls' schools offered music, needlework, and sewing.[21] Curriculums aimed to prepare girls for their future role as housekeeper, wife, and mother.[22] The minister of education was explicit. He feared that too many young women were being educated above their station in life, and suggested that bookkeeping and domestic economy constituted the best basis of female education.[23] In separate schools, with curriculum that moulded life roles based on gender distinctions, girls were not going to reshape their futures dramatically by slightly increasing the average number of years that they spent at school and in the workplace over this period.

Girls then, did become secondary wage earners within the working-class family economy, were increasingly likely to do so over this period, but remained less likely to report a job than were boys. The importance of their contribution to domestic labour, the lower wages they could make in the formal labour market, or an ideological repulsion to girls' labour either within the working class or amongst capitalists, constitute partial explanations for their lower rate of participation. In the absence of interviews or written memoirs, it is important to examine the work patterns of specific families more closely to see what reasons can be deduced from the evidence.[24]

Even among the families apparently in greatest need, sons seem to have been sent out to work in preference to daughters. If any families needed to draw on as many workers as possible, it should have been those headed by the labourers or shoemakers of these wards. In such families, food costs alone for a family with several growing children rapidly outstripped a man's incoming wages. Yet even these families appear to have avoided sending girls out to work, if possible. Among labourer's families in Ste. Anne in 1881, for example, 66 percent of those who had boys over ten reported having a son at work, while only 28 percent of those with girls the same age did so. If older brothers were working, girls generally did not. Girls of age twenty or more would stay at home while a teenage son worked. Their respective roles seem clearly defined. Twenty-six-year-old Ellen Mullin, for example, reported no occupation. Two brothers, aged nineteen and twenty-three worked as carters. Ellen's role was to help her mother with the domestic labour for the three wage earners and her fourteen-year-old younger brother.[25]

In Ste. Anne, even families without sons, or with young sons only, seem to have been either unwilling to send girls to work or unable to find work that was seen as suitable in the neighbourhood. Forty-two-year-old Octave Ethier must surely have had trouble supporting his four daughters aged one to seventeen and his wife on his labourer's wages. Yet neither seventeen-year-old Philomène, nor fifteen-year-old Emma reported having a job.[26]

The girls in labourers' families who did report an occupation fell into two categories. Half were the oldest child, either with no brothers or only brothers who were much younger than they were. Nineteen-year-old Sarah Anne Labor, for instance, was the oldest in a family of six children. The closest brother was only seven. She worked as a soap maker. Her wages, and the fact that the family shared the household with several other families, must have helped make ends meet.[27]

The second group of girl workers in Ste. Anne and St. Jacques came from labourers' families that sent almost all their children to work regardless of gender. Catherine Harrigan, for instance, was fourteen. She worked as a servant. Her two brothers aged fifteen and twenty were labourers like their father. In the family of St. Jacques labourer Damase Racette, four girls aged seventeen to twenty-five were all dressmakers, as was his wife, Rachel. A twenty-seven-year-old son, was a cigar maker.[28] This latter group of families appears the most desperate, perhaps because of recurrent illness, or the habitual drunkenness of a parent. When Commissioners Lukas and Blackeby were examining the work of children in Canadian mills and factories in 1882, they reported finding too many cases in the cities and factory districts where parents with "idle habits" lived "on the earnings of the children, this being confirmed" in their eyes by one instance where three children were at work, having a father as above described.[29] Yet, such a family could simply have been taking advantage of the fact of having more children of working age to make up for years of deprivation on the inadequate wages most family heads could make. Two years later, reports made to the Ontario Bureau of Industries stressed the inadequate wages of family heads as the major cause of children working, while mentioning that dissipation of the husband or father was less often a cause.[30] When a father was chronically ill, or a habitual drunkard, the wages of several children would indeed have been necessary to support a family. The use of daughters and of children aged ten to twelve to earn wages in this minority of labourers' families contrasts with the absence of such workers in other labourers' families, highlighting the relative infrequency of a daughter's work, even among those in greatest need.

Was it in part working-class ideology that kept girls at home if at all possible, seeing the workplace as unfit for them, or was it rather a pragmatic response to the fact that boys wages rapidly outstripped those of girls? Pragmatism, made necessary by the exigencies of daily existence, must certainly have played an important part. It made good sense to have boys earn wages rather than girls, for while young children of each sex might earn a similar wage, once they reached fifteen or sixteen, girls' wages were generally half those of a young man. On the other hand, when there was work available that girls could do, more were likely to report a job. Thus the labourers of St. Jacques were more likely to have daughters at work than those of Ste. Anne. An equal percentage of those with children eleven or over had girls at work as had boys. The fact that nearly 80 percent of these girls worked in some branch of the sewing industry shows how advantage was taken of the availability of this kind of work in the neighbourhood.

Family labour deployment decisions, then, were forges in the context of their own needs, invariably arising partly from the size, age, and gender configurations of the family, as well as from the kind of work in the neighbourhood.

Family labour deployment decisions, then, were forged in the context of their own needs, invariably arising partly from the size, age, and gender configurations of the family, as well as from the kind of work the family head could find. They were realised in relationship with the structure of the local labour market, of job possibilities, and of local wage rates for men and women, boys and girls. And they were influenced by perceptions, ideologies, and gut reactions about what was appropriate for sons and daughters. Thus, it was not just the fact that sewing was available in St. Jacques ward that made this such a popular choice for daughters living in that ward, for putting out could theoretically operate anywhere in the city or the surrounding countryside. It was, I suspect, the very fact that it could be done at home that was crucial. For, while domestic service no doubt took some young women from families in these wards away from their own families and into the homes of others, sewing usually kept daughters working at home.[31]

Home-work offered parents, and mothers in particular, several advantages. Firstly, they could oversee their daughters' work and behaviour, avoiding the individualism that working in a factory might encourage, and skirting the dangers and moral pitfalls that at least some contemporaries associated with factory work for young, unmarried women.[32] More importantly, girls sewing at home, like their mothers, could combine stitching and housework, could take care of younger children, run odd errands or carry water as needed, because they were right there and were always paid by the piece.

The clustering of two to five family members, all seamstresses, commonly found in the census returns for St. Jacques ward suggests very strongly that here was a centre of the home-work that was crucial to Montreal's sewing and shoemaking industries during this period. It was not uncommon to find three to four sisters, ranging in age from eleven to twenty-eight all working, presumably together, as sewing girls. In the Mosian family of St. Jacques ward, for instance, four daughters worked as seamstresses in 1871. The father was a labourer, and although the wife reported no occupation, she probably also did some sewing at home at times.[33] In 1881, the family of Marie and Michel Guigère had reached a relatively secure stage in their family life cycle. With nine children at home aged two to twenty-three, this joiner's family reported seven workers. Four of the girls, aged thirteen to twenty-three were seamstresses, one son worked as a labourer, and the thirteen-year-old son was an apprentice. The girls could combine sewing with helping their mother keep house for other workers, caring for the younger children, shopping, cooking, cleaning, and also looking after her husband's seventy-year-old father who lived with them. Marie too probably helped sporadically with sewing.[34]

Some parents with the liberty to choose must have been reluctant to expose their daughters to the long hours, continual supervision, exhausting work, and brutal forms of discipline that existed in some of Montreal's workshops and factories. Work at home could counteract such factors of "repulsion"[35] in some of the sectors employing girls. Cigar-making factories provided jobs for girls and boys in Ste. Anne and St. Jacques alike. While some manufacturers appear to have been decent men, neither fining nor beating their employees, others, in an apparently desperate attempt to control their youthful workforce resorted to physical violence, heavy fines, even locking up children as they strove to mould this young generation of workers to industrial work. Children, like adults, in these factories worked from six or seven in the morning until six at night, and sometimes later.[36]

Unlike adult males, they were subject to a vast array of disciplinary measures aimed at making them more productive and more responsible as workers. One child reported:

> If a child did anything, that is, if he looked on one side or other, or spoke, he would say: I'm going to make you pay 10 cents fine, and if the same were repeated three or four times, he would seize a stick or a plank, and beat him with it.[37]

Mr. Fortier's cigar-making factory was described as a "theatre of lewdness." There was said to be "no such infamous factory as M. Fortier's . . . nowhere else as bad in Montreal." There, one cigar maker described apprentices as being "treated more or less as slaves."[38] It was the evidence of the treatment of one eighteen-year-old girl that really shocked both the public and the commissioners examining the relations between labour and capital in 1888. Georgina Loiselle described how Mr. Fortier beat her with a mould cover because she would not make the 100 cigars as he demanded.

> I was sitting, and he took hold of me by the arm, and tried to throw me on the ground. He did throw me on the ground and beat me with the mould cover.
> Q.   Did he beat you when you were down?
> A.   Yes, I tried to rise and he kept me down on the floor.[39]

The case of Mr. Fortier's cigar factory was not typical. It created a sensation when the evidence was heard. At least some of the mothers of girls working there got together, perhaps encouraged by Mr. Fortier, to give evidence to counteract the impact of such bad publicity. "I am the mother of a family and if I had seen anything improper I would not have stayed there," explained a Mrs. Levoise. "I have my girl working there."[40]

While conditions in other Montreal factories were not as extreme, there was sufficient evidence of beatings, other draconian forms of discipline and heavy fines to explain why many girls and their parents may have wished to avoid factory labour. In cotton factories there was some evidence of boys and girls being beaten. Furthermore, fines in at least one Montreal cotton factory could reduce pay packages by between $1.00 and $12.00 in two weeks. Work there began at 6:25 AM and finished at 6:15 PM. When extra work was required, employees had to stay until 9 PM, often without time off for supper.[41] There were some perks to work in the textile industry. Nineteen-year-old Adèle Lavoie explained that the girls were accustomed to "take cotton to make our aprons." Apparently this was usually allowed, but on at least one occasion she was accused by the foreman of having taken forty to fifty yards. When a search of her house produced no results, she reported that the foreman returned to the factory to insult and harrass her sister. When she did not produce the cotton, "he stooped at this time and raising the skirt of my sister's dress, he said she had it under her skirt."[42]

Airless, hot, dusty factories, such sexual abuse by foremen, work conditions, and the long hours, were all factors that may have discouraged parents from sending girls into factory work. More significant were the wages they earned. For children under fourteen or so, wages varied little by sex. After that, male and female differentials hardened. Girl apprentices in dressmaking, mantlemaking, and millinery sometimes earned nothing for several years until they learned the trade; then they received around $4.00 a week only. "Girls" in shoe manufactories received $3.00 to $4.00 compared to the $7.00 or $8.00 earned by men. A girl bookbinder made between $1.50 and $6.00 weekly, compared to an average of $11.00 for male journeymen. Even on piece-work, girls and women generally received less than men. In general, wage rates for women were approximately half those of men.[43]

Duties at home and low wages, whether they worked in or outside the home, meant that whereas over this period more and more working-class boys would have reached manhood accustomed to wage labour, their sisters were much more likely to move backwards and forwards between paid work and housework in response to the family's economic needs, and their position in the household. Once boys, and particularly those who had been fortunate enough to acquire a skill in demand in the marketplace, reached their late teens, their earning power might rival that of their father. Wage labour offered such children potential freedom from their family in a way that had not been possible in family economies based on shared work and the inheritance of property. Such freedom was seldom possible for girls, unless they were willing to complement wage labour with prostitution.

AGE, GENDER, AND CHANGING PATTERNS OF RESIDENCE, SCHOOLING, AND DOMESTIC LABOUR

Yet, boys in general do not appear to have taken dramatic advantage of such potential freedom. Nor did girls.[44] In 1861, living with others was still an important stage in the lives of some young people of both sexes. Amongst the seventeen-year-old girls residing in Ste. Anne and St. Jacques, 35 percent were boarding with other families, living with relatives or working and living in as a servant. Twenty years later, only 12 percent of girls that age were not living with their parents, and half of these were already married. Amongst boys aged eighteen 34 percent were not living with their parents in 1861 compared to only 17 percent two decades later. Living longer at home with their parents was a fundamental change in the life cycle of boys and girls alike during this period of industrial expansion.[45]

Behind the percentages of children living with their parents or elsewhere lies a complex history of tension between family needs and individual desires, of children balancing off the advantages of the services offered at home against the relative independence that living with strangers, or even relatives might offer.[46] For all families who had passed through at least fifteen years of budget stretching, house sharing, and debt building while their children were young, the relative prosperity that several workers could offer was to be jealously guarded. It was precisely "because young adults could find jobs" that it "was in the interest of parents to keep their children at home as long as possible."[47] The patterns of residence of children suggest that, whatever conflicts there were overall, in these two wards of Montreal between 1861 and 1881 it was increasingly the parents who were the winners.

The motives behind individual decisions, the weight of traditions of family work, are difficult to grasp in the absence of written records. The factors constraining or encouraging one choice or another are clearer. Most children would have left home once they had a job only if their wages were adequate to pay for lodgings and they felt no commitment to contributing to the family income.[48] Clearly more older boys earned enough to pay for room and board than did girls. Thus, in 1871, when work was readily available, 29 percent of the twenty-three-year-old males living in these wards were boarding or with relatives; 39 percent were living with their parents and 32 percent had married. Amongst girls the same age, the low wages they could make severely limited their options. Only 15 percent were boarding; 41 percent were still with their parents, and 44 percent were already married. The contraction of work and lower wages that accompanied the Great Depression, which hit in 1874, limited the possibility of leaving home to lodge with others or to marry. In 1881, the percentage of twenty-three-year-old boys married had dropped to 25 percent; only 10 percent were boarding or living with relatives. Sixty-five percent remained at home with their parents, presumably pooling resources to survive the difficult times. The depression appears to have hastened the decline of this stage of semi-autonomy. What occurred in subsequent years remains to be determined.

The different roles of boys and girls in the family economy are confirmed in the different patterns of school attendance by age and sex. In general, school and work appear to have been complementary rather than in competition. Some children began school at four years old. By age seven approximately 60 percent of boys and girls were receiving some education. In 1881 this percentage rose to a peak of 78 percent for eight- and nine-year-old boys, and of around 80 percent for girls aged nine to twelve, then fell off rapidly once both sexes reached thirteen. The proportion of children receiving some schooling increased, but not dramatically, between 1861 and 1881. Age, gender, and the economic conjuncture created variations within this overall trend. Most important was the more erratic pattern in the attendance of boys that hints at relationships between age, gender, schooling, and wage labour that require further investigation. Overall the percentage of ten- to fourteen-year-old girls at school increased slowly but steadily from 57 percent in 1861 to 68 percent in 1881.[49] The increase was greater in St. Jacques than Ste. Anne, but the pattern was similar. Amongst boys in each ward, in contrast, the proportion at school was lower in 1871 than any other year, and the proportion of ten- to nineteen-year-olds at work increased. In Ste. Anne, in particular, the factories, workshops, and general labouring jobs attracted growing numbers of these youths. The percentage of fifteen- to nineteen-year-old boys reporting working in that ward increased from thirty-eight in 1861 to sixty-four a decade later. While a certain number of families appear to have taken advantage of boom periods to draw their sons, in particular, out of school, the majority of families appear to have got the best of both worlds. Most working-class boys went to school for varying lengths of time before they reached thirteen or so, and then sought wage labour.

These figures confirm the greater importance of a son's wage contribution to the family economy. Girls' role is clear in the high proportion that continued to report neither a job, nor school attendance. Transformations of the economy and the passage of time were slow to modify this gender difference in the relationship between girls' and boys' schooling, and their roles in the family economy. A study conducted in Quebec in 1942, just before schooling was finally made compulsory in that province, found that among children quitting school before the age of sixteen, 61 percent of girls gave as their reason, "Maman avait besoin de moi," while 50 percent of boys stated, "Ma famille avait besoin d'argent." Only 10 percent of girls gave that reason.[50] The centrality of girls' domestic labour in a different Canadian city, Toronto, is corroborated by evidence showing that potential foster parents in that city at the turn of the century were four times more likely to seek girls than boys, specifically for their usefulness as domestics and nursemaids.[51]

CONCLUSION

Gender was clearly at work in both senses of the word in nineteenth-century Montreal. On the one hand, the labour market was characterised by a sexual division of labour which, despite the rapid and dramatic changes occuring in the period, limited the numbers of jobs where capitalists considered employing women. This was not immutable, as the cases where "girls" were used as strikebreakers made clear. Montreal's labour market included major sectors, particularly sewing and shoemaking, that employed large numbers of girls and women. Yet, the figures of labour-force participation rates for the two wards studied here, suggest strongly that girls and women seldom entered the workforce in proportions equivalent to their brothers or boys the same age, and that over their life courses their participation was totally different.

The reasons why lie at least partially within the workings of the family-wage economy. Working-class families in Montreal clearly both needed and used additional family workers to counteract low wages, and to improve their standard of living. The number of extra workers varied with the skill of the family head, and the worth of that skill in the labour market. Thus, while in good times, skilled workers managed with fewer family workers than the unskilled or those in injured trades, economic depression eroded such superiority. Yet in whatever complex and probably tension-loaded decisions were made about who would seek what kind of work, boys were much more likely to be the auxiliary wage earners than girls.

To explain why brings us, in a sense, to the heart of the debate about the relative importance of patriarchy and capitalism in explaining women's oppression.[52] That the domestic labour of wives has been crucial both to family survival and to women's inequality has long been recognised both empirically and theoretically. But where do daughters fit in? Fathers, one could argue, by keeping girls at home along with their mothers to serve their daily need for replenishment, ensured that the work of all women was viewed as intermittent and secondary to that of the major wage earners.[53] Alternatively, the accent can be put on the nature of specific industries, or more generally on the capitalist labour market, which, by setting women's wage rates at half those of men, made it logical to send boys to work rather than girls.[54] Unequal access to work on the same terms as men thus not only perpetuated women's position in the home, but tragically disadvantaged those single women and widows who alone, or supporting children or elderly parents, had to live on such wages.

Clearly a dialectic is at work here. Neither empirically, nor theoretically, can the workings of patriarchy, or of capitalism be neatly separated from each other.[55] The nature of the interaction between the two and the weight of one over the other will vary historically and geographically. Among Montreal families, decisions were made in part in relation to existing jobs and wage rates, and such decisions perpetuated, reified the idea that women's work was temporary, performed before marriage or in moments of family crisis.[56] Admitting the dialectic adds complexity to the explanation but remains, I suspect, insufficient. It does so, because the emphasis remains on the formal, wage-earning labour market. Domestic labour in the nineteenth century was fundamental to family survival, to the transformation of wages into a reasonable standard of living, and to the reproduction of the working class. Historians have recognised the importance of this job for the working-class wife and mother, the role of daughters has been examined less explicitly.[57] Yet, for nineteenth-century mothers whose children were widely spaced in age, in whose homes technology had made virtually no inroads to lighten their labour, the help of daughters was invaluable. Housewives had no control over the amount of wages the husband earned, and little over how much was turned over to them. Housework was labour intensive and time consuming. One of the only ways in which wives could control the content and intensity of their work was to get children to help. Wherever possible, once girls reached an age where they could be of use to the mother, they were used to babysit, to run errands, to clean, sew, and cook. If this could be combined with wage earning activities, as in the case of home-work in the sewing industry, then such girls did work more formally. If there were no brothers of an age to earn, daughters might work in factories, offices, shops or as domestics. But the need of mothers for at least one helper at home would mean, that the rate of formal labour-force participation for girls would generally be lower than that for boys.[58] Patriarchal ideas within the working class, elements of male pride and self-interest, economic pragmatism and the daily needs of mothers and housewives thus interacted, creating a situation in which most girls served an apprenticeship in domestic labour prior to, or in conjunction with, entering the workforce.[59] In cities and towns where the labour market was completely different, where whole families or women were explicitly sought by employers, this division of labour, indeed, the very institutions of marriage and the family could be modified. The question of how to ensure that the necessary domestic labour was performed, however, would remain fundamental.[60] The working out of roles by gender at home would continue to influence the configurations of gender at work.

NOTES

1. Heidi Hartmann, "Capitalism, Patriarchy, and Job Segregation by Sex", *Signs* 1 (Spring, 1976): 137–69; Judy Lown, "Not So Much a Factory, More a Form of Patriarchy: Gender and Class During Industrialisation" in E. Garmarnikow et. al., *Gender, Class, and Work* (London, 1983); Sonya O. Rose, "Gender at Work: Sex, Class, and Industrial Capitalism" *History Workshop Journal* 21 (Spring, 1986): 113–31; Nancy Grey Osterud, "Gender Divisions and the Organization of Work in the Leicester Hosiery Industry" in Angela V. John, *Unequal Opportunities, Women's Employment in England 1800–1918* (Oxford: Basil Blackwell, 1986), 45–70. Sylvia Walby, *Patriarchy at Work: Patriarchal and Capitalist Relations in Employment* (Minneapolis: University of Minnesota Press, 1986); Ruth Milkman, *Gender at Work: The Dynamics of Job Segregation by Sex during World War II* (Urbana: University of Illinois Press, 1987). For Canadian articles touching the question see: Gail Cuthbert Brandt, "The Transformation of Women's Work in the Quebec Cotton Industry, 1920– 1950" in *The Character of Class Struggle: Essays in Canadian Working Class History, 1840–1985*, ed. Bryan D. Palmer (Toronto: McClelland and Stewart, 1986); Mercedes Steedman, "Skill and Gender in the Canadian Clothing Industry, 1890–1940" in *On the Job: Confronting the Labour Process in Canada*, ed. Craig Heron and Robert Storey (Montreal: McGill-Queen's University Press, 1986), 152–76; Marta Danylewycz and Alison Prentice, "The Evolution of the Sexual Division of Labour in Teaching: A Nineteenth-Century Ontario and Quebec Case Study," *Histoire sociale/Social History* 6 (1983): 81–109; Marta Danylewycz and Alison Prentice, "Teachers, Gender, and Bureaucratising School Systems in Nineteenth-Century Montreal and Toronto," *History of Education Quarterly* 24 (1984): 75–100; Jacques Ferland, "Syndicalisme parcellaire et syndicalisme collectif: Une interpretation socio-technique des conflits ouvriers dans deux industries québecoises, 1880–1914," *Labour/Le Travail* 19 (Spring 1987): 49–88.

2. This argument is obviously not mine alone. It is fundamental to much of the discussion of the workings of patriarchy and to the domestic labour debate, where too often it remains at an abstract theoretical level or based on cursory historical data. It is worth making here because much theoretical work places too much emphasis on either capitalist relations or reproduction and patriarchy, simplifying the complexity of relations between the two, while historical literature on the workplace or the family tend to treat the relation between the two simplisticly.

3. Joy Parr's recent articles offer the first major sustained analysis in which decisions and conditions in the home and in the workplace and the relationship between the two are constantly and systematically examined. See especially "Rethinking Work and Kinship in a Canadian Hosiery Town, 1910–1950," *Feminist Studies* 13, 1 (Spring 1987): 137–62; and also "The Skilled Emigrant and Her Kin: Gender, Culture, and Labour Recruitment,' *Canadian Historical Review* 68, 4 (Dec. 1987): 520–57, reprinted in Veronica Strong-Boag and Anita Clair Fellman, eds., *Rethinking Canada: The Promise of Women's History*, 2nd ed. (Toronto: Copp Clark Pitman, 1991), 33–55. Gail Cuthbert-Brandt does so in a different sense in "Weaving It Together: Life Cycle and the Industrial

Experience of Female Cotton Workers in Quebec, 1910–1950," *Labour/Le Travailleur* 7 (Spring 1981). Mark Rosenfeld's recent article " 'It Was a Hard Life': Class and Gender in the Work and Family Rhythms of a Railway Town, 1920–1950," *Historical Papers* (1988), and reprinted in the volume, carefully unravels how the rhythms of work in the running trades structured the family economy and gender roles in Barrie, Ontario, a railway town.

4. No Canadian works directly confront this question either in the econometric sense in which Claudia Goldin poses it in "Family Strategies and the Family Economy in the Late Nineteenth Century: The Role of Secondary Workers,' in Theodore Hershberg, *Philadelphia, Work, Space, Family and Group Experience in the Nineteenth Century* (New York: Oxford University Press, 1981), 277–310, or in the more feminist and qualitative way that Lynn Jamieson poses it in "Limited Resources and Limiting Conventions: Working-Class Mothers and Daughters in Urban Scotland c. 1890–1925" in *Labour and Love: Women's Experience of Home and Family, 1850–1940*, ed. Jane Lewis (Oxford: Basil Blackwell, 1986), 49–69.

5. Marjorie Cohen makes a similar argument without elaborating on its implications for daughters in stating that "the supply of female labour was limited by the labour requirements of the home." *Women's Work, Markets, and Economic Development in Nineteenth-Century Ontario* (Toronto: University of Toronto Press, 1988), 139. Her insistence on the importance of domestic production and women's work in the home for rural and urban families alike and for an understanding of the wider economy represents an important contribution to economic history as well as to the history of women and the family in Canada.

6. On the average, in the early 1880s, for example, a labourer earned around $1.00 a day, a shoemaker

$1.25, a carpenter $1.50, and various more highly skilled workers anything from $1.75 (blacksmith) up. See Bettina Bradbury, "The Working-Class Family Economy, Montreal, 1861–1881" (Ph.D. diss., Concordia University, 1984), 18; *Canada*, Parliament, Sessional Papers, 1882, Paper No. 4, Appendix 3, Annual Report of the Immigration Agent, 110–11, lists wages in a variety of trades.

7. In this, Montreal and Canada were little different from other cities and countries, nor has much of the discrepancy been eliminated today.

8. The figures used in this paper are derived from research done for my Ph.D thesis, currently under revision for publication. A 10 percent random sample was taken of households enumerated by the census takers in Ste. Anne and St. Jacques in 1861, 1871, and 1881. This resulted in a total sample of 10 967 people over the three decades. They resided in 1851 households and 2278 families as defined by the census takers.

9. For a brief and preliminary examination of how widows of all ages survived, see my "Surviving as a Widow in Nineteenth-Century Montreal," *Urban History Review* 17, 3 (1989): 148–60, reprinted in *Rethinking Canada*, 2nd ed., ed. Strong-Boag and Fellman.

10. These life histories were recreated by tracing families between the censuses of 1861, 1871, and 1881.

11. Mss. Census, St. Jacques, 1881, 17, p. 110.

12. *Iron Moulders Journal*, Jan. and June, 1878, Report of Local 21; *Iron Moulders Journal*, Jan. 1876, Report of local 21 and open letter from local 21 to the editor, cited in Peter Bischoff, "La formation des traditions de solidarité ouvrière chez les mouleurs Montréalais: la longue marche vers le syndicalisme, 1859–1881," *Labour/Le Travail* 21 (Spring 1988), 22. Bischoff suggests, sensibly, that amongst moulders the homogenising experience of these years of depression left them more open to

the idea of including less skilled workers in their union in the 1880s. The widespread appeal of the Knights of Labour could be seen in the same light.

13. In 1861, for example, only 16 percent of those reporting jobs in these two wards were children residing at home; twenty years later nearly one-third of all reported workers were offspring living with their parents. Peter Bischoff found a similar trend amongst moulders. The percentage of moulders for the entire city of Montreal that were sons living with their parents rose from 25 percent in 1861 to nearly 40 percent in 1881. Peter Bischoff, "Les ouvriers mouleurs à Montréal, 1859–1881" (M.A. thesis, Université de Québec à Montréal, 1986), 108.

14. There is not doubt that the wage labour both of young children and married women was under-enumerated. However, as no labour laws existed in Quebec until 1885, and education was not compulsory until 1943, it is unlikely that fear of repercussions would have inhibited parents from responding as it might have elsewhere. It seems fair to assume that the under-reporting of children's jobs, and probably married women's, would have been no greater in Montreal than in other cities of Canada, England, or America, and possibly less.

15. Tamara K. Hareven and Randolph Langenbach, *Amoskeag: Life and Work in an American Factory City* (New York: Pantheon Books, 1978), 262.

16. Caution has to be exercised when using reported jobs for women and children. There is a tendency now in some of the literature on the subject to suggest that gender differentials in work-force participation are largely a result of women's work not being adequately enumerated. While I am sure that some under-enumeration of women's work occurred in Montreal, as elsewhere, I don't think that under-enumeration can explain away the differential. Nor is the phenomenon easy to measure. More

important, I think, was the nature of women's work, which because of its lack of regularity, its more informal nature, was less likely to be reported. On the problem of under-reporting see, in particular, Sally Alexander, "Women's Work in Nineteenth-Century London: A Study of the Years 1820–1850" in *The Rights and Wrongs of Women*, ed. Juliett Mitchell and Ann Oakley (London: Penguin Books, 1976), 63–66; Karen Oppenheim Mason, Maris Vinovskis, and Tamara K. Hareven, "Women's Work and the Life Course in Essex County, Massachussetts, 1880," in Tamara K. Hareven, *Transitions: The Family and the Life Course in Historical Perspective* (New York: Academic Press, 1979), 191; Margo A. Conk, "Accuracy, Efficiency and Bias: The Interpretation of Women's Work in the U.S. Census of Occupations, 1890–1940," *Historical Methods* 14, 2 (Spring 1981): 65–72; Edward Higgs, "Women, Occupations, and Work in the Nineteenth-Century Censuses," *History Workshop* 23 (Spring 1987).

17. Joan Scott and Louise Tilly, *Women, Work, and Family* (New York: Holt, Rinehart and Winston, 1979), 231.

18. Mss. Census, 1861, St. Jacques, 11, p. 7750.

19. By the end of the century the need for this kind of education of daughters was being explicitly preached by Montreal doctors and by church representatives, and was formalised in Quebec with the creation of écoles ménagères after the 1880s. Carole Dion, "La femme et la santé de la famille au Québec, 1890–1940" (M.A. thesis, Université de Montréal, 1984).

20. A. (Père) Mailloux, *Le manuel des parents Chrétiens* (Quebec, 1851, 1910), cited in Carole Dion, "La femme et la santé de la famille," 60–65.

21. L.A. Huguet-Latour, *L'Annuaire de Ville Marie: Origine, utilité, et progrès des institutions catholiques de Montréal* (Montreal, 1877), 165–70.

22. Marie-Paule Malouin, "Les rapports entre l'école privée et l'école publique:

L'Academie Marie-Rose au 19e siè-cle" in *Maîtresses de maison, maîtresses d'école*, ed. Nadia Fahmy-Eid and Micheline Dumont (Montreal: Boreal Express, 1983), 90.

23. Québec, *Documents de la Session*, 1874, "Rapport du Ministre de l'instruction publique," vii.

24. In Lynn Jamieson's study of working-class mothers and daughters in Scotland, which is based on interviews, she makes it clear that mothers made different demands upon boys and girls in terms of the contributions they should make to the family economy. Mothers "pre-occupied with their housekeeping responsibilities" were much more likely to keep girls home from school to help with housework than to encourage boys to go out and earn. If a father died, for example, daughters or sons might enter full-time paid employment, but if a mother died "only daughters left school early to become full-time housekeepers," "Working-Class Mothers and Daughters in Scotland" in *Labour and Love*, 54, 65.

25. Mss. Census, Ste. Anne, 1881, 5, p. 1.

26. Mss. Census, Ste. Anne, 1881, 5, p. 1.

27. Mss. Census, Ste. Anne, 1881, 9, p. 208.

28. Mss. Census, St. Jacques, 1881, 17, p. 340.

29. "Report of the Commissioners Appointed to Enquire into the Working of the Mills and Factories of the Dominion and the Labour Employed therein," Canada, Parliament, *Sessional Papers*, 1882, Paper No. 42, p. 2.

30. Annual Report of the Ontario Bureau of Industries, 1884, cited in Cohen, *Women's Work*, 128.

31. The fact that domestic service was Montreal's leading employment for girls, and that it usually involved living in, complicates this analysis of the work of children. Girls could work away from home as a domestic and contribute their pay to their parents; they would not, however, fig-ure among the average number of workers found in census families, nor would their experience be captured in the proportion of girls having a job. On the other hand, neither is that of any boys who left to find work in construction shanties, lumbering camps, railroad work, etc. The figures given in the text are always the percentages of those living in the ward, and with their parents who reported a job. Those who lived and worked elsewhere are thus always removed from both the numerator and the denominator.

32. On the commissioners' concerns about this see Susan Mann Trofimenkoff, "One Hundred and One Muffled Voices," in Susan Mann Trofimenkoff and Alison Prentice, *The Neglected Majority: Essays in Canadian Women's History* (Toronto: McClelland and Stewart, 1977). How the working class viewed these morality issues requires examination.

33. Mss. Census, St. Jacques, 1871, 6, p. 137.

34. Mss. Census, St. Jacques, 1881, 12, p. 101.

35. Sydney Pollard, *The Genesis of Modern Management: A Study of the Industrial Revolution* (London: Edward Arnold, 1965), 162.

36. *Quebec Evidence*, evidence of Wm. C. McDonald, tobacco manufacturer, p. 529.

37. RCRLC, *Quebec Evidence*, anonymous evidence, p. 42.

38. RCRLC, *Quebec Evidence*, pp. 44–47.

39. RCRLC, *Quebec Evidence*, p. 91.

40. RCRLC, *Quebec Evidence*, evidence of Mrs. Levoise.

41. RCRLC, *Quebec Evidence*, evidence of a machinist, Hudon factory, Hochelaga, pp. 273–74.

42. RCRLC, *Quebec Evidence*, evidence of Adèle Lavoie, pp. 280–82.

43. RCRLC, *Quebec Evidence*, evidence of Patrick Ryan, cigar maker, p. 37; machinist Hudon Mills, p. 271;

Samuel Carsley, dry goods merchant, p. 15; Oliver Benoit, boot and shoemaker, p. 365; Henry Morton, printer, p. 297; F. Stanley, foreman at the Star, p. 331.

44. Here I am referring to the percentage of children at home as opposed to boarding, living with relatives, or living in someone else's house as a servant. The samples taken in each census do not allow me to follow children over time and identify those who actually left home.

45. The same process occurred in Hamilton, and in other cities that have been studied. See Michael Katz, *The People of Hamilton*, 257, 261; Mary P. Ryan, *The Cradle of the Middle Class: The Family in Oneida County, New York, 1790–1865* (New York: Cambridge University Press, 1981), 168–69; Richard Wall, "The Age at Leaving Home," *Journal of Family History* 8 (Fall 1983), 238.

46. For a careful analysis of the relationship between women's wages, costs of board, and decisions about where to live see Gary Cross and Peter Shergold, "The Family Economy and the Market: Wages and Residence of Pennsylvania Women in the 1890s," *Journal of Family History* 11, 3 (1986): 245–66.

47. Paul Spagnoli, "Industrialization, Proletarianization and Marriage," *Journal of Family History* 8 (Fall 1983), 238.

48. Michael Anderson's careful analysis of which children left home shows that boys in Preston, Lancashire, were more likely to do so than girls. He believes children made "a conscious calculation of the advantages and disadvantages, in terms of the standard of living which they could enjoy," based on the wages they could make, their father's wage and the amount they were required to hand over to their parents. *Family Structure*, 67, 127–29.

49. A similar, but greater, increase in girls' school attendance is described for Hamilton by Michael B. Katz and Ian E. Davey in "Youth and Early Industrialization" in *Turning Points: Historical and Sociological Essays on the Family*, ed. John Demos and Sarane Spence Boocock.

50. "Le problème des jeunes qui ne frèquènt plus l'école," *École Sociale Populaire* 351 (April 1941), 26, cited by Dominique Jean, "Les familles québécois et trois politiques sociales touchant les enfants, de 1940 à 1960: Obligation scolaire, allocations familiales et loi controlant le travail juvenile" (Ph.D. diss., Université de Montréal, 1988).

51. "First Report of Work Under the Children's Protection Act," p. 26; "Third Report of Work Under the Children's Protection Act," p. 10, cited in John Bullen, "J.J. Kelso and the 'New' Child-Savers: The Genesis of the Children's Aid Movement in Ontario" (Paper presented to the CHA Annual Meeting, Windsor, Ont., June 1988), 35–38.

52. The usefulness of taking a category of women other than wives and mothers to test the soundness of contemporary feminist theory on this question is clear in the article of Danielle Juteau and Nicole Frenette who start with an examination of the role of Nuns in late nineteenth- and early twentieth-century Quebec, and use their insights to critique much contemporary feminist theory. "L'évolution des formes de l'appropriation des femmes: des religieuses aux "meres porteuses,' " *Canadian Review of Sociology and Anthropology* 25, 2 (1988).

53. One of the great advantages of the domestic labour debate was its recognition of the importance of housework and reproduction of labour power to capitalism. Less clear in much of the writing was the failure of most writers to acknowledge the interest of men in the perpetuation of domestic labour. For an elaboration of this critique see Walby, *Patriarchy at Work*, 18–19.

54. Ruth Milkman criticizes labour-segmentation theory, early Marxist-feminist writing, as well as

Hartmann's description of patriarchy for paying insufficient attention to the effect of industrial structure on the sexual division of labour and struggles over "woman's place" in the labour market. Looking much more concretely than theorists have done at specific industries, she argues that "an industry's pattern of employment by sex reflects the economic, political, and social constraints that are operative when that industry's labour market initially forms." *Gender at Work*, 7.

55. Herein lies the problem of the "dual systems" approach of Hartmann and others. Heidi Hartmann, "Capitalism, Patriarchy and Job Segregation by Sex," *Signs* (1977); Varda Burstyn, "Masculine Dominance and the State" in Varda Burstyn and Dorothy Smith, *Women, Class, Family, and the State* (Toronto: Garamond Press, 1985), Sylvia Walby succeeds better than others in drawing out the links between the two, but insists on their relative autonomy in *Patriarchy at Work*.

56. Canadian historians, whether in women's history or working-class history are only just beginning to unravel this complex, dialectical relationship between the structure of the economy and the needs of the family, in interaction with both capital and labour's definitions of gender roles. It is an unravelling that must continue if we are to understand how gender was at work and continues to work outside the workplace as well as within it.

57. Some of the problems faced by feminist theoreticians grappling with the relationship between women's oppression by males within marriage, their subordination in the labour market, and the wider forces of patriarchy, stem from the assumption that only wives perform domestic labour. This seems to me a profoundly a historical view, and one that downplays the importance of the family as a place of socialization and training.

58. Here would be an example of mothers making choices that made their lives easier, but which in the long run perpetuated, even exaggerated, men's more privileged position in the marketplace. On this see Gerder Lerner, *The Creation of Patriarchy* (Oxford: Oxford University Press, 1986), cited in Bonnie Fox, "Conceptualizing Patriarchy," *Canadian Review of Sociology and Anthropology* 25, 2 (1988): 165.

59. Psychological, Freudian theories about gender identity seem less important here than the practical day-to-day experience in the home and the role model of the mother. Nancy Chodorow, *The Reproduction of Mothering* (Berkeley: University of California Press, 1978).

60. For a superb description of the complex ways in which women in Paris, Ontario—a knitting town where job opportunities for women were much greater than for men—dealt with domestic labour see Joy Parr, "Rethinking Work and Kinship in a Canadian Hosiery Town, 1910–1950," *Feminist Studies* 13, 1 (Spring 1987): 137–62.

HIDDEN WORKERS: CHILD LABOUR AND THE FAMILY ECONOMY IN LATE NINETEENTH-CENTURY URBAN ONTARIO ⬦

JOHN BULLEN

○

The secret of a successful farm, wrote Canniff Haight in 1885, lay in "the economy, industry and moderate wants of every member of the household."[1] Haight was simply repeating the conventional wisdom of the age in his recognition that all members of a farm family including children, contributed to the successful functioning of the household economy. Haight and many of his contemporaries, however, would not have applied the same description to families in urban-industrial centres. The movement of the focus of production from farm to factory, many social analysts believed, decreased the interdependency of the family and offered individual members a greater number of occupational choices.[2] According to this interpretation, a typical urban family relied solely on the wages of a working father and the home management of a mother for its day-to-day survival. This notion of the difference between rural and urban families survived into the twentieth century and surfaced in a number of standard historical works. As late as 1972, for example, Blair Neatby wrote: "The urban family . . . bears little resemblance to a rural family. On a family farm children can make a direct economic contribution by doing chores and helping in many of the farm activities. . . . In the city only the wage-earner brings in money; children . . . become a financial burden who add nothing to the family income."[3] Like many myths of modern civilization, these perceptions of the

⬦ *Labour/Le Travail* 18 (Fall 1986): 163–87. The author would like to thank Michael Piva, Ian Forsyth, Joan Sangster, and Gerald Tulchinsky for their helpful comments on earlier versions of this paper.

urban family rested primarily on outward appearances and vague unfounded suppositions.

In the past fifteen years, social historians have uncovered patterns of urban survival which indicate that many working-class families, like their counterparts on the farm, depended on "the economy, industry and moderate wants of every member of the household," including children, to meet the demands of city life. Several well known primary and secondary sources describe in graphic detail the onerous trials of youngsters as wage-earners in the manufacturing and commercial establishments of large industrial centres such as Montreal, Toronto, and Hamilton.[4] But child labour was by no means limited to factories and shops. Children also performed important economic duties in their homes and on city streets as a regular part of their contribution to the family economy. This article concentrates on youngsters between the ages of seven and fourteen who worked outside of the industrial and commercial mainstream of late nineteenth-century urban Ontario, usually for no wages, but who still contributed in important ways to the day-to-day survival of their families. The latter part of the paper includes a brief examination of the special circumstances of foster children.[5] The article will describe the various types of work children performed, evaluate the contribution youngsters made to the family or household economy, determine the extent to which economic responsibilities affected a child's opportunities for personal development and social mobility, and judge the reaction working children elicited from middle- and upper-class members of society. Such an examination illuminates the social and economic structure of urban-industrial Ontario in the late nineteenth century, and casts light into the shadowy corners of urban poverty, business practices, reform mentality, and class structure.

Urbanization, like its companion, industrialization, marches to its own rhythm; it does not unfold in carefully planned and even measures. In the latter decades of the nineteenth century, Canada's urban population increased at roughly three times the rate of the general population, a pattern that struck stalwarts of agricultural society with worry and despair.[6] *The Globe* acknowledged the trend in 1894, but conceded: "The complaint about the continual movement of population from country to city is a good deal like a protest against the law of gravitation."[7] Urbanization could take several forms. Many sons and daughters of Ontario farmers, victims of land exhaustion and exclusionary inheritance customs, recognized the diminishing promise of rural life and fled to the cities in search of work and spouses with whom to begin their own families. In other instances, immigrant families, mostly from the cities and countryside of Great Britain and continental Europe, settled in Canadian cities in the hope of escaping poverty and oppression. In the latter case, fathers and older sons often emigrated first and sent for remaining family members once employment and residence had been established.

All newcomers to the city discovered an environment and value system starkly different from rural society. While there is no question that life on the farm rarely resembled the bucolic paradise portrayed by romantic novelists, the city's emphasis on materialism, competition, standardization, and consumption constituted virtual culture shock for many recent arrivals. Skilled and unskilled workers alike adjusted their lives to the vagaries of the factory system, the business cycle, and the seasons, in an attempt to eke out a living above the poverty line. All workers lived in fear of unemployment, which struck especially hard in winter when outdoor work was scarce and the higher costs of food and fuel could wipe out a family's modest savings. Poor families huddled together in crowded and ramshackle rental units that lacked adequate water and sanitation facilities. For some demoralized labourers, the local tavern or pool hall provided the only escape from a working life of long hours, dangerous conditions, and abysmally low wages. In the face of these oppressive conditions, workers instinctively turned to the one institution that had served their ancestors so well for generations—their families. Although old rural traditions did not survive the trip to the city completely unscarred, workers still found their most reliable and effective support system under their own roofs. Within this scheme, children played a critical role.

In most working-class homes, children assumed domestic responsibilities before they reached the age of eight.[8] Their first duties usually took the form of assisting in the daily upkeep of the home. At any hour of the day, youngsters could be found sweeping steps, washing windows, and scrubbing floors. In neighbourhoods where dirt roads, animals, wood stoves, coals furnaces, and industrial pollution were common features, keeping a home even relatively clean and liveable could require several hands and many hours of labour. In the absence of fathers whose work kept them away from home ten to fifteen hours per day, six days a week, busy mothers frequently called upon children to make minor repairs to poorly constructed houses.

Other common children's chores contributed in a more direct sense to the day-to-day survival and economic status of the family. Youngsters routinely gathered coal and wood for fuel from rail and factory yards, and fetched water from community wells for cooking and washing. To supplement the family's food supply, children cultivated gardens, and raised and slaughtered animals. What home-produced food the family did not consume itself, children could sell to neighbours or at the market for a small profit. In an age when sickness could spell disaster for a family, youngsters provided care for ill family members and sometimes offered themselves as substitute workers. It was also common for older children to assume the duties of a deceased parent, girls frequently taking up mother's responsibilities and boys stepping into father's shoes. On occasion, parents lent their children's services to neighbours in return for nominal remuneration or future favours. Although youngsters who worked in and around their homes did not normally encounter the dangers associated with industrial life, in at least one case a young Ottawa lad who was gathering wood chips outside of a lumber mill succumbed to his youthful curiosity and wandered into the plant only to meet his death on an unguarded mechanical saw.[9]

Children filled useful roles at home in at least one other crucial area—babysitting. Many working-class families found it necessary to depend on second and third wage-earners to keep themselves above the poverty line. In some cases, especially in families where children were too young for formal employment, economic need forced mothers to set aside their daytime domestic duties and take up employment outside the home. The introduction of machinery in sectors such as food processing and the textile industry created jobs for unskilled female labour, although it also depressed the general wage level and guaranteed that female earnings in particular would remain pitifully low. Such industries, along with retail stores, welcomed this cheap labour force with open arms. Wage-earning mothers, consequently, placed even greater housekeeping and other domestic responsibilities onto the shoulders of their children. Most importantly, mothers enlisted older children to babysit younger siblings in their absence. In cities where day nurseries were available, even the smallest cost proved prohibitive for many working-class families.[10] These duties took on particular importance in households headed by single parents, male and female.

In most cases, children's duties around the home were divided according to sex. Girls more often babysat and attended to housekeeping matters within the confines of the home while boys commonly performed tasks outside the home. This practice was consistent with both rural traditions and the sexual discrimination characteristic of urban life. A typical example can be found in the diary of Toronto truant officer W.C. Wilkinson. Paying a call on the Stone family in 1872, Wilkinson discovered thirteen-year-old Elizabeth cleaning house with her mother while her eleven-year-old brother Thomas was busy helping their father in the garden.[11] Sexual categorization, however, was not impenetrable. Families that lacked children of both sexes simply handed chores over to the most capable and available member. In these instances, domestic necessity conquered sexual stereotyping.

The frequency and regularity with which working-class families called on their younger members to assist in a wide variety of domestic duties highlights the continuing importance of children as active contributors to the family economy. This practice also reveals that working-class families could not rely on industrial earnings alone to provide all the goods and services demanded by urban life. The entrance of mothers into the wage-earning work force undoubtedly disrupted traditional family relations. But the family responded rationally by shifting responsibilities to other members. Single-parent families adjusted in the same manner. Children's chores usually corresponded with a sexual division of labour, except in cases where this was impractical or impossible. Unfortunately, not all observers recognized the significance of youngsters' work in and around the home. Truant officer Wilkinson, for example, complained in 1873 that "in many instances children were kept home for the most frivolous reasons by their parents, such as to run messages, assist in domestic duties, cut wood, and many such reasons that I am compelled to accept, although reluctantly, as the law at present only requires the[ir] attendance four months in the year."[12]

Working-class parents had more pressing concerns than truancy on their minds when they kept children at home to perform important economic duties. In some cases, children's domestic responsibilities included participation in home-centred industries that formed a branch of the notorious "sweat shop" system. The term sweat shop usually described a tiny workplace, sometimes attached to a residence, where a predominantly female and child labour force toiled long hours under contract, or subcontract, producing saleable materials for large retail or wholesale outlets. A federal government inquiry in 1882 found sweat shops "sometimes being in the attic of a four-story building, at others in a low, damp basement where artificial light has to be used during the entire day."[13] The same investigation noted: "The rule, apparently which is observed by employers, is, not how many hands should occupy a certain room or building, but how many can be got into it."[14] The ready-made clothing industry, in particular, depended on sweated labour. In the simplest terms, this work extended and exploited the traditional role of women and girls as sewers for their own families. Workers discovered that they could earn a few extra dollars through this nefarious trade by fulfilling contracts in their own homes, or by bringing home after a regular shift unfinished material produced in a factory or workshop located elsewhere. In both cases, children accounted for a substantial portion of the work force.

The Globe found this to be a common practice among working-class families in Toronto as early as the 1860s:

> Frequently the industrious efforts of a whole family are employed to fill the orders of the employers. Often, in such instances, the child of eight or nine summers is made a source of material help in the construction of the coarser descriptions of men's garments that are now prepared for the ready-made clothing market. In the same way the female head of the house, a group of daughters, and, perhaps, the male members of the family, if no better occupation is available, turn in to assist the father in adding to their means of support.

The same article described one family that worked on clothing contracts sixteen to eighteen hours per day, six days per week.[15]

More than a decade later, in 1882, a federal government inquiry studied the conditions of 324 married female workers. The investigation revealed that 272 women performed most of their work in their own homes. The women explained that in this way they could elicit the assistance of older children and watch over infants at the same time. Of the original 324 women, 255 worked in the clothing industry.[16] Three years later, federal inspector A.H. Blackeby reported that he encountered difficulty amassing information on the wool industry specifically because so much of the work was done in private homes.[17]

In 1896, a petition from the Trades and Labour Congress moved the federal government to appoint Alexander Whyte Wright to undertake a thorough investigation of the sweating system in Canada. Wright visited factories, workshops, and private homes in Halifax, Quebec, Montreal, Ottawa, Toronto, and Hamilton. He found appalling conditions and paltry wages to be the rule in factories and shops, but discovered that workers toiled longer, earned less, and suffered more in their own homes: "When a comparison is made . . . between the condition of the people who work in contractors' shops and the conditions which attend the making of garments in private homes, the advantage is, in a marked degree, in favour of the former system."[18] Wright encountered scores of children working in excess of sixty hours per week in converted bedrooms, kitchens, and living rooms. Home labourers competed with contractors for available work, thus, in Wright's words, "bringing the wages down to the lowest point at which the employees can afford to work."[19] Furthermore, most employers paid by the piece, a practice that encouraged longer hours and a faster pace of work, and discouraged regular rest periods. Wright's report also revealed that home workers occasionally needed to carry damaged materials to the employers, "frequently losing half a day because of having to make an alteration which in actual work only requires a few minutes of time. To avoid this they are often willing to submit to a fine or reduction of wages far in excess of what the making of the alteration would be worth to them."[20] Even in unionized shops where hours of labour were restricted, Wright discovered workers anxious to bring material home to accumulate some precious overtime. "The advantage of having the assistance of their families," he pointed out, "is a further inducement."[21]

Four years after Wright filed his report, a young Mackenzie King undertook a similar investigation on behalf of the postmaster-general. King found sweat shop conditions to be the norm in the carrying out of government clothing contracts: "by far the greatest part of the Government clothing was made by women and girls in their homes or in the shops as the hired hands of sub-contractors. In some cases the different members of the family assisted in the sewing, and in a great many cases, one, two, three or more strangers, usually young women or girls, were brought from the neighbourhood and paid a small sum for their services by the week or piece."[22] Like Wright before him, King discovered that private homes, not factories or workshops, exhibited the harshest working conditions. Children routinely assisted in the sewing process and worked as carters carrying material between home and supply houses. King also reported that home workers were required to supply their own thread, a cost which he claimed composed "a substantial fraction of the gross earnings received."[23] Many shop workers brought unfinished material home at night and completed their work with the help of their families. King concluded: "It was pretty generally conceded that, except by thus working overtime, or by the profits made by the aid of hired help, there was very little to be earned by a week's work."[24]

Home sweat shop workers received no protection from government. Although the Ontario Factories Act of 1884 and the Shops Act of 1888 restricted the age and hours of child workers in industrial and commercial establishments, both pieces of legislation specifically exempted family work from any type of regulation. Thus, in 1900, Mackenzie King could write: "When clothing has been let out to individuals to be made up in their homes, with the assistance only of the members of the household, there was absolutely no restriction as to the conditions under which the work of manufacturer had to be carried on."[25] When the Ontario government's Committee on Child Labor reported seven years later, the situation looked much the same. Wrote the commissioners: "In poor neighbourhoods in cities the practice of employing children [in private homes] is very common. The sweat shop has been termed the nursery of child labour."[26] Unlike Wright and King, these government inspectors seemed not to realize that these conditions were not the creation of cruel parents who enjoyed subjecting their children to long hours of mind-numbing work. The iniquity lay in the callousness of a competitive economic system that mercilessly squeezed workers for the last drop of their labour power while building private fortunes for retail outlet owners, such as the renowned Canadian businessman Timothy Eaton. Business practice, not family practice, underlay this widespread suffering.

The example of the residential sweat shop demonstrates that the rural tradition of family work in the home survived in the city. But new circumstances forced this old custom to undergo a severe transformation. In one sense, the image of parents and children working together invites a comparison to the shared family responsibilities characteristic of rural society. But the urban sweat shop was a long way from the country quilting-bee. Clothing contracts violated the privacy of working-class homes and subjected adults and children to strenuous conditions over which they had little influence. Long hours of tedious labour brought a minimal return. Workers danced to the demands of a consumer market while competing contractors systematically drove wages down. Middlemen turned the sweat shop system into a chain of command that featured lower wages and harder working conditions with each successive downward link. Naturally, children occupied the bottom position in the work hierarchy. Yet it is apparent from the evidence collected by Wright and King that child workers proved to be the decisive factor in the economic feasibility of many contracts. This observation exposes the cruel paradox of child workers in a competitive labour market: the more the sweating system exploited the free or cheap labour of children, the less of a chance adults faced of ever receiving a fair wage for their own work.

In other areas, working-class families used their homes as bases for personal service industries. Young children carried laundry to and from their homes while older siblings assisted in washing and ironing. In cities where young single men and working fathers temporarily separated from their families composed a significant proportion of the population, the services of room and board were always in wide demand. Family-run boarding houses daily called on children to change sheets, clean rooms, serve meals, and wash dishes. Some homes took in extra customers, or "mealers," at the dinner hour, often resulting in several sittings per day. In other instances, children prepared and carried homemade lunches to workers at their place of employment. One Hamilton woman who as a child helped her aunt and uncle operate a boarding house reminisced about her youth with telling detail: "Others were a family. We were a business. . . . I couldn't take friends home. . . . I always seemed to be so busy working that I never had time to really make friends."[27] Although these home-centred industries rose above the conditions of residential sweat shops, child workers still made significant contributions, and sacrifices, on a regular basis.

Reaching beyond the perimeters of the home, many working-class children added to the family coffers through their participation in a variety of street trades. Nineteenth-century families immensely enjoyed socializing in public, and downtown streets bristled with activity and excitement.[28] A police survey of 1887 uncovered approximately 700 youngsters, the vast majority of them boys, who regularly performed, polished shoes, or sold newspapers, pencils, shoelaces, fruit, or other small wares on the streets of Toronto.[29] W. McVitty, chief constable of Ottawa, reported in 1890 that the streets of the capital city supported approximately 175 newsboys but very few girls.[30] Some children, under instruction from their parents, simply begged for money from passers-by.[31] There is plentiful evidence as well of teenage prostitution.[32] Collectively, these youngsters composed a unique and vibrant street culture which occasionally exhibited elements of ritual and hierarchy. Of all the young street vendors, one group stood out—the newsboys.

Newsboys were serious businessmen, not simple charity cases trying to scrape together a few pennies like the other waifs and strays common to city streets. Some of these lads lived on their own in cheap boarding houses or at the Newsboys' Lodging and Industrial Home in Toronto, or its Catholic counterpart, the St. Nicholas Home. These privately run institutions attempted to provide independent newsboys with decent accommodation and moral and industrial training. At the Newsboys' Lodging and Industrial Home, 10¢ per day bought supper, bed, and breakfast, while $1.30 per week fetched full room and board. Many free-spirited boys, however, bristled at the home's regular curfew of 7:00 PM, and extended curfew of 9:00 PM two nights a week, and sought its services only during the most desperate of the winter months. The majority of newsboys lived with their parents and pounded the streets daily as part of their contribution to the family economy. A small percentage of boys delivered door to door, but the greater number worked late into the evenings selling on the street. Some lads worked alone, while more experienced boys headed up teams of sellers. A common trick of a newsboy was to approach a customer with a single paper claiming that it was the last one he had to sell before heading home. If the unwary citizen fell for the con, the newsboy then returned to his hidden pile of papers and repeated the trick. Newsboys stationed themselves near the entrance of hotels, where they undersold the stands inside, and always stood out prominently, along with other young street traders, around the train station.[33] A passive visitor to Toronto, unable to resist the persistent overtures of the newsboys, bootblacks, and fruit vendors, would at least leave Union Station well informed, well polished, and well fed.

In some instances, the earnings of a newsboy shielded a poor family from utter destitution. When W.C. Wilkinson inquired into the absence from school of fourteen-year-old William Laughlan, the lad's mother told him: "the boy was the principle support to the house, the father having been ill for a long time. The boy carried out papers morning and evening."[34] This entry from Wilkinson's diary also indicates the importance of children as substitute wage-earners. In his notebooks, newspaper reporter J.J. Kelso speculated that some newsboys, who he estimated earned between 60¢ and $1.00 a day, fully supported their parents.[35] Despite their importance as wage-earners, the vast majority of newsboys, bootblacks, and other street vendors occupied deadend jobs that promised no viable future employment. Although some business skills could be learned on the street, only a tiny percentage of enterprising newsboys managed to climb the professional ladder. Moreover, the "privation, exposure and irregular life" that characterized the street traders' existence frequently led to petty crime and permanent vagrancy.[36] In the estimation of W.H. Howland, the reform mayor of Toronto, "it was ruinous to a boy to become a newsboy, in nine hundred and ninety-nine cases out of a thousand."[37] J.J. Kelso added: "The profession of selling newspapers is in my opinion pernicious right through."[38]

Newsboys and other young street vendors attracted the attention of a new group of middle-class social reformers and self-styled child-savers. These individuals objected to the presence of so many roughly hewn youngsters on public streets and feared that extensive exposure to the harsher elements of city life would turn vulnerable children into vile and irresponsible adults. This, in turn, would place a greater burden on the public purse through the maintenance of jails and houses of refuge. In an attempt to ameliorate this situation, J.J. Kelso and other leading philanthropists petitioned the Toronto Police Commission in 1889 to adopt measures to regulate the street traders. Kelso and his cohorts succeeded, and the resultant law, enacted in 1890, required newsboys and other vendors under the age of sixteen to apply for a licence, and forbade boys under eight and girls of any age to participate in the street trade at all. To qualify for a badge, a boy had to maintain a clean criminal record, avoid associating with thieves, and attend school at least two hours per day. In addition to having their privileges revoked, violators could be fined or sentenced to the industrial school or common jail. Although over 500 boys applied for licences in the first year, the police failed to enforce the regulations rigorously and the law quickly fell into disuse.[39] Two years later, the Toronto Board of Education established special classes for newsboys, but met with little success. In both cases, reformers failed to recognize the enormous distance between controlled orderliness as prescribed by law and the burden of poverty. Irrespective of the intentions of social legislation, many working-class families depended on the contributions of children.[40] Furthermore, the arguments reformers put forward in favour of regulation revealed a deeper concern with public morality and family values than with the economic circumstances of newsboys and their families. This attitude is especially evident in the extra restrictions placed on girls, the future wives and mothers of the nation. Susan Houston's comment on child beggars is equally applicable to newsboys and other young street vendors: "it was their habits rather than their condition that roused the ire of reformers."[41]

Ironically, middle-class reformers had no farther to look than their own neighbourhoods if they wanted to observe the conditions of child workers. Although little information exists on the work experiences of the natural children of the middle class, there is a substantial body of material that describes the role foster children played in middle-class homes. The care of orphan and vagrant children had always posed a delicate problem for civil authorities. From the early years of Upper Canadian society, officials usually dispensed with parentless and needy youngsters by arranging apprenticeship agreements for them. By the mid-1800s, private charitable institutions such as the Protestant Orphans' Home provided shelter and training for helpless children until placements could be found for them or until they reached an age of independence. By the latter years of the nineteenth century, however, new perceptions of child welfare had emerged. Most reformers now agreed that only the natural setting of a family provided dependent children with a fair opportunity to develop proper social and moral values. Parentless youngsters and those whose natural family settings were found to be unwholesome or inadequate were now to be placed in foster homes where they would be treated as regular members of another family. In this way, reformers hoped to reduce the public cost of child welfare and at the same time prevent the creation of a future vagrant and criminal class. The primary institutional expression of this view was the Children's Aid Society (CAS), the first Canadian branch of which appeared in Toronto in 1891 as a result of the initiative of J.J. Kelso. This approach gained ground in 1893 when the Ontario government sanctioned the activities of the CAS with the passage of the Children's Protection Act and appointed Kelso as the superintendent of neglected and dependent children.[42]

Although the CAS preferred to place its charges in the countryside, in the belief that the wholesomeness and honest toil of farm life would develop moral and industrious habits, a small percentage of older children ended up in lower middle- and middle-class urban homes where they performed the normal roster of domestic duties. Despite the society's efforts to insure that each child placed out would receive elementary education and affectionate treatment, a youngster's ability to perform work around the home often proved to be the decisive factor in his or her placement. In a circular letter dated 15 September 1893, J.J. Kelso instructed CAS agents to be wary of homes that treated foster children as servants, a practice which he admitted was "altogether too common among those who apply for the care of dependent children."[43] A second letter, dated 22 April 1894, warned about parents with young children of their own who used their CAS wards as live-in nursemaids.[44] The demand for child workers also revealed itself through the report of a representative of the Girls' Home in Toronto who stated that her institution received twenty times the number of requests for girls between the ages of ten and thirteen as it did for girls five or six years old.[45]

The CAS must accept partial blame for the numerous instances in which its wards ended up as nothing better than underpaid domestic servants in comfortable urban homes. Although its members unquestionably exhibited genuine concern for the welfare of neglected youngsters, the CAS, like most childsaving agencies of the time, believe fervently that early exposure to work and discipline would guarantee the development of an upstanding and industrious citizenship. The society's literature unambiguously stated that "girls at twelve years of age, and boys at fourteen, should become self-supporting." [46] For children twelve years of age and over, the society used a special placement form that committed the child to domestic service in return for modest payment. The CAS's unbending adherence to the work ethic created a hazy atmosphere that clouded the distinction between healthy work habits and child exploitation. Even if the CAS had developed more stringent regulations pertaining to the type of work children could perform in the home, it would have been impossible to enforce them. Although the Children's Protection Act provided for the creation of local visiting committees with the authority to monitor foster homes, J.J. Kelso reported in 1894 that the province's twenty-five to thirty active committees represented well less than half of the needed number.[47]

Canadian households in search of cheap domestic labour could also look to any one of a dozen or more charitable institutions that specialized in the placement of British children in Canadian homes. From the time that Maria S. Rye arrived at Niagara-on-the-Lake in 1869 with a party of young orphans, the demand for British children always outpaced the supply.[48] By 1879, approximately 4000 British youngsters were living and working with Canadian families.[49] This number would exceed 70 000 by 1919.[50] Like the Children's Aid Society, the British agencies preferred to send children to the countryside, but they also faced an overwhelming demand from city households for older girls to perform domestic work. In most cases, prospective guardians took few measures to camouflage their desire for help around the house. Moreover, correspondence and newspaper advertisements referring to available youngsters frequently emphasized the children's abilities to perform specific domestic tasks.

The best known of the child immigrants are the home children who arrived in Canada under the auspices of philanthropist Dr. Thomas John Barnardo.[51] A second group of children that journeyed to Canada in the late 1880s and early 1890s under the watchful eye of social worker Charlotte A. Alexander, has also left useful records.[52] Alexander primarily handled girls between the ages of ten and fourteen, many of whom found places with families in urban Ontario. Some of Alexander's girls joined in home-centred industries, such as eleven-year-old Jane Busby who helped her mistress produce waistcoats.[53] The vast majority of girls, however, assumed the normal responsibilities of domestic servants or nursemaids. Although an extremely competent and hard-working girl could increase her wages from a starting salary of $2.00 a month to $9.00 after a few years' service, she still earned less than a regular domestic servant. In a letter to a friend, young Maggie Hall described a typical work day:

> I have to get my morning's work done by 12 o'clock every day to take the children for a walk then I have to get the table laid for lunch when I come in then after dinner I help to wash up then I have to give the little boy his lessons then for the rest of the afternoon I sew till it is time to get afternoon tea and shut up and light the gas then by that time it is time for our tea after which I clear away get the table ready for Miss Smith's dinner then put the little boy to bed & after Miss Smith's dinner I help wash up which does not take very long then I do what I like for the rest of the evening till half past nine when we have Prayers then I take Miss Smiths hot water & hot bottle, the basket of silver & glass of milk to her bedroom shut up & go to bed which by the time I have done all it is just ten.[54]

The letter's lack of punctuation perhaps unintentionally corresponds with the rapid pace of Maggie Hall's work day.

The letters among the Charlotte Alexander papers disclose a life of hard and tedious work that offered little in the way of security and opportunity. Alexander negotiated each placement individually, thus failing to insure that her girls would all receive the same treatment. This practice also left many girls at the mercy of particularly demanding guardians. Although Alexander obtained signed indentures for most of her placements, she had no regular visitation system that would allow for verification of the contract. Many guardians complained of the children's rough manners and poor work habits. Others unilaterally altered the terms of the agreement if the girl did not meet their expectations. Extremely dissatisfied customers simply returned unwanted girls to Alexander, or shunted them off to other residences. When children complained of unfair treatment, Alexander encouraged them to be tolerant and reminded them of how fortunate they were to have a position at all. Many children clung to their placements out of fear that another position would present even greater hardships. All girls suffered from a basic insecurity that accompanied the performance of unfamiliar duties in a strange environment. As Joy Parr has stated: "To be young, a servant and a stranger was to be unusually vulnerable, powerless and alone."[55] One letter among the Alexander papers unintentionally projects a vivid image of how onerous life could be for a working child. Lamenting the recent death of a foster child, a friend wrote to Charlotte Alexander on 29 June 1988: "Poor dear little Ada Hees passed away from this cold world—what a happy change for the dear child."[56] In the temporal sense, a more brutally frank assessment of the life of a working child would be hard to imagine.

In private homes and on public streets, children in late nineteenth-century urban Ontario routinely performed a variety of important economic duties that directly contributed to the successful functioning of the family or household economy. Youngsters not only assisted their families in this way, but in many cases provided valuable services to a demanding urban clientele. In working-class neighbourhoods, the widespread practice of child labour exposed the poverty and insecurity that plagued many families that could not rely on industrial wages alone to meet the demands of urban life. At the same time, the use of youngsters as regular or auxiliary workers denoted a family strategy that was both rational and flexible in its response to new and challenging circumstances. In the short term, working-class families could depend on children to add the last necessary ingredient to their formula for survival. In the long term, youngsters paid the price. The most significant of these costs lay in the area of education.

By the latter half of the nineteenth century, most children in Ontario enjoyed free access to primary education. But this held little promise for youngsters whose economic responsibilities at home prevented regular attendance at school. School inspectors repeatedly identified the non-enrollment and irregular attendance of working-class children as the education system's primary problem. A Toronto School Board census of 1863 revealed that of 1632 children between the ages of five and sixteen not registered to attend school, 263, or 16.1 percent, regularly worked at home during the day. Only full-time employment appeared more frequently on the chart as an explanation for non-attendance. This category contained 453 youngsters, or 27.7 percent of the total. Of the remaining 7876 registered students, only middle- and upper-class children posted a record of regular attendance.[57] Ultimately, the irregular school attendance of workers' children exposed the class bias of urban-industrial society. In Hamilton in 1871, for example, Ian Davey has shown that working-class children attended school far less regularly than did the sons and daughters of entrepreneurs. Youngsters from female-headed households occupied the bottom position.[58] Children of the working class were thus denied the full opportunity of personal development and social mobility that regular school attendance offered other youngsters. Although school attendance among working-class children improved near the end of the nineteenth century, youngsters from the middle and upper classes still enjoyed their traditional advantage. Mandatory attendance laws, first passed by the Ontario legislature in 1871 and strengthened in 1881 and 1891, affected the situation little.[59] Even when parents exhibited awareness of attendance laws, which was infrequent, such regulations proved unenforceable and irrelevant to families dependent on children's work.

This view of public education, of course, rests on the premise that working-class children had something tangible to gain by attending school. This is an arguable point in historical circles. Harvey Graff claims that for many children "the achievement of education brought no occupational rewards at all."[60] Michael Katz, Michael Doucet, and Mark Stern offer an identical assessment: "School attendance played no role in occupational mobility."[61] These authors contend that "ascriptive" conditions, such as class, ethnicity, sex, and geographic stability, exerted greater influence on social mobility than did education. This argument, however, largely depends on data drawn from the middle decades of the nineteenth century, a period when neither the public school system nor the urban-industrial labour market had advanced much beyond their formative stages. Early school promoters unquestionably placed greater emphasis on social control than they did on the creation of occupational opportunities for working-class children.[62] By the latter decades of the century, however, less obsessive school boards injected more skill-oriented programs into the educational curriculum, such as bookkeeping and commercial arithmetic.[63] This development occurred at the same time that the urban-industrial labour market began to place a premium on these and other basic academic skills. The rapid growth of the white-collar work force sustains this argument. In 1898, Imperial Oil Canada employed eleven white-collar workers. This number grew to 6000 by 1919. In addition, public service employment in Canada increased from 17 000 in 1901 to 77 000 by 1911.[64] Although policies of social control and other "ascriptive" conditions remained dominant factors in late nineteenth-century society, improvements in school curriculum, coupled with the opening of new sectors in the labour market, increased the value of education for working-class children.[65] Lastly, it can be argued that if education did not provide workers' children with opportunities for upward mobility, it at least offered them lateral mobility in the form of a greater number of occupational choices within their own class.

One further dimension to the school issue warrants brief examination— the question of technical and manual training. By the 1890s, most Ontario schools offered these programs to boys, while girls were invited to study domestic science.[66] School officials claimed that technical and manual training provided boys with practical skills and guaranteed them a secure place in the job market. Trade unionist Daniel O'Donoghue disagreed. Testifying before a royal commission in 1890, O'Donoghue declared that Ontario's labour unions were "unanimously opposed to manual training in the school."[67] In O'Donoghue's estimation, these programs lacked the depth and detail necessary to turn out competent workers. A careful reading of O'Donoghue's testimony, however, reveals that his real concern was that these programs would flood an already crowded labour market, thus driving wages down and threatening the control of the workplace skilled workers had traditionally exercised through strict regulation of the apprenticeship system. Significantly, O'Donoghue did not suggest that the school board improve the quality of its programs. Rather, he recommended that young people be sent to work on farms. Between the lines, one can detect O'Donoghue's hope that this practice would remove these children from the labour market altogether. Moreover, not all unionists shared O'Donoghue's opinion. In 1901, the secretary of the Plumbers' and Gas Fitters' Union sent a letter to the Toronto School Board commending it on its programs of manual training.[68] This position was more consistent with the labour movement's traditional support of general primary education, as evidenced by numerous resolutions and petitions submitted to all levels of government.[69]

Discussions of the actual value of education aside, it appears that most parents believed that their children had something to gain by attending school. This is suggested by the strikingly high enrollment figures recorded by almost all urban school boards. Working-class children dutifully registered for school at the beginning of each semester, but found it impossible to maintain regular attendance in the face of economic pressures at home. In an attempt to combine economic responsibilities with educational opportunities, many working-class families sought, and received, special consideration from local school boards. Inspector James Hughes reported in 1874: "We have in Toronto a considerable number of Pupils who desire to be absent regularly for a part of each day, either as newsboys, or to perform some necessary work at home."[70] J.B. Boyle, Inspector of Public Schools in London, Ontario, reported that parents withdrew their children from school when the family economy demanded extra workers: "Sometimes they become errand boys in shops, or they sell papers, or they do what they can."[71] Lastly, children who attended school irregularly missed the full benefit of the new physical education and health programs most schools offered by the late 1880s.[72]

Children who worked at home or on the street instead of attending school received little compensation in the form of job training. The street trades and sweat shop industries in particular exposed youngsters to elements that were both socially and physically harmful while offering no promise of occupational advancement. Although contractors often relied on the ruse of apprenticeship to encourage home workers to exploit their own children, the only opportunities associated with such labour were missed opportunities. Home-centred enterprises also deprived working-class children of the solace, privacy, and security that most middle- and upper-class youngsters enjoyed as a matter of natural right.

Social legislation and various reform movements had little immediate impact on the conditions of working children. In their attempt to make society safe for middle-class values, and at the same time guard against future costs of public welfare, reformers concentrated more on the symptoms of social maladies than on their causes. Legislation could set standards for proper social conduct, but it did little to relieve poverty. Most reformers, of course, did not view the unequal distribution of wealth and power as the root cause of social problems. In most cases, they preferred to blame the poor for their own condition. W.C. Wilkinson and the Toronto Public School Board, for example, believed that "lack of proper control by parents" was the source of irregular school attendance among working-class children.[73] Yet Wilkinson himself had recorded numerous instances of school-aged children performing important economic duties at home. Wilkinson and his cohorts might have arrived nearer to the truth had they set their sights on business élites whose hold over economic power forced many working-class families to stretch their resources to the limit simply to survive. Even trade unions exercised little influence over the conditions of many working-class families. Indeed, evidence shows that union time restrictions in clothing workshops that paid by the piece forced employees to continue their work at home with the assistance of their families.

New charitable organizations such as the Children's Aid Society unquestionably rescued numerous youngsters from the clutches of poverty and neglect by placing them in the care of benevolent and compassionate foster parents. But records left by the CAS and other child welfare agencies sadly indicate that many foster children ended up as underpaid domestic servants in middle-class homes. In addition to shouldering the burdens common to all working children, these youngsters also bore the cross of class prejudice. While labouring children in working-class homes performed economic duties directly related to their family's survival, foster children provided personal service for the affluent. They were as much a symbol of a successful household as they were a component of it.

One group of historians has argued that "the family is an institution which industrialization shaped by removing the home from the site of the workplace."[74] Most others would agree in principle. Once free from the production-oriented nature of farm life, the family could devote more time to social development and material consumption. Yet for many children from lower-class families, work and home remained one, and the greater social and economic opportunities that allegedly accompanied urban life never materialized. Urban poverty forced many working-class households to apply the rural tradition of shared family responsibilities to meet the challenge of city life. But the transposition was not an easy one. Urban-industrial life provided less insular protection than the farmstead and presented workers with a greater number of competing forces. Consequently, old customs were forced to adapt to new and demanding circumstances. Despite the different pattern of social and economic relations forged by urban life, country and city still shared one common feature: in many lower-class neighbourhoods at least, work in and around the home remained a family affair.

NOTES

1. Canniff Haight, *Life in Canada Fifty Years Ago* (Toronto, 1885), cited in *The Workingman in the Nineteenth Century*, ed. Michael S. Cross, (Toronto, 1974), 34.

2. Late nineteenth-century writers commonly saw their society in transition from a rural–agricultural setting to an urban–industrial one. This simple dichotomy facilitated discussion of new social developments and emphasized the threat to tradition posed by emergent urban-industrial life. Modern historians, taking into account the growth of capitalism and

waged labour, have offered a more complex and sophisticated analysis of social change. Michael Katz, Michael Doucet, and Mark Stern, for example, construct a three-stage paradigm which claims that "North America shifted from a peculiar variety of mercantile–peasant economy to an economy dominated by commercial capitalism to one dominated by industrial capitalism." *The Social Organization of Industrial Capitalism* (Cambridge, MA, 1982), 364. Despite these more complex undercurrents of social transition, most late nineteenth-century workers identified with the rural–urban praxis. Historians develop comprehensive theories of social change over time; workers deal with the realities of life from day to day. This paper focusses on the second set of concerns.

3. Blair Neatby, *The Politics of Chaos: Canada in the Thirties* (Toronto, 1972), 45. E.P. Thompson writes: "Each stage in industrial differentiation and specialisation struck also at the family economy, disturbing customary relations between man and wife, parents and children, and differentiating more sharply between 'work' and 'life.'. . . Meanwhile the family was roughly torn apart each morning by the factory bell." *The Making of the English Working Class* (New York, 1963), 416.

4. See for example *Report of the Commissioners Appointed to Enquire into the Working of Mills and Factories of the Dominion, and the Labor Employed Therein*, Sessional Papers, 9, 15, no. 42, 1882: *Report of the Royal Commission on the Relations of Capital and Labour in Canada* (Ottawa, 1889) (hereinafter *Royal Labour* Commission); *Annual Reports* of the Quebec Department of Labour; and Annual Reports of the Inspectors of Factories for the Province of Ontario. Among secondary sources, see Terry Copp, *The Anatomy of Poverty: The Condition of the Working Class in Montreal 1897–1929* (Toronto, 1974): Bettina Bradbury, "The Family Economy and Work in an Industrializing City: Montreal in the 1870s," Canadian Historical Association *Historical Papers* (1979); Fernand Harvey, "Children of the Industrial Revolution in Quebec" in *The Professions: Their Growth or Decline*, ed. J. Dufresne et al. (Montreal, 1979), reprinted in *Readings in Canadian History: Post-Confederation*, ed. R. Douglas Francis and Donald B. Smith, (Toronto, 1982): Gregory S. Kealey, *Hogtown: Working-Class Toronto at the Turn of the Century* (Toronto, 1974), also reprinted in *Readings in Canadian History*, ed. Francis and Smith; Eugene Forsey, *Trade Unions in Canada 1812–1902* (Toronto, 1982);

Michael J. Piva, *The Condition of the Working Class in Toronto: 1900–1921* (Ottawa, 1979); and Bryan D. Palmer, *A Culture in Conflict: Skilled Workers and Industrial Capitalism in Hamilton, Ontario, 1860–1914* (Montreal, 1979).

5. The youngsters chosen for examination here by no means exhaust all possibilities. Children also worked in institutions such as orphanages, asylums, industrial schools, and reformatories. See Patricia T. Rooke and R.L. Schnell, *Discarding the Asylum: From Child Rescue to the Welfare State in English-Canada, 1800–1950* (Lanham, 1983); Harvey G. Simmons, *From Asylum to Welfare* (Downsview, 1982); Susan E. Houston, "Victorian Origins of Juvenile Delinquency: A Canadian Experience" in *Education and Social Change: Themes From Ontario's Past*, ed. Michael B. Katz and Paul H. Mattingly (New York, 1975); and Susan E. Houston, "The Impetus to Reform: Urban Crime, Poverty, and Ignorance in Ontario 1850–1875" (Ph.D. thesis, University of Toronto, 1974). These children have not been included as subjects of this paper on the grounds that they did not belong to families or households, in the conventional sense of those terms.

6. In 1851, Ontario's rural population stood at 818 541 and its urban population at 133 463. By 1901, at 1 246 969, the rural population was still greater, but the urban population had increased dramatically to 935 978. Source: Canada, Bureau of the Census, *Report on Population*, 1, (1901). In Toronto alone the population increased from 30 775 in 1851 to 144 023 by 1891. Source:Gregory S. Kealey, *Toronto Workers Respond to Industrial Capitalism 1867–1892* (Toronto, 1980), 99.

7. *The Globe*, 1 April 1894.

8. Most of the following examples are drawn from Toronto Board of Education Records, Archives and Museum (hereafter TBERAM), W.C. Wilkinson Diaries, six vols., 1872–74; TBERAM. Management Committee Minutes, 1899–1901; Hamilton

Children's Aid Society, Scrapbook of Clippings, vol. 1, 1894–1961, Hamilton Public Library, Special Collections; Susan E. Houston, "The Impetus to Reform"; and Alison Prentice and Susan Houston, eds., *Family, School, and Society in Nineteenth-Century Canada* (Toronto, 1975).

9. Testimony of John Henderson, manager for J. McLaren & Company Lumber Merchants, Ottawa, *Royal Labour Commission*, Ontario evidence, 1137–39.

10. "Annals of the Poor (The Creche)," *The Globe*, 4 Jan. 1897.

11. TBERAM, Wilkinson Diaries, vol. 2, entry for 7 Oct. 1872.

12. Toronto Board of Education, *Annual Report of the Local Superintendent of the Public Schools* (Toronto, 1874), 45, emphasis added.

13. *Report of the Commissioners Appointed to Enquire into the Working of Mills and Factories*, 4.

14. Ibid., 7. See also *The Globe*, 23 Sept. 1871, and "Toronto and the Sweating System," *The Daily Mail and Empire*, 9 Oct. 1897, part 2.

15. "Female Labour in Toronto: Its Nature—Its Extent—Its Reward," *The Globe*, 28 Oct. 1868.

16. *Report of the Commissioners Appointed to Enquire into the Working of Mills and Factories*, 10–11.

17. "Report of A.H. Blackeby on the State of the Manufacturing Industries of Ontario and Quebec," 18, Sessional Papers, 10, Report 37, (1885), 31.

18. Alexander Whyte Wright, *Report Upon the Sweating System in Canada*, Sessional Papers, 2, 29, no. 61 (1896), 8.

19. Ibid., 9.

20. Ibid., 11.

21. Ibid., 8.

22. W.L. Mackenzie King, *Report to the Honourable the Postmaster General of the Methods adopted in Canada in the Carrying Out of Government Clothing Contracts* (Ottawa, 1900), 10.

23. Ibid., 19.

24. Ibid.

25. Ibid., 28.

26. Ontario, *Report of Committee on Child Labour 1907* (Toronto, 1907), 5.

27. Interview conducted by Jane Synge, cited in Irving Abella and David Millar, eds., *The Canadian Worker in the Twentieth Century* (Toronto, 1978), 98. See also C.S. Clark, *Of Toronto the Good* (Montreal, 1898), 62.

28. Conyngham Crawford Taylor, *Toronto "Called Back" From 1888 to 1847, and the Queen's Jubilee* (Toronto, 1888), 189.

29. Public Archives of Canada (hereinafter PAC), J.J. Kelso Papers, MG30 C97, vol. 4.

30. *Report of the Commissioners Appointed to Enquire into the Prison and Reformatory System of Ontario* (Toronto, 1891), 372–73 (hereinafter *Prison Reform Commission*).

31. See PAC, J.J. Kelso Papers, vol. 4; PAC, Children's Aid Society of Ottawa, MG28 184, Minutes, 1893–1906; and "Industrial Schools," *The Globe*, 4 Nov. 1878.

32. See J.J. Kelso, *Second Report of Work Under the Children's Protection Act for the Year Ending December 31, 1894* (Toronto, 1895), 12; *Hamilton Spectator*, 23 Jan. 1894; C.S. Clark, *Of Toronto the Good*, 136; and *Prison Reform Commission*, Testimony of W.H. Howland, 689; David Archibald, staff-inspector, Toronto Police Force, 701–702; and J.J. Kelso, 724.

33. These descriptions of newsboys are drawn primarily from PAC, J.J. Kelso Papers; *Prison Reform Commission*, testimony of J.J. Kelso, 723–29, and George Alfred Barnett, superintendent of the Newsboys' Home, Toronto, 729–30: Ontario *Report of Committee on Child Labour*; "The Tag System Abortive," Toronto World, 22 Nov. 1890; "The Waifs of the Street," *The Globe*, 18 April 1891; "The Industrial School," *Telegram*, 18 April

1878; "Around Town," *Saturday Night* 10 (21 Nov. 1896); C.S. Clark, *Of Toronto the Good*; J.J. Kelso, *Protection of Children: Early History of the Humane and Children's Aid Movement in Ontario 1886–1893* (Toronto, 1911); and Karl Baedeker, *The Dominion of Canada* (London, 1900). I am indebted to David Swayze for bringing this last source to my attention.

34. TBERAM, Wilkinson Diaries, vol. 5, entry for 9 Dec. 1873.

35. PAC, J.J. Kelso Papers, vol. 8.

36. Ontario, *Report of Committee on Child Labour*, 11.

34. *Royal Labour Commission*, Ontario evidence, 161.

38. *Prison Reform Commission*, 723. Various police chiefs across Ontario upheld the views of Howland and Kelso. See *Prison Reform Commission*, testimony of W. McVitty, chief constable of Ottawa, 372–73, and Lieut. Col. H.J. Grasett chief of police, Toronto, 700. See also Ontario, *Report on Compulsory Education in Canada, Great Britain, Germany, and the United States* (Toronto, 1891), 89.

39. "The Waifs of the Street," *The Globe*, 18 April 1891.

40. Undoubtedly, some newsboys pursued their profession as a matter of personal choice, preferring the small income and independence of the street to the demands and discipline of the school system.

41. Susan E. Houston, "Victorian Origins of Juvenile Delinquency," 86.

42. For a thorough discussion of the new approaches to child welfare, see Rooke and Schnell, *Discarding the Asylum*; Andrew Jones and Leonard Rutman, *In the Children's Aid: J.J. Kelso and Child Welfare in Ontario* (Toronto, 1981); Neil Sutherland, *Children in English-Canadian Society: Framing the Twentieth Century Consensus* (Toronto, 1976): Richard Splane, *Social Welfare in Ontario: A Study of Public Welfare Administration* (Toronto, 1965); Jane-Louise K. Dawe, "The Transition from Institutional to Foster Care for Children in Ontario 1891–1921" (M.S.W. thesis, University of Toronto, 1966); and Terrence Morrison, "The Child and Urban Social Reform in Late Nineteenth-Century Ontario 1875–1900" (Ph.D. diss., University of Toronto, 1971).

43. PAC, J.J. Kelso Papers, vol. 4. Kelso also mentioned this problem in his *First Report of Work Under the Children's Protection Act, 1893 For the Six Months Ending December 31 1893* (Toronto, 1894), 26.

44. Ibid.

45. *Proceedings of the First Ontario Conference in Child-Saving* (Toronto, 1895), 59.

46. J.J. Kelso, *First Report of Work Under the Children's Protection Act*, 27.

47. *Proceedings of the First Ontario Conference on Child-Saving*, 46.

48. See Wesley Turner, " '80 Stout and Healthy Looking Girls,' " *Canada: An Historical Magazine* 3, 2 (Dec. 1975) and "Mis Rye's Children and the Ontario Press 1875," *Ontario History* 68 (Sept. 1976).

49. Ellen Agnes Bilbrough, *British Children in Canadian Homes* (Belleville, 1879).

50. Sutherland, *Children in English-Canadian Society*, 4.

51. A handful of informative monographs on the Barnardo children are now available. The best among them is Joy Parr, *Labouring Children: British Immigrant Apprentices to Canada 1869–1924* (Montreal, 1980). For a more anecdotal approach, see Kenneth Bagnell, *The Little Immigrants: The Orphans Who Came to Canada* (Toronto, 1980); Gail Corbett, *Barnardo Children in Canada* (Peterborough, 1981); and Phyllis Harrison, *The Home Children: Their Personal Stories* (Winnipeg, 1979).

52. PAC, Charlotte A. Alexander Papers, MG29 C58.

53. Ibid., vol. 3, Indexed Register, 1885–93.

54. Ibid., vol. 1, Maggie Hall to Miss Lowe, 13 Feb. 1890.

55. Joy Parr, *Labouring Children*, 82.

56. PAC, Charlotte A. Alexander Papers, vol. 2, Alice Maude Johnson file, Mrs. Coyne to Charlotte Alexander, 29 June 1888.

57. Toronto Board of Education, *Annual Report of the Local Superintendent* (Toronto 1863), 43. To avoid the impression that this period lacked normal youthful playfulness, it should be noted that Toronto truant officer W.C. Wilkinson regularly discovered youngsters engaged in the usual truant shenanigans of fishing, swimming, and attending the races. See TBERAM, Wilkinson Diaries.

58. Ian E. Davey, "Educational Reform and the Working Class: School Attendance in Hamilton, Ontario, 1851–1891" (Ph.D. diss., University of Toronto, 1975), 187.

59. The Ontario School Act of 1871 required children seven to twelve years of age to attend school four months of the year under normal circumstances. In 1881, an amendment to the act required children seven to thirteen years of age to attend school eleven weeks in each of two school terms. In 1885, another amendment reduced compulsory attendance to 100 days per year. In 1891, attendance became compulsory for the full school year for all children between eight and fourteen years of age.

60. Harvey J. Graff, *The Literacy Myth: Literacy and Social Structure in the Nineteenth-Century City* (New York, 1979), 75.

61. Katz, Doucet, and Stern, *The Social Organization of Early Industrial Capitalism*, 197.

62. For discussions of the motivations of early school officials, see Alison Prentice. *The School Promoters: Education and Social Class in Mid-Nineteenth Century Upper Canada* (Toronto 1977); Neil McDonald and Alf Chaiton, eds., *Egerton Ryerson and His Times* (Toronto 1978); and James H. Love, "Cultural Survival and Social Control: The Development of a Curriculum for Upper Canada's Common Schools in 1846," *Histoire sociale/Social History*, 30 (November 1982).

63. See TBERAM, Management Committee Minutes, 1899–1901.

64. Gregory S. Kealey, "The Structure of Canadian Working-Class History," in W.J.C. Cherwinski and G.S. Kealey, eds., *Lectures in Canadian Labour and Working-Class History* (St. John's, 1985), 28.

65. Combining "ascriptive" conditions and educational opportunities, J. Donald Wilson adds another dimension to the school question: "What happened to children in schools, how long they stayed in school, and how much they were influenced by schooling depended to a considerable extent on their ethnic and cultural background." "'The Picture of Social Randomness:' Making Sense of Ethnic History and Educational History" in *Approaches to Educational History*, ed. David C. Jones et al. (Winnipeg, 1981), 36.

66. Douglas A. Lawr and Robert D. Gidney, eds., *Educating Canadians: A Documentary History of Public Education* (Toronto, 1973), 161, and Harvey Graff, *The Literacy Myth*, 210.

67. *Prison Reform Commission*, 739.

68. TBERAM, Management Committee Minutes, 14 Feb. 1901.

69. For numerous examples see Eugene Forsey, *Trade Unions in Canada*. For a more detailed look at labour's view of technical and manual training, see T.R. Morrison, "Reform as Social Tracking: The Case of Industrial Education in Ontario 1870–1900," *The Journal of Educational Thought* 8, 2 (Aug. 1974), 106–107.

70. *Annual Report of the Normal, Model, Grammar and Common Schools in Ontario* (Toronto, 1874), Appendix B, 84. Similar requests with positive

replies can be found in TBERAM, Management Committee Minutes, 1899–1901.

71. *Royal Labour Commission*, Ontario evidence, 604–607.

72. See Sutherland, *Children in English-Canadian Society* and " 'To Create a Strong and Healthy Race:' School Children in the Public Health Movement 1880–1914" in *Education and Social Change*; and Robert M. Stamp, "Urbanization and Education in Ontario and Quebec, 1867–1914," *McGill Journal of Education* 3 (Fall 1968): 132.

73. Archives of Ontario, responses to G.W. Ross's inquiry of July 1895 regarding revisions of the Truancy Act, RG 22, Acc. 9631. Printed Circular no. 47, W.C. Wilkinson, Secretary-treasurer, Toronto Public School Board, to Hon. G.W. Ross, Minister of Education, 8 Oct. 1895. I am indebted to Terrence Campbell, formerly of the Ontario Archives, for bringing this file to my attention.

74. Russell G. Hann, Gregory S. Kealey, Linda Kealey, and Peter Warrian, "Introduction," *Primary Sources in Canadian Working Class History 1860–1930* (Kitchener, 1973), 18.

RETHINKING WORK AND
KINSHIP IN A CANADIAN
HOSIERY TOWN, 1910–1950 ⬦

JOY PARR

o

Historically, both women and men have worked for wages, but the gender balance in the labour force has varied with time and place. Gender has been an integral part of most job descriptions, and gender ideologies have informed personnel policies and labour practices. Workplaces are different when the gender balance on the shop floor is different, and these influences do not stop at the factory gate. The social implications of the prevailing twentieth-century pattern, which favours men in the work force, are familiar: the struggle for a male breadwinner wage, the reinforcement of social patterns that cast women as consumers rather than as producers in the market economy, and the persistent poverty of female-headed households. When women workers constituted the stable majority of the labour force, and jobs for men were in short supply, the social implications of industrial work have been different. This is a study of one such "women's town," Paris, a south-western Ontario hosiery and knit goods centre, in the first half of the twentieth century. It explores the ways in which employers, husbands, daughters, wives, and more distant women kin organized themselves to facilitate lifelong female wage work and the limits to this local adaptation.

Most women have worked both inside and outside the home and expect that getting by will require the deft balancing of these two kinds of labour. Movement between paid and unpaid work occurs partly in

⬦ *Feminist Studies* 13, 1 (Spring 1987). I am grateful to Bettina Bradbury, Meg Luxton, and the members of the Kingston Feminist History Workshop for helpful critiques of the script and to Suzann Buckley, Carol Ferguson, and Brenda Hurd Gadbois for assistance with the project as a whole. The research is funded by the Social Sciences and Humanities Research Council of Canada under the Women and Work Strategic Grants Program.

response to changes in the economy at large and partly as an adaptation to the changes in a woman's family circle.[1] Who would work for pay and who for love and how many would share in the fruits of that labour has depended upon the age and circumstances of others in the household—and upon their sex. Women's labour responsibilities outside paid work have been more pressing and onerous than those of men, even when women have served as the primary wage earners. Communities in which women predominated as wage earners demonstrate clearly the ways in which patriarchal authority cast women as the primary custodians of kin, constrained the allocation of their labour between the household and market economies, and called forth a dependence of female kin upon one another for both domestic help and cash.

When women were the key employees in a town's industries—skilled, crucially situated in the production process, difficult to recruit and to replace—men took on the characteristics of dispensability and irregularity in employment that dual labour market theorists have commonly associated with the secondary sector and with women.[2] As I argue elsewhere, the interaction of industry structure, labour organization, tradition, and technological change created this sex-specific array of entitlement to waged work.[3] The concern here is with how women and men in households, kin groups, and communities formed themselves around this feature of the market economy. Men who stayed in such communities in irregular work, who commuted to jobs elsewhere, or who were among the male minority with secure local employment were members of households where the family income was collectively amassed, not won by a male breadwinner. Similarly, in these households, domestic labour was derived from several sources rather than delegated to a single homemaker. These contingencies evoked some changes in thinking about women's and men's roles and in the practice of domestic gender divisions. They also encouraged female kin to club together, trading domestic labour and determining by mutual advantage who ought to go to the mill and who might better stay home.

This study of a Canadian hosiery town amplifies Gary Saxonhouse and Gavin Wright's observations, based on Japanese and United States textile centres, concerning the essential indeterminacy of the social consequences of industrialization.[4] But although they concentrate on the implications of labour system choice for the sexual division of labour in the mills, the Paris case demonstrates that managers' choice of a predominantly female work force had substantial, though limited, implications for domestic gender divisions as well. Examining a declining textile community where men were leaving and marriage had become an unreliable subsistence strategy, Diana Gittins has noted the importance for women of female kin support systems, flexible patterns of mobility and exchange between paid and unpaid work, and mutual help through coresidence.[5] The evidence presented here suggests that in periods of rapid growth and steady production, wage-earning mothers and daughters shared houseroom and housework among kin, shifting labour resources between the market and the domestic economy to meet their households' needs for cash and care. Finally the

Paris case suggests, in distinction from Saxonhouse and Wright and in accord with Gittins, that both managers recruiting a female labour force and women employees planning to accommodate wage work accepted as outside their agency the patriarchal ideology that made women more responsible for kin and that set definite limits on men's obligations within the household.[6]

In many Canadian resource towns, mining, forestry, and pulp and paper companies establish a work force by recruiting families and large numbers of single men to isolated locations. As the community matures and single men marry, the surplus of women who might wish waged employment becomes acute.[7] In Paris this same pattern developed, but its gender configuration was reversed. Two-thirds of the labour force was female; the town's principal firm, Penman's Company Limited, grew rapidly in the period 1906 to 1928 after the takeover of a local firm by Montreal financial and wholesaling interests.[8] Single women were recruited within the community and in the countryside, but because the town was small and the surrounding tobacco, dairy, and mixed farming district was prosperous, these sources had not met even Penman's smaller late nineteenth-century requirements. Advertisements in small town newspapers from the maritimes to the prairies brought some young women to the company-owned Young Women's Christian Association (YWCA) and local boarding houses. From 1907 to 1928, Penman's supplemented these sources by an assisted passage scheme that brought both single women and families from Britain. Seven hundred workers were recruited under this scheme, principally by agents in the hosiery districts of Nottinghamshire and Leicestershire. Many family members, both female and male, followed in subsequent years. Penman's built company housing for these workers on the streets adjoining their plant sites and at the same time expanded their yarn mill and box factory providing jobs for men who arrived as members of these households.[9] The other firms in the town were much smaller and more irregular employers.[10]

Paris, then, was a "women's town," a good place for women but not a good place for men, even in the early twentieth century. As the years wore on, women stayed at their jobs. They married. Their brothers and sons grew to working age. And the men in textile workers' households had increasing difficulty finding jobs. The problem was not cyclical, a short-term consequence of the postwar recession or the Depression of the thirties, but was structural, a working out of a labour recruitment system that brought to town more women than men. The wider economy, which offered few female employment opportunities, gave women incentives to stay.[11]

For men there were two kinds of jobs in the mills: entry-level work and lifelong work. In the lifelong jobs of spinning, carding, dyeing, boarding, and fixing, turnover was low. These men typically had wives and daughters working in the mills, an adequate merged family income, and few other job options in town.[12] They were protective of their jobs and secretive about the skills they had learned as apprentices in Britain or on the shop floor. By the twenties, younger men were finding their movement from entry-level jobs blocked by men in their forties who would stay on in the mills until their seventies. Managers were unsympathetic to these new employees' demands for better jobs or pay; supervisors had little incentive to mediate disputes between the two groups. All men in the plants except cutters and boarders were required to work nights, without shift differentials, until after World War Two. Even the most skilled men found their bargaining power with the firm limited.[13]

Some male textile workers retrained and took white collar jobs in town. Others started their own businesses or bided their time until local federal government positions became available. Many of the east midlands migrants returned to England. In some cases, however, their wives, daughters, and sisters chose to stay. Most sons left town. By the forties, the popular impression was that there were five women for every man in Paris, that "it was a woman's paradise, but men always had to work out of town." This, indeed, became the most satisfactory solution for men whose wives had secure jobs in the mills—a daily commute to neighbouring centres where metal, woodworking, and electrical industries hired men.[14] Under these circumstances, men became the secondary wage earners in many households. The optimal solution for mill managers was that these men would remove themselves from the local labour market but not so far or to such well-paying jobs that their wives would be tempted to do the same.[15]

Today the mills of Paris are quiet, but during the first half of this century they ran steadily. Heightened tariffs in the early 1930s protected the knit goods industry from the worst effects of the Depression. During the wars the mills were pressed by military orders. By the late 1940s, automobiles and better-heated homes were beginning to reduce Canadians' need for Penman's heavy sweaters and long johns. Still, during the period of 1907 to 1949, Penman's was a dependable employer, with a stable and predominantly female work force, relatively unbuffeted behind a high tariff wall by the cyclical changes of the time.[16]

Girls started work in the mills at a young age, much younger than boys. Most girls began at fourteen because it was the tradition in the hosiery industry, a tradition made of necessity because no one member of the household earned a breadwinner wage. The firm sought out fourteen-year-old female employees, the supervisors sending home messages with kin when they had a job and knew there was a youngster nearing this age in the household. Some girls had their own reasons for complying: the wish to escape school,[17] or to have "all those things girls like to have, clothes and things."[18] Forty percent of those employed in 1936 got their first jobs when they were fifteen or younger; another 26 percent began at age sixteen to nineteen. In mill families, the consensus was that "when you were old enough you were big enough to work."[19] With this earlier entry into steady wage work, girls were initiated into a pattern of relations to their households and the firm, and the local housing and marriage markets, which made their work lives more secure and autonomous than their brothers' while intensifying the obligations they perceived toward kin.

Although the firm actively recruited girls, boys often had to wait about for a job in the mill. Although one-quarter of Penman's male employees in 1936 first had gone to the mill in their early teens, more commonly young men began work there in their late teens or early twenties (see table 1). [20] In the interim, young men worked seasonally on surrounding farms or picked up casual jobs in town. They were aware from their teenage years, from comparing pocket money with their sisters, that in Paris, men's connection with the market economy was more precarious and less lucrative than women's.

TABLE 1 *AGES WORK BEGUN, BY SEX, 1936 AND 1948*

		Flats		Hosiery	
		Women	Men	Women	Men
1936	x	22.11	28.65	21.10	22.51
	sd	10.36	12.04	8.9	9.2
	n	42	88	158	113
1948	x	27.8	33.6	26.10	22.23
	sd	12.4	15.6	12.65	10.62
	n	144	148	237	152

Patricia Hilden, noting that girls started textile work earlier than boys in the north of France, suggests that as "girls fell under the rigid control of factory discipline at an earlier age than most boys" they became more habituated to and compliant with textile workplace regimes. No doubt long days in the mill from an early age narrowed women's horizons. A knitter in the hosiery mill, the wife of a unionist who worked out of town, remembered that "in those days you could get a working permit when you were fourteen and go to work in the mill and that's all some people knew."[21]

But earlier and longer careers in the mills also had other implications. Because the firm needed more female employees than male—particularly experienced employees who were quick, reliable, and accurate—women knew they had more leverage with the boss and comported themselves accordingly. Female employees started younger because the firm's demand for their labour was greater. Girls who took days off for their own good reasons, even against their supervisors' explicit order, returned to find their places waiting. Yet men who had disputes with bosses found themselves out of work. Women may have been more pliant employees than men, although an analysis of their activism in the town's one major labour dispute in the winter and spring of 1949 suggests otherwise.[22] But supervisors were cautious in dealing with women workers, even when they left the plant during shift, typically after disputes over the allocation of well-paying piece work. Thomas Blaney, a master cutter, recalled, "the odd time one of them would walk out and go home, but you daren't take that work and give it to someone else—that had to be there for her to come back, or you would be in trouble then."[23]

The greater autonomy facilitated by their steady wage work was manifested in the housing decisions of young female migrants who came to town. In nineteenth-century Halstead, Essex, Judy Lown has shown a clear connection between the employer's sponsorship of a women's residence, his construction of company housing big enough to accommodate lodgers, and his wish to exert control over the work patterns and morality of female workers. The Waltham boarding system used similar techniques to regulate the lives of women workers in both the United States and Japan. As Patricia Tsurumi has demonstrated, however, in Japan the companies' goals were often frustrated. There, young women left mill work in order to get away from company lodgings and to physically remove themselves from the purview of their employers. In Paris young single women stayed on at work, but once they knew their way about town and felt safe they took steps to evade supervision outside working hours. They did this by establishing themselves in independent households away from the scrutiny of either mill managers or male household heads, and, indeed, single women were more likely to do so than unmarried men.[24]

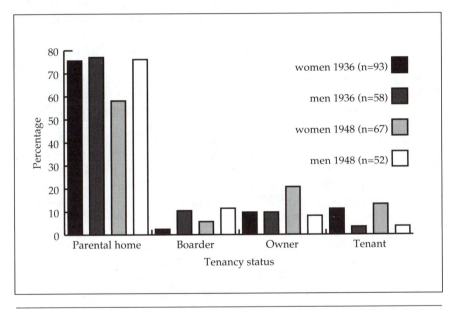

F I G U R E   1   *TENANCY STATUS OF SINGLE EMPLOYEES, ALL MILLS, 1936 AND 1948*

Girls who moved into town to work in the mills usually boarded. Some lived in one of the thirty rooms in the company-owned YWCA.[25] Many women in town took in boarders; some, especially among the east midlands migrants, ran boardinghouses accommodating ten or more mill workers. Conditions for boarders were cramped. Newspaper ads always specified that the terms were two "girls" or "men" to a room. Mildred Hopper, who came to work in the mills from nearby Princeton in 1939 and boarded in four different places before she married ten years later, remembered that "we were three to a room. We all came from the country, knew each other. One would get married and another would move in from the country. We slept together and took our washing with us when we went back to the farm on weekends." Boarding provided modestly priced accommodation and companionship for migrants newly arrived in town, and single men continued to find lodging satisfactory. Its advantages paled, however, for many women.[26]

In 1936, 10 percent of Penman's single employees owned their own homes (see figure 1). The percentages are the same for female and male workers. Although the average age of employed single women and men was the same—twenty-seven—most women, having started to work younger, would have had more time to put money aside. Other single women established independent households in rented quarters. Bachelors rarely became tenants, preferring to continue on as boarders. But there were as many tenants as owners among women known in town as "Miss" in 1936, when only 3 percent of single female mill workers were listed in lodgings. This pattern strengthened over time. In 1948, when only one in ten single men owned or rented his own home, one in three never-married women headed her own household.[27] A large number of single women, principally those without parents in town, bought their own homes and rented houses or apartments, living alone (an unknown circumstance for men) or sharing this accommodation with other single women. These women sheltered kin who came from the English east midlands or the countryside to begin work in the mill, participated actively in the community life, and used their homes as venues for festive gatherings among co-workers.[28]

Single women were not always more residentially autonomous than men, however. In 1936, three-quarters of unmarried mill workers in Paris lived in their parental homes, contributing to the family income. The aggregate statistic is the same for women and men but, broken down by age, a gender divergence emerges.[29] Throughout the period, almost all teenaged mill workers lived at home; the majority in their early twenties were still in their parents' households. But single women were much more likely than men to still be at home when they were over thirty-six[30] (see figure 2).

Why should this be the case? Financial need was acute because of low textile wages and the relatively high incidence of single-headed households in town. Many women lived alone with their children. Some were widowed, deserted, or never-married mothers who moved to Paris with their children because it was a place where they, with help from their teenagers, could assemble a family wage in the absence of a male breadwinner.[31] Other one parent households derived from the stresses of high male unemployment, combined with the presence of stable female employment within the town. Women were reluctant to talk about the domestic tensions engendered when they and their children or they and their siblings were the earners who paid the rent and put food on the table. Absent males merely remained unaccounted for, or were described as having gone away looking for work, or as having returned to England.[32] Mothers alone then needed their wage-earning children at home, but this phenomenon does not account for the gender gap in staying on in the parental household. Approximately one in five of both single women and single men still at home in 1936 and in 1948 lived with single parents.[33]

The answer lies partly in the workings of the local marriage market. When mill workers said that Paris was "a woman's paradise and a hard place for men," they meant that it was far easier for women to find jobs. The search for a spouse, if one were looking, was a different matter.[34] The local marriage market, as an inversion of the local labour market, did not favour women. Hilda Sharp Scott remembered, "As it was more girls than men, if a man got a job at Penman's they thought it was something smart, the girls did—'oh,' they would say, 'we've got another man in town.' " Among older mill workers, many more women than men remained single even in 1948 when cheaper and more readily available transportation made it easier for those men married to women employed in the mills to work out of town.[35]

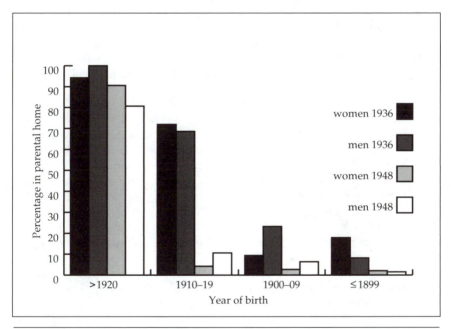

F I G U R E   2   *PROPORTION OF EMPLOYEES LIVING IN PARENTAL HOME, BY YEAR OF BIRTH, 1936 AND 1948*

Of course, as Gittins has observed in her study of a declining Devon woolen town—from which men fled in search of better paying jobs elsewhere—ready access, even to relatively ill-paid textile work, "made women somewhat less dependent upon marriage for survival." And if "marriage partners became more scarce, marriage itself" became "less secure." The "decline in marriage as a source of economic security made more women dependent on work in the formal labour market and upon informal networks

between kin and neighbours."[36] Migrant women, who had distanced themselves to varying degrees from family discipline by leaving home to seek
work, found their steady and rising piece-work earnings sufficient to sustain independent households. Their workplace friendships were emotion-
ally supportive and often the economic foundation for joint households
comprised entirely of women. Many were joined in town by women kin
with whom they were able to share housing and household work and upon
whom they could rely for support in hard times.[37]

Although in many communities, of which the nearby steel town of
Hamilton was one, parents mindful of contributions to the family income
took pains with their grown sons' comforts, an unemployed boy leaving
home took nothing from the family purse. In Paris, where girls' earnings
began earlier and continued more steadily than their brothers' contributions, parents were more likely to attempt to keep daughters at home.
Parents in towns where boys' wages were larger attempted to inculcate a
sense of family responsibility in sons,[38] but the task was easier with daughters. There was a much broader cultural reinforcement for female (than
male) domestic obligations. In a community where women were well paid,
being a dutiful daughter implies both unpaid labour and cash contributions
to kin. It was not unwomanly to take on the responsibilities and satisfac-
tions of a "dutiful daughter," in the way that it might be unmanly to seriously assume the more clouded attribution of dutiful son.

Reinforcing the gendered distribution of familial responsibility in keeping earning daughters at home were the rigorous challenges of female
respectability. A girl leaving home without leaving town seemed to shirk
her primary personal obligations. She also, without sufficient cause, set herself outside the moral scrutiny of the family that unmarried females in particular were understood to require. More mill employees who were
daughters than sons stayed at home unmarried, recognizing that they were
materially better suited to contribute to the family coffers but accepting as
well that both their present sense of well-being as daughters and their
future prospects as wives were best served this way.[39] The deep satisfac-
tions found in being a caring daughter prudently preparing for married life
and conforming to the ideological prescriptions of what a good woman
should be predominate in the woman's recollections of these years in the
parental home.[40]

The average age at marriage among the women interviewed was
twenty-six, twelve years after most had started work in the mill. As Jane
Synge has noted in her study of Hamilton, however, there was more flexibility in the age for marriage than there is now. In Paris, the most frequent
age at marriage was twenty-two. Anne Hedley remembered thinking, "I
was getting on then, we used to say that, at twenty two. Not these days, but
we used to think that then." On the other hand, the late teens was counted
too young, women married at nineteen noting either that they had "rushed
into it" or that "my first was on the way." Another group of female mill
workers married markedly later than twenty-two, in their thirties and forties. Many of these had heavy home responsibilities, a widowed mother, or

ailing parents. Some, having worked for many years, decided to postpone marriage further until they could afford and gain access to a home of their own, sometimes a difficult matter in the postwar housing shortage.[41] One-third of the wives working at Penman's in 1936 were married to men younger than themselves, an atypical pattern that was perhaps a response to the tightness of the local marriage market and perhaps, as Gittens has observed, also emblematic of the greater equality between marriage partners in textile towns.[42]

Penman's female employees worked after marriage and through their early childbearing years and only left paid work after their children grew old enough to replace them as contributors to the household income. In 1936, one-quarter of Penman's female work force aged seventeen to twenty-six was married; 70 percent of those aged twenty-seven to thirty-six were married. The drop comes among women over age thirty-six, only one-half of whom were wives. The pattern is similar in 1948 (see figure 3). Markedly more women gave "home duties" rather than "to be married" as their reason for leaving the mill.[43] In this sense, the pattern of work after marriage in Paris is like that found in the United States in the first third of this century by Mary Cookingham and Martha N. Fraundorf. As Fraundorf has noted, low male earnings "made it necessary for many women with young children to stay in the labour force," and as we have already seen in the case of Paris, "this later substitution of the labour of the children for that of the wife was easier since there were fewer legal and economic barriers to the employment of children, and it was generally considered acceptable behavior."[44]

TABLE 2   PROPORTION OF PENMAN'S WOMEN EMPLOYEES MARRIED, BY BIRTH YEAR, 1936 AND 1948

		1900	1910–19	1900–09	1900
1936	%	13	23	71	53
	n	15	64	21	68
1948	%	59	74	76	47
	n	93	58	38	69

Two further factors sustained this pattern in Paris. Wives' experience in paid work was long and for many satisfying. Going out to work was more familiar, and by community standards more fitting, than quitting to stay at home. Families, the firm, and the community, as we shall see, developed ways to accommodate wives working after childbearing. Between 1936 and 1948, as Penman's female work force grew older, the proportion who were married rose from 40 to 62 percent.

Working while one's children were young was common in the mills although having large families was not. Four out of ten married women at Penman's in 1936 had a child under age five at home,[45] but one-half of the wives working in the mills in 1936 had no children aged five to twenty-one in their households. The average was one, considerably fewer than the mean for similar Ontario towns. Women who married in their thirties and forties rarely had children. In the older work force of 1948, 60 percent of married women had no children aged five to twenty at home, and the average number of children among all married women employees was 0.8.[46] There were economic constraints on having larger families. "Two was enough to keep," Frances Randall said. "In the Depression it was hard to keep them in clothes." More children made it more difficult for a woman to stay on at the mill. There was also some community aspersion toward the fecund. Anne Hedley, a knitter and a Catholic, who thought her family of four too large, noted, laughing in retrospect, "Oh, I had a full house, I thought, I'm ashamed to go out, look at all the children I got. But I got over it, they had lovely curly hair and they loved to go out."

The fit was close between the number of children women had and the number they thought ideal. Gittins also found this pattern in English textile towns, in contrast with mining communities, and attributed the difference to the greater equality and sense of joint responsibility among partners who both worked for wages. Most children were born to mothers in their late twenties, those who married at twenty-two delaying their first pregnancy, those who married later starting their families right away. Working through the first months of pregnancy was common, but most women quit at four and a half months, citing propriety: "You didn't want to be down there when you looked like an elephant."[47]

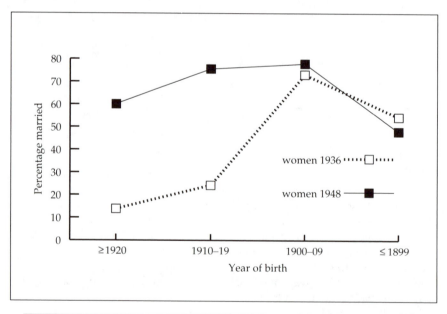

FIGURE 3 *PROPORTION OF FEMALE EMPLOYEES MARRIED, BY YEAR OF BIRTH, 1936 AND 1948*

Principally as a result of childbearing, women's work histories at Penman's were more interrupted than men's. One-fifth of the women in 1936 and one-quarter of the women in 1948 returned to the mills after between two and six periods of absences away; fewer than 7 percent of men had such intermittent work histories. The length of service records of both women and men were, however, considerable and not substantially different by gender: twenty-six years for women and twenty-seven for men in the yarn and knit goods mills, eighteen for women and twenty-five for men in the hosiery mill in 1936. Women's absences for childbearing are often associated in discussions of gender division in the labour force with a short and scant attachment to wage work,[48] but this association is historically contingent. In Paris, exceptionally long and regular work histories among childbearing women were made possible through adaptations by employers, family members, the community, and working mothers.

The knitting industry was vertically integrated through the garment-making stage where most tasks required one worker to each machine and were labeled "women's work." By rating these jobs as piece work, the firm gave women strong incentives to stay or return speedily to work so as to collect on their investment as young day workers and lower-paid piece workers learning the machine. Managers and supervisors also encouraged women to return to the mill after childbearing, visiting them at home or sending word back with kin. They offered flexible hours, afternoon work while young children were sleeping, later starting hours than the 7 AM norm once youngsters were in school, or the option of working on a machine at home. As John Elliott, a supervisor in the hosiery mill, said: "We had lots of work to do and were glad to get it done."[49] Inflexible shop floor regimes for men and the absence of breadwinner wages for any mill worker drove men out of town and kept women at the mill.

The lack of enough local jobs for men and any mill jobs paying breadwinner wages is at the core of why mothers worked in the mills. But it is not the whole of the matter. There was a different logic behind the familial division of labour in town, both within marriage and among kin, particularly female kin. Marriages among mill workers were more egalitarian than the norm. Many domestic tasks were allocated within the household in terms of wage work schedules rather than gender. When husband and wife both worked in the mills for similar remuneration, many aspects of the preparation for wage work became as individuated as collecting the wage.

Men were most likely to turn their hands to cooking. Female kin who did not live together did not, except on festive occasions, prepare meals for one another. Neither was food preparation commonly let to the market. The cooked-food shops of English textile towns were absent in Paris. The resolution of the "meal problem" was internal to the household and more likely than any other domestic labour to be shared by men. The town was small enough that mill workers went home for their lunch hour so that women could get supper "got on the way" at noon. They cooked meat on the weekend to be eaten as leftovers during the week. When they rose in the late afternoon, men who had worked night shift (while their wives worked by day) put on the potatoes and steamed puddings prepared by their wives the night before, and they took full responsibility for their own meals otherwise. One man with a unionized job in a nearby city whose hours were shorter than those at Penman's had dinner on the table by the time his wife returned from the mill. Seasonally employed workers, such as Mildred Hopper's carpenter husband, did both the housework and the meals in winter, just as the seasonally employed fishermen studied by Patricia Connelly and Martha Macdonald took on more household labour when the fishery was slack.[50] Bill paying and grocery shopping were similarly divided in terms of which partner was free at the appropriate time of the day. A redefinition of the sexual division of labour within the household was thus a pragmatic—although limited and patterned—response to daily and seasonal schedules in the market economy.

Even among women whose husbands had been unemployed, sometimes for extended periods, none ever described a spouse assuming responsibility for child care or laundry, the home tasks defined as most onerous. Men played with children, took them on outings; waking night workers looked out for their offspring returning from school. No matter how minimally attached they were to the waged economy, fathers did not, however, change children, bathe them, or assume extended responsibility for their supervision, regarding these tasks as too unpleasant, intimate, or confining. Therefore, when exchanges among female kin were not possible, wage-earning wives turned to the market for help with such domestic labour. Because the mill day began at 7 AM, "awfully early to be taking young ones out," mothers of pre-schoolers looked for older women, no longer able or willing to do mill work, who would come into their homes during the day. Later they relied on neighbours to attend to their youngsters before and after school.

Laundry was, after child care, the real burden in the double day, almost a nightly chore because families had few changes of clothes; the mills were hot and full of floating fibres; and homes, until after World War Two, rarely had indoor toilets. Even in the most egalitarian of households, men did not take on the heavy work of carrying water and pressing wet clothing through wringers perhaps because the end of the process, hanging the wash on lines to dry, had to be done in public view. Bert Russell, who like his wife was a mill worker, shared shopping, cooking, and bill paying, but when faced with laundry told her, "You've got enough work; we'll send it out." A Brantford laundry did a regular business among mill workers in the 1920s and 1930s, making pickups in Paris on Mondays, and deliveries on Wednesdays. Women in town performed the same services, charging twenty-five to forty-five cents per dozen articles, washed, ironed, and returned to the doorstep. There was a trade-off, of course, in contracting laundry out: full mill days and paid domestic help or shortened hours for wages in order to have time for household tasks. Jean Hubbard articulated the dilemma, "sometimes by the time I paid them, they were earning more than I was."[51]

The likelihood that men would share domestic work was thus related to local opportunities for male wage employment in mixed-gender workplaces. However, the firm, although it wished for a stable pool of experienced female employees, had no interest in providing ample jobs for men in town (except during the English family recruitment phase, when male kin without textile skills were found work in the mills so that they could repay their passages). On the contrary, irregularly employed husbands were a strong inducement for women workers to continue at their posts after marriage and though childbearing. Men who found jobs outside Paris typically worked on men-only shop floors with co-workers for whom wage work and preparation for wage work were distinct and sexually segregated and who regarded themselves as breadwinners. Most women said that their husbands would not help at home "unless he was asked," an unsatisfactory foundation for a tightly timed struggle with the double day. Single women remembered days off, when work was slack in the early 1930s, as opportunities for country walks or excursions to Brantford; married women recalled them as "good chances to get caught up on your housework."[52]

The distinctive familial division of labour in the mill community extended beyond household boundaries. In fact, it was the openness with which women ran their own homes and regarded the domestic arrangements of their female kin that sustained women mill workers, providing an essential alternative source of help when there were tasks rejected by husbands as unmanly or when there was no man about the house. Women who shifted daily between paid and unpaid labour from their early teens as wage-earning daughters experienced these two kinds of work as complementary, interdependent, and shared. A different sense of what was time well spent developed among female kin in the mill community. Women were as ready to reallocate their domestic labour between households as they were to reapportion their own labour between home and the mill, in a system of exchange that acknowledged the value of both kinds of labour. In the spring of 1939, knitter Anne Hedley's son was a year and a half; her sister-in-law "had two children and she wasn't going to work, and so she offered, 'I'll mind Peter and that way you can go back to work.'" For the next four years the boy went to his aunt's all week. "She wouldn't let him come home nights, mind you." Anne was back at work and earning but was relieved of the child care aspects of a pressing double day. Her sister-in-law had part of Anne's pay packet, and they shared a sense of accomplishment in the efficiency of the arrangement.

Such agreements were frequent and often initiated by the non-wage-earning relative. They usually terminated when, by consensus, the pooled number of children became large enough to justify two full-time caregivers being out of the labour force. The number for Anne Hedley and her sister-in-law was five. Ida Pelton's mother suggested their sharing scheme, which also involved living together. "They were very busy at Penman's, and we had this baby so my mother said, 'I'm sure you could get a job at Penman's, what you do is what they need. Why don't you come with me and stay,' and so she minded the baby while I worked and I gave her half of my pay." The scheme relieved Ida's mother of the necessity to take out work from the mill, which she found stressful, and allowed Ida to earn higher wages than she could have earned working on a machine at home. They revived the arrangement when Ida's second child was born. Stella Beechey and her husband lived with her mother for eight years after they were married in 1942. During this time their three children were born. Stella returned to work a year after each birth. Her mother took responsibility for child care and cooking; Stella did cleaning and washing at night and on weekends. Her mother used board from Stella's family and her other lodgers to cover her household expenses. When the Beecheys built their own home across the street, Stella's mother continued to be responsible for her grandchildren from 7 AM until after they had eaten supper. These women altered their household to make both staying in the labour force and remaining outside it more bearable, exchanging cash for child care and sharing domestic labour. Through time they adjusted both the nature and the parties to these exchanges and their domestic arrangements, moving between the market and the household economy and into and out of one another's homes.[53]

The domestic division of labour in this "women's town" was not as atypical as the gender configuration of its work force, nor was it consonant with the substantial, often equal, or preponderant contributions women made to the household through intensive wage labour. Given the limited plasticity of domestic gender divisions, women found it easier to develop work and income-sharing arrangements with female relatives. These collaborations depended upon exchanges among women between the market and the household economy and upon flexible patterns of coresidence that opened up the isolated patriarchal household. When female kin were unavailable to help with domestic labour, women mill workers frequently turned for help to the market, finding the boundary between wages and nonwaged work more readily recast than that which separated women from men in the household.

Paris was not a typical manufacturing community, but its unconventionality was made of ordered adaptations, widely accepted by the community and stable over the decades. The example marks the labour practices and domestic forms deriving from the male breadwinner wage for what they are: conventions. It also shows that another way, which relies upon more marital equality and female solidarity, although infrequently recalled, is not uncharted.

NOTES

1. Patricia Connelly and Martha Mac-Donald, in their "Women's Work: Domestic and Wage Labour in a Nova Scotia Community," *Studies in Political Economy* 10 (Winter 1983), analyse the changing allocation of women's work between the home and the labour force as a response to changes in the needs of the external economy. Although I recognize that structural transformations are important factors influencing women's work, the case of Paris suggests that even in a community sheltered by

high protective tariff barriers from the brunt of secular and cyclical change, women's survival strategies involved a continuing reallocation of labour between the market and the household economy.

2. Peter B. Doeringer and Michael J. Piore, *Internal Labor Markets and Manpower Analysis* (Lexington, MA: Lexington Books, 1971); R.D. Barron and G.M. Norris, "Sexual Division and the Dual Labour Market" in *Dependence and Exploitation in Work and Marriage*, ed. Diana Leonard Baker and Sheila Allen (London: Longmans, 1976), 47–69.

3. See Joy Parr, "Disaggregating the Sexual Division of Labour: A Transatlantic Case Study," forthcoming in *Comparative Studies in Society and History*.

4. See Gary Saxonhouse and Gavin Wright, "Two Forms of Cheap Labour in Textile History," *Research in Economic History*, suppl. 3 (1984): 3–31.

5. Diana Gittins's "Marital Status, Work, and Kinship, 1850–1930," in *Labour and Love: Women's Experience of Home and Family, 1850–1940*, ed. Jane Lewis (Oxford: Basil Blackwell, 1986), 251, 253.

6. See Jill Liddington and Jill Norris, *One Hand Tied Behind Us: The Rise of the Women's Suffrage Movement* (London: Virago, 1978); Diana Gittins, *Fair Sex: Family Size and Structure, 1900–1939* (London: Hutchinson, 1982); Judy Lown, "Gender and Class during Industrialisation: A Study of the Walstead Silk Industry in Essex, 1825–1900" (Ph.D. diss., University of Essex, 1983), and "Not So Much a Factory, More a Form of Patriarchy: Gender and Class during Industrialisation," in *Gender, Class, and Work*, ed. Eva Gamarnikow et al. (London: Hutchinson, 1983); Patricia Hilden, "Class and Gender: Conflicting Components of Women's Behaviour in the Textile Mills of Lille, Roubiaux, and Tourcoing, 1880–1914," *Historical Journal* 27 (1984): 361–85; Judith McGaw, " 'A Good Place to Work': Industrial Workers and Occupational Choice: The Case of Berkshire Women," *Journal of Interdisciplinary History* 10 (1979): 227–48; and Patricia Tsurumi, "Female Textile Workers in Early Twentieth-Century Japan," *History Workshop* 18 (1984): 3–27.

7. See Meg Luxton, *More Than a Labour of Love* (Toronto: Women's Press, 1980), 27.

8. In 1901, only 13 percent of the Canadian labour force was female; in 1921, the proportion of women working in manufacturing was 18 percent and falling. In 1931, only 10 percent of women in the work force were married, yet parts of their experience would later be shared by many others. By 1951, 22 percent of the Canadian labour force was female, and 30 percent of these women were married. See Paul Phillips and Erin Phillips, *Women and Work* (Toronto: Lorimer, 1982), 27 and 49, table 2–6; and Julie White, *Women and Unions* (Ottawa: Canadian Advisory Council on the Status of Women, 1980), 8, 37. It is not possible to extract comparable figures for Paris from the aggregate census data, and the Canadian manuscript census is not yet available for the twentieth century. The documentation used here was drawn from reconstructions of the labour force of the mills in 1936 and 1948. The Penman's personnel records, now in the Penman's Archives, Cambridge, Ontario, list last name, maiden name, first name, marital status, birth date, occupation, date for beginning and terminating work for each period worked in the mill, and the reason given each time an employee stopped work. These records exist for all former employees and were sorted to select all those employed in 1936 and 1948. The municipal assessment rolls for 1936 and 1948 are housed in the Paris Town Hall. These records list name, age, household tenure, occupation, marital status, street address, value of house and land, religion,

household size, number of households per dwelling, numbers of children aged five to sixteen and five to twenty-one, annual taxes assessed, and amount of tax in arrears. All employees of Penman's in 1936 and 1948 were searched in the assessment rolls and the two data sets were merged. The statistics cited subsequently are from these two reconstructions.

Two collections of interview transcripts were used. Those conducted in the mid-1970s using municipal funds are located in the Paris Public Library in a collection called "Historical Perspectives" (hereafter cited as HP, after the respondent's name). Transcripts of the fifty-six interviews I conducted in Paris in the summer of 1984 will be deposited in the Queen's University Archives as "Paris Industrial History Project." Those interviews cited here with the pseudonym assigned the respondent, followed by PIHP.

9. *Paris* (Ont.) *Star*, 26 May and 30 June 1920. The east midlands recruitment is discussed in Joy Parr, "The Skilled Emigrant and Her Kin: Gender Solidarities and Family Partition" (Paper delivered at the North American Labour History Conference, Toronto, October 1986).

10. In 1933, Penman's employed 979 in Paris, and the Wincey Mill employed 83. See *Manual of the Textile Industry* (Montreal: Canadian Textile Journal, 1935); Paris Star, 17 and 24 Nov. 1920, 26 Sept. 1929. Interview with Gordon Madden and Martin Hogan, JP, and Charles Harrison, PIHP.

11. On this pattern of female relative immobility in the United States, see Mark Aldrich and Randy Albelda, "Determinants of Working Women's Wages during the Progressive Era," *Explorations in Economic History* 17 (Oct. 1980): 323–41.

12. The average length of service among male Penman's employees in 1936 was twenty-six-and-a-half years; in 1948 it was eighteen years. One-fifth

of the men employed in 1936 had been hired before 1913; 40 percent had joined the firm between 1914 and 1928, and 30 percent of the 1948 male employees had started at Penman's more than twenty years previously [n(1936)=210; n(1948)=301]. Although many men did not return to the mill after wartime service, still, in 1948, 31.3 percent of male hosiery mill workers and 27.2 percent of yarn, sweater, and underwear mill workers had started work at Penman's more than twenty years previously.

13. Lottie Keen, Charles Harrison, Stella Beechey, Anne Hedley, Frances Randall, James Baker, Ellwood Bain, Alice Russell, Robert Fletcher, Bill Edwards, Thomas Blaney, John Hubbard, and Ida Pelton, PIHP; Hilda Sharp Scott and Martin Hogan, HP.

14. Clarence Cobbett, Ida Glass, Charles Harrison, Stella Beechey, Jean Hubbard, May Phillips, Ida Pelton, Ila Graham, Florence Lewis, Robert Fletcher, PIHP; and Hilda Sharp Scott, HP.

15. Saxonhouse and Wright (8) suggest that the precariousness of this balance is key to understanding the labour recruitment difficulties that have contributed to the decline of the textile industry as a whole in North America.

16. *Report of the Royal Commission into the Textile Industry* (Ottawa: King's Printer, 1938), 105; and Thomas Blaney, PIHP.

17. The socially acceptable age for girls to start work became a matter of dispute after 1921 when provincial legislation raised the school-leaving age to sixteen. The municipal council protested the law. In the first four months the legislation was in force, the town police chief issued fifty-one certificates exempting children from its terms, and the council came to regard this as "an easy way to get around the act." Sometimes the police chief resisted, particularly if the applicant was only thirteen, but girls

found he could be persuaded, and the community successfully set its own standard on this matter. See *Paris Star*, 14 June 1922, 10 Aug. and 14 Dec. 1921; and Ida Pelton, PHIP.

18. Olive Cavan, Frances Randall, Florence Lewis, Mildred Hopper, Ila Graham, Stella Beechey, Betty Shaw, Jean Elliot, Ann Eames, Maud Sharpe, and Irene Cobben PHIP.

19. This pattern holds true for the Canadian hosiery and knit goods industry as a whole in 1931, where women comprised 49.6 percent of the labour force but 63 percent of employees under fifteen and under nineteen. See *Report of the Royal Commission into the Textile Industry*, 149. In 1936, all mills, female age start work, n=231; female age start work by year started work, sweater and underwear mills, n=55. In 1948, women, of women employed at the hosiery mill in 1948, 161 had begun in the years 1939–48, 19 percent at fifteen or younger, 41 percent at nineteen or younger. In the sweater and underwear mills, where many seamers were required, young girls continued to be employed in large numbers throughout the period. One-third of the women who started work in these plants before 1914 were fifteen or younger; one-half of those who started in the decade following 1929 were of this age. Alice Russell, Ida Pelton, Mildred Hopper, and Edith Elliot, PIHP.

20. Paul Nelles, PHIP. Among 1936 employees, 39 percent of women and 24 percent of men had begun work in the mills at fifteen or younger. At 95 percent confidence, the differences in the means are significant in 1936 and 1948 for workers in the yarn, sweater, and underwear mills. The 1936 difference is not significant at the hosiery mills; women employed in the hosiery mills in 1948 started work at a significantly later age than men. At the hosiery mill, women who started work in the years before 1939 were younger than men, but many younger males of pre-enlistment age

were recruited in large numbers to replace men leaving for military service in World War Two. Enlistments were less numerous in the yarn, sweater, and underwear mills where men in 1936 were an average of seven years older. In 1936, the mean birth year of employees in the hosiery mill was 1901, n=113.

21. Hilden, 369; *Report of the Royal Commission into the Textile Industry*, 149; Florence Lewis, PIHP.

22. Interview with Madeline Parent, in 1949 a United Textile Workers of America official working in Paris, 4 Dec. 1985. The newspaper record of the strike is gathered together in the Public Archives of Canada, Department of Labour, Strikes and Lockouts File, Penman's 1949, RG 27 467. D.A. Smith, a Paris historian, has brought together interesting interview material on the strike in "The 1949 Strike against Penman's Ltd. of Paris," (March 1981, typescript).

23. Jean Hubbard, John Hubbard, James Baker, Frances Randall, and Thomas Blaney, PIHP.

24. The relationship between male monitoring of female employees and housing forms is discussed in Lown, "Gender and Class," 318–21; Saxonhouse and Wright, "Two Forms of Cheap Labour"; and Tsurumi, "Female Textile Workers."

25. *Paris Star*, 12 May 1920, 2 Feb., 2 Mar., and 4 May 1921, 10 May 1922, 18 Apr. 1923, 9 Jan., 26 Mar., and 2 July 1924, 6 May 1925, 12 May 1926, 11 May 1927, 31 Jan. 1929, 23 Jan. 1930, 5 Feb. 1931. 15 Mar., 8 Feb., and 4 Oct. 1934, 7 Feb. and 14 Nov. 1935, 4 Feb. 1937, 5 Oct. 1939.

26. Hilda Sharp Scott, HP; Lillian Wilson and Mildred Hopper, PIHP.

27. In 1936, all mills—tenancy: men, boarding 10.3 percent, tenants 3.4 percent, owning 10.3 percent, n=58; women, boarding 3.2 percent, tenants 10.7 percent, owning 9.6 percent, n=93. In 1948, all mills—tenancy: men, boarding 11.5 percent, tenants

13.4 percent, owning 20.8 percent, n=67.

28. *Paris Star*, 26 Dec. 1923, 23 Feb. and 10 Aug. 1927, 6 Apr. 1933, 30 May and 6 June 1935.

29. In 1936, all mills—27.6 percent of single women were over age thirty-six, n=94; 20.6 percent of single men were over age thirty-six, n=58; proportion of unmarried workers living in parental home, women 76.3 percent, n=93; men, 77.5 percent, n=58. In 1948, all mills—45 percent of single women were over thirty, n=68; 26.4 percent of single men were over thirty, n=53; proportion of unmarried workers living in parental home, women 59 percent, n=67, men 76.9 percent, n=52.

30. In 1936, all mills—proportion of workers living in parental home when older than thirty-six, women 17.6 percent, n=68; men 8.3 percent, n=108. In 1948, all mills—proportion of workers living in parental home when older than thirty, women 19 percent, n=47; men 9.6 percent, n=42.

31. In 1936, all mills—37.6 percent of female workers lived in single-headed households; 63.8 percent of these households included children, n=170. In 1948, all mills—26.17 percent of female workers lived in single-headed households. Of these households, 47 percent included children, n=256. *Paris Star*, 17 Dec. 1936, obituary for Rebecca Fisher; Irene Cobben, Maud Sharpe, Olive Cavan, and Lillian Wilson (describing her husband's mother), PIHP.

32. The exception is Hilda Sharp Scott (HP) who describes in detail her male kinsmen's decisions to leave town.

33. Proportion of workers living in parental home living in single-headed households, women 18.9 percent, n=74, men 22.4 percent, n=49, all mills in 1936. In 1948, all mills, women 22 percent, n=45, men 17 percent, n=42.

34. There were some suitors in the community who commuted from centres where marriageable women were less numerous. Folktales are legion about young men riding the radial track from Brantford or later cruising about in cars, attracted by the sport of maleness in a woman's town. The young men who filled the YWCA's Sunday afternoon prayer meetings or travelled to attend young people's groups in town churches may have had more serious intentions. *Paris Star*, 21 July 1932; Jean Hubbard, and Charles Harrison, PIHP.

35. Hilda Sharp Scott, HP. In 1936, proportion single among workers over age thirty-six, women 38 percent, n=68; men 11.7 percent, n=102. Although the proportion of older women remaining unmarried had decreased by 1948, the ratio of older single women to men remained great, reduced from four to one in 1936 to two to one in 1948. In 1948, all mills—proportion single among workers over thirty, women 18 percent, n=165, men 9 percent, n=155.

36. Diana Gittins, "Inside and Outside Marriage," *Feminist Review* 14 (1983): 32, and her more recent "Marital Status, Work, and Kinship," 253.

37. *Paris Star*, 29 Aug. 1924, 17 Feb. 1926, 20 July 1927, 1 Nov. 1934, 6 Apr. 1933, and 30 May 1935.

38. The Hamilton example comes from Jane Synge, "Parents and Children in the Working Class," typescript, 40 and 50, part of a large study in progress of family and community in this nearby city. I am grateful to Dr. Synge, Department of Sociology, McMaster University, for sharing this interesting unpublished work with me.

39. Aldrich and Albelda find a similar pattern in their study of textile, silk, and glass workers in the United States. See also Gittins, "Marital Status, Work, and Kinship," 264.

40. Stella Beechey, Jean Hubbard, PIHP; see also Beverly W. Jones, "Race, Sex and Class: Black Female Tobacco Workers in Durham, North Carolina, 1920–1940, and the Development of

Consciousness," *Feminist Studies* 10 (Fall 1984): 449.

41. Synge, 73. For the Paris study, twenty-four married women were interviewed, seven of whom were wed at age twenty-two. Gittins found female factory workers in interwar Britain married on the average at age twenty-four. (*Fair Sex*, 85). Anne Hedley, Ila Graham, Elma Jones, PIHP; Hilda Sharp Scott, HP. There was a woman in town who performed abortions and in 1932 was charged and held on $10 000 bond in connection with the death from acute peritonitis of a twenty-one-year-old woman. But no interviewee mentioned her services. *Paris Star*, 12 May 1932 and 30 Sept. 1937.

42. Lillian Wilson, Maud Sharp, Irene Cobben, Frank Boyle, Mildred Hopper, PIHP; Gittins, *Fair Sex*, ch. 5. In 1936, 18 of the 60 women whose husband's age was known were older than their spouses. By 1948, only 22 wives were older than the 160 husbands whose age was known, 14 percent. Improved transportation provided access to more areas in the search for a spouse and may have made it easier to conform to mainstream prescriptions that husbands be older than wives.

43. One-quarter of the women who worked in the hosiery mill in 1936 gave "home duties" as their reason for terminating their first period of employment at the mill, 15 percent cited "to be married," and 28 percent worked steadily until they retired, n=101. In 1948, 20 percent cited home duties as their reason for leaving Penman's for the first time, 7 percent cited "to be married," and 9 percent worked steadily until retirement, n=187.

44. Martha N. Fraundorf, "The Labor Force Participation of Turn-of-the-Century Married Women," *Journal of Economic History* 39 (June 1979): 416; Mary Cookingham, "Working after Child-Bearing in Modern America," *Journal of Interdisciplinary History* 14 (Spring 1984): 773–92; Elyce J. Rotella, "Women's Labor Force Participation and the Decline of the Family Economy in the U.S." *Explorations in Economic History* 17 (1980): 95–117; Barbara Klaczynska, "Why Women Work," *Labor History* 17 (Winter 1976): 73–87; and Jill Liddington, "Working-Class Women in the North West," pt. 2, *Oral History* 5 (Autumn 1977): 31–45.

45. In 1936, in all mills—average age of female employees thirty, n=200: percent married 40.4 percent, n=168; in 1948, average age of female employees 33.8, n=390; percent married 62 percent, n=258. The Paris assessment rolls list adult household members by name, and both the number of children aged five to twenty-one and the total number of persons in the household. Children under five were assumed to be those unaccounted for. Of the 68 married women employed in all mills in 1936 for whom good household data was found, 40 percent by this inference, had children under age five. In 1948, 26 percent of the 168 married women linked with the tax rolls had children under five living at home.

46. Maud Sharp, Lillian Wilson, Irene Corbett, Olive Cavan, and Mildred Hopper, PIHP. In 1936, average number of children aged five to twenty-one in households of married female mill workers, hosiery 1.16 (n=48), yarn, sweater, and underwear 1.08 (n=18); In 1948, the average number of children age five to twenty-one in households of married female employees was 0.8. In Ontario towns in 1931, with populations of from 1000 to 30 000, the mean household size was 4.16, and the average number of children per household was 1.86. See Canada, *Census*, 1931, *Canadian Family* 12: 37, 169.

47. Gittins, *Fair Sex*, ch. 5; May Phillips, Lillian Wilson, Olive Cavan, Alice Russell, Stella Beechey, and Florence Lewis, PIHP.

48. In 1936, three-quarters of male employees worked for the firm in one continuous period of employment;

another 20 percent returned after one period away, usually occasioned by wartime military service (n=211). The majority of women, 60 percent, also had uninterrupted work terms; another 20 percent left the firm once and returned; the last 20 percent worked between three and seven different periods at the mill. Length of service: hosiery women, n=176, hosiery men, n=119; yarn, sweater, and underwear women, n=55, men=91. Similarly in 1948, 72 percent of men and 53 percent of women worked for the firm in one continuous term; 24 percent of women and only 6.7 percent of men worked between three and seven different intervals, n(men)=296, n(women)=390. See Gary Becker, *The Economics of Discrimination* (Chicago: University of Chicago Press, 1971); Brian Chiplin and Peter Sloan, *Tackling Discrimination in the Workplace: An Analysis of Sex Discrimination in Britain* (Cambridge: Cambridge University Press, 1976); Phillips and Phillips, *Women and Work*, 65–68; Pat Armstrong and Hugh Armstrong, *The Double Ghetto: Canadian Women and Their Segregated Work* (Toronto: McClelland & Stewart, 1975), 141–45; Morley Gunderson and Frank Reid, *Sex Discrimination in Employment* (Ottawa: Labour Canada, 1983).

49. Parr, "Disaggregating the Sexual Division of Labour"; Sam Howell, John Elliot, and Charles Harrison, PIHP. See also Saxonhouse and Wright, "Two Forms of Cheap Labour," 31; and Claudia Goldin, "The Work and Wages of Single Women, 1870–1920," *Journal of Economic History* 40 (March 1980), 87. The same preference for piece-work

among married, knitted-goods employees has also been found in postwar Britain. See R.K. Brown, J.M Kirby, and K.F. Taylor, "The Employment of Married Women and the Supervisory Role," *British Journal of Industrial Relations* 2 (1964): 24. I am grateful to Harriet Bradley, Department of Sociology, University of Durham, for this reference.

50. Kathleen Jenner, Jean Hubbard, Alice Russell, Betty Shaw, Mildred Hopper, Doris Ashley, and Ann Eames, PIHP. See Connelly and MacDonald, 48.

51. Alice Russell and Jean Hubbard, PIHP. *Paris* (Ont.) *Star* listed ads from commercial laundry services and town women offering laundry services, all targeted at mill workers. See 14 and 28 Apr. 1920, 15 Mar. 1921, 25 June 1924, 19 Aug. and 9 Oct. 1924, 31 Mar. 1926, 17 Oct. 1929, 16 Jan., 15 May, 26 June, and 30 Nov. 1930, 31 Dec. 1931, 14 Apr. and 3 Nov. 1932.

52. Hilda Sharp Scott, HP; Ida Pelton, Stella Beechey, John Elliot, Kathleen Jenner, and Alice Russell, PIHP.

53. Anne Hedley, Ann Eames, Ida Pelton, Stella Beechey, and Edith Elliott, PIHP. Note the greater difficulty the women of postwar maritime fishing communities had arranging such exchanges when they relied instead upon their spouses for help in household labour (Connelly and MacDonald, "Women's Work," 64–65). However, there was a similar pattern (to that demonstrated in Paris) of balancing work between the market and household economy according to the needs of the household (58–61).

"IT WAS A HARD LIFE": CLASS AND GENDER IN THE WORK AND FAMILY RHYTHMS OF A RAILWAY TOWN, 1920–1950 ✧

MARK ROSENFELD

○

In December of 1939 Ed Walker was hired as a brakeman by the Canadian National Railways Company (CNR) in Allandale, the railway ward of Barrie, Ontario. This event was not an unexpected one for him. Railway work was part of Walker's heritage—his father had been a conductor and his grandfather a section foreman, overseeing the maintenance of railway track. Having celebrated his twenty-third birthday, Walker was anxious finally to be able to carry on a family tradition. The Great Depression had prevented him from getting work "on the road" and, after completing two years of secondary school, he spent the next five years working in a number of temporary jobs. With the outbreak of war and the need for men to operate trains, Walker's prospects of a career on the railroad were now more assured. His work schedule as a brakeman was nonetheless very irregular. For the next two-and-one-half years, Walker was on the "spare board," replacing brakemen who were off work due to injury, sickness, or the need for rest. There was nothing predictable about where he would be working

✧ Canadian Historical Association *Historical Papers* (1988): 237–79. Many people made helpful comments on previous drafts of this paper. The author would like to thank Ava Baron, Ramsay Cook, Paul Craven, Craig Heron, Greg Kealey, Leora Rissin, Tom Traves, the anonymous readers of *Labour/Le Travail*, and the Toronto Labour Studies Group. I would also like to thank those in the Barrie railway community who graciously agreed to be interviewed and patiently answered my sometimes awkward questions. The responsibility for this paper's shortcomings remain with the author. A doctoral fellowship from the Social Sciences and Humanities Research Council of Canada supported the research of this project, and is gratefully acknowledged.

or the time at which he would be called for work. The tensions created by this type of existence, however, were partially offset by the support and fellowship of workmates in a similar position.

In 1942, Walker left the railway to join the army. Returning home four years later, he resumed his work as a brakeman. That year he also married and bought a house just outside the railway. His wife, a nurse, continued working at the Barrie hospital until the birth of their first child a year later. She then left her job as a nurse to assume full-time domestic work in their home. Except for one brief occasion, she stayed out of the paid-labour force until her children were in their teens, and then resumed nursing on a part-time basis. Walker's frequent absences meant that her responsibilities for the welfare of their family greatly increased. Though promoted to a freight conductor in the late 1940s, her husband still had to work at odd hours and was away from home two or three days a week. Only in 1961, twenty-one years after being hired by the CNR, did he begin work on a regularly scheduled passenger train, which permitted him to be with his family most nights of the week until he retired.[1]

For those of the railway community, Walker's experiences were unexceptional. These were the common patterns of existence for the engineers, conductors, brakemen, and firemen who began operating trains during the Second World War, as well as for their families. There were also many features of Walker's life that were experienced by his father's generation. Though unremarkable to the railroaders of Allandale, the circumstances of Walker's and his father's generation reveal a great deal about the way in which the world of work and its rhythms dominated the lives of men and women in the community.[2] Their experiences also reveal much about the way in which working-class women and men developed strategies, drawing upon the resources of family, friends, union, and community to meet the constraints of their lives.

The constraints they faced were those of both class and gender. Attempts to understand the nature of class relations have had a long, if controversial, history of their own.[3] The study of gender relations, however, has been of more recent vintage. Until the past two decades, gender issues received little attention from historians. Moreover, studies from the 1970s and 1980s that have considered such issues have tended to focus on the experience of women.[4] Histories of men have been largely gender-blind. Most depictions of the past, that strive to be sensitive to the nuances of class relationships among male workers and employers, have not considered the role of gender in shaping class interaction.[5] Yet, as one school of feminist inquiry has convincingly argued, class and gender comprise an integrated system of relations that shapes both the world of women and men and an understanding of that world.[6]

Gender does not simply pertain to the relations between women and men. It plays an important role in class relations among male and among female workers and between workers and employers.[7] The organization of the labour market and the paid (as well as unpaid domestic) work process,

definitions of skill, the exercise of workplace authority, wages, and job status—all are affected by gender. If the structure of work is created out of the
relationship between labour and capital, then the fact that both are gendered deeply influences what takes place.[8]

Analysing the historical constitution and reconstitution of class and
gender relations within a *specific* community can help contribute to a better
understanding of the way in which these relationships *generally* developed
and changed over time. Such analysis also allows for the affirmation, quali-
fication, or challenge of previously held conceptions of these issues. For
example, it is commonly assumed that, within the working class, men have
occupied a position of subordination at work and superordination at home.
Historians have explored the complexities and contradictions of class domination to a greater degree than those of patriarchal domination, however. It
would appear, nonetheless, that complexity and contradiction have characterized gender relations as well. The dimensions of that subordination and
superordination need to be portrayed in fine detail. If wives were subordinate to husbands within the working-class family historically, what were
the contours of that subordination? How was it enforced? Were there areas
where wives could achieve some control and autonomy? If so, why, and to
what effect?

Questions might also be asked about the nature of gender identities and
bonds, and their influence on the formation of class solidarities. Generally,
the literature on male and female bonding argues that ties between men
have been typified by individualism, independence, and competition while
those between women have exhibited the qualities of interdependence, co-
operation, and nurturance.[9] Though it is recognized that the nature of such
bonds has varied according to class and age, these characteristics are still
viewed as the main distinguishing features. Such simple dichotomies, however, seem to belie the intricacy of ties between men and between women,
as recent studies of working-class masculinity, for example, have indicated.[10]
The degree to which concepts of masculinity or femininity have prompted
or undermined solidarity among workers and struggles against class
inequality would also seem to defy any simple generalization. Again, in the
case of working-class masculinity, some sociologists and historians have
stated that concepts of "manliness" have on the whole undermined unity
among workers on the job,[11] while others have suggested that the relationship between class and gender identity has been contradictory and ambiguous. Moreover, the latter observe that gender identities are not immutable;
they can shift in emphasis and meaning as the conditions that shape them
alter.[12] Such studies also underscore the important cognitive and emotional
dimensions of both class and gender identities. To understand the actions of
working-class women and men, one needs to know not only the experiences that helped mould their world view, but also the complex of emotions
that influenced gender and class interaction.[13]

The following study is an oral history that explores the relationship
among work, family, class, and gender in the railway ward of Barrie,

Ontario, as experienced by two generations of engineers, firemen, conductors, and brakemen and their families between the 1920s and the 1950s.[14] It begins with an examination of the structural constraints faced by the men and women of the railroad community, and looks at the world of both paid and domestic unpaid labour. As feminist scholars have emphasized, an examination of the interconnections between these two spheres is essential to an understanding of the forces that shaped the women and men of the working-class community. These interconnections reveal much about working-class reproduction and survival and the social construction of gender.[15] The study considers the implications of such structural constraints for railroaders and their families, and the strategies that were developed in response. It then examines the role of gender identity in shaping relations between husbands and wives, and class relations on the railway, though only certain features of these relationships are investigated. For both the men and women of Allandale, the fact of being working class was experienced in gender-specific ways. Conceptions of masculinity and femininity and of men's and women's "proper sphere"—all shaped and were derived from those experiences. The study concludes with some general comments on the nature of class and gender relations in Allandale over a forty-year period.

o

> On the railroad there was no night or day. (Dave Kingston, conductor, born 1892, hired 1913)

> It's a very poor life. I mean layin' in the bunk houses waitin' to go to work. Waitin' to be called. You're away from home more than you're ever home. . . . I was away 300 days out of 365. (Jim Blythe, engineer, born 1913, hired 1940)

> You never knew from one day to the next what you were going to do. . . . I might go to work at five o'clock in the morning or I might go at midnight. (Norman Crane, conductor, born 1914, hired 1942)

Work, family, and community life in Allandale were profoundly influenced by the railway. The historical recollections of the ward's residents were often prefaced by the comment that "this was a railroader's place." Indeed, until after the Second World War, the economies of Allandale and of Barrie itself were dependent on the railroad—a pattern that had existed since the mid-nineteenth century. Allandale was an important divisional point on both the Grand Trunk Railway (GTR) and its successor in 1923, the Canadian National Railways Company. In a town with a relatively small population and few industries, the railroad was well known as the major employer. Its work force comprised some five hundred employees, approximately 40 percent of whom were running-trades workers.[16] These consisted of what were known as "head-end" and "tail-end" crews of men. The "head-end" was comprised of firemen, responsible for maintaining the steam engine's supply of coal fuel, and engineers who, as former firemen, had gained enough experience and skill to run a locomotive engine. The "tail-end" was comprised of brakemen, responsible, among other duties, for coupling and uncoupling railway cars and switching trains from one track to another, and conductors who, as former brakemen, had gained enough skill and knowledge to oversee and be accountable for the general operation of a train.

To be employed by the railway as a fireman, engineer, brakeman, or conductor was to enter a world where the rhythms of work were in the main chaotic and unpredictable. The hours were long and the work demanded that these men absent themselves from their homes for days, and sometimes for weeks or months. An engineman or a trainman based in Allandale could be moved to any one of a number of terminals that fell within his union's northern Ontario seniority district. Seniority determined the location, amount, and type of work assigned to employees.[17] Most running-trades crews, however, operated freight trains for the greatest part of their career on the road. These trains ran on a twenty-four hour schedule. Passenger trains offered steadier and more predictable hours of work, but only towards retirement were most running-trades workers entitled to operate such trains exclusively.[18]

The rhythms of railway labour were also shaped by cyclical changes in the economy. Work patterns for the generation hired before 1920 were disrupted by the massive layoffs of the Great Depression.[19] Men who had over fifteen years' seniority were laid off for months or longer. Some had to leave their families to work out of terminals located in the far reaches of northern Ontario. Those who normally would have been recruited in the 1930s had to wait until the outbreak of World War II before they were given positions. As the most junior workers, they spent the duration of the war in the north while their families, in many cases, remained in Allandale.[20]

Engine and train crews, however, were able to gain some control over their work rhythms. They could use their elaborate and extensive seniority arrangements and union regulations to intensify their workload. Since pensions were based on the best ten years of earnings, many men chose to labour long hours and take any runs to which they were entitled towards the end of their career when their work schedules should have been the least disruptive. Some also manipulated the payment system where wages were based on the number of miles travelled and quotas were set limiting the miles a worker could accumulate in a month.[21] By exceeding his quota, a running-trades worker not only increased his own workload but also decreased that of others. This type of manoeuvring was not regarded favourably: "Fellas would stay up all night tryin' to figure out a goddamn angle till they get another trip or steal a trip off you or some goddamn thing. . . . They just wanted the money."[22]

Union regulations were also applied in an attempt to regulate the intensity of one's workload in a period before paid holidays and vacations. Crews were allowed to book rest after twelve hours on the job. They could also book off sick in order to be with their families. There were, nevertheless, financial limits to such controls. As one engineer commented, "if you felt like being off, you booked off or you booked sick. Usually they let you off. But years ago when you had a family you couldn't book off because you couldn't afford it. You didn't have the money."[23] The high unemployment of the 1930s also had its effect: "In them days [the 1930s] the unions weren't so strong. And very few booked rest which wasn't good. They'd make you stay on and then penalized you if you made a mistake."[24]

Men also devised informal ways of gaining some limited control over their work rhythms. When summoned to work by the call boy, they would arrange to be absent for the call and this resulted in the next available crew member on the seniority list having to go to work. Some had an arrangement with the call boys that allowed them to get runs which were both profitable and relatively short in duration: "I used them call boys pretty good down there and they used me pretty good too. I got a lot of good trips out of them. . . . I never paid the buggers but when they were stuck I always went. . . . You knew when you worked you'd always get somethin' back. You always did."[25] In addition, when the opportunity arose, engine-crew and train-crew members would try to arrange to work with those who were known to be able to "get over the road" as quickly as possible. Running-trades workers were quite aware of the differences in the skill of their work-mates and often attempted to avoid those who were slow or unsafe.

Despite these stratagems and regulations, however, a large portion of a fireman's, engineer's, brakeman's, and conductor's employment on the rail-road involved uncertain hours, frequent absences from home, and a highly variable supply of work. It was characterized neither by the certainties of industrial shift-work time nor that of "white collar" work. Often the most predictable feature of this work was its unpredictability. Indeed, though work in the running trades offered more economic security than most working-class occupations, it came with a price. The rhythms of labour in the running trades during these decades essentially constituted a special category of industrial work time, incorporating its most disruptive features. Men had to be at work at the designated time; yet at least in the case of most freight runs there was no set time at which work would be over. One could always book off after twelve hours, but there were limitations in doing so. Furthermore, from one day to the next, many workers would not know when work would begin again.[26] Such rhythms could not but have profound implications for the work and non-work lives of these railwaymen and their families.

o

The big burden fell on the women, to look after the home and children, and so on. . . . The boys, both of them grew to realize that there were many things dad couldn't participate in, that mother had to fulfill both functions as both parents. (Ed Walker, conductor, born 1916, hired 1939)

> They really had to adapt. They had to adapt to not only running the family, the home, and it didn't matter what created [a problem], they had to solve it. So they became, well, real pros. There wasn't anything they didn't do. (Elizabeth Burt, born 1918, daughter of a conductor)

Given the chaotic and often unpredictable work rhythms of engine and train crews, it would have been difficult for trains to operate, and for the families of these men to remain intact, without the existence of a particular configuration of gender relations. In Allandale, as with other railway and nonrailway communities of this period, households were constituted and gender divisions shaped according to the predominant twentieth-century pattern. After marriage, husbands were the sole or primary wage earners and their wives were responsible for unpaid domestic labour. There were, however, variations in this pattern between the two generations of families whose husbands or wives were interviewed. The first generation of wives were married by the end of the 1920s, and all worked in the paid labour force or on their family farms before marriage.[27] Upon marriage, they left the paid labour force or farm to assume full-time domestic work in their new homes.[28]

Paid work after marriage was more common for the second generation of wives. As with those of the previous generation, the wives who were married in the late 1930s or early 1940s worked before marriage, in the paid-labour force or on family farms, in occupations that conformed to the sexual division of labour of the time.[29] One-third continued to work outside the home after marriage, before they had their first child. With the arrival of their first child, which was generally within a year or two of marriage, the majority withdrew from the wage-labour force until their children were older.[30] One-third re-entered the paid work force at a later stage of their lives.

There were many interrelated pressures that shaped the after-marriage wage-work patterns of these wives. The economy of Barrie offered little opportunity for the wives of the first generation, most of whom were either residents of Allandale or moved there after marriage.[31] The town's female workforce was small and concentrated into service, clerical, and retail occupations, all of which were notoriously poorly paid. As a result of the Second World War, there were greater work opportunities in town for the wives of the second generation who were from Allandale or moved there in the late 1930s and early 1940s.[32] By then, however, many already had children for whom they were responsible. Unlike the first generation, the majority of wives of the second generation married before their husbands were able to get a position on the railroad. Less than one-third married after their husbands had already taken up railroading.[33]

The rhythms of work in the running trades made it *necessary* that there be a full-time domestic worker in the home after the first child was born. Also, it would have been extremely difficult for a woman to maintain a family on her own income. In view of the fundamental role these women had in providing for their families' well being, there was little economic sense in wives re-entering the wage-labour market while their children were growing up. Re-entry would only have increased the burdens of women already labouring under the time-consuming and often stressful conditions of domestic work.[34]

The ability of engine and train crews to earn enough on their own to support their families for most, if not all, of their career in the running trades allowed wives to assume domestic responsibilities without having to return to the paid work force. Compared to other sections of the railroad labour force, and to most working-class occupations in general, running-trades work was one of the most highly paid. The earnings of these men, however, varied according to occupation and seniority. Firemen and brakemen were paid less per mile than engineers and conductors. The income of junior men improved as they gained seniority and were offered more work and the possibility of promotion.[35]

In spite of these circumstances, earning enough to maintain a family was also at times very difficult for an engineman or trainmen, and this made it necessary for a wife to devise strategies to stretch family income in ways that attempted to avoid her re-entry into the paid labour force. For the generation of wives whose husbands began railway work in the 1920s or before, family income was limited by the layoffs of the Great Depression and a reduced work schedule. In families where the husband started railway work in the late 1930s or early 1940s, previous savings were minimal or nonexistent. As well, in the experience of both generations, family income was limited by a husband's need to pay for living expenses when he was away from home and working in northern Ontario. As the wife of an engineer recalled, "you were keeping two homes going. I was here and he was up [in] Hornepayne and Nakina and money wasn't like it is today. I can remember that if you got fifty dollars every two weeks you thought you were in heaven."[36]

Despite these fluctuations in family income, employment in the running trades still brought greater financial security than most working-class occupations. For the wives of these workers—the majority of whom came from farming or working-class backgrounds—marriage, and particularly marriage to a railroader, also offered more economic security than that of women forced to subsist on the wages paid to female employees in the labour market.[37] As was the case of work in the running trades, however, labouring as a wife and mother in a railroader's family had its price.

In many ways these women faced a situation similar to that of all working-class wives of the period. Like them, they were primarily responsible for all facets of domestic labour—housework, reproduction, and care of dependent children, and of working and dependent adults. Their labour was essential to the maintenance of the family and its wage earners and, within a larger framework, essential to the maintenance of workers as a class and to the economic conventions of industrial capitalism. Their domestic labour was also shaped by the work schedules of their husbands or, if they re-entered or remained in the paid labour market, by the added demands of the "double day."[38] The rhythms of work in the running trades, however, had unique implications for the wives of engine and train crews.

Wives had to juggle the schedules of their own domestic routines to meet those of their husbands. In many cases this involved getting up at odd hours to prepare the meals that husbands would take to work. Dave Kingston's wife had to tend to the needs not only of her husband but also those of her cousin, who boarded with them for almost ten years: "My wife used to have to maybe get up twice in the night. I might go out at one o'clock in the morning and he'd go out at three or four o'clock in the morning. And she'd have to get up and pack that basket."[39] The demands placed on wives to cater both to husband and children could be especially exhausting.

When husbands were home, the rhythms of domestic labour could be actually more chaotic than when they were away for long periods of time. Not only did wives have to prepare a meal at odd hours, but also the irregular sleeping patterns of their husbands meant that children had to be kept quiet while their fathers rested during the day. The long absence of a husband who had to work in the north was, in one sense, easier for a wife. Domestic routines could be organized in a less chaotic fashion, in accordance with a wife's own preferences. Long separations from husbands, nevertheless, also created difficulties for these women. They had primary responsibility for the financial management of the household and for the care of their children. Most working-class wives also had these responsibilities. However, railway husbands were often not around to offer support in instances where such help might have been given. "We were left with everythin'," recalled a conductor's wife. "It seemed always if there was an emergency come up they were on the other end of the line. You didn't have a husband."[40]

After long separations, and even after frequent short absences, family members had to make emotional adjustments. The need to be away from home often meant that running-trades workers had limited contact with their children. When a man came home and was in a position to take on some child care responsibilities, his priorities could differ from those of his wife. The recollections of Joe Mathews, an engineer, underscored the conflicts that could result: "[My wife] more or less brought the children up. I was never home. She'd say once in a while, oh you have to straighten that guy out, one of the girls out. I said listen, I've been away for four days. . . . I want to hug 'em, I don't want to be fightin' with 'em."[41]

As tension managers, wives were expected to deal with the work frustrations of their spouses and those caused by their husband's inability to participate in family events.[42] A certain degree of understanding about railway operations was necessary in order that a wife be able to co-ordinate her own routines with her husband's needs. This understanding was gained through conversations with spouses and other railroaders' wives and, for those who came from railway families, from having observed their fathers on the job. Despite a wife's knowledge and abilities, however, explosive situations could not always be avoided. The intensity of frustration that at least some women could feel was indicated in one wife's comment: "That's the trouble. We all were for our husbands. He's like number one. Like God himself coming in the door and out the door. . . . I used to think for a long time 'You make me so sick I wish to heck he'd run off the track.' Then I prayed like eff that he wouldn't."[43]

Though sometimes exasperated, a railway wife was also keenly aware of her significance to the family's welfare. Household economic management was particularly important to these women. The most common pattern for both generations was that wives would be given their husbands' pay cheque and then would allocate money for groceries, clothing and material to make clothing, furniture, and other essential items. Husbands would then take an allowance or a small portion of their wages for themselves.[44] When two households had to be maintained or in times of economic crisis, some wives augmented family income by offering room and board to single railroaders, by taking in washing for a fee, or by selling knitted goods. Planting vegetable gardens, doing work that might otherwise be purchased on the market, or putting the needs of other family members ahead of one's own were other ways of making ends meet when family resources were limited.[45]

The financial balancing act wives had to perform was both a source of pride and a cause for anguish. When managing finances, these women had autonomy in determining daily expenditures, though this appeared to be less so concerning the purchase of large items. Their position as financial managers was based on a fundamental dependence on their husband's wages. This dependence could have dire consequences if a husband put his own priorities ahead of his family's, and squandered away his pay cheque in gambling and drinking. Most wives, however, were not faced with such a situation. Decisions about household expenditures were often amicably made. Yet, as the wage earner, a husband could also exercise his prerogative and refuse to sanction certain expenses. Rebecca Crane recalled that "it took a lot of years [to work decisions out] because the first few years the man was the boss. There was no question about it."[46] Her comments were echoed by others.

The wives of running-trades workers found themselves in a situation that could be intensely lonely and sometimes exasperating. Their loneliness was not only a product of being separated from their spouses for long periods of time. It was also the result of the work situation of these women. As others have observed, the domestic labour process is isolated, private, and fragmented, and this contrasts sharply with the socialized and integrated process of industrial capitalist production.[47] Wives were quite aware of the conditions shaping their isolation and loneliness, on the whole more so than their husbands.

Though much of their time was spent doing domestic work in the home, wives also had support networks that played a very significant role in aiding them to deal with the isolation and loneliness of their situation. The most important of these networks was that of kinship. For both generations, family provided the material and emotional support that helped both husbands and wives survive the tensions of railroad life. Many wives decided to remain in Allandale rather than move north to join their husbands because of the support offered by their relatives.[48]

Most railroaders had what would technically be considered nuclear family households. The close proximity of kin, however, made the isolation of the household unit more apparent than real.[49] In addition, at specific periods in the life cycle of a number of running-trades workers, the household was extended to include other close family members. Wilma Laidlaw, a conductor's daughter who married a brakeman in 1920, lived with her parents and her brother in an extended family household after marriage. Even after having children, she continued to live with her parents until her husband bought a house across the road from her mother and father. In her extended family situation, housework was done collectively by the women, though "everyone seemed to go their own way, do their own thing" with regard to social activities. Each component of the household was also financially self-sufficient, though family members shared household expenses and collective management, an arrangement that reduced their living costs. When Wilma's husband went to London, Ontario, to work for seven years during the Great Depression she would see her family daily.[50] Wilma Laidlaw's situation was not unique. After they were married, Catherine Roy lived just up the street from her family, Vera Miller took a place next door to her parents, and Rosemary Sharpe settled only a few houses away from her mother and father.[51]

Allandale railway families not only provided emotional and material support, they were also essential in conditioning future railway workers and future railway workers' wives to running-trades work and its rhythms. In the case of the men interviewed, half of whom came from railway families, it was well known that, with a father or uncle in the railway work force, one not only had an important contact that made it easier for a man to get a job on the road. Having a relative on the railroad also allowed a future worker to acquire rudimentary knowledge of the skills and terminology that he would eventually use when hired by the company. It was this type of exposure that was valued by the CNR and its predecessor.[52]

As with sons, daughters were also exposed to their father's work routines. Furthermore, both sons and daughters had experience with the way a father's work rhythms affected family life. Daughters, however, were more likely to be involved with their mother's domestic labour and to hear a great deal more about the anguish and turmoil that their mothers might feel. "My oldest daughter was my sounding board and I talked to her probably before she knew what I was saying," recalled the wife of a conductor.[53] It was certainly felt that a daughter's exposure to railway life equipped her to handle its pressures should she also marry a railroader. Jim Blythe, an engineer, expressed this common belief succinctly: "It was hard for a woman but not for my wife because she was used to it, being the daughter of an engineer. She adjusted to it, but for the other women it was hard to adjust. . . . Had a lot of trouble. Lots of trouble."[54]

Next to the family support network, that established among friends and neighbours and among fellow church members was most important to the wives of running-trades workers. For the most part, friends were the wives of other railroaders, many but not all of whom had husbands working in the running trades. This was true of both generations. Similarly, fellow church members were also from the railway community.[55] Wives looked upon friends and neighbours as a source of help and comfort, especially in emergencies. They would visit one another with their children, thereby creating an informal arrangement of collective child care. Visiting with other wives was a way of combatting loneliness and a form of entertainment. Card parties, community dances, and other social gatherings were also popular forms of entertainment that were important to the support networks railway wives created. Both husbands and wives might participate in these events, but frequently only wives would be involved.

Indeed, there was a gender division of leisure in the railroad community. Many wives of both generations were members of the church women's auxiliaries and, to a lesser extent, the women's branches of union and fraternal organizations. As with the informal networks women created, these auxiliary committees offered them a forum to share their experiences and to break some of the isolation they might experience, especially for those who did not have family in the town. Their participation in such organizations and in informal arrangements was governed, however, by the demands of their domestic work schedule, and especially by their ability to make arrangements for child care.

While others might depend to various degrees on their support networks to deal with the pressures of their situation, they also devised ways to gain some control over the effects of their husband's work schedule on family life. As one historian has observed, "it is within the private sphere that women could wield the most influence over their families. They made effective use of their capacity to argue, nag, manipulate . . . in order to achieve certain demands."[56] Many wives of running-trades workers refused to move their families to northern Ontario when their husbands were sent there to work. In isolated towns such as Hornepayne, Capreol, and Nakina, living conditions were extremely harsh compared to what existed in Allandale. Facilities improved in the 1950s, but still compare unfavourably with those available at home. In light of such conditions, wives stood firm in their commitment to remain in Allandale or in other divisional points in southern Ontario. Given a wife's refusal to move, a husband might pass up a better job in the north to remain with his family when he was allowed to do so, as in the case of senior brakemen and conductors. A conductor's daughter vividly remembered her mother's determination to stay in Toronto: "Our dad, he. . . . started on a passenger [train as a] conductor.

And he wasn't on there very long because he got transferred out to Toronto, from Toronto to North Bay. And my mother says no way would she break her family in Toronto. That was the last thing. So my dad just dropped back to a freight [conductor]."[57] Conversely, some wives insisted that they move up north with their husbands in order to avoid a long separation.

For many wives, a move to northern Ontario would mean the loss of an important family-support network. They were also aware, not only of how conditions in the north would affect their own domestic labour and well being, but also how such conditions might affect the health of their spouses, especially in the harsh winters when much time would be spent outside in temperatures that could fall to as low as minus 35 degrees Celsius.

Some wives pressured their husbands to take every opportunity to get work in the southern Ontario terminals, if their seniority permitted this. Vera Miller's approach was more direct. She used her knowledge of the seniority system and union regulations to have the Allandale station super-intendent bring her husband home, much to her spouse's dismay:

> [I said] why aren't you bringing Peter home? Well, he said, I thought maybe he might just get home and he'd have to go back again. I said that's his worry, not yours. I said, by the way, I said, when Mr. Newton was cut off the railroad, I said, retired, I said that automatically brings a man back. . . . And I said he's still up there. I said what's the point? What did you leave him for? . . . I said you call him back. So he [telephoned the terminal at Hornepayne] and called Peter home. And he never had to go back. Never had to go back. And he could have killed me for it. He said, what did you do that for? I said just because you should have been home, Peter. And I said that's where you should be. And he said, well, I was making good money. I said I don't care how much money you were making. He never had to go back.[58]

Some wives also would meet their husbands at the station on the day they were paid in order to collect their cheques. In certain cases this would pro-vide protection against the spending habits of husbands known for their prowess at drinking and gambling. As the railway would not give the pay cheques directly to the wives, this was one of the few recourses open to women in such situations.[59]

The degree to which women could manoeuvre, however, was still lim-ited. A wife might refuse to move to northern Ontario or to get up at night to make her husband dinner, or she might try to have him come home from the north but she was in no position to prevent the chaotic and disruptive nature of railway scheduling. Her efforts were directed toward *curtailing* the effects of railway work rhythms on family life. Similarly, a wife might develop ways to manage household finances that met the needs of her fam-ily as well as her own needs, but her management was dependent on the wages of her husband.

Running-trades workers were aware of the economic pressures that kept them in the work force as the family breadwinner. These men also derived a certain pride from being able to earn a "family wage."[60] The fact that running-trades workers were the family breadwinners was viewed through a particularly masculine frame of reference. Their situation did not simply reflect economic necessity, but was also a desirable state of affairs. It confirmed their masculinity and underpinned the patriarchal power they might exercise in the family.

As theorists of masculinity have argued, "definitions of masculinity enter into the way work is personally experienced, as a life-long commitment and responsibility. In some respects, work itself is made palatable only through the kinds of compensations masculinity can provide. . . . When work is unpalatable, it is often only his masculinity (his identification with the wage, 'providing for the wife and kids') that keeps a man at work day after day."[61] A male worker views his wages as proof of his ability to endure the harsh working conditions that a woman would supposedly be incapable of surviving. For him, to be the breadwinner of the family is not simply a result of the sexual division of wage labour; it is also a confirmation of his male prowess. It is a prize won "in a masculine mode in confrontation with the 'real' world."[62]

The self-image of running-trades workers as men was bound up in their notion of a wife's place being in the home. For the first generation, this meant after marriage; for the second generation, this meant, if not after marriage, at least after the first child was born. As an engineer's son recalled, "back in those days the women didn't work. If a woman had to go out to work her husband was kinda looked down on because he was supposed to keep her."[63]

A wife working for wages outside the home was, for some men, a threat to the power and privileged position of the male breadwinner in the family, despite the improbability of a wife being able to become economically independent. The comments of one railroader made explicit what others might have also felt but were reluctant to articulate: "My wife never worked outside the house. I don't believe in the woman working. I'm an oldtimer. In the old days that was their place but now it's so much different. A man that starts a little argument [with his wife would be told]: 'Well, I can keep myself. To hell with you.' "[64]

While many railwaymen believed that a woman's place was in the home, their wives did not always concur with this view. Some women, especially of the first generation, resented being told that they had to leave the paid work force upon marriage. Though wives were aware of how wage work for married women reflected badly on their husbands, some were particularly irritated with the way such restrictions were enforced by their employers, and by the railway company itself. To allow married women to work outside the home would give the unwelcome impression that Grand Trunk or CNR wages were insufficient to support a family. Catherine Roy's recollections underscored the irritation that these women felt: "You [were] not allowed [work outside the home after marriage] when you belonged to the CNR in those days. No, you couldn't dare have another job. Your whole life was CNR. . . . The railroad disapproved of it, you see. I don't know how they can run your affairs for you."[65]

Once his wife became a homemaker, a railwayman believed that he was entitled to certain benefits that were compensation for his breadwinning efforts—for example, the right to spend a portion of his time off the job as he pleased. The degree to which a husband might become involved in house-work and child care was limited by his own wage-labour schedule and the time necessary to recover from the demands of his job. Domestic labour was not simply assigned to wives as a result of their husband's work schedule, however. For the vast majority, domestic work was allocated on the basis of gender; it was women's work. In certain instances, husbands might "help out." Some intervened to ease their spouse's workload through the acquisition of home appliances.[66] Some husbands also prepared meals, though generally after their retirement. As well, many practised a division of labour in which they were responsible for house repairs and maintenance.

Domestic labour was, nevertheless, a woman's responsibility from which a husband was exempt unless he chose otherwise.[67] This arrangement was somewhat ironic, however. When away from home, running-trades workers would often cook for themselves and be responsible for keeping their living accommodations clean. The peculiar working conditions of engine and train crews legitimized their involvement in specific elements of what might be considered "domestic labour away from home." When a worker returned to Allandale this labour again became his wife's duty.

Patriarchal practices, however, cannot be seen as simply being imposed on these women (or on these men, for that matter), though impositions certainly did occur. As others have observed, such practices are perpetuated "in the main by consent, by identification with the status quo and a belief in common interests or inevitability."[68] While domestic labour for a railway worker's wife could be stressful, frustrating, and burdensome, much of a wife's identity and pride was bound up in the work she did in the home. "I never wanted to go to work once I had my children," commented an engineer's wife. "I don't know how people can do it really. So I was just like a home person. I wanted to be in the house. I wanted to keep my family. And it never bothered me."[69]

A great deal has been written about the "heroic" elements of working-class masculinity, that enabled a man to survive hostile working conditions through "sheer mental and physical bravery."[70] Similarly, there are also "heroic" elements to working-class femininity that enabled a woman to survive the often conflicting and onerous pressures of domestic labour. Wives of both generations spoke with pride of being able to meet the demands of their situation, though often with great difficulty. They were aware of the essential role they had in the family and its importance, from the smallest matter of family care to the largest.

For a women, not to tend to the needs of family and husband was to call into question her identity as a housewife and mother. It would also call into question the necessity of doing her job well. Wives who drank to excess, or did not provide the "proper care" for children or spouse, or who had extra-marital affairs, were viewed unsympathetically.[71] Husbands who were poor providers, alcoholics, or philanderers were also criticized, though elements of a double standard did exist, especially concerning the question of drinking.

Seeing themselves as wives and mothers, the women of the railway community did not challenge the predominant gender relations of the period. According to their ideological conceptions, a wife's (or at least a mother's) place was in the home—but this was also a necessity. As one railway wife and mother stated, in comments that have been already noted: "I never wanted to go to work once I had my children." Yet underlying this view of herself as a nonwage-working mother and wife was the recognition: "I don't know how people can do it"—that is, raise children and do wage work under conditions in a railway family that would make such a "double day" formidable. In the decades after World War II it became more accept-able for wives without children, or with older children, to work in the paid labour force. Yet, this acceptance was not total. Practical and ideological considerations that pointed to the home as the proper sphere for women also remained strong.[72]

○

The railroad men is a little different from a lot of people. . . . There was togetherness. . . . The railway man was closer because . . . out-side the odd time you'd be off, you'd be together all the time. You'd eat together. You slept together. . . . You'd be together for miles and miles, hours and hours. (Dave Kingston, conductor, born 1892, hired 1913)

We were always brothers. That's what we worked on. (Mike Allen, conductor, born 1915, hired 1941)

The manner in which running-trades workers manoeuvred within the limits of their work and family lives revealed a great deal about their self-image as men. This identity both shaped and was an outgrowth of their work experi-ence. Their view of themselves as breadwinners was conditioned by their class situation, the prevailing gender division of wage labour, and the ideol-ogy of patriarchy. As economic providers they persisted in wage labour for the greatest part of their lives and attempted to ensure economic security for their kin through occupational inheritance.[73] When they intensified their labour by taking all the work they could handle, running-trades workers not only indicated the degree to which economic insecurity might guide their actions, they also revealed how concepts of masculinity, with an emphasis on the role of breadwinning and expectations of competitive indi-vidualism, could fracture unity among workers. Yet, the masculinity they practised was multidimensional and contradictory. It played a role both in promoting and undermining solidarity among workers and opposition to authority at work.

There was much in the lives of enginemen and trainmen to promote a sense of being part of a "brotherhood." Both on and off the job, engineers, firemen, conductors, and brakemen were in close company with fellow workers. When away from their families, married workers returned to the world of single men. Along with their unmarried counterparts, they participated in a bachelor culture of recreation, sanctioned by the particular circumstances of their work.

These men would sleep and eat together in vans or bunkhouses when waiting for a return train, or in hotels or boarding houses when working out of northern Ontario terminals. After rest, and depending on their work schedule, men might go hunting or fishing, if in the north country. Frequently they would play cards, such as poker and "catch"—not the games that were played in the mixed company of card parties at home. The mainstay of conversation was often their work on the railroad. A large part of this recreational culture also involved drinking. As one conductor commented, "booze was mixed up in pretty well every activity they had."[74]

When away from their families, crew members would also go to parties or dances in nearby towns. Freed from the constraints of wife and family and from the view of one's home community, some men threw caution to the wind. "There was a rough old life up there [in the north]," remarked Dave Spalding, an engineer. "A lot of boys got away from their families, you know, and they kinda wooped it up a bit."[75] In the recollections of another railroader, "as soon as the day's work was over it was a hard playin' bunch of fellas."[76]

Wives generally had some knowledge of their husband's recreation away from home, though not necessarily the details. It would appear that these forms of entertainment among men were accepted by wives, except if done to extremes and consequently threatened the security of the family. Tensions did arise at home when workers returned from the world of single men to the world of wife and family and continued to live as if they were still away from home. This was especially true concerning the question of drinking. Some men would spend most of their recreation at home away from the family, drinking in the local bars with their fellow workers. The majority of Allandale's running-trades workers, however, did spend time with their families when at home.

As with their wives, however, there still existed for these workers a gender division of leisure. When in Allandale, engine and train crews by no means completely abandoned the world of men for that of wife and family. Aside from going to a pub with workmates, these men would go together to certain sports events and to monthly union meetings. Many running-trades workers were also members of fraternal organizations in the community. During this period, the Masonic Order was the most popular.[77] In the years before 1930, and especially in the nineteenth century, organizations such as the Sons of England or Scotland, the Oddfellows, and the Orange Order also had a large railway following among Protestant workers.[78] Masonic meetings and events provided these men with the opportunity to get together to discuss lodge affairs as well as events on the railroad. Railroaders became members in order to be with fellow workers and friends, and were often encouraged to join by their supervisors and other workmates.

Participation in such male societies, and in male forms of recreation when at home, was in many respects an extension of the comraderie that was established at work. Away from home, men spent long hours together both on the job and off. In certain respects, co-operation was necessary not only to get a train over the road but also to avoid intensifying the already-existing strains that came with working long, and often irregular, hours under demanding conditions. The friendships established were valued, and for some were important compensations for the disruptions that were part of running-trades work rhythms.

When speaking of fellow workers in the running trades, or on the railroad in general, men used terms such as "brothers," "brotherhood," and "family." These terms of consanguinity were not simply figurative, given the widespread kinship ties that did exist in the railroad labour force. They did underscore, however, a closeness that was felt among crew members. Upon entering the running trades, a man was essentially initiated into what sociologists have termed an "occupational culture," with its own language, accepted forms of interaction, and set of expectations. This was also a male culture where one's masculinity came under scrutiny by seasoned workers.[79] The ability of a new fireman to maintain the necessary supply of coal for the engine's firebox, or the ability of a new brakeman to couple railway cars and "throw" the proper switches, became a test of one's stamina and endurance. The new recruit's lack of detailed knowledge of railway operations, particularly those who had no early exposure to railway work, also became a source of amusement and sport for "old hands."

In this world of male workers, men were often given nicknames based on their particular idiosyncracies. These could be terms both of affection and of friendly (or in some cases not-so-friendly) ridicule, and exhibited a degree of creativity by their originators. Among a number of these, the running-trades work force usually had its "Roarer" ("I was always roarin' about some bastard or something"), "Whiskey Face," "Slippery Dick," "Diamond Jim," "Fats," and "Brandy."[80]

Co-operation and close companionship were important not only "to getting the job done" and to surviving the rigours of work, however. They also provided the basis for collective solidarity in resisting or curtailing the authority of railway officials and supervisors. As those who have studied the labour process of mass-production industries have observed, the formal negotiating power of the union provides only a limited challenge to the discipline of production.[81] In the highly organized running trades, union regulations were an important form of protection. Workers did have some recourse to defending themselves against decisions by officials through grievance procedures (which were stronger in the post-World War II period). Nonetheless, in dealing with authority at work, crew members also relied upon informal means of protecting themselves and challenging the structures of discipline that existed.

A sense of responsibility to fellow workers and to one's companions led workers to protect each other from possible discipline when company regulations pertaining to train operations and the conduct of employees were violated. This most frequently took the form of a "conspiracy of silence" regarding rule violations: "If something happened, you never mentioned it. You just kept quiet. Back in the old days [i.e. in the days of the Grand Trunk Railway] the officials, you know, you could be fired for nothing, practically. They were tough in those days. And the railroad men, especially the running trades, they all worked together. Some guy made an error, you didn't say anything about it.[82] In cases where workers were caught violating regulations, men spoke of company officials offering to limit suspensions from work or to reduce or eliminate the demerit points assigned if the person most responsible was turned in by his workmates. To submit to this form of plea bargaining (by turning company's evidence) was particularly insulting to workers and, for those who did, it represented a betrayal of one's fellow workers and the established code of ethics.[83]

While close co-operation and friendship could exist among Allandale running-trades workers, relations among crew members and between them and the rest of the work force were not as unblemished as the recollections of some railroaders would have them. Faced with the threat of company discipline or the needs of an emergency, workers could "pull together" according to their code of ethics. Nevertheless, generational and occupational tensions and infighting also existed in the running-trades work force, and those tarnished the idealized image of co-operation and comraderie, and revealed another dimension of their working-class masculinity.

For the generation that began work in the 1920s or earlier, relations between junior firemen and brakemen and their more senior engineers and conductors appeared to have been more harmonious than those that existed for the following generation of workers who started during the Second World War. In the experience of the first generation, most firemen and brakemen were in their late teens or early twenties and unmarried when they began, while engineers and conductors were considerably older, with wives and children. Junior crew members would be treated paternalistically, as sons needing guidance and a firm hand when necessary. Bob Lenard, an engineer, had fond recollections of his early years on the railroad: "A lot of the old men, they more or less adopted me. Like I was only a boy compared with them. That time those men were creatin' a family. They were good to me. I haven't got no complaints about any of them."[84]

Given the extent of the kinship ties that existed in the running-trades work force, a young man's entry into railroad work could be seen as a way of reaffirming a bond between kin, between father and son or nephew and uncle. As a new recruit learned his job, the paternal authority of senior crew members came to bear on these young workers, as a source of support, knowledge, and discipline. In this generation's experience, paternalism characterized relations between younger and older workers, and was both a remnant of historical tradition and an outgrowth of the actual kinship bonds that existed in the work force. The railway company saw these familial ties as a *potential* source of discipline, with the actions of sons or nephews reflecting on the reputation of fathers and uncles. The existence of these bonds could also act as a source of solidarity, in resisting or defending workers against company authority, such as in the case of the "conspiracy of silence" that existed on the railroad.

The existence of family ties and paternalistic practices in the work force could as well lead to a rejection of paternalistic relations, as young men came to resist or challenge the authority of their elders. As this first generation of running-trades workers grew older and attempted to apply aspect of the paternalistic practices of their early days on the railroad to the generation that started work in the late 1920s and early 1940s, they met with resistance. There were several reasons why relations between older and younger workers in the experience of the first generation were unlike those of the second generation.

With the outbreak of World War II, the first generation of railroaders was faced with the responsibility of training new men after not having done so for over a decade. These new recruits were also older—many were married and had children, unlike the teenagers and young adults who began running-trades work in the 1920s and earlier decades. Established patterns of work for the first generation were disrupted not only by the introduction of new men but also by the need for the intensification of labour rhythms to meet wartime requirements. In the case of head-end crews, men who had always been firemen and wished to remain so were now forced to become engineers and had to cope with their new jobs as well as with the training of new recruits who might be more technically competent. These new men were perceived as a threat: they were younger and in some respects could better withstand, or appeared better to withstand, the demands of wartime work. Essentially they came to symbolize the turmoil these older men were experiencing during the war years, and their presence could raise awkward questions about an oldtimer's own masculinity.

Workers of the second generation spoke of being ostracized by engineers and conductors of the first generation when they began on the road. These "oldtimers" often would not associate with the new men or would sometimes refuse to work with them, would provide only minimum training and advice, and would strongly criticize new crew members when they made a mistake. Such behaviour was not simply part of the harsh running-trades initiation rite, for those of the first generation had not experienced this treatment to the same degree themselves. Antagonism was not only directed to unrelated members of the work force, but could involve fathers and sons as well. John Heath, who came from a family of railroaders, remembered such conflicts vividly: "When you first started out you ran into these old [crew members]. My father was one of them. They hated to see these young upstarts coming into their territory, you might say. And boy, you had a rough time with those guys. . . . They hated us."[85]

The reaction of many of these recruits was not a passive one, although they were placed in a difficult position of having to work with the "oldtimers" while learning a new job (sometimes on their own) with its attendant uncertainties and vulnerabilities. In addition, company officials apparently took a dim view of oldtimers' refusal to work with new men, especially if this interfered with the training of new recruits. The fact that there were large numbers of men hired during the war alleviated some of the isolation they might feel. These "teddy bears," as they were called by the "oldtimers," drew closer together in light of the similar circumstances they faced. Workers cited incidents of fighting between junior and senior crew members as well as verbal assaults on "oldtimers" who attempted to browbeat the new men. The interaction between crew members could take a very masculine form of confrontation, and was recalled in such terms: "For about two years there used to be fire and hell to pay. Because the young fellas comin' up wouldn't take the BS that was bein' handed to 'em. There was a lot of trouble. Once the older men realized what was goin' on, that they weren't goin' to be the little god anymore, then things changed."[86]

It would appear that relations between these generations of workers did improve as the new men fought back against the authoritarianism of the oldtimers and became proficient in their jobs. In addition, in the postwar period, particularly in the 1950s, many of the oldtimers retired, thereby removing a source of conflict. There could also be tensions, however, between engine crews and train crews as proud engineers and conductors argued with one another about train operations and authority. Such rivalries have been well noted in railway histories and celebrated in literature. In the case of Allandale workers, generational tension between "oldtimer" and "teddy bears" also had elements of occupational rivalry between the head-end and tail-end crews. New firemen would be scorned by conductors and new brakemen would be held in disdain by engineers not only because of generational antagonism but also for reasons of traditional occupational conflict. Workers of the second generation spoke of this conflict being less pronounced among their peer group, in part because of the common hostility all new running-trades workers felt from the "oldtimers." Nonetheless, within this generation, as with the previous one, occupational rivalries could still occur.

Rivalry between the "head end" and "tail end" in certain respects was part of a masculine style of interaction, characterized by playful ridicule and insults that did not necessarily indicate any genuine feeling of antagonism. Engine and train crews could be very friendly with one another and, while some spoke of enginemen having nothing to do with trainmen, many others, especially of the second generation, recalled spending leisure time together both at home and away. There were also instances where junior crew members informally switched jobs among themselves for a period while on a run, though this was against company regulations. A brakeman assigned to the "head end" would "fire" (i.e., shovel coal into the firebox) while the fireman would either take a rest or perform the duties of the brakeman.

A difference in technical knowledge and the meaning these men attached to the concept of skill also underpinned the rivalry between engine and train crews. As theorists of the labour process have argued, skill is not only a technical category but is also an ideological construct that is highly gendered. Definitions of skill are bound up with masculine identities and play an important part in defining the skill level of work performed.[87] Not only has the process of skill definition served to devalue the labour done by women in predominantly female occupations but it has also had an important influence on relations between male workers. To be less skilled was to a certain degree to be less of a man, given the way in which the notion of skill has been infused with the supposed masculine qualities of technical proficiency and competence.

The conflicts that arose between enginemen and trainmen—for example, over speed limits—could become intense when an engineer asserted his belief in the superiority of his technical skills and judgment. That a conductor had jurisdiction over the operation of the entire train could be particularly galling. In the words of one engineer, "[conductors] ran the train, alright. But that engine. Bomb the goddamn train on them. You were in charge of the engine. They could do whatever they liked with that train."[88] Some engineers also were not inhibited in presenting their views to conductors or brakemen: "[Conductors] were largely referred to as the messenger boy. That was the extent of the love between the head end and the tail end. . . . You see some of these fellas [i.e. conductors] come in here on the last trip and oh, are they important. I don't know how they kept the buttons on their coats."[89] This dynamic also played a role in the sectionalism evident between running-trades workers and those who worked in other railway occupations. Engineers, firemen, conductors, and brakemen, who had the most prestigious and autonomous of jobs in the railway labour force, could be accused by those working in the car shop, roundhouse, or the bridge and building department, as comprising a self-important elite that would have little to do with other railroaders. More than a few engine- and train-crew members apparently did little to dispel this accusation.[90]

The nature of the work itself contributed much to both the masculine self-image and practices of these workers. The labour of engine and train crews demanded a great deal of physical effort and endurance. These men had to brave temperatures of extreme heat and cold. Long hours, often limited rest, the uncertainty of weather and track conditions, and the ever-present prospect of accidents that could be fatal—all were an integral part of the job. As theorists of masculinity have argued, the harsh physical demands and mental strains of a working-class occupation can lead men to view their work in terms of "a heroic exercise of manly confrontation with 'the task'. Difficult, uncomfortable or dangerous conditions are seen not for themselves, but for their appropriateness to a masculine readiness and hardiness."[91]

For engine and train crews, a sense of "manly confrontation" with the elements was confirmed by the rhythms and conditions of their labour as well as by the technology they had to operate. Brakemen and conductors noted the skill and physical exertion required to "pull" switches and to couple or uncouple cars, as well as the dangers they courted when doing so. Engineers and firemen proudly spoke of mastering huge locomotive engines and of "breathing life" into inanimate objects. To run an engine at high speeds while pulling a long line of freight or passenger cars gave these men a sense of enormous power. One engineer captured the perspective of many others when he stated: "I loved the engines. I loved power, when I handled power."[92] When diesel engines replaced coal-fired ones in the 1950s, engine crews felt not only a loss of skill but also of some of the qualities of their labour that for them made it a specifically masculine calling. The dirt and sweat involved in feeding coal to a hot firebox, the physical exertion and co-ordination required to operate the steam engine, and the sometimes deafening noise in the cab, were gone.[93]

Paul Willis among others has observed the way in which male workers' "mechanical, sensuous, and concrete familiarity with the tools of production" can mediate both the experience and understanding of the labour process.[94] An engineman might be tired by the demands of needing to be constantly on the move and feel harassed by a supervisor or dispatcher keeping track of his performance or the movement of his engine from a distance. At the same time he could feel exhilarated and be fascinated by the massive and intricate piece of technology he was controlling. For many workers, there was a close identification with the power of the technology they operated. Engineers spoke of this power as an extension of themselves. When discussing the operation of their locomotives they would say that "I got up enough power to make the steep grade" or "I was losing power so I had to cut and run [i.e. disconnect the engine from the rest of the train and go to the nearest coal- or water-storage facility on the line]." It was no coincidence that their descriptions of railway technology and the terminology of train operations were often invested with sexual or gender-specific metaphors and allusions that underscored the close relationship between work and gender identity that existed for engine and train crews. In the lexicon of the railroader an "old girl" was a locomotive, which was always given a title of female gender. When operating his engine an engineer, who would be called a "hogger," "hog jockey," "hoghead," or "whistle pig," might "beat her on the back [i.e. maintain high speed using full engine power] or "maul his pig" [i.e. run an engine at full stroke and throttle]." He would have to "get up steam" in his locomotive until "she was hot [i.e. with enough 'steam up' to run the engine]." Figures of authority and symbols of privilege associated with authority could be given appellations that were meant to symbolize uselessness and impotence, though these workers were quite aware that supervisors were not particularly impotent in the exercise of authority. Division officials might be referred to as "old men," and their private railway cars as "drone cages."[95]

Metaphors of unequal gender relations—of men's domination of women—figured in railwayman's working vocabulary, and these were also employed to describe relations with supervisors. In his analysis of contemporary male workplace culture at Westinghouse, Stan Gray has argued that the language of sex and sexual imagery is used by men to express the reality of class relations. The "sex act is conceived fundamentally as one of exploitation. . . . [It] is used as a model for all forms of exploitation and degradation of people, of which that taking place in production is one."[96]

When officials exercised their power, the terms of domination that workers might employ to describe their mastery of gender-ascribed technology were now used to indicate their own subordination. They were the ones who were now being "mauled" or "beaten." As with workers elsewhere, railroaders might also use explicitly sexual terms to describe authority relations at work. A worker who was given demerit points, suspended, or otherwise disciplined by a superintendent, trainmaster, or master mechanic might speak of being "screwed" or "fucked over" by an official. Supervisors who had a reputation of being particularly harsh, vindictive, or overly zealous were viewed contemptuously, and spoken of in crude terms that referred to aspects of male or female anatomy. Steve Price graphically conveyed the language and metaphors used when appraising company officials: "That's where we got the pricks. Some of the supervisors . . . Old Pete Marwick was a no good bitch. Bill North was a hell of a good guy. . . . Ray Cummings was a rotten little son of a bitch. Sneakin' bastard. Sneakin' around seein' what everybody was doin'. . . . Hal Richards wasn't too bad but he done a lot of dirty goddam tricks too, the son of a bitch."[97]

A mindset that stressed the need to put on a brave front in the face of very difficult or stressful labour conditions was also an important element of these workers' masculinity. Even when admitted, the personal turmoil created by the rhythms of railway labour on work and family life was not discussed at length among fellow workers. This "emotional illiteracy" or inability to express feelings, which was part of a male worker's socialization, was perpetuated by the conventions of work.[98] The fears and insecurities a worker experienced were rarely mentioned, though they might find an acceptable outlet in drinking, arguments, rough play, or fighting. To succumb to such tensions was to be less of a man. Indeed, the pressures of work could be understood as a challenge to one's masculinity rather than as an illustration of the power relations at work, which forced crew members to endure such conditions.[99] Evaluating his work experiences on the railroad, one engineer spoke for many when commenting that he "look[ed] back on things. . . . as sort of successful experiences where you master the job and not let the job get the best of you."[100]

Many workers recalled the harsh conditions they survived with pride and, for some, even with a sense of nostalgia. According to these men, the present generation of running-trades workers would be unable, if not unwilling, to tolerate such circumstances. An emphasis on manly endurance could lead an engineman or trainman to persist in his job when it was neither demanded by supervisors nor safe to do so. Often, workers regarded fatalistically the prospect of being in a major accident. The conventional wisdom among crew members was not to worry about what could not be avoided. Others might repress their fear and believe themselves immune from such a possibility. "You just felt like the same as when I worked in the mine," claimed one man. "Christ, we killed a man every day but ya never thought it was gonna be you. Ya never worried."[101]

In light of the frequent accidents which did occur in running-trades work, many of which involved injury and sometimes death, a fatalistic attitude became one of the means of surviving the tensions of the job.[102] Underpinning the masculinity of these workers was an acceptance of limitations, however uneasy or conditional that acceptance might be. One made the best of a situation and endured what could not be changed. "Making do" could become a virtue in itself. Yet, as with the friendships formed among co-workers, a conception of "manliness" could lead enginemen and trainmen not only to accommodate themselves to the conditions of their labour, but also to challenge authority when its exercise by supervisors impinged on a man's dignity. Such challenges are limited in the sense that they did not fundamentally call into question the relations of power at work, though they might be directed towards containing them to some degree. The demands for a grievance system by the railway unions were motivated not only by the very real need to protect workers from the sometimes arbitrary exercise of officials' authority, but also out of a concern that such treatment was offensive to one's masculine pride. It was this manly pride that proscribed kowtowing to officials and could be a reservoir of aggressiveness in confrontations with authority. Glen McPherson's account of one confrontation captures this style of masculine agressiveness. His comments also underline the rivalries that exist between engineers and conductors and the degree to which confrontations with supervisors could be futile in correcting a perceived injustice:

> The road foreman of engines . . . was criticizing me for pulling this draw bar, [improperly] applying the [engine] brakes at that point. Well, I told him, I was nervy enough to tell him that, "Well, lookit, are you goin' to assess me demerit marks," which he did. He handed me the slip to sign and I wouldn't sign it for him. I says, "I'm not goin' to sign that." I says, "I'm not takin' criticism from you as to how I run an engine. From you, a man who never run an engine." He was a conductor beforehand. . . . The demerit marks went against my record as far as that's concerned.[103]

The nature of a worker's interaction with authority and his willingness or ability to challenge it, however, were also affected by the changing labour conditions of the period. These conditions contributed to what appears to have been a shift in emphasis in the meanings that masculinity had for running-trades workers and a shift in masculine practices themselves. When the sanctions against challenging authority were too great, as was the case during the Great Depression, aggressiveness towards authority was more muted and greater stress was placed on definitions of masculinity that focussed on hard work and endurance. In periods of labour shortage, such as the war years, challenges to authority were less likely to result in dismissal. While a worker's masculinity still emphasized his ability to be "tough," this toughness was also more likely to be practised in relations with senior engineers and conductors (as in the case of new recruits hired during the Second World War) or with officials (as in the case of both generations of workers).[104]

In these "manly" confrontations with supervisors or with each other, workers were not constrained by the presence of women. The work world of the running trades was a male preserve. Historically, women had been excluded from such labour, even during both world wars, when women made limited and temporary inroads into traditionally male occupations. During those wars mainly single women found employment in the railway shops and roundhouses, as well as in the traditional area of office work. They did not work outside the perimeter of the railway station and its maintenance facilities.[105] For the men of the Allandale running-trades labour force, this was both a necessary and preferable state of affairs. Primarily, workers felt that such work would be unfit and unsafe for a woman, married or single: a woman would be unable to withstand the hard physical labour and dangers of the job. Wives also concurred in the view that running-trades occupations were gendered as masculine. Part of the working-class morality of these men and their community was the concept of protecting women from dangerous employment.[106] As one engineman argued, "I wouldn't want any women goin' out when I was runnin'. Their life wouldn't be safe."[107]

Running-trades work could indeed be unsafe, for women or men. The exclusionary arguments of engine and train crews did not, however, simply involve the question of safety and the needs of the family. Aspects of patriarchal privilege would certainly be at stake if women were to enter the running-trades fraternity. Hiring a woman to do a "man's job," particularly a single woman, would deprive a married man of the means to support his family. Aside from the standard defence of the male provider, the nature of running-trades work itself could be invoked in arguing for the exclusion of women. In the running trades, unlike other male occupations into which women were admitted during wartime, it would have been difficult to segregate men and women workers on the job. Given the large amount of time that was spent away from home, separate living facilities would also need to be constructed for female crew members, for reasons of sexual propriety. Such issues had been raised in resisting the entry of women into other areas of the work force; in running-trades work these problems would become especially worrisome and costly to resolve. Moreover it was felt that a woman's own sense of morality would prevent her from seeking employment on the road—no self-respecting woman would do so.[108]

For a woman to become an engineer, fireman, brakeman, or conductor would call into question the ideological conception of these occupations as men's work. Her work in the running trades would make it difficult for a male worker to get a sense of confirmation of his own masculinity. The physical strength and the endurance of harsh and sometimes dangerous conditions demanded by the job could no longer be understood as the unique and special preserve of a man. At the same time, the entry of women into the running trades would constitute an invasion of an important sanctuary of male working-class culture, where men could escape from the constraints of wife and family and be as profane and as rough as they wished, at least when they were not in contact with passengers. It was no coincidence that trainmen stated that the most disagreeable feature of their work on passenger trains was dealing with "the public." While the problems of unruly or dissatisfied passengers were cited as the major source of irritation, it was also the case that these men disliked the constraints placed on their own behaviour, constraints that were absent when working on freight trains. Passenger-train conductors had to wear uniforms that were popularly known as "harnesses," a telling colloquialism that did not refer to the restrictions of a dress code alone.[109]

Theorists of masculinity have argued that male workplace culture can be seen as a form of rebellion "against civilized society's cultural restraints.[110] It was also a domain that had to be protected against representatives of civilizing restraint—women. The presence of women in this world forced men to "clean up their act" and alter the way they behaved with one another. In the presence of women, both on and off the job, running-trades workers did act differently than when just among themselves.[111] Women were not totally closed off from the work-world of engine and train crews. The wives and children of these workers periodically travelled on the trains with their husbands or fathers, and events on the railway were discussed in many running-trades families. Nonetheless, in the presence of women a sanitized image of male work culture would often be conveyed.

The masculinity practised by enginemen and trainmen shared many features with that of other sections of the railway labour force and the male working class in general. As with many workers, these men could be rough and aggressive, "hard drinking" and "hard swearing." In his analysis of contemporary male workplace culture in mass-production industry, Stan Gray has written that male workers worship a self-identity of "vulgar physicalness" where intellectual pursuits and theoretical knowledge are disdained. According to Gray, it is this self-identity that is antithetical to a tradition that spoke of the dignity of labour. The obsessive celebration of physical prowess can be seen as "accepting and then glorifying the middle-class views of manual labour and physical activity as inferior, animalistic and crude."[112] Running-trades workers were certainly proud of their physical capabilities, but their masculinity was not reduced to a simple "self-identity of vulgar physicalness." There was much in the nature of their work—for example, the relative autonomy from direct supervision and the skills demanded of their trade—as well as a rich and proud historical tradition that militated against a view of the labour as inferior or animalistic. These men viewed themselves to be "respectable" and cherished their respectability as did skilled workers within the class as a whole. This was not simple middle-class (or petit-bourgeois) male respectability, though it had many of those features. Its style was too aggressive, direct, and rough for middle-class gentility, nurtured as it was in part at work. Though the exercise of company authority might wound a railwayman's masculine pride and offend his working-class dignity, pride and dignity were also tenacious qualities in the running-trades workers' world.

o

For the men and women of Allandale, the class and gender conditions and relations of the period set limits to what was available and possible. In most running-trades families, husbands were breadwinners and wives were full-time homemakers. This pattern was the response of railway families to the constraints created by the gender division of wage work, running-trades labour rhythms, the prevailing conditions of reproductive labour, and the ideology of patriarchy. Nonetheless, railroaders and their wives also made choices within the limitations of their lives. Some decided that it was better for a family's welfare if a wife remained in Allandale while a husband worked in the north. Others believed that families should stay united. Wives consequently moved to northern Ontario with their husbands. Many men chose to remain running-trades workers despite the disruptive and unpredictable rhythms of their labour. Others, however, could not tolerate the work and sought employment elsewhere in order to support their families. These choices had different implications for the men and women of the community.

The strategies railroad families adopted for survival and well-being revealed some striking continuities. Nevertheless, there were changes as well. Married women of the first generation provided for their family's welfare through their labour in the home. A number of second-generation wives, however, also contributed as secondary wage-earners, at least until they became mothers. During the Great Depression, running-trades families had to abandon temporarily their emphasis on occupational inheritance as a means of providing economic security for the next generation. Men whose career on the railroad belatedly began in the early 1940s were even less able to offer their own sons the prospect of occupational inheritance. With the decline of Allandale as the railway centre and the general contraction of the running-trades work force in the 1960s and 1970s, fathers encouraged their sons to pursue other employment. These strategies both altered and were changed by the constraints of the lives of railway-family members.

Conceptions of masculinity and femininity which informed family strategies also shaped and were moulded by the class and gender relations of the time. Especially in the paid work of railroaders, notions of "manliness" had a rather contradictory influence on labour relations. An emphasis on the breadwinning role and elements of competitive individualism could come into conflict with notions of worker solidarity and the established code of ethics on the job. This was evident in instances when men exceeded their mileage limitations, tried to manipulate their seniority standing, or reported a fellow crew-member's violation of company regulations. An emphasis on masculine hardiness could lead enginemen and trainmen to view the difficult and dangerous conditions of their labour as a test of their manhood and played no small role in relations among workers themselves. Officials would also appeal to such manly virtues when supervising their workers. Yet, being "tough" could as well lead to the challenge of authority and resistance to managerial intimidation when the sanctions were not too great. While a worker's identity as the family provider might foster a dependence on the railway, it might also lead to demands for better wages and working conditions in order to fulfill that breadwinning role.

Within the running-trades "brotherhood," elements of egalitarian and hierarchical relations co-existed.[113] The experience of railroaders hired during the Second World War highlighted the intensity of the conflicts that could arise as claims of equality come up against the paternalistic practices of an earlier generation. Generational conflict and sectionalism between enginemen and trainmen could threaten the solidarity of the brotherhood; yet these men could also stress a united front against officials. Having come up from the ranks, supervisors might claim to remain a "brother" and use that identity with some effect, but the actual power relations on the railroad also served to undermine such appeals.

Running-trades workers themselves played an important role in shaping their gender and class identities. Breaking the conspiracy of silence when faced with company discipline was actively discouraged as unbecoming to both a worker's and a man's dignity. Those who ran afoul of unwritten codes quickly learned accepted practices or were ostracized. In crafting these practices enginemen and trainmen revealed how the strains of individualism in their socialization as men might be contained. The bonds that were formed between these men also revealed many dimensions. Though putting a premium on "toughness," a worker could be supportive and nurturing with his "brothers," too. Independence and interdependence, competitiveness and co-operation, existed uneasily with one another in the bonds of the brotherhood. As the experience of the two generations of railroaders indicated as well, the shaping of gender identities was an on-going process.

Relations between husbands and wives could be equally complex. The family wage earned by a running-trades worker allowed his wife to become a full-time homemaker. The rhythms of railway work and the demands of reproductive labour made her presence in the home a necessity as long as her children were still young. Both the family wage and running-trades work rhythms were also central to the construction of working-class masculinity and femininity in Allandale. The spouses of enginemen and trainmen saw themselves primarily as wives and mothers. Their "proper sphere" was in the home, though this began to shift in the post-World War II period. A husband's self-image as a man was bound up in his breadwinning labour.

His role as economic provider also formed the basis of the power he could exercise in the family. Yet, wives were not simply subordinate to their husbands. They had autonomy in the handling of finances, sanctioned by a husband's frequent absence from home. That autonomy, however, could be undermined when large expenditures were involved. Indeed, the family wage was an arena of conflict and co-operation between men and women.

Wives could also be aggressive with husbands and company officials when the welfare of their family was threatened. At home or in public they challenged the prerogatives of the male breadwinner by refusing to move their families, demanding that their husbands return from the north, and going to the station to take possession of their spouse's paycheque. By their actions these women called into question notions of passive femininity and confronted husbands whose concept of masculinity emphasized the need to be dominant and tough. The results were sometimes explosive.[114] Notions of respectability, however, constrained some wives to maintain their independence within the confines of the home while in public they tended to bolster the masculine image of the spouses.

In the construction of gender identities, material conditions and ideology reinforced one another. Wives had to become self-reliant due to their husband's unpredictable work schedule. Nonetheless, this self-reliance did not extend to mothers working outside the home. Aside from the great hardship involved, a mother's wage work would threaten the respectability, not only of her spouse, but of the whole family as well.

Both men and women of the railway community were quite aware of the material and ideological constraints of their lives. Given the class and gender limitations of the period, they worked out a division of labour based on how their families could best survive. Essentially held together by the railway wife, the family could be a forum where all the tensions of conflicting schedules and pressures were expressed. It could also provide a measure of stability and continuity for a worker who was frequently on the move. Indeed, if the family strategies railroaders adopted were essential to their own well-being, they were the linch-pin of railway operations. Railway families provided a major component of the company's future labour force, early exposure to work rhythms and demands, and a potential source of discipline which operated through kinship networks as sons came to recognize that their actions also reflected on their fathers' reputation. The scheduling of trains was based, among other considerations, on the assumption that enginemen and trainmen could look to their wives for the critical emotional and physical support needed to endure the rigours of work.

The arrangement between husbands and wives was a partnership, though not necessarily of equals. While influenced by concepts of working-class masculinity and femininity, family strategies were conceived and carried out as collective endeavours among members involving emotional and physical burdens for men as well as women.[115] Indeed, as both railroaders and their spouses frequently recalled, "it was a hard life."

NOTES

1. Interview with Ed Walker, born 1916, hired by the CNR in 1939.

2. For the most part, Canadian railway histories have been limited to considerations of railway finance, politics, and economic development. When considering railway workers, they generally have been concerned with union activity and industrial relations, or with the men who actually built the railroads. The different labour processes on the railroad have only recently been closely examined and few studies of the railroad community exist. In those community studies, there is very little analysis of the relationship between the paid-work world of railroaders and the world of unpaid domestic labour maintained by their wives.

3. For example, sample the sometimes heated debates of the past decades that heralded the emergence of the new working-class history in David Bercuson, "Through the Looking Glass of Culture: An Essay on the New Labour History and Working Class Culture in Recent Canadian Historical Writing," *Labour/Le Travail* 7 (1981): 95–112; Gregory S. Kealey, "H.C. Pentland and Working Class Studies," *Canadian Journal of Political and Social Theory* 3, 2 (1979): 79–94; "Labour and Working Class History in Canada: Prospects in the 1980s," *Labour/Le Travail* 7 (1981): 67–94; "Looking Backward: Reflections on the Study of Class in Canada," *History and Social Science Teacher* 16 (Summer 1981): 213–22; Kenneth McNaught, "E.P. Thompson vs Harold Logan: Writing about Labour and the Left in the 1970s," *Canadian Historical Review* 42 (1981): 141–68: S.R. Mealing, "The Concept of Social Class and the Interpretation of Canadian History," *Canadian Historical Review* 46, 3 (1965): 201–18; Terry Morley, "Canada and the

Romantic Left," *Queen's Quarterly* 86 (1979); D. Palmer, "Working Class Canada: Recent Historical Writings," *Queen's Quarterly* 86, 4 (Winter 1979/80): 594–616, and "Listening to History Rather than Historians: Reflections on Working Class History," *Studies in Political Economy* 20 (Summer 1986): 47–84.

4. For example, see the critical comments of Ava Baron in "Technology and the Crisis of Masculinity: The Social Construction of Gender and Skill in the US Printing Industry, 1850–1920" (Paper presented at the 5th UMIST-ASTON Conference on the Organisation and Control of the Labour Process, Manchester, England, 22–24 April 1987).

5. The work of Greg Kealey and Bryan Palmer, for example, does, however, begin to consider such issues. See Gregory Kealey, *Toronto Workers Respond to Industrial Capitalism, 1867–1892* (Toronto, 1980); Bryan D. Palmer, *A Culture in Conflict: Skilled Workers and Industrial Capitalism in Hamilton, Ontario, 1860–1914* (Montreal, 1979); Gregory Kealey and Bryan Palmer, *Dreaming of What Might Be: The Knights of Labor in Ontario, 1880–1900* (Cambridge, 1982). The historical dimensions of class and gender relations for male workers have been explored in some detail in Ava Baron's study of American printers, "Technology and the Crisis of Masculinity," and in Cynthia Cockburn's examination of British printers, *Brothers* (London, 1983). Most studies that address this concern deal with the present and are often written by sociologists. See, for example, Paul Willis, "Shop-Floor Culture, Masculinity and the Wage Form" in *Working Class Culture: Studies in History and Theory,* ed. John Clarke, Chas Critcher, and Richard Johnson (London, 1979), 185–98, 281–82;

Andrew Tolson, *The Limits of Masculinity* (London, 1982); Jeffrey Weeks, *Sexuality* (London, 1986); Stan Gray, "Sharing the Shop Floor" in *Beyond Patriarchy: Essays by Men on Pleasure, Power, and Change*, ed. Michael Kaufman (Toronto, 1987), 216–34; and Michael Yarrow, "Class and Gender in the Developing Consciousness of Appalachian Coal Miners" (Paper presented at the 5th UMIST-ASTON conference on the Organisation and Control of the Labour Process, Manchester, England, 22–24 April 1987). It should be noted that the conceptions of masculinity discussed in this paper refer to *heterosexual* masculinity. See, for example, the comments of Blye Frank on the importance of distinguishing the type of gender identities and practices in "Hegemonic Heterosexual Masculinity," *Studies in Political Economy* 24 (Autumn 1987): 159–70.

6. This approach rejects a "dual systems analysis," which argues that a system of patriarchal gender relations exists apart from that of capitalist class relations. For a sample of the debates that discuss the different conceptualizations of the relationship between class and gender, see, for example, Pat Armstrong and Hugh Armstrong, "Beyond Sexless Class and Classless Sex: Towards Feminist Marxism," *Studies in Political Economy* 10 (Winter 1983): 7–43; Pat Armstrong, *Labour Pains* (Toronto, 1984), 19–48; and Jane Lewis, "The Debate on Sex and Class," *New Left Review* 149 (1985): 108–20.

7. Ava Baron, "Technology and the Crisis of Masculinity," 6–8.

8. For example, the way in which concepts of masculinity have shaped class relations at work is examined in Ava Baron, "Technology and the Crisis of Masculinity"; Cockburn, *Brothers*; Yarrow, "Class and Gender"; Willis, "Shop-Floor Culture"; and Gray, "Sharing the Shop Floor." Whereas Cockburn argues that there is a "sex/gender system," that is separate from the system of class relations, Baron sees class and gender as comprising one integrated system and speaks in terms of a "gendered class."

9. For a discussion of this issue's theoretical and empirical literature, which deals primarily with the present, see Lorette K. Woolsey, "Bonds between Women and between Men, Part I: A Review of Theory," and "Part II: A Review of Research," *Atlantis* 31, 1 (Fall 1987): 116–36.

10. For example, Yarrow, "Class and Gender," and Baron, "Technology and the Crisis of Masculinity."

11. This is indicated, for example, in the studies of Willis, "Shop-Floor Culture," Gray, "Sharing the Shop Floor," and Cockburn, *Brothers*. They underline the contradictory features of working-class masculinity while emphasizing the way it has been used to exclude women from the workplace and from working-class organizations in general.

12. The same can be said of identities based on race, ethnicity, and religion. In "Class and Gender," Yarrow has explored the way in which concepts of manliness have figured in the unity of male Appalchian miners against mineowners and contributed to what he has called a "gender specific class conflict consciousness." Baron's "Technology and the Crisis of Masculinity" and Yarrow's work also bring out the contradictory and changing character of male gender identities in their studies.

13. See Yarrow, "Class and Gender" for a discussion of the emotional and cognitive dimensions of class and gender consciousness.

14. Research for this study is based on a series of interviews with 53 men and women who primarily were either running-trades workers (i.e. engineers, firemen, brakemen, or

conductors), their wives, or their children. In a few cases, those interviewed came from other sections of the railroad workforce but were long-time residents of the railway community. In total, 21 women and 32 men were consulted. Of the women, 5 were wives of engineers (who had previously been firemen), 7 were wives of conductors (who had previously been brakemen), 4 were daughters of conductors, 1 was a clerk who had worked in the Allandale CNR office, 1 was the daughter of a chief clerk, 2 were daughters of a railway crane operator, and 1 was the wife of a carman. Of the men, 16 were engineers (and former firemen), 11 were conductors (and former brakemen), 2 were railway clerks, 1 was a CNR policeman, 1 was a carman, and 1 was a personnel manager. Those interviewed also comprised a total of 32 families of running-trades workers. Eight of those families consisted of husbands and wives who married in the 1920s or earlier. Spouses in the remaining families married mainly in the late 1930s and early 1940s.

The men and women interviewed were not randomly selected and it cannot be simply stated that they were representative of Barrie's running-trades workers or its railroad families of the period. The majority of Barrie railway families noted in the CNR Pensioners' Club files and on the company's mailing list of pensioners was contacted. Those interviewed had been preselected by the basis that they had chosen to remain in Barrie, or to return there. The men interviewed also spent the greatest part of their working lives on the railroad. All had been hired by the CNR before 1948 and remained with the company until their retirement. Many who worked on the railroad in the years under examination were no longer alive and thus could not be interviewed.

15. See, for example, Veronica Strong-Boag, "Keeping House in God's Country: Canadian Women at Work in the Home" in *On The Job*, ed. Craig Heron and Robert Storey (Montreal, 1986), 124–51; Meg Luxton, *More than a Labour of Love* (Toronto, 1980); Bonnie Fox, ed., *Hidden in the Household: Women's Domestic Labour Under Capitalism* (Toronto, 1980); Wally Seccombe, "The Housewife and Her Labour Under Capitalism," *New Left Review* 83 (Jan–Feb. 1974): 3–24; Armstrong and Armstrong, "Beyond Sexless Class"; Armstrong, *Labour Pains*; Elizabeth Fox-Genovese, "Placing Women in History," *New Left Review* 133 (May–June 1982): 52–29; and Bettina Bradbury, "Women's History and Working-Class History," *Labour/Le Travail* 19 (Spring 1987): 23–43.

16. Except for the Great Depression of the 1930s, the size of the workforce seems to have remained stable until the late 1950s. Complete CNR payroll records for the Allandale terminal for this period have not yet been located and relatively detailed census information for Barrie is only available beginning with the 1951 census. That year it was reported that the CNR had a workforce of 380 employees, including express and telegraph workers. These figures might not have included engine and traincrews temporarily working out of different terminals but with a "home base" in Allandale. A number of those interviewed, including the payroll clerk, spoke of a workforce of approximately 500 of which a little less than half were running-trades workers. An occupational breakdown of the Barrie workforce in the 1951 census indicates a similar proportion of running-trades workers. As well, in 1951 the CNR was still the largest industrial employer in the town. Canada, *Census* 1941, vol. VII, table 10; 1951, vol. IV, table 4 and table 17; interviews with Steve Williams, clerk, born 1904, hired 1923; Len Stevens, CNR police, born 1892, hired 1920: Tim Armstrong, clerk, born 1915, hired 1946.

The replacement of coal-fired steam engines with diesel-fuelled ones in the late 1950s, in conjunction with the CNR's program of centralization, dramatically reduced the size of the workforce in the next decade. Other industries setup after the war, such as Canadian General Electric, replaced the railroad as Barrie's major employer. See Spiers, "Technological Change and the Railway Unions, 1945–1972"; Department of Economics and Development, Trade and Industry Branch, *Industrial Survey*, 1966; John Craig, *Simcoe County: The Recent Past* (Simcoe County, 1977), 231–34; Gail Foster, "Industrial Growth in Barrie and Orillia" (B.A. thesis, University of Toronto, 1968); Richard LeGear and John Kearns. "History and Development of Industry in Barrie" (Unpublished paper (OFY Project 4K2419, 1974), copy in Simcoe County Archives), and interviews.

17. Seniority had been in place since the late nineteenth century, when the Brotherhood of Locomotive Engineers, Brotherhood of Locomotive Firemen and Engineers, Order of Railway Conductors, and the Brotherhood of Railroad Trainmen began organizing engine and train crews; see J.H. Tuck, "Canadian Railways and the International Brotherhoods," 21 and passim; Rountree, *The Railway Worker*, 29–30, 216–23, 227–28 and 273; L.A. Wood, *Union Management Cooperation on the Railroad*; Rex Lucas, *Minetown, Milltown, Railtown*, 120–23; W.F. Cottrell, *The Railroader*, 42–59.

18. This is a simplification of what was a very complex system of seniority and promotion. Beginning with the Second World War, fireman and engineers had less control over their promotion and geographic mobility than did, for example, brakemen and conductors. The experience of work rhythms could consequently vary for engine and traincrews. As well, there were regional variations in work rhythms. In the sparsely populated north country, freight and passenger runs were longer and work was steadier and more predictable than in the south.

19. According to G.M. Rountree's calculations, based on annual statistics for all railway lines, road service staff was reduced by more than 40 percent in the 5-year period between 1928 and 1933. Out of a total reduction of 62 000 men, 10 000 were involved in the operation of trains; see G.M. Rountree, *The Railway Worker*, table X, 123 and, in general, 103–36.

20. Interviews with Dave Kingston, conductor, born 1892, hired 1913; Bob Lenard, engineer, born 1901, hired 1918; Tim Reilly, conductor, born 1899, hired 1920; Vera Miller, engineer's wife, born 1906, married 1929; Catherine Roy, engineer's wife, born 1900, married 1923; Ed Walker, conductor, born 1916, hired 1939; Glen McPherson, engineer, born 1909, hired 1942; Don Nelson, conductor, born 1915, hired 1939; Mike Allen, conductor, born 1915, hired 1941.

21. Running-trades workers were paid on a mileage rate basis. Passenger service paid less per mile travelled than freight service since one could "get over the road" and earn one's miles more quickly on a passenger run. As well, engineers and conductors were paid more per mile than fireman and brakemen. A worker was allowed to earn as many miles per month up to a certain quota which increased throughout this period. After reaching that quota one was supposed to stop working for the month and allow others to make up their quota. Rountree, *The Railway Worker*, 74, and interviews.

22. Steve Price, engineer, born 1915, hired 1942.

23. Joe Mathews, engineer, born 1919, hired 1941.

24. Tim Reilly, conductor, born 1899, hired 1920.

25. Steve Price, engineer, born 1915, hired 1942.

26. See, for example, E.P. Thompson's classic statement on the shaping of industrial work time in "Time, Work Discipline and Industrial Capitalism" in *Essays in Social History*, ed. M.W. Flinn and T.C. Smout (Oxford, 1974), 39–77.

27. In my study, 3 of these 8 women had jobs in retail sales, 3 came from farms, 1 worked as an operator for Bell Telephone, and 1 was a nurse.

28. There were 2 exceptions: one woman worked part-time as a nurse before and after her child was born, and another worked in a bakery after her husband retired from the railroad.

29. Of these 24 wives, 4 were in retail or office work, 4 were teachers, 4 worked on family farms, 6 were factory employees, 2 were nurses, 2 were waitresses, 1 was a babysitter, and another a dancer. All but 5 of these women also lived at home before marriage.

30. Only 2 of these 24 wives did not withdraw from the labour force while their children were still young. One worked as a nurse part-time and the other, also a nurse, briefly resumed her job in response to a family financial crisis.

31. This was the case with 6 of the 8 wives interviewed.

32. Nineteen of the 24 wives considered were in this situation.

33. Seven of the 24 wives considered were in this category. Most husbands began railroad work a few years before, or after, marriage.

34. For example, the absence of a state-supported system of child care placed an onus on women to make informal arrangements for the care of their children if they worked outside the home. As Ruth Pierson has observed, while a state-supported system of child care was created during World War II, it was only a temporary measure to allow mothers to enter the paid workforce at a time of wartime labour shortages. Both the provision of child care and tax concessions to married women ended after the war. In the case of the wives of Allandale running-trades workers, there was still little economic incentive for them to take up wartime wage work. See Ruth Pierson, "Women's Emancipation and the Recruitment of Women into the Labour Force in World War II" in *The Neglected Majority*, ed. Susan Mann Trofimenkoff and Alison Prentice (Toronto, 1977), 125–45 and 185–92.

35. Though no complete wage and income date for the Allandale terminal have been located for this period, census figures for Toronto and Hamilton train and engine crews on all railway lines for the period between 1921 to 1951 provide a rough indication of the relatively high earnings of the men. The rate paid per mile was fairly standard in the industry. Canada, *Census*, 1921, vol. III, table 37; 1931, vol. V, table 22 and 23; 1941, vol. VI, table 7; 1951, vol. V, table 23.

36. Vera Miller, engineer's wife, born 1906, married 1929.

37. This is not to say that the motivations for marriage were simply economic, only that the prospects for a woman who remained single and dependent on the wages paid to most women were not very attractive. See, for example, the comments of Luxton, *More than a Labour of Love* (Toronto, 1980), 43–44. Of the 27 wives married to railroaders whose father's occupation is known, 14 came from working-class families, 11 from farming families, and 2 from lower-middle-class families. Concerning those that same from working-class families, 10 were skilled workers, and 7 of these were railroaders.

38. These categorizations of domestic labour are taken from Strong-Boag, "Keeping House in God's Country," 126. See also Luxton, *More than a Labour of Love*. The above generalization is not meant to ignore the differences in the experiences of working-class women. Gender was

experienced in class-specific ways and there were differences within the various sections of the working class, for example, concerning the ability of wives "to make ends meet," the frequency of the need to cope with their husbands' unemployment, and the ways of doing so.

39. Dave Kingston, engineer, born 1892, hired 1913.

40. Evelyn Martin, conductor's wife, born 1915, married 1943.

41. Joe Mathews, engineer, born 1919, hired 1941.

42. See also the observations in Cottrell, *The Railroader*, 73–75, concerning the problem of planning family events.

43. Rosemary Sharp, engineer's wife, born 1924, married 1948.

44. Luxton provides a very interesting analysis of the various ways family finances might be handled in *More than a Labour of Love*, 165–68.

45. See also, for example, the observations of Strong-Boag, "Keeping House in God's Country," 143–44 and, Luxton, *More than a Labour of Love*, 127 and 173–75.

46. Rebecca Crane, conductor's wife, born 1916, married 1937.

47. For example, Luxton, *More than a Labour of Love*, 201–204.

48. Of the 21 families that stayed in Allandale while the husband worked in the north for long periods of time, more than three-quarters had either the wife's or husband's parents or siblings living in the town or nearby. Only 3 wives with relatives in Allandale moved their family north to join their husbands. The remaining 8 of the 32 families considered did not originally come from Allandale and only moved there after the husband worked up north for a number of years.

49. The classic, as well as most problematic, examination of household structure is found in the work of Peter Laslett. See, for example, *The*

World We Have Lost (New York 1965) and Peter Laslett and Richard Wall, eds., *Household and Family in Past Time* (Cambridge, 1972).

50. Interview with Wilma Laidlaw, conductor's wife, born 1900, married 1920; and Val Laidlaw Bates, conductor's daughter, born 1934.

51. Interviews with Catherine Roy, engineer's wife, born 1900, married 1923; Vera Miller, engineer's wife, born 1906, married 1929; Rosemary Sharp, engineer's wife, born 1924, married 1948; Mike Allan, conductor, born 1915, hired 1941; Carol Webster, engineer's wife, born 1918, married 1941; Jim Blythe, engineer, born 1913, hired 1940; and Ed Walker, conductor, born 1916, hired 1939.

52. See also, for example, Cottrell, *The Railroader*, 4–11; Lucas, *Minetown, Milltown, Railtown*, 135–37; Alick R. Andrews, "Social Crisis and Labrador Mobility: A Study of Economic and Social Change in a New Brunswick Railway Community" (M.A. thesis, University of New Brunswick, 1967, 72–73).

53. Jill Allen, conductor's wife, born 1920, married 1939.

54. Jim Blythe, engineer, born 1913, hired 1940.

55. Allandale had a United, an Anglican, and a Presbyterian church within half a block of one another. The congregation of each was almost exclusively composed of railroad families.

56. Franca Iacovetta, "From *Contadina* to Worker: Southern Italian Immigrant Working Women in Toronto, 1947–1962" in *Looking Into My Sister's Eyes: An Exploration of Women's History*, ed. Jean Burnet (Toronto, 1986), 202.

57. Barbara Cruickshank, conductor's daughter, born 1917.

58. Vera Miller, engineer's wife, born 1906, married 1929.

59. Dick Cook, personnel manager, born 1929, hired 1944.

60. The debate over the importance of the "family wage" for working-class survival and for gender relations has been controversial. See, for example, Jane Humphries, "Class Struggle and the Persistence of the Working Class Family," *Cambridge Journal of Economics* 1, 3 (1977): 241–58 and "The Working Class Family, Women's Liberation and Class Struggle: The Case of Nineteenth Century British History," *Review of Radical Political Economics* 9, 3 (Fall 1977): 25–41; Michele Barrett and Mary McIntosh, " 'The Family Wage': Some Problems for Socialists and Feminists," *Capital and Class* 11 (Summer 1980): 51–72 and *Women's Oppression Today: Problems in Marxist Feminist Analysis* (London, 1980); Ruth Milkman, "Organizing the Sexual Division of Labour: Historical Perspectives in 'Women's Work' and the American Labour Movement," *Socialist Review* 10,1 (1980): 95–150; Johanna Brenner and Maria Ramas, "Rethinking Women's Oppression," *New Left Review* 144 (March–April 1984): 33–71; Martha May, "Bread before Roses: American Workingmen, Labor Unions and the Family Wage" in *Women, Work and Protest: A Century of U.S. Women's Labor History*, ed. Ruth Milkman (London, 1985), 1–21.

61. Andrew Tolson, *The Limits of Masculinity*, 48.

62. Paul Willis, "Shop Floor Culture, Masculinity, and the Wage Form," 196–97. See also, for example, Jeffrey Weeks, *Sexuality*, 38.

63. Tim Armstrong, engineer's son and railway clerk, born 1915, hired 1946.

64 Tim Reilly, conductor, born 1899, hired 1920.

65. Catherine Roy, engineer's wife, born 1900, married 1923.

66. For general observations on the availability of domestic technology and its uneven development and application, see Strong-Boag, "Keeping House in God's Country," 130–35 and Luxton, *More than a Labour of Love*, 128–59.

67. On the allocation of domestic work in the household and the benefits derived from wage labour, see also, for example, Luxton, *More than a Labour of Love*, 45 and 163; Tolson, *The Limits of Masculinity*, 68–70 and 81; and Parr, "Rethinking Work and Kinship."

68. Cockburn, *Brothers*, 206.

69. Rosemary Sharp, engineer's wife, born 1924, married 1948.

70. For example, Willis, "Shop-Floor Culture," 189.

71. There was, however, little divorce in this period. Those interviewed commented that divorce might have been more prevalent if it had been more culturally acceptable. As well, for a woman divorce was economically prohibitive and legally difficult. In 1921, only 10 men and women in Barrie (out of a population of 6936) were divorced. In 1951, 37 men and women (out of a population of 12 514) were divorced. Canada, *Census*, 1921, vol. II, table 33; 1951, vol. 1, table 29.

72. Rosemary Sharpe, engineer's wife, born 1924, married 1948.

73. This was especially the case for the generation of workers that began in the 1920s or earlier. The pattern of occupational inheritance, at least for Allendale railway families, appeared to have changed for the generation of sons whose fathers began work during the Second World War. Of the 21 families with sons who might have followed in their father's footsteps, only 4 families had sons who made a career out of railroading. The contraction of the railway workforce beginning in the 1950s, the greater accessibility to postsecondary education beginning in the 1960s, and family encouragement of social mobility directed sons away from a career on the road. It would appear that many, however, did have summer jobs on the railroad.

74. Rusty Brown, conductor, born 1915, hired 1941.

75. Dave Spalding, engineer, born 1911, hired 1941.

76. Rusty Brown, conductor, born 1915, hired 1941.

77. Half of the conductors and two-thirds of the engineers considered in interviews were Masons. The oldest Masonic lodge in Barrie, the Corinthian Lodge, attracted most of the running-trades workers. The few Catholic workers in the running trades belonged to the Knights of Columbus. The involvement of running-trades workers in fraternal organizations and in community affairs, such as the CNR Recreational Association, contrasts significantly with that of the western U.S. train and engine crews Cottrell studies in the 1930s. See W.F. Cottrell, *The Railroader*, 49; 48 and 71–75.

78. See, for example, accounts of meetings of these organizations in Allandale in the late nineteenth and early twentieth century in *Northern Advance and Examiner*. While the Orange Order was strong especially in Protestant Simcoe County's rural areas, it appeared to have had less of a following among the Allandale running-trades workers who began on the road in the late 1930s and early 1940s. A number of these men recalled, however, that their fathers belonged to the Orange Order and that they would participate in the July 12th parades as children.

79. On the masculine aspects of contemporary British male working-class "occupational cultures" in general, see, for example, Tolson, *The Limits of Masculinity*, 451–81; see also Cockburn, *Brothers*; Baron, "Technology and the Crisis of Masculinity"; and Yarrow, "Class and Gender."

80. Herbert Stitt, a former CPR engineer, provides an interesting collection of nicknames of fellow workers in his autobiography, *I Remember* (Toronto, 1983), 99–102.

81. Studies that have examined informal resistance on the factory shop floor are too numerous to mention more than a few. See, for example, Michael Buraway, *Manufacturing Consent Changes in the Labour Process Under Monopoly Capitalism* (Chicago, 1979); Richard Edwards, *Contested Terrain: The Transformation of the Workplace in the Twentieth Century* (New York, 1979); Andrew Friedman, *Industry and Labour: Class Struggle at Work and Monopoly Capitalism* (London, 1977); Huw Beynon, *Working for Ford* (London, 1973); Jim Peterson, " 'More News From Nowhere': Utopian Notes of a Hamilton Machinist," *Labour/Le Travail* 17 (Spring 1986): 169–223.

82. Tim Armstrong, engineer's son and railway clerk, born 1915, hired 1946.

83. The railways had an elaborate system of rules and regulations governing the operation of trains and the conduct of its employees. This was necessary for the purposes of safety and the protection of property and passengers, and as a means of controlling and disciplining the workforce. Rule violators were assigned demerit points. A worker could accumulate 60 points before he was fired. The number of points assigned depended on the gravity of the transgression. One of the most serious offences was drinking on the job, Rule G. Good behaviour and work habits could result in a reduction of dermerit points. In certain cases, the company might also suspend a worker for a period of time instead of firing him. As with the seniority system and other union regulations, the operation of the railway company's system of discipline was not etched in stone. There was room for company officials and supervisors to manoeuvre. On the genesis of the demerit system, and on the evolution of different management styles on American railroads in the nineteenth century, see, for example, Walter Licht, *Working for the Railroad* (Princeton, 1983).

84. Bob Lenard, engineer, born 1901, hired 1918.

85. John Heath, conductor, born 1914, hired 1938.

86. Rusty Brown, conductor, born 1915, hired 1941.

87. For example, Cockburn, *Brothers*, and Baron, "Technology and the Crisis of Masculinity."

88. Steve Price, engineer, born 1915, hired 1942.

89. Rodney Davies, engineer, born 1909, hired 1941.

90. At this point it is difficult to measure the dimensions of sectionalism in the railway workforce. While running-trades workers themselves professed an absence of sectionalism, and attributed it to a previous generation or to the sentiments of the very few, those from other areas of the workforce were more likely to recall the elitism of the running trades. Studies of the railroad workforce have also observed this sectionalism and the resentment of running-trades workers' elitism and "aristocratic" self-image; see, for example, Lucas, *Minetown, Milltown, Railtown*, 119–24 and Andrews, "Social Crisis and Labour Mobility," 77–78.

91. Willis, "Shop-floor Culture, Masculinity and the Wage Form," 196; see also Gray, "Sharing the Shop Floor," 216–34, and Tolson, *The Limits of Masculinity*, 51–81.

92. Skip Johnson, engineer, born 1914, hired 1941.

93. On the way in which technological change also can call into question a worker's masculinity, see the discussion of the printing industry in Cockburn, *Brothers*, 93–190 and Baron, "Technology and the Crisis of Masculinity." As Baron has observed, "deskilling represents a crisis of masculinity, a crisis for men workers simultaneously as men and as workers"; ibid., 9.

94. Willis, "Shop-floor Culture," 191.

95. The terminology analysed here is taken from interviews and from the glossary of terms listed in Cottrell, *The Railroader*, 117–39.

96. Stan Gray, "Sharing the Shop-floor," *Canadian Dimension* (June 1984): 25. This is a longer version of the article published in *Beyond Patriarchy*. See also Tolson, *The Limits of Masculinity*, 60, and Weeks, *Sexuality*.

97. Steve Price, engineer, born 1915, hired 1942.

98. The term "emotional illiteracy" is taken from Tony Eardley, "Violence and Sexuality" in *The Sexuality of Men*, ed. Andy Metcalf and Martin Humphries, (London, 1985), 101. See also Tolson, *The Limits of Masculinity*, 71.

99. See also the comments of Willis, "Shop-Floor Culture"; Gray, "Sharing the Shop Floor"; Tolson, *The Limits of Masculinity*; and Weeks, *Sexuality*.

100. Glen McPherson, engineer, born 1909, hired 1942.

101. Steve Price, engineer, born 1915, hired 1942.

102. All of the running-trades workers interviewed had been in accidents, at least one of which involved a fatality. While some of these were "head-on" or "back-end" collisions, the most common accident with fatalities was a collision with an automobile at a railway crossing.

103. Glen McPherson, engineer, born 1909, hired 1942.

104. Michael Yarrow has also noted shifts in the masculine practices of Appalachian miners in the 1970s and 1980s that were connected to the changing conditions in the coal mining industry; see Yarrow, "Class and Gender."

105. On women's work in the railways and in general during World War I, see James Naylor, "The Woman Democrat" (Unpublished draft), and Paul Phillips and Erin Philips, *Women at Work* (Toronto, 1983), 25.

On the experience of women during World War II, see Pierson, "Women's Emancipation." On the exclusion of women from running-trades work during the period under study, see interviews and Canada. Bureau of Statistics, *Distribution of Occupations by Industry,* 1931 (Ottawa, 1938), table 2; Canada, *Census,* 1951, vol. IV, table 6 for the Allandale railway workforce. On the exclusion of women in the nineteenth century on American railways, see, for example, Licht, *Working for the Railroad,* 214–16, and Ducker, *Men of the Steel Rails,* 72. On the experience of British women in the railway shops during the Second World War, see McKenna, *The Railway Workers,* 96–98.

106. Interviews. For an excellent analysis of protective legislation concerning female and child labour in the early decades of the twentieth century, and of male unionists' motivations for excluding women from areas of work traditionally monopolized by men, see Naylor, "The Woman Democrat." See also the position of the American Federation of Labor in Milkman, "Organizing the Sexual Division of Labor."

107. Jim Blythe, engineer, born 1913, hired 1940.

108. In this period the admittance of women into the running trades was never seriously contemplated by the CNR, the railway brotherhoods, or the men and women of Allandale. These issues were forcefully raised when a few women were hired as running-trades workers in the last decade; see interview with Dick Cook, personnel manager, born 1929, hired 1944.

109. Cottrell, *The Railroader,* 128.

110. For example, Gray, "Sharing the Shopfloor," 225.

111. This was also quite noticeable in interview situations. The language and nature of interaction of these men were influenced by the presence of women. When men were alone or, especially in a group with their former coworkers, the rough and boisterous masculine style of conduct was most evident.

112. Gray, "Sharing the Shopfloor," 226.

113. Michael Yarrow has written that "male subordinates tend to experience relations with other men as involving difficult contradictions between competition and solidarity, between expectations to be subordinate to domineering fathers and yet assert their rights as equals among men and as superordinate to wives and children. Above all is the necessity to maintain membership in good standing in the brotherhood." Yarrow, "Class and Gender," 5.

114. An emphasis on masculine toughness and power in a husband's relationship with his wife and other family members could lead to domestic violence. Its magnitude in Allandale railway families, however, was not revealed in interviews. Such a sensitive topic was difficult to pursue, though some men and women referred to a few husbands who were known to have mistreated their spouses. While court records might provide an indication of domestic violence, most cases would not have been reported in this period.

115. On the issues involved in conceptualizing family strategies, see, for example, Laurel Cornell, "Where Can Family Strategies Exist," *Historical Methods* 20, 3 (Summer 1987): 120–23; Nancy Folbre, "Family Strategy, Feminist Theory," *Historical Methods* 20, 3 (Summer 1987): 115–18; Daniel Scott Smith, "Family Strategy: More than a Metaphor," *Historical Methods* 20, 3 (Summer 1987): 118–20; Louise Tilley, "Beyond Family Strategies, What?" *Historical Methods* 20, 3 (Summer 1987): 123–25.

POSTWAR Families

and Work

FROM CONTADINA TO WORKER: SOUTHERN ITALIAN IMMIGRANT WORKING WOMEN IN TORONTO, 1947–62 *

FRANCA IACOVETTA

o

On Thursday, 16 November 1956, Maria R. and her daughter arrived in Toronto from her peasant farm in Abruzzi. She was met at Union Station by her husband Eneo, who had left her a year previously for work in Toronto. After eating dinner with relatives, she was ushered into her new home—a basement flat in a Calabrian's house. Next day, Maria and Eneo, who took the day off from his Royal York Hotel janitorial job, went to Honest Ed's discount department store to shop for household necessities, including an espresso coffee maker and pots for cooking spaghetti. To Maria's delight, next morning the Santa Claus Parade passed by their Dupont Street home. At seven o'clock Monday morning, Marie went directly to work at a nearby laundry where a sister-in-law had secured her a job as a steampress operator at thirty-seven dollars a week. For twenty years Maria worked at many such low-skilled jobs—sewing, cooking, tending a grocery store and as a cashier—until 1976 when she finally withdrew from the work force to care for her dying husband.[1]

Women played an important role in the immigration of southern Italian peasant families to post-World War II Toronto. Within the patriarchal framework of the family, Italian women performed demanding roles as immigrants, workers, wives, and mothers. Their active commitment to the

* From Jean Brunet, ed., *Looking into My Sister's Eyes: An Exploration in Women's History* (Toronto: Multicultural History Society of Ontario, 1986), 195–222. I would like to thank Ruth Frager, Maragret Hobbs, Daphne Read, Janice Newton, Janet Patterson, Ian Radforth and Joan Sangster for their comments on earlier drafts of this paper. And many thanks to the women I interviewed, whose real names I used not only with their approval but at their insistence.

family helped bridge the move from Old World to New as women's labour, both paid and unpaid, continued to help ensure the survival and material well-being of their families. The transition from *contadina* (peasant) to worker did not require a fundamental break in the values of women long accustomed to contributing many hours of hard labour to the family. As workers, though, they confronted new forms of economic exploitation and new rhythms of work and life imposed by industrial capitalism. Women at home similarly performed important economic and social functions and endured the alienating and racist aspects of urban industrial life. Bolstered by networks of kinfolk and *paesani* (co-villagers) and the persistence of traditional social forms, women not only endured such hardships but displayed a remarkable capacity to incorporate their new experiences as working-class women into traditionally rooted notions of familial and motherly responsibility.

This article will consider three aspects of southern Italian women's role in postwar immigration: Old-World conditions, chain migration, and early living and working conditions in Toronto. Based on documentary research and interviews, the conclusions presented here are tentative and exploratory. While the essay focusses on women's activities and perceptions, an attempt also has been made to provide the structural contexts—political, economic, social, and familial—in which those experiences took place.

Following the long interruption caused by government restrictions, the Great Depression and the Second World War, Italian immigration resumed on a major scale once again in the late 1940s and 1950s. Millions of temporary and permanent emigrants travelled to continental Europe, North and South America, and Australia. Between 1951 and 1961, overseas emigrants numbered over one million; 250 000, or 25 percent of them, settled in Canada. A target city after 1951, Metropolitan Toronto alone attracted some 90 000, or 40 percent, of the total Italian immigration to Canada in this period.[2]

Women and children comprised a substantial proportion of the influx. Over 81 000 women aged fifteen and over arrived in Canada from 1951–61. Between 25 000–30 000 women, many with children, settled in Toronto. Young, married women sponsored by their husbands and families predominated.[3] After 1952, for example, "dependent" women and children accounted for 40–54 percent of the annual wave of Italians into the country. In a typical year, 1958, dependent women alone comprised almost 35 percent (or 6064) of the total adult population (17 381). And they made up over 70 percent of the number of total adult females (8515).[4] Most women were former peasants from the Mezzogiorno—the southern agricultural regions of Abruzzi-Molise, Basilicata, Campagnia, Puglia, and Calabria. Peasants from the south accounted for nearly 60 percent of the total Italian immigration to Canada in this period.[5]

As southern European Catholics, these women were the target of nativist hostilities. Anticipating the postwar influx of non-British immigrants, the Anglican church in 1941 depicted southern Europeans as "amenable to the fallacies of dictatorship, less versed in the tradition and art of democratic government," and better suited to the hot climate and fragile political structures of Latin America.[6] The British Dominions Emigration Society dismissed northern Italians as communists and southerners as unsatisfactory settlers.[7] Provincial officials, who worried about increasing numbers of Jews and Catholics entering Protestant Ontario, co-operated with manufacturers in recruiting skilled tradesmen exclusively from Great Britain.[8] Even federal immigration officials who did recruit from Italy focussed on the inferiority of southern Italians, whom they portrayed as backward and slovenly, and they worried that these peasants significantly outnumbered their more "industrious" northern compatriots. "The Italian South peasant," one official wrote, "is not the type we are looking for in Canada. His standard of living, his way of life, even his civilization seems so different that I doubt if he could ever become an asset to our country."[9]

Immigration officials interested in recruiting Italian male labourers did not expect the married peasant women to work and so they paid no attention to her. (By contrast, they welcomed some 16 000 females, mostly single northerners, who arrived as trained domestics, hairdressers, and seamstresses.[10]) A 1950 reciprocal agreement between Canada and Italy that removed customs duties on bridal trousseaus entering either country at least recognized women's role in setting up a home in the new society. But it also reflected notions about married women's prescribed roles as wife and mother and reinforced the assumption that married southern Italian women were dependent upon their men and could make no real contribution to Canadian society.[11]

o

Contrary to contemporary assumptions that women were little more than part of the male newcomer's cultural baggage—a view some male scholars have also adopted—southern Italian women were active agents in family migration. A consideration of their role must begin with life in the Old World.

Southern peasants did not come from a background of isolated, closed villages, nor were they completely self-sufficient subsistence farmers isolated from a market economy and ignorant of the world beyond their village. Typically, southern Italians resided in hilltop agro-towns or villages (*paese*) situated in the region's mountainous terrain. Daily, the town's peasants (*contadini*) and agricultural labourers (*braccianti*) walked long distances to the scattered fields and landed estates below. With populations that numbered in the thousands, towns were characterized by complex social structures and class divisions evident in the presence of gentry, middle men and professional notaries as well as bureaucrats, artisans, peasants, agricultural labourers and the unemployed poor.[12] One women, Assunta C., for instance, described her home town of San Paulino in Campagnia as main-taining various commercial and retail and food services, blacksmith and tai-lor shops and a train station. People located in village fragments and hamlets had access to larger urban centres.[13]

Various long-term factors produced Italy's infamous "southern prob-lem" and made life brutal for its residents. The heat and aridity of summer, followed by heavy but sporadic winter downpours, resulted in poor irriga-tion and soil erosion. Though more southerly areas also grew fruits, olives, nuts and poor-quality wine, peasants relied heavily upon wheat and other grain crops. Hilly and mountainous terrain precluded mechanization and encouraged traditional labour-intensive farming techniques that relied upon an ox or cow, a few simple tools and brute strength.

Another serious handicap was the highly fragmented nature of peasant holdings. Outside the latifundia, gentry-controlled estates were divided into small tenancies rented or sold to peasants who simultaneously might own, rent and even share-crop numerous small and widely scattered plots of questionable soil quality. This further discouraged mechanization or intensive cultivation and reinforced undercapitalized and labour intensive methods of faming. The region's "natural" poverty was exacerbated by decades of political neglect as successive government failed to provide irri-gation, develop industry, and institute land reforms; and it contrasted sharply with the industrialized and agriculturally more prosperous North.[14]

Though tied to underproductive plots, *i contadini* were also part of a larger market economy; they engaged in regional trade networks and par-ticipated in a cash economy on a local, national, and international scale. Peasants had economic and social connections to the surrounding regions and urban centres where they exchanged money for goods and services. Maria L., who came from a village in Molise too small to sustain artisan or retail activity, noted how family members frequently visited the nearby town to buy shoes and tools or call for the doctor. The women I interviewed said that their families had regularly sold surplus wheat, eggs, and vegeta-bles to co-villagers and residents in nearby villages who came to their home. A women from the Vasto-Giardi area near Campobasso in Molise, Assunta Ca., sold eggs door to door in her village. And women also pur-chased linens and cloths from travelling merchants.[15]

The very poverty of the South, which made total subsistence impossible for peasants, compelled families to pursue economic strategies that drew them further into a cash economy. Peasant families effectively supplemented meagre farm incomes by sending out members, usually men, on temporary sojourns as wage workers. Hiring themselves out as day labourers on the landed estates (*giornalieri*), many men found seasonal work in the local or regional economy. Other men, such as the fathers of Maria R. and Vincenza, found outside employment as seasonal woods workers.[16] Others sought jobs in agriculture, railway construction and in the building trades either on the Continent or overseas. These activities and the cash remittances families received brought them into contact with highly industrialized economies around the world—a pattern that intensified during the decade following the Second World War.[17]

Although scholars debate definitions of the nuclear and extended family, they agree that the family is the most important economic and social unit to peasants, and that it provided the basis of peasant solidarity in the South. Familial allegiances were sufficiently strong to exclude membership in other institutions and (apart from some exceptional cases of peasant protests and experiments in peasant communism) communal or collectivist associations. Even the celebration of local feasts took on familial forms.[18]

As the basic mode of production and social organization, the peasant family relied upon the maximum labour power of every member of the household, and each person was expected to sacrifice individual needs and contribute to the family's survival. Women interviewed described typical workdays by focussing on how every member performed a necessary task. Some, such as Julia, recalled how the relentless work of farming was made more enjoyable by the camaraderie of family and kinfolk: "we worked so very hard . . . we get up at the crack of dawn to go to work in the *campaign* [fields] but we singing . . . happy because we're together."[19] Beyond the privileged sphere of close family, members of the extended *familiari*— cousins, aunts, uncles and in-laws—also shared this mutual trust and help when it did not interfere with the priorities of the family. (In practice, however, conflicts often occurred.) Nevertheless, such status was denied to all others except *i compari*— non-relatives who gained admittance to the *familiari* through the ritual kinship of godparenthood (*comparagio*). Extreme familialism in the South also involved a distrust of others and constant gossiping about others' misfortune, though people did share a spirit of loyalty to their native village or town and its residents (*campanelismo*).[20]

With respect to women, the literature focusses on the twin themes of sexual segregation and subordination. The patriarchal organization of the southern Italian family and society and the cultural mores of the South did impose heavy restrictions on the choices and behaviour of women. As women interviewed remarked, "honourable" women did not accompany men from outside the household in public unless chaperoned. During local dances, Sunday afternoon visits in the piazza, and at religious festivities, young adults socialized under the watchful eyes of their elders. The very concept of familial *onore* (honour) so valued by Italians rested in large part upon the sexual purity of wives, daughters, and sisters and men's success in guarding the virtue of their women and in playing the predominant role of family breadwinner. Linked to prevailing notions of male self-esteem and dominance, an almost obsessive fear that women might engage in pre- and extra-marital sex, and thereby bring shame to their entire family, was central to women's oppression in southern Italy. Constant supervision of their activities was the inevitable result.[21]

Male privilege was exercised widely within the public sphere. Men were freer to socialize and lead the religious and social feasts celebrated within the village. Considered the family's chief decision maker, the male head acted as the family's representative in its dealings with the outside world. This included making annual rental payments to absentee landlords, journeying out of the region in search of work, or acting as the main marriage negotiator for children—a task that carried a highly visible profile. Assunta C.'s father, for example, spent two weeks consulting people, including the local cleric and doctor, before granting final approval to his daughter's prospective husband.[22]

Nevertheless, a model of male dominance/female submission is ultimately too simplistic to account for the experiences of peasant women in the Mezzogiorno. It ignores the complexity of gender relations in Italy and serves to underestimate the importance of female labour to peasant family production. The dictates of the household economy regularly drew women outside of the home to participate in agricultural production. Though the supposed "natural" link between women and domestic labour persisted, women's work roles included domestic and farm duties. And both involved back-breaking efforts.[23]

Domestic responsibilities included cooking, cleaning, and child care, as well as weaving, sewing clothes and, especially during the winter slack period, producing embroidered linens and crocheted tablecloths for bridal trousseaus. Such labours were time consuming and arduous. As Maria L. explained, doing laundry involved fetching water from the town well to boil and then soaking the items for an hour before carrying them to a nearby stream where they were rinsed and laid out on the rocks to dry. Cooking over open wood stoves was hot and dirty work, and the stoves required constant maintenance and cleaning.[24]

Women and girls also farmed—clearing the plots, sowing and planting, hoeing and sharing in the overall work of the summer grain harvest, a project that drew on help from kinfolk and neighbours. At home, women might supervise the threshing and perform the winnowing process. During the autumn ploughing, women transported manure from barns to the various field plots. Though the actual task of breaking the ground usually involved several men equipped with basic hand tools and an ox or cow, women also performed this exhausting work. All season long, they travelled back and forth between the town and the fields, carrying food and supplies in baskets on their heads. Female members helped in other ways as well. They grew vegetable gardens, fed the animals and herded them into grazing areas scattered among the family fields. Women made cheese from goat and sheep milk and often sold the surplus locally. In southern regions, women and children picked olives, nuts, and fruits growing on their land, or they picked for large landowners in exchange for a portion of the produce. Girls and boys in coastal towns brought home smelts and other small fish. Women made vegetable and fruit preserves and prepared meats, and they helped collect fuel wood from communal lands. Young women might be sent to the local seamstress to learn pattern making and sewing or might train as a hairdresser. Though there were few non-agricultural job opportunities, some families sent single daughters away to work in domestic service or in garment, textile and silk factories of the region. There, they lived in chaperoned boarding houses and regularly sent their wages home. Particularly in the latifundia regions, increasing numbers of "peasant" women after the war engaged in part-time agricultural wage labour.[25]

Distinctions between women's and men's work roles were often blurred—a vital point frequently ignored by scholars. When large numbers of men from the South were conscripted into the Italian army during World War II, for example, women ran the family farms. Similarly, wives, sisters, and daughters compensated whenever men worked in the paid labour force.[26] It was also linked to the size and character of households. When there were several women in one household, younger females were released from domestic work for field work or, as in Pina's case, a seamstress apprenticeship in town. As a single woman, Maria R. often worked in the fields with her parents, grandfather, and brother since her grandmother stayed home and took charge of daily house chores. Assunta C. noted life after marriage was actually easier because she no longer divided her time between work and field duties; she now stayed at home while her husband and in-laws farmed. By contrast, Dalinda, who lived alone with her husband, performed all the domestic labours herself and shared the field work with her husband.[27]

Nor can we assume that patriarchal structures and values in effect to subordinate women meant that they were passive victims with no basis for exercising power. Scholars have stressed the importance of men's public role and have made much of women's tendency to act modestly in mixed company and to claim to outsiders that they speak and act in their husband's or father's name. This can be very misleading, for it is within the private sphere that women could wield the most influence over their families. They made effective use of their capacity to argue, nag, manipulate, disrupt normal routine, and generally make life miserable for men in order to achieve certain demands.[28]

In *Women of the Shadows*, a grim look at postwar southern Italian women, Ann Cornelisen captured the public/private dynamic in her description of a married woman who had been supporting her elderly parents. When asked who made the family's decisions, the woman claimed she consulted with her parents. But when Cornelisen confronted her with the fact she did not usually confer with her parents, she responded: "The Commandments say honour thy father and thy mother, don't they? No reason to let any one know what happens inside the family." Another woman endured months of verbal and physical assault from her husband before convincing him to work in Germany in order to raise funds for their son's hospital care. In fact, she even secured the necessary work permit.[29] Mothers also acted as their children's mediators, as did Julia's mother, who sent instructions to her husband in Argentina in 1955 to grant formal approval to their daughter's marriage plans because *she* favoured it.[30]

Far from Ann Bravo's model of lonely, isolated peasant women with a truncated self-identity, women's close identification with their family did not preclude bonds of friendship with other women.[31] Joint labour projects between households permitted women to work together and, during breaks, to chat and gossip. Women performed many chores—such as laundry and shelling beans—outside the house in the company of other women. Within households, in-laws collectivized domestic and field labour and often became close friends. Not all women were natural allies; they could be suspicious of, and cruel to, each other.[32] But there were also numerous opportunities for women to establish friendships and many did so. With the exception of Maria S., whose father had discouraged friendships, all the women interviewed had confided in close women friends back home and most had chosen long-time girlfriends to be their children's godmothers.[33] As the family's social convener arranging visits, meals, and gifts between kinfolk and *paesani*, women placed themselves at the centre of wide networks of family, kin, and friends.[34] Men were also subjected to community sanctions should they squander the family resources or prove to be inadequate providers, and at home husbands frequently conceded to women's demands.[35] Though gender relations reflected patriarchal precepts, they were far more complex than had hitherto been acknowledged. Even victims of abuse refused to be totally submissive wives.

○

No longer compelled by fascist policies to remain in their home region, Italians after the war escaped worsening conditions in the South—the further pulverization of land-holdings, rising unemployment, inadequate housing, sanitation, and drinking water, and extensive malnutrition and disease. Attracted to the city's boom economy and pulled by the dynamic of chain migration, many of them arrived in Toronto.[36] The poorest residents of the Mezzogiorno—landless agricultural labourers and the unemployed urban poor—did not figure prominently among the influx, however. Rather peasants, who had owned, rented or share-cropped various plots of land, sold their surplus crops and perhaps accumulated savings, predominated. They comprised 75 percent of adult Italian immigrants to Canada during the 1950s.[37] All the women interviewed came from such families and each stressed how her family, though poor, was considerably better off than the *braccianti* and unemployed. Assunta C. recalled how poor and malnourished women in town used to beg for the water in which she had boiled beans so they could feed their babies. Assunta Ca.'s husband had even lent money to relatives and friends.[38] Far from a strategy to deal with abject poverty, emigration served to offset the dwindling opportunities of peasants, especially newly married couples, to improve property holdings. In this way, they avoided loss of status and obtained family property elsewhere.[39]

Women were often denied a formal voice in the decision of the family to emigrate, largely because migration was linked to men's work opportunities, a pattern reinforced by immigration policies in Canada and elsewhere. By making use of informal mechanisms of persuasion, women nonetheless sought to influence the timing and target of migration. Desperate to marry and leave war-torn Fossocessia, Molise, Maria S. persuaded an initially very hostile fiancé that, after their marriage in 1948, they should join her married sister in Toronto.[40] Against her parent's wishes, a spirited Iolanda, who was a hairdresser apprentice from Miamo, Abruzzi, joined two brothers in Toronto in 1956.[41] Other women could not negotiate their own future. The parents of a large southern Calabrian family in Rocella Ionica sent Pina, two sisters, and a brother to Toronto in order to raise money for their butcher shop and the father's medical bills.[42]

On the other hand, many married women shared with their husbands the desire to immigrate to Toronto. They believed in the "dream of America" and were convinced that several years of hard work would secure wealth and a comfortable life for them. Assunta C. recalled how she had always been impressed by the sojourners who had returned to the home town wealthier men. Others received encouraging letters from friends and family and travelled to join them.[43]

Immigration occurred in a comparatively ragged fashion and, led by young, married men who benefited from kinfolk-arranged sponsorship and accommodation, the process frequently involved the temporary fragmentation of families. Nicolletta met her husband during his periodic visits home to Pescara while working in Belgium coal mines in 1951–54. Soon after they married in 1954, her husband returned to Belgium and, in 1956, a pregnant Nicolletta joined him. Upon receiving news a male cousin had sponsored her husband to Canada, the family returned home, and her husband left immediately for Toronto. In 1961 after her husband had sponsored his father and youngest sister, Nicolletta and daughter finally arrived in Toronto.[44]

Although after 1951 it became more common for women to accompany their men to Toronto, many women continued to stay behind while husbands explored opportunities overseas. Significantly, women were familiar with economic strategies that involved the temporary breakup of the family unit but which secured its long-term survival. Many had experienced the absence of fathers and brothers who had emigrated temporarily outside of Italy and had served in the war.[45] Even so, loneliness and hardship ensued, especially for women whose marriage and separation followed closely together. This also led to a further blurring of traditional gender-linked work roles. With only occasional help from her father and brother, Dalinda ran the farm in Vasto-Giardi, Molise, for two years while rearing two small children, including a son born just two days before her husband's departure in 1951 for a Quebec farm. Immediately after their marriage in Mountarro, Calabria, Vincenza's husband left for several years to work in agricultural and railway repair jobs in Switzerland. He made two brief visits in two years but respected his familial obligations by sending money home regularly. He returned home only to accompany a brother to Toronto; one year later, he called for his wife and child. Initially opposed to joining her husband permanently in Toronto, Julia eventually gave in because she felt responsible for her daughter's unhappiness: "my little girl she call 'daddy, daddy' every day . . . she say, 'mommy why we don't go see daddy; mommy, mommy she's a devil, she not let me see my daddy.' Oh, she make me cry every day."[46]

Travelling alone or with female kin or husbands, southern Italian women benefited from family-linked chain migration that acted as a buffer against the alienating features of immigration. A ticket was financed in a variety of ways—a father's savings, money sent home by a husband, cash raised from a woman's sale of household furniture and the Canadian government's Assisted Passage Loan Scheme. Women experienced their first direct confrontation with government bureaucracy when they visited the crowded consulate in Rome for processing and medical examinations. Six months later, they embarked upon the two-week sea voyage and the train ride from Halifax to Toronto's Union Station.

Women's reaction to leaving home and to the trip varied. Some cried, others felt optimistic about prospects in Canada. While some enjoyed the food and dancing aboard ship, others feared their children might fall overboard or disturb passengers by crying in the cabin at night. At Halifax, they feared being separated from their children. When Dalinda arrived on a cold November day in 1953, she was embarrassed by her lightly clad sons and feared she might be considered a bad mother. The train ride through eastern Canada evoked concern as the scattered woodframe houses resembled more the poverty of home that the expected wealth of the New World. But Toronto brought familiar faces and relief, and women settled with their men in the growing southern Italian enclaves in the city's east and west ends and within College Street's Little Italy.[47]

At home and at work, southern Italian immigrant women contributed to the welfare of their working-class families now struggling to survive in Toronto. Their domestic activities and their participation in the paid labour force will be discussed separately.

In order to understand women's domestic duties, a discussion of immigrant households is necessary. They consisted primarily of two types: an extended familial arrangement in which one or more relatives owned the house and other residents paid rent, or a flat rented from non-kin or even non-Italian landlords who normally resided on the main floor. Given their intense clannishness, fewer emotional benefits could be derived by newcomers who rented separate quarters from strangers. Women resented daily infractions of their privacy, and mothers were highly protective of their children. "With the children is very hard to live in . . . another people's house," explained Vincenza. "You have to live in freedom . . . other people they get too frustrated for the children . . . is not fair." She detested three years spent in a tiny third-floor flat near Christie and Bloor streets: "I was think it was gonna be different. I was living worse than over there [Italy]. I live in a third floor . . . two kids after six months . . . and a kitchen in the basement. . . . I wanna go back home. But the money was gone, the furniture was sell, nothing was left." Julia, however, so resented her landlord's complaints regarding water and electricity bills and her child's ruining the hardwood floors that she made her husband move to better quarters within a month of her arrival in Toronto.[48]

By contrast, the *familiari* set-up held greater opportunities for social bonding between kinfolk. A central feature of Italian immigration was the remarkable extent to which family, kin, and *paesani* boarded together temporarily and the high turnover rate of boarders within any particular household. Boarding served an economic and psycho-cultural function for newcomers; it provided boarders with cheap rents, homeowners with savings to put towards mortgage payments, and everyone with an opportunity to engage in "fellow-feeling-ness."[49] It held practical advantages as couples passed on household and baby things, and the group took on labour-intensive projects such as wine-making and the annual slaughter of a pig. Women preferred this arrangement, and several commented on how remarkably rare serious outbursts were in a household containing up to twenty people. A Molisana woman who lived for several years in a crowded Dupont Street house, Ada, even claimed those early years were special times when *parenti* united during hard times. "We cared more for each other then than now," she added.[50]

Far from huddling indiscriminately, the dynamics of these crowded households reflected a deep-seated sense of propriety and were largely organized according to nuclear families. At supper, for instance, families sharing a kitchen ate at different or overlapping times as each woman, who alone was responsible for her family's meals, awaited her husband's arrival from work before heating her pot of water for pasta. Individual families shared private quarters and, while several women might be entrusted to do the grocery shopping, each family paid for its share of the supplies.[51]

Whatever the household structure, women at home performed crucial economic roles. Like other working-class women, they stretched limited resources and found ways to cut costs and earn extra cash. To the benefit of industrial capitalism, women's labours daily replenished the male breadwinner and fed, clothed, and raised children. In extended households, they served extra menfolk who were unmarried or had not yet called for their wives, as well as elderly parents and in-laws. Maria S., who stayed home to raise three children, divided her days between doing her housework, which included gardening and sewing, and helping her sick married sister who lived nearby.[52] Since some households lacked refrigerators until the late 1950s or early 1960s, women purchased daily perishables such as milk and bread. Without washing machines and often with access only to hotplates located in otherwise unfinished basements, basic chores were time consuming and arduous.[53]

Women cut living costs by growing vegetables and grape vines and by preserving fruits and vegetables. With pride Assunta C. recalled how she had produced most of the family's food: "I did everything, tomatoes for sauce, pickles, olives. I did pears, peaches, apricots, everything we eat. We bought the meat from the store and I make sausages and prosciutto." Maria S. saved money by shopping at a large farmer's market at the city limits. Others earned additional cash by taking in boarders or extra washing and many baby-sat for working relatives—all of which increased domestic chores.[54]

Moreover, the wife frequently acted as the family's financial manager, allocating funds for groceries, furniture, and clothing, paying bills, and depositing savings in the bank or putting them towards mortgage payments.

Several women described how at the end of each week their husbands would hand over their pay cheques. In Maria S.'s words, "My husband bring the money home and give it to me and he say, 'You know what you're doing, take care of the money'. . . . I tried save money, and I did. After three years we buy a house." Women considered this task to be of the utmost importance. Though men later usurped this role when finances and investments grew more complex, it also suggests that women's influence at home, especially during the critical early years, was considerable. Certainly, when families were merely surviving men relied upon women's resourcefulness to help make ends meet.[55]

Extended households also let women collectivize housekeeping and exchange confidences. Women who were at home all day—one nursing a newborn, another sewing clothes, and another unemployed—frequently shared domestic chores. For over a year Vincenza lived with a sister-in-law and their children while their husbands worked out of town on a mushroom farm. She babysat the children while her in-law worked as a hospital chambermaid, and each night they shared the cooking and clean-up duties. Similarly, three single working sisters daily shared cooking and cleaning tasks, and on week-ends they rotated laundry, shopping, and housekeeping.[56]

Many women also made friends with non-related Italian and even non-Italian women in their neighbourhood. Maria S. and her sister befriended several Ukrainian and Jewish women in their neighbourhood. In spring and summer they spent hours outside talking, and they made a point of celebrating each other's birthday. At home with her own and her cousin's children, Assunta C. spent afternoons with a neighbour who also baby-sat children. Each would alternate working in her garden or house while the other supervised the children.[57]

Whether at home or in the factory, urban industrial life evoked anxiety and fear in women who no longer enjoyed the protection of the *paese*. Several women recalled the fear of going out alone at night, the mocking looks of native Torontonians, and even the experience of being robbed in their own homes.[58] Daily they confronted prejudice. Marie S. recalled crying all the way home after being laughed out of a department store one day in 1949 when she could not make herself understood by the saleswomen. (She had wanted to purchase socks and work pants for her plasterer husband.) Interestingly, this incident spurred her on to learn English. While returning from a weekend visit with relatives in New York City, a misunderstanding at the border resulted in the jailing of Pina and her sister for ten days in Buffalo until an American aunt hired an Italian-speaking lawyer who cleared up the confusion.[59]

Mothers also feared for their children's safety at school where outbursts regularly occurred between Anglo-Saxon and Italian schoolmates, especially boys. They worried about being called poor mothers by doctors, school nurses, and teachers. When school authorities sent home a girl suspected of having lice, her family became totally distraught and immediately took her to the hospital. Marie L., who gave birth to a premature son the morning after she arrived in Toronto, was afraid to leave him in the hospital for fear he would die. As she noted, the comfort traditionally provided by the village midwife had been abruptly cut off and impersonal institutions put in her place.[60]

Women's anxieties were well founded, for racism permeated postwar Toronto society. Fearing the loss of the city's British and Protestant character, native Torontonians could be very cruel to the new Jewish and Catholic immigrants of the 1940s and 1950s.[61] Women worried about police harassing their men as they congregated outside churches or clubs to chat with *paesani* as they had at home. Though some noted the kindness of certain strangers, they resented being stared at while riding the streetcars, or being treated like ignorant children.[62] Racism could run deep. In a 1954 letter to Ontario Premier Leslie Frost, a Toronto Orangeman wrote: "In regards to the Immigration to this country of so many Italians the place around here is literally crawling with these ignorant almost black people. . . . [and] so many landing in this country with TB disease." While he saved his worst criticism for young Italian men suspected of being "armed with knives and . . . continually holding up people and especially ladies near parks and dark alleys," the writer expressed total distaste for foreign-speaking Catholic men and women and called for a stop to immigration from a Vatican-controlled and disease-infested Italy.[63]

Many southern Italian women contributed to their family's finances by entering the paid labour force. They were part of the dramatic postwar increase of women in general, including married women, who entered the Canadian work force. In 1961 almost 11 percent of over a million working women in Canada were European-born, of whom Italian-born women comprised over 17 percent. Some 15 percent of the over 100 000 working women in Ontario were European-born with the Italian-born making up 20 percent of the total. In Toronto, 16 990 Italian women made up 7 percent of the 1961 female labour force. Working women, most of whom were probably postwar immigrants, accounted for 30–38 percent of the total Italian adult female population in Canada as well as Ontario in 1961; for Toronto this was nearly 40 percent. And these statistics do not take into account money raised by women at home.[64]

While Canadian-born women swelled the ranks of white-collar work, immigrant women provided cheap, unskilled, and semi-skilled female labour, suggesting that female migration from Europe after the war helped Canadian employers keep down labour costs. With the approval of employers who considered them hard-working and docile, Italian women in Toronto took on low-skilled, low paying jobs normally offered to immigrant women lacking English-language and other marketable skills beyond some domestic training. These included garment piece-work at home, operating steampresses, sewing and novelty-making machines, packaging, bottling and labelling, cafeteria work and domestic service.[65]

Manufacturing and domestic service were the largest employers of European-born women in Canada and Ontario in 1961. Almost 57 percent of over 32 000 Italian women workers in Canada were in manufacturing, particularly clothing (50 percent), food, and beverage (11 percent), textiles (12 percent), leather goods (6.2 percent), and unskilled factory work (6.6 percent). In service, where 28 percent of the total were located, nearly 76 percent of them were domestic servants. For Ontario, over 20 000 Italian women workers were similarly concentrated in manufacturing (50 percent) and service (31 percent). In the former category, they included leather cutters and sewers (38 percent), tailoresses (22 percent), food-processing workers (14 percent), and unskilled factory workers (10 percent). Over 61 percent of the personal service workers were housekeepers, waitresses and cooks; 28 percent were laundresses and dry-cleaners.[66]

Whether a woman worked outside the home depended on various factors such as a husband's attitude, child-bearing, availability of baby-sitters, and work opportunities. Alone, with menfolk, or in groups of female kin, women in search of work headed for the garment and light manufacturing areas of the city, where they went door to door asking for jobs. It took Pina four months of searching with her brother, who worked nights as a bowling alley janitor, before she found work packaging men's socks in a Spadina garment factory. Following an unsuccessful two-month search, Dalinda sewed children's clothes at home for five cents a garment until a cousin landed her a factory job several months later. Many women benefited from kin-networking at the work place as already-employed women would arrange positions for incoming relatives.[67] Scholars have stressed how these occupational enclaves eased men's concerns about women working outside the home by providing traditional checks on female behaviour,[68] but the women themselves preferred to emphasize the utility of kinship ties and the camaraderie of the work place. Several said they would have worked wherever they found suitable jobs, and some, such as Ada and Marie L., found work for a time in ethnically mixed work places.[69]

Italian women's paid labour was part of a well-articulated working-class family strategy for success, one most often measured in terms of home ownership. Female wages helped support families through periods of seasonal male unemployment, especially for the men in construction and public works or out of town on farms, in mines, or on government building projects. Women's earnings paid for daily living expenses, such as groceries, clothing, and household necessities, while men's pay cheques went into savings and toward buying houses and other investments. Characterized by low wages and high turnover, their work experience also reflected the gender inequalities of the postwar occupational structure. Predictably, the desire of capital for cheap workers and of immigrant working-class families for additional earnings were inextricably linked.[70]

Like many unskilled male and female workers, Italian women worked long hours at either monotonous or hazardous jobs that were physically demanding. Women employed in the drapery and clothing factories endured poor ventilation and high humidity, as well as speed-ups and close supervision. Women assembling items in plastics factories put up with dust and foul-smelling fumes. Laundry work required much sorting and carrying, and steampresses made the workplace almost unbearable in summer. Italian women in factories also confronted the new time and work discipline of industrial capitalism and the impersonal relations between employers and workers. On the other hand, the daily experience of the workplace, where Italian women learned to speak English from co-workers and sometimes forged friendships with non-*paese* and non-Italian women, may also have had a broadening impact on women hitherto confined to the household. By contrast, domestic workers cleaning house for middle-class clients toiled in total isolation from the rest of working women.[71]

During the 1950s and early 1960s, Italian women workers did not express an articulated political response to their exploitation as female workers. This was linked to their low status as cheap and unskilled labour and to the barriers of language and ethnicity erected between women in the workplace. Another major factor was the isolation of domestic workers. Household duties also kept women away from organizing meetings, and many were unsure about union organizers who visited their shops. Since joining a local might endanger their jobs, they feared compromising their main goal of helping the family's finances. Moreover, southern Italians were concentrated in industries characterized by high concentrations of unskilled female workers and high labour turnover rates. As a result, relatively few joined unions.[72]

Familial priorities, especially the duties of newly married women to bear and raise children, helped shape the timing and rhythm of women's participation in the labour force. Some women, such as Virginia, a trained seamstress from Pescara, Abruzzi, who worked for three years in a Spadina Street bathing-suit factory until she had her first child, never returned to work after starting families. Others, such as Assunta C., did not work until all their children reached school-age. Ten years after her arrival in Toronto in 1959 Assunta C. found work in a crest-making factory. Having worked for several years, Vincenza withdrew from the labour force for six years between 1960 and 1966 to rear her children before returning to domestic service.[73]

Significant numbers of Italian women, however, regularly moved in and out of the labour force. They moved from one type of factory work to another, and from factory work to service jobs such as cafeteria and chambermaid work as well as fruit and vegetable picking. Frequently women left jobs as a protest against poor working conditions and pay. Ada quit work as a shirt packager after losing some overtime hours, but in only a few weeks she secured work as a bow-machine operator for a factory producing wrapping and party accessories. Husbands sometimes urged their wives to quit. In 1963 Maria L. quit work as a Royal York Hotel chambermaid to appease her husband who disliked her cleaning up for strangers and working on Sundays, even though his father and sister also worked at the hotel. Several years earlier, however, Maria had spontaneously quit her job in a

Woolworth's cafeteria when management shifted her into a more stressful job in inventory. That time her husband had immediately approved of her quitting, even though he had found her the job in the first place.[74]

Most often, women left work temporarily to fulfill family obligations—having children, tending to a family crisis, or resettling the family in a new home. Shortly after Angella immigrated with her parents in 1958, for example, she worked as a seamstress in a Spadina Street bathing-suit factory and continued to work there for two years following her marriage in 1959. One year later, she left to have a child and then returned in 1962 to similar work at a sportswear and leather factory on College Street. Three years later she left to have her second child and then returned to the same job two years later. Following the family's move to Willowdale, a Toronto suburb, she secured work in a local plastics factory, which she left in 1971 to have her third child, only to return six months later. In 1973 she suffered a slipped disc at work, which kept her out of the labour force for ten years.[75]

When baby-sitting could not be provided by female kinfolk or *paesane*, many Italian women put off work until a sister, in-law, or cousin became available to watch the children. (These relatives might themselves be recent immigrants or new mothers.) Mothers who hired landladies or neighbours often felt uneasy about leaving their children with "strangers" unconnected to them by links of kin or village. Maria L. recalled how each morning she hated leaving her crying and clinging son with the landlady downstairs. Suspecting that her son was being neglected by the baby-sitter, who had young children of her own, Marie stopped working for over a year (with her husband's approval) until her mother's arrival in the city in 1959 gave her the confidence to re-enter the work force. Opting for a different solution, Julia and Vincenza worked as domestic servants while they had pre-school youngsters and brought the children to their clients' homes.[76]

Nor did outside work reduce the burden of housekeeping. Although men performed certain tasks, such as stoking the coal furnace, shovelling outside snow and perhaps watching children briefly while their wives shopped or cleaned, working women were responsible for the household chores, even during periods of male unemployment. Indeed, other women often watched the children while their mothers performed domestic tasks. This double burden hung heavily on the shoulders of Maria L., who for over a year combined full-time work as a steampress operator with caring for a son, a husband, and his father and two brothers. "Oh poor me," she recalled, "full-time work . . . wash, clean, cook . . . I did all that! I was really just a girl, nineteen years old and thin, thin like a stick. I had four men, a baby. I was with no washing machine. I would go down to the laundry tub. . . . Then I had to cook and I had to work. And it was not only me." Julia probably voiced the frustration of many working women when she said: "Of course he should help in the house. My back I hurt it at work, it hurts to wash the floor, pick up the clothes. But what you gonna do? Can't have a fight every day about it so I do it. But no it's not right!"[77]

Notwithstanding the obstacles to unionization, assumptions regarding Italian women's alleged docility and their outright hostility to unionization may be exaggerated. At a time when female militancy in the work place was not pronounced, it is not surprising that Italian immigrant women did not became politicized during the 1950s. Nor is there any reason to assume they should have felt any sense of working-class solidarity with their Canadian-born sisters, especially white-collar workers. Some women explained that for years the topic of unionization had never come up in the work place. Employers no doubt also took advantage of ethnic and cultural divisions among new arrivals.

In contrast to Italian women radicalized by their participation in the wartime Resistance movement—women who became socialists and communists and who, by the early 1960s, spearheaded Italy's modern feminist movement with the creation of Unione Donne Italiane—most southern peasant women who came to Toronto had little if any prior experience with industrial work and the traditions of worker protest.[78] (There were communists in the South. They included former landless *braccianti* who benefited from land reforms initiated under Italy's postwar reconstruction program as well as peasants, though probably none of the local élites, Italian women perhaps understood instinctively the exploitative relations between employers and workers, and many were truly angered by the injustices they suffered as working immigrant women. Even Julia, an anti-unionist, dismissed what she considered ruling-class rhetoric that portrayed Canada as a land of limitless opportunity. "Why feel grateful?" she said. "We really suffered for what we got. I have four back operations. I have to leave my kids alone and work. . . . And we don't live like kings and queens. I work hard for what I got." Moreover, increasing numbers of women grew to support unionization over the years not only because higher wages further helped their families but because they identified improved working conditions and health benefits won during the sixties and early seventies with a recognition of their labour and with self-respect. In Dalinda's words, "Sure we should get more money, we work hard for it, we leave our kids, come home tired, do the dirty jobs.[79]

The entry of southern Italian peasant women into Toronto's postwar labour force reflected a pattern of continuity, for women had been important contributors to the peasant family economy in the Mezzogiorno. Traditional values that stressed the obligation of all family members to contribute to the family's well-being eased the transition into Toronto's industrial economy. Since women's work was already justified in terms of peasant survival, no dramatic change in values was needed to allow these immigrant women to work outside the home. Women themselves argued that they were accustomed to working long and hard for the family. "I went to work to help out the family," was a common response. Given the scarcity of resources accessible to southern Italian immigrant families newly arrived in Toronto during the 1940s and 1950s, additional wages earned by women, including those at home, amounted to an effective familialist response.[80]

To a remarkable degree, southern Italian families preserved traditional cultural forms and familial arrangements and thereby resisted disintegration. Problems confronted by working women were often handled effectively within the context of family and kinship networks. Even so, women's entry into an urban, industrial work force did not occur without considerable strain and difficult adjustments, especially for married women. These strains reflected a dialectical process by which southern Italian peasants became transformed into working-class families. Their familial and collectivist behaviour was not simply the expression of traditional peasant culture; it also reflected their new economic position as working-class families coping with conditions of scarcity and restriction under industrial capitalism. This held particular significance for working Italian women, a fact ignored by scholars who view Italian immigrant women exclusively in terms of family and home. How demands of family and work conflicted with but also complemented each other also required consideration.[81]

Motivated by a commitment to family, southern Italian women linked their self-identification as women and mothers to the paid and unpaid labour they performed for the benefit of parents, husbands, and children. Whether at home or at work, they took on dirty and difficult jobs and cut costs wherever possible. In the process they developed a conception of feminine respectability that was rooted in both their peasant and immigrant working-class experiences, and that expressed the pride of women who saw themselves as indispensable to their family. Stripped of notions of reserved femininity and delicate demeanour, it also contrasted sharply with postwar middle-class models of womanhood.[82] While the nature of their labour was largely transformed when they entered Toronto's industrial economy, southern Italian women's paid and unpaid work remained critical to the daily survival of their newly arrived families in postwar Toronto.

NOTES

1. Interview with Maria Rotolo.

2. Samuel Sidlofsky, "Post-War Immigrants in the Changing Metropolis with Special Reference to Toronto's Italian Population" (Ph.D. diss., University of Toronto, 1969), ch. 1; Franc Sturino, "Family and Kin Cohesion among South Italian Immigrants in Toronto" in *The Italian Immigrant Woman in North America*, ed. Betty Boyd Caroli, Robert F. Harney, and Lydio F. Tomasi, (Toronto, 1978); A.T. Bouscaren, *European Economic Migrations* (The Hague, 1969).

3. Sidlofsky, "Immigrants," 97–110; Sturino, "Family and Kin," 288–90; Freda Hawkins, *Canada and Immigration: Public Policy and Public Concern* (Montreal, 1972), 47–48;

Jeremy Boissevain, *The Italians of Montreal: Social Adjustment in a Plural Society* (Ottawa, 1970), 10.

4. Department of Citizenship and Immigration, *Annual Report*, 1950–62, tables indicating dependents and intended employment, my calculations.

5. "White Paper, Canadian Immigration Policy," 1966, cited in Hawkins, *Canada*, 9–10; Sturino, "Family and Kin," 291; Sidlofsky, "Immigrants," 97–101. See also Istituto Centrale di Statistica, *Annuario Italiano* (Rome, 1951–60).

6. Public Archives of Ontario (hereinafter PAO), Ontario, Department of Planning and Development, Immigration Branch Files (hereafter IBF), "The Bulletin Council for Social Service,"

no. 104, Church of England of Canada, 15 Oct. 1941, pp. 15–91. I would like to thank Donald McCloud at the PAO for making these materials available to me.

7. PAO, IBF, E.H. Gurton, Canadian Manager, British Dominions Emigration Society, Montreal, to Ontario Immigration Branch, 1 June 1951, 2b.

8. A departmental memo to the minister responsible for Immigration, William Griesinger, was critical of the federal government for not attracting more British immigrants and advised him that Ontario must secure federal help in its effort to maintain a racial and religious balance in the province, "preferably one British to four others . . . any preference to British is given simply because they are our greatest source of skilled help and a minimum readjustment [sic] to our way of life." PAO, IBF, F.W. Stanley to William Griesinger, 28 Nov. 1950; see also Griesinger to Stanley, 30 Oct. 1950; the *Telegram* (Toronto), 27 Dec. 1950 (clipping); see also files on the 1951 plan to recruit British tradesmen for Ontario manufacturers.

9. Public Archives of Canada (hereafter PAC), Immigration Branch Records (hereafter IR), vol. 131, Laval Fortier to acting Commissioner of Immigration Overseas, 4 Oct. 1949.

10. Department of Citizenship and Immigration, *Annual Report*, 1950–61, tables on intended occupation, my calculations.

11. PAC, IR, vol. 131, Department of External Affairs Statement, 29 March 1950; A.D.P. Heeney Memo, 30 March 1950; House of Commons, *Debates*, 28 March 1950, p. 1208.

12. Rudolf Vecoli, "Contadini in Chicago: A Critique of the Uprooted," *Journal of American History* 51 (1964); Robert Foerster, *The Italian Emigration of Our Times* (Cambridge, 1919); Rudolph Bell, *Fate and Honour, Family and Village: Demographic and Cultural Change in Rural Italy Since 1800* (Chicago, 1979).

13. Interview with Assunta Capozzi and Maria Lombardi.

14. Bell, *Fate and Honour*, 123–48; J.P. Cole, *Italy: An Introductory Geography* (New York, 1974); Alan B. Mountjoy, *The Mezzogiorno* (London, 1973).

15. Interview with Maria Lombardi and Assunta Carmosino; also interviews with Maria Rotolo, Assunta Capozzi, Maria Sangenesi, Marie Carmosino, and Dalinda Lombardi-Iacovetta.

16. Interviews with Maria Rotolo and Vincenza Cerulli.

17. Interviews with Salvatore and Josephine D'Agostino and Julie Toscano. See also Robert F. Harney, "Men Without Women: Italian Migrants in Canada, 1885 to 1930" in *Italian Immigrant Women*; his "Montreal's King of Italian Labour: A Case Study of Padronism," *Labour/Le Travailleur* 4 (1979); Bruno Ramirez, "Workers Without a 'Cause': Italian Immigrant Labour in Montreal, 1880–1930" (Paper presented to the Canadian Historical Association, Annual Meeting, 1983).

18. On South Italian peasants, general monographs include: Edward Banfield, *The Moral Order of a Backward Society* (Illinois, 1958); Jan Brogger, *Montavarese: A Study of Peasant Society and Culture in Southern Italy* (Oslo, 1971); Constance Cronin, *The Sting of Change: Sicilians in Sicily and Australia* (Chicago, 1970); John Davis, *Land and Family in Pisticci* (London, 1973); Joseph Lopreato, *Peasants No More! Social Class and Social Change in an Underdeveloped Society* (San Francisco, 1967).

19. Interview with Julia Toscano.

20. Vecoli, "Contadini"; Bell, *Fate and Honour*, 2–3, 72–76; Leonard W. Moss and Stephen C. Cappannaro, "Patterns of Kinship, Comparaggio and Community in a South Italian Village," *Anthropological Quarterly* 33 (1960).

21. See Brogger, *Montavarese*, 106–20; Cronin, *Sting*, ch. 4; Bell, *Fate and Honour*, 90, 120–23; Ann Cornelisen, *Women of the Shadows: A Study of the Wives and Mothers of Southern Italy* (New York, 1970); Virginia Yans-McLaughlin, "Patterns of Work and Family Organization: Buffalo's Italians" in *The Family in History: Interdisciplinary Essays*, eds. Theodore R. Rabb and Robert I. Rotberg and her *Family and Community: Italian Immigrants in Buffalo, 1880–1930*, 180–217. Also interviews with Ada Carmosino, Maria Lombardi, Marie Carmosino, Dalinda Lombardi-Iacovetta, and others.

22. Interview with Assunta Capozzi.

23. Interviews. Also, Ann Bravo, "Solidarity and Loneliness: Piedmontese Peasant Women at the Turn of the Century," *International Journal of Oral History* 3 (June 1982); Brogger, *Montavarese*, 41–50, 106–109; Miriam Cohen, "Italian-American Women in New York City, 1900–1950: Work and School" (Paper presented to the American Studies Association, San Antonio, Texas, 1975); Cornelisen, *Women*, 71–129; Columba Furio, "The Cultural Background of the Italian Immigrant Woman and Its Impact on Her Unionization in the New York City Garment Industry" in *Pane e Lavoro: The Italian American Working Class*, ed. George E. Pozzetta, Donna Gabaccia, "Sicilian Women and the 'Marriage Market': 1860–1920" (Paper and discussion at the Sixth Berkshire Conference on the History of Women, June 1984); Simonetta Piccone Stella, *Ragazze del sud* (Rome, 1979).

24. Interview with Maria Lombardi, Assunta Capozzi, Dalinda Lombardi-Iacovetta.

25. Interviews. Yans-McLaughlin, *Family*, 26–27; Bell, *Fate and Honour*, 130–33; Sydney Tarrow, *Peasant Communism in Southern Italy* (New Haven, 1967). On an earlier period, see also Louise A. Tilly and Joan Scott, *Women, Work, and Family* (New York, 1978).

26. Interviews with Julia Toscano, Marie Sangenesi, Ada Carmosino, Maria Carmosino, and Josephine D'Agostino.

27. Interviews with Josephine D'Agostino, Marie Rotolo, Assunta Capozzi, and Dalinda Lombardi-Iacovetta.

28. Brogger, *Montavarese*, 41–109, Bell, *Fate and Honour*, 120–28. On men's role in feasts, see, for example, Enrico Cumbo, "The Feast of the Madonna del Monte," *Polyphony* 5, 2 (Fall/Winter 1983). See also Ernestine Friedl, "The Position of Women: Appearance and Reality," *Anthropological Quarterly* 40 (1967).

29. Cornelisen, *Women*, 222—24, 57–93; see also Vincenza Scarpaci, "La Contadina, The Plaything of the Middle-Class Woman Historian," Occasional Papers on Ethnic and Immigration Studies, Multicultural History Society of Ontario (Toronto, 1972); and her "Angella Bambace and the International Ladies Garment Workers Union: the Search for an Elusive Activist" in Pozzetta, *Pane e Lavoro*.

30. Cronin, *Sting*, 78; interview with Julia Toscano.

31. Bravo, "Peasant Women."

32. See especially Cornelisen, *Women*; Bell, *Fate and Honour*; Banfield, *Backward Society*. See also Sydel Silverman, "Agricultural Organization, Social Structure, and Values in Italy: Amoral Familialism Reconsidered," *American Anthropologist* 70 (Feb. 1968).

33. Interviews with Maria Sangenesi, Dalinda Lombardi-Iacovetta, Marie Lombardi, Ada Carmosino, Maria Rotolo, Assunta Capozzi.

34. Interviews; Gabaccia "Sicilian Women." Most studies deal with Italian women almost exclusively in terms of family and home. See for example, Vaneeta D'Andrea, "The Social Role Identity of Italian-American Women: An Analysis of Familial and Comparison of Familial and Religious Expectations" (Paper

presented to the American Italian Association, 1980); Harriet Perry, "The Metonymic Definition of the Female and Concept of Honour Among Italian Immigrant Families in Toronto" in *Italian Immigrant Women*. At the Columbus Centre in Toronto, Samuel Bailey recently described Italian women in prewar Argentina, New York, and Toronto as living in insular worlds defined by the particular block on which they resided with their children and families. By contrast, men identified more easily with the larger ethnic community. The implication is that women stayed at home and played no role in the ambience of the ethnic enclave.

35. Harney, "Men Without Women."

36. Mountjoy, *Mezzogiorno*, 32–36; Tarrow, *Peasant Communism*. See also Carlo Levi, *Christ Stopped at Eboli* (New York, 1946). On chain migration see, J.S. MacDonald, "Italy's Rural Structure and Migration," *Occidente* 12, 5 (Sept. 1956); J.S. MacDonald and L.D. MacDonald, "Chain Migration, Ethnic Neighborhood Formation and Social Networks," *Millbank Memorial Fund Quartery* 13 (1964); Harvey Choldin, "Kinship Networks in the Migration Process," *International Migration Review* 7 (Summer 1973). On Toronto, see, Sidlofsky, "Immigrants"; Sturino, "Family and Kin"; his "Contours of Postwar Italian Immigration to Toronto," *Polyphony* 6, 1 (Spring/Summer 1984).

37. Hawkins, *Canada*, 47–48. See also "White Paper," 9–10.

38. Interview with Assunta Capozzi and Assunta Carmosino.

39. On an earlier period, see: Joseph Barton, *Peasants and Strangers: Italians, Rumanians and Slovaks in an American City, 1890–1930*; John Bodnar, "Immigration and Modernization: the Case of Slavic Peasants in Industrial America," *Journal of Social History* 10 (Fall 1976); Yans-McLaughlin, *Family*, 33–36; Harney and Scarpaci, eds., *Little Italies in*

North America (Toronto, 1983). See also John Baxevanis, "The Decision to Migrate," in his *Economy and Population Movements in the Peloponnesos of Greece* (Athens, 1972), 60–75.

40. Interview with Maria Sangenesi.

41. Iolanda Marano interviewed by Pina Stanghieri.

42. Interview with Josephine D'Agostino.

43. Interviews with Maria Carmosino, Maria Lombardi, Assunta Capozzi, Vincenza Cerulli, Dalinda Lombardi-Iacovetta.

44. Nicoletta DeThomasis interviewed by Rosemary DeThomasis.

45. Julia Toscano's father, for example, spent her entire girlhood outside the country—in Albany from 1936–38, Germany 1938–39, and Argentina for six years after the war. For a discussion of the impact of men's immigration on home life in Italy see: Harney, "Without Women"; N. Douglas, *Old Calabria* (New York, 1928).

46. Interview with Dalinda Lombardi-Iacovetta, Vincenza Cerulli, and Julia Toscano.

47. Interviews. On postwar settlement, see Sidlofsky, "Immigrants"; Sturino, "Family and Kin" and his "Postwar Immigration."

48. Interview with Vincenza Cerulli and Julia Toscano. Also with Josephine D'Agostino.

49. Harney, "Boarding and Belonging," *Urban History Review* 2 (Oct. 1978). On the importance of kin and boarding for an earlier period see also: Michael Anderson, *Family Structure in Nineteenth Century Lancashire* (Cambridge, 1971); John Modell and Tamara K. Hareven, "Urbanization and the Malleable Household: An Examination of Boarding and Lodging in American Families," in Hareven, ed., *Family and Kin in Urban Communities, 1700–1930*, ed. Tamara K. Hareven (New York, 1977); and her "Family Time and

Industrial Time: Family and Work in a Planned Corporate Town, 1900–1924," ibid.

50. Interviews with Ada Carmosino, Maria Rotolo, Maria Lombardi, Maria Sangenesi, Maria Carmosino, Dalinda Lombardi-Iacovetta.

51. Ibid.

52. Interview with Maria Sangenesi. See also *Canadian Ethnic Studies*, Special issue on Ethnicity and Femininity, 1981.

53. Interview with Dalinda Lombardi-Iacovetta, Maria Lombardi, Ada Carmosino, Maria Rotolo, Josephine D'Agostino. All of them obtained appliances several years after their arrival.

54. Interview with Assunta Capozzi and Maria Sangenesi; also with Assunta Carmosino. See also labour force statistics indicating Italian-born women who took in washing, boarders and children. Canada, *Census* 1951. Others, of course, went unrecorded (tables on Canada and Ontario).

55. Of course, working women might also perform this role. Interview with Maria Sangenesi, Maria Rotolo, Vincenza Cerulli, Maria Lombardi, Ada Carmosino, Julia Toscano, and Josephine D'Agostino.

56. Interviews with Ada Carmosino, Maria Lombardi, Dalinda Lombardi-Iacovetta; also with Vincenza Cerulli and Josephine D'Agostino.

57. Interview with Maria Sangenesi and Assunta Capozzi.

58. Dalinda Lombardi-Iacovetta was robbed one day in 1953 while she was at home with her two children doing garment piece-work. The thief, who came to the door, armed with a knife, got away with two weeks' pay—twenty dollars.

59. Interview with Maria Sangenesi and Josephine D'Agostino.

60. Interview with Maria Lombardi (Maria reported on the story above, in which a cousin by marriage was involved); also with Dalinda Lombardi-Iacovetta, Maria Rotolo, Ada Carmosino. Also, in conversation with several Italian-born men who attended elementary and secondary school in Toronto during the 1950s. All stressed backyard brawls in which they engaged and the embarrassment of being put behind in school grade level because of language difficulties.

61. See, for example, *Debates*, 13 June 1950; Margot Gibb-Clarke, *Globe and Mail*, 20 Oct. 1984, 18; Sturino, "Postwar Immigration to Toronto" (Paper given to the Colombus Centre, 1984).

62. Interviews. Also interviews with Salvatore D'Agostino, Camilo Schiuli, and Salvatore Carmosino.

63. PAO, IBF, F.J. Love to Premier Leslie Frost, 1 Sept. 1954. See also response; H.K. Warrander to J.L. Love, 2 Sept. 1954. Following an explanation that the Ontario government carried out "a very small selective type of immigration programme . . . [having] to do only immigrants from the United Kingdom, it added: "Other immigrants . . . are dealt with by the Federal Government departments and I am therefore sorry to say that we have no control over that type of immigrant or whether or not he comes here in a healthy condition."

64. Canada, *Census*, 1951. The figures for Toronto were provided by Statistics Canada researchers. On postwar women and work see: Pat and Hugh Armstrong, *The Double Ghetto* (Toronto, 1978); Julie White, *Women and Unions* (Ottawa, 1980).

65. Ibid. See also Sheila McLeod Arnopolous, *Problems of Immigrant Women in the Canadian Labour Force* (Ottawa, 1979); Laura C. Johnson with Robert C. Johnson, *The Steam Allowance: Industrial Home Sewing in Canada* (Toronto, 1982); Monica Boyd, "The Status of Immigrant Women in Canada" in *Women in Canada*, ed. Marylee Stephenson, (Don Mills, 1977); Anthony Richmond, *Immigrants and Ethnic Groups in Metropoli-*

tan Toronto (Toronto, 1967). For useful theoretical discussions of immigrant and migrant women see: "Why Do Women Migrate? Towards Understanding of the Sex-Selectivity in the Migratory Movements of Labour," *Studie Emigrazione* 20 (June 1983); Annie Phizacklea, ed., *One Way Ticket.*

66. Canada, *Census*, 1951, my calculations.

67. Interviews with Josephine D'Agostino, Dalinda Lombardi-Iacovetta, Maria Rotolo; also with Maria Lombardi, Maria Carmosino, Vincenza Cerulli, Julia Toscano, Ada Carmosino.

68. See, for example, Yans-McLaughlin, "Family"; Sturino, "Postwar Immigrants."

69. Interviews especially with Maria Lombardi and Ada Carmosino.

70. Interviews; Bettina Bradbury made this argument for an earlier period on working-class families in Montreal. See her "The Fragmented Family: Family Strategies in the Face of Death, Illness and Poverty, Montreal, 1860–1885" in *Childhood and Family in Canadian History*, ed. Joy Parr (Toronto, 1982).

71. Interviews. Studies on working women in Canada include Ruth Frager, "No Proper Deal: Women Workers and the Canadian Labour Movement, 1870–1930" in *Union Sisters: Women in the Labour Movement*, ed. Lynda Briskin and Linda Yanz, (Toronto, 1984); Joan Sangster, "The 1907 Bell Telephone Strike; Organizing Women Workers," *Labour/ Le Travailleur* (1978), reprinted in *Rethinking Canada: The Promise of Women's History*, 2nd ed., ed. Veronica Strong-Boag and Anita Clair Fellman, (Toronto, 1991); Wayne Roberts, *Honest Womanhood* (Toronto, 1976).

72. White, *Women and Unions.*

73. Virginia interviewed by Tina D'Accunto; interview with Assunta Capozzi and Vincenza Cerulli.

74. Interview with Ada Carmosino and Maria Lombardi.

75. Angella interviewed by Tina D'Accunto; similar patterns emerged for Dalinda Lombardi-Iacovetta, Maria Rotolo, Maria Carmosino, Marie Lombardi.

76. Interview with Maria Lombardi, Julia Toscano, and Vincenza Cerulli; also with Dalinda Lombardi-Iacovetta, Maria Rotolo, and Assunta Carmosino.

77. Interview with Maria Lombardi and Julia Toscano.

78. Judith Adler Hellman, "The Italian Communists, the Women's Question, and the Challenge of Feminism," *Studies in Political Economy* 13 (Spring 1985); M. Jane Slaughter, "Women's Politics and Women's Culture: The Case of Women in the Italian Resistance" (Paper presented to the Sixth Berkshire Conference on the History of Women, June 1984); Margherita Repetto Alaia, "The Unione Donne Italiane: Women's Liberation and the Italian Workers' Movement, 1945–1980" (Paper presented to the Sixth Berkshire Conference on the History of Women, June 1984). On the South see, for example, Jane Kramer, *Unsettling Europe* (New York, 1972); P.A. Allum, "The South and National Politics, 1945–50" in *The Rebirth of Italy 1943–50*, ed. J.S. Woolf (New York, 1973).

79. Interview with Julia Toscano and Dalinda Lombardi-Iacovetta.

80. On an earlier period see Scott and Tilly, *Women, Work, and Family.*

81. Bodnar, "Modernization and Immigration."

82. See, for example, Betty Frieden, *The Feminine Mystique* (Harmondsworth, 1965).

TWO HANDS FOR THE CLOCK: CHANGING PATTERNS IN THE GENDERED DIVISION OF LABOUR IN THE HOME [◇]

MEG LUXTON

O

When I first got a job, I just never had any time, what with looking after the children and the housework. But now my husband has started to help me. He cooks and picks up the kids and is even starting to do other stuff! What a difference! Before, I used to feel like the second hand on the clock—you know, always racing around. Now, with his help, it feels like there are two hands for the clock—his and mine—so I get to stop occasionally.

More and more married women with young dependent children are employed outside the home. Studies conducted in the early and mid-1970s suggested that when married women took on paid employment, their husbands did not respond by increasing the amount of time they spent on domestic labour. These studies reached the general conclusion that married women were bearing the burden of the double day of labour almost entirely by themselves.[1]

Underlying women's double day of labour is the larger question of the gendered division of labour itself. The gendered division of labour, and particularly women's responsibility for domestic labour, have been identified as central to women's oppression in the capitalist societies as a whole, and specifically to women's subordination to men within families.[2] Women's changing work patterns have posed questions sharply about domestic labour: What is actually being done in the home? Is it sufficient? Who is actu-

---

◇ *Studies in Political Economy* 12 (Fall 1983). This paper reports the results of research carried out in Flin Flon, Manitoba, in 1981. All the quotes cited in this paper without references are from interviews conducted as part of that research.

ally doing it? Who should be doing it? This in turn has raised further questions about the existing unequal power relations between women and men.

In the paid labour force, some women's groups, particularly within the union movement, have organized campaigns centred on such specific issues as equal pay and equal access to jobs. Their efforts are a challenge to the existing divisions of work between women and men.[3] Such changes in the definition and distribution of women's work raise the question of whether or not attitudes toward the gendered division of labour in the family household are also being challenged. Has there been any comparable redefinition of men's work roles? And further, has there been any redistribution of work inside the family household? As women learn to drive electrohauls, shovel muck, and handle the heat of coke ovens, are men learning to change diapers, comfort an injured child, or plan a week's food within the limits imposed by a tight budget?

A recent Gallup poll on the sharing of general housework is suggestive. The poll, conducted across Canada in August 1981, reports that during the years 1976 to 1981, Canadians changed their opinions substantially about whether husbands should share in general housework. When asked the question, "In your opinion, should husbands be expected to share in the general housework or not?" 72 percent responded "yes" in 1981 as compared with 57 percent in 1976. Only 9 percent (11 percent of all men and 7 percent of all women) replied that men should not share the work.

However, changes in attitudes do not necessarily indicate changes in behaviour. The Gallup poll goes on to suggest that there has apparently been little change in what husbands do. It also implies that women and men disagree on the extent to which men are helping regularly. In 1976, 44 percent of men polled said they helped regularly with housework, while in 1981, 47 percent said they did. By contrast, in 1976, 33 percent of women polled said men regularly helped while in 1981, 37 percent of women polled said men regularly helped.[4]

FLIN FLON REVISITED

In 1976–77 I investigated women's work in the home through a case study of one hundred working class households in Flin Flon, a mining town in northern Manitoba.[5] Five years later, in 1981, I carried out a follow-up study to discover whether or not changes had occurred over the preceding five years. As Flin Flon is a small, fairly remote, single-industry town, it is not a Canadian pace setter. Changes occurring in Flin Flon probably indicate more widespread developments. While this case study does not dispute the finding of earlier studies (that when married women get paying jobs they continue to do most of the domestic labour), it does suggest that the situation is considerably more complex than had previously been perceived. It illustrates some of the factors underlying the emergence of the different patterns of attitudes and behaviours reflected in the Gallup poll. It also shows that in some working-class households, important changes in the division of labour are beginning to occur, as women exert pressure on their husbands to take on more domestic labour.

In the first study, I interviewed women of three generations. The first generation set up households in the 1920s and 1930s, the second in the 1940s and 1950s, and the third in the 1960s and 1970s. With just a few exceptions, women of the third generation were the ones with young children under the age of twelve. Just over half the women interviewed had held paid work outside the home for some period after their marriage. None of them, however, had worked outside the home while their children were young. Most had worked for pay before their children were born, but then had not worked for pay again until the children were of school-age. Regardless of whether or not they held paid jobs outside the home, these women identified themselves primarily as housewives and considered domestic labour their responsibility. They generally maintained that they did not expect their husbands to help with domestic labour. Those few men who did some work were praised as wonderful exceptions.

In the follow-up study I sought out only women of the third generation and was able to locate forty-nine of the original fifty-two. In striking contrast to the previous study, I found that these women, all of whom had children twelve years of age or less, were for the most part working outside the home for pay. Over half of these women had pre-school children, and nineteen had had another baby between 1976 and 1981. Despite their continued child care responsibilities, forty-four women had full-time employment. Of these, fourteen said they would prefer to be in the home full-time; nine said they would prefer part-time paid work; and almost half (21) said they were satisfied with the situation they were in. Four women had part-time paid work. Of these, two were satisfied while one wanted, but had not yet been able to find, a full-time paid job. One wanted to return to full-time domestic labour, but could not afford to quit her job. Only one women was still working full-time in the home and she said she was there by choice.

What emerged from the interviews was that regardless of whether or not they wanted to be employed, these women were changing their identification of themselves as being primarily housewives. As one of the women who was working for pay full-time, but who wished she could stay at home, put it:

> I am a housewife. That's what I always wanted to be. But I have also been a clerk for four years so I guess I'm one of those working mothers—a housewife, a mother and a sales clerk.

Given the demands of their paid work, these women were forced to reorganize their domestic labour in some way. Both interviews and time budgets showed that the attitudes women have towards their work responsibilities (both paid and domestic) affect the way they reorganize domestic labour. A key factor was the extent to which they were willing to envisage a change in the gendered division of labour inside the family household.

Labour-force participation did not necessarily reflect their approval of "working mothers." In 1981 all of the women were asked what they thought about married women who had dependent children and who worked outside the home. Seven flatly opposed it under any circumstances, although all of them were in that situation. Nine did not think it was right for them personally, although they felt such a decision should be made on an individual basis. Eight women said it was fine if the women needed the money, although they opposed mothers working outside the home for any other reasons.[6]

In contrast, over half of the women interviewed (25) maintained that mothers with dependent children had every right to work outside the home if they wanted to. Many of them (14) went further and argued that it was better for mothers to be working outside the home. For these women, economic need was only one of several valid reasons that women would take paid employment.

There was a direct correspondence between the attitudes these women expressed toward paid employment for mothers and their views on the gendered division of labour in the home. All of the women were asked who they thought should be responsible for domestic labour. Their responses show three distinct strategies in balancing the demands of domestic labour, paid employment, and family. I have identified these distinct positions, based on their conceptualization of appropriate gender relations, as follows:

1. separate spheres and hierarchical relations;
2. separate spheres and co-operative relations;
3. shared spheres and changed relations.[7]

SEPARATE SPHERES AND HIERARCHICAL RELATIONS

Seven respondents (14 percent) advocated a strict gender-based division of labour. They flatly opposed women working outside the home because doing so would both violate women's proper role and detract from their ability to do domestic labour. These women argued that men, as males, were breadwinners and were "naturally" also household or family heads. Women were to be subordinate to their husbands—this was described by several women as "taking second place to my husband." They argued that women's wifely duties included acquiescence in relation to their husband's demands and putting their families' needs before their own. These women maintained that they themselves held paid jobs outside the home only because their earnings were crucial. They intended to stop work as soon as the "emergency" was over.

They insisted that their paid work must never interfere with their ability to care for their husbands and children or to run their households. Because they assumed that domestic labour was entirely women's responsibility, they did not expect their husbands to help. They maintained that boy children should not be expected to do anything at all around the house and argued that they were teaching their girl children domestic labour skills, not because the mothers needed help, but as training for the girls' future roles as wives and mothers. Accordingly, these women sustained the full double day of labour entirely by themselves.

To deal with the contradiction between their beliefs and their actions, these women worked even harder at their domestic labour. In what appears to be a rigorous overcompensation, they actually raised their standards for domestic labour. They were determined to behave as though paid work made no difference to their domestic performance. Many of them insisted, for example, that every evening meal include several courses made from scratch as well as home-made desserts.

As a result, these women set themselves up in a never-ending vicious circle and ran themselves ragged. Their fatigue and resulting irritability and occasional illnesses only served to convince them that their original prognosis was correct: paid employment is bad for women and harmful to their families.

SEPARATE SPHERES AND CO-OPERATIVE RELATIONS

Seventeen women (35 percent) said that women and men are different. Each gender moves in a separate sphere and marriage, in uniting a women and man, requires co-operation between the two spheres, with each person pulling his or her own weight. These women considered it acceptable for women to "help out" by earning money when necessary but, they argued, women's real work was in the home.

There were two identifiable currents within this general position. Nine women advocated full-time domestic labour for themselves though they agreed that might not be the best option for all women. These women maintained that they should not be working outside the home because they thought it interfered with their family responsibilities. While they were more flexible in their attitudes than those in the first group of women, they argued generally for the maintenance of the gendered division of labour. Particularly in their childrearing attitudes and behaviour, they adhered to a strict notion that boys should not be expected to engage in domestic labours while girls should be encouraged to do so.

Like the first group of women, these women also did most of the domestic labour on their own. Their way of trying to cope with the enormous strain this created, however, was to ease up their standards for domestic labour. They were much more willing to purchase "convenience foods" or to eat in restaurants. They talked about doing less around the house and about feeling vaguely disappointed that they could not keep their place nicer. They were, however, prepared to accept that they could not work outside the home and continue to do full-time domestic labour as well.

Taking a slightly different approach, eight women stated that paid work was acceptable for women with children, if the woman's income was necessary for her household economy. While these women also indicated that they were in favour of maintaining a traditional gendered division of labour, they often engaged in contradictory practices. They would argue that domestic labour was women's work, but in day-to-day activities they frequently asked their husbands to lend a hand, and they all expected their boy children as well as the girls to learn and take on certain domestic tasks.

To a large extent, it appears that the discrepancy between their beliefs and their behaviour lies in an experienced necessity. Unlike those who argued for hierarchical relations, these women were unwilling to become "superwomen." They acknowledged the pressures on them and were willing to ask for help. The extent to which they asked for, and received, assistance varied from household to household. In most cases, children had assigned chores such as washing the dishes or setting the dinner table which they were expected to do on a regular basis. Husbands were not assigned regular jobs but were usually expected to "lend a hand" when they were specifically asked.

TOWARDS SHARED SPHERES
AND CHANGING RELATIONS

Twenty-five women—just over half the sample (51 percent)—stated that regardless of necessity, women with young children had the right to paid employment if they wanted it. For them, wives and husbands were partners who should share the responsibilities for financial support and domestic labour. They supported the idea of changing the division of labour and in practice they were instituting such changes by exerting increasing pressure on their husbands and children to redistribute both the responsibility for, and the carrying out of, domestic labour. As it is these women who are challenging the existing ideology and practice of the gendered division of labour, and especially the place of women and men in the family home, I want to look more closely at the changes they have enacted in the last five years.

A REDISTRIBUTION OF LABOUR TIME

While the women who argued for separate spheres were defending a gendered division of labour within the household, statements made by the third group reflected the trends indicated in the Gallup poll. When these twenty-five women were asked in the 1976 study if they thought husbands should help with domestic labour, most agreed that they did not expect their husbands to do anything, although six said their husbands actually did help. By 1981, however, they unanimously insisted that husbands should help out and all said their husbands did some domestic labour on a regular basis.

An examination of time budgets for these households shows that men have in fact increased the amount of time they spend on domestic labour. By themselves, the figures seem to be quite impressive; men increased their domestic labour time from an average of 10.8 hours per week in 1976 to 19.1 hours in 1981—an increase of 8.3 hours.

By contrast, in 1976 full-time housewives spent an average of 63 hours per week on domestic labour while women working a double day spent an average of 87.2 hours per week working, of which 35.7 hours were spent on domestic labour. In 1981, women doing both jobs averaged 73.9 hours per week of which 31.4 hours were spent on domestic labour. This is a decrease of only 4.3 hours per week. While one would not expect a direct hour for hour substitution for one person's labour for another, there is a discrepancy between the increase in men's work and the relatively insignificant reduction in women's work. Women on an average were spending 12.3 hours a week more than men on domestic labour. Furthermore, there is a discrepancy between the women's insistence that domestic labour should be shared equally and the actual behaviour of household members. These discrepancies generate considerable tension between wives and husbands—tension which reflects the power struggle inherent in the redistribution of domestic labour.

WOMEN AND MEN'S DOMESTIC LABOUR

The women who want their husbands to be more involved have developed a variety of strategies and tactics with which to get the men to take on more work. These range from gentle appeals to fairness or requests for assistance to militant demands for greater (or equal) participation. In a few cases, women discussed the situation with their husbands and they mutually agreed on a sharing of tasks that both partners considered fair and reasonable. In the majority of cases, however, negotiations appeared to be out of the question. Instead the couples seemed locked into tension-generating, manipulative power struggles.

For the women, the impetus to change comes first from the pressures of their two jobs. It is fuelled further when they compare their experiences with those of their husbands. Some contrasted their own working time at home with their husband's leisure time. "I come home from work dead tired and I still have to cook and be with the kids and clean up. And he just lies around, drinking beer, watching TV and I get so mad, I could kill him."

Others compared the standards their husbands expected from their wives with those the men held for themselves. They noted that when living alone, some men kept their households immaculately clean; others lived in a total mess. Whatever their standards for themselves, when the women were around, men changed their behaviour, altered their expectations and pressured women to meet male standards.

> When my husband is on his own, he's quite happy to live in a pig sty. Mess doesn't bother him. But the minute I get back he insists that he can't live in the house unless it's spotless.
>
> Before we were married he lived on his own and his place was so clean and tidy. But as soon as we got married, he somehow never felt he could clean up. It was all up to me.

Despite the obvious interest these women have in redistributing domestic labour, and despite their motivating anger, there are numerous forces operating that make it difficult for women to insist that their spouses actually share the work. Because inequalities in the division of labour are based on male power, when women demand equalization of the work, they are challenging that power. Some women were afraid that if they pushed for more male participation, they would provoke their husbands' anger and rage. At least one woman said her husband had beaten her for suggesting he help with domestic labour.

While there is evidence to suggest that when women have paid employment they increase their own power in marriage, all of these women earned considerably less than their husbands. As a result, the men retained economic power (breadwinner power). Men can also use their greater earnings as a justification for not doing domestic labour. They often argued that with their earnings they discharged the responsibility to the household. Under present circumstances it is up to the individual women to initiate changes in the patterns of domestic labour. For many, economic dependency makes it difficult to challenge their husbands.

Furthermore, the actual task of getting men to do domestic labour is often difficult. If women want their husbands to begin doing domestic labour, they must be prepared to take responsibility not only for overcoming male resistance but also for helping the men overcome both the accumulated years of inexperience and the weight of traditional assumptions about masculinity. Generally, the women assumed that their husbands were unfamiliar with domestic labour and therefore neither knew what needed doing nor had the necessary skills to carry out the work. Taking on this training of resisting and unskilled workers is often in itself an additional job.

When men do start doing domestic labour, women begin to lose control. Domestic labour has traditionally been the one sphere of female control and power. For most women, the kitchen is the closest they ever come to having a "room of one's own." It is difficult for many women to relinquish this, particularly if they are not compensated for that loss by gains made elsewhere—for example in their paid work. While the women were uniformly pleased that their husbands had increased their contribution, they were troubled by the way domestic labour was being redistributed.

MEN AND DOMESTIC LABOUR

That men increase the amount of time they spend on domestic labour does not in itself convey much about changing work patterns. Most significantly, it was still assumed that women were primarily responsible for domestic labour and that men were "helping out." When women do domestic labour they often juggle several tasks at once. One of the ways that men have increased the amount of time they spend on domestic labour is by taking over some of that simultaneous work. Many women reported that their husbands were willing to watch the children while the women prepared dinner or did other household chores. While such actions obviously relieved some of the pressures and tensions on women, they did not reduce the amount of time required of women for domestic labour.

Often when men (and children) took on certain tasks, they ended up generating even more domestic work. A number of women indicated that their husbands cooked, but when they did so they seriously disrupted the orderliness of the kitchen, emptying cupboards to find something and not putting things back or using an excessive number of dishes in the preparation. Another commonly cited example was that when men agreed to look after the children, they actually paid more attention to their visiting friends or the TV. Unattended, the children ran "wild" through the house so that when the woman returned she had to spend a great deal of time tidying the house and calming the children. Further, many women pointed out that getting their husbands to do domestic labour required a considerable amount of their time and energy. Sometimes, women argued, it took more work to get the man to do the work than it did to do the work themselves.

Furthermore, men tended to take over certain specific tasks that had clearly defined boundaries. They did not take on the more nebulous, on-going management tasks and they rarely took responsibility for pre-task planning. For example, a number of men did the grocery shopping on a regular basis but they insisted that the women draw up the basic list of things needed. Some men would do the laundry, if all the dirty clothes were previously collected and sorted and if the necessary soap and bleach were already at hand.

A recurring theme throughout the interviews was that men preferred jobs that involved working with machinery. A number of men were willing to do the vacuuming because they enjoyed playing with the vacuum cleaner. One women described how her husband had refused to cook until they purchased a food processor. After that he was forever reading the recipe book and planning new techniques for meal preparation. Several women noted that their husbands had increased their participation in meal preparation after they bought microwave ovens. The redistribution that is occurring is selective. The husbands tend to take the path of least resistance. The trend has been for men to take on those tasks that are the most clearly defined, or sociable and pleasant ones, while leaving the more ill-defined or unpleasant ones to the women. Repeatedly women noted that their husbands had taken on reading the children a bedtime story and staying with them until they fell asleep, thus "freeing" the women to wash the dishes and tidy the kitchen. Men were often willing to feed their infant children or take older ones to the park, but on the whole they would not change soiled diapers or wash their children's hair. They would wash the dishes but not the kitchen floor or the toilet. One man would vacuum the living room rug but refused to do the stairs because they were too awkward.

A number of women expressed concern about this pattern. They noted that when men took on the more pleasant aspects of domestic labour, they were left with the most onerous and boring tasks. They were particularly concerned when the man took on more of the playtime with children. As one women expressed it:

> I'm really glad he's spending more time with the children. They really enjoy it. But it's beginning to make me look like the meany. Daddy plays with them and tells them stories and other nice things while I do the disciplining, make them wash up, tidy their toys and never have time to play because I'm cooking supper.

One of the most significant transformations of men's involvement in domestic labour has been in the area of child care. While most fathers have always spent some time with their children, particularly with older children, increasingly they are doing more of the day-to-day caregiving, especially with younger children. Perhaps the most significant change of all has been with the birth process itself.[8] In 1976 only four out of twenty-five men had been present at the birth of at least one of their children. However, of the babies born between 1976 and 1981, ten of the nineteen new fathers had been present at the birth (and only two of these were of the original four). The wives indicated that they felt very strongly that having their husbands involved in the birth also drew the men into the whole process of pregnancy, child birth and infant care. Men who were willing to attend the birth were subsequently more inclined to get up at night with the baby, to take over certain feedings and to be generally more involved with their small babies.

Despite this very promising shift, women were still responsible for overall child care. All twenty-five women said it was up to them to arrange day care for their children when they worked outside the home. If the child care arrangements fell through on any particular day, it was the women who had to get time off work to stay home, although this can in part be explained by her lower pay and in part by his unavailability when underground.

Furthermore, men "baby-sat" their own children—something that women never did. The implication of this typical reference was that the children were the responsibility of the mother, and the father "helped out." This attitudinal difference was often carried out in behaviour as well. Women repeatedly described situations where men would agree to watch the children, but would then get involved in some other activity and would ignore the children. As children grew up, they learned from experience that their mothers were more likely to be helpful, and so they would turn to the woman rather than the man for assistance, thus actively perpetuating the traditional division of labour.

The ambivalent and often reluctant way in which these men have moved into domestic labour reflects a combination of valid reasons and invalid excuses. In "The Politics of Housework," Pat Mainardi describes with biting sarcasm the various forms of male resistance developed in response to a wife's attempt to share housework:

> (Husband): "I don't mind sharing the work, but you'll have to show me how to do it."
> Meaning: I'll ask a lot of questions and you'll have to show me everything every time I do it because I don't remember so good. And don't try to sit down and read while I'm doing my jobs because I'm going to annoy the hell out of you until it's easier to do them yourself.[9]

Flin Flon women described various forms of male behaviour that were obviously intended to resist attempts to draw them into domestic labour. The majority of resisters took a subtle approach (passive resistance) similar to the ones satirized by Mainardi. One woman described how their kitchen sink was directly in the centre of the kitchen counter. Normally the draining board sat on the left-hand side and the dirty dishes were stacked on the right. Her husband maintained he was unable to do the dishes as he was left-handed and the sink was designed for right-handed people. Some women talked suspiciously of the way household machinery "broke down" when their husbands tried to use it. Several women told of incidents where their husbands agreed to do the work but then repeatedly "forgot" to do it, complained when the women "nagged" them about it, and finally told the women to do it themselves if they did not like the way the men did it. One man explained his position quite clearly :

> Look, I'm not interested in doing stuff around the house. I think that's her job, but since she's working she's been on my back to get me to help out so I say "sure I'll do it." It shuts her up for a while and sometimes I do a few things just to keep her quiet. But really, I don't intend to do it, but it prevents a row if I don't say that.

For men to take on domestic labour meant that they had to give up some of the time they had previously spent on their own enjoyments. Within certain limits this may not be much of a sacrifice, but at some point a man's increasing involvement in domestic labour starts eroding his ability to engage in other activities he values highly. There is a substantial difference between washing dishes and watching TV and in having to come home early from drinking with one's mates at the pub because one has to cook dinner.

Because the majority of men have, until recently, not been expected to do domestic labour, they have not been taught either implicitly, the way girls learn via their dolls and play kitchens, or explicitly, through "helping" mother or in home economics classes. As a result, they often lack knowledge and are unskilled and awkward. Working at a job for which one is ill-prepared often generates feelings of anxiety, inadequacy and incompetence that are easily translated into a generalized reluctance to continue the job.

Some men expressed a willingness to do domestic labour but they were afraid that if it were publicly known that they did "women's work," they would be subjected to teasing and ridicule. One man, for example, quite enjoyed doing the vacuuming. However, there were no curtains on the windows, so the interior of the house was visible from the street. As a result, he did the vacuuming on his knees so that no one would see him! Other men were willing to do tasks inside the house but steadfastly refused to do those tasks that were "women's work" outside in public (hanging washing on the line, for example).

This fear of public ridicule was illustrated by two neighbours. Both families visited together frequently, and the men were friends. They also did a considerable amount of cooking and cleaning. Both, however, insisted that their wives not let the other couple know of the extent to which the men did domestic labour. The fear of public ridicule may reflect a deeper fear. When wives insist that men move into an area that has traditionally been defined as "women's work," men face a challenge to their conventional notions of femininity and masculinity. This may arouse deep psychological and emotional resistances, and stimulate anxiety and fear.

Because most couples are unable to negotiate openly a redistribution of labour, they often get locked into tension-producing manipulations. This was illustrated rather graphically by the story one women told about how she "got" her husband to do the laundry.

She began by explaining that she felt it was only right that he do some of the domestic labour once she started working full-time outside the home. She asked him to help her and he agreed in principle, but he did not do anything. When she asked him to do things like cook supper or wash the dishes he would regularly say that he was going to, but then he would put it off indefinitely so that she ended up doing it all. She decided that she needed to teach him to do one specific task on a regular basis. Laundry, she estimated, would be an appropriate job for him, so she figured out what the discrete tasks involved in doing the laundry were.

The first day she left the laundry basket of sorted clothes sitting at the top of the basement stairs. As he was going down to his workroom she asked him to take the laundry down and put it on top of the machine. She repeated this several times until he automatically took the basket down without being asked. "Once he had done that a few times I knew he'd taken it on regular so I was ready to move on to the next step." She then asked him, as he went down with the basket, to put the laundry into the machine. Once that was learned, she asked him to put in the soap and turn the machine on. "Finally it got so he would regularly carry the laundry down, put it in and turn it on. I never even had to ask him. So then I began getting him to pick up the dirty clothes." Eventually, after more than six months of careful, though unstated strategizing on her part, the man was doing all the work involved in laundry. "Now he does it all regular. I think I will train him to do the dishes next."

While neither of them discussed what was going on, the husband by participating in the process gave his tacit acceptance of the new division of labour. However, because the work was being redistributed by manipulation rather than negotiation, the process only served to exacerbate the already existing tensions between the spouses. It did not engender greater respect or affection between the two. By "tricking" her spouse, the women had relieved some of the burden of her work but she was contemptuous of him for the way he took it over:

> What a fool. If I'd have asked him, he would have refused. If I'd begged and pleaded he would have said he'd do it if he knew how, but would have said he didn't know how and so couldn't. So I fooled him and now he does it. But the whole thing's really stupid.

For his part the husband refused to discuss what was occurring. The wife's interpretation was bitter:

> Things are changing in our life. My job has forced us to do things differently. But he will not talk about it. So I play tricks and hate him and I think he must resent me—but I don't know because he won't tell me. So things change but I don't know what it means. Sometimes I think men are really stupid, or they hate women or at least there's no point trying with them.

CONCLUSION

This case study suggests that changing patterns of paid employment are creating a crisis in the way labour is currently distributed and accomplished in the family household. It illustrates the ambiguities reflected in the Gallup poll findings and shows that these ambiguities arise from serious problems in the way domestic labour is changing. It also suggests that the ideologies of "family" are very strong and play a central part in the way most people organize their interpersonal relationships and their domestic lives.

Because people tend to evaluate their experiences in light of existing social explanations and ideologies, the response of Flin Flon women can be set in a broader context. The three perspectives expressed reflect ideologies that are currently prominent.

Those women who put forward a "separate spheres and hierarchical relations" position were defending the traditional conservative view which locates women inside the family, subordinates women's interests to men's, and places priority above all on the preservation of the breadwinner husband/dependent wife nuclear family.

Because the beliefs these Flin Flon women held conflicted directly with the activities they engaged in, they were compelled to mediate the contradiction. Their attempts to defend a strict gendered division of labour forced them deeper into the hardship of the double day. Their actual experiences highlight the conditions under which support for right-wing "pro-family" reform movements is generated, for in their opinions, it is their paid work that creates the problem.

Those women who argued for "separate spheres and co-operative relations" were expressing a classic liberal view of appropriate female/male relations in the family. This "different but equal" perspective echoes the maternal feminism of some early twentieth-century theorists. It is also found in many sociologists of the family such as Young and Wilmott, who argue that marriages are now symmetrical or companionate.[10]

Those women who argued for "shared spheres and changing relations" were expressing contemporary feminist views which hold that the existing gendered division of labour is a major factor in women's oppression. In challenging the way work is divided in the home, they are questioning the existing relationships between women and men, and between children and adults. Discussing existing family relationships, Hartmann has argued that "Because of the division of labour among family members, disunity is thus inherent in the 'unity' of the family."[11]

This study suggests that a large-scale social transformation is occurring as traditional patterns are eroding and new ones are emerging, but to date the change has been acted out on the level of the individual household, and may, in the short run, be intensifying family disunity. What emerged from these interviews was the total isolation both women and men felt. Women involved in active, collective organizing to change the division of labour in the paid work force have the women's liberation movement, the trade union movement, Status of Women committees, and sometimes the law and other organizations or institutions such as the Human Rights Commissions, to back them up. In contrast, women challenging the gendered division of labour in the home do so on an individual basis. Similarly there is a complete lack of social and material support for men with regard to domestic labour. Very few unions have won paternity leave, for example, so it is very difficult for new fathers to get time off work to be with their new children. This makes it very difficult for men actually to take equal responsibility for their infants.[12] Accordingly, any man who takes on domestic labour places himself at odds with current social practices. It takes a certain amount of self-confidence and courage to do so.

As a result, the majority of respondents implied that they considered that the changes in their domestic division of labour were specific to their individual households. They perceived these changes not as part of a large-scale transformation in the patterns of work and family life, but as a personal struggle between them and their spouse. Such a perception only exacerbated the tensions between women and men.

As material conditions change and new ideologies emerge, many individuals and families are floundering, trying to decide what they want, how to get it, and most problematically, how to resolve conflicts between various possibilities and needs. There are currently no social policies or clear-cut, developing social norms to provide a context in which individuals can evaluate their own actions. Instead, there are several contending ideologies and related social movements, such as the "pro-family" movement and the women's liberation movement.[13] While these movements articulate positions on what female/male relations should entail, they rarely organize to provide support for women to achieve the desired end. The current situation is thereby generating a great deal of confusion and often pain and interpersonal conflict, especially between women and men.

Finally, this study demonstrates that until the exclusive identification of women with domestic labour is broken, there is no possibility of achieving any kind of equality between women and men. If the necessary labour is not redistributed, women end up with a dramatically increased work load. Unlike earlier studies, the findings of this research suggest, that despite all the problems, some working-class women are contesting male power and challenging male privilege and some men are responding by assuming responsibility for domestic labour.

NOTES

1. Heidi Hartmann, "The Family as the Locus of Gender, Class, and Political Struggle: The Example of Housework," *Signs* 6, 3 (Spring 1981): 377–86.

2. Rayna Rapp, "Family and Class in Contemporary America: Notes Towards an Understanding of Ideology," *Science and Society* 42 (Fall 1978): 278–301; Michelle Barrett, *Women's Oppression Today* (London 1980); Michelle Barrett and Mary MacIntosh, *The Anti-Social Family* (London, 1983).

3. Deirdre Gallagher, "Getting Organized in the CLC" in *Still Ain't Satisfied: Canadian Feminism Today*, ed. Maureen Fitzgerald, Connie

Guberman, and Margie Wolfe (Toronto, 1982); Debbie Field, "Rosie the Riveter Meets the Sexual Division of Labour" in ibid.

4. Canadian Institute of Public Opinion *Gallup Report* (Toronto, 7 Oct. 1981), 1–2.

5. Meg Luxton, *More than a Labour of Love: Three Generations of Women's Work in the Home* (Toronto, 1980).

6. The problem here, however, lies in trying to determine what constitutes economic need. All of these women (24) maintained that they were working outside the home for economic reasons, because their families needed the money. In all likelihood, this is true. However, it may be that these women, like most employed housewives who have been studied, also have non-economic reasons for accepting paid employment. Economic necessity is a more socially legitmated reason and some of these women may be dealing with the contradictory feeling they have toward their family obligations and their pleasure in employment by convincing themselves and others that they are only working because they "have to."

7. There were no obvious sociological factors that might explain the differences in opinion and behaviour. While a large-scale survey might reveal correlations between these different strategies and such factors as political or religious affiliation, ethnicity, and husbands' attitudes, at least among this group of women, and given the available data, no such patterns emerged.

It is also important to point out that while these three approaches are typical, they are not the only available options. Some women have fully egalitarian relations with the men they live with; others live alone with other women.

A creative strategy was developed by one couple (not included in the study). The man worked a forty-hour week in the mines; the woman was a housewife. They determined mutually what work she was responsible for during a forty-hour week. She did child care while he was at work, as well as heavy cleaning and certain other chores. The rest of the domestic labour—child care, cooking, cleaning, laundry, shopping—they divided equally between them. As a result, each worked a forty-hour week at their own work and shared all remaining labour.

8. It seems to me that the involvement of men in the actual birth of their children is of enormous significance—something that has not yet been appreciated or studied.

9. Pat Mainardi, "The Politics of Housework" in *Sisterhood is Powerful*, ed. Robin Morgan (New York 1970), 449–50.

10. Nellie McClung, *In Times Like These* (1915; Toronto 1972); Michael Willmott, *The Symmetrical Family* (London 1973).

11. Hartmann, "Family as Locus," 379.

12. In Quebec the unions of CEGEP teachers have won paternity leave. This has made it possible for some men to take equal responsibility for infant care.

13. Susan Harding, "Family Reform Movements: Recent Feminism and its Opposition," *Feminist Studies* 7, 1 (Spring 1981): 57–75.

MARRIAGE LAW AND
MARRIAGE RITUALS

MARRIED WOMEN'S PROPERTY LAW IN NINETEENTH-CENTURY CANADA ⬦

CONSTANCE B. BACKHOUSE

◯

English common-law rules that transferred the property of women to their husbands upon marriage were part of the larger package of laws emigrants from England brought to Canada. These harsh rules left Canadian women in a most unenviable position—the equitable precedents that had evolved in England to prevent the most glaring instances of abuse had less impact in Canada where courts of equity developed slowly and sporadically, and many individuals had no practical access to their jurisdiction. The need for reform of married women's property law was made even more pressing because of an apparently high rate of wife abandonment, that left women without the benefit of matrimonial support, yet still subject to the disabilities of coverture.

These conditions inspired nineteenth-century Canadian legislators to forge new laws relating to married women's property. This article will trace the development of the laws enabling women to hold and dispose of their property while married. It will not deal with dower, curtesy, a married woman's right to make a will, or the laws relating to spousal life insurance. This article will also be restricted to the common-law provinces, and will not attempt to describe the married woman's property rules applicable under the civil-law system of Quebec.

⬦ *Law and History Review* 6, 2 (Fall 1988): 211–57. I would like to express my appreciation to Rosemary Coombe, Kate Hughes, Elizabeth Seto, and Catherine Fedder, who provided research assistance with this article. Funds from the Social Humanities Research Council of Canada and the Law Foundation of Ontario were invaluable in completing the manuscript for this article.

For purposes of analysis, Canadian legislation can be divided into three distinct waves of reform.[1] The waves, however, are not entirely separable, and they overlap in time, and, indeed, in some cases within a single statute. The first wave of statutory enactments dealt only with emergency situations, where marital breakdown had occurred and married women were desperate to reclaim control of their own assets. Far from attacking the doctrine of marital unity, however, these statutes served only to provide backup protection from the legal system where the husband had improperly absented himself.

The second wave of legislation can more clearly be characterized as an encroachment on common-law principles. These statutes established "separate estates" on the part of all women, which insulated a married woman's property from her husband and his creditors, but failed to bestow broader dispositive powers. The acts were essentially protective measures, designed to function as a form of debtor relief in a harsh economic climate.

The legislative leadership that Canada exhibited during the first two-thirds of the nineteenth century had considerably dissipated by the later decades. England passed a statute in 1870 setting the tone for a belated set of Canadian enactments that slowly began to introduce truly egalitarian measures. Ironically in 1868 English legislators had called upon the example of earlier Canadian legislation to assist them with married women's property reform, and then Canadian legislators slavishly copied the resulting 1870 Married Women's Property Act. This third wave of statutes attempted to grant married women control of their earnings, as well as dispositive powers over their separate property. Ambiguous wording and restrictive judicial interpretation necessitated extensive additional enactments to accomplish significant reform, but substantial progress was eventually achieved. By the close of the century, most Canadian wives would be entitled to property rights markedly greater than those held by their sisters in the early nineteenth century.

THE RECEPTION OF MARRIED WOMEN'S PROPERTY LAW IN CANADA: COMMON LAW AND EQUITY

The doctrine of marital unity, through which married women lost most of their rights to property, entailed a "suspension of the independent existence of the wife, and an absorption by the husband of the woman's person and all her belongings."[2] So wrote Clara Brett Martin, Canada's first woman lawyer, who noted the irony of the marriage ceremony, in which the husband solemnly promised to endow his wife with all his worldly goods. With veiled sarcasm, Martin (who, incidentally, never married) attributed the injustice of this situation to the common-law tradition that Canadians had inherited from England. "This notion of the unity of husband and wife," she wrote in 1900, "meaning thereby the suspension of the wife and the lordship of the husband, seems to have been particularly agreeable to the whole race of English jurists, tickling their grim humor and gratifying their very limited sense of the fitness of things."[3] Canadians acquired this legal doctrine province by province as part of the process whereby the common law was received into the English colonies.[4]

The common-law rules extricating a married woman from her property have been outlined in their full complexity by many authors.[5] In brief, upon marriage, all personal property belonging to the wife, including wages, vested absolutely in her husband.[6] Although a married woman did not lose the ownership of her real estate, she did forfeit her authority to manage the property or receive the rents and profits from it—all of which flowed by right to her husband during the marriage.[7] Married women were legally incapable of contracting, of suing, or of being sued in their own names—a not insignificant disability for women who wished to engage in trade and commerce.[8] Indeed, women were only permitted to carry on business separately from their husbands if they had their spouses' consent to do so.[9]

These harsh rules caused considerable distress to married women. In 1853, James Whibby abandoned his wife, Mary, and four children in Newfoundland, leaving them to survive upon their own resources. For thirteen years, Mary Whibby worked slavishly, taking in washing and scrimping and saving to make ends meet. The court lauded Mrs. Whibby on her "industrious and thrifty" ways, and noted with astonishment that at the time of her death in 1868, she had managed to save $1000. Given the remarkably slender earning capacity of women in the nineteenth century, this was no mean feat. Upon his wife's death, James Whibby returned to claim these monies, and a son contested his entitlement. Chief Justice Sir H. W. Hoyles concluded that although the common-law rule "work[ed] in this case very hardly," James Whibby was entitled to his wife's wages.[10]

The rule that incapacitated married women from litigating on their own behalf also created peculiar problems in some cases. In Campbell v. Campbell in 1875, Eliza Campbell attempted to bring a lawsuit in Toronto against James Campbell, a relative of her husband, for damages for slander. James had apparently accused Eliza of committing adultery, which had resulted in her husband's turning her out of their home. Since Eliza was still a married woman, she was forced to join her husband as a co-plaintiff in the slander suit.[11] Robert Campbell, convinced of his wife's guilt, took the stand and gave evidence on behalf of the defendant, testifying he fully believed in the veracity of the charge. Perhaps sympathizing with Eliza's unenviable legal position, the jury awarded the plaintiff $1000 of the $10 000 damages claimed. However, the award was set aside by the review court, which accepted Robert Campbell's evidence over Eliza's protestations of innocence.

An 1892 Nova Scotia case, Kieley v. Morrison, illustrated the futility of seeking to enforce the common-law rule that a husband was responsible for providing his wife and children with necessaries. In 1889, Mr. Kieley abandoned his wife, Margaret, and their two children after brutally beating Margaret. He left her penniless, and in a desperate attempt to support herself and her children, Margaret sold the family bull. Justice Charles Townshend concluded that Margaret had no authority to sell the bull: "Now when the husband does not provide [necessaries], or when he leaves home, and abandons his wife without making proper provision for such wants, the law gives the wife the husband's credit, and enables her to make him liable to the extent of such requirements. It has never yet been decided, however, that the wife is at liberty to sell and dispose of her husband's chattels and effects for such reasons. She has no implied authority, even in order to obtain necessaries, to part with his property."[12] The courts, however, did not explore the difficulties married women experienced in finding shopkeepers who would agree to accept their credit. Indeed, an earlier Ontario decision concluded that a wife who was no longer residing with her husband forfeited even the implied authority that a married woman had at common law to pledge her husband's credit for necessaries.[13] The prospects of a deserted woman actually obtaining financial support from her runaway husband were remarkably bleak.

The glaring injustice of the common-law rules had become apparent as early as the late sixteenth century in England where the courts of chancery developed a body of equitable precedents that undermined the doctrine of coverture and improved the status of married women.[14] Antenuptial and postnuptial contracts and trusts (or marriage settlements) appeared as devices to permit a married woman to keep some property apart from her husband for her "separate use." Marriage settlements could be created by the woman herself, her father or other relatives, friends, or her husband.[15] Property could be settled in the trust before or after marriage, safe from the husband's control, by conveying nominal ownership to a trustee who was directed to manage the property for the benefit of the married woman.[16] Initially, courts of chancery would only recognize such agreements where there was some particular need for protection, in cases where the husband was away at sea or had abandoned his wife, or where he was a conspicuous spendthrift; later such trusts were enforced regardless of the circumstances of the marriage.[17] By the mid-eighteenth century, courts began to accept the validity of contracts made without the intervention of a trustee, at first appointing the husband as nominal trustee, and later eliminating the need for any trustee at all.[18] The consent of the husband to the creation of the settlement was a prerequisite until the mid-eighteenth century, when this too was abandoned.[19] The terms of the settlement dictated the rights a married woman had over this separate property—sometimes she was given full dispositive powers and in other cases she was restricted to obtaining the income from the property only.[20]

In Canada, the rules of equity appear to have had very little impact on married women's property rights. Certainly the courts of chancery were by no means as well established as in England. In Ontario, for example, equitable agreements were judicially unenforceable until the Court of Chancery was first set up in 1837.[21] Although some individuals apparently executed equitable documents regardless, they were dependent upon voluntary compliance or an ad hoc system of arbitration to resolve disagreements.[22] In the maritime jurisdictions, there seems to have been somewhat greater access to judicial relief. The governor of each colony, through his royal prerogative as keeper of the Great Seal, was authorized to excercise the powers of the chancellor. In Nova Scotia, the governor actually exercised this informal equitable jurisdiction from 1749, first with the assistance of his council, and later through the auspices of a number of professional lawyers.[23] New

Brunswick and Prince Edward Island followed a similar procedure.[24] It is tempting to dismiss this early jurisdiction as rather primitive. C.J. Townshend, writing of Nova Scotia in 1900, dispelled this assumption, noting that the early enforcement of equitable justice was procedurally and substantively in conformity with that of other equity courts in the period and accounted for a relatively large share of the judicial business of the province.[25] Less is known about the western provinces, although their supreme courts appear to have been capable of equitable jurisdiction from the outset.[26]

Access to enforcement mechanisms was, of course, only one of the problematical aspects. The bar seems to have been relatively short on practitioners experienced in equity principles, thus hampering those who wished to draft marriage settlements with professional assistance.[27] Interestingly Norma Basch's research on New York has uncovered a number of "do-it-yourself" law manuals that included forms for setting apart specific items and small amounts of cash in marriage settlements.[28] One wonders whether similar guides may have existed to aid enterprising Canadians of the same period. The sheer expense of tying up estates in trust settlements may have been the biggest hurdle. George Smith Holmested, writing at the turn of the century, concluded that for Canadians, marriage settlements were "as a rule enjoyed by the few only who could indulge in [this] luxury. . . . To the ordinary run of married women they were a dead letter."[29]

No detailed research has yet attempted to quantify the number of women who tried to insulate their property through marriage settlements in nineteenth-century Canada. By way of comparison, Lee Holcombe has estimated that only 10 percent of the marriages in nineteenth-century England invoked trust settlements.[30] Marylynn Salmon concluded that between 1 and 2 percent of the couples marrying in South Carolina between 1785 and 1810 created separate estates.[31] An examination of all the reported cases on married women's property in nineteenth-century Canada indicates that at least some women did enjoy marriage settlements, and that these did provide some degree of protection for their property.[32] In many cases, the settlement appears to have been made at the insistence of the woman's parents, who wished to bestow gifts of property upon their daughter, but wanted to preserve it from the husband for the future benefit of their daughter and potential grandchildren.[33] In other cases, the principal parties appear to have been the main instigators of the agreement, at times evidencing a fairly mercenary view of the marital bond.[34] Widows were often involved in such arrangements, generally seeking to preserve their own control over assets they had amassed from a former marriage or during the interim widowhood.[35]

Equity did not always provide effectual relief, however, even where women had the benefit of lawful separate estates. In the Toronto case of Rice v. Rice in 1899, the evidence showed that Rebecca Rice's father had set up a separate estate for her in his will, but that she had used the money for family expenses, keeping no separate account of these expenditures. Her husband later became insolvent, and when his wife sought repayment of the loans she had made from her separate estate, the court disallowed the repayment as a fraud on her husband's creditors. Chief Justice John D. Armour stated: "A wife having property settled for her separate use is entitled to deal with the money as she pleases. If she directly authorizes the money to be paid to her husband he is entitled to receive it and she can never recall it."[36] Indeed, even valid settlements could be subverted with ease.

And of course, some women had no access to equity at all, and their plight was the most severe. One such victim was Hannah Snider, wife of Henry Nolan of the township of Colchester, Canada West.[37] In 1824, Hannah's father, anxious about his daughter's husband, "a man of unsteady habits," conveyed to her a life estate in fifty acres of land. Since no court of chancery would be established in the jurisdiction until 1837, the land was not transferred as Hannah's "separate property," and her husband obtained by common law the right to manage the property and enjoy its income. After a short period of time, Henry abandoned his wife, but not his interest in the land, which he continued to lease for his own profit until he sold it outright in 1856. Left without any means of support, Hannah continued to live in the neighbourhood for the thirty years after her husband left her, "dependent more or less on the charities of those who were acquainted with her, having none of the comforts of the home which her father hoped he had provided for her."[38] Although the colonial courts were helpless to protect Hannah's interests for thirty years, upon her husband's death in 1864 they held that her life interest reverted, and she regained the property at the expense of the individual to whom her husband had sold it.

These cases illustrate that real and substantial suffering attended the importation of the English legal system to Canada and make the need for reform abundantly clear.

LEGISLATIVE REFORM OF MARRIED WOMEN'S PROPERTY LAW

THE FIRST WAVE: MARRIAGE BREAKDOWN LEGISLATION

Since it was marriage that incapacitated women from controlling property, it is not illogical that the first statutes that began to return property rights to married women dealt with situations in which the marriage itself was in trouble.[39] Even at common law, special exemptions had evolved before the turn of the eighteenth century to protect women in such situations. Blackstone had noted that where a husband "had abjured the realm, or [was] banished," he was legally disabled from controlling his wife's property, and she was consequently restored to the status of *feme sole*.[40] This narrow exception was to prove inadequate for the needs of the developing colonies, where the lure of vast expanses of unsettled land caused many men to desert their families and relocate anonymously in relatively unpopulated areas. The same geographic realities that caused some Canadian jurisdictions to expand access to divorce, created a demand for legislation to restore property rights to married women who had been abandoned.

The Maritime Provinces initiated this wave of legislation, following upon the lead of a number of American states.[41] In these provinces, the lure of travel combined with the perils of the sea to breed marital instability. Indeed, marriage breakdown seems to have been a concern of some magnitude in the Maritime Provinces, for they had also been the first to introduce legislation opening access to divorce.[42] The first married women's statute was enacted in 1851 in New Brunswick.[43] An Act to Secure to Married Women Real and Personal Property Held in Their Own Right provided that a married woman who was deserted or abandoned could sue for debts or damages in her own name, notwithstanding any discharge or release from her husband to the contrary.[44] A married woman who was deserted "or compelled to support herself" was authorized to retain any property she accumulated as a result of her own labour, safe from the control of her husband or his creditors.[45] The New Brunswick Legislature expanded upon these rights in 1869. The group of women protected was increased to include any married woman living separate from her husband "not wilfully and of her own accord."[46] The powers such women held over their property were also expanded to include the right to dispose of it, by will or otherwise, without the consent of their husbands.[47] This right was clarified in 1874 to include property acquired prior to desertion as well as afterward.[48]

Following closely upon the heels of its neighbouring province, Prince Edward Island enacted legislation in 1860 that practically duplicated the 1851 New Brunswick statute.[49] In 1866, Nova Scotia also passed legislation along this line, but it appears to have been modelled upon an English precedent, rather than upon the earlier New Brunswick or Prince Edward Island versions. The Nova Scotia statute provided that where a married woman was deserted by her husband without reasonable cause, and where she was "maintaining herself by her own industry or property," she could apply to the Supreme Court for an order protecting any property she acquired after the desertion from her husband and his creditors.[50] Upon the granting of such an order, she would be placed in the position of a *feme sole* with respect to her rights to dispose of the property, to contract, to sue, and to be sued.[51] Should her husband or his creditors ignore the court order, the married woman was permitted to sue for restoration of the property wrongfully detained, plus a penalty of a sum equal to double the value of such property.[52] Although the focus on deserted wives was reminiscent of the earlier New Brunswick and Prince Edward Island statutes, the Nova Scotia Legislature chose to follow the procedure for protecting deserted wives set out in the English Matrimonial Causes Act of 1857.[53]

One western colony also enacted legislation to protect the property of women whose marriages were in difficulty. In 1862, the Vancouver Island Legislature passed a statute similar to the Nova Scotian and English enactments,[54] perhaps in reaction to the Fraser River gold rush, which began in 1858 and caused a boom and bust effect. During this period, the population of Victoria swelled to twenty thousand and then collapsed to three thousand, undoubtedly leaving Vancouver Island with a large number of abandoned wives and children.[55]

Statutes enacted during the first wave of reform were never intended to endow women with the right to financial autonomy. Their goal was far more limited—to provide temporary relief for families in crisis. Canadian judges, who were called upon to interpret and apply the legislation, viewed this limited extension of married women's property rights with favour. The 1867 New Brunswick case of Abell v. Light provided an excellent illustration of the need for such legislation and one judge's sympathy with its intent.[56] Mrs. Abell's husband was a seaman who had become insane after a number of "misfortunes" befell him; he was confined to the provincial lunatic asylum. Mrs. Abell had been left destitute, and she attempted to support herself and her three children by running a boardinghouse in Saint John. One of her boarders refused to pay her for his lodging, and she issued a lawsuit against him in her own name, relying upon the 1851 New Brunswick statute. The defendant argued that the plaintiff could not avail herself of the legislation because technically there had been no desertion or abandonment. Since at common law a married woman had no authority to wage litigation in her own name, he argued that the claim should be denied.

Chief Justice William L. Ritchie refused to accept this argument and pointed out that denying this woman the right to sue on her own behalf would "place her in . . . a helpless position [and] entirely frustrate the humane intention of the Legislature. . . . " The judge noted that the cruel necessity of the woman's plight was obvious, and that since she lacked a husband to support her, she should be assisted by the law in her efforts to provide for her fatherless children. He also pointed to the respectability of her occupation, concluding: "There is certainly no more legitimate way by which a married woman, left destitute and compelled to support herself, could acquire property than by keeping a boardinghouse."[57] Nevertheless the judicial perspective was clear: legislation expanding married women's property rights in emergency situations where there was no husband around to exercise his marital prerogative was socially beneficial and should be enforced with rigour.

When the marriage breakdown was less clear, judges could be surprisingly less supportive of the legislation. The 1880 Nova Scotia case of Sinclair v. Wakefield provides a good example of this type of situation.[58] Frederick Wakefield deserted his wife, Emily, in 1872. She subsequently opened a school in Halifax and under the terms of the 1866 Nova Scotia statute she obtained a court order protecting her earnings from her husband and his creditors. This order established Emily Wakefield as a full individual in the eyes of the law, providing her with full legal rights over her property, the right to contract, and the right to sue and be sued. In 1876, her husband returned and the couple reconciled and took up common residence again. Emily and her husband cosigned a rental agreement with their landlord, and when the couple defaulted the landlord sued Emily for the unpaid rent, probably assuming she was the better prospect for judgment recovery. The landlord relied upon section seven of the legislation, which provided that the court order of protection (which made Emily responsible for her contracts) was to remain in force "until reversed or discharged." Since neither event had transpired, the landlord must have felt reasonably safe in bringing the lawsuit against a married woman.

Despite the clear wording of the act, the Supreme Court of Nova Scotia concluded that the resumption of cohabitation had abrogated the order, especially since the rental agreement postdated the reconciliation and the landlord was aware that the couple was living together again.[59] "The spirit of the English law is to discourage anything like the separation of the interests of husband and wife," commented Justice Alexander James. Temporary emergency relief for married women was one thing, but bestowing separate property rights upon women who resided with their husbands was quite another, regardless of what the letter of the law might specify. The absurdity of providing married women with independent rights over their property tickled the judge's fancy, and he speculated upon the "ludicrous results" that would follow from such a state of affairs:

> If the contention on the part of the plaintiff in this case be sustained, a man and his wife may live together for half a lifetime, in the face of the public, fulfilling towards each other all of the duties of the married life, and yet each of them capable of doing business on his or her separate account, each capable of suing and being sued separately, and neither of them in any way responsible for the acts of the other in business transactions. They may conduct rival commercial establishments; one may get rich while the other is drifting into hopeless, and perhaps, discreditable insolvency, while they are living in the same house, dining at the same table, and, when the toils of the day are over, sharing the same couch of repose. They may give credit to each other, and use each other's notes, accept each other's bills, and in case of disagreement they may sue each other at law, seize each other's property under execution, or incarcerate each other's bodies in jail for debt; or, on the other hand, they might inaugurate a happier state of affairs and one more calculated to preserve connubial harmony, by entering into partnership under the firm of A B & Wife, that is, if they did not happen to quarrel when they were going home at night over the division of the day's profits.[60]

The limits of judicial tolerance were clear: as long as the home was abandoned by the husband and father, a married woman could exercise limited forms of authority over her property. The prospect of her doing so when her spouse was at her side was nothing other than patently ridiculous.

In summary, none of the "first wave" statutes heralded an acceptance of the right of married women to financial autonomy. As conceived by the legislators and applied by the judges, they were meant to provide emergency relief where the head of the household had absconded or become incapacitated from serving as the manager of family property. The statutes embodied an attempt to make the broken family a more efficient economic unit, and to preserve the community from the need to provide public support for abandoned women and their children. In fact, care of the children may have been the primary interest. The enactments were not meant to challenge the authority of the patriarchal family, but merely to serve as a last resort for the family in crisis. Rather than providing married women with proprietary equality, they reinforced the concept of female subordination. When a husband defaulted upon his marital responsibilities, a married woman was authorized to obtain equivalent protection at the hands of a paternalistic legal system. However, by securing to some married women the right to control their property, even in limited circumstances, these statutes provided the first legislative recognition of the failure of the common-law rules. They would in turn be superseded by legislation that began to chip away at the premise of coverture.

THE SECOND WAVE: "PROTECTIVE LEGISLATION"

A second wave of legislation enacted across Canada between 1851 and 1884 purportedly addressed the rights of *all* married women, not just those deserted or abandoned by their husbands. Although an 1872 Ontario statute is commonly cited as the first such statute in Canada,[61] in fact, the 1851 New Brunswick statute discussed in the preceding section really deserves this acclaim. In addition to its provisions regarding deserted and abandoned wives, the 1851 statute had one section that was drafted to apply to all women, and that designated the real and personal property of a married woman, whether accumulated before or after marriage, to be "owned as her separate property," and exempt from responsibility for the debts and liabilities of her husband.[62] No dispositive powers seemed to attend this separate estate; indeed, the act itself added that this property could not be conveyed or mortgaged without the full consent of the married woman—something that would have been redundant if the married woman had had the right to dispose of her property as she pleased.

The impetus behind this legislative thrust may have come from the United States.[63] The province had set up a codification and consolidation committee in 1848 to revise all of its statutes. In the course of its investigation, the committee had examined American legislation, and thus must have been familiar with some of the reforms issued there. The 1851 statutes represented a culmination of the committee's work.[64] The actual wording of the New Brunswick statute, however, did not correspond to any of the American state legislation then in existence, suggesting an entirely indigenous interest in the issue. The real motivation may have been economic in nature. From the late 1840s until late 1851, New Brunswick experienced a financial crisis due to poor harvests, the reduction in British timber preferences, and the repeal of the Corn Laws. The resulting confusion brought with it tight credit, falling prices, sudden bankruptcies, and generally disturbed business conditions.[65] The New Brunswick act seems to have been part of a package of legislation intended to deal with harsh economic times. Another statute, passed the same day, purported to facilitate the confirmation of bankruptcies.[66]

The debtor-relief rationale explains why the statute did not endow women with dispositive control over their property. Married women were to be restricted to enjoying the profits from their separate property, and not permitted to sell or otherwise dispose of their assets. The intent was to *protect* their property from misuse in the hands of the husband, and the assets were insulated from seizure by the husband or his creditors. The goal was to rescue at least some family assets from attachment by creditors in times of economic emergency. The legislators had no intention of altering the traditional rules of coverture in any radical fashion. Women were still viewed primarily as homemakers, expected to care for their husbands, children, and family resources. It was quite natural, in an era of growing acclaim for motherhood, that their property should be given special protection to preserve it from seizure in the event of family emergency.[67]

There were sporadic, unsuccessful attempts throughout the 1850s to enact similar legislation in Nova Scotia,[68] but it was Ontario that managed to pass the next statute in 1859.[69] A number of early attempts, beginning in 1856, had proved fruitless, but under the determined leadership of the Honorable Malcolm Cameron, success was achieved.[70] The impetus behind the passage of this more expansive act seems to have been more complex than in New Brunswick. Certainly economic woe formed some of the genesis for the legislation. Crop failures accompanied by land and railway speculation had developed into a full-fledged financial crisis in 1857 and 1858.[71] Another statute passed at the same time included measures to abolish imprisonment for debt.[72] Debtor-relief was not the entire goal, however. Cameron, a fervent member of the temperance movement, linked the legislation directly to family misery caused by alcohol. "The object," he claimed, "was to relieve married women from imposition and injustice on the part of their worthless, drunken husbands."[73] The preamble of the statute made no mention of economic difficulties, but expressed concern about women's rights: "Whereas the law of Upper Canada relating to the property of married women is frequently productive of great injustice, and it is highly desirable that amendments should be made therein for the better protection of their rights."

Feminist initiative seems to have played at least some role here. It is generally assumed that the organized women's movement did not appear in Canada until 1876,[74] but Mary Jane Mossman, examining the genesis for the 1859 act, uncovered records of a series of petitions presented by Elizabeth Dunlop and other women to the Legislative Assembly between 1852 and 1857.[75] The *Globe* published portions of one of the petitions on 9 January 1857. The female lobbyists were claiming that by the act of marriage, "a woman . . . is instantly deprived of all civil rights. . . . " Placing women's property and earnings in the "absolute power" of their husbands "occasion[ed] manifold evils becoming daily more apparent." Although the women argued that the suffering extended "over all classes of society," the lower classes were at particular risk: "[M]uch more unequivocal is the injury sustained by women of the lower classes for whom no [marriage settlements] can be made. . . . The law in depriving the mother of all pecuniary resources . . . obliges her in short to leave [her children] to the temptations of the street, so fruitful in juvenile crime."[76] The reasoning here combines an interesting blend of women's rights and children's welfare concerns.

Interjurisdictional borrowing may also have prompted the action. Cameron told his fellow legislators that "a similar law had for a great period been in successful operation in the different States of the Union and in the Eastern Provinces."[77] Certain features of the statute were similar to its New Brunswick predecessor. Proximity to Quebec with its civil-law community-property system may also have inspired the legislative amendments to the common law.[78] One of the earliest Canadian commentators on the legislation attributed it to the example set by neighbouring states such as New York and Vermont.[79] In contrast, the Ontario judiciary seems to have believed the critical influence was English. Justice Adam Wilson attributed the 1859 statute to a report issued by the Law Amendment Society in England in 1856.[80] This powerful group of legislators and law reformers convinced Sir Erskine Perry to introduce a bill into the House of Commons in 1857 that might have given married women full dispositive powers over their property. The bill was not passed, and instead a limited form of relief was provided to women who were divorced or separated from their husbands.[81] The influences of other jurisdictions must have played some part in the Ontario reform, but it would be misleading to categorize this development as a "copycat" response. There was no wholesale adoption of legislative precedents from the American, English, and other colonial jurisdictions. Instead, the Ontario Legislature undertook a deliberate and principled task of borrowing and combining various concepts to create a truly indigenous product.

Reflecting its multifarious origins, the substantive provisions of the Ontario statute were far from uniform. The legislators wanted to expand the rights of married women, but were equivocal about how far this reform should go. The statute authorized a married woman to "have, hold and enjoy [her property] in as full and ample a manner as if she continued sole and unmarried," which appeared to grant full autonomy.[82] Provisions that seemed to fly in the face of this sentiment followed. Unless a married woman's husband was absent from the province, he was to be joined in any legal proceeding in which she was involved.[83] Furthermore a husband's entitlement to his wife's and children's earnings was to remain unchallenged unless a court issued an order of protection to the contrary. Such orders could only be granted in extreme circumstances, such as the husband's lunacy, imprisonment, habitual drunkenness, or desertion.[84] The ambiguities inherent in these reform measures soon spread beyond New Brunswick and Ontario. Legislation passed in British Columbia, the Northwest Territories, Manitoba, and Nova Scotia contained similar evidence of confusion.[85]

The ambivalence embodied in the "second wave" statutes meant that their reform potential was open for speculation. The editors of the *Upper Canada Law Journal*, for their part, believed the legislation might prove to be a revolutionary force. Commenting on the 1859 Ontario act, the editors complained:

This is what the bill before us does. It makes every married woman possessed of property, real or personal, *quoad* the property, independent of and separate from her husband. She may do with it as she pleases. She may enjoy it in "as full and ample a manner as if she continued sole and unmarried." She may make separate contracts— she may make devises and bequest—she may fancy her good man "down among the dead men" and govern herself accordingly in all matters of property and civil rights. This is we fear going *too* far as an experiment.[86]

The actual scope of the legislation, however, fell to the judges to determine. In their hands the statutes were systematically stripped of their potential, and the dramatic transformation in married women's property rights forecast by the law editors was halted in its tracks. The judges ensured that the second wave statutes would be properly characterized as "protective" legislation, rather than measures to enhance women's proprietary autonomy.

The majority of judges made no secret of their preference for the common-law rules governing married women's property. One year after the passage of the 1859 Ontario statute, Chief Justice William Henry Draper pronounced what would become the authoritative statement regarding the judicial interpretation of the legislation: "Every provision [in this legislation] is a departure from the common law. And so far as is necessary to give these provisions full effect, we must hold the common law is superseded by them. But it is against principle and authority to infringe any further than is necessary for obtaining the full measure of relief or benefit the act was intended to give."[87] Five years later, fondly recalling the "honest rule of the common law," Justice John Hawkins Hagarty remonstrated: "We never sufficiently appreciate the broad wisdom and justice of the common law until we come to apply the provision[s] of a statute like this to the realities of every day life."[88] After becoming Chief Justice by 1870, Hagarty was even more forthright. The "will of the Legislature," he admitted, was adamantly opposed "to some of our strongest views as to the wisdom of the common law so largely superseded by this Statute."[89]

These sentiments underlay what amounted to a virtual nullification of most of the terms of the legislation. In 1860, Chief Justice Draper had to consider whether several oxen, alleged to be the property of a married woman, should be available to satisfy her debts. Outlining the common-law position, the judge noted that "marriage operate[d] as an absolute gift in law to the husband, of all the goods and chattels and personal property of the wife." Despite the clear wording of the statute, the judge concluded that this situation had not been abrogated by the legislation: "I do not perceive that any of these provisions, either in letter or spirit, require us to hold that chattel property which belonged to the wife before marriage is not, by the marriage, placed in the hands, and under the protection, of the husband, though no longer subject to his debts, or to his disposal."[90]

This interpretation practically erased any prospect of increasing the control of married women over their property. The sole function of the legislation, as the court saw it, was protective. It was meant to preserve the property from alienation by the husband or seizure by his creditors. Interestingly, the result in this particular case was far from unwelcome to the married woman involved. She managed to avoid responsibility for a promissory note she had signed. The larger impact, however, was substantially detrimental to the interest of married women who were thereby restricted in their ability to get personal credit or assume contractual liability.[91] Realizing that married women could not be held liable for their property transactions, few business people would voluntarily agree to deal with them.

Other decisions consistently ruled against the interests of married women when determining which assets actually constituted "separate property." Apart from outright gifts, which could easily be identified as belonging to the donee, most property was held to belong to the family, and thus, the husband. Farm equipment and livestock were regularly attributed to the husband, a result that severely limited the quantity of property married women were assumed to own in a predominantly rural economy.[92] The 1865 Ontario case of Lett v. Commercial Bank of Canada provides a good illustration.[93] Fanny Lett's father had settled a farm in Blenheim and the rents and profits it generated upon his daughter "for her separate use." She and her husband, Dr. Stephen Lett, managed the farm; when he fell into debt, the bank seized horses, cattle, sheep, and farming equipment to satisfy their claim. Fanny's lawyer argued that these assets had been purchased with money from her farming venture, and that they should be protected from seizure under the terms of the 1859 statute.[94] Disagreeing, the court concluded that these goods had been reduced into the possession of her husband, and had thus become liable for his debts. Expressing concern for the rights of the husband in such cases, Justice Hagarty remarked that to accept Fanny Lett's argument "would involve very serious and inconvenient results." Chief Justice Draper summed up:

> The evidence shews the farm is worked by the husband, and without any evidence he is to be deemed the head of the establishment, having the rights and subject to the liabilities of the master of the family . . . . If in the present case she bought the different things to enable the husband to carry on the farm for his own benefit, and that of his wife and family, they are in my opinion liable to satisfy his debts. . . . I am not inclined to hold that because the wife has separate estate, we are to treat the husband as her agent, clerk or farm bailiff, having the interest of a servant or employee; nor. . . that he is a mere dependent on her bounty, and owns none of the property which he or those working on the place use in its cultivation.[95]

The ability to make a legal contract was critical to women who wished to engage in business ventures, make investments, obtain credit, or operate with any autonomy. Yet the judges flatly concluded that married women had no such power. In Kraemer v. Gless, Chief Justice Draper made short shrift in the 1859 Ontario legislation: "This statute does not alter the power of a married woman to make contracts; she is not enabled to bind herself, while a *feme covert*, more than she could before it was passed."[96]

In an 1865 decision, Chief Justice Draper held that the legislation had also had no impact on married women's power to convey their land: "[W]e are clearly of opinion this statute has not changed the law as to the conveyance by married women of their real estate. It enables a married woman to have, hold, and enjoy her real estate free from the debts and obligations of her husband, but it leaves the law as to the conveying such estate untouched. Except where the statute directly interferes, we apprehend the law as to husband and wife continues as it was before. . . . "[97]

Three years later, in Royal Canadian Bank v. Mitchell, Vice-Chancellor John Godfrey Spragge tackled the question of whether the right of married women to the "enjoyment" of their property under the act invested them by implication with the *jus disponendi*, the right to convey or dispose of their property.[98] Concluding that the act had withheld the *jus disponendi*, Spragge argued that the whole tenor of the act was to protect married women, rather than to expose them to the vagaries of the marketplace: "The general scope . . . of the Act is to protect and free from liability the property, real and personal, of married women; not to subject it to fresh liabilities."[99]

Chancellor Van Koughnet extended this ruling in Chamberlain v. McDonald in 1868 to cover personal property; married women were denied the right to contract with or dispose of their personal property as well as their real estate.[100] One year later, Chief Justice William Buell Richards struck the typical judicial stance in Wright v. Garden—if the legislature wished to bestow rights upon married women, it would have to do so in words that would permit of no alternate interpretation.[101] Lacking "express authority" to contract, married women would not be granted such rights by any judicial implication. That same year, in Balsam v. Robinson, Justice John Wellington Gwynne provided his own rationale for these restrictive rulings.[102] He spoke first with concern about the importance of "peace [inside] the marriage state," arguing that to give married women absolute power over their property would permit them to dispose of their assets "against the will and advice" of their husbands. When it came to the balance of power between husband and wife, Canadian judges were loathe to disrupt the traditional patriarchal arrangement. To allow a married woman to conduct business in her own name, speculate for profit, and deal with her property independently would pose a significant threat to the hierarchical marriage. To the extent that they could delay this from happening, the Canadian judges were only too happy to intervene.

Next, Justice Gwynne addressed what he referred to as the "true interests" of married women. Somewhat paternalistically, he suggested that placing unfettered power in the hands of married women would permit them to jeopardize their estate:

> If it should prove to be the law, that the words in the Act, which vest all her real and personal property in herself, *"free from the debts and obligations* of her husband, and from his control and disposition *without her consent,"* are to be construed as giving *to her* absolute control and disposition *without his consent.* I fear the result may be to deprive her of the benefit of his advice and protection, while

relieving her property from his obligations and control, and may expose her to the contrivances of designing persons, who may persuade her to make bargains and dispositions of the property highly prejudicial to the joint interests of herself and her husband.[103]

In the judge's frank estimation, business sense was a gendered attribute.

A few judges raised their voices in dissent at this point. Vice-Chancellor Oliver Mowat was quite supportive of the 1859 statute, and he did not hesitate to label the common law "somewhat barbarous" with respect to married women's property.[104] He spoke out in 1868 to warn that he saw "great difficulty" arising from the rulings of his colleagues that married women had no *jus disponendi*, particularly with respect to personal property. He cautioned: "Money and many other descriptions of personal property cannot be enjoyed at all without being disposed of, and to require the consent of the husband to the disposition by the wife, of any of her personal property would . . . be to make her subject to his control, which is what the statute says shall not be."[105]

Adam Wilson soon joined Mowat and voiced his unequivocal support for the legislation. Applauding the "mental and moral capacity" of married women, Wilson argued in 1869 that the legislature had intended "to establish [a married woman's] individual entity and to attach those rights to it in law which she was in fact capable of exercising." An "enlightened" new system of law, the statute had "purposely subverted . . . the harsh and unreasonable rules of feudal times."[106] Wilson was prepared not only to dissent from the decisions of his colleagues, but to challenge expressly the logic of their holdings. Kraemer v. Gless was, he insisted, "a judgment opposed to the object and principle of the statute."[107] With respect to married women's personal estate, Wilson was adamant in asserting that this property was "at the complete disposal of the wife in this country." With respect to her real estate, Wilson would have preferred to grant a married woman full control over this as well. However, in light of other legislation stipulating that a husband's consent was necessary for a valid conveyance of real estate, he concluded that married women could not dispose of their land solely on their own. He made no secret of the fact that he thought the latter legislation incomprehensible, since it "practically nullifie[d] the beneficial purpose" of the married women's property act.[108] Apart from this imposed restriction, he urged his colleagues to do their duty, "to give effect to a statute which was so manifestly intended to have been the Married Women's Bill of Rights."[109]

Mr. Frederic Eustache Barker of the New Brunswick Supreme Court also dissented from the majority rulings. Relying upon slightly different wording in the 1877 New Brunswick Married Woman's Property Act, Justice Barker held a married woman liable for a contract she had negotiated for repairs to the Royal Hotel in Moncton, which she operated. The New Brunswick statute had enacted the rule that a married woman's property should "vest in" her as property held to her separate use, and Justice Barker concluded that these words granted married women the power of disposal by implication. Although no express language bestowed a specific *jus disponendi* upon married women, Justice Barker was prepared to assert that "no special words were necessary for this purpose."[110] A strong dissent to Barker's opinion was registered by Justice Daniel L. Hanington who argued that the legislators had never contemplated such a result when they passed the statute.[111] This decision was reversed in short order by the Supreme Court of Canada. Chief Justice Sir Henry Strong articulated the traditional judicial perspective:

> [The New Brunswick legislation] indicates that [a married woman's] enjoyment of her property shall be free from the control of her husband, and that it shall not be liable to her husband's debts, [but] it does not indicate that she shall have the power of binding it, encumbering it, and disposing of it as if she were an unmarried woman. This certainly does not do away with the disability of a married woman to alienate her freehold lands or to enter into contracts which would at common law be absolutely void.[112]

Apart from Mowat, Wilson, and Barker, the majority of Canadian judges seemed determined to sabotage the second wave of married women's property legislation. They stripped it of all potential for establishing equality between men and women. They ensured that the statutes would function solely as "protective" legislation, to safeguard family property from loss in times of economic emergency. They were prepared to deny husbands some of their traditional rights over their wives' property, at least to the extent that they might dissipate the estate. They were by no means equally ready, however, to increase a married woman's rights over her property accordingly. Married women's property was to be *protected*, not *set at liberty* for unrestricted commerce.[113]

To some extent, one can attribute these decisions to the fact that the legislation itself was ambivalent. The second wave of statutes was by no means a clear women's rights measure, despite Adam Wilson's attempt to characterize the Ontario enactment as such. However, judicial conservatism must be singled out as a critical factor. Research has revealed that Canadian judges effectively held back progress for women in many areas of nineteenth-century law. In the field of child custody awards, they deliberately minimized the impact of legislation intended to increase mothers' rights.[114] In judgments relating to alimony upon separation or divorce, they repeatedly upheld as ideal a marital relationship in which wives behaved with submissive obedience to the dictates of their husbands.[115] They narrowly interpreted criminal legislation to ensure that only women of unblemished character and dependent status were protected from forcible rape.[116] In decisions concerning tort, they frequently voiced concern over women's propensity to fabricate stories of seduction in order to extort money from victimized men.[117] Evidence from various fields has brought forth a clear pattern of jurisprudence in which it appears that nineteenth-century Canadian judges were fearful of women, hostile towards their independence, and anxious to restrict them within the confines of a subordinate domestic role. Their interpretations of this second wave of married women's property legislation must be assessed in this context. Although it is true that the legislators could have drafted the statutes less equivocally, it was the judges who were primarily responsible for the slowness of married women's property reform in the nineteenth century.

THE THIRD WAVE: EGALITARIAN LEGISLATION

The third wave of legislation was the first to challenge directly the domination of the doctrine of marital unity. Egalitarian legislation encompassed statutes that authorized women generally to retain control of their own wages, attempted to grant them various entrepreneurial powers such as the right to contract, sue, and conduct business, and bestowed upon them the ability to dispose of their real and personal property as they saw fit.

While Canada had had an innovative record in enacting "marriage breakdown" and "protective" laws in the early decades of the century, it fell markedly behind in the third wave of reform legislation. A spirit of legislative creativity, ably demonstrated in earlier decades, seems to have stultified by the 1870s and 1880s. In its place, a distinctly colonial mentality took root, and subservience to English precedent seems to have superseded any sense of Canadian identity.[118] The key to the passage of the first "egalitarian" statutes in Canada was the enactment of England's first Married Women's Property Act of 1870, which served as a model for subsequent Canadian statutes.[119] Interestingly, English legislators were fully aware of Canada's earlier lead in the field. During the debates on the 1870 statute, Canada was singled out as an example of pioneering reform, and the Honorable John Rose, finance minister of Canada, apparently was called before an English parliamentary committee to be questioned about the Canadian experience. Rose testified that the experiment had been successful, and that Canadians had no desire to return to the old common-law system.[120] Canadian legislators who enacted egalitarian legislation after 1870, in most cases drafted their statutes upon the imperial example, seemingly unaware that this constituted a complete about-face. The first egalitarian statute, passed in 1872 in Ontario, was widely agreed to be based upon the 1870 English act.[121] This trend would expand to encompass every common-law province in the country by the end of the century.[122] This change seems not to have been restricted to legislation on married women's property, but was part of an overall transformation affecting Canadian legal education, judicial interpretation, and legal thought in general.[123] However, it was strikingly apparent in the field of married women's property reform where a colony, that had independently forged ahead of the mother country, took on a decidedly imitative and quiescent character in the decades following confederation.

There were several other factors that might also account for the passage of egalitarian legislation. In part, these statutes must have been a response to the recalcitrant behaviour of Canadian judges, who had robbed earlier statutes of much of their reform potential. In part, they were also a response to the economic impasse that had been created by the judicial rulings. The "protective" decisions had consigned married women's property to a legal "twilight zone."[124] No one knew who had the absolute dispositive control over it. Anxious to clarify this matter and to regularize credit relations in a modernizing economy, legislators moved to lift the restrictions judges had attached to married women's property.[125]

The first issue that reached the judiciary related to the *jus disponendi*. Despite statutory wording that seemed to extend such powers, lawyers continued to argue that this authority was still lacking in married women. Merrick v. Sherwood dealt with this point almost immediately after the 1872 Ontario statute had been passed.[126] Section 1 of the Ontario act had provided that "any married woman shall be liable on any contract made by her respecting her real estate, as if she was a *feme sole*." Section 9 provided that "any married woman may be sued or proceeded against separately from her husband in respect of any of her separate debts, engagements, contracts, or torts as if she were unmarried." Concluding that this legislation made married women liable for their own contracts, Justice Gwynne conceded that "no language could be more explicit . . . for the purpose of shewing the intention of the Legislature to be to assimilate the status of a married woman identically to a *feme sole*." It seemed that the court was finally going to yield to legislative direction.

One year later, Justice Gwynne felt forced to reconsider. A Mrs. McGuire of Whitby, Ontario, had apparently left her husband "without any just cause" according to the court, merely three years after their marriage. She demanded that he return to her a horse and carriage and household furniture that had belonged to her before the wedding. Mr. McGuire refused, insisting that his wife should return home and fulfill her marriage vows if she wished the use of her property. Relying upon section 9 of the Ontario statute, which provided that married women were entitled to sue in their own names to recover their separate property "against all persons whomsoever," Mrs. McGuire sued her husband in trover. Adam Wilson conducted the trial, and despite his typical support for married women's property rights, he found this scenario a bit much. He ruled for the husband, holding that Mr. McGuire's refusal to return the property was not sufficient evidence of a wrongful deprivation of goods.

Mrs. McGuire moved to have the verdict set aside, and the final decision was rendered by Justice Gwynne. He reminded the litigants that as long ago as 1869 he had expressed concern that the married women's property legislation would be destructive to the peace of the marriage state. He speculated as to the horrifying ramifications of holding in favour of the wife in this case: "[A] married woman [would have] . . . a right to treat her husband as a trespasser whenever he, although in the house in which they live together, intermeddles with any property which was her separate property before the marriage in a manner which she objects to . . . [and] a married woman [could] when she pleases, prosecute her husband as a trespasser if he continue in *her* house after having received orders from her to leave it."[127]

Referring to Wilson's previous opinions, which had been so opposed to those by the rest of the judges, Justice Gwynne sarcastically remarked that Wilson and his supporters had incorrectly designated the statute "the Married Woman's Bill of Rights"; instead it should more aptly be characterized as "Acts for the emancipation of married women at their own pleasure from all the obligations of the married state, and to enable them notwithstanding to retain the exclusive enjoyment of all rights of property of a *feme sole*."[128] While admitting that a "literal construction" of the statute would seem to bestow upon women an "absolute power of disposition" over their property, he yet refused to so rule, holding that the legislature could not have intended any such thing. Astutely ignoring his earlier decision in Merrick v. Sherwood, Justice Gwynne concluded that a married woman's personal chattels were placed at marriage into the hands of her husband "for the mutual use, convenience, and enjoyment of both husband and wife during the marriage." A married woman had no power to remove these goods and dispose of them at her pleasure, he decided. The legislation had served only to prevent a husband from disposing of such property without his wife's consent—a *jus protegendi* (or power of retaining) rather than a *jus disponendi*.[129]

Attempting to rationalize the narrow construction, the court in Darling v. Rice argued that the 1872 Ontario statute was intended to effect a procedural reform, rather than a substantive amendment. Referring to a married woman's right to contract, the court concluded that she was still by no means the equal of a *feme sole*. Before a creditor could recover against a married woman, it was necessary to show that at the time the contract was made she had a separate estate, and that at the time the action was tried, she still had the same separate estate. Despite the legislative provisions that made married women liable to be sued separately from their husbands as if they were unmarried, in respect of any of their separate debts, engagements, contracts, or torts, Justice Thomas Moss ruled: "I think the object of this provision was to render it unnecessary any longer to join her husband as a defendant, when a suit was brought upon any separate engagement or contract binding upon her. In my opinion it should not be construed as extending her power to contract, but as defining the procedure which may be adopted when a suit or proceeding is conducted against her upon a contract or engagement, on which she is liable."[130]

The 1878 case of Brown v. Winning widened this a bit, recognizing that the legislation authorized a married woman to contract "in respect of some separate employment in which she was engaged," but specifically added that the legislature had not "empowered a married woman, in all cases, to contract as if she were a *feme sole*."[131]

Taking his customary heterodox stand, Wilson was prepared to stand apart from his fellow judges on this issue. He argued in Wagner v. Jefferson in 1876 that the proper interpretation of the 1872 statute authorized a married woman to contract "whether she has separate estate or not." "The liability of a married woman," he insisted, "[was] of a personal nature, not dependent upon her possession of a separate estate."[132] His views did not change over time. In 1882, he extended this ruling to hold that a married woman who was carrying on business could also be sued without regard to separate estate. Registering some sense of despair at his colleagues' consistent refusal to agree with him on these questions, he lamented: "I do not hope . . . to change the mind of any one who has fixed and determinate views upon the construction of this statute as opposed to my own, any more than I can hope to have my own opinion changed upon this subject as I read the statute."[133]

Justice Wilson pointed out that to continue to shelter married women from liability for their contracts would systematically thwart all business opportunities for them. Without credit, he continued, it was impossible to conduct business in a modern economy and what creditor would agree to contract with a married woman when the courts repeatedly refused to enforce liability against them?[134]

In 1881, John Douglas Armour also removed himself from the ranks of the majority and sided with Wilson on this matter.[135] In a long and sarcastic judgment, he intimated that the actual goal of the legislature was substantially at odds with the legislative intention "extracted by the judicial process." He ridiculed the traditional interpretation developed by the courts, alleging that this position was totally illogical:

> [The interpretation of the majority] produced this—that when the Legislature there said that any married woman might be sued or proceeded against, it did not intend that any married woman might be sued or proceeded against, but only that any married woman who had separate estate, and that separate estate only of a particular quality, might be sued or proceeded against; nor did it intend that any married woman so having such separate estate of such a particular quality might be sued or proceeded against, but only that such separate estate of such a particular quality might be proceeded against; and that when the Legislature . . . used the words "as if she were unmarried," it did not intend to use those words, and that section should be read as if they were struck out.[136]

Justice Armour seems to have taken this position out of an interest in creditors' rights, rather than a genuine interest in women's rights per se. That same year in Griffin v. Patterson he explained:

> I endeavoured to point out in my feeble way, in Clarke v. Creighton, a very few of the very many curious legal results that have arisen from the construction put upon . . . the Married Women's Property Act, 1872. The practical results of it have been particularly disasterous to creditors. There are hundreds, I might say thousands, of cases throughout Ontario in which the husband has contrived that the wife shall own everything; she is wealthy, he is worthless; his creditors are set at defiance, because by the construction, to which I have adverted, her property is not of that particular quality of separate estate which will permit them to have a remedy against it.[137]

It is interesting that in many of these cases, the plaintiffs who were arguing for an expansive interpretation of the legislation were creditors rather than women's rights proponents. The motivation of credit regularization seems to have been central to the development of married women's property rights.

In the latter decades of the nineteenth century, more judges seem to have been willing to endorse Justice Wilson's views. Certainly this was true in Manitoba, where Chief Justice Thomas Warlaw Taylor expressly accepted the construction Wilson had placed upon the married women's property legislation, when he considered how to interpret the Manitoba Woman's Act of 1872. A Mrs. McManus had been operating a boardinghouse, lodging twenty-six men who worked for the Canadian Pacific Railway at the Capell station. She had contracted for certain goods with which to run this business, and then tried to avoid liability by arguing that as a married woman, she was only liable to the extent of her separate property. Chief Justice Taylor pronounced himself "prepared to construe [the Manitoba legislation] in a wide and liberal manner," in direct contrast to the decisions of the majority of the Ontario judges, whose construction had "narrow[ed] [the] effect" of the Ontario statute, and largely defeated what Taylor "[conceived] to have been the intention of the Legislature." He concluded: "The whole object of the Legislature on this subject seems to be to extend the powers of married women in dealing with their property, to enable them to contract, and be contracted with in business transactions, and as a consequence of these extended powers to subject them to the ordinary liabilities, and to give those dealing with them the same remedies against them, as against other contractors and debtors."[138]

The judicial deadlock continued in Ontario, however, and in 1884 the legislature stepped in again. At least with respect to the *jus disponendi*, the legislature was unequivocal. Statutorily reversing McGuire,[139] the amending statute provided that a married woman could "acquir[e], hold . . . and dispos[e] . . . of any real or personal property as her separate property, in the same manner as if she were a *feme sole*. . . . " Furthermore she was authorized to contract, sue, and be sued with respect to her separate property, "in all respects as if she were a *feme sole*"; her husband, the act continued, "need not be joined with her." Finally, the act noted that a married woman was entitled to protect her property, using the same remedies a *feme sole* would have, "against all persons whomsoever, including her husband."[140]

In 1892, the Supreme Court of Canada was forced to recognize that the 1884 statute had effected significant change. Chief Justice Henry Strong conceded: "This act of 1884 greatly enlarged the power of disposition of married women. . . . Thenceforth married women were completely emancipated from their husband's control both as regards the enjoyment and the disposition of their real estate."[141] However, some restrictions still remained. The courts continued to insist that before a married woman could make a binding contract, she had to have some separate property.[142] Men, on the other hand, were permitted to make binding contracts regardless of their possession of property.[143] It took legislation again to dismantle this hurdle. In 1897, the Ontario legislature stipulated that a married woman who contracted was deemed to bind her separate property, whether or not she possessed any separate property at the time of the contract. Such contract bound all separate property she might at the time or thereafter possess.[144]

The same wave of statutes that gradually increased the rights of married women to dispose of their property also granted them control of their wages.[145] Traditionally women had been required to seek a court order permitting them to retain their earnings during coverture. Such orders were typically issued only in extreme circumstances—such as desertion, or a husband's habitual drunkenness, imprisonment, or lunacy.[146] Beginning with Ontario in 1872, wives were empowered to hold their "wages and personal earnings . . . and any acquisitions therefrom . . . free from the debts or dispositions of the husband." The legislation specifically authorized married women to dispose of their wages without their husbands' consent, as if they were *femes sole*.[147] British Columbia, the Northwest Territories, Manitoba, and New Brunswick followed suit in 1873 and 1895.[148] Nova Scotia required that before a married woman was authorized to retain her own earnings, her husband had to register his written consent. Otherwise a court order of protection was necessary to give a married woman control of her own wages.[149] Prince Edward Island remained the most backward jurisdiction with respect to married women's wages. Court orders of protection continued to be required throughout the nineteenth century.[150]

Even in the more progressive jurisdictions, litigants remained somewhat confused about the extent of the statutory reform regarding wages. An 1874 Ontario case challenged the section of the 1872 statute that purported to grant married women control over their earnings.[151] The defendants in the case were lumberers in the Lindsay area, and they had authorized a Mr. McCandy to hire labourers for their shanty. McCandy had hired his wife as a cook, and the two of them had moved into the shanty together. When the defendants failed to pay the wages owing, Mrs. McCandy filed suit. The defendants argued that Mrs. McCandy, a married woman, had no right to sue for wages on her own. Although the 1872 legislation had disposed of the need for a court order of protection, they insisted that married women were only entitled to their wages in situations where the court would traditionally have granted an order of protection. Since the McCandy's were living together, and there was no evidence of drunkenness or other such disablement on the part of the husband, the defendants claimed that the legislation could not assist Mrs. McCandy to recover. That such an argument could be made in the face of express legislation granting married women full control over their wages indicates how narrowly some advocates expected the bench to interpret the reform statute.

Chief Justice J.H. Hagarty felt constrained to deny the defendants' claim, and he concluded that the 1872 legislation must be construed to grant married women the right to their earnings under all circumstances. The explicit wording of the statute left him no other choice. He did, however, voice some personal consternation over the outcome of the case:

> It may startle a good many lawyers to be told that our construction of the Act enables a woman, living with her husband, to claim her daily or other earnings as her separate property, and sue for and recover them in her own name, and invest the proceeds in furniture or anything else she pleases. It is rather destructive of the old-

fashioned ideas of community of interest, and community of exertion and labour, for the maintenance of a family. We are not responsible for the consequences of an Act of the Legislature, we can only try to ascertain its true meaning.[152]

The same reluctance to recognize married women's claim to their own earnings appeared in a Manitoba case in 1900.[153] Mrs. Doidge, a married woman, had taken Richard Kingdon, a longtime family friend, into her home to nurse him through a terminal illness. Upon his death seven weeks later, she sued his estate for the wages she alleged he had agreed to pay her for this service. The court was hard-pressed to determine whether this constituted part of Mrs. Doidge's domestic responsibilities or whether it involved special work separate from household chores. If the former, the court determined that the right to these services belonged to the husband, and Mr. Doidge would have the only right of action against Kingdon's estate. If the latter, Mrs. Doidge would be empowered to sue in her own name under the Manitoba statute of 1881.

Carefully dividing the work as he saw fit, Justice John Farquhar Bain concluded that the nursing attendance necessitated by a long and serious illness "could not be considered to be part of the ordinary household work," and might "very properly be held to be wages and personal earnings." As regards the meals, however, Justice Bain determined that the foodstuffs were originally the property of the husband, and the preparation of means could not be considered to be outside the realm of typical household labour. The right of action for these remained in the husband alone.[154] The judges obviously retained a very restricted conception of women's work. Anything akin to domestic responsibilities in the home was scrutinized circumspectly before permitting it to be classified as wage labour.[155] The normal ways in which women earned extra money in the nineteenth century—from taking in boarders to selling eggs and butter— would have been characterized by the courts as too closely associated with household tasks to constitute separate earnings.[156]

The third wave of married women's property legislation also expanded the rights of *femes coverts* to carry on business in their own right. Ontario set the precedent in 1872 when it provided that the profits of a married woman amassed from any occupation or trade "which she carried on separately from her husband," or derived from any literary, artistic, or scientific skill, were to be held, enjoyed, and disposed of without her husband's consent.[157] Similar provisions were enacted in every province except Prince Edward Island before the turn of the century.[158] The vast bulk of the litigation that followed these statutes revolved around the issue of whether the married woman was indeed conducting the business "separately" from her husband. Not surprisingly, the courts were very conservative in their consideration of this question.

In 1877, the Upper Canada Court of Queen's Bench dealt with a claim by Jemima Harrison that her farm crops, livestock, and equipment should not be seized for her husband's debts.[159] She held the title to the farm, which her husband had transferred to her in return for her agreement to bar her dower with respect to other property. The couple lived on the farm and when William Harrison fell into financial difficulties, his creditors attempted to seize the farm assets. Jemima Harrison argued that although her husband worked on the farm, he did so as her agent, and that in reality she carried on the enterprise separately. Holding that the creditors should succeed here, Chief Justice Robert Alexander Harrison indicated that he had little sympathy with such an argument: "Attempts, however ingenious, to convert the wife to a farmer into "the husbandman," and the husband into her mere servant, agent, or manager, so as to enable him to live on the farm, work the farm, derive his support from it, and do so in defiance of his creditors, are not to be encouraged." Indeed, it seemed that the Chief Justice had great difficulty conceiving how a farming enterprise could ever be conducted without a husband's assistance. "If the occupation or trade be such that a wife cannot carry it on without the husband's active co-operation or agency," he added, "it is not easy to discover in what sense it can honestly be called an occupation or trade, carried on by her 'separately from her husband.' "[160]

The issue was raised again in Murray v. McCallum in 1883.[161] David Murray, a notorious spendthrift, lost all of his money at the horse races, and his farm was sold for debt. Concluding that she could no longer rely on her husband, Elizabeth Murray had taken her small savings, borrowed some money, and purchased a hotel-tavern in Owen Sound, which she managed with several other partners. They hired David Murray for fifteen dollars a month to work as bartender. When David again ran into financial embarrassment, his creditors tried to seize Elizabeth Murray's hotel assets, arguing that because David was involved in the business, the property was not protected by the 1872 legislation. Although the decision did not evoke complete agreement on the bench, Justice George W. Burton concluded that David Murray's duties as bartender deprived the business of its separate character. Indeed, he suggested that only a limited range of businesses such as dressmaking, millinery, singing, acting, and other artistic occupations were meant to be encompassed by the legislation.[162]

The tragedy that could ensue from such rulings was starkly illustrated in an 1894 case, Streimer v. Merchant's Bank.[163] A Manitoba farmer, J. Streimer, had had his farm and crops seized for debt in 1892, leaving him, his wife, and their nine children poverty-stricken. Helena Streimer, his wife, then managed to purchase a substitute quarter-section of land with money she borrowed from friends and relatives, and the wages of one of her daughters. J. Streimer was sickly and too ill to do much more than give instructions to the family about how to manage the farm. Nevertheless, Streimer, his wife, a fifteen-year-old daughter, and a ten-year-old son harvested a crop in 1893. J. Streimer's creditors kept their eyes on the situation, and immediately attempted to seize the proceeds. Helena argued that the crop was hers.

Noting that the case constituted one of "great hardship," Justice Joseph Dubuc admitted that all Helena Streimer was trying to do was to "provide [for] and support her family . . . after being left penniless, with a sickly husband." Nevertheless he ruled that the grain belonged by right to the creditors, because the farming venture could not be characterized as a separate business of the wife's. J. Streimer's involvement in the harvest and the fact that the crop had been cut with his farm implements was sufficient evidence for Justice Dubuc to rule against Helena's defence.[164]

It took legislative reform to change the outcome of most of these cases. In 1887, the Ontario Legislature deleted the stipulation that a married woman's business had to be carried on "separately" from her husband in order to shelter it from his debts and grant her dispositive control over the proceeds. From then on it was necessary to prove only that the husband had "no proprietary interest" in the business.[165] In 1895, Justice Featherstone Osler ruled that this signified simply an "interest as owner" or "legal right or title."[166] By the end of the century, most married women gained the right to control the profits from their entrepreneurial ventures.

For women in Prince Edward Island, this right was not realized until the twentieth century, and for married women in Nova Scotia, such rights were conditional upon their husbands' granting written consent. An 1894 Nova Scotia case pointed out how such restrictions could work to the disadvantage of women. Ida Adams, who was living apart from her husband, James, had purchased and was operating a licensed tavern in Bridgewater. She had failed to register the necessary document indicating that her husband consented to her carrying on the business. The court concluded that lacking James Adams's written consent, all of the business assets belonged to him and could not be dealt with by Ida without his authorization.[167]

Apart from these anomalies, the last wave of legislation gradually released women's property from the restricted position it had been placed in as a result of judicial reluctance to recognize married women's property rights. The majority of the judges continued to express concern over the prospect of treating married women as the equal of men with respect to property relations, but successive legislative amendments ultimately left them little choice. The rights of creditors to seek satisfaction for family debts eventually outweighed the perceived need to protect married women's assets from seizure during time of financial crisis. By the turn of the century, married women were finally empowered to control their property in most respects as men had done from time immemorial.

CONCLUSION

The nineteenth century witnessed a dramatic transformation in the property rights of married women in Canada. From a position of virtual powerlessness in 1800, married women gradually amassed significant control over their real and personal property, wages, and business profits by 1900. The change was initiated by the provincial legislators, who accomplished this reform through three successive waves of married women's property enactments. These statutes seem to have been generated by distinctive and sometimes conflicting goals. Some were motivated by a paternalistic desire to provide women with a limited form of income as an emergency measure when the marriage was no longer functioning. Others expressed protective impulses, in which legislators sought to preserve married women's property from seizure for their husbands' debts. Some were also meant as egalitarian measures, to increase the status of married women with respect to their property. The later legislation seems to have been enacted largely as a form of self-imposed genuflexion on the part of an imitative subservient colony to an imperial power. To the extent that the last wave was viewed as a substantive reform, the goal seems to have been to regularize creditors' rights, by subjecting married women to the same property laws that governed everyone else.

It fell to the judges to determine how to apply these waves of statutory reform. Seemingly in agreement with the motivation of the first statutes, Canadian judges enthusiastically enforced their provisions in a broad and general manner. The second and third waves of legislation met with quite a different fate. Scornful of the legislative goals and palpably concerned about the dangers such reform measures posed for the Canadian family, the majority of judges deliberately embarked upon a campaign of statutory nullification. They consistently refused to grant women the *jus disponendi* over their property. They restricted a married woman's right to contract. They refused to recognize domestic labour as work done for separate wages. They narrowly construed what constituted "separate" property, and what constituted a "separate" business undertaking, giving married men control over the vast bulk of family assets and business ventures.

These rulings were issued within a frame of reference that the judges believed was critical for the maintenance of peaceful and harmonious marital relations. The nineteenth-century Canadian family was never to be viewed as a partnership of equals, where both spouses were permitted to contribute independently to the well being of the domestic unit. To the contrary, the hierarchical family the judges idealized required that married women be rigorously restricted from exercising control over their property. The autonomy that full married women's property rights would have given Canadian wives was an appalling prospect to nineteenth-century judges. Their beliefs and prejudices about women, property, and the nature of marriage prompted an archly conservative approach. Not until the end of the century would their rulings be supplanted by successive legislative amendments that ultimately put an end to the judicial foot-dragging and catapulted Canadian married women into the modern era.

Formally entitling married women to the same rights over property as men, the law would now appear to be egalitarian and even-handed. Actual access to resources and wealth, of course, would remain markedly skewed in favour of men. Property allocation would continue to be gender-imbalanced despite theoretically equal entitlements. It leaves one to wonder whether the battle to obtain formal property rights for married women, a struggle that engaged so many for so long, was the best choice that feminists of the nineteenth century could make. One is left speculating whether the petitioning women, like Elizabeth Dunlop, would have been satisfied with the outcome of their activism.

NOTES

1. Richard Chused's analysis of the waves of married women's property statutes passed in the United States laid the groundwork for other scholars attempting comparable periodization. While the Canadian data are distinguishable, it is useful to note Chused's findings in the United States. He concludes that the first wave was based upon debtor-relief, the second upon the establishment of separate estates over which the wife had little dispositive control, the third to give women control over their own wages, and, finally, in the second half of the nineteenth century, enactments that more comprehensively granted dispositive powers over married women's property. See R. Chused, "Married Women's Property Law 1800–1850," *Georgetown Law Journal* 71 (1983): 1359; Chused, "The Oregon Donation Act of 1850 and Nineteenth-Century Federal Married Women's Property Law," *Law and History Review* 2 (1984), 77.

2. C.B. Martin, "Legal Status of Women in the Provinces of the Dominion of Canada (Except the Province of Quebec)," in *Women of Canada: Their Life and Work*" (1900), 37.

3. Ibid.

4. See A.H. Osterhoff and W.B. Rayner, *Anger & Honsberger Law of Real Property* (1985), vol. 1, ch. 3, for an account of the reception of English common law in Canada.

5. For one of the most readable, accurate, and complete accounts, see L. Holcombe, *Wives and Property: Reform of the Married Women's Property Law in Nineteenth-Century England* (1983), ch. 2. See also W. Blackstone, *Commentaries*, 1: 430–33; 2: 433–36; R.T. Walkem, *The Married Women's Property Acts of Ontario* 1–4 (1874); G.S. Holmested, *The Married Women's Property Act of Ontario* 1–6 (1905); N. Basch, *In the Eyes of the Law: Women,*

Marriage and Property in Nineteenth-Century New York (1982), 17–20, 54–55; P.A. Rabkin, *Fathers to Daughters: The Legal Foundations of Female Emancipation* (1980), 19–37, 121–22 B.L.S. Bodichon, *A Brief Summary in Plain Language of the Most Important Laws Concerning Women, Together with a Few Observations Thereon* (1854); R.S.D. Roper, *A Treatise on the Law of Property Arising From the Relation between Husband and Wife*, 2d ed., (1826).

6. This and the following statements regarding common-law rules have been drawn from the various sources listed in note 5. Some exception to this proposition existed for personal property characterized as "paraphernalia," that is, clothing and personal ornaments. "Choses in action" or personal claims such as debts owed by one individual to another did not vest in the husband until he reduced them into his possession.

7. A married woman was not entitled to alienate her own lands, despite her technical retention of ownership, without her husband's reciprocal consent.

8. Married women were given very limited rights to contract for necessaries as agents of their husbands.

9. In medieval times, some married women had been permitted the status of "separate trader," and given full property rights of spinsters, but by the mid-nineteenth century, this situation prevailed only in the City of London.

10. Whibby v. Walbank (1869), 5 Nfld. R. 286 (S.C.) Since Mary Whibby's son had directly contributed to his mother's savings by paying her some of his wages, the court did award a portion of the savings to the son, but did not thereby disentitle the husband from his wife's earnings.

11. Campbell et ux. v. Campbell (1875), 25 U.C.C.P. 368 per John Wellington Gwynne, J. Although legislative reform had given married women certain rights to their separate property by this time, the lawyers involved argued that they had no rights regarding name or reputation, and thus the old common-law rules continued to hold regarding the necessary joinder of a married woman's husband.

12. Kieley v. Morrison (1892), 24 N.S.R. 327 at 329.

13. See Zealand v. Dewhurst (1873), 23 U.C.C.P. 117 per Thomas Galt J., at 122.

14. Basch, *In the Eyes of the Law*, 21; Chused, "Married Women's Property Law," 1386. For the best general description of equitable jurisdiction regarding married women's property see Holcombe, *Wives and Property*, and M. Salmon, *Women and the Law of Property in Early America* (1985), ch. 5. See also Basch, *In the Eyes of the Law*, 72–111; Rabkin, *Fathers to Daughters*, 21–36; Walken, *Married Women's Property Acts*, 4–11; Holmested, *Married Women's Property Act*, 6–7; Salmon, Marriage Settlements, 1730–1830," *William and Mary Quarterly* (3rd ser.) 39 (1982), 657–684.

15. Holcombe, *Wives and Property*, 39.

16. Ibid.

17. Ibid.

18. Salmon, "Women and Property," 660.

19. Chused, "Married Women's Property Law," 1386.

20. Holcombe, *Wives and Property*, 41–42.

21. An Act to Establish a Court of Chancery in this Province, 7 Wm. IV (1837), c. 2. The lieutenant governor of the province had, in theory, jurisdiction as chancellor, but never exercised these rights. B. Laskin, *The British Tradition in Canadian Law* (1969), 13.

22. This statement is based largely upon assumption. Salmon's superb research in *Women and the Law of Property*, chs. 4 and 6, has uncovered data showing that Americans drafted and signed equitable contracts regardless of the absence of formal enforcement machinery and resorted to arbitration to settle disputes in the last resort. While no specific evidence has yet been discovered in Canada, Elizabeth Brown (who has written the best account of equity jurisdiction in nineteenth-century Upper Canada) has found that even *after* the creation of a court of chancery, parties were having their cases decided by arbitrators rather than submitting to the vagaries of chancery. My conclusion is that this pattern of behaviour likely predated the establishment of the court in 1837. E. Brown, "Equitable Jurisdiction and the Court of Chancery in Upper Canada," *Osgoode Hall Law Review* 21 (1983): 275, 291.

23. This informal jurisdiction was "regularized" in 1825 when the Master of the Rolls was formally appointed as chancellor. C.J. Townshend, "History of the Court of Chancery in Nova Scotia," 20 *Canadian Law Times* (1900): 14, 37, 74, 105 at 14–16 J.D. Blackwell, "William Home Blake and the Judicature Acts of 1849," in *Essays on the History of Canadian Law*, ed. Flaherty (1981), 1: 38–39; Brown "Equitable Jurisdiction," 276.

24. New Brunswick formally appointed a Master of the Rolls in 1838, and Prince Edward Island in 1848. Laskin, *British Tradition*, 13.

25. Townshend, "History of Court of Chancery," 75–77. He noted that the procedures of the Irish Court of Chancery appeared to be the model.

26. Laskin, *British Tradition*, 12.

27. Even after the creation of a court of chancery in Ontario the press complained that only a few legal practitioners in Toronto truly understood

the system. Blackwell, *Commentaries,* 164, 167.

28. Basch, *In the Eyes of the Law,* 109. Suzanne Lebsock has also done research on separate estates in Petersburg, Virginia, in the eighteenth and nineteenth centuries and concluded that it was a "fairly simple procedure" that did not require a lawyer. Lebsock, *The Free Women of Petersburg: Status and Culture in a Southern Town, 1784–1860* (1984), 59–60.

29. Holmested, *Married Women's Property Act,* 6.

30. Holcombe, *Wives and Property,* 46.

31. Salmon, "Women and Property," 663. Salmon's additional research into the use of marriage settlements in colonial Maryland also indicates the scarcity of such agreements in early America. Salmon, "The Legal Status of Women in Early America: A Reappraised," *Law & History Review* (1983), 149. Lebsock has complied similar data on Petersburg, Virginia. Prior to 1820, she has noted, separate estates were rare but each decade brought substantial growth in the number of such agreements. Lebsock, *Free Women of Petersburg,* 52–59.

32. See, e.g., the Nova Scotia case, Routledge v. Routledge (1897), 30 N.S.R. 151.

33. The cases frequently refer to arrangements by which fathers attempted to grant land and money to their daughters—by mail or otherwise—for their separate use. See, for example, Routledge v. Routledge (1897), 30 N.S.R. 151; Rice v. Rice (1899), 31 O.R. 59 (Div. Ct.). The Ontario case of Hilcock v. Button (1881), 29 Chy. R. 490, per William Proudfood, V.C., makes mention of the usual purpose of settlements: to protect the married women's property from the improvidence of the husband, for her benefit and the benefit of her children.

34. In one remarkable case the court was forced to delve into the rea-

sons why a prospective bridegroom would settle property upon his fiancée, where the husband's creditors alleged that the transaction was merely a ruse to defeat their claims. In Stuart v. Thomson (1893), 23 O.R. 503 (Q.B.)

35. See, e.g., Pemberton v. O'Neil (1851), 2 Chy. R. 263; Fenton v. Cross (1858), 7 Chy. R. 20; Dorsey v. Dorsey (1898), 29 O.R. 475.

36. Rice v. Rice (1899), 31 O.R. 59 (Div. Ct.) at 55.

37. Nolan v. Fox (1865), 15 U.C.C.P. 565, per William Buell Richards, C.J.

38. Ibid., 576.

39. This discussion will omit consideration of married women's property rights upon divorce, since such women were no longer "married." It will concentrate, instead, upon abandonment, desertion, and cruelly treated women who were still legally bound to the marriage.

40. Blackstone, *Commentaries,* 1: 431, 433.

41. Chused describes a string of Alabama private bills in the 1820s granting deserted wives *feme sole* status, followed by general legislation in the 1840s for the benefit of deserted women as a whole. Chused, "Married Women's Property Law," 1405–7.

42. An account of the Canadian early divorce legislation can be found in C. Backhouse, "Pure Patriarchy: Nineteenth-Century Canadian Marriage," *McGill Law Journal* 31 (1986): 264. Nova Scotia enacted its first divorce legislation in 1758, New Brunswick in 1791, and Prince Edward Island in 1833.

43. 14 Vict. (1851), c. 24 (N.B.). The statute also contained two provisions that would put it within the second wave of "protective legislation" and it will be discussed under that heading as well. See also R.S.N.B. 1854, vol. 1, c. 114.

44. Ibid., sec. 3.

45. Sec. 5. Ibid.,

46. An Act in Addition to Chapter 114, Title XXX, of the Revised Statutes Of the Real and Personal Property of Married Women, 32 Vict. (1869), c. 33 (N.B.), sec. 1.

47. Ibid., sec. 2.

48. An Act Relating to the Real and Personal Property of Married Women, 37 Vict. (1874), c. 23 (N.B.) The act however specifically exempted certain property from its provisions. It was not to apply to any property acquired *from one's husband* during marriage, or *earned* during marriage and before desertion. See also C.S.N.B. 1877, c. 72.

49. An Act to Protect the Rights of Married Women, in Certain Cases, 23 Vict. (1860), c. 35 (P.E.I.) sec. 1 & 2. The only distinction was that the Prince Edward Island legislation may have intended to grant somewhat larger rights to deserted wives. The New Brunswick statute granted women control over property accumulated as a result of their own labour, where they were "compelled to support" themselves. The Prince Edward Island statute did not restrict this right to earnings, but included "any property," that was then to "vest" in the woman, "and be at her disposal and not subject to the debts, interference or control of her husband" (sec. 2).

50. An Act for the Protection of Married Women in Certain Cases, 29 Vict. (1866), c. 33 (N.S.), sec. 1 & 2. See also R.S.N.S. 1873 (4th ser.), c. 86.

51. Ibid., sec. 2 & 5.

52. Ibid., sec. 4.

53. See Matrimonial Causes Act, 20 & 21 Vict. (1857), c. 85 (Eng.). The English influence seems to have been well-known amongst the Nova Scotian legal community. In Sinclair v. Wakefield (1800), 13 N.S.R. 465, the plaintiff's lawyer would later argue that this act (as later incorporated into R.S.N.S., c. 86) was "iden-

tical" in various provisions with the English statute 20 & 21 Vict., c. 85. The English statute was considered a great disappointment by a group of feminists led by Barbara Leigh Smith Bodichon, who had begun an active lobby for improved married women's property rights in the 1850s. The success of the partial reform was attributed to the campaign of Caroline Norton, whose own marital separation had caused her to call for protection for separated women, but not for universal married women's property rights. See *Selected Writings of Caroline Norton* (1978); D.M. Stetson, *A Womans Issue: The Politics of Family Law Reform in England* (982); Holcombe, *Wives and Property*, 50–109.

54. An Act to Protect the Property of a Wife Deserted by her Husband, 1862, *Public General Statutes of the Colony of Vancouver Island 1859–1863*, c. 51, at 20. The act allowed a deserted wife to seek an order of the court to protect any money or property she may have acquired after her husband's desertion, free from her husband and his creditors. If after such an order a husband seized his wife's property, he was liable not only to restore the specific property, but also to pay her an amount of money equal to double the value of the property seized.

55. M. Ormsby, *British Columbia: A History* (1985), 135ff.

56. Abell v. Light (1867), 12 N.B.R. 96 (S.C.), per William J. Ritchie.

57. Ibid., 100–101. Mrs. Abell's remedy was more circuitous than might appear from the initial decision. A later case indicated that Mrs. Abell, still attempting to collect the debt due from her boarder, detained the defendant's goods. He had her arrested and she subsequently sued him for malicious prosecution and false imprisonment. She was granted £500 in damages. See (1868), 12 N.B.R. 240 (S.C.)

58. Sinclair v. Wakefield (1880), 12 N.S.R. 465.

59. Justice Robert L. Weatherbe dissented from the majority decision, holding that the clear wording of the statute permitted no other result.

60. Sinclair v. Wakefield at 470, per Alexander James, J.

61. See, e.g., S. Altschul and C. Caron, "Chronology of Some Legal Landmarks in the History of Canadian Women," *McGill Law Journal* 21 (1975), 477; M.E. MacLellan, "History of Women's Rights in Canada" in *Cultural Tradition and Political History of Women in Canada* (1971), 4.

62. 14 Vict. (1851), c. 24 (N.B.), sec. 1.

63. The American states had enacted similar legislation somewhat earlier, beginning in Arkansas in 1835 and Mississippi in 1839. By the end of the Civil War, almost every state and territory had moved to protect married women's property from their husbands' debts. Despite the multiplicity of legislative initiatives, there was little verbatim copying between jurisdictions, suggesting that there was no unified leadership behind this wave of enactments. The insightful analysis that American scholars have brought to bear on these statues suggests a number of factors had combined to create the impetus behind the reform. Economic motivation to provide debtor-relief to families in times of financial crisis, the interests of fathers to pass legacies from one generation to another intact, the movement for codification, the concerted attack on the equity court system, feminist agitation, and cross-fertilization from neighbouring community-properties regimes such as Louisiana, Texas, and Florida have all been suggested. See Chused, "Married Women's Property Law"; Warbasse, "Changing Legal Rights"; Basch, *In the Eyes of the Law*; *Fathers to Daughters*; and E. Griffith, *In Her Own Right: The Life of Elizabeth Cady Stanton* (1988), 43.

64. See Preface to *Statutes of New Brunswick*, 1858.

65. See W.D. Easterbrook and H.G.J. Aitken, *Canadian Economic History* (1980), 243, 245, 354–55; W.S. MacNutt, *New Brunswick: A History*, 1784–1867 (1963), 329, 330, 345.

66. An Act to Authorize the Confirmation of Certificates of Bankruptcy in Certain Cases, 14 Vict. (1851), c. 23 (N.B.).

67. Along with this growing cult of motherhood came greater rights over child custody and more restrictions on access to abortion and birth control. See C. Backhouse, "Shifting Patterns in Nineteenth-Century Canadian Custody Law" in *Essays on the History of Canada*, ed. Flaherty, 212, and "Involuntary Motherhood: Abortion, Birth Control and the Law in Nineteenth-Century Canada," *Windsor Yearbook of Access to Justice* 3 (1981): 61. Chused has made the direct link between these developments and greater married women's property rights in the American context. See Chused, "Married Women's Property Law," 1414–24.

68. Philip Girard, who is presently conducting research on married women's property in nineteenth-century Nova Scotia, has discovered that a number of bills were introduced, beginning in 1855. Interestingly the first bill was a verbatim copy of the 1848 New York Act. See his unpublished manuscript "The Law Reform Movement in Mid-Nineteenth Century Nova Scotia."

69. An Act to Secure to Married Women Certain Separate Rights of Property, 22 Vict. (1859), c. 34 (P.C.). See also C.S.U.C. 1859, c. 73.

70. Bills were presented in 1856 and 1857 and again in 1859. Early versions of the 1859 bill were more radical than that finally passed. Married women were permitted to keep all their personal earnings.

This provision was struck out before enactment. See S. Kierans, *The Family Matters* (1986), 51–57.

71. See Easterbrook and Aitken, *Canadian Economic History*, 371, 373; E.J. Middleton and F. Landon, *The Province of Ontario—A History* (1927), 1: 347.

72. See An Act to Extend the Provisions of the Act for the Abolition of Imprisonment for Debt, 22 Vict. (1859), c. 33 passed the same day.

73. The *Globe*, 10 March 1859.

74. This date marks the founding of the first suffrage organization in Toronto. C. Cleverdon, *The Woman Suffrage Movement in Canada* (1974), 20. The organized temperance movement had reached both Ontario and New Brunswick by the late 1840s, and may have set the climate for receptivity to married women's property reform, although no records have been located of specific lobbying on this issue by temperance groups. C.L. Bacchi, *Liberation Deferred? The Ideas of the English-Canadian Suffragists, 1877–1918* (1983), 70–76. In the United States, active temperance societies had not only preached abstinence, but also lobbied for individual property rights for wives so that women could earn and keep incomes separate from alcoholic husbands. See Griffith, *In Her Own Right*, 77.

75. Personal correspondence from Mary Jane Mossman, 1985–87. Professor Mossman has kindly made available to me the following details. Elizabeth L. Hawley "and others" delivered a petition in 1856 requesting an act similar to the one in New York State (*Journals of the Legal Council* 1856). The Journal Index 1852–66 indicates Anne Macdonald "and other ladies" brought forward a petition for an act to secure married women's property rights in 1852–53, and possibly again in 1854–55 and in 1856. Elizabeth Dunlop "and others" brought forward a petition in

1857 (see Journal Index 1852–66) for an act to render the property of married women free from the control of their husbands. This seems to have been one petition among many, but hers is the only name specified.

76. The *Globe, Women's Rights Petition*, 9 Jan 1857, 1.

77. The *Globe*, 10 March 1859.

78. G. Blaine Baker has noted that mid-nineteenth-century Upper Canadian lawyers exhibited great interest in French and Lower Canadian legal literature and were well aware of legal trends in jurisdictions other than England. In this vein, it is interesting to note that New Brunswick also had a large French-speaking population. G.B. Baker, "The Reconstruction of Upper Canada Legal Thought in the Late-Victorian Empire," *Law and History Review* 3 (1985): 219.

79. Holmested, *The Married Women's Property Act*, sec. 8, referred to the 1840 Vermont statute, the 1848 New York statute, and the 1857 Massachusetts statute.

80. In Wright v. Garden (1869), 28 U.C.Q.B. 609 at 619, Justice Wilson claimed that the Ontario legislation "was introduced no doubt to give effect to the report and recommendation of the society for the amendment of the law made in 1856 and published in the *Law Magazine*, vol. 1, N.S. 391 and in other contemporaneous publications."

81. For an account of this reform campaign and its eventual defeat, see Stetson, *A Woman's Issue*, 50–80; Holcombe, *Wives and Property*, 91; V. Ulrich, "The Reform of Marital Property Law in England in the Nineteenth Century," *Victorian University of Wellington Law Review* 9 (1977): 22. Canadians were well aware of these English developments. The editors of the *Upper Canada Law Journal* reprinted in 1857 an article from the English *Law Magazine and Law Review* that

recounted the great public furor over Perry's bill. Interestingly, the journal made no reference to the existence of similar pressure groups in Canada. The same editors made short shrift of the radical English proposal, and left no doubt that they believed married women's property reform should be restricted to situations where marriage breakdown had occurred. "The Married Woman Question," *Upper Canada Law Journal* (1857), 143–45, (1858), 107–8.

82. Section 1 provided that: "Every woman who shall marry after the passing of this Act without any marriage contract or settlement, shall and may, notwithstanding her coverture, have, hold and enjoy all her real and personal property, whether belonging to her before marriage or acquired by her by inheritance, devise, bequest or gift, or as next of kin to an intestate, or in any other way after marriage, free from the debts and obligations of her husband, and from his control or disposition without consent, in as full and ample a manner as if she continued sole and unmarried, any law, usage or custom to the contrary notwithstanding: provided that this clause shall not extend to any property received by a married woman from her husband during coverture."

83. 22 Vict. (1859), c. 34 (P.C.) sec. 19.

84. Section 6 listed the situations in which an order of protection of earnings *might* be issued: "Any married woman having a decree of alimony against her husband, or any married woman who lives apart from her husband, having been obliged to leave him for cruelty or other cause which by law justifies her leaving him and renders him liable for her support, or any married woman whose husband is undergoing sentence of imprisonment in the Provincial Penitentiary, or in any gaol for a criminal offence, or any married woman whose husband from

habitual drunkenness, profligacy or other cause, neglects or refuses to provide for her support, and that of his family, an any married woman whose husband has never been in this Province, or any married woman who is deserted or abandoned by her husband, may obtain an order of protection."

85. British Columbia enacted legislation proclaiming that the real estate of a married woman was to be "held and enjoyed by her for her separate use, free from any estate or claim of her husband." The restriction to real estate was novel, and an 1887 amendment brought personal property into the new regime. The other features of the 1873 statute seem to have been inspired by the 1870 English Married Women's Property Act, more properly considered under the "third wave" of legislative reform, and will be discussed under that heading. An Act to Extend the Rights of Property of Married Women, 36 Vict. (1873), c. 29 (B.C.); C.S.B.C. 1877, vl. 1, c. 117 (B.C.); 46 Vict. (1883), c. 18 (B.C.); 50 Vict. (1887), c. 20 (B.C.).

The Northwest Territories (then including what would become the provinces of Alberta and Saskatchewan) passed an act essentially duplicating the 1873 British Columbia statute in 1875. The North West Territories Act, 1875, c. 49, sec. 58 & 52, as printed in E.H. Oliver, *The Canadian North-West: Its Early Development and Legislative Records* (1915), 1086–87. It was not until 1889 that married women in the Northwest Territories were given separate property rights over personal property: An Ordinance Respecting the Personal Property of Married Women, Ord. No. 16 of 1889 (N.W.T.).

Manitoba adopted the 1859 Ontario legislation practically verbatim in 1875. Additional provisions are more accurately characterized as "third wave" legislation, and will be discussed under that section. An Act Respecting Separate

Rights of Property of Married
Women, 38 Vict. (1875), c. 25
(Manitoba); C.S.M. 1880, c. 65.

Nova Scotia was the last jurisdiction to adopt "second wave" legislation. (Prince Edward Island went
directly from marriage breakdown
legislation to the "third wave"
reform.) The Ontario model seems
to have been the major influence
for the Nova Scotian model,
although there were some distinctive features. An entirely novel
provision disentitled married
women who were guilty of adultery from any protection under the
act. Of the Property of Married
Women, R.S.N.S. 1884 (5th Ser.) c.
94.

86. *Upper Canada Law Journal* (1858),
107. The editors were quick to suggest that a form of "marriage
breakdown" legislation would
have been preferable: "It is a delicate, and it may be unsafe, thing to
enact that husband and wife shall
no longer by one but two persons.
The dependence of the wife upon
the husband has long been recognized as a guarantee of connubial
felicity. The absolute dependence
may in some cases work hardship.
Why not then proceed by making
provision for exceptional cases
instead of making exceptional
cases the basis of general legislation." Ibid.

87. Kraemer v. Gless (1860), 10
U.C.C.P. 470 at 475.

88. Lett v. Commercial Bank of Canada
(1865), 24 U.C.Q.B. 552 and 561–62.

89. Corrie v. Cleaver (1870), 21
U.C.C.P. 186 at 188–89.

90. Kraemer v. Gless, 472 and 475.

91. Basch, *In the Eyes of the Law*, 215,
has developed this point in connection with her research on married
women's property in New York.

92. Ibid., 212, where she notes that
similar rulings occurred in New
York. "Such enterprises as boarding houses and farms, businesses
frequently operated in the family's

place of residence and closely
related to women's customary
domestic duties, were often constructed as belonging to the husband."

93. Lett v. Commercial Bank of Canada.
Fanny's lawyer urged "with great
force, that a married woman
[could] not 'have, hold and enjoy'
her personal property 'in as full
and ample a manner as if she were
sole and unmarried,' if she [could]
not buy what she please[d] with
her own money, and have flocks
and herds and ships and ware-
houses of her own, as a single
woman might."

94. Lett v. Commercial Bank of
Canada, 562.

95. Ibid., 559.

96. Kraemer v. Gless, 473. Nor, he
added, (474) could a married
woman wage litigation alone.
"Even for a cause of action accru-
ing . . . before coverture," he stipulated, "the husband must be
joined."

97. Emrick v. Sullivan (1865), 25
U.C.Q.B 105 at 107.

98. Royal Canadian Bank v. Mitchell
(1868), 14 Chy. R. 412.

99. Ibid., 419.

100. Chamberlain v. McDonald (1868),
14 Chy R. 447.

101. Wright v. Garden (1869), 28
U.C.Q.B. 609.

102. Balsam v. Robinson (1869), 19
U.C.C.P. 263.

103. Justice Gwynne's statements were
in obiter.

104. Balsam v. Robinson, 269.

105. See Fraser v. Hilliard (1869), Chy.
R. 101 at 102; Chamberlain v.
McDonald, 449–50.

106. Wright v. Garden, 623–24.

107. Ibid., 625. See also Wilson's judgment in Halpenny v. Pennock
(1873), 33 U.C.Q.B. 229, in which he
rendered a liberal interpretation of
the statute.

108. Wright v. Garden, 618–19, 624. The other legislation referred to was 22 Vict. (1859), c. 35 (P.C.), sec. 6.

109. Wright v. Garden, 624.

110. Lea v. Wallace (1896), 33 N.B.R. 492 (S.C.). The statute in question was C.S.N.B. 1877, c. 72.

111. Ibid., 542.

112. (1897), 28 S.C.R. 595.

113. This pattern of judicial rulings seems not to have been restricted to Canada, since others have described similar responses in the United States and England. Warbasse, "Changing Legal Rights," 237; Basch, *In the Eyes of the Law*, 206–207; K.E. Thurman, "The Married Women's Property Acts" (LL.M. diss. University of Wisconsin, 1966); See also A. Sachs and J.H. Wilson, *Sexism and the Law* (1978), 77–78.

114. See Backhouse, "Shifting Patterns."

115. See Backhouse, "Pure Patriarchy."

116. See. C. Backhouse, "Nineteenth-Century Canadian Rape Law, 1800–1892," in *Essays on the History of Canadian Law*, ed. Flaherty, 200.

117. See C. Blackhouse, "The Tort of Seduction: Fathers and Daughters in Nineteenth-Century Canada," *Dalhousie Law Journal* 10 (1986).

118. The United States, it should be noted, also preceded Canada at this stage of legislative reform. Beginning in the late 1840s and early 1850s, American statutes entered what I have categorized as the "third wave." See Chused, "Married Women's Property Law," 1398, 1424; Chused, "Oregon Donation Act," 77–78; Warbasse, "Changing Legal Rights," 245. This situation was no different from that which existed during the first and second waves of reform, however. The key change was the English innovation.

119. 33 & 34 Vict. (1870), c. 93 (Eng.), as amended by 37 & 38 Vict. (1874), c. 50 (Eng.).

120. Rose also testified regarding the married women's property system in Lower Canada, based on French law and the Custom of Paris prior to the Code Napoleon. *Hansard Parliamentary Debates*, 3rd ser., vol 201 (1870), 885; (1877), 235, 75–76; Ulrich, "Reform of Matrimonial Property Law," 22. Australian legislators would similarly make reference to Canadian innovation in their decision to reform married women's property law in the 1870s. See R. Teale, ed., *Colonial Eve: Sources on Women and Australia 1788–1914* (1978), 165; J. Mackinolty, "The Married Women's Property Acts" in *In Pursuit of Justice: Australian Women and the Law 1788–1979*.

121. An Act to Extend the Rights of Property of Married Women, 35 Vict. (1871–72), c. 16 (Ont.). See also R.S.O. 1877, c. 135. Although the language of the two statutes was similar in many respects, the Ontario statute placed slightly more emphasis upon freeing the married women's earnings from her husband's debts, perhaps a vestigial holdover from the earlier protective slant.

122. The western provinces were next to enact egalitarian legislation. British Columbia, in 1873, passed virtually an exact duplicate of the 1872 Ontario statute. An Act to Extend the Rights of Property of Married Women, 36 Vict. (1873), c. 29 (B.C.); see also An Act Respecting the Property of Married Women, 50 Vict. (1887), c. 20 (B.C.). The latter was a virtual duplicate of the 1884 Ontario act, with a few additional provisions. See also R.S.B.C. 1897, c. 130.
  The Northwest Territories partially followed suit in 1880. See An Act to Amend and Consolidate the Several Acts Relating to the North-West Territories, 43 Vict. (1880), c. 25 (D.C.), sec. 57–62. The 1880 act was a virtual duplicate of the 1872 Ontario statute, except that it was missing a few sections relating to life insurance and stockholding.
  Manitoba was the only western province with any innovative

spirit. Its first married women's property statute, passed in 1875 was largely protective in nature, but included several egalitarian provisions that seem not to have been duplicated in exact words in any other Canadian or English jurisdiction. The statute appeared to grant married women significant dispositive power over their real estate, and the right to sue and be sued in their own names, without joining the names of their husbands. The novel sections seemed to conflict in part with the foregoing protective sections of the act and would therefore seem to have been the product of some confusion over how extensively married women's property rules should be reformed. By 1881, however, it appears that the Ontario model had by and large supervened, and various sections of the 1872 statute were imported into Manitoba. A 1900 enactment, with some drafting distinctions, similarly introduced much of the substance of the 1884 Ontario legislation. An Act Respecting Separate Rights of Property of Married Women, 38 Vict. (1875), c. 25 (Manitoba). An Act to Amend Certain of the Acts Forming Part of the Consolidated Statutes of Manitoba, 44 Vict. (1881), c. 11 (Manitoba), sec. 75–81; 48 Vict. (1885), c. 28 (Man.); 49 Vict. (1886), c. 13 (Man.); 53 Vict. (1890), c. 17 (Man.); R.S.M. 1891, vol. 11, c. 95; 63–64 Vict. (1900), c. 27 (Man.).

The maritime jurisdictions, which had been the first to initiate the marriage breakdown wave of legislation, were the last to enact egalitarian provisions. Nova Scotia passed a rather unusual piece of legislation in 1884, which seems to have been borrowed in part from Ontario and in part from England, and which embodied a very restricted set of egalitarian reforms. Some provisions appear to have been truly indigenous, indicating that this was no matter of routine legislative copying, but a deliberate response to matters of purely regional concern. Before a married

woman was authorized to retain her own earnings, her husband had to register his written consent, a proviso not required in any other Canadian or English jurisdiction. Otherwise a traditional court order of protection was necessary to give married women control over their wages. Only after a court order of protection was issued, or a husband's consent was registered, were married women entitled to contract, sue, and dispose of their property on their own authority. In all other cases, husbands also had to be joined in any litigation arising out of their wives' property or torts. Of the Property of Married Women, R.S.N.S. (1880) (5th ser.), c. 94: 60 Vict. (1897), c. 37 (N.S.); 61 Vict. (1898), c. 22 (N.S.) Eleven years later New Brunswick fell in line with the other Canadian provinces and passed an act very similar to the 1884 Ontario precedent. An Act Respecting the Property of Married Women, 58 Vict. (1895), c. 24 (N.B.).

Prince Edward Island was the last jurisdiction to enact egalitarian legislation in 1896. An Act Relating to the Separate Property and the Rights of Property of Married Women, 59 Vict. (1896), c. 5 (P.E.I.) The act was apparently sparked by a petition in 1895 from a group of women demanding reform. This is particularly interesting, since Prince Edward Island had little in the way of organized suffrage forces. In fact, Cleverdon has described a "general indifference to the question of women's political rights" in Prince Edward Island. Cleverdon, *Woman Suffrage Movement*, 198, 201. In one important aspect, Prince Edward Island continued to lag behind the rest of the country. The statute specifically denied married women the right to their own earnings unless a traditional court order of protection was granted (sec. 4). The fact that virtually every other feature of the Ontario legislation was adopted, save for the matter of wages, indicates exceptional anxiety over the prospect of wage-earning wives.

123. For an incisive and thought-provoking account of this development, see G.B. Baker, "Reconstruction of Upper Canada Legal Thought," 219.

124. I am indebted to Suzanne Lebsock, who first coined this phrase in *Free Women of Petersburg*, 85.

125. For good discussions of this economic rationale in the American context, see ibid., 85; Basch, *In the Eyes of the Law*, 39, 126, 226; E. Van Tassel, "Women, Property and Politics in Nineteenth-Century Law," Reviews in *American History* 2 (1983): 378.

126. Merrick v. Sherwood (1872), 22 U.C.C.P. 467. See also Brooks v. Brooks (1896), 2 T.L.R. 289, where the court held that Ord. No. 20 of 1890 (N.W.T.) had given married women the *jus disponendi*, although the judge seemed uncertain whether this was a wise legislative decision, at 293, per Lt. Col. Hugh Richardson.

127. McGuire v. McGuire (1873), 23 U.C.C.P. 123 at 125–26.

128. Ibid., 126 and 129.

129. Ibid., 130, 132, 135, 136.

130. Darling v. Rice (1876), 1 O.A.R. 43 at 52. See also Holmested, *Married Women's Property Act*, 20.

131. Brown v. Winning (1878), 43 U.C.Q.B. 327 at 331; per Robert Alexander Harrison, C.J.

132. Wagner v. Jefferson (1876), 37 U.C.Q.B. 55 at 557–58. This statement was made in obiter.

133. Berry v. Zeiss (1882), 32 U.C.C.P. 231 at 241.

134. Ibid., 238–39.

135. Eight years later, Chief Justice Armour distinguished himself by articulating a strong belief that husbands and wives should have equal rights in marriage in Quick v. Church (1893), 23 O.R. 262 (Q.B.). In this decision, he held that a married woman should have the right to bring an action for criminal conversation just as her husband had tra-

ditionally had. This was a very bold decision, for which there was no English or Canadian precedent, and it was soon reversed in Lellis v. Lambert (1897), 24 O.A.R. 653.

136. Clarke v. Creighton (1881), 45 U.C.Q.B. 514 at 524, Armour, J., in dissent.

137. Griffin v. Patterson (1881), 45 U.C.Q.B. 536 at 555.

138. Wishart v. McManus (1884), 1 M.L.R. 213 (Q.B.) at 224 and 228.

139. While the legislation did not deal specifically with a married woman's right to enjoy her own property upon separation, it did reverse McGuire to the extent that that case had determined that a married woman did not have a *jus disponendi* over her personal property. See Holmested, *Married Women's Property Act*, 19, for his analysis of this point.

140. 47 Vict. (1884), c. 19 (Ont.), sec. 2, 11.

141. Moore v. Jackson (1892), 22 S.C.R. 210 at 223.

142. Palliser v. Gurney, 19 Q.B.C. 519; Stogdon v. Lee, [1891] 1 Q.B. 661. The requirement stipulated that this separate property had to exist at the time the married woman made the contract.

143. Holmested, *Married Women's Property Act*, 28.

144. 60 Vict. (1897), c. 22, sec. 1; Holmested, *Married Women's Property Act*, 28–29.

145. Interestingly, at common law, a husband was required to consent to his wife's working outside the home for wages. Since the new legislation said nothing about this, at least one legal commentator concluded that a husband's consent was still necessary in order for a married woman to earn in the employ of another. Clara Brett Martin wrote in 1990: "For example, should she go out as a domestic, he could serve her employer with notice to discontinue her services, and should her employer

refuse, the husband would be entitled to an action for harbouring. The reason given is that a wife might put an end to the matrimonial relationship without his consent, and for no fault of his, a power which it is said could not have been the intention of the Legislature to confer upon her." C.B. Martin, "Legal Status of Women," 98.

146. See, e.g., 22 Vict. (1859), c. 34 (P.C.), sec. 6.

147. 35 Vict. (1871–72), c. 16 (Ont.), sec. 2.

148. See 36 Vict. (1873), c. 29 (B.C), sec. 2; The North-West Territories Act, 1875, c. 49, saec. 49; 44 Vict. (1881), c. 11 (Man.), sec. 75; 58 Vict. (1859), c. 24 (N.B.), sec. 5.

149. 47 Vict. (1884), C. 12 (N.S.), sec. 37–52, 57–60.

150. 59 Vict. (1896), c. 5 (P.E.I.), sec. 4 provided that such orders could be granted in the following circumstances: (1) where a married woman had a decree for alimony; (2) where she lived apart from her husband having been obliged to leave him for cruelty or other cause that by law rendered him liable for her support; (3) where the husband was a lunatic or undergoing sentence of imprisonment; (4) where the husband from his habitual drunkenness, profligacy, or other cause neglected or refused to support his wife and family; (5) where the husband had never been in the province during coverture; (6) where the husband had deserted or abandoned his wife; (7) where the husband resided outside of the province.

151. McCandy v. Tuer (1874), 24 U.C.C.P. 101.

152. Ibid., at 104.

153. Doidge v. Mimms (1900), 13 M.L.R. 48 (Ct. of K.B.).

154. Ibid 57–58. The case was sent back for a new trial on the question of whether the defendent had undertaken to pay for such services.

155. See also Young v. Ward (1896), 27 O.A.R. 423 at 127, where Chancellor J.A. Boyd commented that "the act of taking in one lodger into the family home can hardly be classed under the heading of 'employment, trade, or occupation.' "

156. Basch has found a similar response on the part of New York judges: see Basch, *In the Eyes of the Law*, 216. See also Rabkin, *Fathers to Daughters*, 140.

157. 35 Vict. (1871–72), c. 16 (Ont.), sec. 2.

158. 36 Vict. (1876), c. 29 (B.C.), sec. 2; The North-West Territories Act, 1875, c. 49, sec. 49; 44 Vict. (1881), c. 11 (Man.), sec. 74; 58 Vict. (1895), c. 24 (N.B.), sec. 5; 47 Vict. (1884), c. 12 (N.S.) sec. 52–60.

159. Harrison v. Douglass (1877), 40 U.C.Q.B. 410.

160. Ibid., at 415. But see Plows v. Maughan (1877), 42 U.C.Q.B. 129, in which Chief Justice Harrison ruled differently where the couple did not actually live on the wife's farm.

161. Murray v. McCallum (1883), 8 O.A.R. 277.

162. Ibid., at 291–92. The trial judgment had concluded that the assets were exempt from the husband's creditors, and since the appeal court was evenly split in its decision, the trial judgment was allowed to stand. Chief Justice Spragge and Justice Cameron ruled in favour of Elizabeth Murray, while Justice Berton and Justice Patterson ruled against. Manitoba judges were no more prepared to recognize the autonomy of married women's business ventures than their Ontario brothers were. Chief Justice Taylor, who had taken an unusually broad interpretation with respect to the *jus disponendi* issue, was unequivocal about using a narrow construction when it came to the matter of

women's business affairs. "There is to be no departure from the rules of the common law further than is warranted by the statute," he concluded and subjected a married woman's business assets to seizure by her husband's creditors. In this case the married woman had gone into business as a partner with her husband's brother. Capital had been contributed by each in equal shares; the husband had contributed nothing. But since the husband managed the business and drew a weekly salary from it, Chief Justice Taylor concluded that the business was not carried on separately from the husband. Merchants Bank v. Carley (1892), 8 M.L.R. 258 at 261.

163. Streimer v. Merchants Bank (1894), 9 M.L.R. 546.

164. Ibid., 548, 550, and Slingerland v. Massey Manufacturing (1894), 10 M.L.R. 21.

165. 50 Vict. (1887), c. 7 (Ontario), sec. 22.

166. Cooney v. Sheppard (1895), 23 O.A.R. 4 at 6.

167. Rodenhiser v. Cragg (1894), 27 N.LS.R. 273. This case did not actually involve a husband–wife dispute. Ida Adams had been convicted of a violation of the Liquor Licence Act, and in order to escape the warrant of seizure, she attempted to sell the business to her sister. Officials still seized her household furniture, beer, candies, tobacco, pipes, etc. Adams's sister sued the officials, and lost when the court determined that since the property really belonged to James Adams, his wife had no right to sell it.

THE JUNE BRIDE AS THE WORKING-CLASS BRIDE: GETTING MARRIED IN A HALIFAX WORKING-CLASS NEIGHBOURHOOD IN THE 1920s◇

SUZANNE MORTON

○

On Wednesday 16 June 1926, Sadie McGrath married Thomas Corney at 6:30 AM at St. Joseph's Roman Catholic Church in Halifax, Nova Scotia. McGrath, who until her marriage was employed as a telephone operator, wore a white wedding gown and veil as her father accompanied her down the aisle to organ music. The newspaper account, published that evening in one of the city's papers, focussed on the bride. The presence of the groom, an employee of the Canadian National Railway, was only noted.[1] After a ceremony attended by many friends, Sadie and Thomas may have gone to a commercial studio for photos, then returned to the bride's parents' home for a wedding breakfast shared with immediate relatives.

The marriage of a telephone operator and a railway employee was important in their own personal history but is also important to the historian because the public nature of the event offers insight into an aspect of the working-class experience outside the workplace. Working-class Canadians faced many changes in the 1920s, both at work and beyond, as the growth of mass culture and consumption shifted priorities and muted class boundaries. Yet, continuities remained. A distinct working-class culture did not disap-

◇ This paper has not been previously published. The revision to an earlier form of this paper, presented to the Canadian Historical Association in Quebec City, 1989, was supported by a post-doctoral fellowship from the Social Sciences and Humanities Research Council of Canada. I am grateful to Bettina Bradbury and to Janet Guildford and her students at Saint Mary's and Dalhousie Universities for their comments.

pear. Examination of the rituals surrounding weddings allows us to see the mingling of tradition and continuity in the lives of young working-class women and men.

This paper looks at the ways in which the respectable working class of one Halifax neighbourhood married in the 1920s, examining how changes in the workplace and in the importance of consumption in the private sphere influenced this important ritual. It seeks first to determine whether there were changes in the role of romance and views about marriage. Secondly it examines the culture and practices that were developed surrounding weddings in women's workplaces. The final section explores the rituals of the marriage ceremony within the working-class community. Like the newspaper descriptions of weddings, this paper focusses on the bride. It also follows popular custom by discussing only young couples, who represented the vast majority of those who wed.

The study of weddings in the 1920s is of significance for at least three reasons. Firstly, according to the 1921 census, more Canadians were married than at any previous time. In 1920, over 91 percent of men and just under 90 percent of women over the age of sixty-five were currently or had been married.[2] In contrast with the nineteenth century, when celibacy, especially among women, had been fairly high, getting married had become a nearly universal experience for Canadians. Secondly, the 1920s was a decade in which the institution of marriage came under much public scrutiny and discussion. Issues such as marital law, divorce, companionate marriage, and the overall purpose of marriage were very much in the public sphere.[3] Finally, weddings were one of the few public events where women played the leading role. Women, so often invisible to the historian in other spheres, were at the centre of public attention as brides.

At the core of this study are the 486 weddings performed between 1919 and 1929 in the three churches located near the Halifax working-class neighbourhood of Richmond Heights. Parish records were available for St. Mark's Anglican and United Memorial churches. Information on the 149 marriages performed at St. Joseph's Roman Catholic Church was gathered from newspaper accounts.[4] Undoubtedly, this study misses many of the weddings performed at St. Joseph's, but the available sample is sufficiently large to incorporate most trends. Newspaper descriptions and announcements of the weddings of Richmond Heights residents who married at other churches outside the neighbourhood are also incorporated for additional insights.

The neighbourhood where most of the brides and grooms resided was by no means ordinary. Located at the north end of the Halifax peninsula, the area around Richmond Heights was devastated in the 1917 Explosion. Most of the inhabitants in the 1920s were living in new homes rented from the post-explosion relief agency. The area served by the three parishes could generally be described as respectable working class. It was largely populated by the families of men whose craft skills had once secured them a privileged position in the community. Low immigration levels meant that this Anglo-Celtic community was remarkably homogeneous and almost exclusively Nova Scotian-born. Men in the community were primarily employed in transportation or construction. As the decade advanced, they were increasingly likely to be found in either the service sector—serving the military or the municipality—or in trade, working in warehouse and distribution positions.

Married women with husbands who were capable of finding employment rarely worked outside the home. Their single daughters, sisters, and nieces sought some form of wage labour upon leaving school. With the economic recession of the early 1920s, manufacturing positions for women, like employment at Moir's confectionary, declined. By the latter part of the decade, half of the employed neighbourhood women worked in lower white-collar occupations as sales clerks, telephone operators, and stenographers.[5] This economic and occupational transformation affected the way people lived and perceived the world at the most basic of levels, including how they felt about and went about getting married.

ROMANCE AND MARRIAGE

The idea of romance itself is historically constructed, reflecting the values and beliefs of individuals in specific times and places. Karen Lystra's recent work suggests that for middle-class heterosexuals in nineteenth-century America, privacy, individualism, and a search for meaning increasingly characterized romance.[6] Peter Ward, examining the same period in Canada, and working largely with middle-class records, has suggested that a love match was the goal of people of all backgrounds, and that "the rituals of Canadian romance had little to do with class."[7] Ward appears to sever any connection between rite and material reality. Neither romance nor marriage meant exactly the same thing to a middle-class Victorian as it did to a Halifax telephone operator in the 1920s. Nor did they necessarily mean the same thing to younger and older Haligonians. In the female, working-class Halifax version of romance in the 1920s, opportunities for consumption and escape appear to have been major components. The connection between romance and consumption was a product of the times and of these youths' lives. In a study of marriage and divorce in California, Elaine Tyler May concluded that "The cultivation of romance was not cheap; it required the free time and abundance that only a mature industrial system could provide."[8] Increased free time, some discretionary income among young people, and the commercialization of leisure meant that working-class romance in Halifax became associated with spending money. This started with movies and candy and culminated in the costs of a wedding.[9]

After the First World War, public discussion regarding the purpose of marriage increased. Heightened expectations of the private sphere were corollaries of a new home-centredness among working-class men. Marriage and the relationship with a spouse were expected to provide greater personal satisfaction. The new perceptions were apparent to Robert and Helen Lynd, in their 1920–25 study of Muncie, Indiana. There they found that most people believed "romantic love" was the only legitimate basis for marriage.[10] Yet, there was not a unanimous consolidated ideology surrounding marriage that young Richmond Heights couples could adopt. Traditional images of marriage as a holy hierarchy ordained by God competed with the newer concept of romantic love, which suggested a diminished desire to defer gratification to a heavenly afterlife. Like consumption, romantic love focussed on immediate individualistic self-gratification and personal fulfillment.

While this modern vision of marriage gained strength, traditional views also persisted. Rev. George Ambrose, the rector at St. Mark's Anglican Church, articulated the older view in the debate surrounding the use of *obey* in the Anglican service.

> The Anglican Church has ever stood for things tried and proved, and the patriarchal government of the home is one of these things. Instances of unworthy men to whom this government has been given do not alter the fact that the ideal home, with a wise and loving father, a loving and obedient wife, and dutiful and respectful children, is the picture and the type of all good government. Let the word "obey" be omitted and the word "honor" naturally follows it into oblivion; whilst "love" in its true sense cannot exist in a family without a head, without respect and without obedience. It is for men to recognize their responsibilities in the "Holy State of Matrimony"; to realize the very high position in regard to their families, in which God has placed them, and to make themselves worthy of honor and obedience.[11]

Ambrose's vision of marriage was most likely to prevail among older couples who continued to uphold a relationship based on obedience and service. Sixty-one-year-old Jane Anderson, for example, was praised in her obituary for her faithful attendance to her dying husband.[12] Certainly, there had always been households in which genuine affection bound husband and wife. In two of the rare wills left by neighbourhood residents, this sentiment was conscious as wives were referred to as "beloved."[13] Nonetheless, the purpose of marriage had partially shifted from the procreation and raising of children to personal fulfillment and the promotion of happiness for the spouses.[14] At the same time, working-class marriage continued to a large extent as a financial partnership. Wives were necessary to transform and extend a husband's wages into a form that could sustain the family.[15] This skill might include budgeting or a more complex reproduction of labour in terms of cooking, housekeeping, shopping, child care, health care, and community social service. This mutual economic dependence, still present in working-class marriages, did not conform to either Ambrose's image of a family patriarchy or the modern goal of "romantic love." In Halifax, the romantic ideal and the economic function of marriage co-existed uneasily.

Although the romantic and the economic were not easily reconciled, the idea of companionate marriage clearly did make inroads into Richmond Heights. While it is impossible to measure the extent of these inroads, changes in leisure activities confirm the presence of the new ideals surrounding companionate marriage. In her study of American fraternalism, Mary Ann Clawson has noted that social relations between men and women shifted in the early twentieth century with the expansion of commercial activities—dance halls, amusement parks, and movies—that encouraged mixed-sex participation. Companionate marriage also encouraged a more sexually integrated social life and the rise of married-couple leisure.[16] In Richmond Heights during the 1920s, though men continued to participate in exclusively male social activities, there does appear to have been a growing emphasis on couples sharing leisure after courtship and marriage. Indeed, an important aspect of the new home-centredness among the working class was the increased likelihood that men and women would engage in leisure activities together.

The public discussion of marriage and the appeal of romance across class lines was reflected in the prominence of weddings in the media. The ceremonies of glamorous Hollywood stars like Mary Pickford and Douglas Fairbanks attracted much attention in the popular press. Haligonians were keenly interested in these events, particularly when some local connection could be boasted, as in Nova Scotian-born dancer Ruby Keeler's marriage to singer Al Jolson. The colonial legacy of the city was clear in the fascination for royal romances and weddings. Haligonians participated vicariously in the endless matchmaking for the Prince of Wales. They celebrated the wedding of his sister Princess Mary to Viscount Lascelles in 1922, then of his brother, the Duke of York, to Lady Elizabeth Bowes-Lyon the following year.

The romantic mood of the decade had been launched with the royal wedding of "Princess Pat" in 1919. Princess Patricia of Connaught offered Canadians a special connection to royalty. She was the granddaughter of Queen Victoria, daughter of a former Governor General and honorary colonel of the famous Princess Patricia Canadian Light Infantry. The romance surrounding this "love match" between a Princess bride and a commoner captured the imagination of Haligonians who felt a special sense of participation in the romance because of the Canadian connection.[17] Part of the light-hearted celebration that surrounded this wedding in 1919 was no doubt linked to the sheer joy people felt as peace replaced war. Indeed, the escapism and the quest for, and preoccupation with, personal fulfillment might be explained as a reaction to the sacrifices and horrors of war. Certainly Haligonians were not alone in absorbing these new values. They were but part of a continent-wide movement toward new ideas.

One of the most obvious ways in which people consumed romance was at the movies. While many movies were preoccupied with romantic themes, their portrayal of weddings is of particular interest here. The Moncton *Daily Times* in July 1922 advertised Marion Davis starring in *The Bride's Play*, "a fascinating picture about Brides and Weddings" with "some of the most gorgeous scenes you have ever seen in any pictures."[18] The 1930 Joan Crawford picture *Our Blushing Brides* evoked similar fantasies.[19] Novels and short stories reinforced and promoted the romantic ideal and fantasy presented in the movies. The editor of *Maclean's* advised a group of Canadian authors that his magazine desired "short stories of romance and adventure and love stories in a lighter vein."[20] Magazines provided romantic stories because of reader preference. In 1927 a Glace Bay widow, Charlotte Pouson, wrote to Annie Buller, business agent for *The Worker*, declining Buller's offer to provide communist reading material for her sixteen-year-old daughter as the girl was "working hard in a store and I am sorry to say her mind is on love stories at the present."[21] The growth of mass circulation magazines in which many of these love stories appeared reflected the growth in advertising dollars. It was no coincidence that the romantic ideal presented in movies and magazines coincided with increased consumption. The mention of brides seemed to attract money.

For those involved, marriage meant a transition from romantic consumption to household consumption, with the wedding itself the major point of consumption between the two, different because it was financed, at least in part, by the family. The money spent on the actual wedding, including dresses, flowers, photos, and gifts, did not compare with the tremendous expenditure involved in establishing a new home. Local advertisers recognized the importance of spending on both the wedding and the new household with an annual wedding supplement produced by the *Evening Mail*. The supplement included gift ideas, etiquette, and fashion as well as hints for setting up housekeeping. One local flower shop dependent on the wedding trade used a hard-sell approach that suggested there was only one type of legitimate wedding. The newspaper copy read, "No wedding is complete without flowers. You know this, so it is only a question of the right kind of flowers."[22] The bride herself was also courted in her new role as a potentially powerful consumer. National brand-name products aimed advertisements explicitly at her potential anxieties and needs as a newly-wed. Robin Hood flour, for example, warned that "many a marriage ship has gone on the rocks because of soggy doughnuts."[23] The importance of the bride as a consumer would increase with the expansion of advertising. By 1934, the cult of the bride had reached such proportions in North America that it could attract the advertising dollars to support *Bride*, a marketing magazine for prospective customers/brides.[24]

While American magazines like *Bride* might appeal to the wealthy, advertisements in local newspapers focussed on the local, working-class clientele. Working-class daughters who held clerical positions before marriage were particularly attractive customers. Advertisers believed that their office experience had exposed them to modern technology and had heightened customer expectations. In 1925, the local power company placed a revealing advertisement in the weekly Halifax labour newspaper addressed "To the Business-Girl Bride," which compared typewriters, filing cabinets, and stamping machines in the office to gas appliances in the kitchen. The announcement noted that "office work hasn't been drudgery to them and neither should housework prove tedious." The purchase of a gas range, the ad promised, could be made "without the immediate sacrifice of pretty things you want for other parts of the house."[25]

ROMANCE AND WOMEN'S WORKPLACE CULTURE

This explicit link between the office and the bride reflected the new realities of work in this period. It also would have made sense for young female working-class readers. For the single young woman of the 1920s, the most important place for the consumption of romance was the workplace.[26] Increasingly over the first decades of the twentieth century, that workplace was not in the manufacturing sector, or in the service sector but in retail and clerical occupations[27] (see table 1). The decline of both domestic service and female employment in manufacturing transformed the work experience of many women. Instead of working alone under the supervision of their mistresses, or in noisy, dirty factories, girls clustered together in quieter, cleaner offices and shops. As waged employees, such women enjoyed an independence unattainable by those in service. Furthermore, as they received all of their earnings in income rather than in a combination of cash and subsistence, they represented a much more powerful pool of consumers.

TABLE 1   FEMALE EMPLOYMENT IN HALIFAX BY ECONOMIC SECTOR

	1911 (%)	1921 (%)	1931 (%)
Manufacturing	23.00	13.03	3.92
Transportation	1.67	5.72	2.85
Trade	16.54	19.38	12.93
Professional	11.23	14.96	13.99
Service	17.58	12.16	11.51
Domestic service	28.93	21.91	22.54
Clerical⬦		12.65	27.79
Other	1.05	.19	4.47

⬦ There is no category for clerical work before 1931. The number given for 1921 represents some women involved in transportation, construction, and finance.

Source: Government of Canada, *Census*, 1911, 6: 326–35; 1921, 4: 382–99; 1931, 2: 31; 5: 572–75, 688–89; 7: 267–77.

Women under the age of twenty-five, in particular, were less and less likely to work in domestic service. These young women embraced the new opportunities in office and sales work. Work in stores, offices, restaurants, and factories made such women much more visible on public streets than were domestic servants whose places of work were generally dispersed throughout more quiet and affluent residential neighbourhoods. The public nature and growing geographical concentration of women's work in the 1920s probably created an exaggerated impression of the number of employed women, feeding the image of the "new working woman."

These new kinds of workplaces also permitted the development of a collective workplace culture, for their communal nature inadvertently promoted a sociability that would have been impossible in isolated private homes.[28] The elevated status associated with office and sales work allowed young single women of slightly different backgrounds to mix at the workplace. Unlike the private home or the factory, the office and the shop brought the daughters of the lower-middle and working classes together and facilitated some exchange of behaviours and attitudes. This mixing of classes in the office, with little differentiation in responsibilities, treatment, or appearance, offered some young women an experience unique from that of other family members. The narrow range of employment opportunities available for women tended to de-emphasize barriers between middle- and working-class women, while accentuating the "femaleness" of specific occupations. In these occupations, the common experience of being female and young fostered a workplace culture in which romance held a central place. Young women shared an interest in discussing boyfriends, clothes, evening entertainment, and the romances of their fellow workers. The fixation with boyfriends was partly rooted in the economic reality that, for these wage-earning women, men were necessary to provide financial access to popular entertainment.[29]

In this situation, marriage not only represented the culmination of romance, but it also brought adult status and freedom from parental control. The focus on marriage in this work-based culture of romance encouraged getting married at a relatively early age. At St. Mark's, the only church for which age data is available, the average ages of the couples in the twenty-four marriages in 1921 was 25.6 for men and 25.3 for women. Although the sample is small, these working-class men appear to have married younger than the national average of twenty-eight years. Local women, in contrast, who well may have delayed marriage slightly in order to continue working and accumulate some savings, were slightly older than the 24.3 average for Canadian women.[30] While the national difference in age between men and women was not reflected at the local level, women generally married younger than men, a reflection of their romantic expectations of marriage and the financial responsibility that men assumed following their wedding. Respectable working-class men did not marry until they were in a position to support a family.[31]

Specific work-related marriage customs developed in those jobs where young women were concentrated, including textile and knitting mills and office work.[32] Showers acted as a peer recognition of the event and had a particular importance in the female workplace as marriage usually meant departure from work. Some showers were held in the office, the bride's desk "artistically decorated" with pink and white wedding bells, streamers, flowers, and kewpie dolls.[33] Occasionally these decorated desks provided an opportunity to link work experience directly to the wedding. One future bride spent her last day at work sitting under "three mischievous Kewpies each representing one year of Miss Gates' term of service with the company."[34] Company welfare organizers at Moir's incorporated showers into their social program for female office and production employees. Moir's employees held a dance and buffet-lunch shower for twenty-five couples for a three-year employee, Margaret Jackson. This shower was not typical as it included men, and was large enough to have live music provided by the Moir's company orchestra.[35] Only the bride was given gifts, even though the groom was present. Surprise kitchen, grocery, or linen showers on week-nights were the norm. The in-house Maritime Telephone and Telegraph *Monthly Bulletin* captured the atmosphere of one company kitchen shower as it described a decorated room and co-workers waiting for the arrival of the guest of honour. "Jolly little kewpies, glowing rosily in their conventional attire under the pink-shaded candles peered roguishly through festoons of pink hearts and clusters of pink blossoms at the mass of femininity below them engaged in an almost futile struggle to keep hushed." Once the future bride entered, she was presented with a "big clothes basket filled with all conceivable kitchen articles."[36] Showers provided an additional opportunity to consume, and they assisted the engaged couple with the expenses involved in establishing a new home. They also allowed fellow workers to participate directly in the wedding ritual in an environment removed from the bride's family.

The intrusion of workplace culture into wedding celebrations was not the only link between work and weddings. While reports on weddings in the newspapers often did not describe the attire of the bride, they rarely failed to mention where the bride and groom had been employed. Custom and eti-quette also seemed to dictate that the gift communally offered to the bride or groom from co-workers be specified in the announcement. For example, Sadie McGrath received an electric lamp from the staff at Maritime Telephone and Telegraph.[37] Wedding gifts from fellow employees were often very gen-erous. Men at the Canadian National Railway repair shops, who were pre-dominantly skilled workers, received large items of furnishing such as a mahogany parlour suite or a sofa-bed.[38] Unskilled workmates offered grooms less extravagant household items such as a Morris chair or a clock.[39]

Brides' workmates' generosity was even more astounding given their lower wages, limited spending money, high turnover rates, and relatively short number of years spent working together. Co-workers most often gave the bride a chest of silver flatware or a silver tea service. Both gifts were genteel luxury items, symbols of respectability. Communal gifts made sense economically. They also demonstrated the importance workmates attached to the wedding and perhaps their hopes to soon be on the receiving end. Brides who were moving from Halifax after the wedding were likely to receive a cheque, sometimes in a travel bag, to assist with expenses in set-ting up a new household in a new city.[40] New consumer durables such as electric lamps and irons were also presented occasionally.[41]

The workplace not only provided a source of wedding gifts but could also play a role in the introduction of couples. Work offered many women the opportunity to meet prospective husbands. In her study of working-class youths in Hamilton, Ontario, Jane Synge concluded that "social life and marriage chances would be seriously impaired should she have to stay home and care for an ailing mother or younger siblings."[42] Maritime Telephone and Telegraph in the June 1923 *Monthly Bulletin* referred to one of their departments as "the University of Intending Brides." A year later, when two employees were getting married, the editor commented that:

> It is pleasant to reflect that Miss Graves' intimacy with payrolls has given her an experience that will be invaluable to her as a house-keeper. It will be difficult for Gordon Frost, should he ever be inclined that way, to "pad his vouchers" when accounting for the contents of his fortnightly pay envelope.[43]

While suggesting that husbands sometimes hid some of their wages from their wives, this observation also reinforced the notion that pre-marriage work experience better prepared a woman for her real life-long career as a housewife and mother. Since marriage changed most women's economic role and removed them from the paid public labour force, it made sense that the workplace would play such a large role in the wedding. The importance of the wedding for women was in part a result of the identity change she experienced as she become someone's wife.

CEREMONIES AND RITUALS

Weddings continue to be one of the most important and symbolic of the multitude of rituals of modern urban industrial society. John Gillis argues in his study of British marriages between 1600 and the present, that a "new ceremonialism" emerged surrounding British working-class weddings in the twentieth century. He suggests that "when people lose control over vital aspects of their lives, they seek ways to compensate symbolically, thereby gaining a measure of subjective satisfaction by interpreting and expressing events in their own idiom."[44] Gillis links the importance of an elaborate ceremony with the wishes of women, but fails to tie their emphasis on ritual to the fact that, as a group, they were experiencing great changes during this period. In Halifax in the 1920s, changes in women's workplace culture appear to have influenced not only the period leading up to the wedding, but the wedding rituals themselves.

The wedding ceremony, which transformed most women's economic role, was a mixture of the sacred and the secular for all classes. Civil ceremonies were not permitted in Nova Scotia until 1962, so the wedding acted as one of the many intersections of church and state. In the early twentieth century, Canadian couples also had to comply with increased state intervention restricting who could wed by means of licensing, registration, and the establishment of an age of consent.[45] The rituals and practices surrounding the actual wedding ceremony also reflected an amalgamation of economic circumstances with culture and with the tradition within the established religious and civil-legal framework. The way people chose to celebrate their marriage revealed something of their present economic circumstances, inherited traditions and customs, and future aspirations.

The number of weddings in a given year coincided with economic conditions. In 1920, sixty-eight weddings were performed at the three working-class churches, while during the years 1924–27, the number of weddings never exceeded thirty-seven annually. In 1929, the number had risen again, and at least fifty-two weddings were held. Although the 1920 high probably included some delayed weddings of World War I veterans, the average and mean ages of brides and grooms at St. Mark's tended to be low, suggesting that few grooms were returned men. Of much more significance in accounting for the unusually large number of weddings in 1920 was the relative prosperity, which contrasted with the rest of the decade. An economic depression began in the summer/fall of 1920 and arguably continued until the Second World War, with a temporary improvement around 1929. The depression of the 1920s affected the young adults of Halifax, who left the city in great numbers searching for employment in Boston, Detroit, or Central Canada. Some of these young men and women returned to marry, but announcements of weddings occurring in Boston were also common in Halifax papers.[46]

Outmigration influenced the way in which people married and probably the meaning of the wedding ceremony itself. While there were many examples of newlywed couples living with one set of parents or setting up housekeeping on the same street as kin, it was also common for the wedding to mark the permanent departure of the couple from Halifax. John Gillis has argued that British working-class weddings did not emphasize the separation of the bride from her family but rather reinforced the continued relationship and importance of family.[47] Certainly the importance of family was evident in Halifax weddings. Fathers gave away their daughters and, in the father's absence the bride's mother accompanied the bride down the aisle and gave her away.[48] However, for the many Halifax couples who left the city immediately after the ceremony, separation from family must have been associated with marriage.

While the decisions whether to wed and where to live after the wedding were influenced by practical phenomena such as outmigration and economic fluctuations, older myths and traditions permeated the choice of the month, the day of the week, and the time of the day to wed. In all three parishes, June was the most popular month in which to be married. The next most popular months were September and October. These selections can be explained in part by tradition, but also by the practical limitations of Halifax weather. For some unknown reason, members of St. Joseph's were less likely to marry in October than were Protestants in the same neighbourhood. Custom and church law combined to make March the least popular month of marriage. Roman Catholic cannon law forbade the blessing of marriage in Lent and Advent except by special dispensation "for some just reason."[49] A traditional prohibition against marriages in Lent in the Protestant churches continued long after any prohibitive church law was abolished. The adage "Marry in Lent and you'll live to repent" continued to have some meaning in people's lives.[50] In contrast, there appears to have been little reluctance among adherents at St. Mark's and United Memorial to marry in December during Advent. The traditional aversion to marrying in May continued: folk sayings such as "Marry in May, And rue the day" and "From marriages in May, All bairns die and decay" continued to influence betrothed couples to wait until June.[51]

The days that couples in this working-class neighbourhood chose to marry conform to the residual folk traditions in the following rhyme.

Monday for health, Tuesday for wealth,
Wednesday the best day of all
Thursday for crosses, Friday for losses,
Saturday no day at all.[52]

Of the 253 weddings for which the day of the week is known, fully one-third occurred on a Wednesday. The next most popular days of the week were Tuesday and Monday; indeed almost one-third of Catholic couples chose Tuesday as their wedding day. Only ten and thirteen weddings were held on Friday and Saturday respectively. Not surprisingly, no weddings were recorded on Sunday. Oral traditions and superstitions surrounding when weddings should take place clearly continued well into the twentieth century in spite of the inroads mass culture was making into other wedding day rituals.

The time of day when the wedding occurred was closely tied to religious practices. For Roman Catholic weddings, the nuptial mass had to be held before noon and without breaking the fast. This meant that weddings at St. Joseph's regularly occurred as early as 6:00 AM.[53] Despite the early hour, these weddings could be complete with organ, choir, a decorated church, and a large public attendance.[54] Marriages were sometimes held early in the morning at United Memorial and at St. Mark's, although this was usually so the couple could depart on the morning train. In the Protestant churches, particularly Anglican St. Mark's, large public weddings were occasionally held in the middle of the afternoon during the work week. This suggests that some employers were still flexible enough to excuse their employees temporarily in order to attend community weddings. Afternoon weddings were, however, more common outside working-class neighbourhoods, and the proclamations of newspaper etiquette columns concerning the fashionable nature of the "high noon" wedding had little impact on the marrying habits of working-class Halifax.[55] Most big public Protestant working-class weddings were held in the evening so that like the early morning Catholic weddings they did not interfere with the work day.

For Catholic weddings, the location of the ceremony was also determined by religious custom. All blessed Roman Catholic marriages were performed in the church. Ceremonies at St. Joseph's that were not held in the sanctuary usually indicated a mixed marriage. Such interdenominational weddings within the Catholic Church suggest that many young people may not have confirmed to parental wished in their selection of marriage partners.

The meaning of a church wedding for Protestants was much more ambiguous. The decline of the house wedding for Protestant working-class couples was probably the most important trend occurring in the 1920s. A survey of the Halifax newspapers before the First World War showed that Protestant weddings held in churches were large formal affairs and seldom involved working-class couples.[56] While house weddings did continue in the 1920s, they were more and more likely to be held in a more public forum. The smallest and least formal Protestant working-class Haligonian weddings were held in the manse or rectory. Large working-class weddings, which had once been held in the home, were now moved into the very public forum of the church.

The growth of the public wedding reflected important changes in the community and social structure. Firstly, women's peer groups took on increased importance with changes in the female labour market. Peers and friends probably adopted some of the emotional support roles previously offered by the family. Yet, despite their increased importance, they were not yet integrated into the ceremony as bridesmaids and maids of honour. Secondly, the public wedding held in the church celebrated the end of life in one sphere and the beginning of life in another. For weddings not only marked the normal end of paid employment for women, but also the end of a public life that few women in previous generations had shared. From the beginning of school attendance through to marriage, working-class women lived in the public sphere. Upon marriage, with few exceptions, women ceased public work and concerned themselves with the establishment of the private world of their new home.[57] Finally, church weddings also reinforced the idea of a society where class distinctions were minimal. Working-class men and women could mimic the activities of middle- and upper-class couples. This was a superficial imitation in Halifax. Small informal middle-class weddings continued to be held in private homes, while the working class increasingly chose churches, perhaps for the very practical reason that their homes were smaller than middle-class counterparts and could house fewer guests.

Marrying in the public sphere generated new pressures. One woman who grew up in the neighbourhood stressed the importance of public standards when she described her own wedding in the early 1940s: "I had to get a book on etiquette. . . . If you are going to have a church wedding if it's not proper you're just a laughing stock."[58] The widespread extent of similar concerns in the 1920s is behind the staggering success of etiquette manuals such as Emily Post's, which topped the American nonfiction best sellers list in 1923.[59]

Ironically, romance, which supposedly emphasized the experience of the individual, helped foster a uniformity of acceptable behaviour; propriety and respectably were connected to the illusion of classlessness. Genteel behaviour and attitudes, once associated with only the highest echelons of society, were now apparently accessible by means of a mass culture to be borrowed and discarded at will by anyone wishing to acquire their related status. The illusory nature of this classlessness is clear in studying the wedding photos published on the social page of the *Evening Mail*.[60] In 1929 a photo of a marriage at St. Mark's appeared, suggesting that the local convention that only the wealthier, South End wedding photos were printed had been shattered. It had not. This was the only wedding from the three churches that was published during the 1920s. Working-class engagement announcements very seldom appeared in newspapers, and those that did were never accompanied by a photo of the future bride on the social page which was standard in the case of most middle- and upper-class announcements.

A white wedding was increasingly the classless and seemingly universal ideal, fostered by contemporary bridal etiquette books, which offered little choice but white. According to one book, "even at the simplest home wedding, and when the bride perhaps is passed her first youth, the white gown, the orange blossoms, and the filmy veil are essential outward signs of all the precious sentiment that characterizes this most important event of her life."[61] The white silk gown, veil, and a bouquet of orange blossoms were constructed as the "traditional" bridal costume, offering the comfort of custom and the illusion of class mobility and prestige to brides beginning their new identity.[62] Yet this tradition only extended to a generally privileged group in the previous century.[63] Before the 1920s, most brides wore a new evening gown in whatever colour best suited them so that it could be used later as a best dress.[64] Folk rhymes suggest the variety of possibilities.

> Married in red, you'll wish yourself dead.
> Married in blue, he will always prove true.
> Married in white, you've chosen all right.
> Married in green, not fit to be seen.
> Married in brown, you'll live out of town.
> Married in black, you'll wish yourself back.
> Married in grey, you'll live far away.
> Married in pink, your spirits will sink.[65]

Despite modern etiquette, older customs and economic reality continued to influence the choices women made about the colour of their outfit. Blue wedding gowns were still the most popular choice in this working-class neighbourhood during the 1920s. In the cases where the colour of the bride's dress was mentioned, seventy-one women wore blue, while only fifty wore white. Brown and pink were tied for a distant third, with nineteen brides each wearing shades of these colours. The familiar wedding saying "Something old, something new, something borrowed, something blue" may have influenced the choice of colour. Many, like young working-class Québécoises marrying around the same period who consciously chose a colour that they could wear on other occasions, simply could not afford to spend a lot of money on something that would be worn only once. Reusable gowns or more practical travelling suits were the most popular attire for these brides.[66] Traditions surrounding weddings were clearly in flux as old proscriptions and superstitions regarding colour, day, month, and time mingled with new norms that were promoted by industry. Those who could afford to do so did seem increasingly to have married in white.

The wedding ring was more than a consumer durable; it played a central role in the religious ceremony. Most women over the age of twenty-five probably wore a plain gold band on the third or fourth finger of their left hand as a permanent reminder of their wedding and a public declaration of their status. Apparently the engagement ring was fairly widespread among the Halifax working class by the turn of the century, for it was common for women under the age of thirty-five to accompany the wedding band with a gold-plated diamond solitaire or a ruby with two small diamond chips on either side.[67] The appearance of the engagement ring reflected the relative affluence of the skilled working class, the very effective marketing of diamonds, and the increased importance of the engagement period. In England after the war, engagements grew longer and, according to Gillis, took on some of the characteristics of the pre-industrial betrothal.[68]

The engagement ring was probably more vulnerable to economic recession than the other wedding custom that increased with affluence—the honeymoon.[69] The honeymoon for working-class Haligonians usually meant the chance to visit family living elsewhere. The newly married couple might visit a married sister in Boston or Toronto or family still residing in rural areas of the province.[70] Railway employees were particularly mobile as they were free to travel on pass. While the importance of friends and family in the post-wedding tour is reported to have declined in the latter half of the nineteenth-century among middle-class North Americans, for many working-class Halifax couples visiting family remained a major honeymoon choice. Ellen Rothman has argued that among middle-class Americans, the need to affirm romantic love by sending the newlyweds off alone together superseded any need to reinforce community and family bonds.[71] The emphasis placed on romantic love may not have been as important for working-class couples. For this group of Haligonians who experienced high levels of mobility and migration, the honeymoon offered some the rare opportunity to visit relatives, affirming either their rural origins or their links with family attracted to the greater economic opportunities beyond Nova Scotia. Staying with relatives may also have been the only kind of holiday many of them could afford.[72]

The location of the wedding breakfast was influenced by the presence of family and their economic resources. While etiquette books decreed that this function should never be hosted by the groom's family, the Halifax community was not so arbitrary.[73] The bride's family usually hosted the reception, inviting the couple's immediate family. Small receptions were apparently common probably because homes were small and economic resources limited. Occasionally newspaper accounts stressed the meagre number of guests, probably to prevent offence to friends not included. In the absence of the bride's parents or their inability to act as hosts, receptions were held by almost anyone claiming a relationship or friendship with the couple. Less frequently, the couple themselves hosted the reception in their new home.[74] Only one description of a wedding specifically mentioned a dance being held in connection with the celebration, a custom popular in the city's more affluent neighbourhoods.

CONCLUSION

Unlike the public wedding ceremony, the reception carried the bride into the private world of home and family. Working-class women moved from worker to wife. The wedding was the rite of passage marking the end of public adolescent production and the beginning of private adult consumption. The persistence of older rituals and customs surrounding weddings reflected the risks, vulnerability, and uncertainties involved in marriage. Old traditions were complemented by new rituals that reflected the economic transitions in Halifax in the 1920s, the expansion of mass consumption across North America, and the evolution of a new young female work culture. These rituals changed weddings, creating a commercialized public celebration that increasingly incorporated peers into the place of family.

For female work-based peer groups, the consumption of romance appeared to offer an escape. Movies and mass circulation magazines assisted in the formation of a mass culture that portrayed romance in uniform, consolidated images that young women desired to replicate. These new ideas emphasized the relatively recent link between romance and marriage for the working class and disturbed the traditional economic understanding of marriage. The tightly defined universal etiquette that was fabricated around weddings was juxtaposed with the economic and social realities of family, unemployment, and outmigration. Weddings continued to hold meanings that were specific to the respectable working class. Yet the commercial construction and promotion of romance made these weddings more and more like others all over North America, fostering an appearance of class homogeneity that muted the undertones of class variance. The result was a move toward the ideal universal and classless image of a June bride in white.

Men and women like Sadie McGrath and Thomas Corney freely consumed the ideology of mass culture, adopting some of the superficial forms, customs, and conventions associated with other classes in society. Yet they did not necessarily accept the accompanying bourgeois ideology, nor could they afford the same kinds of celebrations. A growing number of these women went into marriage with the experience of earning their own money and having shared a new workplace culture in offices and shops in which engagements, showers, and weddings were given a prominent place. Despite some shared rituals, working-class weddings in Halifax were not like those of wealthier Haligonians. Romance, ceremony, and customs cannot be disconnected from everyday experience, material reality, and ideological beliefs. The place where they married, the number of people attending the reception, and the type of honeymoon set working-class weddings apart. Beneath the uniformity of the increasingly conventional and apparently classless white wedding gown lay real differences. Old traditions merged with new work-related practices. The words of etiquette manuals and magazines had to be reconciled with economic reality.

NOTES

1. *Evening Mail* (Halifax), 16 June 1926.

2. John Herd Thompson with Allen Seager, *Canada 1922–1939: Decades of Discord* (Toronto, 1985), 5; Canada, *Census*, 1921, 2:115.

3. James G. Snell and Cynthia Comacchio Abeele, "Regulating Nuptiality: Restricting Access to Marriage in Early Twentieth-Century English-speaking Canada," *Canadian Historical Review* 69, 4 (Dec. 1988): 466–89; James G. Snell, "Marital Cruelty: Women and the Nova Scotia Divorce Court, 1900–39," *Acadiensis* 18, 1 (Autumn 1988): 3–32; Emily Murphy, "Compassionate Marriage: From the Point of View of Mother and Child," *Chatelaine* (May 1928), 3. See also J.G. Snell, "Marriage Humour and Its Social Functions, 1900–39," *Atlantis* 11, 2 (Spring 1986): 70–85, and Mary Vipond, "The Image of Women in Mass Circulation Magazines in the 1920s" in *The Neglected Majority: Essays in Canadian Women's History*, ed. Susan Mann Trofimenkoff and Alison Prentice (Toronto, 1977), 116–24.

4. United Memorial was formed after the Explosion in 1917 when the Methodist and Presbyterian congregations joined together to create a union church, which entered the United Church in Canada upon its formation in 1925. The sample of available weddings is from the *Evening Mail* (Halifax), 1 Jan. 1919 to 31 Dec. 1929 and Public Archives of Nova Scotia (PANS), Micro: Churches: Halifax: St. Mark's Anglican, Marriages, and PANS Micro: Churches: Halifax: United Memorial United Church, Marriages. The records of the Catholic Diocese of Halifax are not open to the public for this period.

5. For details on Richmond Heights during this period see Suzanne Morton, "Men and Women in a Halifax Working-Class Neighbourhood during the 1920s" (Ph.D. diss., Dalhousie University, 1990).

6. Karen Lystra, *Searching the Heart: Women, Men, and Romantic Love in Nineteenth-Century America* (Oxford, 1989).

7. Peter Ward, *Courtship, Love, and Marriage in Nineteenth-Century English Canada* (Montreal, 1990), 174.

8. Elaine Tyler May, *Great Expectations: Marriage and Divorce in Post-Victorian America* (Chicago, 1980), 62.

9. Anglican Rev. L.J. Donaldson criticized the amount of money spent on movies and candy as diverting savings from furnishing new homes. *Evening Mail*, 3 Jan. 1921.

10. May, *Great Expectations*, p. 62; S. Lynd and Helen Merrell Lynd, *Middletown: A Study of Contemporary American Culture* (New York, 1928), 114–15.

11. *Evening Mail*, 21 March 1922.

12. Ibid., 29 June 1919.

13. PANS, RG 48, 366, vol. 16 Halifax County Wills, 1919–1925, 9704, 367, vol. 17, 11251, Halifax County Wills, 1925–1929. A total of 13 wills were found for 1919–1931 by residents of Richmond Heights.

14. May, *Great Expectations*, 71, 90.

15. See Meg Luxton, *More than a Labour of Love* (Toronto, 1980); Veronica Strong-Boag, "Keeping House in God's Country: Canadian Women at Work in the Home" in *On the Job: Confronting the Labour Process in Canada*, ed. Craig Heron and Robert Storey (Montreal, 1986); Ellen Ross "'Fierce Questions and Taunts': Married Life in Working-Class London, 1870–1914," *Feminist Studies* 8, 3 (Fall 1982): 575–602, and Elizabeth Roberts, *A Woman's Place: An Oral History of Working-Class Women, 1890–1940* (Oxford, 1984).

16. Mary Ann Clawson, *Constructing Brotherhood: Class, Gender and Fraternalism* (Princeton, 1989), 263.

17. *Evening Mail*, 25, 26 Feb. 1919; *Acadian Recorder* (Halifax), 26 Feb. 1919.

18. *Daily Times* (Moncton), 5 July 1922.

19. Mary P. Ryan, "The Projection of a New Womanhood: The Movie Moderns in the 1920s" in *Our American Sisters: Women in American Life and Thought*, ed. Jean E. Friedman and William G. Shade (Boston, 1976), 369.

20. Thompson, *Canada*, 166.

21. Archives of Ontario, RG 4 Attorney General Series C-3, File 3188/1931 "B" *Worker* correspondence; 5B009; 27 Jan. 1927; Charlotte Pouson to Annie Buller.

22. *Evening Mail*, 16 May 1919.

23. *Evening Mail*, 24 Oct. 1927.

24. Marcia Seligson, *The Eternal Bliss Machine: America's Way of Wedding* (New York, 1973), 41.

25. *The Citizen* (Halifax), 29 May 1929.

26. Veronica Strong-Boag, "The Girls of the New Day: Canadian Working Women in the 1920s," *Labour/Le Travail* 4 (Fall 1979): 131–64; Graham Lowe, "Women, Work and the Office: The Feminization of Clerical Occupations in Canada, 1901–31" in *Rethinking Canada: The Promise of Women's History*, ed. Veronica Strong-Boag and Anita Clair Fellman (Toronto, 1986), 107–22.

27. Workplace participation should not be primarily regarded in terms of the number of working women, for the percentage of Canadian women in the total labour force increases only gradually between 1911 and 1931 and the percentage of Halifax women in the local labour force actually declined. In 1911, nearly a third of the total Halifax labour was female, but by 1921 this percentage had fallen to just over a quarter, increasing to only 26.9 percent in 1931.

28. Discussions of women's work culture appear in Kathy Peiss, *Cheap Amusements: Working Women and Leisure in Turn of the Century New York* (Philadelphia, 1986); Susan Porter Benson, *Counter Cultures: Saleswomen, Managers, and Customers in American Department Stores,* *1890–1940* (Urbana, 1986); and Leslie Woodcock Tentler, *Wage-Earning Women: Industrial Work and Family Life in the United States, 1900–1930* (New York, 1979).

29. Peiss, *Cheap Amusements*, 51–55.

30. Ellen Gee, "Fertility and Marriage Patterns in Canada 1851–1971" (Ph.D. diss., University of British Columbia, 1978), 168.

31. Based on his British sources, Gillis found that the unskilled married younger than the skilled. John R. Gillis, *For Better or Worse: British Marriages 1600 to Present* (New York, 1985), 289.

32. Sallie Westwood describes textile industry rituals in England in 1970s as has Joy Parr for Paris, Ontario, in the 1920s and 1930s. Sallie Westwood, *All Day Every Day: Factory and Family in the Making of Women's Lives* (London, 1984); Joy Parr, *The Gender of Breadwinners: Women, Men, and Change in Two Industrial Towns, 1880–1950* (Toronto, 1990). In her study courtship and wedding customs in Swansea, Wales, in the late 1960s, Diana Leonard found work-leaving rituals were most frequent and elaborate in situations with "a lot of young women working together." Diana Leonard, *Sex and Generation: A Study of Courtship and Marriage* (London, 1980), 145–46.

33. Dalhousie University Archives (DUA), Maritime Telephone and Telegraph, *Monthly Bulletin*, June 1924.

34. *Monthly Bulletin*, June 1920.

35. *Evening Mail*, 18 June 1927.

36. *Monthly Bulletin*, May 1920: For other example of showers see *Monthly Bulletin*, June 1924; *Evening Mail*, 28 May 1919; 3 June 1920; 28 June 1921; 5 Nov. 1924, etc.

37. *Evening Mail*, 16 June 1926.

38. *Evening Mail*, 8 Sept. 1919; 13 Sept. 1922.

39. *Evening Mail*, 16 June 1920; 28 Sept. 1926; 16 Nov. 1927.

40. *Evening Mail*, 24 Oct. 1924; 28 Sept. 1926.

41. *Evening Mail*, 16 June 1926; 1 Sept. 1925; 16 June 1920; 8 Aug. 1923.

42. Jane Synge, "Young Working-Class Women in Early Twentieth Century Hamilton: Their Work and Family Lives" in *Proceedings of the Workshop Conference on Blue Collar Workers and their Communities*, ed. A.H. Turrintin (Toronto, 1976), 139.

43. *Monthly Bulletin*, June 1924.

44. Gillis, *For Better or Worse*, 260.

45. Snell and Abeele, "Regulating Nuptiality."

46. For example, see *Evening Mail*, 15 March 1924.

47. Gillis, *For Better or Worse*, 285.

48. For example, see *Evening Mail*, 3 July 1925; 17 Aug. 1926; 5 Jan. 1927.

49. Leo G. Hinz, *The Celebration of Marriage in Canada: A Comparative Study of Civil and Canon Law Outside the Province of Quebec* (Ottawa, 1957), 156.

50. David Cressy, "The Seasonality of Marriage in Old and New England," *Journal of Interdisciplinary History* 16, 1 (Summer 1985): 7.

51. William S. Wals, *Curiosities of Popular Customs and of Rites, Ceremonies, Observances, and Miscellaneous Antiquities* (Philadelphia, 1925), 680–81. The persistence of this belief was also seen in a 1923 disappointed contingent of Lowland Scottish brides, who worried that the delay of their Canadian arrival meant they would be married in the "unlucky" month of May. Jim Wilkie, *Metagama: A Journey from Lewis to the New World* (Toronto, 1987) 80. The aversion to May weddings conflicted with practical factors such as leases which typically began 1 May. Morton, "Men and Women," 55.

52. Edith Fowke, *Ring Around the Moon* (Toronto, 1977), 85.

53. For example, *Evening Mail*, 22 July 1919; 28 June 1921; 25 April 1923; 12

Sept. 1924; 29 June 1926; 16 Aug. 1927. Lucia Ferretti describes a similar pattern among working-class couples in Montreal a decade earlier in "Mariage et cadre de vie familiale dans une paroisse ouvrière montréalise: Sainte-Brigide, 1900–1914," *Revue d'histoire de l'Amérique française* 39, 2 (Autumn 1985): 233–51.

54. For example *Evening Mail*, 28 May 1919; 19 Aug. 1919; 28 June 1921; and 17 Aug. 1922.

55. *Evening Mail*, 30 April 1920.

56. The survey examined wedding announcements that appeared in the *Evening Mail* and the *Acadian Recorder* in June 1910, and assumptions are based upon the place of residence of participants.

57. Most women ceased paid labour upon their marriage although by the end of the decade it was becoming increasingly common to stay at work until the birth of the first child. *Monthly Bulletin*, Aug. 1927.

58. Interview with Mrs. Gladys McTier, July 1988, Ottawa.

59. Alice Payne Hackett, *Seventy Years of Best Sellers, 1895–1965* (New York, 1967), 127.

60. *Evening Mail*, 20 Sept. 1929.

61. Emily Holt, *Encyclopedia of Etiquette: A Book of Manners for Everyday Use* (New York, 1921), 264.

62. Diana Festa-McCormick, *Proustian Optics of Clothes, Mirrors, Masks and Mores* (Saratoga, CA, 1984), 128.

63. Gillis, *For Better or Worse*, 285.

64. Alison Laurie, *The Language of Clothes* (New York, 1983), 186.

65. Fowke, *Ring Around the Moon*, 86.

66. Denyse Baillargeon, "Travail domestique et crise économique: les ménagères montréalaises durant la crise des annéees trente," (Ph.D. diss., Université de Montréal, 1990), 183.

67. PANS, MG 27, vol. 3, #1, Halifax Explosion, List of Unidentified

Dead; for example see nos. 27, 68, 86, 107, 114, 138, 336, 353, 459, 476, 1074, 1105.

68. Gillis, *For Better or Worse*, 281. See Edward Jay Epstein, *The Rise and Fall of Diamonds* (New York, 1982) regarding the mass marketing of the diamond engagement ring in the United States.

69. Gillis, *For Better or Worse*, 296.

70. For example, *Evening Mail*, 12 July 1922; 8 and 9 June 1929.

71. Ellen Rothman, *Hands and Hearts: A History of Courtship in America* (Cambridge, MA, 1984), 175–77, 280.

72. A similar pattern is described by Denyse Baillargeon among working-class Montreal couples who visited relatives in the Quebec country-side and in the United States. "Travail domestique," 186.

73. *Evening Mail*, 30 April 1920.

74. *Evening Mail*, 26 Feb. 1920.

section

6

FAMILIES AND THE STATE

"THE WHITE LIFE FOR TWO": THE DEFENCE OF MARRIAGE AND SEXUAL MORALITY IN CANADA, 1890-1914*

JAMES G. SNELL

O

The years before World War I witnessed a rising fear that the family and the home, the central institutions of the social order, were experiencing increasing pressures and showing signs of considerable tension.[1] Indeed, there is strong evidence that, as a result of such phenomena as industrialization, rural depopulation, and urbanization, the character of the family and the home was changing markedly in the second half of the nineteenth century. It is not surprising that these changes created serious strains within the nuclear family and that one manifestation of these strains was breakdown in marriages among Canadians. As a result of such breakdowns, and even more as a result of fear or disintegration of marriages, reformers and leaders in Canada began to act, especially after the turn of the century, to reinforce the institution of marriage. In particular, Canadian leaders pressed for a stronger role by the state in defending marriage and in punishing any deviations from the moral code and social order associated with marriage.

The anxieties apparent regarding marital and sexual morality were a product of much broader concerns regarding society in general. A recent history of the anti-prostitution movement in the United States during this time period argues convincingly that prostitution was "a master symbol, a code word, for a wide range of anxieties engendered by the great social and historical period"; the perceived crisis regarding prostitution represented really a much more extensive crisis in sexual and "civilized morality."[2] In Canada, it can be argued, marriage breakdown operated as a similar, negative symbol. Marriage represented a code of moral and sexual behaviour

* Histoire sociale/Social History 16, 31 (May 1983): 111–28.

which was felt to have long ordered society; marriage breakdown, on the other hand, symbolized a wide variety of conduct that was considered immoral, anti-social, and unacceptable. This link between marital conduct and sexual morality was reinforced by the fact that (with one minor exception) adultery was the only recognized ground for divorce in Canada.

Marriage, including by definition proper or moral sexual activity, was considered to be a legitimate and fit subject for consideration by the state and by leaders of society. The institution of marriage represented the divinely ordained method or ordering the home, of controlling and legitimizing passion and sex, of structuring relations between males and females, and of procreating and nurturing the future generation. As the legal cornerstone of the home and family, marriage was a basic means by which the state might influence the character of and conduct in the home. By examining some of the fears and anxieties articulated by middle-class spokesmen it is possible to gain insight into attitudes toward sexuality, views of male and female character and social roles, and perceptions of the home and the family.

o

It is clear that the number of divorces in Canada was rising. During the 1890s the number of divorces changed little, averaging just twelve per year. Early in the new century, however, a gradual increase set in, so that in the first decade of the twentieth century there were 26.3 divorces per year, on average. In the first five years of the second decade the rise continued, there being an average of 54.6 divorces per year. Compared with the number of divorces in other countries or with what was to happen in later years in the Dominion, the Canadian divorce rate was extremely low. In relative and local terms, however, it was increasing. Given that the average number was more than doubling each decade, it is understandable that articulate Canadians were concerned.[3]

Far more difficult to deal with in numerical terms is desertion. For a variety of reasons, abandonment of home and family was the "poor man's divorce." But it is one of those social phenomena which generally goes unreported. Social reformers and church leaders at the time certainly thought that desertion was a significant social problem. Petitions (more often than not from members of the working class) to the Department of Justice represented desertion was a major form of marriage breakdown, on an individual basis. Law reports give numerous specific examples of desertion, usually involving cases of bigamy or of criminal non-support, or in petitions for alimony. General statistics, however, are more difficult to come by. In 1912 a police magistrate in Montreal estimated that he dealt with four or five cases a day concerning husbands' non-support of their families, but how many of these cases involved desertion? The number of children admitted to the care of the Children's Aid Society of Winnipeg because of desertion by parents rose markedly in the years prior to World War I: in

1911 and 1912, sixty-two children (representing 13 percent of the total wards in those years) had come to the Society because of parental desertion. This figure represents, presumably, only those cases where both parents had abandoned the home, though not likely at the same time; how many deserted children were left at home with the remaining parent?[4]

While to the modern eye these numbers do not appear very great, nevertheless many people at the time certainly thought they had sufficient proof to stir leaders in Canadian society to action. Marriage and the family were perceived to be weakening, undermined by general causes such as urbanization, but also by an increasing immorality as demonstrated by such "sins of the flesh" as prostitution, adultery, and cohabitation outside marriage, and by a diminishing sense of responsibility on the part of individuals as shown by non-support, desertion, and divorce.[5] A major method of dealing with these problems and of reinforcing the institutions of marriage and the family was to call on the power of the state. If old-fashioned respect for the sanctity of the sacrament of marriage and for long-standing standards of moral conduct was no longer sufficient to maintain the integrity of the marital home, then various facets of the law should be employed to put a halt to the disintegration of Canadian marriages.

The state was already directly involved in the granting of divorces. In all but three provinces (Nova Scotia, New Brunswick, and British Columbia) divorces could be obtained only by act of the Dominion Parliament on an individual basis; the federal legislature thus directly controlled divorces for the vast majority (82.8 percent in 1911) of the population. The parliamentary process was lengthy (over a year) and expensive (at least $1000), and presented parliamentarians with serious philosophical and moral problems. A few "voices in the wilderness" argued before the House of Commons for the establishment of divorce courts across the country in order to reduce the cost and the time involved, to enforce a strictly judicial procedure, to reduce individual publicity, and also to rid Parliament of a troublesome and touchy issue. Such arguments were generally met with hostility. Instead, it was strongly felt to be in the national interest that divorce remain difficult to secure. Writing on behalf of the Conservative Government in 1896, Sir Charles Tupper defended the prevailing parliamentary method of divorce:

> There has been a very general feeling among our public men of both sides, that, notwithstanding individual cases of hardship which cry for immediate redress, divorce should not be made too easy to obtain. That is why the Government of Canada has not established a divorce Court, and the same reason will I think continue to operate in the same direction.[6]

This policy was maintained by succeeding governments.

During the first decade of the twentieth century a scattered number of backbenchers in the House of Commons raised the question of establishing divorce courts. The arguments presented to defeat such a proposal (such motions never came to a vote) were quite consistent. In 1901 Prime Minister Laurier commented that there was no public support for the passage of a divorce law in Canada, likely because of the bad example set by the United States where, he said,

> divorces are not to be desired. For my part I would rather belong to this country of Canada where divorces are few, than to belong to the neighbouring republic where divorces are many. I think it argues a good moral condition of a country where you have few divorces, even though they are made difficult—a better moral condition than prevails in a country where divorces are numerous and made easy by law . . . I am glad to say that as a rule they [divorces] are not favoured, that they are discouraged, and that fact speaks well for the moral condition of our people.[7]

The absence of any federal Canadian legislation dealing with divorce was thus argued to be a healthy sign, proof of the stability of the Canadian family. The same attitude was manifested by Senator James Gowan, the long-time Canadian Chairman of the Senate Divorce Committee. Congratulating Sir Wilfrid Laurier on his prompt action to crush any move toward the establishment of divorce courts, Gowan (himself a retired County Court judge of good reputation) asserted:

> the establishment of Divorce Courts in my judgement would be fraught with peril to the morals and best interests of our Country— the home and the family being the very essence of a healthy community, the sacredness of marriage [is] scarcely to be over estimated. I had the great satisfaction when in the old Country of being able to boast the fact that divorce was *no part of the laws of Canada*.[8]

Section 91 (26) of the British North America Act gave the Dominion Parliament exclusive jurisdiction over marriage and divorce. Reasoning such as that demonstrated by Laurier and Gowan, however, resulted in the deliberate absence of any Dominion legislation regarding divorce in general. The first minor legislation on the subject was not passed until 1926, and it was not until 1968 that the first general divorce law was enacted in Canada.

In the meantime, parliamentary divorces were defended as right and proper. Perhaps most articulate of this general sentiment was E. A. Lancaster, a lawyer and Conservative member of Parliament for Lincoln, Ontario, 1900–1916. Divorce was a serious issue and had "a bad effect on the country," he claimed.

> Where will this country come to in twenty-five years if we are going to grant divorces simply because some woman has been disappointed in regard to her husband, and comes here and asks for a dissolution of her marriage because she made a mistake when she married? The whole social fabric of the country would go to pieces.

Anyone asking Parliament for a divorce was seeking a special privilege, rather than the enforcement of a basic right, Lancaster continued. Therefore it was incumbent on the petitioner "to show something in the interest of the state, not in the interest of herself or of her husband only."

We may build all the Grand Trunk Pacifics we like, we may debate free trade or protection, we may grant autonomy to all the provinces from Vancouver to Halifax, we may pass all the laws on a business basis we like, but if we interfere unnecessarily or recklessly in the relations between man and wife, we will go a long way towards undermining the morality of this country, and if our laws tend to produce such a result and break up homes we had better repeal them and build up a system of laws more suited to a sound condition of public and private morality.

To grant divorces for anything but the most serious causes would have the effect, Lancaster alleged, of instructing the youth of Canada that there was no longer anything sacred in the marriage tie. The only acceptable ground for divorce was "that the continuance of the marriage would be a scandal and an injury to the community." To dissolve a marriage on any other grounds was "doing great harm to the country, setting a very bad example and causing a very bad state of affairs."[9]

There were many people both in and out of Parliament who agreed with Lancaster.[10] The moral fabric of Canada was considered to be vitally at stake in the relations between husband and wife. The extent to which these relations could be controlled and maintained on a lofty plateau reflected the moral character of the country. The maintenance of individual marital bonds thus symbolized the preservation of virtue and rectitude in all Canadians and upheld the model for intersexual relations, a beacon in a world all too darkened by sin and selfishness.

In short, the restrictive system of parliamentary divorces offered considerable advantages. The parliamentary procedure allowed divorce for those few people with enough money and influence (who might otherwise exert real pressure for divorce reform) while maintaining the marital bonds of the overwhelming majority of the population. Divorce through individual legislation made it easier to avoid having any general divorce act. The net result of all this was a very small number of divorces and thus apparent proof of the stability of Canadian marriages and of the morality in Canadian homes. Legislative divorce (as opposed to judicial divorce) was defended as being restrictive and highly supportive of marriage and morality.

Yet even those advocates of divorce reform often argued that change would be more restrictive and more conducive to public morality. One member of Parliament claimed that a federal divorce law would establish uniform conditions and would thus potentially be more restrictive. Another reasoned that judicial divorces would result in reduced public exposure of individual sins, as opposed to the parliamentary process in which the cleaning staff each night avidly read the minutes of the Divorce Committee and took some of the papers home where the children might be exposed to the lurid details. Finally, a legal journal asserted that costly divorces effectively permitted immoral husbands or wives "to sin with practical impunity," whereas inexpensive divorces would inhibit adultery and promote morality.[11] What change was contemplated was often aimed at restricting divorce or at making it less attractive. For example, Senator Cloran, an Irish

Catholic from Montreal, introduced the Evils of Divorce Restriction Bill in 1913, designed to give Parliament the right in a divorce case to restrict the guilty spouse from remarrying.[12]

In such a setting it is no coincidence that the divorce jurisdiction of the Supreme Court of British Columbia came under direct challenge. The Court's jurisdiction had in fact been in doubt for a number of years. In 1877 the Chief Justice of the province, in a dissenting opinion (Sharpe v. Sharpe), had held that the Court had no authority to deal with divorce, but two fellow judges ruled otherwise. Fourteen years later the Court's power to hear divorce cases was reaffirmed (Scott v. Scott), only to be brought into question again in 1896 (Levey v. Levey). In none of these cases was there an appeal beyond the province's boundaries. Finally, in 1907 Mrs. Mary Watts petitioned for a dissolution of her twenty-nine-month-old marriage. Judge Clement directed counsel to argue before him as to the power and jurisdiction of the Supreme Court to grant a divorce. Counsel for the appellant, for the respondent, and for the Attorney-General of British Columbia appeared, and all argued that the Court did indeed have jurisdiction. Nevertheless, Judge Clement held otherwise, dismissing the case for want of jurisdiction. This time the decision was appealed directly to London, where the Judicial Committee of the Privy Council set aside the judgment, thus confirming the Court's jurisdiction.[13] The challenge to the judicial divorce process had thus failed, but it is one more indication of the tendency toward a restriction of divorce.

Indeed, in divorce procedure no change had occurred at all in the two decades preceding World War I. There had, however, been an increasing discussion of divorce as the number of legal dissolutions of marriage rose both in Canada and elsewhere. This discussion served simply to entrench the restrictive and defensive philosophy regarding divorce. The interests of society at large were more vital than those of the individual and thus the state had every right to impose its own attitudes and values concerning divorce, even though, as Sir Wilfrid Laurier put it, individuals might suffer.

Although no change took place regarding divorce in Canada, considerable effort was exerted in the area of criminal law in order to inhibit various factors associated with marriage breakdown. Two major developments helped to establish the character and focus of this effort. The codification of Canadian criminal law in 1892 gave interested persons a visible target. Equally important was the decision during the 1890s that Parliament, rather than the courts, would be the principal source of ongoing change in the criminal law. Reform groups thus were provided with, as they saw it, a vehicle for social change (the Criminal Code) and a means to put their ideas into law (Parliament). When combined with a basic belief that "positive social goals could be achieved by negative means, that is, by prohibiting certain kinds of behaviour,"[14] the stage was set for strengthening of marriage and the family through an attack on marital and sexual misconduct. As one leading reformer, D. A. Watt, put it: "the public conscience is, for the most part, created and maintained by statute law, and by scarcely anything else."[15]

Indeed, during the drafting of the original Code, the Department of Justice was subjected to rather intensive pressure from the Society for the

Protection of Women and Children with a view to including various sexual offences in the new legislation. The Society, led by D. A. Watt, printed and distributed two pamphlets, while Watt and his colleagues wrote to the Minister and Department nineteen times between 1889 and 1892. Making use of social purity and criminal code literature from the United States and the United Kingdom, the Society pointed to the social evils present in young girls and immigrant women from seduction and abduction, and to crush the operation of brothels and the procuration of underaged females. As a result of this pressure, "Canada's Criminal Code of 1892 had and retains the most comprehensive system of offences for protecting young women and girls from sexual predators."[16]

Social purity advocates did not rest content, however. In the two decades following passage of the Criminal Code, reformers both in and out of Parliament pushed repreatedly to buttress existing sections, to expand others, and to make more severe the penalties attached to offences linked to marriage and sexual morality. The original Code contained many clauses that might be associated with marriage breakdown. Bigamy and polygamy were obvious sections, but they attracted only limited interest and only minor alteration. In 1892 the Code extended Canadian courts' jurisdiction over bigamous marriages by making anyone who had committed bigamy outside the Dominion liable to conviction if the person, being a British subject and a Canadian resident, had left Canada with the intent of such a commission. This extension of the Code to cover extra-territorial acts was upheld by the Supreme Court of Canada in 1897. Writing with the majority, Justice John Gwynne held that control over such affairs was essential if the central government was to have a meaningful role within the Canadian constitution. Furthermore:

> Bordering as Canada does upon several foreign States, in many of which the laws relating to marriage and divorce are loose, demoralizing and degrading to the marriage state, such legislation as is contained in the above sections of the Criminal Code seem[s] to be absolutely essential to the peace, order and good government of Canada, and in particular to the maintenance within the Dominion of the purity and sanctity of the marriage state.[17]

Even the judiciary was caught up in defence of marriage.

Related to these marital offences were the broader issues of adultery and extra-legal cohabitation.[18] According to Canadian law, cohabitation was illegal when it involved conjugal union with a person who a) was married to someone else or b) lived or cohabited with someone else in a conjugal union. Even if this section were enforced across the country, it would not prohibit two otherwise unattached adults of opposite sex from living together. There was no law in the Dominion prohibiting adultery, except in New Brunswick where an old pre-Confederation statute remained unrepealed though seldom used.[19]

Adultery and extra-legal marriage were felt to be all too frequent in turn-of-the-century Canada. As a factor in divorce cases and in unofficial divorce petitions,[20] adultery was dominant—although since adultery was the only recognized ground for divorce, this is to be expected. A number of spokesmen felt, as well, that extra-legal marriages were increasingly common. A clergyman in the Niagara Peninsula wrote to his member of Parliament regarding "wrongful co-habitation and open adultery":

> You undoubtedly know, from knowledge of conditions in your town, as I do of similar conditions here, how widespread and growing is the above evil. And not only in our respective communities, but all over the Dominion, this evil is making inroads upon our moral system, and standing out as a degrading object lesson to our young people.[21]

Some reformers, such as Sir Robert Borden's Minister of Justice and a Presbyterian minister in Port Arthur, Ontario, linked the problem to groups of recent foreign immigrants.[22] Another Ontario cleric's complaint gives a good indication of the character of the reformers' concerns:

> Heres [sic] a case. A man has a double house. He lives alone in one half, a woman whose husband is alive but absent has rented the other half. It is a common thing to see her in his half alone with him, and even she is admitted into his apartments late at night. Must clean living persons endure the stench of such conduct? It is commonly known and admitted that their relation is bad.[23]

Although the offending couple conformed at least to some of the outward forms demanded by society in that they had separate accommodation, local social leaders were outraged by their conduct. The state had a clear right and duty to intrude into the bedrooms of the nation.

As of 1904 there were demands to have the Criminal Code deal with these matters. A County Court judge in Ontario drafted a clause to broaden the application of the bigamy section and to include extra-legal marriage within the definition of bigamy. The Presbyterian Church called for inclusion of "adultery and lewd cohabitation" as punishable offences within the Criminal Code; supporting resolutions came in from several synods and presbyteries. Branches of the Woman's Christian Temperance Union and the Young Women's Christian Association, the Police Magistrate of Winnipeg, the Moral and Social Reform Council of Canada, and the Plenary Council of the Roman Catholic Church all joined in the chorus clamouring for punishment of adultery and extra-legal marriage. The pressure was such that the Department of Justice did look into the possibility of legislating in this regard.[24] Wisely, however, the Government forswore passage of what would surely have been an unenforceable law.

There were, however, some legal changes which could be made. In particular, punishment for various sorts of sexual immorality could be reinforced, thus attacking adultery indirectly and giving strength to the belief that only within the institution of marriage was sexual activity morally acceptable. Some demand was heard for an expansion of the definition of incest to include step-parents and step-children, but no changes in the legislation were made.[25] Many of the pleas regarding punishment of adultery also asked for legislative action against "the social evil" or "white slavery"—prostitution.[26] In 1913 section 216 of the Code was rewritten, expanding the definition of procuring to include any female and dropping the previous exclusion of "common prostitutes" and of women "of known immoral character." Also the punishment for procuring was dramatically increased: in 1909 the potential term of imprisonment was raised from two to five years, and this was raised again in 1920 to ten years; in 1913 whipping was added as an additional penalty for second or subsequent convictions. That same year the definition of a keeper of a "disorderly house" was expanded to include employees, being a "found in" became a criminal offence, and landlords or tenants became liable if premises under their control were used for purposes of prostitution.[27] That such changes were part of a movement to defend the institution of marriage was made clear by Rev. J. G. Shearer, founding secretary of the national Moral and Social Reform Council. In an American tract on white slavery, Shearer described a married man in Vancouver "who—untrue to the solemn marriage vows taken upon him—continually resorted to a den of vice, regardless of his sacred duties owed his wife or children." It was sad to say, he continued, but "there are thousands of married men who, like this one, soon forget their pledges at the marriage alter."[28] If Shearer and his fellow reformers had their way, such men would be forced back to the conjugal bed.

Legislative action was also taken to protect young women from men's lust. In 1900 several sections were changed or added to the Criminal Code. The crime of seduction had always applied only to females "of previously chaste character." Now the accused male was required to shoulder the onus of proof of previous loss of the seduced female's chastity. As well, the legal term "guardian" was explicitly and broadly defined, particularly regarding responsibilities to females under a guardian's charge: the minimum legal age for carnal knowledge of a girl was raised from sixteen to eighteen; and the section protecting females suffering from imbecility or insanity was broadened.[29] At the provincial level several legislatures acted to facilitate civil suits for seduction. Manitoba in 1892 and the North West Territories in 1903 adopted a pre-Confederation Upper Canadian statute to this effect; in Prince Edward Island in 1895 failure to comply with the judgment in such a suit became punishable by up to nine months' imprisonment.[30]

Over one particular section of the Criminal Code regarding seduction there was extended debate. Section 183, dating from 1892, declared it a criminal offence for an employer or manager in a factory, mill or workshop to seduce or have "illicit connection with" any female under age twenty-one and of previously chaste character who was under his direction. For the next twenty years pressure was exerted to widen the places of work named in the law. Shops or stores were proposed for inclusion in 1896, and were added in a rewriting of the section in 1900.[31] More vocal were pleas for the inclusion of domestic servants, one of the most vulnerable groups of female employees. However, the reformers met with considerable opposition from the legislators. Members of Parliament and senators were concerned lest any such law leave the employers of female domestics open to invidious blackmail, despite the fact that section 684 of the original Code made corroborating evidence mandatory in seduction charges. Worried more about the reputations of middle- and upper-class males than with the abuse of young females, the politicians dismissed demands for such a reform.[32]

These efforts and new legislation represent the various attempts to use the law to circumscribe extra-marital sexual activity.[33] Any opportunity for sexual activity outside marriage was regarded not only as sinful on an individual basis, but also as a destructive force within society as a whole. If both the opportunity and the attractiveness of extra-marital sex could be reduced, then men would be persuaded to expend their sexual energies in their homes and with their wives.

It remains to examine attempts to coerce husbands more directly to stay at home and to accept their responsibilities as "breadwinners." Evidence of considerable concern regarding desertion and non-support does not appear until 1908–1909, but over the following years much attention was directed to these problems. Some legislation was already in place; it was, for example, a criminal offence to fail to provide the necessities of life for one's wife or children under age sixteen, if the negligence resulted in death, danger to life or permanent injury. As well, in Ontario—but in no other provinces—there was a Deserted Wives' Maintenance Act, first passed in 1888. The measure allowed a deserted wife for the first time to apply on behalf of herself, with or without a family, for a court order requiring her husband to pay up to five dollars a week in support payments. In 1897 the definition of a deserted wife was enlarged to include a wife living apart from her husband because of his refusal or neglect to support her.[34]

There were obvious deficiencies in these measures, and reformers were quick to point them out. Neglect or non-support in and of themselves were not criminal offences; to become so they had to entail death or danger or permanent injury.[35] What about desertion where such results did not occur, where the husband deserted and repudiated his familial responsibilities but his wife and children were able, though barely, to struggle on? What about the husband who allowed charitable societies or city welfare agencies to assist his family while he avoided his duties? What of the husband who refused to work or who removed himself from the local court's jurisdiction, and thus could or would make no support payments? Finally, what of the husband who sat in jail, fed, clothed and sheltered, while his wife and children suffered the cruelties of climate and poverty in this country?

To deal with these weaknesses in the law, reformers pressed the federal government vigorously. The Associated Charities of Toronto established an interdenominational committee to examine the problem and to propose reforms. The committee met a number of times, secured legal and expert advice, consulted both the federal and provincial Attorney-General's departments and the local police department, and submitted proposed amendments to the Criminal Code, which the committee then urged the federal government to adopt.[36] The work of the committee attracted attention elsewhere. The Local Council of Women and the National Council of Women, the Charity Organization Society of Montreal, the Associated Charities of Saint John, the Brandon Charity Organization, several court officials and politicians, and the Associated Charities of Winnipeg all came to the support of the Toronto committee's work. The Winnipeg society was particularly active, sending its General Secretary, J. H. T. Falk, to Ottawa and elsewhere on at least two occasions and generally pressing hard to have the Code amended. Other major groups, such as the Moral and Social Reform Council and the Methodist Church's Department of Temperance and Moral Reform, argued for similar legislation.

The pressure worked. In the Department of Justice the pleas fell on sympathetic ears. One official noted on a request submitted by the Associated Charities of Winnipeg: "These outside gentlemen do not realize that in no place is the heart more wrung with the sufferings of the innocent wives & children . . . than in this Department."[37] In 1913 the Criminal Code was amended in a major way. The definition of non-support was considerably extended by omitting any reference to death, danger, or permanent injury; mere failure to provide the necessities of life was now sufficient for conviction. As well, cohabitation was defined as *prima facie* evidence that the man was lawfully married to the woman involved; if a man had in any way recognized children as being his own that would be *prima facie* evidence that they were his legitimate children. Both of these changes tended to force responsibility for support on the common-law husband. Finally, summary conviction for non-support was now made possible.[38]

Reformers viewed the changes as a great step forward, although the law was still not all that they sought. The Government had not, for example, accepted the proposal that a husband convicted of non-support be set to work while in jail and that the proceeds from that work be used directly to support his family. Nevertheless, any "wife-deserter" could now be readily punished for his sins. As well, in some provinces deserted wives' maintenance legislation, similar to that in Ontario, had been adopted: in British Columbia in 1901 and Saskatchewan in 1910. J. J. Kelso, the long-time Ontario Superintendent of Neglected and Dependent Children, arranged for the printing of a flyer publicizing the new changes in the Criminal Code. Under a picture of Britannia protecting little children behind her shield, Kelso declared: "As this amendment to the Code was granted at the urgent request of many officials and social workers, its enforcement should not be neglected. The preservation of the home is the foundation principle of all social endeavour."[39]

This rising concern over non-support and the changes in the law were reflected in the criminal statistics. Charges for non-support, which averaged 131.2 per year during 1900–1909, jumped dramatically to 196 in 1912, a 49.4 percent increase, and then to 531 in 1913, a 170.9 percent increase over the previous year, before settling back to around 174 charges per year. The number of convictions followed a similar pattern, rising 33.3 percent to 68 convictions followed a similar pattern, rising 33.3 percent to 68 convictions in 1912, and then in 1913 vaulting to 394, a 479.4 percent increase over the previous year before falling to around 100 convictions per annum in the years immediately thereafter.[40]

What of the international boundary? Associated with the movement to amend the Criminal Code regarding desertion and non-support was a desire to make these extraditable offences. An Order-in-Council to this effect was approved in April 1915, but the Convention involved was not ratified by the American Senate.[41]

One further attempt was made to control the behaviour of men. Not only were they to stay at home and expend their sexual energies "properly," they were also not to beat their wives, a problem which some social leaders considered to be serious. No man should be allowed physically to mistreat a female. In a discussion of whipping as a form of corporal punishment, members of the House of Commons in 1909 castigated wife-beaters; there was considerable support for, as the Prime Minister put it, giving a "man . . . a taste of his own medicine." In Ontario in 1897, legislation was amended to include within the definition of a deserted wife any woman living apart from her husband because of repeated assaults or other acts of cruelty. To cope with the problem nationally the Criminal Code was amended. Section 292 dealing with indecent assault was expanded in 1909 to punish any male who "assaults and beats his wife or any other female and thereby occasions her actual bodily harm."[42] Since assault causing bodily harm was already dealt with elsewhere in the Code and entailed harsher punishment, the value of this new legislation is doubtful. However, the desire to protect wives and to specify proper behaviour between husband and wife is significant.

o

Regulation of marital and sexual conduct at this time is part of a broader theme discussed by other historians. Angus McLaren has recently indicated the repressive tendencies of the state and of social leaders regarding abortion, and has pointed out how this repression coincided with apparently changing societal practices. In an important paper in 1970 Michael Bliss opened up a new area of research for Canadians in a stimulating analysis of turn-of-the-century attitudes toward sexuality: Bliss revealed a widespread concern among leaders within Canadian society for control over sexuality and for repression of extra-marital or "unnatural" sexual activity.[43] Canadians working for "social purity" were concerned enough about the negative developments within society to organize, in 1905–1906, the Canadian Purity-Education Association. This organization was simply a manifestation of an existing and rising concern for the moral and social "hygiene" of Dominion society. The Association complemented such existing groups as the Montreal-based Society for the Protection of Women and Children and parallelled in time and in character similar developments in the United States.[44] Both Americans and Canadians noted signs that moral and sexual attitudes and codes of conduct were altering, along with much else in society. In an attempt to maintain some stability and to gain reassurance as to traditional values and behavioural codes, articulate members of North American society were speaking out and acting against any change.

Yet the very reaction revealed change. The public discussion of sexuality and of sexual conduct contributed meaningfully to "the breakdown of the conspiracy of silence" regarding sexual matters.[45] In the open debate of such issues, the sacramental or religious character of the questions was weakened and their secular aspects became more important. As well, by articulating a code of moral and sexual conduct these reformers were setting up an ideal type which was not always compatible with the parallel ideal of a happy marriage in which mutual obligations and responsibilities were fully respected. Indeed, a rationale was being developed and legitimized for marital dissolution, a rationale which would come to be increasingly adopted in the future. What would happen when one was forced to choose between maintenance of a marriage in which at least one of the partners was guilty of immoral conduct and the dissolution of that marriage in order to demonstrate that such conduct could not properly be tolerated within marriage? In the following decades in Canada, as ideals of sexual, moral, and marital conduct came increasingly to be articulated, the possibility of acceptable marital dissolution would come, albeit slowly, to be legitimized.

It was in the courts of the land where the conflict between these two ideals first became apparent. While politicians and social reformers could discuss various principles in the abstract, the courts were forced to apply the resulting laws to specific cases. The consequence, in the early twentieth century, was much ambivalence, as the judiciary tried to cope with the conflicting pressures. On the one hand, adulterous conduct could be enough to relieve the other spouse of marital obligations, as for example in Montreal in 1902. Mrs. H. applied for a judicial separation and moved out of the matrimonial home. In receipt of alimony from her husband, she took up residence elsewhere in the city and became "the kept mistress of a married man." On learning of this, the husband discontinued the alimony and his wife sued, but the courts eventually supported the husband because of the wife's improper behaviour.[46] On the other hand, a wife's neglect of some of her marital obligations was not sufficient to absolve the husband of his duty to maintain her. One Mr. Karch, a machinist in Hespeler, Ontario, was considered by the court to be an industrious, good man who, while living at home, had provided properly for his family. Over time Mrs. Karch had shown evidence that she generally neglected her husband (for example, by not preparing his meals) and "was not as considerate as a wife should be of her husband's welfare." While Mr. Karch tolerated this conduct for many years he eventually left his home in 1911 "because of her lack of interest in him and her nagging and scolding," particularly over monetary matters. The court's ambivalent attitude was clearly indicated in the judge's conduct of the case and in his decision.

At the trial I urged the parties to make a further effort to bring their differences to an end, so that the home should not in any sense be broken up, and I intimated that I would withhold judgement for a time to see if they could effect a reconciliation. I have not heard that this has been accomplished. The case is an unfortunate one, happening as it does between people possessed of all the possibilities of making a comfortable home.

The wife had done nothing to abrogate her right to support payments, and in the separation she was awarded alimony of five dollars weekly. At the same time the judge made clear his assessment that the fault in this marriage breakdown lay largely with the wife, to whom he recommended a "self-examination . . . [of] her own behaviour." "I do not think that this is a case where great liberality should be displayed in making her an allowance," he commented, and then went on to award to the husband both custody of the two children and possession of the marital home.[47]

The courts of the land were thus very much involved in applying and in reacting to the attitudes and values articulated by the social reformers. The sanctity of the marital contract and the incumbent responsibilities were repeatedly upheld, as for example in the refusal to recognize foreign divorce decrees or in the refusal to claim jurisdiction in annulment.[48] The question of whether a spouse was willing to resume cohabitation in the marital domicile was frequently a critical test in awarding alimony.[49] Desertion or adultery or some other form of unacceptable conduct could be ground for denial of important rights, such as dower rights.[50] At the same time there seems to have been a rising tendency in the courts, in the years leading up to World War I, to define laws and procedural or evidential rules in such a way that conviction for sexually related criminal offences became easier.[51]

This activity by the courts was parallelled by increased attention elsewhere. The arrest and conviction rates for crimes involving marital or sexual misconduct were rising steadily throughout the period; in many cases the conviction rate was outstripping the increase in arrests and the overall rate of population growth. Much of this increase can be explained by two factors. First, the courts and Parliament by widening the law had facilitated prosecution. Second, public concern and a stronger articulation of public standards of morality were becoming more evident, as reflected in social gospel and moral reform movements of the time. When one examines the reported criminal statistics in detail, this factor becomes more apparent, as the geographical incidence of charges laid is so consistently disproportionate that cultural values and perceptions must be used to help explain the distribution.[52] Similarly, a recent study of prostitution in Calgary found in the immediate prewar year a distinct increase in public concern and police action aimed at removal from the city both of the prostitutes themselves and of those who made use of their services.[53] Thus it was that the courts, police forces, and public attitudes all combined to create a more punitive environment regarding offences against marriage and sexual morality.

Not only did punishment of extra-marital sexual activity become more severe and more certain, but in the courts and elsewhere there was a general sense that more basic problems were even more crucial. Marriage was believed to be in trouble; the home was in need of protection. "A true home," asserted a Methodist report, "is the result of two spirits blending and becoming one. It is a spiritual union rather than otherwise. The Christian home is an atmosphere."[54] That atmosphere was perceived by many observers to be threatened by a variety of problems, for which there were several convenient symbols. Late in 1911 the Ontario Woman's Christian Temperance Union in convention passed a resolution attacking "Mormonism" and recommending:

> That violation of the marriage laws be made punishable under the Criminal Code and that we entreat the Legislators to so safeguard this country in all matters of marriage and Divorce that the purity & sanctity of the home may remain inviolate.[55]

Given the fact that Mormon practices of "plural marriage" had been specifically prohibited within the Criminal Code as early as 1892 (section 278), what these women and others like them seem really to have wanted was a reassertion of the basic values and practices associated with marriage and the home. The defensive attitude regarding the home which the resolution displayed was widespread. Little or no attempt was made to understand marriage breakdown. Apart from occasionally mentioning immigration or specific ethnic or religious groups, no basic social factors (apart from class) were discussed, much less analysed. Instead, it was simply taken for granted that all breakdowns were wrong and sinful, destructive of the family and the home. Therefore all evils that might lead to marriage breakdown must be subject to punishment. As one Canadian purity reformer put it, " 'The White Life for two' has to be insisted upon."[56]

Canadians certainly did not ignore marriage breakdown, but they did refuse to believe that, or to consider whether, part of the problem might lie in the institution itself. Instead, influential leaders sought simply to suppress or to punish any deviations from "acceptable" practice. Canadians were able to admit that there was a problem but were unable to deal with it positively. As the incidence of marriage breakdown rose during the twentieth century, this inability to deal realistically with the problem became increasingly important. Possibly this relatively unthinking response by Canadian leaders was a reflection of the continuing sensitive character of sexuality as a topic. Repression and punishment were easy because they demanded little or no thought. Rather than seek the varied causes of marital breakdown, which would have opened up an issue with which Canadians were not yet ready to cope, they simply reinforced existing values and standards.

Not surprisingly, given the prevailing stereotypes of males and females, there was a strong sexist bias in the attitudes and legislation regarding

marriage breakdown and sexual morality. Adultery was relatively tolerated as a male vice and this was reflected in divorce legislation. While a
husband was required to prove only adultery on the part of his spouse, a
wife had to prove both adultery and either desertion or cruelty. In other
areas of law as well, men were seen to be the more sinful element, and the
criminal statistics appeared to bear out and reflect such a perception.
Desertion was more often than not referred to as "wife desertion"; the
Criminal Code punished husbands who neglected their families, but not
wives. Physical abuse of wives was punishable in law, but the possibility of
physical abuse of husbands was a matter for joking in the House of
Commons.[57] The result was that complaints and legislation tended to deal
with causes as they related to males and results as they related to females.
The consequent imbalance in concern and awareness was entrenched in law
and attitudes.

As well, there was a distinct class bias to the perceptions and legislation
dealing with marriage breakdown. Desertion and non-support were attacked
so vigorously because they were felt to be particularly prevalent among the
lower class. Workers, it was feared, had not fully accepted such middle class
concepts as familial responsibility and husband-as-breadwinner. It was therefore necessary to employ the broader powers of the state to impose these concepts. Similarly, some of the legislation reflected class bias. In most of
Canada, divorce was available only for the upper strata of society; legal dissolution of marriages remained unavailable to the lower strata that could not be
trusted to use such a "privilege" wisely. Another example of such class distinctions was the debate over seduction of female domestics.

The movement to defend marriage and sexual morality originated as a
response among the increasingly assertive middle class to the social and economic turmoil and disruption of the late nineteenth and early twentieth centuries, when so much of what was valued in society seemed to be threatened.
In particular, that central institution of civilization, the family, was felt to be
in jeopardy. Spokesmen for the middle class articulated traditional values
regarding the family and morality, using a new vehicle (or at least an existing
vehicle in a relatively new way)—the state—to enforce and entrench those
values. The movement was similar, for example, to prohibition, which by the
end of the nineteenth century had moved from temperance to total abstinence and which now sought to employ the power of the state much more
forcefully. No longer could the ideals of marriage or sexual morality or sobri-
ety be left simply as ideals. Instead, an articulate and aggressive middle class,
making use of new-found experts such as J. J. Kelso or J. H. T. Falk, set out to
assert and enforce through the power of the state the values felt to be essential if modern society were to cope successfully with the new forces and
problems that it faced. The evidence suggests not only that the movement to
defend marriage and sexual morality was successful in strengthening the
law, but also that the police forces and the courts responded positively to the
new laws and the basic values and ideals therein. The defence of marriage
and sexual morality in the period 1890–1914 went hand in hand with such
child-centred reform movements as those associated with public health, juve-

nile courts, children's aid, and "new" education. All were part of a massive thrust to stabilize and strengthen the institution of the family.

NOTES

1. N. Sutherland, *Children in English-Canadian Society* (Toronto: University of Toronto Press, 1976); T. R. Morrison, "The Child and Urban Social Reform in Late Nineteenth Century Ontario" (Ph.D. diss., University of Toronto, 1971); A. Jones and L. Rutman, *In the Children's Aid: J. J. Kelso and Child Welfare in Ontario* (Toronto: University of Toronto Press, 1980).

2. M. T. Connelly, *The Response to Prostitution in the Progressive Era* (Chapel Hill: University of North Carolina Press, 1980), 6–10.

3. The annual number of divorces is listed in the *Canada Year Book 1921* (Ottawa: Dominion Bureau of Statistics, 1922), 825. By way of contrast the Canadian population as a whole increased by 11.1 percent in 1891–1901 and 34.1 percent for 1901–11.

4. Public Archives of Canada (hereinafter PAC), Records of the Department of Justice, Central Registry Files, RG 13, A 2, vol. 178, p. 514, S. C. Leet to C. J. Doherty, Montreal, 16 March 1912; ibid., statistics of the Children's Aid Society of Winnipeg, 1903–12.

5. See, for example, C. S. Clark, *Of Toronto the Good* (Montreal, 1898).

6. PAC, Sir Charles Hibbert Tupper Papers, MG 27, I D 16, vol. 16, p. 7725, Tupper to W. Hull, (n.p.), 8 April 1896.

7. Canada, Parliament, *House of Commons Debates* (hereafter *Commons Debates*) 54, 1 (1901): 1422–23. See also *Commons Debates* 58, 1 (1903): 573–74.

8. PAC, Sir Wilfrid Laurier Papers, MG 26 G, vol. 5, pp. 1576–80, J. R. Gowan to Laurier, Barrie, Ont., 28 March 1903 (PAC reel C-799).

9. *Commons Debates*, 72, 4 (1905): 6276, 6283, 6347–49, 6357; 76, 3 (1906): 5447–52, 6043; 102, 5 (1910–11): 8977–78.

10. See, for example, *Canada Law Journal* 42 (1906), 56, 259; *Commons Debates*, 72, 4 (1905); 6279, 7623–24, 6364; 92, 4 (1909): 6071–73; 102, 5 (1910–11): 8971–73.

11. Ibid., 54, 1 (1901): 1421–22; 58, 1 (1903): 575; *Canada Law Journal* 35 (1899): 530–31.

12. L. Cobon, "The Senate's Select Committee on Divorce, 1888–1914: An Unintentionally Progressive Body" (Honours Thesis, University of Guelph, 1982), 31.

13. *Canada Law Journal* 32 (1896): 139–41, 319–22; *Watts v. Watts, Appeal Cases* (1908): 573–79. Judicial divorce was commonly considered to be a process permitting more divorces; it is thus possible to see the challenge to the Court's jurisdiction as a move to restrict the number of divorces.

14. R. C. Macleod, "The Shaping of Canadian Criminal Law, 1892 to 1902," Canadian Historical Association *Historical Papers* (1978), 64–75. In this and several other respects the reform discussed in this article follows the pattern of "coercive reform" suggested in J. R. Gusfield, *Symbolic Crusade* (Urbana: University of Illinois Press, 1963).

15. D. A. Watt, "The Canadian Law for the Protection of Women and Girls, with Suggestions for Its Amendment and for a General Code" in *The National Purity Congress: Its Papers, Addresses and Portraits*, ed. A. M. Powell (New York: American Purity Alliance, 1896), 437.

16. G. Parker, "The Origins of the Canadian Criminal Code" in *Essays in the History of Canadian Law*, ed. D. H. Flaherty (Toronto: University of Toronto Press, 1981), 268.

17. In re Criminal Code Sections relating to Bigamy, *Supreme Court Reports* 27 (1897): 481. See also *Canada Law Journal* 37 (1901): 805; Canada, *Statutes*, 6364 Victoria, c. 46, s. 3; PAC, RG 13, A 2, vol. 169, p. 1362.

18. Extra-legal marriage is defined here as a man and woman living together as though they were married but without actually having gone through a legal form of marriage.

19. Canada, *Revised Statutes*, 1906, c. 146, s. 310 (b); PAC, RG 13, A 2, vol. 160, p. 303; vol. 1920, p. 348.

20. Various archival collections of government ministries, officials, and representatives contain a large number of letters from a wide variety of Canadians seeking dissolution of their marriage or permission to remarry. I refer to these as unofficial divorce petitions.

21. PAC, RG 13, A 2, vol. 157, p. 1330, Rev. F. C. Walling to F. R. Lalor, Cayuga, Ontario, 8 Nov. 1909.

22. Ibid., vol. 150, p. 204, Rev. S. C. Murray to the Minister of Justice, Port Arthur, Ontario, 30 Jan. 1908; *Commons Debates* 111, 5 (1912–13), 10073.

23. PAC, RG 13, A 2, vol. 1915, p. 892, Rev. F. J. Clarke to the Minister of Justice, Cardova, Ont., 16 June 1908.

24. Ibid., vol. 130, p. 185; vol. 150, p. 204; vol. 157, p. 1330; vol. 160, p. 303; vol. 1920, p. 348; PAC, Laurier Papers, vol. 593, pp. 160902–3 (PAC reel C-881), Rev. S. D. Chown to Laurier, Toronto, 14 Oct. 1909; vol. 598, pp. 162111–12, 162183–85, 162257–58 (reel C-882); vol. 599, pp. 162517–18, 162522–23, 162665 (reel C-883). The involvement of temperance-related organizations is natural, given their long-standing emphasis on alcoholism's negative impact on the family.

25. PAC, RG 13, A 2, vol. 130, p. 185, C. W. Colter to C. Fitzpatrick, Cayuga, Ont., 19 Feb. 1904.

26. See also ibid., vol. 179, p. 729.

27. Canada, *Statutes*, 8–9 Edward VII, c. 9, s. 2; ibid., 10–11 George V, c. 43, s. 18; ibid., 3–4 George V, c. 13, ss. 9–13. Punishment of an inmate or habitual frequenter of a common bawdy house had been defeated in 1903; see *Commons Debates* LX, 3 (1903): 7490. Also reflective of the rising concern regarding prostitution was that the annual criminal statistics in 1910 began to record the charges and convictions for procuration and that immigration authorities were trying to deport landed immigrants who had been convicted of being an inmate of a disorderly house; see Re Margaret Murphy, *Canadian Criminal Cases* 17 (1910): 103–107.

28. Rev. J. G. Shearer, "The Canadian Crusade" in *Fighting the Traffic in Young Girls*, ed. E.A. Bell (Chicago: National Bible House, 1911), 356.

29. Canada, *Statutes*, 63–64 Victoria, c. 46, s. 3 (regarding ss. 183A, 186A, 187, and 189).

30. Ontario, *Revised Statutes*, 1887, c. 58; Manitoba, *Statutes*, 55 Victoria, c. 43; Alberta, *Consolidated Ordinances*, 1915, c. 117; Saskatchewan, *Revised Statutes*, 1909, c. 139; Prince Edward Island, *Statutes*, 58 Victoria, c. 5.

31. Canada, Statutes, 63–64 Victoria, c. 46, s. 3; Commons Debates, 42, 2 (1896): 6499–500.

32. Ibid., 46, 1 (1898): 2886–87; 52, 2 (1900): 6321–22; 111, 5 (1912–13): 10072, and 6 (1912–13): 11605–07, 12138; Canada Parliament, *Senate Debates*, 1913: 1003–04. The House of Commons alone did pass such a change in 1913; the clause, dropping all restriction as to specific places of work, eventually passed into law in 1920 (Canada, *Statutes*, 10–11 George V, c. 43, s. 5).

33. Other sorts of state coercion were also developed at this time and in this regard. Among the grounds for which film censors of the four western provinces agreed in 1919 that movies should be condemned was:

"Scenes showing men and women living together without marriage, and in adultery." (See D. F. Bocking, "Saskatchewan Board of Film Censors, 1910–1935," *Saskatchewan History* 24 (1971): 59).

34. Canada, *Revised Statutes*, 1906, c. 146, s. 242; Ontario, *Statutes*, 51 Victoria, c. 23; 60 Victoria, c. 14, s. 34; R. N. Komar, "The Enforcement of Support Arrears," *Reports of Family Law*, 1st series, 19 (1975): 165–69.

35. See, for examine, The King v. Wilkes, *Canadian Criminal Cases* VI (1906): 226–31.

36. PAC, RG 13, A 2, vol. 178, p. 514: S. Arnold to A. B. Aylesworth, Toronto, Ontario, 28 October 1910, and enclosures; E. Bayly to the Minister of Justice, Toronto, 27 Jan. 1911; S. Arnold to C. J. Doherty, Toronto, 27 Nov. 1911; "Desertion and Non-Support"; and *passim*.

37. Ibid., J. H. T. Falk to F. H. Gisborne, Winnipeg, Man., 6 May 1911.

38. Canada, *Statutes*, 3–4 George V, c. 13, s. 14; *Commons Debates* 111, 5 (1912–13): 10072–73. Also, in 1911 the Ontario Deserted Wives' Maintenance Act was amended, facilitating court action and raising the maximum support to ten dollars weekly. See Ontario, *Statutes*, 1 George V, c. 34, s. 2.

39. PAC, RG 13, A 2, vol. 256, p. 307; Saskatchewan, *Revised Statutes*, 1920, c. 154; British Columbia, *Statutes*, 1 Edward VII, c. 18; Komar, "Enforcement," 168.

40. Calculated from Canada, Department of Trade and Commerce, "Criminal Statistics, 1912–1915," Appendix to the *Report of the Minister of Trade and Commerce* (Ottawa: King's Printer, 1913–16).

41. PAC, RG 13, A 2, vol. 178, p. 514; vol. 256, p. 307.

42. Ibid., vol. 152, p. 833, Rev. R. H. Murray to A. B. Aylesworth, Halifax, N. S., 2 June 1908; *Commons Debates* 89, 1 (1909): 561–70; Canada, *Statutes*, 8–9 Edward VII, c. 9, s. 2; Ontario, *Statutes*, 60 Victoria, c. 14, s. 34. See also PAC, RG 13, A 2, vol. 169, p. 1362; University of Western Ontario, D. Mills Papers, box 4287, Letterbook II (1898–99), p. 451, J. D. Clarke to M. Marshall (Secretary, Society for the Protection of Women and Children, Montreal), (n.p.), 21 Jan. 1899.

43. A. McLaren, "Birth Control and Abortion in Canada, 1870–1920," *Canadian Historical Review* 59 (1978): 319–40; J. M. Bliss, " 'Pure Books on Avoided Subjects': Pre-Freudian Sexual Ideas in Canada," Canadian Historical Association, *Historical Papers* (1970): 89–108.

44. Ibid., 105–107; Toronto District Woman's Christian Temperance Union, *Reports and Directories*, 1895–96 to 1914–15; Rev. C. W. Watch, "Social Purity Work in Canada" in Powell, *Purity Congress*, 272–78; Watt, "Protection of Women," ibid., 437–51; J. C. Burnham, "The Progressive Era Revolution in American Attitudes toward Sex," *Journal of American History* 59 (1972–73): 885–908; D. J. Pivar, *Purity Crusade: Sexual Morality and Social Control, 1868–1900* (Westport: Greenwood Press, 1973).

45. Connelly, *Response to Prostitution*, 18–19.

46. H. v. H., *Canadian Criminal Cases* 6 (1902): 163–66. cf. Moon v. Moon, *Dominion Law Reports* 6 (1912): 46–47.

47. Karch v. Karch, *Dominion Law Reports* 4 (1912): 250–52.

48. See, for example, Prowd v. Spence, *Dominion Law Reports* 10 (1913): 215–16; Re Chisholm, *Dominion Law Reports* 135 (1913): 811–13; The King v. Woods, *Canadian Criminal Cases* 75 (1903): 226–39.

49. See, for example: Karch v. Karch, *Dominion Law Reports* 4 (1912): 250–52; Standall v. Standall, *Dominion Law Reports* 7 (1912): 671–74; Ney v.

Ney, *Dominion Law Reports* 11 (1913): 100–104; Brizard v. Brizard, *Dominion Law Reports* 16 (1914): 55–60.

50. See, for example, Re Auger, *Dominion Law Reports* 5 (1912): 680–86; Re S., *Dominion Law Reports* 3 (1912): 896; Ney v. Ney, *Dominion Law Reports* 11 (1913): 100–104; Miller v. Miller, *Dominion Law Reports* 16 (1914): 557–58.

51. It would be interesting to know whether the terms of conviction became any harsher at the same time. See T. L. Chapman, "Sexual Deviation in British Columbia: A Study of Offences Against Morality and Chastity, 1890–1920" (Paper presented at the B.C. Studies Conference, Simon Fraser University, Oct. 1981).

52. For non-support over the fifteen years, 1900–1914, Ontario accounted for fully 80.7 percent of the charges laid and York County (including Toronto) alone for 51 percent of the national total; by contrast, the province of Quebec accounted for 8.2 percent and Montreal for 3 percent. In the case of indecent assault, 55.4 percent of the total charges were laid in Ontario (17 percent in York County) while 10 percent were laid in Quebec (3.4 percent in Montreal).

53. J. Bedford, "Prostitution in Calgary 1905–1914," *Alberta History* 29 (1981): 1–11.

54. Methodist Church of Canada, Department of Temperance and Moral Reform, *Principles, Problems, Programme in Moral and Social Reform* (n.p., 1911), 35.

55. PAC, RG 13, A 2, vol. 169, p. 1362. The annual reports of the Methodist Church's Department of Temperance and Moral Reform echoed in these years the concern that Mormon teachings and practice of polygamy "have become a menace to Canada and Canadians"; see *Principles, Problems, Programme*, 38.

56. Watch, "Social Purity Work in Canada," 278.

57. *Commons Debates* 89, 1 (1909): 565–67. Similarly, it was held in Alberta that only females could be convicted of being inmates of bawdy houses; see The King v. Knowles, *Canadian Criminal Cases* 21 (1913): 321–22.

FAMILY ALLOWANCES AND FAMILY AUTONOMY: QUEBEC FAMILIES ENCOUNTER THE WELFARE STATE, 1945–1955 *

DOMINIQUE JEAN

O

Among the many transformations affecting Western families during the twentieth century, historians agree that the advent of the welfare state is of major importance. Yet the impact of new social policies has been difficult to isolate from the general movement towards a better standard of living or from the changing demands of the economy upon families. This paper seeks to assess the impact of one major policy of the postwar welfare state— family allowances—on the economic and social autonomy of Canadian families. It is based largely on analysis of the rich array of documents existing in the archives of the government departments in charge of implementing the program. These allow a reconstitution of the process of policy formation, shed some light on the diverse interests involved, and allow a critical reading

* I am grateful for financial assistance from the Social Sciences and Humanities Research Council of Canada and the Graduate Studies Faculty of l'Université de Montréal in the preparation of this paper. I would like to thank Bettina Bradbury for her direction and Nicole Neatby and Harold Benenson for their comments and suggestions. Help was offered by Bennett McCardle and Sheila Pawl of the Federal archives, National Archives of Canada, by John Taylor of the Department of National Health and Welfare Library, by Pierre Ostiguy of the Official publications section, Canadian National Library and by John McCann, responsible for the enforcement of the Access to Information Act of the Income Security Programs, Health and Welfare Canada. Earlier versions of this paper were presented at the Social Science History Association 1987 Meeting and at the "Séminaires libres" of the History department of l'Université de Montréal. The conclusions of this piece are now part of my Ph.D. thesis, "Familles québécoises et politiques sociales touchant les enfants, de 1940 à 1960: obligation scolaire, allocations familiales et travail juvénile" (Université de Montréal, 1988).

of the declared intentions of politicians. Furthermore, studies conducted by the agents of the welfare state combined with written exchanges between the state and its "clients" allow us to describe the enforcement of welfare measures and to assess the economic and political impact of the program on Canadian families.

The study of the family allowances inaugurated in 1945 offers an interesting window into the history of Canadian families and their relation with the welfare state, because they were the first universal measure of social security in the country. On one hand, state agents and social workers were particularly curious about the impact of such a novelty, so they undertook many investigations of the impact and the use made of the allowances. On the other hand, families were especially conscious of this new intervention of the state in their lives. The first part of this paper outlines the major goals articulated by politicians and the various social groups that promoted family allowances. The second part focusses on the ideology of the family that pervaded the program. Next, I analyse the educational campaign, which was the main public tool of intervention in family consumption patterns, and contrast these intentions with the program's effects on the incomes and expenditure patterns of rural and urban families. Finally, I describe the struggle for the indexation of allowances, an episode that helps to explain family practices and the political leverage of poor clients of the welfare state. The first sections of the paper address Canada as a whole, while the discussion of the effects of family allowances on families focusses on the province of Quebec.

WHY WERE FAMILY ALLOWANCES ENACTED IN 1944?

A convergence of factors prompted the passage of family allowances legislation in Canada at the end of the Second World War. While Canadian scholars still debate their relative importance, they agree on four major influences. First, there were immediate political objectives. The approach of a federal election hastened the Liberal government's adoption of this politically potent policy. During the war years many proposals for comprehensive social security had been drafted in Canada, and their endorsement by the CCF considerably threatened the Liberal government. By launching the program just before the elections, the government could send money into 1 400 000 households, thus proving that it sought to avoid the return of harsh prewar economic conditions. Mackenzie King could also remain vague as to the adoption of other measures popularized by the *Report on Social Security for Canada* of 1943, particularly health insurance and a comprehensive employment policy. This strategy placed the opposition Conservatives, in the difficult situation of denouncing the electioneering character of the measure while voting unanimously in favour of it.[1]

Politicians also expected the program to reinforce the popularity of the federal state among citizens, particularly in post-conscription Quebec. Cheques and educational pamphlets repeatedly reminded beneficiaries that "Family allowances are paid by the federal government."[2] At the same time, the allowances program was one of the many means by which the federal government tried to widen its jurisdiction. By making family allowances non-contributory, Mackenzie King used federal spending power to circumvent the provincial responsibility for welfare. The program, once implemented, gave the prime minister strong bargaining power in postwar federal–provincial meetings. He justified his proposal of federal appropriation of income taxes by citing the costs of national public welfare programs. Quebec Premier, Maurice Duplessis, a promoter of provincial autonomy, fully appreciated the threat of centralization brought by federal family allowances. However, his opposition was launched too late and soon decreased as the political danger of fighting such a popular measure became clear.[3]

A source of conflict between French and English MPs was the decreasing size of the benefits after the fourth child, a feature unique in the history of family allowances. French-Canadian MPs were especially anxious to enhance the links between family allowances and fertility, which had already been suggested in the 1931 census monograph on the family. They relied on two decades of Catholic campaigns for family allowances in the name of the *"famille nombreuse."* This made it easy for English Canadians to accuse Mackenzie King of paying "baby bonuses" to the French-speaking electorate. To prevent the debate over family allowances from dividing along ethnic lines, the government reduced the allowance paid after the fourth child. Yet, perhaps in the face of declining fertility rates in Quebec and the widespread satisfaction with the program, objections to equal allowances for all children did not last long. The decreasing rate was abandoned in 1949 without any debate.[4]

A second goal of family allowances was to stimulate the postwar Canadian economy. The government wanted to avoid an unemployment and production backlash similar to the postwar crisis of 1919–1922. Ministers assumed that family allowances would promote consumption, fuelling a sustained demand for goods, stabilizing the national economy and preventing the national revenue from dropping. Giving families money to spend for clothes, shoes and food for their children would stimulate the most vulnerable Canadian enterprises, especially factories that had been fully mobilized for soldiers' needs during the war. Certainly the program responded to requests of the Canadian Manufacturers Association to increase citizens' purchasing power. In this way, family allowances would indirectly contribute to raising the level of employment.[5]

The promoters of family allowances promised additional economic advantages. They would free other social programs from the dilemma of having to adjust rates to family size and would ensure a regular income for children, independent of fluctuations in a father's earnings.[6] This was all the more important since other contemporary reforms concerning children, including compulsory schooling in Quebec and new limitations on child labour conflicted with the working-class practice of supplementing a father's wage through children's earnings.[7]

From the government's point of view, the allowances also appeared to solve the problem of inadequate wages for urban workers, especially those with large families. In Quebec, many members of the Catholic Church had long proposed family allowances, both because of their advantages for large families and their concordance with the concept of a "fair wage" elaborated in the encyclicals *Rerum Novarum* (1891) and *Quadragesimo Anno* (1931).[8] Most Canadian unions, in contrast, opposed allowances, fearing they would allow employers to maintain salaries below the level necessary to raise a family.[9] Indeed, during the war a committee of the National Labour Board had investigated industrial conflicts and had suggested the introduction of family allowances as a way of maintaining low salaries. Prime Minister Mackenzie King clearly had this advantage in mind. In public, however, he preferred to argue that allowances could provide workers with the material base for greater negotiating power.[10]

Family allowances, according to at least some liberal rhetoric, represented "a step towards the eradication of misery and fear."[11] Some liberal MPs proclaimed that the number of children in families was the major cause of poverty. For Minister of National Health and Welfare Brooke Claxton, the size of families was the primary cause of want:

> The greatest single factor in creating differences between one family in Montreal and another family in Montreal—or even between one family in Montreal and one family in Toronto—is neither their wages nor their health; it is the number of their children. Taken by and large across the great bulk of the population, nothing so much affects the relative economic position of the family than the number of their children. This is why this measure is introduced at this time; it is an endeavour to correct that disparity by attempting, in part of course, to bridge the gap between wages and the number of children.[12]

The allowances could provide a minimum of welfare to everybody, "equal advantages in the battle of life," in the words of the 1944 speech from the throne.[13] In doing so they would ease the economic pressure of raising a family so that children, all too often seen as a burden—would instead become a source of pleasure.[14]

In 1945, politicians had to answer the mood of a hopeful electorate for whom the idea of universality was becoming popular, thanks to the sense of community generated by the war effort and the campaigns for a "social minimum," "social security," and "freedom from want" that were then being launched in many Western societies. Until 1945, Canada had never embarked on a universal program of assistance. Relief programs to the poor had required investigation of the recipients' need. The old-age pension scheme of 1927 was a means-tested measure. So were the numerous provincial relief schemes of the Depression, which had been partly funded by the federal government, and the various provincial programs of allowances for needy mothers.[15]

The third purpose, a concern for children's welfare, combined with these political and economic goals to shape the family allowances policy. The program addressed families as agents of social reproduction who had to be maintained and encouraged, in part to ensure defence and an adequate labour force. Social surveys conducted during the Depression and medical examinations of soldiers during the war had awakened the authorities to the poor physical condition of young people. In 1942 the armed forces had rejected 28 percent of volunteers and conscripts because of their physical unsuitability. Two years later, the proportion had risen to 52 percent.[16] The government expressed its concern clearly: Canada's three and a half million children were the most important component of the country's future wealth. The Liberals compared state intervention through family allowances to the more generally accepted subsidies to private enterprises. Only a few conservative thinkers denounced this equation of children with human capital. To Montreal economist François-Albert Angers, it was nothing less than fascism.[17]

The fourth immediate purpose of the government in launching family allowances was to promote the return of married women workers to their homes after the war. Early in the conflict, the government had attempted to attract married women into the labour market. The proportion of wives in the female labour force increased from 10 percent in 1939 to 35 percent in 1944. But the cabinet feared that returning soldiers would glut the labour market. By stressing the importance of their domestic role, the government not only encouraged married women to leave the labour force, it also appeared to meet the demands of feminists and reformers for recognition of women's domestic labour. Indeed, Paul Martin stated that family allowances were "a long overdue tribute to the mothers of Canada."[18] But payment to mothers was a matter of some contention, especially in Quebec where it was opposed by the conservative elite. A group of social scientists, asked by the provincial government in 1944 to write a report on the desirability of allowances in Quebec, had proposed to send the cheque to both parents, to acknowledge both the patriarchal character of the Quebec Civil Code and the democratic evolution of families. But the feminist leader of the struggle for the cheque in the name of the mother, Thérèse Casgrain, recalled that she "knew perfectly well that by tacit agreement it was generally the wife who handled the family budget." She was backed in her victorious fight by the Catholic Union of Agricultural Producers and the Canadian and Catholic Confederation of Labour.[19]

In sum, the Liberal cabinet invested family allowances with all the expectations generated by larger reconstruction schemes popular during the war. Not only were the allowances to help families with children, they were supposed to maintain a high level of employment in the country and enhance the health of its citizens. The program was launched with the promise of ensuring equality of opportunity for all children and of freeing Canadians from a major cause of poverty.

THE THIN LINE BETWEEN PROMOTING FAMILY AUTONOMY AND SUPERVISING FAMILY SPENDING

Beyond these immediate economic, political, and demographic objectives, politicians harboured ideals of family life that shaped the content of family allowances legislation. By attempting to solve the problem of poverty with family allowances, the government placed families at the centre of its welfare interventions. The family, according to King's speech from the throne, was the basis of national life, and children within it were entitled to a minimum of welfare. When the material basis to which families were entitled was threatened by an economic system in which most depended on salaries to survive, the state had a responsibility to help. King affirmed that "if it is want that has been brought about through no fault of the individual himself, but because of an existing industrial system, which the state permits to exist, then that want should be met in some way by the agency of the state itself."[20] In Canada, as in many other Western countries, increased consciousness of the family problems posed by dependence on wages was crucial in the development of a more active welfare state.[21]

Yet most politicians still believed strongly in individual responsibility. The debate over what form allowances were to take highlighted the conflicting visions about individual and state responsibilities. Conservatives questioned the wisdom of making cash payments to families, arguing that because the government could not be assured that these benefits would be spent for the welfare of children, the money would be better used for the improvement of welfare services to children.

Liberal MPs insisted that families were a better agency to take care of children than any services the federal government could fund. To prove that parents were dependable, these politicians invoked, among other things, maternal instinct, parental love, and scientific studies of the quality of nutrition per level of income. They argued that mothers had proven their reliability during the war mobilization on the home front and by their good management of federal allocations to soldiers' dependants.[22] Such reasoning was in line with the spirit of the Marsh Report, which had stated that:

> Canadians believe not only in the family, but in a strong measure of individuality. There must be reasonable leeway for parents' decision in the expenditure of the budget for their children. It is an impossible situation to imagine that all guidance and all services should be provided by non-family authorities. The virtue of a standard endowment of benefit in cash is that it becomes part of the normal family income, which is left to the parent to expend.[23]

Similarly, in 1944 in Quebec, the report on allowances prepared by social scientists for the short-lived Liberal government of Adélard Godbout, had supported payments in cash because they fostered initiative and upheld the superiority of family services to children over state services.[24]

By promoting cash payments, Liberal MPs could argue that their confidence in parents' autonomy was greater than that of their opponents. They used the same weapon to dismiss Conservative MPs suggestions of allowances in kind. Liberals proclaimed that they meant to break away from such degrading practices. According to Brooke Claxton, choosing payments in kind would involve

> going back to such set-up as was adopted by a former administration during the worst period of the depression. It led to every kind

of effort to get around the regulations; it reduced the self-respect of the recipients; it was a reversion to the days when the rich man took a basket of necessaries to the poorer people in his city. . . . [This] will not be accepted by the people in Canada."[25]

Yet there were real limits to the Liberals' professed confidence in parents' sense of responsibility for the welfare of their children. Promoters of allowances believed that parents had to assume some of the economic responsibility for their offspring. Thus, rates of allowances were set at a level under the actual cost of raising children. During the war the government estimated this cost at $14 to $20 a month per child in Canadian urban areas, but the actual family allowances ranged from $6 to $9 according to the child's age.[26] Higher payments, the government thought, might deter parents from working or, worse, encourage procreation "for gain." One reassured civil servant proclaimed that the low purchasing power of the monthly cheque would ensure production of children for "pleasure, rather than profit."[27]

Although ministers had argued against too much supervision of family spending, they did want to ensure that allowances were spent for their intended purpose. Even CCF members such as House Leader J.W. Colwell, admitted the necessity of accounting for the effects of public spending and of ensuring that the allowances would be used for food, clothes, and other important items.[28] In this they were supported by the Canadian Council of Welfare for whom supervision constituted the condition of success of family allowances.[29] Similarly, Brooke Claxton declared that "it is not enough just to pay this money out"; the government had to convince parents "to spend it in the best possible way for the benefit of their children."[30] To that end, the law specified that parents had to spend these sums exclusively for their children, and it allowed the minister and his department to stop payments in cases of misuse.[31] In order to monitor the efficiency of the program, the government initiated a series of studies into the uses people made of their allowances.[32]

Most MPs saw education as the most acceptable way of ensuring that the allowances were spent for the welfare of children. For Liberals, publicity was a preventive measure. Educational material sent with the monthly cheque would influence parents who were, in their view, not ill-intentioned but ill-informed. Middle-class women's groups had long emphasized the advantages of a campaign of education aimed at poor mothers, and many commented on the benefits of sending educational literature along with cheques.[33] Conservative MP, Ellen Louks Fairclough's description of working-class families is typical of the faith placed in education:

Today, there are families living in two and three rooms in many municipalities in this country. Under the conditions which prevail in housing, they are living in quarters in which there is no adequate provision for food storage so it is necessary for them to live from hand to mouth. . . . Owing to this situation, the money which is going into these homes, ostensibly for the care of these children, is being spent on the most expensive type of food that the home-maker can buy. It is being spent on that food because, in many instances, the mother of the family does not realize there is a better way in which to spend that money.[34]

The 1944 Quebec report on family allowances also stressed the neces-sity of popular education, as did many social workers. Montreal business-man Gérard Parizeau even suggested that the church join the government in the educational campaign.[35]

Some Liberal MPs showed a lack of confidence in parents' spending habits, not unlike the mistrust displayed by Conservative proponents of payment in services. Manitoba Liberal J.P. Howden, for instance, warned his colleagues that a family might save the money while depriving children of necessary goods. In the end, the law would reflect this element of mis-trust. When misuse was suspected, officials could investigate families. Conservative MP Gordon Graydon pointed in vain to the contradiction between this clause and Liberals' statements about family autonomy over expenses. The conservative economist François-Albert Angers also opposed investigation in the name of the very principle of family independence the Liberals had defended during the debate over cash payments. Angers saw no more reason to tell parents how to spend their allowances than to tell them how to spend their salaries.[36]

The government's mistrust was the product of many biases, which quickly compromised the initial message of universality. Opposition MPs were quick to point out that rich families had not been subjected to such public scrutiny when tax deductions for children were established in 1919. King's answer was that rich citizens who paid income taxes deserved more privileges than citizens who did not. Suspicion was directed more at poor fathers than poor mothers. One reason for promoting payment of the allowances to the mother was to keep the money out of the hands of unem-ployed or drinking husbands. When it came to native parents, politicians showed their lack of confidence in a series of strict regulations. True, for selected native groups the economic autonomy of the families remained a strong government goal: family allowances entitlements could be converted into "rifles, boats and other hunting and fishing equipment . . . in these cases where a reasonably large credit has accumulated. . . , thus increasing the capacity of self-reliance." Administrators of family allowances and at the Department of Indian Affairs initiated a plan whereby allowances could be used to finance up to 80 percent of the price of fishing boats. A minority of "Indians" (21 percent in 1949) and the majority of "Eskimos" received allowances in kind. Families could chose from a list of eligible items pre-pared in collaboration with the Department of Indian Affairs. Public ideals regarding the well-being of children were clearly those of mainstream, white society. The program made powdered milk and cereals for babies semi-mandatory and gradually introduced other nutritive foods, and, later, children's clothing.[37]

In summary, new parameters were to shape the relationship between the state and families over the welfare of children. Cash payments symbolized the end of a particularly degrading form of relief. Universal allowances also marked the advent of a type of assistance that was not means tested. But the government kept some measure of control over the beneficiaries through its right to suspend misused payments and through the promotion of specific forms of spending. Only a close study of the reality of such aspects of the program can help to evaluate the extent of government control and whether the anti-poverty goals of the legislators were realistic.

THE MANY MESSAGES OF THE EDUCATIONAL CAMPAIGN

The task of devising the content of the educational campaign fell to the civil servants. Between 1945 and 1955, the Information Division of the Department of National Health and Welfare disseminated propaganda proclaiming the benefits and the desirable uses of family allowances. In the literature that arrived with their cheques parents were invited to consider images of ideal family spending patterns, roles, and attitudes promoted by their government. In both scale and means this educational campaign recalled the war propaganda on the home front. This was no coincidence. The Wartime Commission of Information contributed to the launching publicity.

In the literature makes clear that, from the bureaucrat's point of view, the main agent of the domestic economy was the mother and wife, "a wise women [who] regards housekeeping as a profession and prepares and follows plans as carefully as an engineer draws and follows his blueprints for a bridge. . . . She is not only the planner but the purchasing agent and the maintenance man." Mothering was represented as a full-time occupation, a message consistent with the government's desire to return married women workers to their homes after the war. While the distribution of power over the decisions within the family was not explicitly prescribed, husbands were depicted as sole breadwinners whose involvement with the program was limited to tasks like filling in the application form or planning long-term expenses.[38]

In keeping with the program's major concern, children were at the centre of the family activities and choices depicted in the literature. Unlike earlier pamphlets produced by Social Catholics promoting family allowances in Quebec, campaign illustrations seldom showed more than two children.[39] Spending the allowances to prolong children's education and dependency was encouraged, but parents were also advised to avoid spoiling their offspring. Giving them an allowance as they grew up or encouraging them to save for their own bicycles were presented as good ways to make them "self-reliant and responsible about money." Government officials saw this lesson as the key to the reproduction of values in a subsequent generation. Young citizens would be ready to raise progeny of their own in a responsible fashion, having themselves learned that "things have value and that dolls' carriages and baseball bats, chesterfields and motor cars do not grow on trees. . . . someone has to earn them." In this way propagandists reconciled the two roles of the family: protecting children while training them for independence.[40]

The ambivalence exhibited in pamphlets regarding the ideal way to spend allowances indicated there was some recognition of the socio-economic diversity of families. Some pamphlets seemed to address families with economic difficulties, showing "how to get the most value from the food you buy with your family allowance," how to spend the cheque wisely, or "how to get more for your money." For this group the literature emphasized "necessities" as well as occasional crucial expenses like medicine or visits to the doctor or dentist. The campaign also addressed comfortable families by promoting the investment of this "extra" money in a "fuller life": piano lessons, bicycles, sports equipment, summer camps. The dual rhetoric echoes the politicians' hesitations about the vocation of the family allowances as a "minimum" or a "supplement."[41]

The booklet *You and Your Family* made explicit the distinction between families of the "lower income brackets" and others. Another government booklet, *Speaking of Family Allowances*, portrayed three imaginary families in different socio-economic positions. It invited the reader to meet the Gagniers who used their allowances for vaccinations, vitamin D, skates for the son Jean, and a journey to the countryside for Suzanne, the daughter. Their neighbour, a widow by the name of Mme Leduc, needed "each cent of her son's allowance; when the cheque does not arrive, things become complicated." She used most of the allowances for clothes. Finally, it introduced her friends, the Sauvés. They "couldn't allocate a large part of the allowances to these things [that exclusively concern the development of children], and would preferably spend them on more milk, school supplies for the eldest girl, visits to the dentist and exceptionally on the piano lesson of their son who was gifted."[42]

Yet this occasional tendency to make a distinction between families according to their socio-economic level was more than offset by the more widespread tendency to confuse them. The government's literature emphasized budgeting and saving. All families were equally exhorted to adopt these practices, whatever the amount, whatever the period of saving. Comfortable families were warned to save for periods of illness or economic difficulty. *You and Your Family* extolled planning as a remedy for poverty:

> It may mean that you do without new shoes for another month, or that the family eat more baked beans and less meat, but somehow find the money within your means for entertainment and do not let the children do without something they really need just to make this extravagance possible.[43]

Poorer families were depicted as capable of imitating their richer neighbours' spending on matters that meant a lot to them, if "they consciously save[d] in order to do it." Similarly, the farmers' weekly, *La Terre de Chez Nous*, encouraged its readers to save the allowances. Families were already accustomed to wartime propaganda exhorting them to save. The war finished, the new objective of delayed spending for consumer goods reflected the government's preoccupation with a smooth transition towards a peacetime economy.[44]

In publishing pamphlets that tended to show all families sharing similar economic problems, civil servants of the Information Division acted as if they confused the promises of equality attached to family allowances with the realities of Canadian life. In the meantime, other branches of the Department of National Health and Welfare were conducting studies into the efficiency of the program. They were discovering unexpected levels of poverty. These studies began to paint a picture of poor families that made the educational campaign look irrelevant and that called into question the feasability of the initial objectives of family allowance legislation.

UNRAVELLING OF THE REAL IMPACT OF ALLOWANCES ON FAMILIES

When the first cheques were distributed in the summer of 1945, prognoses were still oscillating between the likes of conservative nationalist François-Albert Angers, who feared that an "esprit de lucre" would penetrate the households of the beneficiaries of family allowances, and of Communist MP Fred Rose, who sardonically predicted that beneficiaries would not deposit the cheque in a bank or spend them on luxury goods or overseas travel: "They will bring them to the store."[45] The Department of National Health and Welfare was eager to know how the money was being used, and it initiated investigations in various areas of the country. The social policy makers and high civil servants of the 1940s were influenced by the general development of social science in Canada. Even when they had not trained in social science departments themselves, they hired many prominent scholars to conduct studies of family allowances. Policy makers and civil servants hoped such studies would improve their knowledge about the Canadian family, thus increasing their own power and legitimizing Liberal intervention in family welfare with proof of the positive impact of the legislation.[46]

These surveys unexpectedly uncovered a significant proportion of Canadian families living in poverty. On the average, as predicted, the allowances represented a small part of family incomes. From 1945 to 1957, benefits amounted to $5 to $8 per child, depending on his or her age; Canadian families received an average allowance of $16.07 per month during these years. In 1945–46, the net total of payments in the province of Quebec amounted to a minimum of 3.5 percent of family income. However, these averages hid a diversity of situations. For some, the allowances brought an improvement in economic conditions. As table 1 reveals, rural families, large families, and low-income urban families saw major proportional gains in their income.[47]

TABLE 1 *FAMILY ALLOWANCES AS A PERCENTAGE OF TOTAL FAMILY INCOME*

Area	Family allowances as % of family income	Number of families in sample	Character of families in the sample
Montreal 1947[a] Families with		79	Helped by the child welfare agency of
2 children	7	(49)	South-West Montreal;
Families with			nuclear[+] with 2 or 3
3 children	12.0	(30)	children.
Montreal 1948[b]	19	30	Working-class fathers; poor ward; nuclear;
Gaspé-Nord 1945–46[c]	18	115	Diversified sources of income; nuclear; reachable by means of regular transportation.
Nicolet 1947–48[d]	16	66	Distant from large urban market, areas with francophone majority; randomly selected; derive at least half of their income from farm.
Prairies 1947[e] Northern		416	Distant from large urban market;
Saskatchewan	20		randomly selected;
West-central			derive at least half
Saskatchewan	14		of their income
West-central			from farm.
Alberta	14		
Maritimes 1947[f] Families with		114	From 1 to 5 children;
1 child	3◊		Mother, father, and
Families with			maximum of one
5 children	13◊		boarder; annual income: $650–$3000.
Income of $2800 and over	6◊		
Income between $1600 and $1999	5◊		

◊ When income tax is excluded from the income, these four proportions are lowered respectively to 0.9, 12.5, 1.6, and 6 percent.

+ In the table, "nuclear" means husband and wife present and nuclear family without the presence of extended kin.

Sources:

a R. Blishen, J. Crawley, and J.E. Pearson, "Family Allowances in Montreal; A Study of their Uses and Meaning in a Selected Group of Wage Earning Families" (M.A. thesis, McGill University, 1948), 52. The survey calculated income from "take-home pay" (i.e., salary minus income tax and other taxes).

b Thérèse Roy, "Influence économique et sociale des allocations familiales" (M.A. thesis Université de Montréal, 1948), 35.

c Thérèse Légaré, *Conditions économiques et sociales des familles de Gaspé-Nord, Québec* (Faculté des sciences sociales, Université Laval, May 1947), 129–32.

d M.A. Macnaughton and G. Lafléche, *Preliminary Report on Distribution and Use of Family Allowances Payment in Nicolet County, Québec, 1947–48* (Ottawa: Economic Division, Marketing Service, Department of Agriculture, 1936, NAC, RG 29, R233/105–13/5), 12. The "cash living expenses" considered here do not include the part of the income devoted to capital investments and repayment of debt.

e M.A. Macnaughton and J.M. Mann, *Distribution and Use of Family Allowances Payments in Three Areas of the Prairie Provinces*, supplement to M.A. Macnaughton and M.E. Andal, *Changes in Farm Family Living in Three Areas of the Prairie Provinces from 1943–43 to 1947* (Ottawa: Economic Division, Marketing Service, Department of Agriculture and Department of National Health and Welfare in co-operation with the Universities of Alberta and Saskatchewan, King's Printer, 1949, publication 815, Technical Bulletin 69), 85. The cash living expenses considered here do not include the part of the income devoted to capital investments and repayment of debt. When the whole income is considered, the proportions are lowered to 4.6 and 8 percent respectively. Areas are listed from the poorest (Saskatchewan north) to the wealthiest (Alberta centre-west).

f Derek Griffin, *Family Budgets of Wage-Earners in Four Maritime Communities, 1947* (Halifax: Institute of Public Affairs, Dalhousie University, 1952), 81, 83, 84. Only extreme cases of income and number of children were precise in the original table

The aggregated results of four studies of the effects of the program are reported in table 1 and form the basis of this section. None of the studies observed rigorous methods of sampling. To be representative, they would have had to consider family size, income level, ethnic origins, and distribution by age and sex. Yet, when interpreted with care, they clearly demonstrate the different ways in which family allowances modified the family economy and family strategies among rural families, and among poor and more comfortable urban families.[48]

To the Liberal leaders, who had believed that state help was necessary mainly to correct the inadequacies of the industrial wage system, the level of relief that family allowances brought to rural families might have come as a surprise. Families in rural areas spent most of their funds on essential goods like food and clothing, as table 2 shows. This was true in the grain-growing Prairies, in the Quebec dairy farming area of Nicolet, and in the mixed lumbering and farming area of North Gaspé. The level of relief brought to rural areas equalled that in poor urban sections. Because of the scarcity of cash income in farming households, the ideals of budget planning and delayed spending were even less attainable for rural parents than for their urban counterparts. Rural families were less likely than urban ones to save their allowances or to invest them in insurance. Rural income depended on fluctuating staples prices, which bred constant insecurity.

In some cases, the addition of new cash income could even change the working patterns of a family, bringing it closer to the nuclear ideal envisaged by the Department of National Health and Welfare. Not used to having much monetary income, farming, fishing, and lumbering families interviewed by social workers saw their cash income rise by 16 percent to 18 percent. In some areas, the regular payment lowered farmers' reliance on lumbering, if the testimony of this manager of a forestry enterprise is credible:

TABLE 2   PATTERNS OF EXPENDITURE OF FAMILY ALLOWANCES
(Percentage of Families Mentioning Each Type of Expenditure)

Sample	Clothing	Food	Education	Recreation	Insurance	Savings	Medical care	Number
Quebec City[a]	63	30	29	12	35	19	33	172
Montreal 1947[b]								
Total	89	42	——— 4 ———		19	24	39	79
Income below $1800	87	53	——— 2 ———		——— 30 ———		45	53
Income $1800 and above	92	19	——— 8 ———		——— 31 ———		27	26
Montreal 1948[c]	80	63	7			17	23	30
Gaspé-Nord[d]	62	34	10		——— 6 ———		20	115
Nicolet[e]	72	54	31		——— 26 ———		18	65
Prairies[f]								
Total	77	59	20	19		16	22	277
Northern Saskatchewan	85	71	22	22		8	23	
West-central Saskatchewan	68	72	12	16		25	28	
West-central Alberta	77	53	25	20		18	17	

Table 2 continued

Sample	Clothing	Food	Education	Recreation	Insurance	Savings	Medical care	Number
Canada[g]								
Families with 1 to 2 children	39	14	——10——		20	16	14	1749
Families with 3 to 4 children	42	24	——18——		13	8	21	
Families with more than 5 children	49	32	——23——		12	3	30	
Canada[h]	66	37	——23——		10	15	16	319

Sources:

a   Maurice Tremblay, Albert Faucher, and J.-C. Falardeau, *Family Allowances in Quebec City. Report of a Study in the Faculty of Social Sciences of Laval University*, trans. Department of National Health and Welfare (Quebec, 1951, NAC, RG 29, R233/100-63-2), 42.

b   Blishen, Cawley, and J.E. Pearson, "Family Allowances in Montreal," 64, 93. Unfortunately, results on insurance and savings are not consistent from one page to the other.

c   Roy, "Influence économique et sociale des allocations familiales," 45.

d   Légaré, *Conditions économiques et sociales des familles de Gaspé-Nord*, 133–34.

e   Macnaughton and Laflèche, *Preliminary Report on Distribution and Use of Family Allowances Payment in Nicolet County*, 10.

f   Macnaughton and Mann, *Distribution and Use of Family Allowances Payments in Three Areas of the Prairie Provinces*, 82.

g   Research Division, Department of National Health and Welfare, "The Use of Family Allowances Payments by Canadian Families" (Ottawa, unpublished), quoted by J.C. Vadakin, *Children, Poverty and Family Allowances* (New York: Basic Books, 1968), 104.

h   NAC, RG 29, 1934, R233/110/13. Results of the "Ten Families Surveys" conducted by civil servants of the regional offices of family allowances in various cities of the country. I could not get a precise idea of their methodology.

TABLE 3 PERCENTAGE DISTRIBUTION OF FAMILIES ACCORDING TO THEIR USE OF FAMILY ALLOWANCES

Area	Exclusively for children under 16	Into general family budget	Partly for children under 16, partly for other members of family	Undefined	Total	Number
Quebec City[a]	65	24	11	–	100	213
Montreal[b]						
Total	46	20	34	–	100	
Income below $1800	42	21	38	–	100	79
Income above $1800	54	19	27	–	100	53
Gaspé-Nord[c]	63	34	–	3	100	115
Nicolet[d]	33	50	5	12	100	65
Prairies[e]						
Total	38	34	24	4	100	277
Northern Saskatchewan	34	41	23	2	100	
West-central Saskatchewan	40	33	25	3	100	
West-central Alberta	40	26	26	8	100	

Table 3 continued

Area	Exclusively for children under 16	Into general family budget	Partly for children under 16, partly for other members of family	Undefined	Total	Number
Canada[f]						
Families with 1 or 2 children	43	38	19	–	100	1749
Families with 3 or 4 children	34	45	21	–	100	
Families with more than 5 children	28	46	26	–	100	

Sources:

[a] Tremblay, Faucher, and Falardeau, *Family Allowances in Quebec City*, 37.

[b] Blishen, Cawley, and Pearson, "Family Allowances in Montreal," 56.

[c] Légaré, *Conditions économiques et sociales des familles de Gaspé-Nord*, 133–34.

[d] Macnaughton and Laflèche, *Preliminary Report on Distribution and Use of Family Allowances Payment in Nicolet County*, 8.

[e] Macnaughton and Mann, *Distribution and Use of Family Allowances Payments in Three Areas of the Prairie Provinces*, 81.

[f] Research Division, Department of Health and Welfare, "The Use of Family Allowances Payments by Canadian Families," 104.

the program is interfering with the recruitment of labour. It is the practice of the Canadian lumber industry in Quebec and Ontario to hire men for logging in the northern woods for the winter season. In the past, farmers have been available for this work in their off seasons and have been willing to leave their homes to get the needed cash income. The eastern lumber industry found it difficult in the winter of 1945–46 to obtain their seasonal labour supply and believes that this is because the cash income received through the family allowances eliminated the incentive for these men to leave their families during the winter months for employment in the "bush."[49]

The use of, and perhaps the need for, child labour could similarly decrease. Family allowances pushed farming communities to send children to school, as payments were suspended when the compulsory school attendance law was not respected. They gave parents some means to dispense with child labour. When American anthropologist Horace Miner examined the rural parish of St-Denis de Kamouraska at the end of the 1940s he observed that family allowances, together with new sources of cash income, rising agricultural prices, and other government programs, had allowed farmers to buy their first agricultural machines. This had freed children from farm labour.[50] Increased cash income and the greater need for capital expenditures may explain in part why rural families were more likely to spend the allowance for the whole family than were their urban counterparts (see table 3).

Rural children clearly benefitted a good deal from family allowances. Yet the results of the program fell far short of politicians' expectations, largely because they had counted on a level of economic autonomy that was absent from many households. In the elaboration of social policies, Canadian governments had long considered that the mythical self-sufficiency of families in rural areas was available to all citizens. The Montpetit Commission, established by the Quebec government during the Depression to consider the question of social insurance, had used this argument to justify the rejection of a family allowance policy. Its rationalization had been that rural families did not need allowances and that allowances to urban parents would encourage rural depopulation.[51]

To be fair, some promoters of family allowances had taken a step away from these assumptions. A long-time promoter of the allowances, Jesuit Léon Lebel, stated in 1927 that, "one has to be blind not to realize that the majority is far from benefitting from a living standard superior to the conditions of urban workers. Only poets, now, can celebrate the charm of country living." In the House, during the debates of 1944, MP G.E. Wood had proclaimed: "I am inclined to think that this is one of the first measures in which the farmer has been permitted to share alike with urban folks." Wood hoped allowances would enable farm families to afford better and more varied diets and that increased nutrition would promote the growth of robust children. One year before, Leonard Marsh had proposed that family allowances would maintain rural families in agriculture and compensate them for their disadvantages in schooling, job placement, and health-care institutions.

Similarly, Prime Minister Mackenzie King had alluded to the lack of social services in rural areas, but he had hoped that rural families would be comfortable enough to use the allowances for more than the basic needs: "Combined with the floor under farm prices, family allowances will give real social security to rural Canadians for the first time in [their] history."[52]

In reality, family allowances were used mostly for more immediate needs. One-fifth of rural families reported using their benefits for basic medical and dental care, a proportion comparable to that among workers' families in poor sections of Montreal. Yet, in more than three-fifths of the families interviewed by Légaré in rural Gaspésie in 1946 neither the mother nor the children had ever received medical care. In 60 percent of the cases, no doctor had delivered the children. The educational literature may have improved hygiene in some families even in the absence of medical care. Mothers in Saint-Octave, a newly settled community in Gaspésie with poor medical services, began to use the government booklet *The Canadian Mother and Child*, which was advertised in the family allowances educational campaign.[53] In the Beauce region, allowances enabled mothers to afford food and medical care that was better for the health of their progeny, as their MP, Dr. Poulin, explained to the Commons:

> In the practice of my profession, in the country, I have been able to see . . . the way this money is used. Often, in my office, mothers bring their small children of every age, and ask me to examine them, even if they don't consider them to be sick, to know if there was not something they could do to better their health. After an examination, and a prescription if need be, these mothers are proud to take from their purse their family allowances cheque and to tell me that it allows them to take good care of their children.[54]

Poulin was so enthusiastic about these effects of the allowances that he suggested raising them to replace proposed public health insurance.

Allowances also permitted mothers in rural areas north of Montreal to diversify the diet of their families. One merchant reported that his clients were able for the first time to buy oranges for their children: "Yesterday, oranges were golden fruits for rich people, rare fruits that children only discovered once a year in their Christmas sock . . . if their bad behaviour had not transformed it into a potato!" These were not isolated occurrences. Social workers across Canada reported that rural children fared better as a result of improved diet.[55]

Family allowances represented the first form of public social assistance many Canadian rural families encountered. The program fulfilled many of its promises to rural children: better health, a closer family life, and a prolonged dependency. However, these improvements were far from sufficient to improve their standard of living to the level of the majority of the country. Their parents soon discovered that universality did not mean economic equality for children, or the end of poverty.

Another new clientele of the universal welfare state was the middle class. Unfortunately, the aggregate data of most of the studies don't allow for an analysis weighted by levels of income. However, examination of interviews conducted for the "Ten Families Surveys" in Montreal and Quebec City permits some economic analysis.[56]

Many well off parents came to see the program as insurance, and this was in line with the expectations of the government. They were already receiving a tax deduction for dependants, so the new program didn't have much effect on their total income. They "hesitated to apply . . . and finally decided to in case of possible sickness or unemployment." Thus, they got a monthly payment that the federal government recovered, in whole or in part, through income tax.[57]

Some wealthy parents chose not to apply to the program. Among those interviewed, several mentioned their disappointment at having to return part of the allowances in taxes; one family opposed allowances altogether on this ground. They "considere[d] Family Allowances a nuisance for families having an income over $3000.00." Journalist Jeanne Grisé-Allard of the Jesuit monthly *Relations* discovered that some middle-class parents felt embittered by the lack of consideration the federal government showed for the hardships of raising children. These parents may well have felt there was a stigma attached to accepting state benefits. Others considered their own acceptance of a universal measure a necessary step for the benefit of poorer classes, "a good reform for poor families."[58] In January 1947, the government began to encourage richer families to apply by deducting $100 of their taxable income for each child eligible for family allowances, and registrations increased accordingly.[59]

While allowances did not significantly enrich such relatively comfortable families, they could provoke a slight realignment of economic power from fathers to mothers, an unintended consequence of the government's campaign to bring mothers who had held jobs during the war back to their families. Middle-class women had more control over the allowances than over tax deductions from their husbands' incomes. The McGill enquiry discovered that as family incomes rose, so did the husband's degree of control over spending.[60] For some of these man, the transfer of power that accompanied family allowances constituted a governmental interference in their affairs. One angry father of four, earning $3491 annually, wrote to a Quebec City newspaper in 1949 challenging the right of any representative of the federal government to usurp the right of a father to decide which part of surplus salary should be dedicated to his children's advantage.[61] The divergent interests of mothers and fathers in wealthier families may explain why it was a middle-class woman, Thérèse Casgrain, who led the campaign in Quebec for the payment to the mother and why it was a group of middle-class men who opposed the idea in the name of paternal authority.

In urban areas, the allowances had the greatest impact on families where the father's income was inadequate or non-existent. The widow Leduc presented in the governmental education campaign accurately depicted a lived reality. Nineteen of the 116 families interviewed in the "Ten Families Surveys" had no father–husband breadwinner. An even larger proportion of those families benefitting from the salary of the father at the time of the enquiry had faced this situation previously when the breadwinner had been sick, unemployed, or had deserted them. In one case, the father had returned to school using the privileges offered to veterans. Like Mme Leduc, each of these families "needed every cent of the allowance. . . . " For the family of a sick inspector and a mason who was only employed periodically, allowances were sometimes the only source of income. In one-quarter of the "Ten Families Survey" sample, the federal program supplied more than a one-third of the monthly income.[62] Housekeepers described the allowances as "very welcome" for they gave "a new sense of security." In this context the program truly realized one of its goals: ensuring a minimum family income.

Family allowances were not the only welfare support available to families without a male breadwinner. But those interviewed compared the new benefit favourably with older types of help they had received, such as needy mothers' allowances and private charities. The rigid conditions surrounding needy mothers' allowances excluded many families. One woman "applied for Needy Mothers' Allowances but the uncertainty of [her husband's] illness made her ineligible. . . . Family Allowance of $24.00 was the only income of which she was certain. As she discussed a budget, the fact that she had it, and had a right to it, seemed to restore some of her self-assurance."[63] Needy mothers' allowances were too low to raise children. Thus the family allowances represented 35 percent of the income of one needy Montreal mother who had four children under sixteen.[64] Some families interviewed were receiving income benefits from contributory welfare schemes, available to the members of the most stable sectors of the work force. These included unemployment insurance for the breadwinner, or for older children, a father's private pension scheme, and a veterans' allocation. When such families had many children, family allowances made a crucial difference. One family with six children under the age of sixteen received almost $40 from the allowances, a major complement to the $60 the father was receiving in unemployment insurance. Another family with five children under sixteen lived on the monthly salary of $39 earned by one older son and the $27 family allowance cheque.

Family allowances alone were not sufficient to allow all families without a male breadwinner to attain the life promoted in the publications of the Department of National Health and Welfare. Many families without an earning father could not offer children the prolonged dependency and the constant care of a mother at home. Most relied on the work of older children or of the mother outside the home.[65] Many of these families shared their living quarters with other people, either by taking in lodgers, living in the house of the grandmother without paying rent, or living in a boardinghouse. Their domestic arrangements were often far from the ideal. An extreme example was that of the wife of a mason who worked irregularly. She was planning to move to a smaller, cheaper flat and to place her seven children in institutions. Had the McGill survey not been so restrictive in the selection of its sample, its investigators would also have met many families who took in lodgers or lived with in-laws. Nearly one-half of the 3331 families under the care of the Child Welfare Association of Montreal in 1947 (the association from which subjects were chosen) had such living arrangements.[66]

The government had predicted that allowances would help families purchase essential goods, and at least two-thirds of the families interviewed did spend their allowance on clothes. Clothing dealers were quick to grasp the opportunity. Dalfen's of Montreal advertised prices reduced by 10 percent for all goods bought with a family allowance cheque. One-tenth of the families interviewed in south-west Montreal had a department store account that was financed by the allowances. Some salespeople even scheduled their monthly collection according to the rhythm of the allowance cheques. And a few zealots among them threatened to report mothers to the government if they did not continue to buy their products. The Regional Office of family allowances countered by asking the Quebec bishops to have a letter read in every church warning the public about these tactics.[67] Increased ability to purchase clothes for children had an indirect impact on family roles. Firstly, spending for ready-made clothes relieved some mothers of domestic production, even though many still knitted and sewed new clothes or altered old ones to save money. Grandmothers, sisters, and even more fortunate neighbours could assist them in this task. Secondly, clothes could make the difference between regular and sporadic school attendance. Finally, clothes meant more than comfort. They symbolized one's economic background, often a source of shame or pride. The McGill investigation found that 37 percent of the families believed the allowances had improved the quantity or quality of their clothing.

The studies also showed that legislators' expectations of the relief allowances would bring to children in large families were too high. In such families, allowances were not sufficient to improve clothing for all members. Thérèse Roy wrote after her interviews with the wives of French-Canadian workers that in families of seven or more children it was often still impossible for mothers to provide adequate winter clothing for all the school children or even the most basic of clothes for preschoolers. She concluded her report by recommending the abolition of the decreasing rate of allowances for fifth and subsequent children. Countering the prime minister's justifications for the reduced rate, she contended that "it is difficult to believe that the clothes of the first four children can still be of use when the thirteenth and the fourteenth children are born." Clearly the political goal of muting ethnic conflict had prevailed over the socio-economic goal of alleviating poverty.[68]

Food expenditure figured second among the uses that families reported making of the allowances. Actually, the use of some or all of the allowances for food was probably greater than reported if we consider that some women may well have been ashamed of mentioning it. The food purchased was not the kind that would add surplus vitamins to the children's diet but was the essential staples of the family meal. Purchase of food was mentioned most often among the lowest income families, especially in large households.[69]

The government had not predicted that allowances would be used for rent, but one-fifth of the labourers' households studied in the eastern Montreal sample used their allowances either for rent or for repayment of debts. The regularity of the allowance income and the timing of its arrival influenced its allotment. Mothers' spending on rent showed a capacity for planning worthy of the government's propaganda. They "considered that this solution was most practical, because they were always sure to get, usually at mid-month, their cheque of family allowances from which they can immediately take out the amount of the rent." It's worth noting that the monthly allowance exceeded the cost of rent for over half the tenant families for whom the survey listed rents.

Unfortunately, this new ability to buy necessities soon diminished. Rising prices aggravated by the termination of price controls in 1947 rapidly depreciated the value of allowances. As early as 1948, only one-third of those studied in south-western Montreal believed that the quantity or quality of their diets had increased since the beginning of the program. Family allowances might cushion the spiralling cost of living, but they could not offset it. One year later, 90 percent of Montreal women interviewed by Roy testified that, while it had been possible to buy more milk, fruit, and vegetables when allowances were first initiated, at current prices mothers had to be content with diminishing quantities of these foods. In 1951, nine of the 214 families in the Quebec City study mentioned that the allowances did not even pay for milk; half found the allowance insufficient.[70] Macro statistics verify what mothers knew. While the payment levels had stayed the same, the consumer price index had risen by 55.2 percent between 1945 and 1955. The cost of clothing and food had increased even more quickly, by 74 percent and 80 percent respectively. As a result, allowances of $5 and $8 in 1955 were worth only $3.16 and $5.07 respectively in 1951 dollars. To have maintained their initial value, the government would have had to increase these payments to $8 and $13.[71]

About one-third of the urban families receiving allowances used them to pay for medical care. Medical expenditures apparently had more to do with urgent care than with the forms of prevention promoted in the educational campaign. Few parents had anticipated making this a primary use of the fund. In the "Ten Families Surveys," seven of the 116 mothers reported having had to pay for an operation; five purchased medicine or the services of a doctor or a dentist when the children fell sick; eight others used the allowances for health care of an unspecified nature. Only one family made an explicit reference to prevention—the purchase of tonics. Many doctors adjusted their fee instalments to the allowance rates.[72] This practice suggests that the new welfare measure helped stabilize the income of these professionals, many of whom had suffered during the Depression. Indeed, it may have contributed to the decrease in the approval of public health insurance among doctors after the war, yet another way in which family allowances could have delayed the adoption of universal health care in Canada.

In sum, many urban families could not use the allowances "as an extra." For them, consumption of "surplus" goods was impossible however much they tried to plan their spending.[73] The panacea promoted in the government's leaflets was beyond their reach. This does not mean that poorer families were unable to adopt long-term economic strategies, only that their patterns of delayed expenditure differed from those of more comfortable families. The wish parents in general had expressed most clearly was to save their allowances. Findings on actual savings practices are difficult to interpret. In Montreal, labourers' families did not mention saving. In southwestern Montreal and Quebec City, where the background of the families interviewed was more varied, one-quarter of parents put at least part of their allowances in the bank. But this doesn't mean that the alternative was possible only for rich. The Quebec City enquiry suggests almost the opposite. There, "the proportion of families depositing the allowance money in saving accounts was relatively higher in 'poorer' wards."[74] This phenomenon suggests a pattern of small-scale deposits, similar to that found by Paul Johnson in nineteenth-century England. Then, workers' families put away cash on a short-term basis to stabilize consumption and to save for major expenditures.[75] Wealthier families could be more confident in their future capacity to meet large expenditures and needed less short-term planning.

Insurance, another form of saving, was also important for families at all socio-economic levels. Despite government reluctance, one-third of the Quebec City households and one-fifth of those in Montreal devoted a part of the allowance to insurance policies. In Quebec City, insurance represented the second most important type of expenditure. Monthly payments varied from $1 to $3 per child and thus could consume up to 50 percent of the allowance. In the wake of salespeople and doctors, insurance agents "would call just after the dates when the family allowance cheques were due."[76] Family allowances encouraged the spread of insurance into the poorer parts of eastern Montreal, according to Roy. She commented that "this is a very nice initiative allowed by family allowances and which did not exist before, at least amongst the families whom we have interviewed." Roy expected this practice to enlarge educational opportunities. However, parents did not always gear insurance toward education. In three-fifths of the Quebec cases, they insured the life of their children; only in another fourth did parents buy endowment policies in which the capital could be recovered to pay for the children's schooling. As some life-insurance policies could terminate and be reimbursed in part when the child arrived at a certain age, insurance was used as a form of saving.[77]

The government not only continued to promote ideals more in tune with the spending habits of wealthier families, it also tried to discourage practices like investing allowances in insurance because they jeopardized hopes for immediate consumption. Ministers had relied, after all, on poor people's high propensity for spending. When insurance companies advertising policies for children directly addressed the family allowances beneficiaries, Deputy Minister of Welfare George Davidson warned them that he wished to avoid campaigns, either in terms of high-pressure salesmanship of consumer goods or in terms of savings investments, insurance, etc., that will have the effect of diverting the Family Allowances moneys into unwise spendings, or even into unwise savings and hoarding, during the deflationary period of the postwar years when the interest of the country may call for a policy of encouragements to spending rather than encouragements to saving.[78]

Four years later, when the need for increasing consumer demand diminished, the research department of the ministry kindly agreed to a request for information from the Bank of Montreal, which was preparing publicity to encourage the saving of family allowances for children.[79]

Sociologist Maurice Tremblay and his colleagues denounced life insurance on the child's behalf as selfish behaviour on the parents' part, because "in such a case, it is the parents of the child who, if the latter dies, are financially protected."[80] It would be interesting to study the extent to which life-insurance policies for children provided security for mid-twentieth-century Quebeckers. In reality, payments by installments such as those accepted by doctors, department stores, and itinerant sales agents, were convenient ways of budgeting for poor urban families. For these poor families,

> the unpredictability of income and expenditures made some financial provision for the future essential. The way most households chose to cope with the problem was by committing a set portion of income each week to financial planning. . . . Small regular deductions were not missed in the way a lump-sum would be, and they imposed a degree of external discipline on the saving scheme. Willpower was seldom strong enough to permit accumulation in a week when money for food and rent was short, but the power of contract often was.

The debtors saw in the regular family allowances sums that could easily be kept aside for repayment. However, Canadian politicians, bureaucrats and social scientists, like the British middle classes studied by Paul Johnson, did not "appreciate that in small scale borrowing, saving or spending on durable goods, workers were demonstrating not their fecklessness but their true desire for financial stability."[81]

On the whole, social workers painted a picture of the realities of Canadian family life that was darker than the one projected by most MPs during the debates over family allowances. The series of investigations drawn on above, combined with daily contacts with poor families, led many employees of regional offices of the Department of National Health and Welfare to believe that "family allowances were not too much of a good thing . . . We may safely assume that the monies are currently spent by the parents who, in the great majority, are in need of this 'extra' income."[82] Canadian society numbered more of the Sauvés, the family portrayed in the

Speaking of Family Allowances booklet who spent their allowances on the most basic food and supplies for the children, than the Gagniers who spent it on extras. Many families benefitted from the program in unexpected ways. Family allowances permitted poor families both rural and urban to buy essential food and pay their rent more easily. Some had the means to pay for emergency medical care for the first time. Mothers both in poor and better-off families gained some economic power and autonomy from this monthly cheque.

These were important gains for individual families. Family allowances did not, however, succeed in realising the greater socio-economic promises pronounced at the time of their enactment. Equality of economic opportunities for children, a minimum of welfare for young Canadians and an end to poverty remained dreams. This was not only because of the conflict between these goals and other immediate political objectives, but also because policy makers' lack of knowledge about or unwillingness to admit the causes and extent of poverty in Canada had led them to invest the program with an illusory potential, and the educational campaign with unattainable ideals.

Politicians and bureaucrats had distinguished realistically between the different uses wealthier and poorer families would make of allowances, but they had underestimated the amount of real poverty. They had underrated the economic instability of rural and urban working-class families. It is difficult to decide which part of this attitude we should attribute to ignorance, and which part we should explain by their unwillingness to question the adequacy of salary levels in Canada and to enact the truly distributive welfare programs proposed in the reconstruction plans drafted during the war. What is certain is that once the results of the inquiries about family allowances were published, it was no longer possible to pretend that the elimination of poverty could be achieved through the allowances alone. Economic autonomy based on the salary of a father obviously remained unattainable for many, and this knowledge probably encouraged politicians to build support for the welfare programs of the years to come.

In the meantime, the unrealistically high expectations that had been so widely broadcast threatened to have a negative impact on the morale of poor parents. At times, the Department of National Health and Welfare's illusory standards could trigger feelings of inadequacy or guilt. McGill social workers reported that some interviewees in south-west Montreal seemed to feel that they were not using the family allowances as they "were supposed to be used." The researchers believed that "this attitude may well have arisen from emphasis in family allowances publicity on the use of money for children specifically while mothers usually bought food for the whole family, rather than separate family members."[83] The educational campaign added another voice to the growing number of directives aimed at parents from both the booming publicity for consumer goods and popular psychology. Family allowance propaganda may have contributed to the blurring of ideas about child raising, increasing some parents' uneasiness about their child-rearing capacities.[84]

EPILOGUE: THE STRUGGLE FOR THE INDEXATION OF FAMILY ALLOWANCES AND THE POLITICAL ROLE OF FAMILIES

What does the history of the implementation of family allowances mean for our understanding of the impact of the welfare state on Canadian parents and children? A range of theories has addressed the question of the relationship between families and the state. The "social administration" approach to social policies and the functionalist tradition of family sociology have proposed a bottom-up model that relies on a strong faith in the workings of liberal democracy. According to these approaches, a consensus emerged in the twentieth century in which the state was called upon to assume new tasks, either to fit the new needs of an industrial-urban society or to take over traditional family responsibilities that families could no longer manage.[85] In reaction to this consensus-politics view, which was too uncritical of the rhetoric of policy makers, historians of the "social control" school have crafted a top-down model. They describe an authoritarian and bourgeois state, progressively dispossessing passive families of traditional functions and imposing its morality on them.[86] In the simplest versions of this view, the apparent generosity of the state is an illusion: the economic and political elites of post-industrial societies conceded some measure of social security to maintain their power and control and avoid public disorder.

Family allowance policy can be interpreted using either of these models. In terms of the democratic-liberal idea, the program brought the anticipated electoral rewards, helping King return to power in 1945. The Liberal Party continued to hold the federal majority until 1957. During the decade following the implementation of the allowances, the popularity of the program increased from 49 percent to 90 percent in Quebec public opinion polls, despite the decrease in the real value of allowances.[87] As late as 1971, married women in Quebec viewed more generous family allowances as the most important of six measures proposed to them by demographers to help them with their family responsibilities.[88] Virtually none of the Canadian families interviewed by social workers and government officials on the effects of allowances explicitly opposed state intervention in family matters. Those that did, did so either because they felt they could raise their children alone or because they suspected that the public authorities expected something in return.[89] There seemed, then, to be a consensus about the need for such policy, based on the fact that these regular and predictable sums of money responded to real needs, strengthening the economic basis of many families in both rural and urban areas and injecting needed money into the postwar economy.

On the other hand, many elements of social control can be discerned both in the enactment and the enforcement of family allowances. Without question the desire to intervene materially and ideologically in family economies existed among politicians and public servants in the 1940s. And while the forms of control were mild compared to the investigation apparatus brought to bear on those living on relief during the Depression, one family in seven hundred was inspected for alleged misuse of allowances during the first decade of the program. Authorities proposed a change in payment provisions for one-third of those investigated.[90] Moreover, family allowances opened the realm of domestic consumption to state influence. Liberal ministers' ideas on the social role and economic priorities of the family conflicted with the actual values of poor families. They did not endorse poor families' ways of planning or their traditional income strategies. The unrealistic rhetoric promoting ways of spending and the failure to index allowances to the rising cost of living left many poor parents with a sense of disillusionment. Comparison of parents' hopes regarding the use of allowances and of their actual expenditures certainly reveals a lot of frustrations. The government's broken promises renewed poorer parents' sense of economic powerlessness.

There was consensus about the usefulness of family allowances, yet its implementation also involved the desire to control. Thus neither the consensus politics nor the social control theory is adequate to fully understand family allowances.[91] A more recent theoretical trend—a revision of the social control approach—can be of help. Historians of nineteenth-century education have begun to describe families as having their own distinct cultures and beliefs, which led them to resist state intrusions. Such work rehabilitates the concept of family autonomy and focusses attention on families' opposition to government control.[92] This kind of more dialectical approach opens up the possibility of studying the internal dynamic of families and of observing them in interaction with the state.

The history of family allowances suggests we could push this model further and give greater weight to the role of families in policy formation. The idea of family resistance, which may be sufficient to explain nineteenth-century social policies, does not adequately account for the history of a universal program in the mid-twentieth century. There was definitely more to these allowances than electoralism through cash benefits, more than an illusory resolution of the economic problems of the mid-1940s in favour of elites. Family allowances may have been a cheap version of reconstruction plans popular during the war; they may have been an easier way to intervene in the economy than by regulating enterprises. The cabinet felt that the population would not let them get away with less. If Canadians were to lend their support to the Liberals in the 1945 elections, they wanted to be reassured that the party cared for the general economy. Universal child benefits were the necessary minimum the government had to enact to maintain its legitimacy. Means tests would "not be accepted by the people in Canada."[93]

Parents did not vanish from the political arena once allowances became policy. Some of the disillusionment concerning the diminishing purchasing power of the allowances surfaced in the House of Commons in the demands of specific groups. By the end of the 1940s, two major labour councils were among the many groups asking for the indexation of the allowances. In a major campaign held between July 1954 and May 1955, several unions, 327 municipal or school councils and various other associations again requested indexation. Nearly three thousand Canadian citizens signed petitions making the same request. Over subsequent years some opposition MPs also called for indexation. Quebec MP Lionel Bertrand received so many letters asking for a rise in the amount of family allowances that he could not answer them all.[94] In 1951, the tireless Father Léon Lebel deplored that:

> given the actual price of milk—19 cents for a pint—the monthly allowance of $5.00 given for children of less than six years does not even pay for the pint of milk that doctors recommend as the daily requirement for children and adolescents to ensure the normal development of their body. . . . The allowances are ineffective in helping workers' families in large cities.[95]

Concerns about child welfare backed by pressures from recipients were not sufficient in themselves to win the indexation of allowances.[96] By the mid-1950s, the government no longer feared a fall in the demand for goods. Postwar prosperity had been ensured, and ministers shifted their focus to policies of economic management aimed at promoting the health of enterprises rather than of children. The threat of a CCF victory was vanishing, and the "Government Party" could afford to be less sensitive to public demands. Assessing the impact of family allowances in 1955, R.H. Parkinson, chief supervisor of welfare services related to the program, confidently declared that they had accomplished almost everything expected. Liberal ministers countered the mounting pressure for indexation with budgetary arguments largely absent a decade earlier: the government didn't have enough money; family allowances already represented one-fourth of the social security budget; linking the program to the cost of living would threaten the program itself; Canada still offered more than other countries.[97]

But there was more to the unwillingness of the government to index allowances than simple economics. Members of cabinet now feared that their own welfare promises might feed an ever increasing stream of claims on the state. Ministers began to hint at a new type of abuse of state help. Speaking in the House of Commons, Paul Martin, minister of health and welfare, suggested that it would be regrettable to give people the impression that there was no limit to what the government could do in this domain.[98] Civil servants of the Department of National Health and Welfare, who quickly saw the devastating effects of inflation, dealt with the politicians' lack of willingness by adjusting their propaganda. The annual report in 1947–48 acknowledged that family allowances might only have maintained rather than improved the standard of living, but "the increase in the cost of living would have had a far worse impact without family allowances." In 1951, the draft of a pamphlet of the nutrition division still pretended that for $5 per month per child, "you can be sure that your child receives the two foods that are needed most to improve the diets of Canadian children. 1. Milk: at least one pint daily. 2. Vitamin D. . . . That still leaves some money for other foods." Such blind optimism may explain why the government never printed this pamphlet; instead, a new brochure told families how to get more for their money but refrained from alluding to the purchasing power of the allowances.[99]

To complete an explanation of the impact of family allowances on Canadian families, we need to reject monolithic approaches to the study of the state. The state was and is a diverse and changing institution that is not a simple tool of economic elites but reflects the existing levels of social tension, power, and class conflict within a society, while still maintaining a certain logic of its own.[100] Seeing the state in this way encourages the study of specific state actions or policies, following laws at different stages of their life, and allowing for some autonomy among civil servants, cabinet members, MPs, lobby groups, and electors.[101] From such a point of view, families can be seen not simply as the objects of policy, but also as political agents, able to influence the implementation of some laws by resistance or promotion at the local level and able to shape the larger political process of the country. With this more flexible idea of a dialectic relationship between families and the state, the two institutions can be considered as co-existing actors, as dynamic and complex systems of reproduction that can influence each other.[102]

In the end, the interests of Liberal politicians prevailed. The failure to respond to a widespread demand for improved welfare is sufficient to challenge the model of consensus politics, but our interpretation should not stop at this critique. Parents who had voted for the Liberal Party in 1945 were not the victims of authoritarian bourgeois manipulations. They did not experience economic constraints passively. While the propaganda surrounding the enactment and the distribution of allowances fostered unrealistic expectations and generated a sense of alienation among some poor parents, it also led parents to incorporate the idea of an adequate allowance into their concept of their rights as Canadians. In putting forward the idea that the state had a financial responsibility for the economic welfare of all children, the government had set a new threshold for families' claims in the future. The history of family allowances does not fit the idea that increasing state activity automatically lowered family responsibilities, a concept found in some of the literature. This study shows a more complex history, where a particular program did not automatically dispossess parents from their traditional functions but might lead them to enlarge their concepts of their rights as citizens.[103]

NOTES

1. J.L. Granatstein, *Canada's War: The Politics of the Mackenzie King Government, 1939–1945* (Toronto: University of Toronto Press, 1990), 397, 406. For the way in which the King government surrounded most proposals of the Marsh report, see Michiel Horn, "Leonard Marsh and the Coming of the Welfare Sate in Canada: A Review Article," *Histoire sociale/Social History* 9 (1976): 197–204; Frank Breul, "The Genesis of Family Allowances in Canada" *The Social Service Review* 27, 3 (1953): 276–77.

2. See, for instance, Service de l'information, Ministère de la santé nationale et du bien-être social, *En parlant des allocations familiales* (Ottawa: King's Printer, 1950); Quebec Regional Office of Family Allowances (hereinafter ABRQ), 40-13, vol. 1.

3. Dominique Jean, "Les parents québécois et l'État canadien au début du program des allocations familiales: 1944–1955," *Revue d'histoire de l'Amérique française* 40, 1 (1986): 89–92.

4. Débats de la chambre des communes, 1944, p. 5740, 5564. Since this study was conducted in French, most references to the Debates of the House of Commons use the French version, referred to henceforth as Débats. Only when a direct quote was involved did I go back to the English version. They were following the lead of the leading British expert on social policy matters, Sir William Beveridge; A.J. Pelletier, "La famille canadienne," in Canada, Bureau fédéral de la statistique, *Recensement du Canada*, 1931, 12: 189–90; Débats 1944, pp. 5564, 5567, 5619, 5569, 5633; 1947, p. 4451; 1952, p. 1779; See Leon Lebel, s.j., Les allocations familiales: solution du problème des familles nombreuses (Montreal: École sociale populaire, no. 159–60, 1927); Gérard Forcier, o.m.i., Les allocations familiales: Savez-vous ce qu'elles sont? (Ottawa: Centre social de l'Université d'Ottawa, 1944); Robert Lévesque and Robert Mignier, *Camilien et les années vingt suivi de Camilien au Goulag, cartographie du Houdisme* (Montreal: Éditionds des Brûlés, 1978), 84. Other pro-natalist statements came from some western MPs of all parties. Débats 1944, p. 5704, 5633, 2790. See also, from the Maritimes, pp. 5695, 5563. The same ethnic differentials long blocked Canadian measures on family planning. Angus McLaren and Arlene Tigar McLaren, *The Bedroom and the State: The Changing Practices and Politics of Contraception and Abortion in Canada, 1880–1980* (Toronto: McClelland and Stewart, 1986) 13; Débats 1949, p. 2548. No MP publicly endorsed conservative social worker Charlotte Whitton's view that allowances punished those responsible attitudes towards family planning. See "The Family Allowances Controversy in Canada," *The Social Service Review* 18, 4, p. 432.

5. Débats 1944, pp. 5619–20; 1946, pp. 2790, 5333.

6. Leonard Marsh, *Report on Social Security for Canada* (Toronto: University of Toronto Press, 1975), 201; D.H. Stepler, *Les allocations familiales au Canada* (Montréal: École sociale populaire, no 362, 1943), 4–5. Jane Lewis, "Dealing with Dependency: State Practices and Social Realities, 1870–1945", in *Women's Welfare: Women's Rights* (London: Croom Helm, 1983), 22.

7. Dominique Jean, "Le recul du travail des enfants au Québec entre 1940 et 1960: une explication des conflits entre les familles pauvres et l'État providence," *Labour/Le travail* 24 (Fall 1989).

8. Abbé Émile Cloutier, "Le salaire et la famille" in *Capital et Travail*. *Semaines sociales du Canada*, IIIe session (Ottawa: Bibliothèque de l'Action française, 1922) 150–74; Lebel, *Les allocations familiales*; Alfred Charpentier, "La question ouvrière" 19–39; in *Program de restauration sociale* (Montréal: École sociale populaire, no. 239–240, 1933), 19–39; R.P. Archambault, s.j., *Pour restaurer la famille* (Montreal: École sociale populaire, no. 371, 1944), 25–27; Forcier, *Les allocations familiales*.

9. Stepler, *Les allocations familiales*, 12; Jacques Rouillard, *Les syndicats nationaux au Québec de 1900 à 1930* (Quebec: Presses de l'Université Laval, 1979), 169, 247; Tremblay, Faucher, and Falardeau, *Family Allowances in Quebec City*, 73, 74.

10. Brigitte Kitchen, "Wartime Social Reform: The Introduction of Family Allowances," *Revue canadienne d'éducation en service social* 7, 1 (1981): 29–54; Breul, "Genesis of Family Allowances."

11. Débats 1944, p. 5559.

12. Debates of the House of Commons, 1944, p. 5726. Débats 1944, p. 5932;

see also 1944, p. 5553, and Stepler, *Les allocations familiales*, 8-12.

13. Débats 1944, pp. 2, 5739, 5531.

14. Débats, 1944, pp. 5552, 5740, 5528, 5529, 5603; *Santé et bien-être social Canada*, July 1948.

15. Dennis Guest, *The Emergence of Social Security in Canada* (Vancouver: University of British Columbia Press, 1981), 110.

16. Débats 1944, pp. 11, 5529–30; Guest, *Emergence of Social Security*, 129–31.

17. Débats 1944, pp. 5593, 5603. See also Léon Lebel, *Le problème de la famille nombreuse: Sa solution: les allocations familiales* (Montreal: Le Devoir, 1928), 17; François-Albert Angers, "Les allocations familiales fédérales de 1944," *L'Actualité économique* 21, 3 (1945), 229.

18. Geneviève Auger and Raymonde Lamothe, *De la poêle a frire à la ligne de feu: La vie quotidienne des Québécoises pendant la guerre '39–'45* (Montreal: Boréal Express, 1981), 160; Ruth Roach Pierson, *They're Still Women After All: The Second World War and Canadian Womanhood* (Toronto: McClelland and Stewart, 1986), 216, 220; Debates, 1944, p. 5402.

19. J.C. Falardeau, Maurice Tremblay, Maurice Lamontagne, Roger Marier, Jean-Pierre Després, "Mémoire sur les allocations familiales" (préparé à la requête d'un comité de la Commission permanente du Conseil supérieur du travail de la province de Québec, mai 1944, Manuscript document, Bibliothèque du ministère du Travail), 56–57; Thérèse Casgrain, *A Woman in a Man's World* (Toronto: McClelland and Stewart, 1972), 113. Interestingly, the French version also alludes to her sense of fighting for a cause that women of Quebec wanted her to endorse: "je savais parfaitement que le mandat existait, et qu'en général c'était la femme qui administrait le budget familial"; Thérèse F. Casgrain, *Une femme chez les hommes* (Montreal: Éditions de l'Homme, 1971), 170–74.

20. Debates, 1944, p. 5336. For other Liberals, Débats 1944, pp. 5692 and 5565.

21. Eli Zaretsky, "The Place of the Family in the Origins of the Welfare State," in *Rethinking the Family: Some Feminist Questions*, ed. Barrie Thorne and M. Halom (New York: Longman, 1981), 195.

22. Débats 1944, pp. 5692, 5532, 5557, 5628, 5631, 5698, 5600, 5932.

23. Marsh, *Report on Social Security*, 199.

24. Falardeau et al.,"Mémoire sur les allocations familiales," 23–24.

25. Debates, 1944, p. 5726.

26. Marsh, *Report on Social Security*, 201–202.

27. "What They Are Saying about Family Allowances," CBC *This Week* Program, ABRQ, Publicité, 40-15; Débats 1944, p. 5555; see also Falardeau et al., "Memoire sur les allocations familiales," 39–40; Brigitte Kitchen, "The Family and Social Policy" in *The Family: Changing Trends in Canada*, ed. Maureen Baker (Toronto: McGraw-Hill Ryerson, 1984), 178–97 180.

28. Débats 1944, pp. 5636, 5637, 5923; 1946, p. 2786.

29. Débats 1944, p. 5600.

30. Débats 1945, p. 3604.

31. Statuts du Canada, 8 GEO VI, art. 5.

32. See especially the comments on the surveys in Canada, Department of National Health and Welfare, Information Division, *You and Your Family* (Ottawa: King's printer, 1949), 4. These studies constitute the main source for the last part of this article.

33. Débats 1946, pp. 2787–88.

34. Débats 1946, 2787–88; Débats 1944, p. 5558, Debates 1950, pp. 3914-3915.

35. Falardeau et al.,"Memoires sur les allocations familiales," 58; Stepler, "Les allocations familiales," 6. Thérèse Roy, "Influence economique et sociale des allocations familiales" (M.A. thesis, Université de Montréal, 1948), 59, 5–6 Gérard Parizeau, "Fait d'actualité. Les allocations familiales," *Assurances* 12, 2 (1944): 85–87.

36. Débats 1944, p. 5948, 5538; Angers, "Les allocations familiales," 250.

37. Débats 1944, p. 5932; Parizeau, "Fait d'actualité," 86; Débats 1944, pp. 5556, 5946; 1946, pp. 2787–88; Research Division 1953, NAC, RG 29, 1932, R233/100, 1–2, pt. 1; Rapport annuel du ministère de la Santé nationale et du Bien-être social 1949–1950 (thereafter RAMSNBES), pp. 105–106; 1950–1951, p. 88; A.M. Willms, "Setting Up Family Allowances," (M.A. thesis, Carleton University, 1962).

38. *You and Your Family*, 27, 10, 19.

39. *En parlant des allocations familiales*, 9; Advertisement for family allowances published in *La Terre de chez nous*, 20 June 1945, p. 19; Canada, Ministère de la Santé nationale et du bien-être social, Économisez les vivres, 1946, NAC, RG 29, Education and Nutrition-Cooperation with F.A. re Inserts, 109, 180-26-15.

40. *You and Your Family*, 26; Hervé Varenne, "Love and Liberty, la famille américaine contemporaine," in *Histoire de la famille*, ed. André Burguière (Paris: Armand Colin, n.d.), 420–21.

41. Débats 1944, pp. 5231, 5233, 5593, 5698, 5740; 1947, p. 4462.

42. *You and Your Family*, 4, 21; *Speaking of Family Allowances* (Ottawa: King's Printer, 1950).

43. *Speaking of Family Allowances*, 21–22.

44. Roger De Bellefeuille, "Les allocations familiales et la jeunesse agricole," *La Terre de chez nous* 1 (Aug. 1945). See also *Revue Desjardins* 6

(June–July 1945): 102; Economisez les vivres Canada, Ministère de la Santé nationale et du bien-être social, Allocations familiales, Charte de l'enfance, 1945, "What They Are Saying about Family Allowances," 7.

45. Angers, "Les allocations familiales," 234; Débats 1944, p. 5620.

46. For a similar development in Australia, Rob Watts, "Family Allowances in Canada and Australia 1940–1945: A Comparative Critical Case Study," *Journal of Social Policy* 16, 1 (1987): 44. See also Innes de Neufville, "Production de connaissances et processus de planification," *Revue internationale d'action communautaire* 19, 55 (Spring 1988): 189.

47. Statistiques Canada 1976, pp. 246, 248, 530, 535.

48. Undated Memo to Mr. Willard, NAC, RG 29, 1934, R233/100/13; John Modell, Patterns of Consumption, Acculturation, and Family Income Strategies in Late Nineteenth-Century America" in *Family and Population in Nineteenth Century America*, ed. Tamara K. Hareven and Maris A. Vinovkis (Princeton: Princeton University Press, 1978), 206–24.

49. Edward Schwartz, "Some Observations on the Canadian Family Allowances Program," *Social Service Review* 20, 4 (1946) 471.

50. Horace Miner, *St-Denis: A French-Canadian Parish* (Chicago: University of Chicago Press, 1963), 258–60, 267–69.

51. Stepler, *Les allocations familiales*, 26–27.

52. Lebel, *Le problème de la famille nombreuse*, Debates 1944, p. 5504; Stepler, *Les allocations famiales*, 26–27; Debates 1944, p. 5337.

53. Thérèse Légaré, *Conditions économiques et sociales des familles de Gaspé-Nord, Québec* (Faculté des sciences, Université Laval, May 1947), 83, 74.

54. Débats 1949, deuxième session, p. 180. My translation.

55. Jeanne Grisé-Allard, "Les allocations familiales: Un chèque bien employé," *Relations* 7, 92 (1948): 240. My translation. Schwartz, "Some Observations," 451–73; Légaré, "Conditions économiques et sociales," 52; Nora Fox, "Family Allowances in Northern Ontario," *The Social Worker* 15, 3 (1947).

56. ABRQ, Surveys and Studies, 40–20, vol. 1. I was able to locate 116 interviews.

57. Ten Family Surveys 1948; R. Blishen, J. Cawley, and J.E. Pearson, "Family Allowances in Montreal: A Study of their Uses and Meaning in a Selected Group of Wage-Earning Families" (M.A. thesis, McGill University, 1948), 100; Canada, Statutes, 9 Geo VI, c. 23, art. 9; Canada, Department of National Health and Welfare, Information Division, *Family Allowances and Income Tax* (1946).

58. Grisé-Allard, "Les allocations familiales," 240; Ten Family Surveys 1946.

59. Canada, Statutes, 10 Geo VI, c. 55.

60. Blishen, Cawley, and Pearson, "Family Allowances in Montreal," 54–55.

61. Donat-C. Noiseux, *L'Action catholique*, 19 April 1949, in ABRQ, 42-8, vol. 1, paper clippings. The newspaper clipping itself is not dated.

62. See also Roy, "Influence économique et sociale," 35.

63. Agnes Tennant, "Family Allowances Story," *The Social Worker* 15, 3 (1947): 27–28.

64. Roy, "Influence économique et sociale," 35–39.

65. The surveys found a low proportion of mothers who worked outside the home, but this is not surprising according to Quebec standards. The number may have been influenced by the methods of the inquiries. Mothers were less easy for the interviewers to find.

66. Blishen, Cawley, and Pearson, "Family Allowances in Montreal," 41.

67. *La Presse*, 14 Dec. 1950, found in ABRQ, 42-8, vol. 1, paper clippings; Blishen, Cawley, and Pearson, "Family Allowances in Montreal," 74, 75, 92, 93; Rapport annuel du service de bien-être du Bureau régional du Québec 1950–1951, NAC, RG 29, Annual Reports. FA Division, 1283, p. 14.

68. Roy, "Influence économique et sociale," 25, 44.

69. Blishen, Cawley, and Pearson, "Family Allowances in Montreal," 79–82.

70. Blishen, Cawley, and Pearson, "Family Allowances in Montreal," 82–84, 106. At the beginning, the newness of the program and the newness of inflation sheltered the government from criticism. The "Ten Families Surveys" conducted in 1945–46 suggest that families welcomed the allowances precisely because they helped meet the high cost of living (10 percent of the mothers interviewed mentioned it); Roy, "Influence économique et sociale," 53; Maurice Tremblay, Albert Faucher, and J-C Falardeau, *Family Allowances in Quebec City: Report of a Study in the Faculty of Social Sciences of Laval University*, trans. Department of National Health and Welfare (Quebec, 1951).

71. A. Asimakopoulos, "Section J: Prices Indexes." in M.C. Urquhart and K.A.H. Buckley, *Historical Statistics of Canada* (Toronto: Macmillan, 1965), 304, (series J147-152); Débats 1952, p. 1776; 1951, Second Session, p. 220.

72. Blishen, Cawley, and Pearson, "Family Allowances in Montreal," 92.

73. Indeed, only one-fourth of the Quebec City families kept budgets, although the researchers could not link the practice to a particular level of income; Tremblay, Faucher, and Falardeau, *Family Allowances in Quebec City*, 17.

74. Ibid., 17. The reason why poor Montrealers did not mention savings is still puzzling to me. It could be that Légaré's questions did not address this type of savings.

75. Paul Johnson, *Saving and Spending: The Working Class Economy in Britain, 1870–1939* (London: Oxford University Press, 1985).

76. Blishen, Cawley, and Pearson, "Family Allowances in Montreal," 93.

77. Roy, "Influence économique et sociale," 47; Tremblay, Faucher, and Falardeau, *Family Allowances in Quebec City*, 45.

78. Letters to the Montreal Board of Trade, The Trust Companies Association of Ontario and to a firm in Toronto 1945, NAC, RG 29, Acc. 82-83/152, 260-8-1.

79. Correspondence between Willard and Sheldon 1949, NAC, RG 29, 1934, R233/100/13.

80. Tremblay, Faucher, and Falardeau, *Family Allowances in Quebec City*, 33.

81. Johnson, *Savings and Spending*, 220–21.

82. RABRQ, 1950–1951, p. 12.

83. Blishen, Cawley, and Pearson, "Family Allowances in Montreal," 79–82. Enquirers did not agree on the significance of spending for the whole family or for children specifically. On one hand, Blishen, Cawley, and Pearson believed that poorer families could less easily spend the sums separately, a behaviour they explained by the "pressures of everyday needs" (p. 55). On the other hand, Tremblay, Faucher, and Falardeau found parents in the poorer sections of Quebec City spending allowances specifically for the children. They inferred that meagre incomes prompted a stricter budget allotment among family members. (*Family Allowances in Quebec City*, 29).

84. Arlene Skolnick, "Public Images and Private Realities: The Family in Popular Culture and Social Sciences" in *Changing Images of the Family*, ed. Virginia Tufte and Barbara Myeroff (New Haven: Yale University Press, 1979), 297–318.

85. See for instance Serge Mongeau, *Évolution de l'assistance au Québec* (Montreal: Éditions du Jour, 1967); Guest, Emergence of Social Security; P.T. Rooke and R.L. Schnell, *Discarding the Asylum: From Child Rescue to the Welfare State in Canada, 1800–1950* (Boston: University Press of America, 1983), 389–413.

86. Michel Pelletier and Yves Vaillancourt, *Les politiques sociales et les travailleurs*, Cahier I, *Les années 1900–1920* (Montréal, 1974, published by the authors); *Les politiques sociales et les travailleurs*. Cahier II, *Les années '30*. (Montréal, 1975). Jane Ursel, "The State and the Maintenance of Patriarchy: A Case Study of Family, Labour and Welfare Legislation in Canada," in J. Dickinson and B. Russel, ed., *Family, Economy and the State* (Toronto: Garamond, 1986), 150–91.

87. Granatstein, *Canada's War*; Canadian Institute of Public Opinion, "Gallup Poll of Canada. 90 p.c. in Favor of Family Allowances," *Toronto Star*, 12 March 1955.

88. Jacques Henripin and Evelyne Lapierre Adamcyk, *La fin de la revanche des berceaux: qu'en pensent les Québécoises?* (Montreal, Presses de l'Université de Montréal, 1974), iii. Collection "Démographie canadienne."

89. Three cases in Blishen, Cawley, and Pearson, "Family Allowances in Montreal," 96–105; six cases in MacNaughton and Mann, *Distribution and Use of Family Allowances*, 91.

90. Jean "Les parents québécois," 80-81.

91. Sarah Eisenstein, *Give Us Bread But Give Us Roses: Working Women's Consciousness in the United States, 1890 to the First World War* (London: Routledge and Kegan Paul, 1983), 2–11; Zaretsky, "Place of the Family."

92. Philip Corrigan and Bruce Curtis, "Education, Inspection and State Formation: A Preliminary Statement," Canadian Historical Association *Historical Papers* (1985): 156–71; Bruce Curtis, *Building the Educational State: Canada West, 1836–1871* (London: Falmer Press and Althouse Press), 1988; Maurice Crubellier, *L'enfance et la jeunesse dans la société française, 1800–1850* (Paris: Armand Colin, 1979), 223. Louise A. Tilly and Myriam Cohen, "Does the Family Have a History: A Review of the Theory and Practice of Family History," *Social Science History* 6, 2 (Spring 1982). Tamara Hareven, "Les grands thèmes de l'histoire de la famille aux États-Unis," *Revue d'histoire de l'Amérique française* 39, 2 (Fall 1985).

93. Brooke Claxton in Debates, 1944, p. 5726.

94. Roy, "Influence économique et sociales," 120; See also the secretary of one Confédération des travailleurs catholiques du Canada union mentioned in Eugène L'Heureux, "Allocations familiales," *L'événement journal*, 18 July 1951, found in ABRQ, 42-8, vol.1, paper clippings; Davidson to Willard, 1955, NAC, RG 29, 1933, R233-100-1-6; Knowles and Lockhard and Jackman in Débats de la Chambre des Communes, 1948, pp. 5488 and 5890–91 respectively; Poulin, ibid., 1949, Deuxième session, p. 180; Poulin, ibid., 1951, Première session, pp. 2266–67; Poulin, Argue, and Brown, ibid., 1951, Deuxième session, pp. 148–49, 220 and 776 respectively; Dubé, Poulin and Argue, ibid., 1952, pp. 1983, 3138, 1775–77 respectively; Bertrand and Argue, ibid., 1953, pp. 2959 and 1182–204 respectively; Argue, Girard, and Dupuis, ibid., 1954, pp. 1354, 328, 352. In 1953, Argue even presented a proposal to raise the family allowances to compensate for the increase in the cost of living.

95. Léon Lebel, "Notre système d'allocations familiales," *Relations* (April 1951), 93. My translation. See also

L'Action catholique, 8 July 1955, found in ABRQ, 42-8. vol. 1, paper clippings.

96. This invalidates Bernice Madison's thesis about the program ("during the following decade, the economic objectives receded, and the social welfare objectives emerged which have since been the predominant ones") in "Canadian Family Allowances and Their Major Social Implications," *Journal of Marriage and the Family* 26, 2 (May 1962): 140. See John MacNicol's analysis of the same problem in Great Britain: *The Movement for Family Allowances, 1918-1945: A Study in Social Policy Development* (London: Heinemann, 1980).

97. "Ten Years of Family Allowances," *Canadian Welfare* 31, 4 (1955), 199.

98. Débats 1952, p. 1783, my translation. See also 1948, p. 5488; 1954, pp. 1371, 1378.

99. RAMSNBES, 1947–1948, p. 96; 1946–1947, p. 76. My translation; NAC, RG 29, 109, 180-26-15.

100. Kenneth Finegold and Theda Skocpol, "State, Party, and Industry: From Business Recovery to the Wagner Act in America's New Deal" in *State Making and Social Movements: Essays in History and Theory*, ed. C. Bright and S. Harding (Ann Arbor: University of Michigan Press, 1984), 152–92; James Struthers, *No Fault of their Own: Unemployment and the Canadian Welfare State, 1914–1941* (Toronto: University of Toronto Press, 1983); Alvin Finkel, "Origins of the Welfare State in Canada" *The Canadian State: Political Economy and Political Power*, ed. Leo Panitch (Toronto: University of Toronto Press, 1977), 344–70.

101. John Carrier and Ian Kendall, "Social Policy and Social Change: Explanations of the Development of Social Policy," *Journal of Social Policy* 2, 3 (1973): 209–24 and "The Development of Welfare States: The Production of Plausible Accounts," *Journal of Social Policy* 6, 3 (1977): 271–90; Elwood Jones,

"Dependency and Social Welfare," *Journal of Canadian Studies/ Revue d'études canadiennes* 14, 1 (1979): 1.

102. Martine Segalen, "La révolution industrielle: du prolétaire au bourgeois" in *Histoire de la famille*, ed. André Burguière et al. (Paris: Armand Colin, 1986), 411; Asa Briggs, "The Welfare State in Historical Perspective," in *The Collected Essays of Asa Briggs*, vol. II (Urbana: University of Illinois Press, 1985), 177–211 (the article was first published in 1961); John Carrier and Ian Kendall, "Categories, Categor-izations and the Political Economy of Welfare," *Journal of Social Policy* 15, 3 (1986): 315–32; James Dickinson and Bob Russel, "The Structure of Reproduction in Capitalist Society" in *Family, Economy and the State*, ed. J. Dickinson and B. Russell (Toronto: Garamond, 1986), 1–20; Brigitte Kitchen, "The Family and Social Policy," in *The Family: Changing Trends in Canada*, ed. Maureen Baker (Toronto, McGraw-Hill Ryerson, 1984), 178–97.

103. See also the warnings of Segalen, "La révolution industrielle," 411.

FURTHER READING

○

With the exception of the first section, I am limiting this bibliography to monographs and collections of essays. Readers should be able to mine the footnotes of the articles included in the collection and the journals listed below for further references.

BIBLIOGRAPHIES AND HISTORIOGRAPHICAL ESSAYS ON OR RELATED TO FAMILY HISTORY

Anderson, Michael. *Approaches to the History of the Western Family, 1500–1914* (London: Macmillan Press, 1980).

Bellingham, Bruce. "The History of Childhood Since the 'Invention of Childhood': Some Issues in the Eighties," *Journal of Family History* 13 (1988).

Bradbury, Bettina. "Women's History and Working-Class History," *Labour/Le Travail* 12 (1987).

Bradbury, Bettina. "Femmes et Familles," *Guide d'histoire du Québec*, ed. Jacques Rouillard (Éditions du Méridien, 1991).

Gaffield, Chad. "Children, Schooling, and Family Reproduction in Nineteenth-Century Ontario," *Canadian Historical Review* 57, 2 (1991).

Hareven, Tamara. "Family History at the Crossroads," *Journal of Family History* 12, 1–3 (1987).

Hareven, Tamara. "Les grands thèmes de l'histoire de la famille aux États-Unis," *Revue d'histoire de l'Amérique française* (hereinafter RHAF), 39, 2 (1985).

Rapp, Rayna, et al., "Examining Family History," *Feminist Studies* 5 (1979).

Ségalen, Martine. "Sous les feux croisés de l'histoire et de l'anthropologie: La famille en Europe," *RHAF* 39, 2 (1985).

Stone, Lawrence. "Family History in the 1980s: Past Achievements and Future Trends," *Journal of Interdisciplinary History* 12 (1981).

Tilly, Charles. "Family History, Social History, and Social Change," *Journal of Family History* 12, 1–3 (1987).

Tilly, Louise A. "Women's History and Family History: Fruitful Collaboration or Missed Connection?" *Journal of Family History* 12, 1–3 (1987).

Tilly, Louise, and Miriam Cohen. "Does the Family Have a History? A Review of Theory and Practice in Family History," *Social Science History* 6 (1982).

JOURNALS

Histoire sociale/Social History
Journal of Family History
Journal of Interdisciplinary History
Journal of Marriage and the Family
Journal of Social History
History Workshop
Labour/Le Travail
Revue d'histoire de l'Amérique française

SELECTED NON-CANADIAN MONOGRAPHS

Accampo, Elinor. *Industrialization, Family Life, and Class Relations. Saint Chamond, 1815–1914.* Berkeley: University of California Press, 1989.

Anderson, Michael. *Family Structure in Nineteenth Century Lancashire.* Cambridge: Cambridge University Press, 1971.

Aries, Philippe. *Centuries of Childhood: A Social History of Family Life.* New York: Vintage, 1962.

Flandrin, Jean-Louis. *Families in Former Times: Kinship, Household and Sexuality.* Cambridge: Cambridge University Press, 1979.

Davidoff, Leonore, and Catherine Hall. *Family Fortunes: Men and Women of the English Middle Class, 1780–1850.* Chicago: University of Chicago Press, 1987.

Gordon, Linda. *Heroes of Their Own Lives: The Politics and History of Family Violence.* New York: Viking, 1988.

Grossberg, Michael. *Governing the Hearth. Law and the Family in Nineteenth-Century America.* Chapel Hill: University of North Carolina Press, 1985.

Hareven, Tamara. *Family Time and Industrial Time: The Relationship between the Family and Work in a New England Industrial Community.* New York: Cambridge University Press, 1982.

Laslett, Peter, with Richard Wall, eds. *Household and Family in Past Time.* Cambridge: Cambridge University Press, 1972.

Lewis, Jane ed. *Labour and Love: Women's Experience of Home and Family, 1850–1940.* Oxford: Basil Blackwell, 1986.

McFarlane, Alan. *Marriage and Love in England, 1300–1840.* Oxford: Basil Blackwell, 1986.

Mitterauer, Michael, and Reinhard Sieder. *The European Family.* Oxford: Basil Blackwell, 1982.

Ryan, Mary P. *Cradle of the Middle Class: The Family in Oneida County New York, 1780–1865.* New York: Cambridge University Press, 1981.

Shorter, Edward. *The Making of the Modern Family.* New York: Basic Books, 1975.

Smith, Bonnie. *Ladies of the Leisure Class: The Bourgeoises of Northern France in the Nineteenth Century.* New Jersey: Princeton University Press, 1981.

Stansell, Christine. *City of Women: Sex and Class in New York, 1789–1860.* Urbana: University of Illinois Press, 1987.

Stone, Lawrence. *The Family, Sex and Marriage in England, 1500–1800.* New York: Harper and Row, 1977.

Tilly, Louise A. and Joan W. Scott. Women, Work, and Family. New York: Holt, Rinehart and Winston, 1978.

CANADIAN MONOGRAPHS

Anderson, Karen. *Chain Her By One Foot: The Subjugation of Women in Seventeenth-Century New France.* New York: Routledge, 1991.

Backhouse, Constance. *Petticoats and Prejudice: Women and Law in Nineteenth-Century Canada.* Toronto: Women's Press, 1991.

Bradbury, Bettina. *Working Families: Daily Survival in Industrializing Montreal.* Forthcoming.

Brown, Jennifer S.H. *Strangers in Blood: Fur Trade Company Families in Indian Country.* Vancouver: University of British Columbia Press, 1980.

Cohen, Marjorie. *Women's Work, Markets, and Economic Development in Nineteenth-Century Ontario.* Toronto: University of Toronto Press, 1988.

Le Collective Clio. *L'Histoire des femmes au Québec depuis quatres siècles.* Montreal: Les Quinze, 1982. Translated by Roger Gagnon and Rosalind Gill as *Quebec Women. A History.* Toronto: Women's Press, 1987.

Dandurand, Renée B. *Des Mères sans alliances: Monoparentalité et désunions conjugales*. Ville Saint-Laurent: Institut québécois de recherche sur la culture, 1988.

Dechêne, Louise. *Habitants et marchands de Montréal au XVIIe siècle*. Paris: Plon, 1974.

Eichler, Margrit. *Families in Canada Today: Recent Changes and Their Policy Consequences*, 2nd ed. Toronto: Gage 1988.

Gaffield, Chad. *Language, Schooling, and Cultural Conflict: The Origins of the French-Language Controversy in Ontario*. Montreal: McGill-Queen's University Press, 1987.

Gagan, David. *Hopeful Travellers: Families, Land, and Social Change in Mid-Victorian Peel County, Canada West*. Toronto: Ontario Historical Studies Series, 1981.

Gauvreau, Danielle. *Québec. Une ville et sa population au temps de la Nouvelle France*. Sillery: Presses de l'Université du Québec, 1991.

Graff, Harvey. *The Literacy Myth: Literacy and Social Structure in the Nineteenth-Century City*. New York: Academic Press, 1979.

Greer, Allan. *Peasant, Lord and Merchant: Rural Society in Three Quebec Parishes, 1740–1840*. Toronto: University of Toronto Press, 1985.

Henripin, Jacques. *La Population canadienne au début du XVIIIe siècle: nuptialité, fécondité, mortalité infantile*. Paris: Presses universitaires de France, 1954.

Houston, Susan, and Alison Prentice. *Schooling and Scholars in Nineteenth-Century Ontario*. Toronto: University of Toronto Press, 1988.

Iacovetta, Franca. *Such Hardworking People: Women, Men, and the Italian Immigrant Experience in Postwar Toronto*. Forthcoming.

Katz, Michael B. *The People of Hamilton, Canada West: Family and Class in a Mid-Nineteenth-Century City*. Cambridge: Harvard University Press, 1975.

Katz, Michael B., Michael Doucet, and Mark J. Stern. *The Social Organization of Early Industrial Capitalism*. Cambridge: Harvard University Press, 1982.

Lemieux, Denise, and Lucie Mercier. *Les Femmes au tournant du siècle, 1880–1940. Ages de la vie, maternité et quotidien*. Ville Saint-Laurent: Institut québécois de recherche sur la culture, 1989.

Lévesque, Andrée. *La Norme et les déviantes: Des femmes au Québec pendant l'entre deux guerres*. Montreal: les éditions du remue-ménage, 1989.

Lindstrom-Best, Varpu. *Defiant Sisters: A Social History of Finnish Immigrant Women in Canada*. Toronto: Multicultural History Society of Ontario, 1988.

Luxton, Meg. *More than a Labour of Love: Three Generations of Women's Work in the Home*. Toronto: Women's Press, 1980.

McLaren, Angus, and Arlene Tigar McLaren. *The Bedroom and the State: The Changing Practices and Politics of Contraception and Abortion in Canada, 1880–1980*. Toronto: McClelland and Stewart, 1986.

Murray, Hilda Chaulk. *More than 50%. Woman's Life in a Newfoundland Outport, 1900–1950*. St. John's: Breakwater Books, 1979.

Parr, Joy. *The Gender of Breadwinners: Women, Men and Change in Two Industrial Towns, 1880–1950*. Toronto: University of Toronto Press, 1990.

Parr, Joy. *Labouring Children: British Immigrant Apprentices to Canada, 1869–1924*. Montreal: McGill-Queen's University Press, 1980.

Prentice, Alison, Paula Bourne, Gail Cuthbert Brandt, Beth Light, Wendy Mitchinson, and Naomi Black. *Canadian Women: A History*. Toronto: Harcourt Brace Jovanovich, 1988.

Snell, James. *In the Shadow of the Law: Divorce in Canada, 1900–1939*. Toronto: University of Toronto Press, 1991.

Strong-Boag, Veronica. *The New Day Recalled: The Lives of Girls and Women in English Canada, 1919–1939*. Toronto: Copp Clark Pitman, 1988.

Sutherland, Neil. *Children in English-Canadian Society: Framing the Twentieth Century Consensus.* Toronto: University of Toronto Press, 1976.

Van Kirk, Sylvia. *"Many Tender Ties." Women in Fur Trade Society, 1670–1870* Winnipeg: Watson & Dwyer Publishing Ltd., 1980.

Ward, Peter. *Courtship, Love, and Marriage in Nineteenth-Century English Canada.* Montreal: McGill-Queen's University Press, 1990.

COLLECTIONS OF ARTICLES AND DOCUMENTS

Arnup, Katherine, Andrée Lévesque, and Ruth Roach Pierson, eds. with Margaret Brennan. *Delivering Motherhood: Maternal Ideologies and Practices in the Nineteenth and Twentieth Centuries.* London: Routledge, 1990.

Burnet, Jean, ed. *Looking Into My Sister's Eyes: An Exploration in Women's History.* Toronto: Multicultural History Society of Ontario, 1986.

Conrad, Margaret, Toni Laidlaw, and Donna Smyth, eds. *No Place Like Home: Diaries and Letters of Nova Scotia Women, 1771–1938.* Halifax: Formac, 1988.

Cook, Ramsay, and Wendy Mitchinson, eds. *The Proper Sphere: Woman's Place in Canadian Society.* Toronto: Oxford University Press, 1976.

Dickinson, James, and Bob Russel, eds. *Family, Economy and State: The Social Reproduction Process Under Capitalism.* Toronto: Garamond Press, 1986.

Eid, Nadia Fahmy, and Micheline Dumont, eds. *Maîtresses de maison, maîtresses d'école: Femmes, famille et éducation dans l'histoire du Québec.* Montreal: Boréal Express, 1983.

Light, Beth and Joy Parr, eds. *Canadian Women on the Move, 1867–1920.* Toronto: New Hogtown Press, 1983.

Light, Beth, and Alison Prentice, eds. *Pioneer and Gentlewomen of British North America.* Toronto: New Hogtown Press, 1980.

Light, Beth, and Ruth Roach Pierson, eds. *No Easy Road: Women in Canada 1920s to 1960s.* Toronto: University of Toronto Press, 1990.

Luxton, Meg, and Harriet Rosenberg. *Through the Kitchen Window: The Politics of Home and Family.* Toronto: Garamond Press, 1986.

Mandell, Nancy, and Ann Duffy, eds. *Reconstucting the Canadian Family: Feminist Perspectives.* Toronto: Butterworths, 1988.

Parr, Joy, ed. *Childhood and Family in Canadian History.* Toronto: McClelland and Stewart, 1982.

Prentice, Alison, and Susan E. Houston, eds. *Family, School and Society in Nineteenth-Century Canada.* Toronto: Oxford University Press, 1975.

Ramu, G.N., ed. *Marriage and the Family in Canada Today.* Scarborough, Ont; Prentice-Hall, 1989.

Rooke, Patricia T., and R.L. Schnell. *Studies in Childhood History: A Canadian Perspective.* Calgary: Detselig Enterprises; 1982.

CONTRIBUTORS

○

Constance Backhouse teaches law at the University of Western Ontario. She has published many articles on women and the law. Her book *Petticoats and Prejudice* is a major study of women and the law in nineteenth-century Canada.

Gérard Bouchard is director of SOREP at l'Université de Québec à Chicoutimi. He and his co-workers have published extensively on methodology and on the history of the families of the Saguenay.

Bettina Bradbury teaches women's history, family history, and economic history at l'Université de Montréal. She is the author of *Working Families: Age, Gender, and Daily Survival in Industrializing Montreal*.

Jennifer Brown teaches in the history department at the University of Winnipeg. She is author of *Strangers in Blood: Fur Trade Company Families in Indian Country*.

John Bullen defended his Ph.D. at the University of Ottawa on "Children of the Industrial Age: Children, Work, and Welfare in Late Nineteenth-Century Ontario," in the spring of 1989, shortly before he was killed in a car accident.

Marie-Aimée Cliche is author of *Les pratiques de dévotion en Nouvelle-France: comportements populaires et encadrement ecclésial dans le gouvernement de Québec* and of several important articles based on research in the judicial archives.

Chad Gaffield teaches family history and Canadian history at the University of Ottawa. He has published many articles on the history of education and the family, and is author of *Language, Schooling, and Cultural Conflict: The Origins of the French-language Controversy in Ontario*.

Franca Iacovetta is the author of *Such Hardworking People: Italian Immigrants in Postwar Toronto*. She teaches history at the University of Toronto.

Dominique Jean teaches history at Carleton University. Her major publications focus on the relationship between families and the state in the post-World War II period.

Yves Landry teaches historical demography at l'Université de Montréal and is a member of the Programme de recherche en démographie historique. He has published widely on the historical demography of New France and is the author of *Orphelines en France, pionnières au Canada: les Filles du roi au XVIIe siècle*.

Meg Luxton teaches in the social science department at Atkinson College, York University. She has made a vital contribution to our understanding of the role of women's domestic labour. Her major work is *More than a Labour of Love: Three Generations of Women's Work in the Home.*

Suzanne Morton recently completed her Ph.D. in history at Dalhousie University. She has published several articles on different aspects of working-class history in the Maritimes.

Joy Parr's most recent work, *The Gender of Breadwinners: Women, Men and Change in Two Industrial Towns, 1880–1950* won the John A. Macdonald prize for the best book in Canadian history published in 1991.

Marilyn Porter teaches sociology at Memorial University of Newfoundland. She is author of *Home, Work and Class Consciousness.*

Mark Rosenfeld recently completed his Ph.D. in history at York University. His article published in this volume is drawn from that research. He currently has a postdoctoral fellowship to study masculinity.

James Snell teaches history at the University of Guelph and is the author of *In the Shadow of the Law: Divorce in Canada, 1900–1939.*

Sylvia Van Kirk teaches history and women's studies at the University of Toronto. She is author of *"Many Tender Ties": Women in Fur Trade Society, 1670–1870* and many articles on women in western Canada.

An honest attempt has been made to secure permission for all material used, and if there are errors or omissions, these are wholly unintentional and the Publisher will be grateful to learn of them.

Yves Landry, "Le choix du conjoint en situation de déséquilibre des sexes: le cas des filles du roi au XVIIe siècle," printed with the permission of the author.

Marie Aimée Cliche, "Filles-mères, familles et société sous le régime Français," *Histoire sociale/Social History* (May 1988): 39–69. Reprinted with the permission of the journal.

Sylvia Van Kirk, "'The Custom of the Country': An Examination of Fur Trade Marriage Practices" in *Essays on Western History*, ed. L.H. Thomas (Edmonton: University of Alberta Press, 1976), 49–68. Reprinted with the permission of the author.

Jennifer S.H. Brown, "A Cree Nurse in a Cradle of Methodism: Little Mary and the Egerton R. Young Family at Norway House and Berens River" in *First Day, Fighting Days: Women in Manitoba History* (Regina: Canadian Plains Research Center, 1987), 19–40. Reprinted with the permission of the Canadian Plains Research Center.

Gérard Bouchard, "Les systèmes de transmission des avoirs familiaux et le cycle de la société rurale au Québec, du XVIIe au XXe siècle," *Histoire sociale/Social History* 17, 34 (Nov. 1984): 34–60. Reprinted with the permission of the journal.

Chad Gaffield, "Canadian Families in Cultural Context: Hypotheses from the Mid-Nineteenth Century," Canadian Historical Association *Historical Papers* (1979): 49–70. Reprinted with the permission of the journal and the author.

Marilyn Porter, "She Was Skipper of the Shore Crew: Notes on the History of the Sexual Division of Labour in Newfoundland," *Labour/Le Travail* 15 (Spring 1985): 105–23. Reprinted with the permission of the editor. © Canadian Committee on Labour History.

Bettina Bradbury, "Gender at Work at Home: Family Decisions, the Labour Market and Girls' Contributions to the Family Economy" in *Canadian and Australian Labour History*, ed. Gregory S. Kealey and Greg Patmore (Sydney: Australian-Canadian Studies, 1990): 119–40. Reprinted with the permission of the editor of the Australian Society for the Study of Labour History and Committee on Canadian Labour History. © Canadian Committee on Labour History.

John Bullen, "Hidden Workers: Child Labour and the Family Economy in Late Nineteenth-Century Urban Ontario," *Labour/Le Travail* 18 (1986): 163–88. Reprinted with the permission of the editor. © Canadian Committee on Labour History.

Joy Parr, "Rethinking Work and Kinship in a Canadian Hosiery Town 1919–1950," *Feminist Studies* 13, 1 (Spring 1987): 137–62. Reprinted with permission.

Mark Rosenfeld, "'It Was a Hard Life': Class and Gender in the Work and Family Rhythms of a Railway Town," Canadian Historical Association, *Historical Papers* (1988): 237–79. Reprinted with the permission of the journal and the author.

Franca Iacovetta, "From *Contadina* to Worker: Southern Italian Immigrant Working Women in Toronto, 1947–62," in *Looking into My Sister's Eyes: An Exploration in Women's History*, ed. Jean Burnet (Toronto: The Multicultural History Society of Ontario, 1986), 195–222. Reprinted with the permission of the Multicultural History Society of Ontario.

Meg Luxton, "Two Hands for the Clock: Changing Patterns in the Gendered Division of Labour in the Home," *Studies in Political Economy* 12 (Fall 1983). Reprinted with permission.

Constance B. Backhouse, "Married Women's Property Law in Nineteenth-Century Canada," *Law and History Review* 6, 2 (Fall 1988): 211–57. Reprinted with permission of the journal and the author.

Suzanne Morton, "The June Bride as Working-Class Bride: Getting Married in a Halifax Working-Class Neighbourhood in the 1920s," printed with the permission of the author.

James Snell, "The White Life for Two: The Defence of Marriage and Sexual Mora[...] Canada, 1890–1914," *Histoire sociale/Social History* 16, 31 (May 1983): 111–30. Repr[...] with the permission of the journal.

Dominique Jean, "Family Allowances and Family Autonomy: Quebec Families Encou[...] the Welfare State, 1945–1955," printed with the permission of the author.

James Snell, "The White Life for Two: The Defence of Marriage and Sexual Morality in Canada, 1890–1914," *Histoire sociale/Social History* 16, 31 (May 1983): 111–30. Reprinted with the permission of the journal.

Dominique Jean, "Family Allowances and Family Autonomy: Quebec Families Encounter the Welfare State, 1945–1955," printed with the permission of the author.